CONSTRUCTION LAW SERIES

ARCHITECTS AND ENGINEERS

THIRD EDITION

James Acret
of the Santa Monica Bar

WEST GROUP
Bancroft-Whitney • Banks-Baldwin • Clark Boardman Callaghan
Lawyers Cooperative Publishing • WESTLAW® • West Publishing

Copyright © 1977, 1979, 1980, 1981, 1982, 1983, 1984, 1985, 1986, 1987, 1988, 1989, 1990, 1991, 1992, 1993 by McGraw-Hill, Inc. All rights reserved. Printed in the United States of America. Except as permitted under the United States Copyright Act of 1976, no part of this publication may be reproduced or distributed in any form or by any means, or stored in a data base or retrieval system, without the prior written permission of the publisher.

Revised edition of *Architects and Engineers, Second Edition* by James Acret (Shepard's/McGraw-Hill 1984)

2 3 4 5 6 7 8 9 10   SHXX   9 3 2 1 0 9 8

Library of Congress Cataloging in Publication Data

Acret, James.
   Architects and engineers.

   Includes index.
   1. Architects—Malpractice—United States.
2. Engineers—Malpractice—United States. I. Title.
KF2925.3.A92   346.7303'3   84-5314
ISBN 0-07-172438-9   347.30633

ISBN 0-07-172438-9

ARER3

Information has been obtained by Shepard's/McGraw-Hill, Inc. from sources believed to be reliable. However, because of the possibility of human or mechanical error by our sources, Shepard's/McGraw-Hill, Inc., or others, Shepard's/McGraw-Hill, Inc. does not guarantee the accuracy, adequacy, or completeness of any information and is not responsible for any errors or omissions or for the results obtained from use of such information.

   The Sponsoring Editor for this book was Chris Kloeris, the Legal Editor was Laurel Cohn, and the Construction Law Publisher was Mary Kay LaRue.

Shepard's Construction Law Series

California Construction Law Digests
California Construction Law Manual, Fourth Edition
Construction Arbitration Handbook
Construction Industry Formbook, Second Edition
Construction Law Digests
Construction Litigation Handbook
Florida Construction Law Manual, Second Edition
Illinois Construction Law: Manual and Forms
Insurance Coverage of Construction Disputes
New York Construction Law Manual
Texas Construction Law Manual, Second Edition

For Mandy

For Mandi

Acknowledgments

Thanks are due to Sharon Smith, who prepared the manuscript with her usual efficiency and devotion, and to Thomas Wogan for exemplary research and editing.

Contents

Summary

Acknowledgments

1 Liability for Negligence

2 Liability for Intentional Torts

3 Liability Arising from Statute

4 Liability Arising from Contract

5 Liability for Estimates

6 Liability Arising from Warranty Law

7 No Damage Cases

8 Liability Arising from Agency

9 Defenses

10 Damages

11 Limitations

12 Indemnity

13   Insurance

14   Arbitration

15   Trial and Hearing Techniques

Appendixes
Tables
Index

Detailed

Acknowledgments

1   Liability for Negligence
    §1.01   Malpractice
    §1.02   Duty versus Negligence
    §1.03   Standard of Practice
    §1.04   —Not a Warrantor
    §1.05   —Reasonable Skill and Knowledge
    §1.06   —Conventional Standard Criticized
    §1.07   —Conventional Standard Applied
    §1.08   —Required Duty
            Engineer's Duty
            Architect's Duty
            Contract Standards
    §1.09   No Insurer
            Architect Liable
            Liability Limited by Fee Size
    §1.10   Failure to Warn
    §1.11   Intrinsically Dangerous
    §1.12   Nondelegable Duty
    §1.13   Negligent Misrepresentation
            Inducement
    §1.14   Negligence
            Reasonable Care Standard

§1.15	—Contract versus Tort Liability
	Setoff Allowed
§1.16	—Negligence and Breach of Contract
§1.17	—Reasonable Skill Required
	No Guarantee
	Reasonable Skill
	Proximate Cause
	Foreseeability
§1.18	—Privity of Contract
	Old Rule
	Rejection of the Defense
	Lack of Duty
	Economic Loss Rule
§1.19	—Expert Testimony
	Expert Testimony Required
	Qualifications of Expert
	Expert Testimony Not Required
§1.20	Liability to Third Parties—Contractors
	Negligent Review by Architect
	Subcontractor versus Engineer
§1.21	—Developers and Construction Lenders
	Architect Not Liable to Lender
§1.22	—Workers
	Worker versus Architect
	Worker versus Engineer
	Owner Not Liable
§1.23	—Invitees, Patrons, and Occupants
§1.24	—Sureties and Indemnitors
§1.25	—Other Remote Parties
	Subsequent Purchasers
	Sub-Subcontractor
	Bondholder
§1.26	Liability Arising from Real Estate Law

2 Liability for Intentional Torts
§2.01 Fraud
Fraudulent Misrepresentation
False Payment Certificate
Fraudulent Concealment
§2.02 Conspiracy
§2.03 Conflict of Interest
§2.04 Slander
Qualified Privilege
Innocent Construction Rule
Libel Per Se
Qualified Immunity
Litigation Privilege
§2.05 Interference with Contract
Requirement of Malice
Agency Defense
Immunity of Arbitrator
Tortious Interference
Litigation Privilege
Privilege Not Shown
Statute of Limitations
Privity of Contract Defense
§2.06 Trespass
§2.07 Bad Faith
§2.08 Conversion

3 Liability Arising from Statute
§3.01 Inspection and Supervision
§3.02 Licensing Statutes
Surveyors
Limitations
Expert Witness
Collapse
Nonlicensure Prevents Recovery of Fee
Design-Build Contract

- §3.03 Failure to Comply with Building Code
  - Negligence Per Se
  - Illegality
  - Negligence
  - Compliance Defense
  - Nondelegable Duty
  - Trade Practice
  - Workers Injured
- §3.04 Safe Place Statutes
- §3.05 "Scaffold Acts"
- §3.06 Safety Regulations
  - Evidence of Standard of Care
  - Workers Injured
- §3.07 Intentional Diversion of Water
- §3.08 Copyright
- §3.09 Seals

4 **Liability Arising from Contract**
- §4.01 Breach of Contract and Negligence
  - Duties Imposed by Contract
  - Implied Conditions
  - Lack of Privity Defense
  - Duty Arises from Contract, Lack of Privity No Defense
  - Exculpatory Clause
  - Specific Performance
  - Contract Duty versus Contributory Negligence
- §4.02 Design Compliance Defense of the Designer-Builder
- §4.03 Contract as Creating Duty
  - Third-Party Beneficiary versus Duty Created by Contract
  - Subrogation
  - Active Negligence
  - Economic Loss
  - Privity
  - Surety's Indemnitee Protected
  - Contractor versus Engineer

Exculpatory Clause Is Defense to Third-Party Action
Workers Injured
No Duty to Worker
No Contractual Duty
Joint Venture
§4.04   The Duty to Supervise
No Duty to Workers
Patron
Duty Is Found
§4.05   Third-Party Beneficiary
Owner Is Third-Party Beneficiary
Owner Not Third-Party Beneficiary
Contractor Is Third-Party Beneficiary
Contractor Not Third-Party Beneficiary
Remote Owner Is Third-Party Beneficiary
Remote Owner Not Third-Party Beneficiary
Workers Not Third-Party Beneficiaries
Lenders Not Third-Party Beneficiaries
§4.06   Safety Engineering
Voluntary Safety Inspections
Insurance Carrier Not Liable
§4.07   The Power to Stop the Work
Common Law Obligation
Agency
Architect's Lack of Authority

5   Liability for Estimates
§5.01   The Pervasive Problem
Substantial Accuracy
§5.02   Recoverability of Fee
Major Changes
Niggardly Damages
§5.03   Duty to Establish Budget
Budget Established by Law

CONTENTS xvii

    Guess versus Estimate
    No Budget Established
§5.04 Misrepresentation
    Misrepresentation Voids Contract
    Damages for Misrepresentation
    Estimate of Fee
    Intentional Misrepresentation
§5.05 Breach of Contract
    Parol Evidence Rule
    Quantum Meruit Recovery
    Intentional Breach of Contract
    Prevention of Performance
    Measure of Damages
§5.06 Willful Overrun
§5.07 Negligence
    Contributory Negligence
    Expert Testimony Required
§5.08 Parol Evidence Rule
    Parol Evidence Received
    Parol Evidence Contradicts Contract
    Uncertainty of Contract
    Oral Condition
    Parol Evidence Refused
§5.09 Substantial Accuracy
    Insubstantial Error
    Substantial Error
    Quantum Meruit Recovery
§5.10 Redesign
    No Warrantor
    Project Abandoned
§5.11 Exculpatory Clauses
§5.12 Contributory Fault of Owner
    Unjust Enrichment
    Cost Increases by Owner

§5.13 Waiver
Purported Waiver Ambiguous
§5.14 Unjust Enrichment
§5.15 Benefit-of-the-Bargain Damages
Fraud Theory
Measure of Damages Criticized
Tenant's Damages
§5.16 Out-of-Pocket Damages
§5.17 Loss-of-Fee Damages
Effect of *Quantum Meruit* Damages

6 Liability Arising from Warranty Law
§6.01 Generally
§6.02 Express Warranty
Warranty versus Misrepresentation
Strict Liability versus Express Warranty
§6.03 Implied Warranty
Warranty Implied in Favor of Owner
Benefit-of-Bargain Damages Inapplicable
Implied Warranty of Builder
Statute of Limitations—Privity
Warranty Found
Damages
§6.04 Strict Liability
Privity Defense
Justification for Strict Liability
§6.05 —Mass Home Builders
§6.06 —History of the Doctrine
§6.07 —Architects
Strict Liability Rejected
§6.08 —Engineers
Engineer Not Strictly Liable
§6.09 —Application Criticized

7 No Damage Cases
§7.01 Generally

§7.02   Mental Anguish
§7.03   Economic Damage

8   **Liability Arising from Agency**
    §8.01   Generally
            Delegation of Duties of Agent
            Agent versus Independent Contractor
            Design-Build
            Liability for Acts of Agent
            Agency Relationship
    §8.02   Owner Bound by Acts or Knowledge of Agent
            Knowledge of Architect Attributed to Owner
            Torts of Agent
            Actual Knowledge
            Estoppel
            Extra Work
            Collusion with Owner
            Negligent Approval of Estimates Exonerates Bond
            Agent for Design
            Limitation on Authority of Agent
    §8.03   Owner Not Bound by Acts of Architect
            Independent Contractor
            No Right of Control
            Agent for Transaction
            Arbitrator, Not Agent
    §8.04   Agency Relationship as a Defense to the Architect
    §8.05   Liability for Acts of Consultant
            Nondelegable Duty
    §8.06   Liability of Partnerships and Corporations

9   **Defenses**
    §9.01   Generally
    §9.02   Privity of Contract
            Foreseeability
            Doctrine of Invitation

§9.03 —Rejection
Warranty
§9.04 Economic Loss
§9.05 —Continuing Application of Privity Defense
§9.06 Completion and Acceptance
§9.07 Patent Defect
§9.08 Immunity—Architect as Arbitrator
§9.09 —Application
§9.10 —Criticism
§9.11 No Duty
Defense Rejected
§9.12 Architect No Insurer
§9.13 No Causation
§9.14 Assumption of the Risk
§9.15 Contributory Negligence
§9.16 Comparative Negligence
Apportionment and Comparative Negligence
§9.17 —Application
§9.18 Reliance on Information Furnished by Others
§9.19 Approval by Building Department
§9.20 Waiver and Estoppel
Failure to Complain
Estoppel Rejected
Waiver and Estoppel Accepted
§9.21 Approval by Owner
Approval Accepted as a Defense
§9.22 No Supervision
Duty to Supervise
§9.23 No Control
Reverse Application
§9.24 —Methods of Construction
§9.25 —Application
Vitality of the Defense
Assumption of Responsibility by Conduct
Details of Construction

§9.26 —Rejection
Supervisory Power
Positive Protective Duty
Summary
§9.27 Defective Work Concealed
§9.28 Deviation from Plans
§9.29 Exculpatory Clauses
Architect as Drafter of Contract Documents
Contract Documents
Public Contracts
Standard Forms
§9.30 —Application
Claims by Sureties
Claims by Contractors
Claims by Owners
Claims by Workers
Defense Rejected
§9.31 —Criticism
§9.32 Exclusive Remedy
§9.33 Privilege
§9.34 Sovereign Immunity
§9.35 —Application
§9.36 —Rejection
§9.37 Release
Release of Joint Tortfeasor
Release of Principal Releases Agent
§9.38 Accord and Satisfaction
§9.39 No License
§9.40 Other Forms of Illegality
§9.41 Res Judicata and Collateral Estoppel
§9.42 Other Defenses
Nonfeasance versus Misfeasance
Compliance with Statute
Act of God
Lack of Federal Jurisdiction
Percolating Waters

Superseding Cause
Riparian Law
Compliance with Contract
Duplicate Recovery
Statute of Frauds

10 Damages
§10.01 Generally
Approaches to Damages
Consequential Damages
Market Value
§10.02 Cost of Correction of Public Project
§10.03 —Private Project
Cost Saving or Value
Betterment
Cost of Correction
Cost of Repair
Moorman Doctrine
§10.04 Negligent Survey
Difference Minus Fee
Lost Profit Denied
§10.05 Convenience, Comfort, and Enjoyment
§10.06 Development of Out-of-Pocket Damages
§10.07 —Application
§10.08 Cost of Correction Uneconomic
§10.09 Rental Value
Rent versus Interest
Rent Plus Interest
§10.10 Economic Loss
Economic Loss Awarded
Flawed Jury Instruction
Moorman Doctrine
Doctrine Rejected
Conflicting Decisions

§10.11 Mental Anguish
§10.12 Punitive Damages

11 Limitations
§11.01 Generally
Estoppel
Compendium
Criticism
§11.02 Applicable Period
Damage to Project
Contract
Contract Statute Applied
Contract versus Malpractice
Malpractice
Design versus Malpractice
Contract and Tort
Tort
Tort versus Contract
Tort versus Contract versus Property Damage
Third-Party Beneficiary
Economic Loss
Negligence Statute Applied
Bodily Injury
Professional Service
Statute of Repose versus Negligence
Indemnity
§11.03 Accrual—Negligent Act
New York Rule
§11.04 —Time of Completion
§11.05 —When Damage Occurs
Payment as Damage
Criminal Prosecution
§11.06 —Discovery Rule
§11.07 —Statutes of Repose
Bodily Injury
Discovery Extension

Fraud Claim
Auto Accident
Completion of Services
Contract Action
Latent Defect
Retrospective Effect
Statute of Repose Does Not Extend Time to Sue
§11.08 —Constitutional Considerations
A Box Score
Constitutionality of Statute Upheld
Statute of Repose Held Unconstitutional
§11.09 —Statute of Repose Applied
Indemnity Action
Completion of Construction
Improvement to Real Property
§11.10 —Application of Statute Rejected
§11.11 Continuous Services
Attempted Repairs
Continuing Inspections
Assurances of Repair
Professional Assurances
Contractor Does Not Rely on Architect
Gap in Services
§11.12 Arbitration
§11.13 Remedial Efforts

12 Indemnity
§12.01 Generally
§12.02 Contractual Indemnity
Subrogation to Indemnity
No Indemnity for Architect
Indemnity against Architect
Joint Negligence
Attorneys Fees
Architect Indemnifies Owner

                Mechanics Lien
                Contractor Indemnifies Engineer
                No Indemnity for Economic Damages
                No Omission, No Indemnity
                Ambiguous Clause
§12.03 Indemnity against Own Negligence
        Narrow Construction
        Broad Construction
§12.04 Statute Annulling Indemnity Provision
§12.05 No Contribution
        No Joint Fault
§12.06 Implied Equitable Indemnity—Development
        Early Development: Active/Passive
        Active/Passive Distinction
        No Duty, No Indemnity
§12.07 —Sought from Architect or Engineer
        Active/Passive
        Indemnity Based on Implied Warranty
        Numerous Factors
        No Indemnity to Active Tortfeasor
        Disproportionate Fault
        No Indemnity Where Both Parties Negligent
        No Indemnity for Parties in pari delicto
        Indemnity for Defective Design
        Negligent Approval
        Active or Affirmative Negligence
        "Primary" Fault
        Joint Fault
        No Duty
        Indemnity Enforced
§12.08 —Sought by Architect or Engineer
        Active/Passive
        Architect Actively Negligent
        Contractor Indemnifies Architect
        Nonfeasance Is Active Negligence

More versus Less Negligent
Indemnity to Actively Negligent Engineer
Architect versus Supplier
Fault Destroys Right to Common Law Indemnity
Vouching In
Contribution Permitted
Exclusive Remedy Defense
Release Bars Indemnity
Required Relationship
No Duty of Contractor to Engineer
Independent Wrongs—No Indemnity
Common Wrong
Contribution Statute—Economic Loss
§12.09 Limitations
Statutes of Repose
Other Statutes

13 Insurance

§13.01 Generally
§13.02 Comprehensive Liability Coverage
Comprehensive versus Professional Insurance
Breach of Contract Enforced
Professional Services Exclusion
Insurance Extended by Contract
Bad Faith
§13.03 Professional Services Exclusion
Claim Covered
Claim Excluded
Duty to Defend Not Excluded
Exclusion Applied
§13.04 Exotic Coverage
Wrapup Policy
Builders Risk
§13.05 Subsurface Exclusion

§13.06　Professional Liability Insurance
　　　　Slander Claim Covered
　　　　Duty to Notify Carrier
§13.07　Duty to Defend
　　　　Late Presentation of Claim
　　　　Multiple Claims
　　　　Known Error or Omission
　　　　Intentional Wrongdoing
§13.08　Claims Made during Policy Period
　　　　Claim after Policy Expired
　　　　Notice to Excess Carrier
　　　　Tardy Notice
　　　　Wrong Address
§13.09　—Application
　　　　Claims Made
　　　　Insurer's Duty of Disclosure
　　　　Late Report
　　　　Discovery versus Occurrence Policy
　　　　Claim by Telephone
　　　　Prior Knowledge of Claim
　　　　Lack of Written Notice
　　　　Late Report
§13.10　—Policy Arguments
　　　　Freedom of Contract
§13.11　Settlement by Insured
§13.12　Responsibility of Carrier Where Insured Loses or Forgives Fee
§13.13　Deductible
§13.14　Waiver and Estoppel
§13.15　Excess Clause
　　　　Excess Clause versus *Pro Rata* Clause
§13.16　Subrogation

14 Arbitration
- §14.01 Generally
  - Architect as Arbitrator
- §14.02 Right to Compel Arbitration
  - Architect versus State
  - Limited Scope
  - Stay of Litigation Pending Arbitration
  - Broad Scope
  - Arbitration Agreements Unenforceable
  - Arbitration Agreements Enforceable
  - Third-Party Beneficiary
- §14.03 Waiver
  - AAA Rule
  - Pursuit of Discovery
- §14.04 Conditions Precedent to Arbitration
- §14.05 Multiple Parties
  - Collateral Estoppel
  - Consolidation
  - Anti-Consolidation Clause
- §14.06 —Joinder and Consolidation
  - Joint Arbitration Ordered
  - Collateral Estoppel
- §14.07 —Vouching In
- §14.08 Selection of Arbitrator
- §14.09 Conduct of Arbitration Hearing
- §14.10 Considerations in Selecting Arbitration
  - Time
  - Appeal
  - Expense
  - American Arbitration Association Fees
  - Postponement Fees
  - Additional Hearing Fee
  - Hearing-Room Rental
  - Refund Schedule
  - Other Cost Factors
  - Privacy

    Discovery
    Legal Error
    Evidence Rules
    Statute of Limitations
    Provisional Remedies
    Multiple Parties
    Expertise
    Lawyers
    Pretrial and Settlement
    Other Factors
  §14.11 Mediation
  §14.12 Enforcement of Award
  §14.13 Vacation of Award

15 Trial and Hearing Techniques
  §15.01 Generally
  §15.02 Fact Summary
  §15.03 Delay Chart
  §15.04 Witness Outline
  §15.05 Document File
  §15.06 Deposition Summary
  §15.07 Expert Witnesses
    Local Standard Not Established
    Expert from a Different Profession
    Safety Expert
    Hypothetical Questions
    Expert Relies on Hearsay
    Attorney Work Product
    Attorney-Client Privilege
    Qualifications of Expert
  §15.08 Law Notes
  §15.09 "Trial Book"
  §15.10 Proposed Award

  Appendix A Persons Protected
    Owner

Remote Owner
Tenant
Neighbor
Patron
Lender
Third Party
Vehicle Occupant
Infant
Worker
Contractor
Subcontractor
Surety
Architect
Supplier

Appendix B   Fact Situations
Septic, Sewer
Underground Obstruction
Cave-In
Soils
Slab
Bulge
Collapse
Mechanical Heating, Ventilating, and Air Conditioning
Mechanical
Roof Leak
Leaks
Explosion
Cracks
Fire
Glass Door
Falling Object
Flood and Storm Water
Dam Burst
Fall

Bodily Injury: Third Party
Traffic Accident
Asphyxiation
Electrocution
Defective Plans
Multiple Defects in Plans
Plans Violate Code
Negligent Selection of Contractor
Delay
Safety Inspection
Dirt Estimate
Bribery
Misrepresentation
Extra Work
Payment Certificate
Survey
Water and Percolation Tests
Miscellaneous

Appendix C   Contract Forms

Tables
　Cases
　Statutes

Index

Liability for Negligence

1

§1.01 Malpractice
§1.02 Duty versus Negligence
§1.03 Standard of Practice
§1.04 —Not a Warrantor
§1.05 —Reasonable Skill and Knowledge
§1.06 —Conventional Standard Criticized
§1.07 —Conventional Standard Applied
§1.08 —Required Duty
Engineer's Duty
Architect's Duty
Contract Standards
§1.09 No Insurer
Architect Liable
Liability Limited by Fee Size
§1.10 Failure to Warn
§1.11 Intrinsically Dangerous
§1.12 Nondelegable Duty
§1.13 Negligent Misrepresentation
Inducement
§1.14 Negligence
Reasonable Care Standard
§1.15 —Contract versus Tort Liability
Setoff Allowed
§1.16 —Negligence and Breach of Contract
§1.17 —Reasonable Skill Required
No Guarantee
Reasonable Skill

	Proximate Cause
	Foreseeability
§1.18	—Privity of Contract
	Old Rule
	Rejection of the Defense
	Lack of Duty
	Economic Loss Rule
§1.19	—Expert Testimony
	Expert Testimony Required
	Qualifications of Expert
	Expert Testimony Not Required
§1.20	Liability to Third Parties—Contractors
	Negligent Review by Architect
	Subcontractor versus Engineer
	Subcontractor versus Architect
§1.21	—Developers and Construction Lenders
	Architect Not Liable to Lender
§1.22	—Workers
	Worker versus Architect
	Worker versus Engineer
	Owner Not Liable
§1.23	—Invitees, Patrons, and Occupants
§1.24	—Sureties and Indemnitors
§1.25	—Other Remote Parties
	Subsequent Purchasers
	Sub-Subcontractor
	Bondholder
§1.26	Liability Arising from Real Estate Law

§1.01 Malpractice

Although the subject of malpractice has a well-defined inner structure, its periphery is amorphous. *Malpractice* is commonly defined as a dereliction from professional duty or a failure of professional skill or learning that results in injury, loss, or damage.

The standard of care applicable to architects and engineers is the same as for other professionals, including lawyers, accountants, and others furnishing skills and services for compensation. That standard requires reasonable care and competence, although the professional does not guarantee correct or even the best professional advice, but merely reasonable care and competence.[1]

---

[1] Delmar Vineyard v Timmons, 486 SW2d 914 (Tenn Ct App 1972).

The classic definition of the standard has been questioned. It is anomalous that a layperson should be held to a higher standard of care than a professional. As pointed out by Professor Curran, the law requires of the layperson more than average conduct—it requires average *prudent* conduct.[2] This is up the scale from average. However, for professionals, the law seems satisfied with average or minimum acceptable conduct, and just in case that is too high, allowance is sometimes made for the locality where the defendant practices. Ordinarily, a jury cannot judge this standard, only a professional can. Thus, the question of liability often turns on the credibility of expert witnesses.

The study of malpractice as a field of law is, indeed, largely the study of a special form of negligence. The amorphous boundaries of the subject, where the law is growing and developing, enclose such topics as intentional torts, statutory duties, duties voluntarily assumed by contract strict liability, and liability derived from breach of warranty as developed in the law of sales. The term *architect* as used in this work includes all design professionals who work on buildings and real estate, namely engineers, draftsmen, designers, surveyors, and, to the extent that they participate in the design function, contractors and manufacturers.

The following cases involving malpractice are presented as illustrations of the well-defined inner structure and the amorphous periphery of malpractice outlined above.

In *Spielvogel v Merrill Lynch, Pierce, Fenner & Smith, Inc*,[3] a pedestrian alleged that she was felled by a gust of wind on an open plaza surrounding an office building near the World Trade Center in New York. The building had been completed in 1971 and was designed and constructed in strict compliance with city codes and building regulations. No similar accidents had ever been reported. Summary judgment in favor of the building designer was AFFIRMED. The plaintiff utterly failed to demonstrate any evidence of a design or construction defect that created a dangerous condition that caused her injuries.

In *La Bombarde v Phillips Swager Associates*,[4] the administrator of the decedent's estate filed a wrongful death action against an architect for damages resulting when the decedent, while an inmate at a county jail, hung himself from a grill that was part of the jail's heating and air conditioning system. HELD: an architect owes a duty of care to persons likely to use a structure and must design the structure so that it is safe for its intended use. However, an architect is under no duty to design a jail cell without grills on the heating and

---

[2] Curran, *Professional Negligence—Some Current Comments*, 12 Vand L Rev 535 (1959).
[3] 127 AD2d 532, 512 NYS2d 75 (1987).
[4] 130 Ill App 3d 896, 474 NE2d 942 (1985), *appeal denied* (May Term 1985).

air conditioning system. It would not be reasonable to expect an architect to remove all fixtures that might be used by prisoners to aid in the commission of a suicide.

In *Richards & Associates v Boney*,[5] a subcontractor filed an action against an architect who had instructed the owner not to make a final contract payment of $37,000 to the subcontractor. The subcontractor had made a claim of $519,000 against the owner for delay. The architect advised the owner not to make the final payment until the subcontractor dropped the claim. HELD: after the subcontractor completed its work, the architect had no further duty to the subcontractor. The advice to the owner was not architectural in nature and the architect breached no architectural duty.

§1.02 Duty versus Negligence

Within the analysis of architect's malpractice exists a classic and confusing debate: Does liability require the presence of both duty and negligence, or is duty merely one of the components of negligence? In *Palsgraf v Long Island Railroad*,[6] Judge Cardozo said that negligence is not actionable unless it involves the invasion of a legally protected interest, the violation of a right. Quoting from Pollock: "Proof of negligence in the air, so to speak, will not do."[7] Thus, according to the majority in *Palsgraf*, it is for the law to say whether the defendant is under a duty to protect the plaintiff, and then for the jury to determine whether the defendant was negligent.

According to the minority in *Palsgraf*, once it is determined that an act is negligent, it is no longer necessary to look to see if there was a duty. *Duty* is just an element in determining the existence of negligence, and if an architect is negligent and the plaintiff is harmed, the architect is liable.

The minority view was followed in holding an architect liable for economic loss suffered by a tenant supermarket despite lack of privity. The architect had argued that there was no privity of contract since the architect had been employed by the building owner rather than by the tenant. The plaintiff alleged that the architect failed to diagnose the condition of subsoil, causing the supermarket floor to settle unevenly so that the premises became untenable. The architect's demurrer was overruled. The Wisconsin Supreme Court AFFIRMED.[8] A tenant may have a good cause of action against an architect

---

[5] 604 F Supp 1214 (EDNC 1985).
[6] 248 NY 339, 162 NE 99, *reargument denied*, 249 NY 511, 164 NE 564 (1928).
[7] F. Pollock, Torts 455 (11th ed).
[8] AE Inv Corp v Link Builders, Inc, 62 Wis 2d 479, 214 NW2d 764 (1974).

not in privity. In fact, "[p]rofessionalism is the very antithesis to irresponsibility to all interests other than those of an immediate employer."[9]

On the other hand, following the majority concept in *Palsgraf*, the Supreme Court of Louisiana reversed a trial court judgment for wrongful death on the ground that the architect had *no duty* to a worker who was scalded to death when a boiler exploded for lack of a thermostat or a relief valve. The contract documents required the thermostat and the pressure relief valve on the boiler, but the subcontractor mistakenly installed these devices on a hot-water storage tank; therefore, as soon as the boiler was fired, an explosion was inevitable. The architect's contract with the owner required that the architect furnish supervision to reasonably insure strict conformity with the contract documents, but the court held that this merely meant the architect had a duty to the owner to see that the overall job would comply with the contract documents before acceptance of the building. The architect had no duty to inspect the hot-water system during its installation in order to protect workers from a potential explosion.[10]

In a similar ruling, the Supreme Judicial Court of Massachusetts held that the designer of a septic system is under no duty to prevent an occupier of land from suffering mental anguish caused by a flood of sewage.[11]

In *Wicks v Milzoco Builderse, Inc*,[12] four homeowners brought an action alleging negligence, breach of implied and express warranties, and strict liability against a surveyor hired to set boundary lines of lots and lay plans for the sewage and drainage lines in a housing development. The court concluded that the *degree of foreseeability* that the surveyor's improper performance will lead to the plaintiffs' injuries determines whether there is a *duty* imputed to the surveyor. The court ruled that the homeowners' complaint stated a cause of action in negligence since the surveyor reasonably should have foreseen that faulty preparation of drainage plans could result in water damage to homes in the development.

In another case based on the issue of foreseeability, *Mears Park Holding Corp v Morse, Diesel, Inc*,[13] a lender, having foreclosed its deed of trust, filed an action against an architect who had been employed by a real estate developer who had gone into default. The lender alleged negligent performance by the architect of its duties to the developer. The court dismissed the action against the architect. AFFIRMED. Design professionals who breach their professional duties are liable in negligence only to those who foreseeably rely upon their

---

[9] *Id* 769.

[10] Day v National United States Radiator Corp, 241 La 288, 128 So 2d 660 (1961).

[11] McDonough v Whalen, 365 Mass 506, 313 NE2d 435 (1974).

[12] 291 Pa Super 345, 435 A2d 1260 (1981), *vacated on other grounds*, 503 Pa 614, 470 A2d 86 (1983).

[13] 427 NW2d 281 (Minn Ct App 1988).

professional services. The possibility that the architect's activities would have injured the lender following the developer's default was too remote to be foreseeable.

§1.03 Standard of Practice

The classic statement of the architect's standard of practice is found in *Coombs v Beede*.[14]

> The responsibility resting on an architect is essentially the same as that which rests upon the lawyer to his client, or upon the physician to his patient, or which rests upon any one to another where such person pretends to possess some skill and ability and some special employment, and offers his services to the public on account of his fitness to act in the line of business for which he may be employed. The undertaking of an architect implies that he possesses skill and ability, including taste, sufficient to enable him to perform the required services at least ordinarily and reasonably well; and that he will exercise and apply in the given case his skill and ability, his judgment and taste, reasonably and without neglect. But the undertaking does not imply or warrant a satisfactory result. It will be enough that any failure shall not be by the fault of the architect. There is no implied promise that miscalculations may not occur. An error of judgment is not necessarily evidence of a want of skill or care, for mistakes and miscalculations are incident to all the business of life.[15]

The court had instructed the jury that:

> [I]f Mr. Coombs was explicitly told, in addition to the other things, that the building he was designing must not cost over $2,500, that he was to make plans and specifications for a building to cost not over that, why, then, Mr. Coombs, the plaintiff, should have either made plans accordingly, or frankly told Mr. Beede that he could not do it, and declined to do it. If he undertook to make plans with that restriction made to him specifically, why, then he must do it before he can recover any pay.[16]

The Maine Supreme Judicial Court held that the instruction was misleading, since it punished plaintiff for what might have merely been an honest mistake or miscalculation. The ruling implied a guarantee or warranty.

---

[14] 89 Me 187, 36 A 104 (1896).
[15] *Id* 105.
[16] *Id* 107.

Although the parties could have made such a contract, there was no convincing evidence that they had done so.

Even if the defendant's version of the facts were true, and the plaintiff undertook to make plans for a house to cost no more than $2,500, if the plaintiff acted in good faith and exercised its skill and ability in an endeavor to bring about that result, that is all that could have been expected or required. If the house could have been built for less than $2,700 (as it was), it could hardly have been called a failure. Plaintiff was willing to make alterations to which the defendant would not consent. Therefore, the architect was entitled to recover the fee.

An architect is not expected to have perfect knowledge of all possible building conditions. In *Seiler v Ostarly*,[17] the heaving and settlement of a foundation slab caused extensive damage to a triplex. The cause was found to be *expansive clay*, which was unique to the particular job site. No other building in the area had exhibited similar phenomena. The court held that an architect hired merely to prepare line drawings was not obliged to make the type of extensive studies that would have been necessary to disclose the presence of expansive clay. The architect had inquired of the building department whether pilings were necessary and was informed that they were not; moreover, the architect had constructed apartments in the immediate neighborhood and encountered no problems. Therefore, the architect had utilized the skill and care customarily employed by architects.

In a suit for wrongful death, the administratrix of the estate of a junior high school student filed an action against a board of education alleging that the student died because of exposure to friable asbestos. The board filed a third-party action against the design architect. The architect's motion for summary judgment was GRANTED. The involvement of the architect in the project ended in 1959; therefore, the professional standard of care was to be measured as it existed at the end of 1959. In 1959, the use of asbestos in a school building was not inconsistent with professional standards. The architect could not reasonably have been expected to have known the deleterious effect of asbestos.[18]

In another suit for wrongful death, plaintiffs alleged that consulting engineers were responsible for defective design and construction which caused a body of water to form in a highway median. Plaintiffs contended that the standing water promoted the deterioration of a tree that fell onto the highway, striking the victim's automobile. HELD: the record did not contain evidence that the consulting engineers failed to follow accepted standards of interstate highway construction. The consulting engineers were not responsible for

---

[17] 525 So 2d 1207 (La Ct App 1988).
[18] Barnett v City of Yonkers, 731 F Supp 594 (SDNY 1990).

designating which trees presented a hazard and which should be removed. Further, the evidence failed to show that the ponding caused the tree to fall.[19]

In *Clark v City of Seward*,[20] the standard of practice was defined as follows:

> In performing professional services for a client, an engineer has the duty to have that degree of learning and skill ordinarily possessed by reputable engineers, practicing in the same or a similar locality and under similar circumstances.
>
> It is his further duty to use the care and skill ordinarily used in like cases by reputable members of his profession practicing in the same or a similar locality under similar circumstances, and to use reasonable diligence and his best judgment in the exercise of his professional skill and in the application of his learning, in an effort to accomplish the purpose for which he was employed.

HELD: there was no evidence to show that the engineer failed to adhere to the standard.

In *Daniel, Mann, Johnson & Mendenhall v Hilton Hotels*,[21] judgment was entered in favor of a hotel owner and against an engineer for a sum in excess of $1 million. The jury's verdict was not supported by expert testimony. HELD: the court properly instructed the jury that the surveyor's liability was founded upon an implied duty to perform in a workmanlike manner. In this case, performance was a matter of surveying from fixed monuments for the location of caissons (several of which were misplaced), and the issue was not so complicated as to require expert testimony. The conduct was within the common knowledge of laypersons, and it was not necessary to require the jury to measure the surveyor's conduct against the standard of an ordinarily skillful surveyor under similar circumstances. The case shows that liability may be predicated in part upon a finding that a surveyor breached an implied duty to perform in a workmanlike manner.

The order of priority that governs inconsistencies in a description of land is: (1) natural monuments or landmarks; (2) artificial monuments and established lines, marked or surveyed; (3) adjacent boundaries or lines of adjoining tracts; (4) "calls" for courses and distances; and (5) designation of quantity. It has been held that a surveyor should not rely on an extended fence line.[22]

An architect was not guilty of professional negligence when a veal feeding facility that it designed was shut down because the industrial waste level produced by the plant had an excessive biochemical oxygen demand level. The

---

[19] Bullard v State Dept of Transp & Dev, 413 So 2d 606 (La Ct App 1982).
[20] 659 P2d 1227 (Alaska 1983).
[21] 98 Nev 113, 642 P2d 1086 (1982).
[22] Spainhour v B. Aubrey Huffman & Assocs, 237 Va 340, 377 SE2d 615 (1989).

owner considered its feeding techniques to be a trade secret and did not disclose them to the architect. The architect may have had a duty to advise its client of industrial waste problems, but was not negligent for failing to warn the owner about potential problems created by a secret process. "An architect does not owe a fiduciary duty to its employers; rather, the architect's duties to its employer depend upon the agreement it has entered into with that employer."[23]

In *City of Urbandale v Frevert-Ramsey-Cobes, Architects-Engineers, Inc*,[24] architects designed an indoor pool and recreation center for a city. Moisture retention caused walls and the roof to deteriorate. A jury found both parties at fault. Total damages were $130,000; judgment was entered against the architects for $65,000. AFFIRMED. Questions of negligence, contributory negligence, and proximate cause are for the jury.

In *Weill Construction Co v Thibodeaux*,[25] an architect was employed by oral contract to design a skating rink. Drainage problems occurred. In an action by the owner against the architect, a judgment in favor of the architect was AFFIRMED. In the absence of an express contractual provision to the contrary, an architect is not liable for faulty or defective plans unless the problems are caused by neglect in exercising skill or care. Evidence supported the trial court's conclusion that the drainage design conformed with local community standards.

§1.04 —Not a Warrantor

"In the absence of an express contractual agreement to the contrary, an architect's obligation does not imply or guarantee a perfect plan. . . ."[26]

It has been held that an architect is not a warrantor of its plans and specifications and is not liable for construction faults due to defects in plans if the plans were supported by the standard of common knowledge upon such matters at the time. In *City of Mounds View v Walijarvi*,[27] the court stated:

> The undertaking of an architect implies that he possesses skill and ability, including taste, sufficient to enable him to perform the required services at least ordinarily and reasonably well, and that he will exercise and apply in a given case his skill and ability, his judgment and taste, reasonably and

---

[23] Strauss Veal Feeds, Inc v Mead & Hunt, Inc, 538 NE2d 299, 303 (Ind Ct App 1989), *transfer denied* (Feb 8, 1990).

[24] 435 NW2d 400 (Iowa Ct App 1988).

[25] 491 So 2d 166 (La Ct App 1986).

[26] Frischertz Elec Co v Housing Auth of New Orleans, 534 So 2d 1310, 1316 (La Ct App 1988), *writ denied*, 536 So 2d 1236 (La 1989) (architect did not provide contractor with information about conditions concealed within walls in city housing renovation project).

[27] 263 NW2d 420 (Minn 1978).

without neglect. But the undertaking does not imply or warrant a satisfactory result. . . . [A]doption of the city's implied warranty theory would in effect impose strict liability on architects for latent defects in the structures they design. . . . [However,] even in the present state of relative technological enlightenment, the keenest engineering minds can err in their most searching assessment of the natural factors which determine whether structural components will adequately serve their intended purpose. Until the random element is eliminated in the application of architectural sciences, we think it fair that the purchaser of the architect's services bear the risk of such unforeseeable difficulties.[28]

In *Lukowski v Vecta Educational Corp*,[29] the decedent fell from some bleachers at a basketball game. The widow claimed that the architect negligently failed to specify adequate lighting. HELD: the law provides that absent a special agreement, an architect does not imply or guarantee a perfect plan. The responsibility of an architect does not differ from that of a lawyer or physician. An architect that possesses requisite skill and knowledge, and that in the exercise thereof has used its best judgment, has done all the law requires. The architect is not a warrantor of its plans and specifications. The result may show a mistake or a defect, despite the exercise of the required reasonable skill.[30]

In *Ressler v Nielsen*,[31] a building designed by an architect was defective in several respects: water pipes installed in the ventilating system froze and burst; steam pipes laid under the cement floor in the basement sprung leaks; and radiators placed near a plate glass window caused a window to break. The court held that the architect is not a guarantor of plans and specifications in the absence of special agreement. "Liability rests only on unskillfulness or negligence, not upon mere errors of judgment."[32] Neither does an engineer warrant the accuracy of plans and specifications.[33]

Another example is found in *530 East 89 Corp v Unger*,[34] in which the contract provided: "We will make every effort to satisfy all requirements.

---

[28] *Id* 423-24. *See also* Paxton v Alameda County, 119 Cal App 2d 393, 259 P2d 934 (1953); Bayshore Dev Co v Bonfoey, 75 Fla 445, 78 So 507 (1918); Pittman Constr Co v City of New Orleans, 178 So 2d 312 (La Ct App), *appeal denied*, 248 La 434, 178 So 2d 274 (1965). *See generally* Annotation, 25 ALR2d 1085 (1952).

[29] 401 NE2d 781 (Ind Ct App 1980).

[30] *Id* 786.

[31] 76 NW2d 157 (ND 1956).

[32] *Id* 162.

[33] Bates & Rogers Constr v North Shore Sanitary Dist, 92 Ill App 3d 90, 414 NE2d 1274 (1980), *aff'd*, 109 Ill 2d 225, 486 NE2d 902 (1985).

[34] 54 AD2d 848, 388 NYS2d 284 (1976), *aff'd*, 43 NY2d 776, 373 NE2d 276, 402 NYS2d 382 (1977).

Under no circumstances do we imply a guarantee." HELD: the city building department's refusal to approve the plans did not establish a cause of action against the architect, where the contract specifically negated any guarantee.[35]

Where an architect's plans are grossly defective, and the defects cannot easily be remedied, the architect is entitled to no compensation for its services.[36]

The mere fact that an injury, even a fatal injury, has occurred does not establish the presence of a design defect. In *McDermott v TENDUM Constructors*,[37] a mail handler at the New York Bulk and Foreign Mail Center was killed while using an extendable conveyor that had been rolled into the trailer portion of a tractor-trailer. Summary judgment for the defendant architectural firm was AFFIRMED. The architectural firm was fully responsible for planning and designing all aspects of the facility; nevertheless, the plaintiff failed to make a prima facie case showing that there was any design defect in the extendable conveyor which the architectural firm designed.

In *Friendship Heights Associates v Vlastimil Koubek AIA*,[38] the owner brought an action against the architect, contractor, painting subcontractor, and paint manufacturer when painted concrete surfaces began to peel badly within three months of application. The first coat of paint peeled after the second coat had been applied. The second coat adhered to the first coat and also to the concrete in instances where it was applied directly to the concrete instead of to the first coat. It was apparent that something about the second coat caused the first coat to peel. The owner, however, was unable to show why the peeling occurred.

The architect testified that, before specifying paint, he visually inspected the premises and determined what type of paint had been applied previously. The architect also testified that he had consulted with the paint manufacturer before specifying the paint, but conflicting testimony strongly indicated that this consultation had not occurred until after the repainted surfaces began to peel. HELD: the owner demonstrated that the architect breached professional duty, but the owner did not demonstrate that the breach caused the damage. "An architect does not, by agreeing simply to perform work for a client, guarantee the ultimate results, only that he or she will perform with the requisite degree of care and skill."[39]

---

[35] *See also* American Sur Co v San Antonio Loan & Trust Co, 44 Tex Civ App 367, 98 SW 387 (1906).

[36] Dunne v Robinson, 53 Misc 545, 103 NYS 878 (1907) (plans did not include dimensions; figures and scales were incorrect; other unskillful omissions and inaccuracies made the plans unusable).

[37] 211 NJ Super 196, 511 A2d 690 (1986).

[38] 573 F Supp 100 (D Md 1983), *revd on issue of expert witness*, 785 F2d 1154 (4th Cir 1986). *See* §1.19.

[39] *Id* 105.

§1.05 —Reasonable Skill and Knowledge

In a professional negligence action, the plaintiff "bears the burden of presenting evidence which establishes the applicable standard of care, demonstrating that this standard has been violated, and then developing a causal relationship between the violation and the harm complained of."[40]

A surveyor's standard of care is "that degree of care and skill which a surveyor of ordinary skill and prudence would exercise under the same or similar circumstances."[41] The standard of practice for surveyors is a *national standard*, not a local or regional one. (The surveyor was negligent for failing to ascertain the use to which the survey was to be put, and negligent in certifying that he had carefully surveyed the property when he had not actually done so.)

Contrast the rule of an early case, *Hubert v Aitken*,[42] in which the court stated that the test of an architect's competence was the ability to apply reasonable skill and knowledge to all of the elements of the project under construction.

> The architect who undertakes to construct a house that is to be heated by steam is groping in the dark unless he knows how large a chimney is required. It is as necessary that the architect should know what is needed to make the steam heating apparatus serviceable, as it is that he should know how sewer gas is to be kept out of the house. No one would contend that at this day an architect could shelter himself behind the plumber, and excuse his ignorance of the ordinary appliances for sanitary ventilation by saying that he was not an expert in the trade of plumbing. He is an expert in carpentry, in cements, in mortar, in the strength of materials, in the art of constructing the walls, the floors, the staircases, the roofs, and is in duty bound to possess reasonable skill and knowledge as to all these things; and when, in the progress of civilization, new conveniences are introduced into our homes, and become, not curious novelties, but the customary means of securing the comfort of the unpretentious citizen, why should not the architect be expected to possess the technical learning respecting them that is exacted of him with respect to other and older branches of his professional studies? It is not asking too much of a man who assumes that he is competent to build a house at a cost of more than $100,000, and to arrange that it shall be heated by steam, to insist that he shall know how to proportion his chimney to the boiler. It is not enough for him to say, "I asked the steamfitter," and then throw the consequences of an error that may be made upon the employer who engages him, relying upon his skill. Responsibility cannot be shifted in that way.

---

[40] Bell v Jones, 523 A2d 982, 987 (DC 1986).
[41] *Id* 987.
[42] 15 Daly 237, 2 NYS 711 (CP 1888), *affd*, 123 NY 655, 25 NE 954 (1890).

The court did not refer to the terms *average, ordinary*. The court imposed a much higher and more intimidating standard: that of expert, reasonable skill and knowledge in all trades, even down to the proportioning of chimneys to boilers.

In *AF Blair Co v Mason*,[43] the court concluded that architects and engineers must exercise that degree of professional care and skill which is customarily employed by others of the same profession, located in the same general area. Negligence was not established because no evidence was introduced to show the degree of professional care and skill that prevailed in the community. The dissenting opinion criticized the majority's reliance upon the *locality rule*, suggesting that a nationwide standard now applies to all professions.

§1.06 —Conventional Standard Criticized

The conventional standard of care in architect malpractice cases has been criticized by Professor Curran:[44] Why should the professional be held only to average conduct, when the man in the street is held to average *prudent* conduct? Why too should the professional be given the additional benefit of the *locality* criterion, which holds the professional only to the standard of practice which prevails in his or her community? Professor Curran notes that an unfortunate consequence of the *average, ordinary* test is the fact that a jury, unaided, cannot judge the standard. Only a professional can. Questions of professional negligence are a contest of expert witnesses, with the jury judging the credibility of the expert witnesses rather than the conduct of the architect. For example, in a Utah case, the defendant's witnesses testified that it was good practice to use a two-inch coupling to attach a 12-pound valve to the bottom of a natural gas compressor tank. The plaintiff's witnesses testified that it was not good practice. Judgment for the plaintiff was AFFIRMED. The jury has the prerogative to believe which witnesses they choose.[45]

Justice Cardozo, discussing negligence, said "standards of prudent conduct are declared at times by courts, but they are taken over from the facts of life."[46] In judging professionals according to *average, ordinary* conduct, the courts have departed from Cardozo's facts of life. The person in the street held to a standard of average prudent conduct justly and universally expects a professional to be held to a higher standard. The professional is educated for it (often at public expense) and paid for it (at the client's expense).

---

[43] 406 So 2d 6 (La Ct App 1981), *cert denied*, 410 So 2d 1132 (La 1982).
[44] Curran, *Professional Negligence—Some Current Comments*, 12 Vand L Rev 535 (1959).
[45] Uinta Pipeline Corp v White Superior Co, 546 P2d 885 (Utah 1976).
[46] Pokora v Wabash Ry, 292 US 98, 104 (1934).

The courts have probably accepted average, ordinary conduct upon the consideration that it would be anomalous if the majority of practitioners could be culpable. However, courts should not exclude this possibility. No profession should be permitted to set itself above the law and to define its own canons of liability. Thus it was laid down by Judge Learned Hand in *The TJ Hooper*.[47]

> There are, no doubt, cases where courts seem to make the general practice of the calling the standard of proper diligence. . . . Indeed in most cases reasonable prudence is in fact common prudence, but strictly it is never its measure; a whole calling may have unduly lagged in the adoption of new and available devices. It never may set its own tests, however persuasive be its usages. Courts must in the end say what is required; there are precautions so imperative that even their universal disregard will not excuse their omission.[48]

By the same token, the fact that the conduct of a professional is *below average* should not of itself constitute malpractice. It is possible for a whole profession to become unreasonably *prudent* to the public detriment, as, for example, to require unnecessary or harmful laboratory tests, or to refuse to design a building because of a remote or insubstantial risk of earthquake. The jury should be permitted to find conduct prudent although it is below average, and negligent although it is above average.

In *Henry v Britt*,[49] an engineer designed a swimming pool drain in violation of state board of health rules and regulations. HELD: such design was negligent despite expert testimony that the engineer exercised the same skill and diligence as other engineers of ordinary skill and training in the community.

§1.07 —Conventional Standard Applied

Courts do, indeed, make their own judgments of professional standards in architect malpractice cases without expert testimony. In *Martin v Board of Education*,[50] an architect designed a culvert to carry 100 cubic feet per second more storm water than the peak runoff from any rainstorm during the preceding 73 years. A freak storm on August 10, 1963, overloaded the culvert, flooding a nearby residence. The court affirmed a summary judgment for the architect, holding that there was no question of fact to be determined by a jury since the injury to the plaintiff was not foreseeable. The decision was not

---

[47] 60 F2d 737 (2d Cir 1932).
[48] *Id* 740.
[49] 220 So 2d 917 (Fla Dist Ct App), *cert denied*, 229 So 2d 867 (Fla 1969).
[50] 79 NM 636, 447 P2d 516 (1968).

predicated upon a weighing of expert testimony as to average conduct, but on the court's own conclusion as to the negligence of the architect.

Generally, an architect is not an insurer and is not required to prepare perfect plans. If hired to supervise construction, the architect is only required to use reasonable care and diligence in seeing that the work is properly done.[51] However, the court noted in *Kleb v Wendling* that: "It is the architect's duty, when superintending or overseeing the construction of a building, to prevent gross carelessness or imperfect construction. Mere detection of defective workmanship does not relieve him of a duty to prevent it."[52]

A lenient standard of practice was applied in a case where the architect designed a retaining wall to support an excavation adjoining federal property. The retaining wall collapsed, damaging the government sidewalk. The government filed an action against the owner. The court held that the owner could not be liable for any negligence of the architect, since the architect was not negligent. The architect examined similar projects in other parts of the city and consulted with other architects about the design. Therefore, although the architect's judgment as to the type and size of wall required might have been defective, it was not negligent. Since the architect was not negligent, the landowner was not responsible.[53]

In a similar case, an engineer designed a foundation piling for a city incinerator project. Because of serious, latent, unstable soil conditions, the piles were displaced. The engineer then prepared new plans for remedial pile work and employed a floating concrete slab for foundation purposes. The contractor warned that the slab might settle, but the engineer ignored the warning and proceeded with the plan. The slab did settle, causing damage. All the expert testimony asserted that the engineer met the required standard since the degree of settlement was unpredictable. HELD: the engineer was not guilty of professional negligence.[54]

In a New York case, an architect certified interim payments to a masonry contractor at a time when the height and appearance of the windows and the stoop were defective and the masonry contractor had failed to follow the plans. A referee held that the architect had devoted the customary amount of time and care to supervision of the project and that variations from the plans were not caused by its negligence. This decision was upheld by the court of appeals, which stated that the architect fully performed the duty and was entitled to compensation.[55]

---

[51] Kortz v Kimberlin, 158 Ky 566, 165 SW 654 (1914).

[52] Kleb v Wendling, 67 Ill App 3d 1016, 385 NE2d 346 (1978).

[53] United States v Peachy, 36 F 160 (D Ohio 1888).

[54] Pittman Constr Co v City of New Orleans, 178 So 2d 312 (La Ct App), *appeal denied*, 248 La 434, 179 So 2d 274 (1965).

[55] Petersen v Rawson, 34 NY 370 (1866), *revd*, 15 NY Sup Ct 234 (1857).

16   LIABILITY FOR NEGLIGENCE

In *Plant v R.L. Reid, Inc*,[56] the widow of a deceased employee filed an action against an engineer for failure to specify safety devices. Plaintiff claimed that the engineer was negligent in "failing to specify a guard to shield the nip point of the head pulley in plans and specifications for modifying the bulk loading facility at the State Dock."[57] HELD: "If the standards of the profession in 1964 required engineers to include safety features in all plans and specifications and if to meet established safety standards a guard was required, Reid could be found to have breached its duty in not specifying such guards."[58]

In *Weston v New Bethel Missionary Baptist Church*,[59] the court, quoting *Wells v City of Vancouver*,[60] stated: "An engineer or designer is guilty of negligence if he fails to apply the skill and learning which is required of similarly situated engineers or designers in his community."[61]

§1.08   —Required Duty

Engineer's Duty

An engineer's duty is to exercise such care, skill, and diligence as people engaged in the engineering profession ordinarily exercise under like circumstances. However, the engineer is not an insurer that the contractor will perform properly in all respects. It merely has a duty to exercise reasonable care to see that the contractor follows the contract documents.

An engineer, by contract, was required to inspect and supervise work during the course of construction of a bridge project. After completion, cracks appeared in two walls and it was revealed that pilings which were intended to carry a load of 15 tons would only support 7 to 13 tons. The engineer had inspected the project two or three times daily. The engineer tried to have the contractor keep records of the driving of all the piles, and although it was not present when the defective pilings were driven, it was assured by artisans who had been reliable in the past that they had been driven to the required depth. This evidence was sufficient to support a verdict which allowed the engineer to recover its fee.[62]

In *National Housing Industry v E.L. Jones Development Co*,[63] a subdivider employed an engineer to prepare subdivision plans. The subdivider showed the plans to the plaintiff, who later purchased the land for development. The

---

[56] 365 So 2d 305 (Ala 1978).
[57] *Id* 305.
[58] *Id* 305.
[59] 23 Wash App 747, 598 P2d 411 (1978).
[60] 77 Wash 2d 800, 467 P2d 292 (1970).
[61] 23 Wash App at 752, 598 P2d at 414.
[62] Cowles v City of Minneapolis, 128 Minn 452, 151 NW 184 (1915).
[63] 118 Ariz 374, 576 P2d 1374 (1978).

plaintiff then discovered that development would require importing 20,000 cubic yards of fill, and that an adjoining property owner would not permit surface drainage across the adjoining land. HELD: based on expert testimony, the standard of care in Phoenix did not require a subdivision engineer to include cut and fill estimates as a standard part of services. The engineer met the standard of care in preparing the subdivision plans and was not liable for the additional expense of importing fill.

The Supreme Court of Iowa has held that an engineer employed by a city to design a city sewer project owed no duty to property owners adjoining the sewer's right-of-way. When the contractor excavated for the sewer without providing for support of the adjoining property owner's land, the adjoining land settled and damage to a building resulted. The engineer's contract with the city made the engineer responsible for any apparent defects or deficiencies in the contractor's completed work. However, the purpose of this provision was to protect the city rather than adjoining landowners. The contract also provided for on-site review of the work, but this was to protect the city from substandard work and not to protect the public from potential damage. The contractor had the power to control construction methods; the engineer merely had quality control of the contractor's completed work. The engineer did not owe a duty of care to others and was not responsible for the contractor's negligence. Judgment for the property owner and against the engineer for 30 per cent of damages was REVERSED. (The court affirmed an award of compensatory and punitive damages against the contractor: the contractor had excavated to a depth below the footings of the neighbor's building without providing sheeting that could have prevented the damage.)[64]

Architect's Duty

In a case in which a building settled after construction, a jury found that the plaintiff architect was entitled to recover a fee. The Oregon Supreme Court AFFIRMED,[65] holding that an architect is held to act with reasonable diligence in performing its duties, and if the architect meets this standard of care, it is not liable for damages if the results of the work are unsatisfactory. There was sufficient evidence to support the jury's verdict. The architect did not guarantee satisfactory results.

In *MacIntyre v Green's Pool Service, Inc*,[66] the owner alleged that the architect did not give proper advice on the selection of a general contractor, did not advise the owner properly as to when and how progress payments should be made, and

---

[64] Shepard Components, Inc v Brice Petrides-Donohue & Assocs, 473 NW2d 612 (Iowa 1991).
[65] White v Pallay, 119 Or 97, 247 P 316 (1926).
[66] 347 So 2d 1081 (Fla Dist Ct App 1977).

did not advise the owner to record a notice of commencement of work of improvement. As a result, the contractor abandoned the job and many subcontractors and material suppliers recorded mechanics liens. HELD: there was no evidence that these obligations "fall within the duties ordinarily assumed or placed upon an architect by custom and practice."[67]

The Virginia Supreme Court has found that the standard of practice requires an architect to know the setback requirement of the local building code.[68] It has been held that an architect complies with the requisite standard for inspecting a construction project by visiting the job twice daily, once before the beginning of the day's work and again after the day's work is complete.[69] A number of cases have recognized that where a project is unusual or complex, the architect may not be liable even if the results are unsatisfactory.[70]

In *Travelers Indemnity Co v Ewing, Cole, Erdman & Eubank*,[71] the architect contracted with Rutgers University to serve as executive architect for the construction of a student dormitory and to provide all necessary architectural and engineering services. The dormitory was to consist of modules manufactured at the contractor's plant. After less than a year of performance, the contractor filed a petition in bankruptcy. The contractor's surety finished the job, as required by the performance bond, and filed an action against the architect as subrogee of the owner's cause of action.

The architect made periodic visits to the factory and executed certificates authorizing progress payments. When the trustee in bankruptcy claimed title to all of the materials and work in progress, the surety had to arrange for another contractor to complete the project. The surety alleged that the architect should have advised the owner that it could have protected itself against the possibility of bankruptcy by employing such options as field warehousing or bonded warehouses. The trial court entered judgment for the surety. REVERSED. (1) The question of whether the defendant measured up to the standard of care expected of reasonably prudent architects is a mixed question of law and fact and is, therefore, subject to review on a plenary basis. (2) Although it is true that an architect may be liable for failing to provide information to the client, the omitted information must be within the special knowledge of design professionals. (3) The unsupported opinion of the plaintiff's expert witness is insufficient to impose on architects "a duty to inform their clients about matters

---

[67] *Id* 1083.

[68] Bott v Moser, 175 Va 11, 7 SE2d 217 (1940).

[69] Chiaverini v Vail, 61 RI 117, 200 A 462 (1938).

[70] *See, e.g.*, Bonadiman-McCain, Inc v Snow, 183 Cal App 2d 58, 6 Cal Rptr 52 (1960) (dirt on subdivision grading project expanded instead of shrinking; client "lost" 1 out of 33 lots); Surf Realty Corp v Standing, 195 Va 431, 78 SE2d 901 (1953) (complicated sliding steel ballroom roof; cantilevered tracks).

[71] 711 F2d 14 (3d Cir 1983), *cert denied*, 464 US 1041 (1984).

that have yet to be recognized as within the special expertise of design professionals."[72] The case does not involve an unsophisticated and helpless consumer. The owner was represented by a deputy attorney general who had extensive experience in construction. The authority never indicated that it expected the architect to point out potential legal pitfalls in the proposed arrangement, and it is far from clear that an architect would believe that it had a duty to inform the legal counsel of its client about such matters. "It seems an inefficient allocation of professional responsibilities to hold architects liable for not alerting lawyers to the legal ramifications of the bankruptcy of a contractor."[73]

Contract Standards

The terms of a contract between an architect and an owner may impose their own standard of practice. In a Louisiana case, an engineering firm employed an incompetent as resident engineer. As a result, there were hundreds of defects in the project. The court stated that the "skill usually exercised by others of its profession in the same general area" standard did not apply. The duties imposed by the terms of the contract applied.[74]

§1.09 No Insurer

An architect does not guarantee a satisfactory result; it is not an insurer. This concept is of no use in producing a rational analysis of liability. It is a makeweight comment added to the opinion after the court has decided that the architect should win.[75]

Although, in one case, the architect instructed a worker to observe obvious safety precautions, this did not transform the architect's role from "one as an on-site coordinator to one as an on-site baby-sitter."[76]

In *Three Affiliated Tribes of the Fort Berthold Reservation v Wold Engineering PC*,[77] a water system froze. HELD: the design engineer did not guarantee satisfactory results, only that it would exercise that degree of skill and care exercised in the profession. The design of the system met that standard of care.

In *Gilchrist v City of Troy*,[78] parents brought an action against an architect for injuries sustained by a child when struck by a hockey puck at a city arena. The

---

[72] *Id* 18.

[73] *Id* 18.

[74] Town of Winnsboro v Barnard & Burke, Inc, 294 So 2d 867, 877 (La Ct App 1974).

[75] *See, e.g.*, Cowles v City of Minneapolis, 128 Minn 452, 151 NW 184 (1915).

[76] Teitge v Remy Constr Co, 526 NE2d 1008, 1041 (Ind Ct App 1988).

[77] 419 NW2d 920 (ND 1988).

[78] 113 AD2d 271, 495 NYS2d 781 (1985), *affd*, 67 NY2d 1034, 494 NE2d 1382, 503 NYS2d 717 (1986).

trial court denied the architect's motion for summary judgment. REVERSED. Plaintiff alleged that failure to provide screening along the side of the arena where the child was watching an amateur hockey game constituted negligence. HELD: the duty to protect spectators is discharged by providing screening behind the goals, as long as the screening is sufficient to provide protection for as many spectators as may want to seek shelter.

Architect Liable

It seems that in some cases the courts do make the architect an insurer of satisfactory results. In one case, a contractor attached one end of a beam to a stud partition and floored it over before the architect could inspect it. This violated the building code and ultimately caused the floor to settle. The architect was liable to the owner despite concealment of the defect by the construction company.[79] Similarly, in a California case, the architect spotted an inferior grade of roof sheathing when it was delivered to the job site and condemned it. By the time of the architect's next visit, the contractor had installed, tarred, and graveled the sheathing. A worker was injured when he broke through the roof. The court held that a jury could have found that the architect was negligent for failure to make another inspection before the defect was concealed.[80]

However, where an electrician slipped and fell on an icy ramp on a job site, the appellate court AFFIRMED a dismissal due to insufficient evidence, stating that the architect's only duty in the absence of privity was to refrain from active negligence.[81]

Liability Limited by Fee Size

One court looked to the amount of the fee and the method of payment to determine whether the defendant was an insurer. The plaintiff was considering the purchase of two lots and employed the defendant at $10 per hour to drill test holes to check for the presence of fill. Defendant reported that the depth of fill was 12 to 16 inches, when in fact it was 3 to 6 feet. The court held that the plaintiff had a good cause of action for deceit and negligence, but not for breach of warranty or strict liability. The defendant was selling service and not insurance. Thus, the measure of damage was the difference between the value of the lots and what plaintiff paid for them, rather than the excess foundation cost.[82]

---

[79] Straus v Buchman, 96 AD 270, 89 NYS 226 (1904), *affd*, 184 NY 545, 76 NE 1109 (1906).

[80] Paxton v Alameda County, 119 Cal App 2d 393, 259 P2d 934 (1953).

[81] Hamill v Foster-Lipkins Corp, 41 AD2d 361, 342 NYS2d 539 (1973).

[82] Gagne v Bertran, 43 Cal 2d 481, 275 P2d 15 (1954). *Accord* Morrison-Maierle, Inc v Selsco, 186 Mont 180, 606 P2d 1085 (1980); Gravely v Providence Partnership, 549 F2d 958

Unlike a manufacturer, an architect does not impliedly guarantee that its work is fit for its intended purpose; rather, the architect impliedly promises to exercise that standard of reasonable care required of members of the profession.[83]

§1.10 Failure to Warn

A claim against an architect may be phrased as *failure to warn*, which some lawyers have imprecisely labeled a *new tort*. The correct analysis is that failure to warn of danger is a fact to be considered in determining whether the conduct of the architect was negligent. If an architect owes a duty of care to some person, then that duty might be discharged by preventing the danger from occurring, by correcting a dangerous condition once it has occurred, or by warning or ordering the person to stay away from the area of danger.

A worker who was injured when a ditch collapsed alleged that the architect had a duty to warn. HELD: the architect did not retain any control over the construction methods employed by the contractor and therefore owed no duty to the contractor's employees.[84]

In a Washington case, workers were injured when a form broke spilling them into the Columbia River along with 200 tons of wet concrete. They alleged failure to adequately supervise construction, failure to halt construction when a hazardous condition existed, and failure to warn. The appellate court upheld a verdict for the plaintiffs on the ground that the architect negligently failed to comply with a statute which required supervision in checking of concrete forms to prevent collapse.[85]

Failure to warn was rejected as a premise of liability where the *architect* claimed that the manufacturer of roofing material had a duty to warn against failure of material. The manufacturer had approved the original roof design and represented that its product would be waterproof; thereafter, the architect changed the design and notified the manufacturer, which failed to warn against the change. The court said that the architect relied on its own professional judgment in changing the design of the roof system, and that no duty to warn arises unless a product is unreasonably dangerous.[86]

(4th Cir 1977) (hotel guest injured in fall on spiral staircase); Ryan v Morgan Spear Assocs, 546 SW2d 678 (Tex Civ App 1977) (defective soils analysis and foundation).

[83] Klein v Catalano, 386 Mass 701, 437 NE2d 514 (1982).

[84] Seeney v Dover Country Club Apartments, Inc, 318 A2d 619 (Del Super Ct 1974).

[85] Loyland v Stone & Webster Engg Corp, 9 Wash App 682, 514 P2d 184 (1973), *review denied*, 83 Wash 2d 1007 (1974).

[86] Standhardt v Flintkote Co, 84 NM 796, 508 P2d 1283 (1973).

Failure to warn was accepted as a potential cause of action against a design engineer in *Russell v GAF Corp.*[87] The plaintiff worker was injured after stepping on a sheet of corrugated asbestos cement that was being installed as a ceiling in the Lincoln Memorial. The sheet shattered, and the worker fell through. Evidence showed that the manufacturer recommended that planks or chicken ladders be used during installation to distribute weight, but this had not been done. A safety expert testified that it was important to warn workers of the danger of stepping on the material, since it was very brittle and a small crack or flaw could reduce its strength to the breaking point. The expert pointed out a section of the National Building Code (BOCA) which provides that the architect has a responsibility to identify in the drawings all specified prefabricated materials and their physical properties. The expert then gave the opinion that the designer should have transferred the information in the manufacturer's instructions to the drawings.

The court held that this testimony was sufficient to establish a question for the jury and, on that ground, REVERSED the trial court which had directed a verdict for defendant.

A failure to warn claim was made against a registered land surveyor who was employed by a property seller to perform a high water and percolation test. The test was properly made, and a report supplied to the seller. The seller then sold lots to purchasers, without revealing that the percolation test report showed that fill would be required before a septic system could be installed. The purchasers brought suit against the surveyor, alleging fraud and violation of the Massachusetts Consumer Protection Act.[88] Plaintiffs alleged that the surveyor had a duty to warn them about prospective problems with their lots. The superior court dismissed the suit and was AFFIRMED. Nondisclosure does not constitute fraud where there is no duty to speak. The surveyor did not participate in the negotiations of the sales, nor did he make any misrepresentations.[89]

In *Francisco v Manson, Jackson & Kane, Inc*,[90] a 10-year-old boy died from a fall off a diving board at a school swimming facility. A jury verdict in favor of the parents against the architect was AFFIRMED. The architect had a duty to warn the school district of risks involved in using the diving board. Intervening negligence of the school district did not relieve the architect of liability.

The California Attorney General opines that a registered engineer who is retained to investigate the integrity of a building and determines that there is an imminent risk of serious injury to the occupants has a duty to warn the

---

[87] 422 A2d 989 (DC 1980).
[88] Mass Gen Laws Ann ch 93A (West).
[89] Nei v Boston Survey Consultants, Inc, 388 Mass 320, 446 NE2d 681 (1983).
[90] 145 Mich App 255, 377 NW2d 313 (1985), *appeal denied* (Jan 28, 1986).

occupants of the danger. The engineer should discharge this duty even if the owner requests that the engineer treat the results of the investigation as confidential.[91]

§1.11 Intrinsically Dangerous

The courts sometimes predicate liability on a theory that a design is *intrinsically dangerous*. This basis of liability developed as an exception to the now abandoned rule that an architect owed no duty to protect a person from harm after the completion and acceptance of a structure in the absence of privity of contract.[92]

Courts have also stated that an owner is not liable for the acts of the architect which cause injury to a third party unless the project is intrinsically dangerous. The architect is an independent contractor, and the construction of an ordinary building is not intrinsically dangerous.[93]

It has been argued in a dissenting opinion that a supervising engineer should be liable for injuries suffered from a cave-in caused by inadequate shoring, since trenching is an inherently dangerous activity, and the contractor is not motivated to take adequate precautions for the safety of employees, because the contractor's liability is limited to the payments prescribed under the workers' compensation statutes.[94]

§1.12 Nondelegable Duty

Is an architect liable for failure to protect against a risk created by an independent contractor? The answer is *yes*. Indeed, most cases dealing with liability arising out of the architect's supervision of construction will be found to be of this nature. Under circumstances where a peculiar risk of harm exists, or where a statute requires the architect to provide safeguards, it has been held that duty to protect the plaintiff is nondelegable.[95]

In an Oregon case, a pedestrian was injured when a masonry wall was blown down by high wind, landing on the pedestrian. The structural engineer who

---

[91] Cal Atty Gen Op, 85 Op 208 (1985).

[92] Hunt v Star Photo Finishing Co, 115 Ga App 1, 153 SE2d 602 (1967) (remote tenant versus architect; roof collapse).

[93] White v Green, 82 SW 329 (Tex Civ App 1904) (brick building collapsed, damaging plaintiff's adjoining property).

[94] Wells v Stanley J. Thill & Assocs, 153 Mont 28, 452 P2d 1015 (1969).

[95] Stilson v Moulton-Niguel Water Dist, 21 Cal App 3d 928, 98 Cal Rptr 914 (1971) (peculiar risk of harm to workers); Johnson v Salem Title Co, 246 Or 409, 425 P2d 519 (1967) (statutory duty imposed by building code which provided "buildings and structures . . . shall be designed . . . to resist wind pressure"); Restatement (Second) of Torts §424 (1968).

24   LIABILITY FOR NEGLIGENCE

had designed the wall was not a defendant. The court held that the architect was liable because the wall did not comply with the requirements of the uniform building code. Since the building code was enacted for the protection and safety of the public, the architect was liable for the error of the structural engineer, even though the engineer was an independent contractor. The fact that the architect did all it reasonably could (by employing a competent engineer) was no defense. That is the essence of the doctrine of *nondelegable duty*.[96]

In *Mayor & City Council v Clark-Dietz & Associates-Engineers*,[97] a city filed an action against an architect/engineer and a contractor for damages that occurred when a protected levee surrounding the site of a wastewater treatment plant collapsed. The architect/engineer defended on the basis of the contractor's express warranty. HELD: an architect's duty to exercise professional engineering judgment is nondelegable; therefore, the owner's reliance on information supplied by specialty firms or other third parties was legally irrelevant.

§1.13   Negligent Misrepresentation

An architect may be liable for negligent misrepresentation in the preparation of contract documents, drawings, surveys, and test data, and in the placement of survey monuments.

In *Rozny v Marnul*,[98] a survey plat contained an express representation: "This plat of survey carries our absolute guarantee for accuracy." The survey was prepared for S & S Builders, which sold to Nash, who sold to the plaintiffs. The plaintiffs relied on the survey, and as a result, their driveway and garage encroached. The court held that the plaintiffs may recover for misrepresentation despite lack of privity since: the surveyor voluntarily made the guarantee; the surveyor knew the plat would be relied upon by others; the potential liability was restricted to a relatively small group of practitioners; an innocent purchaser should not carry the burden of the surveyor's professional mistakes; and this holding would promote caution among surveyors.

Courts have held that mere nondisclosure is not sufficient to constitute misrepresentation. In *Nei v Boston Survey Consultants, Inc*,[99] the surveyor had no relationship to lot purchasers and therefore had no duty to warn them about potential problems created by a high water table.

An early case, *Niver v Nash*,[100] related misrepresentation to warranty. A counterclaim alleged that the architect represented that it was competent and

---

[96] Johnson v Salem Title Co, 246 Or 409, 425 P2d 519 (1967).
[97] 550 F Supp 610 (ND Miss 1982), *appeal denied*, 702 F2d 67 (5th Cir 1983).
[98] 43 Ill 2d 54, 250 NE2d 656 (1969).
[99] 388 Mass 320, 446 NE2d 681 (1983).
[100] 7 Wash 558, 35 P 380 (1893).

that the building would be first class and well lighted, that the representations were untrue, and that the building was neither well lighted nor first class. HELD: the representations amounted to a warranty. The architect was an expert, representing itself as fully qualified to judge such matters, whereas the plaintiff had no such qualifications. The counterclaim stated a good cause of action.

In contrast, in *Rosos Litho Supply Corp v Hansen*,[101] the court stated that the Uniform Commercial Code is inapplicable to the provision of professional services; therefore, the owner had no warranty remedy against its architect for economic loss. The court went on to say that there is no other implied common law or statutory warranty applicable to an architect's services.

In a case that is of doubtful authority under current legal thinking, a court held that there can be no liability for negligent misrepresentation in the absence of privity of contract.[102] In an opposite holding, a general contractor alleged that an engineer, employed by a landowner, misplaced offset stakes upon which the contractor relied. The court held that the contractor, despite lack of privity, could recover either on a theory of intentional misrepresentation, on a theory of reckless misrepresentation, or on a theory of negligence.[103]

In *Robert & Co v Rhodes-Haverty Partnership*,[104] an engineer issued a report about the condition of a building. The report allegedly contained misrepresentations that could be used to persuade prospective purchasers to buy the building. The trial court held that the engineer was liable only to the party to whom the report was made. REVERSED. Lack of privity does not shield an engineer from liability to third persons whom the engineer should foresee may rely on a report.

It has been held that a statement of opinion will not support a cause of action for negligent misrepresentation. In *Jones v McGuffin*,[105] homebuyers were shown a 13-year-old house with some cracks in the ceiling and walls. The buyers instructed a real estate broker to obtain a structural engineering report. The engineer issued a letter report to the broker: "The house appeared to be

---

[101] 123 Ill App 3d 290, 462 NE2d 566 (1984).

[102] Bilich v Barnett, 103 Cal App 2d Supp 921, 229 P2d 492 (1951) (sewer contractor versus engineer employed by property owner to prepare grade sheets which were inaccurate).

[103] Craig v Everett M. Brooks Co, 351 Mass 497, 222 NE2d 752 (1967). *See also* Roberts v Karr, 178 Cal App 2d 535, 3 Cal Rptr 98 (1960) (surveyor reported 51,000 cubic yards of excess dirt, actually only 15,802 cubic yards; HELD: plaintiff had a good cause of action for negligence and deceit); Dysart-Cook Mule Co v Reed & Heckenlively, 114 Mo App 296, 89 SW 591 (1905) (plaintiff alleged that architect negligently designed and supervised construction of a mule barn, then asked for an instruction that architect could be liable for misrepresentation in preparing plans for a building different from that contracted for; HELD: no evidence of misrepresentation; therefore, the instruction was properly refused); Harbor Mechanical, Inc v Arizona Elec Power Co-op, Inc, 496 F Supp 681 (D Ariz 1980).

[104] 250 Ga 680, 300 SE2d 503 (1983).

[105] 454 So 2d 509 (Ala 1984).

in excellent structural condition except for some minor cracks in the south end ... I could find no evidence that these cracks were caused by foundation movement.... In my opinion, these cracks do not represent any major problem and are of little consequence."

After they had taken possession, the owners immediately noticed that the cracks had widened considerably and that new cracks had appeared. It was determined that the foundation had moved and the *fix* required underpinning with 24 piers at a cost of $12,300. The jury brought in a verdict in favor of the owners and against the engineer and broker for $20,000, including mental anguish and cost of repair. REVERSED. Alabama Code §6-5-101 (1975) defines *legal fraud* as "misrepresentations ... made willfully ... and acted on by the opposite party...." HELD: "It is axiomatic that mere statements of opinion are not material facts upon which actions for legal fraud can be maintained."[106]

In *Donnelly Construction Co v Oberg, Hunt & Gilleland*,[107] a contractor filed an action against an architect for negligent misrepresentation on the ground that erroneous plans resulted in increased costs of construction. HELD: the contractor stated a cause of action in negligent misrepresentation, although there was no privity between the contractor and the architect (citing Restatement (Second) of Torts §552 (1968)).

Inducement

In the leading case of *Gagne v Bertran*,[108] Justice Traynor held that a soil tester who was employed at $10 per hour would be liable for deceit for stating (with reference to fill) "nothing to worry about, okay, 12 to 16 inches is about all,"[109] when in fact the lot contained 3 to 6 feet of fill. This was a representation of fact, and not an innocent misrepresentation, and the defendant knew that the plaintiff would alter its position in reliance on the representation.

In a South Carolina case, an action for negligent misrepresentation against an architect was supported by evidence that the architect induced a property owner to enter into a contract for architectural services by stating that the architect's design would qualify for tax-exempt bond funding.[110]

In *Haberman v Washington Public Power Supply System*,[111] it was held that bondholders who had contributed to financing nuclear power plants stated a good cause of action against design engineers when they alleged that statements

---

[106] *Id* 512.
[107] 139 Ariz 184, 677 P2d 1292 (1984).
[108] 43 Cal 2d 481, 275 P2d 15 (1954).
[109] *Id* at 483, 275 P2d at 18.
[110] Gilliland v Elmwood Properties, 301 SC 295, 391 SE2d 577 (1990).
[111] 109 Wash 2d 107, 744 P2d 1032 (1987).

in the prospectus accompanying the bond offering included misrepresentations by the engineers as to structural feasibility. Here, the engineers knew that their statements would be used to induce the reliance of prospective investors.

§1.14 Negligence

Of the many legal theories used as a foundation for liability for malpractice of architects, negligence is by far the most frequently found in the decisions. Where negligence is mentioned as a foundation of liability, it is often coupled with some other theory of liability (breach of contract, fraud, interference with contract relations, or statutory duty) or some discrete variety of negligence (misrepresentation or failure to warn).

The conduct of an architect's representative, even if negligent, will not support a judgment unless the conduct was the proximate cause of the plaintiff's injury.[112]

In *Crawford v Gray & Associates*,[113] a surveyor erroneously prepared a plat that revealed "no servitudes, easements or rights-of-way." After the building slab was poured, it was discovered that a 9-by-12-foot corner of the building rested on a right-of-way held by the state. The surveyor asserted that the plaintiff improperly assumed that the right-of-way was 30 feet wide rather than 50 feet wide. This fact, the court held, did not diminish the surveyor's duty to question the existence of the right-of-way and to properly reflect it on the survey plat. Therefore, the surveyor's negligence was the legal cause for plaintiff's harm.

In *Miller v City of Broken Arrow Oklahoma*,[114] a contractor filed an action against a city for breach of contract and delay damages; the city filed a third-party complaint, seeking indemnity from its engineer. A judgment of $22,500 against the engineer was AFFIRMED. The project called for installation of sewer lines. When the contractor encountered unstable muddy areas, the engineer issued a change order requiring the use of crushed rock to stabilize the area. When this failed, the contractor repeatedly requested advice from the engineer, but was told only to "keep trying." The city, following the engineer's advice, terminated the contractor's performance. HELD: "an architect may be held liable for a failure to exercise reasonable care and professional skill in the preparation and execution of plans."[115] The contractor repeatedly sought help from the engineer, to no avail. "Not only did they act unlawfully, it was completely rude to just ignore these letters, time after time after time the

---

[112] Belgum v Mitsuo Kawamoto & Assocs, 236 Neb 127, 459 NW2d 226 (1990).
[113] 493 So 2d 734 (La Ct App), *writ denied*, 497 So 2d 1013 (La 1986).
[114] 660 F2d 450 (10th Cir 1981), *cert denied*, 455 US 1020 (1982).
[115] *Id* 458.

contractor almost praying for help."[116] REMANDED for the trial court to determine additional costs that should be assessed as damages against the engineer.

The contractual and professional relationship between architect and client can give rise to two distinct causes of action: one contractual, and one for professional malpractice.[117]

In *Burrows v Bidigare, Bublys, Inc*,[118] an arbitrator awarded $10,003 to physicians and against an architectural firm as compensation for water seepage, rot, and delamination in portions of a glass curtain wall. The physicians attempted to modify the award to include the individual architects who were employed by the firm. The court held that liability could be imposed only upon proof that an individual personally committed a negligent or wrongful act or directly supervised one. Here, the decision of the arbitrator did not establish which of the architects was personally at fault.

In *Gilbert Engineering Co v City of Asheville*,[119] a contractor filed an action against an engineer alleging negligence. The contractor encountered numerous problems in completing a water and sewage treatment facility and finally completed the project 283 days late. HELD: there was no evidence to indicate that delays were caused by any fault in design by the engineer. Judgment of $7,358 against engineer REVERSED.

In *Westmount International Hotels, Inc v Sear-Brown Associates Professional Corp*,[120] it was held that an engineer who advised owners that a ballasted roof would not meet state building code requirements should go to trial on the issue of whether it was employed by the owner to give its professional judgment as to whether the roof *could* be installed or *should* be installed.

An architect was not liable to homeowners for damages that resulted from improper surface drainage in a subdivision project, since the contract between the architect and the developer did not create a duty on the part of the architect to establish minimum foundation grade levels.[121]

In *Pearce & Pearce, Inc v Kroh Brothers Development Co*,[122] judgment was entered in favor of an owner and against an architect who was held to be solely responsible for property damaged by water leakage. The architect had negligently failed to include flashings on the plans and specifications for a medical office complex.

---

[116] *Id* 458.

[117] Robinson Redevelopment Co v Anderson, 155 AD2d 755, 547 NYS2d 458 (1989). *Also see* §1.15.

[118] 158 Mich App 175, 404 NW2d 650 (1987).

[119] 74 NC App 350, 328 SE2d 849, *review denied*, 314 NC 329, 333 SE2d 485 (1985).

[120] 65 NY2d 618, 480 NE2d 739, 491 NYS2d 150 (1985).

[121] Ferentchak v Village of Frankfort, 105 Ill App 2d 474, 475 NE2d 822 (1985).

[122] 474 So 2d 369 (Fla Dist Ct App 1985).

Reasonable Care Standard

Reasonable care was found to be the standard where the architect designed and supervised the construction of a brick hotel building. The walls cracked, assertedly because of a defective foundation. The court found that the architect was obligated to see to it that the building was constructed with reasonable care. This required the architect to cause the foundation to be sufficiently deep or otherwise protected to prevent settling which would cause the walls to crack. The court declared: "A house is not constructed with reasonable care, the foundations of which are so defective as to cause the walls to crack."[123]

In *Century Ready-Mix Co v Campbell School District*,[124] architect approved replacement of a concrete subcontractor with a new subcontractor, when the original subcontractor's concrete had failed pressure tests. Original subcontractor filed an action for negligence and malpractice. HELD: Architect owed no contractual duty to subcontractor, and did not fail to use reasonable care in obtaining or relaying information to the owner.

§1.15 —Contract versus Tort Liability

One of the earliest cases in the field of architect malpractice, *Pierson v Tyndall*,[125] illustrates a point that is present to one degree or another in every case of malpractice where the plaintiff is the architect's client: Is the negligent conduct also a breach of the contract of employment? And if it is, will contract doctrine, or tort doctrine, be used to determine liability and damages?

In *Pierson*, an architect brought an action against a client to recover fees for the design and supervision of a building project. The client attempted to offset damages for alleged negligence in the preparation of the plans and in the supervision of construction. The court said that an architect is held to a duty to exercise the care and skill expected of architects. The architect raised the defense that the client had paid a contractor in accordance with certificates for payment issued by the architect and was thereby estopped from offsetting the alleged damages. Such conduct, in legal theory, might be contributory negligence (the owner contributed to the damage by making payments for improper work) or, in the lexicon of contract law, it could be proved on the issue of mitigation of damages. The court held that the trial court should have instructed the jury that payment with full knowledge of faulty work would not preclude the client from offsetting damages against the architect's fee. Such payments

---

[123] Schreiner v Miller, 67 Iowa 91, 24 NW 738 (1885). *See also* Trinity Area School Dist v Dickson, 223 Pa Super 546, 302 A2d 481 (1973).
[124] 816 P2d 795 (Wyo 1991).
[125] 28 SW 232 (Tex Civ App 1894).

could be considered on the issue of damages but would not totally bar recovery. Although the court spoke in terms of negligence, since facts constituting contributory negligence did not bar the client from asserting the offset, it seems that the case was decided upon principles of contract law. Indeed, the architect's action for the fee was a contract action, not a tort action.

Setoff Allowed

In *Hubert v Aitken*,[126] the distinction between negligence and breach of contract was clearly drawn. The architect had agreed to design and supervise the construction of an apartment building. After occupancy, it was discovered that the chimney flues were not large enough for the purpose designed; they had to be replaced at a cost of $1,000. The architect filed suit to recover a fee, and the owner filed a counterclaim for damages resulting from the architect's negligence.

The owner contended that the act of negligence also constituted a breach of contract. Contract doctrine holds that a breach of contract by one party excuses performance by the other. Therefore, the owner argued that because of the breach, the architect could collect no fee.

The court pointed out that the plans prepared by the architect were complete in all details, including the chimney, and the fact that the design of the chimney was negligent should not be sufficient to defeat all recovery on the contract since all of the obligations undertaken were performed. Therefore, the owner was entitled to a $1,000 setoff (for the cost of replacing the chimney flues), and the architect was entitled to recover the fee.

In *Lindeberg v Hodgens*,[127] an architect sued a homeowner for the balance of a professional fee, and the homeowner alleged that negligence barred any recovery at all, even though the architect may have substantially performed the obligations of the contract. The homeowner complained that the architect supervised the project poorly, as evidenced by a shrinkage of woodwork. The trial court defense verdict (denying the architect any part of the fee) was REVERSED. An architect who contractually assumes a duty of supervision must exercise due care and if negligent, the employer obtains a cause of action for damages in recoupment and counterclaim. Such negligence is not a complete bar to the architect's action for a fee.

In another early case, *Corey v Eastman*,[128] Justice Holmes indulged in a mixture of negligence, contract, warranty, fraud, and deceit language in holding an architect liable. An architect induced a client to make a progress payment to

---

[126] 15 Daly 237, 2 NYS 711 (CP 1888), *affd*, 123 NY 655, 25 NE 954 (1890).
[127] 89 Misc 454, 152 NYS 229 (Sup Ct 1915).
[128] 166 Mass 279, 44 NE 217 (1896).

a builder even though the client protested that the work accomplished did not comply with the requirements of the contract documents. Holmes said, as a consequence of the architect's employment contract, the architect was tortiously liable for negligently made erroneous statements and imprudent advice. The holding was based on the same principle that under a warranty, an erroneous statement was a deceit by the old common law even without negligence.

In a Texas case, an architect designed a residence which, after allowing for the setback required by the city, would not fit on the lot. It admitted error in plotting the width of the lot. The court of appeal REVERSED a directed verdict for the architect. The architect's admission of a mistake in the plans was sufficient to raise a jury issue with respect to negligence.[129]

In another Texas case, an engineer filed suit against a municipal utility to recover payment for engineering fees. The utility asserted a counterclaim alleging that the engineer's plans were not prepared in a good and workmanlike manner and did not meet the standards of reasonable engineering practice. The Supreme Court of Texas held that once the engineer introduced evidence that it complied with the requirements of the contract, it was not necessary for the engineer to go on and disprove its own negligence. The architect was entitled to a presumption that the work performed was "good and workmanlike" until the contrary was proven by the utility.[130]

Many states do not allow recovery for economic loss in negligence cases. (Economic loss is diminution in the value of property, cost of repair or replacement, lost profit, lost business opportunity, and similar consequential damages.)[131] If contract or warranty law, rather than negligence law, is applied to the case, then economic loss may be recovered.

Contract and tort liability often arise out of the same fact situation. In *Tamarac Development Co v Delameter, Freund & Associates, PA*,[132] a developer sued an architect for damages resulting from defective grading of a trailer court. The developer testified that the parties had an oral agreement that the architect would insure that the grading was accurate. The architect argued that no breach of contract was involved and the cause of action was for negligent failure to use reasonable care. The trial court granted a summary judgment on the ground that the tort statute of limitations had expired. REVERSED. The record shows that the oral contract called for a specific result, namely, proper grading. The testimony supported an action for breach of implied warranty to inspect and supervise the project in a workmanlike manner.

---

[129] Newell v Mosley, 469 SW2d 481 (Tex Civ App 1971).
[130] Coulson & CAE, Inc v Lake LBJ Mun Util Dist, 734 SW2d 649 (Tex 1987).
[131] Moorman Mfg Co v National Tank Co, 91 Ill 2d 69, 435 NE2d 443 (1982) (crack developed in a steel plate in a grain storage tank).
[132] 234 Kan 618, 675 P2d 361 (1984).

§1.16 —Negligence and Breach of Contract

The same act, of course, can constitute both negligence and a breach of contract. In *Willner v Woodward*,[133] the court seemed to consider the contract as one of the factors in determining whether or not the architect was negligent. The plaintiff homeowner directly employed a plumbing company to design and build the heating and air conditioning system in a house designed by defendant architect. The system was a disaster. It did not work. The ducts filled with water. The homeowner filed suit against the architect for negligence in failure to properly review the design of and supervise the installation of the system. Summary judgment for the architect was REVERSED. The Virginia Supreme Court held that the evidence raised questions of fact as to whether or not the architect undertook, as a part of the contract, to approve the heating and air conditioning system and to supervise its installation. If the architect did so undertake, it would have been held to perform that duty with reasonable skill, and the issue of negligence should have been presented to the jury for determination.

In *Navajo Circle, Inc v Development Concepts Corp*,[134] condominium owners and their association filed an action against architects, alleging that they negligently supervised construction and subsequent repairs of a condominium roof. The court held that the complaint stated a good cause of action. It was true that there was no privity of contract between the architects and the plaintiffs; however, the issue was whether the injury resulted from defendants' violation of a legal duty owed to plaintiffs.

> The duty owed by a defendant to a plaintiff may have sprung from a contractual promise made to another; however, the duty sued on in a negligence action is not the contractual promise but the duty to use reasonable care in affirmatively performing that promise. The duty exists independent of contract. Existence of a contract . . . is not an exclusive test of the existence of that duty. Whether a defendant's duty to use reasonable care extends to a plaintiff not a party to the contract is determined by whether that plaintiff and defendant are in a relationship in which defendant has a duty imposed by law to avoid harm to the plaintiff. . . . Where it is foreseeable that the plaintiff will suffer the injury sued on, the supplier of a service has a legal duty to use reasonable care to avoid unreasonable risks to that plaintiff in performance of his service.[135]

---

[133] 201 Va 104, 109 SE2d 132 (1959).
[134] 373 So 2d 689 (Fla Dist Ct App 1979).
[135] *Id* 691.

In *Hotel Utica, Inc v Armstrong*,[136] owners sued architects, in separate counts, for breach of contract and negligence. The trial court dismissed the breach of contract count, and the jury returned a defense verdict on the negligence count. HELD: it was error to dismiss the breach of contract count. The owner may sue for the malpractice of an architect both in contract and in negligence. Of course, the owner is then entitled to only one recovery for damages arising out of the same facts and circumstances.

In a Louisiana case, the plaintiff employed a surveyor to *confirm* an earlier survey. A note on the survey declared that the tract contained 13.16 acres; the surveyor did not check the acreage computation. The correct area was 11.26 acres. The owner bought the property for $6,840 per acre. The court held that the owner was entitled to recover an overpayment of $3,600 per acre on a negligence theory. Even though the surveyor was liable for negligence, it was still entitled to a fee for its services which were in all other respects satisfactory and from which plaintiff derived benefit. Thus, the negligence theory prevailed over the breach of contract theory. A material breach of contract would have destroyed the surveyor's entitlement to recover any fee, while negligence would merely establish an offset against the fee.[137]

An architect or engineer may be liable to a general contractor for economic loss for breach of a common law duty of care. In *Davidson & Jones, Inc v New Hanover County*,[138] the court held that where breach of a contract results in foreseeable injury to persons so situated by their economic relations and community of interests as to impose a duty of due care, liability will arise from the negligent breach of the common law duty of care flowing from the parties' working relationship.[139]

In *Balagna v Shawnee County*,[140] plaintiff's decedent was killed when an unshored, unbraced trench collapsed. The project architect was employed under a contract that did not impose any responsibility for the safety of workers at the job site. However, the architect had actual knowledge that safety standards require shoring of open trenches. Furthermore, the architect had actual knowledge that the prescribed safety precautions were not being followed at the

---

[136] 62 AD2d 1147, 404 NYS2d 455 (1978).

[137] Jenkins v J.J. Krebs & Sons, 322 So 2d 426 (La Ct App 1975), *writ denied*, 325 So 2d 611 (La 1976). *See also* Reighard v Downs, 261 Md 26, 273 A2d 109 (1971), *appeal after remand*, 265 Md 344, 289 A2d 299 (1972) (surveyor determined area to be 22.075 acres, but area was actually 19.58 acres; HELD: a surveyor must exercise that degree of care which one of ordinary skill and prudence would exercise under similar circumstances).

[138] 41 NC App 661, 255 SE2d 580, *review denied*, 298 NC 295, 259 SE2d 911 (1979).

[139] *See also* Caldwell v Bechtel, Inc, 203 US App DC 407, 631 F2d 989 (1980) (engineer agreed to perform safety engineering services. Worker suffered injury by inhalation of silica dust; HELD: a contract entered into with another may impose an obligation sounding in tort to act in such a way that a noncontracting party will not be injured).

[140] 233 Kan 1068, 668 P2d 157 (1983), *revd on other grounds*, 11 Kan App 2d 357, 720 P2d 1144 (1986).

time when the accident occurred. HELD: such actual knowledge created a duty for the architect to take reasonable action to prevent injury to the worker. Summary judgment for architect was REVERSED.

In *Hanna v Huer, Johns, Neel, Rivers & Webb*,[141] two employees of a subcontractor were injured when a steel tie joint fell from the upper level of a building that was under construction. The injured workers alleged that the architect was guilty either of breach of contract or of negligence. HELD: under the contract documents, it was the responsibility of the contractor, not the architect, to provide and enforce safe working conditions. The general duty to "supervise the work," included in the American Institute of Architects (AIA) Document A201, General Conditions, created a duty on the part of the architect to ensure that the building was constructed according to plans and specifications. However, absent a clear assumption of the duty to be responsible for job site safety procedures, the architect was not liable for the contractor's failure to adopt or enforce the procedures.

§1.17 —Reasonable Skill Required

The court in *Conklin v Cohen*[142] set forth the standard of skill required of an architect:

> An architect may be liable for negligence in failing to exercise the ordinary skill of its profession, which results in the erection of an unsafe structure whereby anybody lawfully on the premises is injured. . . . Architects are under a duty to exercise such reasonable care, technical skill and ability, and diligence as is ordinarily required of architects in the course of their plans, inspections and supervisions during construction, for the protection of any person who foreseeably and with reasonable certainty might be injured by the failure to do so.[143]

No Guarantee

While an architect is required to exercise reasonable skill, it does not guarantee a satisfactory result. In an early case, when a building settled, it was necessary to shore up the walls using jack screws at an expense of $1,700. The owner refused to pay the architect's fee and alleged that negligence caused the building to settle. HELD: an architect is free from liability if it acts with reasonable diligence; if the architect meets this standard it is not liable for

---

[141] 233 Kan 206, 662 P2d 243 (1983).
[142] 287 So 2d 56 (Fla 1973).
[143] *Id* 61.

damages, even if the results of the work are unsatisfactory. The jury found that the architect was not negligent (even though the building settled) and, therefore, was entitled to its fee.[144]

While an engineer does not warrant the accuracy of plans and specifications, a subcontractor stated a cause of action when it alleged failure to use reasonable care in designing electrical switch gear.[145]

Reasonable Skill

The Iowa Supreme Court, in a fee suit, upheld an owner's counterclaim that an architect had prepared drawings in a negligent manner. An architect is duty bound to furnish plans and specifications prepared with a reasonable degree of technical skill.[146]

Proximate Cause

"The duty of the architect is to use the standard of care ordinarily exercised by members of that profession, taking into account the foreseeable use of the building and persons or property that might be injured thereby."[147]

The negligence of an engineer does not entitle the client to damages unless it is the proximate cause of a loss. (Plaintiff employed an engineer to check plaintiff's design of viaduct shoring. The engineer failed to discover a design defect. Although negligent, the conduct did not cause the loss, since the shoring system had already been fabricated, and plaintiff would have been required to take corrective measures regardless of whether the engineer discovered the defect.[148])

Foreseeability

To be actionable, the negligence of the architect must be the proximate cause of damage to the plaintiff. In *Minor v Zidell Trust*,[149] a motorist, attempting to park on the second level of a parking facility, lapsed into unconsciousness. His car surged forward over a 7-3/4-inch curb and through a 3-foot brick wall, finally landing on the street below. The motorist filed an action against the architect, alleging negligent design of the wheel curb and the wall behind it. Summary judgment for defendant was AFFIRMED. The alleged negligence

---

[144] White v Pallay, 119 Or 97, 247 P 316 (1926).

[145] Bates & Rogers Constr v North Shore Sanitary Dist, 92 Ill App 3d 90, 414 NE2d 1274 (1980), *affd*, 109 Ill 2d 225, 486 NE2d 902 (1985).

[146] Trunk & Gordon v Clark, 163 Iowa 620, 145 NW 277 (1914).

[147] Karna v Byron Reed Syndicate No 4, 374 F Supp 687, 689 (D Neb 1974) (motel guest injured after colliding with glass door).

[148] Pacific Form Corp v Burgstahler, 263 Or 266, 501 P2d 308 (1972).

[149] 618 P2d 392 (Okla 1980).

was not the proximate cause of the injury. The motorist's lapse into unconsciousness was so "unusual and extraordinary an event as to merit recognition as unforeseeable in law."[150]

An engineering firm was not entitled to summary judgment when it was responsible for making recommendations for the cleanup and control of toxic waste, since material questions of fact existed as to whether employees who thereafter worked at the job site were within the class of persons foreseeably harmed by the negligence of the engineering firm. The engineer had issued a report representing that all remedial actions had been taken and that only traces of toxic substances remained on the employer's property. Approximately four years later, a regulatory agency conducted a site inspection and found heavy contamination.[151]

§1.18 —Privity of Contract

Old Rule

For decades, the lack of privity of contract has served as a defense where the plaintiff was not the owner. In *Geare v Sturgis*,[152] the descendant's administrator alleged that an architect negligently designed the roof and balcony of the Knickerbocker Theatre in Washington, causing the decedent's death when the roof and balcony collapsed. The court held, with many citations, that neither a contractor nor an architect is liable for injuries arising after the completion of the building and its acceptance by the owner; otherwise, there would be no end to suits. The true proximate cause of the injury was considered to be the fact that the owner maintained a defective building, rather than the negligence of the architect or contractor.

Rejection of the Defense

During the decade of the 1950s, most courts abandoned the defense of privity and held that architects would be liable for damages caused by their negligence, in common with other defendants. In *Pastorelli v Associated Engineers, Inc*,[153] the plaintiff, a patron in the clubhouse at a racetrack, was injured when a heating duct fell. The duct had been attached by hangers to a 7/8-inch ceiling rather

---

[150] *Id* 394.
[151] Henshaw v Edward E. Clark Engrs-Scientists, 490 So 2d 161 (Fla Dist Ct App 1986).
[152] 56 App DC 364, 14 F2d 256 (1926), *overruled*, Hannah v Fletcher, 97 US App DC 310, 231 F2d 469 (1956).
[153] 176 F Supp 159 (DRI 1959).

than to the ceiling joists. The architect had been employed to supervise the contractor's work. The contract required first-class workmanship and called for the ducts to be securely supported from the building in an approved manner. The court held that the architect was under a duty to exercise care for the benefit of future patrons of the building, and that the negligence of the architect was the proximate cause of the plaintiff's injury.

In *Colbert v Holland Furnace Co*,[154] a husband contracted with a furnace company to install a hot air furnace, which was guaranteed for five years. After a year, the wife stepped on a grating which gave way, causing serious injury. Plaintiff filed an action alleging that the furnace company was negligent because it used old, weak, brittle, and unsafe cleats to support the grating. A verdict for plaintiff was AFFIRMED. The court acknowledged that there was no privity of contract between the wife and the furnace company, and that the lack of privity would usually absolve an independent contractor from liability to a third party after completion and acceptance by the employer. However, *an exception to the rule applies where it is obvious from the nature of the item that any defect would be likely to result in injury.*

In *American Fidelity Fire Insurance Co v Pavia-Byrne Engineering Corp*,[155] an engineering company employed to inspect the work of a contractor and issue payment certificates, was found liable to the surety on a contractor's performance bond. The engineering company was not a party to the contract between the city and the contractor; therefore, the surety could not have recovered on a contract theory. However, the engineering company was liable to the surety for damages caused by its negligence. The degree of care owed by an engineer to a surety company is the same as that owed to the owner. Evidence demonstrated that the engineering company violated its duty to skillfully inspect the work as it progressed and to properly calculate the estimated value of the contractor's work for the purpose of paying the contractor's monthly estimates. In spite of the lack of privity, the engineering company's failure to carefully perform this duty made it liable to the surety for overpayments made by the city in reliance on the payment certificates.[156]

In *Moore v PRC Engineering, Inc*,[157] a worker was injured in a fall from a beam. Under its contract with the owner, the engineering firm had a contractual duty to ensure that the job was done safely. HELD: defendants may be liable for negligence notwithstanding the absence of privity.

---

[154] 333 Ill 78, 164 NE 162 (1928).

[155] 393 So 2d 830 (La), *writ denied*, 397 So 2d 1362 (La Ct App 1981).

[156] *See also* Detweiler Bros v John Graham & Co, 412 F Supp 416 (ED Wash 1976); Quail Hollow East Condominium Assn v Donald J. Scholz Co, 47 NC App 518, 268 SE2d 12 (1975), *review denied*, 301 NC 527, 273 SE2d 454 (1980).

[157] 565 So 2d 817 (Fla Dist Ct App 1990).

Most courts continue to hold that an architect's liability does not depend on privity. The tort analysis focusing on duty, foreseeability, and negligence is applied in professional malpractice cases.[158]

In *Hughes-Bechtol, Inc v State*,[159] the court held nexus between a contractor and an architect can serve as a substitute for privity when seeking recovery of economic damages under a tort theory.

Lack of Duty

The defense that there is no privity of contract between the design professional and the plaintiff still has vitality in some courts. In *Carlotta v T.R. Stark & Associates*,[160] a neighbor filed suit against the property owners and their surveyor for continuing trespass and for negligent preparation of a boundary survey. The surveyor's demurrer was sustained. AFFIRMED. The plaintiffs could not maintain an action against the surveyor on grounds of negligence, since the survey was prepared at the request of their neighbors. The surveyor who lays out a disputed boundary line owes no duty of care to an adjoining landowner who does not rely on the survey.

In *Breiner v C&P Homebuilders, Inc*,[161] a subdivision project caused an increased flow of surface water over the land of neighboring strawberry growers. The growers filed an action against the borough and its engineers, alleging that building permits were issued by the borough after the engineers approved the subdivision plan without protecting the growers against rainwater runoff. HELD: the borough had no duty to landowners in an adjacent township. The engineers carefully performed their duty toward the borough itself and owed no duty to the growers; therefore, the trial court judgment against the engineers was REVERSED.

Economic Loss Rule

"Economic loss" refers to a diminution in value of a particular product caused by the product itself, such as the failure of the product to function as represented. The economic loss doctrine makes tort remedies unavailable to persons whose only injury is a loss in their expectations for a product. (Engineer was granted a summary judgment in an action brought by owner for cost to repair improperly designed equipment.)[162]

---

[158] Ferentchak v Village of Frankfort, 121 Ill App 3d 599, 459 NE2d 1085 (1984), *affd in part, revd in part*, 105 Ill 2d 474, 475 NE2d 822 (1985).

[159] 124 BR 1007 (Bankr SD Ohio 1991).

[160] 57 Md App 467, 470 A2d 838 (1984).

[161] 536 F2d 27 (3d Cir 1976).

[162] Wausau Paper Mills Co v Charles T. Main, Inc, 789 F Supp 968 (WD Wis 1992).

In *Floor Craft Floor Covering, Inc v Parma Community General Hospital Assn*,[163] the Ohio Supreme Court decided (four to three) that a contractor may not sue an architect for economic loss in the absence of privity. The contractor contended that the project architect (who was employed by the owner) had prepared a defective design, thus requiring the contractor to repair flooring that was damaged after it was installed. HELD: tort litigation of economic losses could upset contractual allocation of risks. The dissenting justices objected to the resurrection of the doctrine of privity of contract as providing a defense to architects and engineers in economic loss cases. The dissent stated that, in at least 21 states, courts have held that the absence of contractual privity *does not* shield design professionals from liability for malpractice that causes economic loss.

In *E.C. Goldman, Inc v A/R/C Associates*,[164] a roofing subcontractor sued roofing consultants who had been employed by a school district to evaluate the condition of a roof built by the subcontractor. The consultant recommended that the board withhold payment. The subcontractor demanded arbitration against the board and obtained an award of $63,639. The subcontractor then sued the consultants. HELD: the consultants were outside the chain of construction and were not responsible for the design or construction of the roof. They simply gave their opinion to the board. There was no privity of contract, and the subcontractor was not an intended beneficiary of the consulting contracts. In preparing their expert report, the consultants had no duty to the subcontractor and, thus, were not liable for any negligence in preparing their report. (The dissent argued that subcontractor was an intended third-party beneficiary.)

In *Wood Brothers Construction Co v Simons-Eastern Co*,[165] a contractor filed an action against the project designer-supervisor of a wood energy system plant, alleging damages for delay. Summary judgment for designer-supervisor was AFFIRMED. The claim for negligent supervision arose out of the contract between the owner and the designer-supervisor. The contractor was not entitled to recover damages for delay from the designer-supervisor in the absence of privity of contract.

§1.19 —Expert Testimony

Expert Testimony Required

Proof of professional negligence of an architect often depends upon expert testimony.[166] The plaintiff must show a failure to exercise the degree of care

---

[163] 54 Ohio St 3d 1, 560 NE2d 206 (1990).
[164] 543 So 2d 1268 (Fla Dist Ct App), *review denied*, 551 So 2d 461 (Fla 1989).
[165] 193 Ga App 874, 389 SE2d 382 (1989), *cert denied* (Jan 25, 1990).
[166] See discussion in §1.06.

that would be exercised by the ordinary, average architect in the locality. For example, when a natural gas compression station was destroyed by fire, the plaintiff's experts testified that the fire probably resulted from a rupture in a tank, caused by dislodgement of a valve which was attached to the tank by a swage fitting. The plaintiff's expert blamed the architect for erroneous design: the valve should have been supported. The defendant's experts testified that the design complied with good practice. Verdict against the architect was AFFIRMED.[167]

A South Carolina case has held that in a case of architectural malpractice, there can be no finding of negligence in the absence of expert testimony to support it.[168]

In a New York case, a new tenant, a paraplegic, was burned by placing his feet in bathwater without first testing the temperature. HELD: the tenant provided no expert testimony as to its claim of professional negligence, and summary judgment was, therefore, properly granted.[169]

In *Bartak v Bell-Gallyardt & Wells, Inc*,[170] the decedent fell when a piece of fiberboard roof decking gave way under his weight. No expert testimony was offered as to the standard of architectural practice. The court REVERSED the jury verdict against the architect in this wrongful death action. "[T]here can be no finding of negligence unless there is expert testimony to support it, because laymen would be unable to understand highly technical architectural requirements without hearing other architects testify as to those requirements."[171]

In *Herkert v Stauber*,[172] Mazer-Stauber Associates (M-S), an architectural service corporation, contracted to design and build an apartment building. M-S also agreed to provide all architectural and engineering documents necessary to obtain Farmers' Home Administration financing for the project. The plaintiff alleged that M-S was guilty of a breach of contract because M-S failed to provide the documents. The court refused to impose liability. The plaintiff did

---

[167] Uinta Pipeline Corp v White Superior Co, 546 P2d 885 (Utah 1976).

[168] Gilliland v Elmwood Properties, 301 SC 295, 391 SE2d 577 (1990).

[169] Tirella v American Properties Team, Inc, 145 AD2d 724, 535 NYS2d 252 (1988).

[170] 473 F Supp 737 (DSD 1979), *revd*, 629 F2d 523 (8th Cir 1980).

[171] A number of cases have recognized the rule that expert testimony is required to establish failure of an architect to conform to professional standards: Ponce de Leon Condominiums v DiGirolamo, 238 Ga 188, 232 SE2d 62 (1977) (surface water runoff); Dresco Mechanical Contractors, Inc v Todd-CEA, Inc, 531 F2d 1292 (5th Cir 1976) (boiler explosion): Noble v Worthy, 378 A2d 674 (DC 1977) (infant fall from balcony); 530 East 89 Corp v Unger, 43 NY2d 776, 373 NE2d 276, 402 NYS2d 382 (1977) (delay in responding to building department's objections); National Hous Indus v E.L. Jones Dev Co, 118 Ariz 374, 576 P2d 1374 (1978) (failure to disclose requirement of 20,000 cubic yards of fill on subdivision plan); Seaman Unified Sch Dist No 345 v Casson Constr Co, 3 Kan App 2d 289, 594 P2d 241 (1979) (the common knowledge that water runs downhill was insufficient to interpret the technically complicated plans; therefore, expert testimony was required).

[172] 106 Wis 2d 545, 317 NW2d 834 (1982).

not prove that the breach related to *professional services*. The record did not contain evidence that it was the normal practice of professional architects to assist a client in obtaining financing for a construction project. Plaintiff also failed to provide expert testimony establishing the standard of care owed by a professional who attempts to perform services beyond his or her experience or training.

In *H. Elton Thompson & Associates, PC v Williams*,[173] a verdict was entered against an architect for damages sustained when a lake filled with silt and mud deposited by surface water runoff during and after construction of a new school. The plaintiff failed to introduce expert testimony as to the standard of care required of an architect. The holding was REVERSED. Expert testimony is required to establish the boundaries of professional conduct, and the jury may not speculate as to the standard against which to measure the acts of a professional.

In a Louisiana case, a city incinerator project incurred severe damage because of settlement. The foundation piles were displaced by serious latent unstable soil conditions. The engineer designed additional piling to correct the condition but went forward with the installation of a floating slab despite warnings from the contractor. The slab did settle and damage occurred. The court held that the engineer was not responsible for the damage, since all of the expert testimony indicated that the degree of settlement which occurred could not have been predicted beforehand.[174]

In *Watson, Watson & Rutland/Architects, Inc v Montgomery County Board of Education*,[175] the board of education alleged that an architect was guilty of negligent inspection, the result of which was that a school received an inadequate roofing system. The board recovered judgment of $24,813 on its breach of contract claim against the architect. REVERSED. The board had the option to select continuous on-site inspection, or (at a lesser fee) general site inspections to be performed by the architect. (Article 8, American Institute of Architects (AIA) Contract). The board selected general site inspections. HELD: under the contract, the architect had the obligation to make "reasonable inspections." The nature and extent of the duty of an architect who agrees to perform such inspections are not of common knowledge; therefore, expert testimony would have been required to sustain the judgment.

In *Nelson v Commonwealth*,[176] an architect first designed and then administered construction of a 550-bed teaching hospital on the campus of Virginia Commonwealth University. Construction was delayed for one year and seven

---

[173] 164 Ga App 571, 298 SE2d 539 (1982).

[174] Pittman Constr Co v City of New Orleans, 178 So 2d 312 (La Ct App), *appeal denied*, 248 La 434, 179 So 2d 274 (1965).

[175] 559 So 2d 168 (Ala 1990).

[176] 235 Va 228, 368 SE2d 239 (1988).

months. A number of experts in the field of *construction administration* testified, but none testified so as to establish the standard of care in the architectural profession for the administration of construction contracts. No expert testified that the architects failed to perform their administrative duties with reasonable technical skill. Judgment awarding the state $1,286,750 was REVERSED on the ground that the practice of architecture is sufficiently technical to require expert testimony to establish the standard of care and any departure therefrom.

In *McKee v City of Pleasanton*,[177] the plaintiff slipped on coping tile used around the edge of a swimming pool and was injured. In an action against the designer of the pool, summary judgment for the designer was AFFIRMED. The plaintiff failed to present evidence that use of the coping material violated standards of professional practice in the architectural and engineering community.

In *Sams v Kendall Construction Co*,[178] a subcontractor alleged that an architect was negligent in drafting and interpreting a contract provision that established a *carpet allowance*. The court HELD that the plaintiff failed to establish a cause of action, because no expert witness testimony established the appropriate standard of care for the community or that the architect's conduct fell below such standard.

In *Donnell & Froom v Baldwin County Board of Education*,[179] the Board of Education alleged architect had failed to exercise professional care, skill, and diligence in recommending payment for a change order. The Board presented no expert testimony regarding the standard of care. Judgment against architects REVERSED.

Qualifications of Expert

In *Overland Constructors, Inc v Millard School District*,[180] a dispute arose between a contractor and a school district as to who was responsible for payment of utility charges. The architect determined that the contractor was responsible. The trial court overruled the architect and held the school district responsible. The school district then sought indemnity from the architect. HELD: the school district failed to call an expert witness to testify as to the standard of conduct. Therefore, it was not established that the architect was negligent in failing to specify in the contract documents which party would be

---

[177] 242 Kan 649, 750 P2d 1007 (1988).

[178] 499 So 2d 370 (La Ct App 1986).

[179] 599 So 2d 1158 (Ala 1992). *See also* D'Annunzio Bros v New Jersey Transit Corp, 245 NJ Super 527, 586 A2d 301 (1991) (malpractice claim against engineer must be supported by expert testimony).

[180] 220 Neb 220, 369 NW2d 69 (1985).

responsible for utility charges. While matters of *common knowledge* may be resolved without the aid of expert testimony, *the issue of professional care in the preparation of contract documents is not within the knowledge of a lay juror.*

A trial court abused its discretion when it refused to qualify as an expert capable of rendering an opinion on the cause of paint delamination a witness who held a master's degree in chemical and ceramic engineering and a doctorate in silicate sciences. Although the witness may have lacked practical experience, the witness was qualified because of education, knowledge, and training. The same court also abused its discretion by refusing to allow an expert witness, qualified as an architect and a structural engineer, to testify concerning the standard of care required of an architect who drafted specifications for a building repainting project.[181]

An architect who was a defendant in a controversy arising out of the failure of a roofing system contended that only an architect should be permitted to testify as to the standard of practice applicable to an average competent architect. HELD: it was proper for the trial court to admit testimony of a civil engineer who had a great deal of experience in the roofing industry.[182]

To the extent that plans and specifications are intended to be read and interpreted by nonarchitects, a nonarchitect may express an opinion as to those plans and specifications.[183]

In *Keel v Titan Construction Corp*,[184] an architect designed a solar energy system for a home. The system did not work properly and, as a result, some of the pipes froze and burst. The homeowner replaced the entire system. The homeowner called as an expert a professor of physics who had developed an early interest in solar energy, had supervised the development of a solar collector in 1956, had attended numerous workshops and seminars dealing with solar energy, and had participated in a solar energy course at MIT. HELD: plaintiff's expert was eminently qualified to offer its opinions as to the suitability of the architect's plans. The expert's conclusion that the failure of the system was caused by improper design was sufficient to support recovery either in breach of contract or in tort.

An architect/engineer did not violate professional standards by failing to foresee the need for baffles on window air conditioners, where a mechanical engineer testified that the only technique for assuring proper performance of the units would have been trial and error.[185]

---

[181] Friendship Heights Assocs v Koubek, 785 F2d 1154 (4th Cir 1986).

[182] School Dist No 11 v Sverdrup, Parcel & Assoc, 797 F2d 651 (8th Cir 1986).

[183] Prichard Bros v Grady Co, 436 NW2d 460 (Minn Ct App 1989), *review denied* (May 2, 1989).

[184] 721 P2d 828 (Okla Ct App 1986).

[185] R.G. Wood & Assocs, 85-1 BCA (CCH) 17,898 (1985).

In *Wagner v Modulars by Design, Inc*,[186] homeowners employed engineer A to plan a sewer system. The system failed to pass inspection, so they turned to engineer B. The homeowners withheld payment from engineer B, who filed an action to collect its fee. On a motion for summary judgment, the homeowners submitted testimony from engineer A that engineer B was the negligent party. Summary judgment for engineer B was AFFIRMED. Conclusionary statements are insufficient to defeat a motion for summary judgment.

In *Tomberlin Associates Architects, Inc v Free*,[187] the question was whether a civil engineer was qualified to supply expert testimony as to the professional responsibilities of an architect. Landowners brought an action against an architect claiming its plans had caused their property to be damaged by mud and silt from an adjoining construction site. The jury awarded compensatory and punitive damages against the architect. AFFIRMED. An architect is qualified to perform engineering services incidental to the practice of architecture and, in this case, the architect contractually bound itself to render civil engineering services. Accordingly, the architect's conduct was to be judged by civil engineering standards and the civil engineer was competent to introduce such testimony.

Expert Testimony Not Required

The Supreme Court of Montana has determined that a trial court is not necessarily bound by the testimony of an expert witness.[188] Many cases have recognized that expert testimony is not required to evaluate whether professional malpractice has occurred.[189]

In a 1987 Louisiana case, a contractor filed an action against an architect alleging delay and inefficiency in remodeling the state capitol building caused by the architect's failure to discover a metal X-brace. The court held that since the architect could have found the X-brace by reference to the original plans of the building, the architect was negligent and, furthermore, the negligence could be inferred by a layman without the requirement of expert testimony.[190]

---

[186] 163 AD2d 676, 558 NYS2d 194 (1990).
[187] 174 Ga App 167, 329 SE2d 296 (1985), *cert denied* (May 1, 1985).
[188] Morrison-Maierle, Inc v Selsco, 186 Mont 180, 606 P2d 1085 (1980).
[189] Seiler v Levitz Furniture Co, 367 A2d 999 (Del Super Ct 1976) (failure to protect warehouse from obvious flood danger); Hull v Enger Constr Co, 15 Wash App 511, 550 P2d 692, *review denied*, 87 Wash 2d 1012 (1976) (specification of threshold that caused plaintiff to fall when heel became lodged in water-return). *See also* 530 East 89 Corp v Unger, 43 NY2d 776, 373 NE2d 276, 402 NYS2d 382 (1977) (recognizing rule); Lawyers Title Ins Co v Carey Hodges & Assocs, 358 So 2d 964 (La Ct App 1978) (surveyor erroneously located drainage structure on parcel A, actually located on parcel B); Chaplis v Monterey County, 97 Cal App 3d 249, 158 Cal Rptr 395 (1979) (architect's failure to recognize need for special use permit was within the scope of ordinary conduct and did not require expert testimony).
[190] M.J. Womack, Inc v House of Representatives of State, 509 So 2d 62 (La Ct App), *writ denied*, 513 So 2d 1211 (La 1987).

In *Cipriani v Sun Pipe Line Co*,[191] the court held that expert testimony was not required since the matter under consideration was simple, and the lack of ordinary care was obvious and within the range of comprehension of the average juror. The defendant township engineer had issued a permit for a cable company to excavate in a state highway, although the engineer had reason to know there was a gas line under the highway, and although the engineer had no authority to issue permits for excavations in state highways.

In *Daniel, Mann, Johnson & Mendenhall v Hilton Hotels*,[192] the engineer incorrectly laid out the location of several caissons, which were to be surveyed from fixed monuments. No expert testimony was offered as to the standard of practice, and the jury was merely instructed that the engineer was under an implied duty to perform in a workmanlike manner. HELD: expert testimony was not required, since the conduct involved was within the common knowledge of laypersons.

In *Hogan Exploration, Inc v Monroe Engineering Associates*,[193] an engineer certified the location of a gas well drill site, even though the engineer had never visited the site. The well was drilled in the wrong quarter section, on property that did not belong to the engineer's client. The plaintiff failed to offer expert testimony as to the standard of care for engineers in the area. HELD: the conduct of an engineer may be so unprofessional and so clearly improper, so manifestly below reasonable standards, as to constitute a prima facie case of either lack of the requisite degree of skill or failure to exercise such skill.[194]

In *Zontelli & Sons v City of Nashwauk*,[195] it was held that a court may properly find an engineer to be negligent without expert testimony. The engineer drastically underestimated concrete quantities for a sewer construction project, falsely represented that the highway was a municipal rather than a state highway, misled bidders as to the thickness and strength of concrete, and failed to indicate that construction was governed by certain state requirements. Preliminary inquiries and basic care could have avoided these inaccuracies, which could have properly been evaluated without expert testimony.

In *Paragon Engineering, Inc v Rhodes*,[196] a contractor alleged that a surveyor so negligently staked the boundaries of a retention basin that the contractor, who excavated the basin in accordance with the staking, produced a product that was only one-half the size called for by the contract documents. The owner refused to pay the contractor for its work and the contractor filed an action against the surveyor. HELD: although expert testimony is ordinarily required

---

[191] 393 Pa Super 471, 574 A2d 706 (1990), *appeal denied*, 527 Pa 668, 593 A2d 843 (1991).
[192] 98 Nev 113, 642 P2d 1086 (1982).
[193] 430 So 2d 696 (La Ct App 1983).
[194] *See* Annotation, 3 ALR4th 1023 (1981).
[195] 373 NW2d 744 (Minn 1965).
[196] 451 So 2d 274 (Ala 1984).

to establish the standard of care for a professional, here the unchallenged testimony of nonexpert witnesses was admissible where the witnesses were knowledgeable and experienced with respect to surveying practices.

In *Huang v Garner*,[197] it was HELD that it was not necessary to introduce expert testimony regarding the standard of professional care. (An architect failed to comply with the requirements of the state building code. Failure to comply with statutory requirements is negligence per se.)

§1.20 Liability to Third Parties—Contractors

Negligent Review by Architect

A series of cases has held that an architect can be liable for negligent practice which damages a contractor or subcontractor. In *United States v Rogers & Rogers*,[198] the prime contractor on a school project filed an action against the government's architect. Some of the concrete furnished by a subcontractor was not up to specification, but this was not brought to the prime contractor's attention until after the concrete had been incorporated into the building. As a result, the architect stopped the job while corrective measures were taken, all to the delay and damage of the prime contractor. Under the architect's contract with the government, the architect was obliged to review test reports of the concrete in bents (preformed structures, which when hoisted into place form the skeleton of the building). The contractor alleged that the architect negligently failed to properly review and interpret the test reports and allowed the incorporation of the bents into the structure. The court said that the doctrine of privity of contract no longer protects an architect from liability to a third party for negligent performance of a contractual duty:

> The determination whether in a specific case the defendant will be held liable to a third person not in privity is a matter of policy and involves the balancing of various factors, among which are the extent to which the transaction was intended to affect the plaintiff, the foreseeability of harm to him, the degree of certainty that the plaintiff suffered injury, the closeness of the connection between the defendant's conduct and the injury suffered, the moral blame attached to the defendant's conduct, and the policy of preventing future harm.[199]

The court said that the position and authority of the supervising architect are such that the architect ought to labor under a duty to the prime contractor to supervise the project with due care:

---

[197] 157 Cal App 3d 404, 203 Cal Rptr 800 (1984).
[198] 161 F Supp 132 (SD Cal 1958).
[199] *Id* 135.

Altogether too much control over the contractor necessarily rests in the hands of the supervising architect for him not to be placed under a duty imposed by law to perform without negligence his functions as they affect the contractor. The power of the architect to stop the work alone is tantamount to a power of economic life or death over the contractor. It is only just that such authority, exercised in such a relationship, carry commensurate legal responsibility.[200]

Rogers & Rogers represents something of a high point in the imposition of liability on architects. The contractor, in effect, was awarded damages for its own breach of contract: the incorporation of inferior bents was a breach of the contract between the contractor and the owner; but, the contractor was allowed to transfer liability to the architect on the theory that the architect's negligence caused the contractor to breach the contract. However, should the contractor not have at least equal responsibility with the architect to prevent its own breaches of contract?

A similar claim was allowed to stand against an engineer where, in a roundabout way, it was held that an engineer could be liable to a contractor for the contractor's own breach. The contractor installed a water line under a river. The line was damaged in an unrelated dredging operation because it had not been buried as deeply as called for in the contract documents. There was evidence that the pipe was four to six feet higher than designed, and that the engineer used an improper method (a man in a boat with a stick) to measure the depth. On demand of the county, the pipeline contractor repaired the damage, but the county refused to pay for the repair work. The contractor then filed suit against the county for the cost of repair, and the county filed a third-party complaint against the engineer for negligent supervision. Directed verdict for the engineer was REVERSED. There was sufficient evidence of negligence on the part of the engineer to go to the jury. Thus the engineer, in effect, became liable for the contractor's breach of contract.[201]

The original bidding documents for a school renovation project provided that bidders would include $9,000 in their bids to cover the costs of contingencies. The $9,000 contingency clause was later removed from the contract documents by an addendum mailed to all bidders. The school district rejected all bids because of budget considerations and the project was re-bid. A bidder noticed

---

[200] *Id* 136.

[201] Lee County v Southern Waters Contractors, Inc, 298 So 2d 518 (Fla Dist Ct App 1974). *See also* Palm Bay Towers Corp v Crain & Crouse, Inc, 303 So 2d 380 (Fla 1974); A.R. Moyer, Inc v Graham, 285 So 2d 397 (Fla 1973); Detweiler Bros v John Graham & Co, 412 F Supp 416 (ED Wash 1976) (subcontractor versus architect); E.C. Ernst, Inc v Manhattan Constr Co, 551 F2d 1026 (5th Cir 1977), *cert denied*, 434 US 1067 (1978) (electrical subcontractor v architect for delay in approving submittals, modifying drawings, and making decisions).

that the architect, this time, had failed to remove the $9,000 contingency. The bidder called the architect for clarification and was informed that the contingency would again be removed by addendum. However, the addendum was never mailed; therefore, the bidder's bid was $9,000 lower than it would have been had the bidder included the contingency. Judgment against the architect for $9,000 was AFFIRMED. The contractor expected to be told the truth, and the architect intended that the contractor accept the statement as true. Although the contractor was negligent in failing to carefully read the addendum that was issued, the contractor's negligence "pales when compared to the negligence of [the architect] in failing to make the planned correction of their specifications."[202]

In *Farrell Construction Co v Jefferson Parrish*,[203] the court held that Louisiana case law recognizes the existence of a duty of care owed by an architect to persons not in privity with the architect, including a contractor employed by the city to perform work according to allegedly defective drawings, plans, and specifications which impeded the progress of the work.

In *E.C. Ernst, Inc v Manhattan Construction Co*,[204] it was held that a general contractor was entitled to recover delay damages from an architect, when delay resulted from the architect's defective plans and specifications and from the architect's procrastination in making decisions.

The Florida Supreme Court has held that if the supervising architect is negligent in the preparation of contract documents, and this proximately causes damages to the contractor, the contractor has a good cause of action against the architect. The architect is held to a duty of care to the contractor even if there is no direct contractual relationship, and since the contractor may foreseeably be injured or suffer economic loss as the proximate result of negligent conduct by the architect, a cause of action exists even in the absence of privity of contract.[205]

In *Magnolia Construction Co v Mississippi Gulf South Engineers, Inc*,[206] a contractor employed by a city for construction of a sewer project claimed that the engineer negligently prepared plans and specifications and negligently supervised and inspected the project. After approving 18 requests for partial payment, the engineer determined that grades were not established in accordance with the plans, and final payment was, therefore, withheld. The court of appeal held that summary judgment in favor of the engineer was inappropriate since the contractor presented genuine issues of material fact as to the duty owed

---

[202] Godrey, Bassett & Kuykendall Architects, Ltd v Huntington Lumber & Supply Co, 584 So 2d 1254, 1259 (Miss 1991).

[203] 693 F Supp 490 (ED La 1988).

[204] 551 F2d 1026 (5th Cir 1977), *cert denied*, 434 US 1067 (1978).

[205] A.R. Moyer, Inc v Graham, 285 So 2d 397 (Fla 1973).

[206] 518 So 2d 1194 (Miss 1988).

by the engineer to the contractor as defined by the engineer's contract with the city.

In *Malta Construction Co v Henningson, Durham & Richardson, Inc*,[207] the court held that an engineer who supplied information to a contractor for construction of post-tensioned bridges had a duty of care to the contractor who relied upon such information.

In a New York case, *Northrup Contracting, Inc v Village of Bergen*,[208] it was held that for a contractor to recover against an engineer there must be a "relationship of contractual privity . . . or a relationship sufficiently intimate to be equated with privity. . . ."[209] The engineer was retained by the village to design a wastewater collection project. The contractor utilized plans and specifications and test borings prepared by the engineer to determine subsurface conditions in preparing its bid. The contractor encountered excessive subsurface water and filed a claim with the engineer for additional compensation. Processing of the claim was denied and the contractor was advised to move to another part of the job. The contractor terminated performance, protesting delay caused by the engineer's dealing with the water problem. HELD: the contractual responsibility of the engineer to the village established a relationship between the contractor and the engineer. "It was [the engineer's] continuing supervision, the negligent manner in which it was performed, and the tortious interference with [the contractor's] contract . . . that caused [the contractor] to suffer damages."[210]

A general contractor relied on plans prepared by project engineers in submitting a bid to perform a construction contract. The contractor suffered damages because of subsurface debris and filed an action against the project engineer and architect, alleging that they were contractually obligated to supervise the work of a wrecking company which had been employed to prepare the site for construction. The engineer and architect had received notice, through soil test reports, of the existence of subsurface debris, but failed to disclose the existence of the debris in the final plans and specifications. HELD: (1) plaintiff stated a good cause of action for negligent misrepresentation despite lack of privity, since the architect and engineer supplied false information and it was foreseeable that the general contractor for the project could be injured by reasonable reliance on such false information; (2) architects and engineers are liable to a general contractor for failing to accurately describe construction requirements, even in the absence of privity, where such accuracy

---

[207] 694 F Supp 902 (ND Ga 1988).
[208] 139 Misc 2d 435, 527 NYS2d 670 (Sup Ct 1986).
[209] *Id* at 437, 527 NYS2d at 671.
[210] *Id* at 438, 527 NYS2d at 671-72.

is vital to the bidding process; and (3) claims of negligent supervision could not be maintained absent privity.[211]

In *Linde Enterprises, Inc v Hazelton City Authority*,[212] engineer was to provide design and supervision for the reconstruction of a dam. Judgment in favor of the prime contractor and against the engineer in the amount of $26,607.66. REVERSED. Contractor claimed it suffered damages because of faulty specifications and negligent supervision. HELD: Pennsylvania courts have long held that privity between parties is required to maintain an action for professional negligence. There was no indication in the contract that contractor was a third-party beneficiary of the contract between the city and the engineer.

When an engineer's failure to make proper calculations could foreseeably create a risk of harm to a third-party general contractor responsible for applying the specifications to the job, the engineer could be held liable to the contractor.[213]

In *Carroll-Boone Water District v M&P Equipment Co*,[214] a contractor built a concrete wastewater intake structure. It was necessary to remove rock near the completed intake structure in order to convey water into the system. The contractor proposed tunneling, but the engineer required blasting and prepared plans for three shots. The final shot damaged the structure. HELD: the engineer's fault was 100 per cent; the contractor was entitled to judgment against the engineer.[215]

Where the contractor also designs a project, it may be liable to the owner for negligent design. The fact that the owner's engineer approves the plan does not absolve the contractor from liability.[216]

In *C.W. Regan, Inc v Parsons, Brinckerhoff, Quade & Douglas*,[217] the contractor failed to impose liability on the project engineer when a tunnel project was flooded. As a result of an unusual spring tide, water entered a highway tunnel project from three sources: one was controlled by the plaintiff contractor, the second was controlled by the engineer and a fellow contractor, and the third was partly controlled by the plaintiff contractor and a fellow contractor, but approved by the engineer. There was no duty on the part of the engineer to specify how the bulkheads should be caulked; the evidence indicated that this was a construction detail within the province of the contractor. Any

---

[211] Gulf Contracting v Bibb County, 795 F2d 980 (11th Cir 1986).

[212] 602 A2d 8978 (Pa Super Ct 1992).

[213] Bacco Constr Co v American Colloid Co, 148 Mich App 397, 384 NW2d 427 (1986).

[214] 280 Ark 560, 661 SW2d 345 (1983).

[215] *See also* French v Jinright & Ryan, PC Architects, 735 F2d 433 (11th Cir 1984).

[216] *See* Simpson Bros v Merrimac Chem Co, 248 Mass 346, 142 NE 922 (1924) (plaintiff designed and built underground concrete fuel oil storage tank; it was designed negligently and floated).

[217] 411 F2d 1379 (4th Cir 1969).

negligence of the engineer in performing inspection did not relieve the contractor from liability for its own acts. The engineer's motion for directed verdict should have been granted.[218]

When a severe cloudburst caused a creek to flood, floating aeration tanks in a sewer project, the contractor recovered a verdict against the engineer on the ground that the engineer had failed to provide a sufficient dike to prevent flooding.[219]

Lack of privity has served as a defense in some contractor versus engineer cases. Where a contractor alleged that an engineer negligently misrepresented the amount of excavation necessary to perform an airport job, the engineer successfully argued that since there was no privity of contract between the engineer and the contractor, there was no liability.[220] Reaching a similar result in *Harbor Mechanical, Inc v Arizona Electrical Power Co-op, Inc*,[221] the court held that a contractor has no action for negligence against an engineer in the absence of a clause in the contract between the engineer and owner creating a duty to protect the contractor from damage.

A general contractor for construction of an office building filed an action against the architect alleging negligence in performing the architect's duties under the architect's contract with the owner. There was no contractual relationship between the architect and the general contractor. The court held that the general contractor could not recover in a tort action against an architect for economic loss arising from the architect's alleged breach of contract with the owner.[222]

Subcontractor versus Engineer

In a subcontractor versus engineer case, it was held that the engineer could be liable for negligent inspection which resulted in a breach of contract by the subcontractor. The engineer was employed by a school district to furnish continuous batch plant inspection of concrete to be installed in a school project. The inspector assisted the employees of the subcontractor in mixing the concrete and used the wrong admixture. The court held that the engineer was liable even though under no contractual duty to participate in the mixing of the concrete: a duty of ordinary care may arise out of a voluntarily assumed relationship. Therefore, the engineer's motion for nonsuit should have been denied.[223]

---

[218] *Id.*
[219] Schlitz v Cullen-Schlitz & Assocs, 228 NW2d 10 (Iowa 1975).
[220] Delta Constr Co v City of Jackson, 198 So 2d 592 (Miss 1967).
[221] 496 F Supp 681 (D Ariz 1980).
[222] Blake Constr Co v Alley, 233 Va 31, 353 SE2d 724 (1987).
[223] Walnut Creek Aggregates Co v Testing Engrs, Inc, 248 Cal App 2d 690, 56 Cal Rptr 700 (1967).

A Georgia court held that a subcontractor stated a good cause of action against an engineer when the subcontractor alleged that the engineer failed to note a gas pipeline on drawings, as a result of which the subcontractor's equipment struck the line, causing explosion and fire damaging the equipment. Summary judgment for the engineer should not have been granted, since some of the expert testimony indicated that proper procedure for the engineer would have been to note the presence of the line on the drawings.[224]

In *Waldor Pump & Equipment Co v Orr-Schelen-Mayeron & Associates*,[225] a subcontractor alleged that the engineering firm negligently prepared and interpreted specifications so as to reject sludge pumps supplied by the subcontractor. HELD: engineer was liable for negligence causing damage to subcontractor who foreseeably relied upon, and was harmed by, the engineer's drafting and interpretation of specifications.

An architect owes subcontractors, within reason, a duty to properly inspect the work and specify corrections if required to secure the architect's approval of the subcontractor's work.[226]

A subcontractor installed piles for a hospital addition. The specifications required the architect's approval of the mix design to be provided by the subcontractor. The mix submittal was returned by the architect with the notation "furnished as noted." Test piles constructed with the mix failed load tests. The architect orally directed the subcontractor to proceed with the production of piles with a promise of written confirmation that was never received. HELD: the hospital owed a duty to the subcontractor, since the contract between the hospital and the general contractor was intended to, and foreseeably would, affect the subcontractor. The hospital could have prevented the subcontractor's loss either by not approving the mix or by acting reasonably when difficulties arose. (The architect was not a party to the appeal.[227])

In *Mayor & City Council v Clark-Dietz & Associates-Engineers*,[228] the city filed an action against the architect and against the contractor for damages resulting from failure of a protective levee surrounding the site of a wastewater treatment plant. The contractor filed a cross-complaint against the architect-engineer. HELD: the architect-engineer breached its contractual duty to the city to provide an adequate design. In so doing, it breached a tort duty to the contractor

---

[224] Chastain v Atlanta Gas Light Co, 122 Ga App 90, 176 SE2d 487 (1970). *See also* Ogle v Billick, 253 Or 92, 453 P2d 677 (1969) (county engineer negligently supervised road condition; after posts supporting handrail at stairway collapsed, plaintiff fell).

[225] 386 NW2d 375 (Minn Ct App 1986).

[226] Hartford Elec Applicators of Thermalux, Inc v Alden, 169 Conn 177, 363 A2d 135 (1975).

[227] Berkel & Co Contractors, Inc v Providence Hosp, 454 So 2d 496 (Ala 1984).

[228] 550 F Supp 610 (ND Miss 1982), *appeal denied*, 702 F2d 67 (5th Cir 1983).

and was therefore liable to the contractor for extra construction expense proximately caused by the negligent design.[229]

In *Lutz Engineering Co v Industrial Louvers, Inc*,[230] the court held that a subcontractor had no right to recover damages from a project engineer for deficiencies in the subcontractor's own shop drawings. The supplier to the subcontractor prepared shop drawings for large louvered panels that were to be installed as part of the heating and ventilation system. The engineer employed by the contractor was responsible for reviewing the shop drawings. The shop drawings were rejected because they did not meet an air-leakage requirement. The supplier resubmitted corrected drawings which still did not correct the air-leakage problem. The subcontractor passed the drawings on to the contractor without comment; the drawings were returned "approved" by the engineer. After installation, the louvers leaked in the wind and rain. Judgment against engineer for negligence and approving resubmitted shop drawings was REVERSED. The engineer did not owe a duty of care to the subcontractor. The subcontractor attempted to use the engineer's resources, talent, and expertise in order to meet the subcontractor's own contractual responsibilities. The subcontractor had no right to do so. Under its contract with the contractor, the subcontractor assumed complete responsibility for its work. It had no right to transfer that responsibility to the engineer because the engineer failed to discover errors on the subcontractor's own shop drawings.

In a Louisiana case, the plaintiff subcontractor had convinced the architect to use a special butyl rubber seal to prevent leakage in a complex roofing system which consisted of two interlocking domes with skylights at the apex of each dome. When the roof leaked, the owner filed suit against the roofing contractor, who sought indemnity from the material supplier and the architect. The court pointed out that the owner might have a good case against the architect, but the subcontractor could not recover from the architect, since the subcontractor actively induced the architect to specify the faulty materials in the first place.[231]

In *John W. Johnson, Inc v Basic Construction Co*,[232] it was held that a subcontractor could not recover damages from an architect who directed the

---

[229] Cases have held an architect liable for damage to property of neighbors: *see, e.g.,* Seaman v Castellini, 415 SW2d 612 (Ky 1967) (flooding from storm sewer); or of a subsequent home buyer, see Swett v Gribaldo, Jones & Assocs, 40 Cal App 3d 573, 115 Cal Rptr 99 (1974) (home purchaser versus soil engineer; soil settlement). *See also* Stuart v Crestview Mut Water Co, 34 Cal App 3d 802, 110 Cal Rptr 543 (1973) (fire damage to homes and owners' water system; HELD: allegations were sufficient to withstand demurrer); Bodin v Gill, 216 Ga 467, 117 SE2d 325 (1960) (grading plan changed drainage pattern and destroyed neighbor's topsoil, lawn, flowers, and shrubs); Covil v Robert & Co, 112 Ga App 163, 144 SE2d 450 (1965) (T-joint slipped from 24-inch pipe causing millions of gallons of water to flow onto plaintiff's land).

[230] 585 A2d 631 (RI 1991).

[231] New Orleans Unity Socy of Practical Christianity v Standard Roofing Co, 224 So 2d 60 (La Ct App), *rehg denied*, 254 La 811, 227 So 2d 146 (1969).

[232] 139 US App DC 85, 429 F2d 764 (1970).

prime contractor to cancel the subcontractor's subcontract. Evidence showed that the subcontractor abandoned work because the contractor would not make a commitment for additional payments; therefore, the architect's direction did not actually cause the contractor to discharge the subcontractor.

In *Richards & Associates v Boney*,[233] a subcontractor made a claim against an owner for $519,000 for delays. The architect advised the owner not to make the final payment of $37,000 to the subcontractor until the subcontractor released its claim. The subcontractor then sued the architect, claiming damages flowing from the architect's wrongful advice. HELD: after the subcontractor had finished its work on the project, the architect had no further duty to the subcontractor. Moreover, the advice given by the architect was not *architectural* in nature and the architect breached no architectural duty.

An architect can be liable to a third person not in privity if there exists an economic relationship or community of interest which imposes a duty of due care. Where a breach of contract results in foreseeable injury to these third parties, liability will arise from the negligent breach of the common law duty of care flowing from the parties' working relationship.[234]

Subcontractor versus Architect

In *McElvy, Jennewein, Stefany, Howard, Inc v Arlington Electric, Inc*,[235] subcontractor recovered judgment against architect after alleging negligent interpretation of contract provisions. REVERSED. Architect had been employed by the city for design and construction of the Tampa Bay Performing Arts Center. Subcontractor requested substitution of electrical equipment supplier, which substitution was denied by the city based on the architect's advice. HELD: where plaintiff lacks privity of contract, the architect can be liable in tort to a subcontractor only where the architect had the duty to supervise contractual performance. Here, the duties of the architect were merely advisory. The final decision as to the interpretation of the contract rested with the city.

§1.21 —Developers and Construction Lenders

It has been held that an engineer owes a duty of care to a real estate lender. In a California case, the plaintiff had loaned money to a developer to construct homes in a subdivision. The defendant soil engineer conducted soil tests. After the houses were finished, differential settlement caused foundations to fail, as well as other damages. The plaintiff filed suit on the theory that the negligence

---

[233] 604 F Supp 1214 (EDNC 1985).

[234] Davidson & Jones, Inc v New Hanover County, 41 NC App 661, 255 SE2d 580, *review denied*, 298 NC 295, 259 SE2d 911 (1979).

[235] 582 So 2d 47 (Fla Dist Ct App 1991), *rehg denied* (July 11, 1991) (per curiam).

§1.21 DEVELOPERS & CONSTRUCTION LENDERS 55

of the soil engineer had impaired the value of the trust deeds which stood as security for the loans. Since a negligent engineer can be liable to a purchaser of real property, the court found reason to extend similar liability to a mortgagee when the negligence impairs the security interest.[236]

In *Browning v Maurice B. Levien & Co*,[237] an architect undertook to supervise construction of an apartment complex for the bank which loaned plaintiff money to finance the cost of the building. The architect inspected construction at the time of each progress payment request and certified compliance with the plans and specifications. The plaintiff owner sued the architect for overcertification of payments. An architect that contracts to perform services is liable for damages proximately caused by its negligence to anyone who might reasonably be foreseen to rely on its services. The plaintiff owner was such a party. The trial court erred in charging the jury that the owner could be contributorily negligent for failing to examine the books and records, as there was no evidence presented that such an examination would have revealed overcertification by the architect.

In another case involving a construction loan, the complaint alleged that the negligence of the engineers in performing inspections and rendering reports on work completed caused the mortgagee to overpay loan proceeds to the developer-mortgagor. HELD: reversing the lower court; it was reasonably foreseeable that the mortgagee would rely on the certification of work completed to issue loan proceeds and that negligent certification could therefore injure the mortgagee. Multiparty mortgage notes with the lender, borrower, and endorser are common instruments in the financing of real estate developments. The engineer's negligence caused the lender to disburse loan proceeds which would not otherwise have been allocated; these disbursements contributed to the deficiency which the lender sought to recover. (The case was dismissed without prejudice on alternate grounds.[238])

The soil engineer was not liable in *Swett v Gribaldo, Jones & Associate*,[239] where the engineer pointed out in the report:

> It is imperative, therefore, that any proposed construction on the five subject lots be reviewed by this office for approval and/or modification.... This certification... does not include any finish lot grading which may have been (or may be) required for residential construc-

---

[236] United States Fin v Sullivan, 37 Cal App 3d 5, 112 Cal Rptr 18 (1974). *See also* Cooper v Jevne, 56 Cal App 3d 860, 128 Cal Rptr 724 (1976) (condominium purchaser versus architect, project designed in a substandard manner and in violation of building codes; city inspectors could also have been liable for passing project which violated code).

[237] 44 NC App 701, 262 SE2d 355, *review denied*, 300 NC 371, 267 SE2d 673 (1980).

[238] Hobbs v Florida First Natl Bank, 406 So 2d 63 (Fla Dist Ct App 1981), *dismissed without opinion*, 412 So 2d 466 (Fla 1982).

[239] 40 Cal App 3d 573, 115 Cal Rptr 99 (1974).

tion. . . . The lots are hereby certified complete to rough grade and are now ready for final lot grading and/or residential improvements. Any such grading required, and of course the residential foundation construction itself, must be made in accordance with the requirements of our Soil Investigation Report, or acceptable methods, approved in writing by this office.[240]

The evidence showed that the subdivider went ahead with fine grading and foundation work without further consulting the soil engineer, and the fine grading changed the slope and the compaction. There was no evidence of negligence; therefore, the engineer could not be liable.

> [T]hose who sell their services for the guidance of others in their economic, financial, and personal affairs are not liable in the absence of negligence or intentional misconduct. . . . [T]he services of experts are sought because of their special skill. . . . [T]hose who hire such persons are not justified in expecting infallibility, but can expect only reasonable care and competence. They purchase service, not insurance.[241]

An engineer who was employed by a developer to provide engineering for a mobile home park obtained a building permit from the city, but failed to apply for a permit from the Department of Health and Environmental Control. The engineer, nevertheless, allowed the developer to proceed with construction, while concealing objections lodged by the department. HELD: the engineer was liable for the costs of bringing the project into compliance. Had it not been for the engineer's numerous breaches of contract, the department would have issued the permit and approved the project.[242]

Architect Not Liable to Lender

A developer employed an architect to prepare drawings for a project. The contract between the developer and the architect prohibited assignment of the contract without written consent. The developer defaulted on its loans to the lender and transferred title to the project to the lender in lieu of foreclosure. The developer attempted to assign its rights and causes of action to the lender, who then filed suit against the architect. The court held that the attempted assignment was invalid and that the lender was not an intended third-party beneficiary under the contract. Moreover, architects who breach their professional duties are liable in negligence only to those who foreseeably relied upon

---

[240] *Id* at 576, 115 Cal Rptr at 102.
[241] *Id* at 576, 115 Cal Rptr at 101.
[242] Foxfire Village, Inc v Black & Veatch, Inc, 304 SC 366, 404 SE2d 912 (Ct App 1991), *cert denied* (Aug 15, 1991).

their professional services. The possibility of liability to the lender following the developer's default and foreclosure was too remote to be foreseeable.[243]

§1.22 —Workers

Worker versus Architect

An architect may be liable for injuries to workers on the job. The widow of a deceased worker filed an action against an architect who had designed and supervised the construction of a building. The decedent was killed by the collapse of a wall which was supported by iron tubular girders resting on cast-iron pillars. The collapse occurred when workers were attempting to raise the pillar supporting a girder on which the wall rested. They employed jack screws, a method previously approved by the architect and successfully used to raise another pillar. The architect was not present when the collapse occurred. HELD: the verdict for plaintiff was AFFIRMED. The architect argued that it should not be liable for mere nonfeasance. The court accepted that rule in general but found that the evidence showed the architect was guilty of positive misfeasance either in approving an improper method for raising the pillars or in designing defective girders.[244]

Where an excavation caved in, killing a worker, the architect had the duty to inspect the work and the authority to stop the job. The project engineer had pointed out to the architect the fact that the excavation was unshored and was cracking because of wet clay. The architect agreed that the condition was dangerous and would be corrected, but the cave-in occurred nevertheless. The court held that liability for negligence resulting in death may be based on the supervisory activities of the architect, and privity of contract is not a prerequisite to liability. The descendant was in a zone of risk created by the architect's failure to act.[245]

In *Alexander v City of Shelbyville*,[246] a worker was killed when a sewer trench caved in. The contract between the city and the engineer provided that the engineer was to "determine compliance with the plans and specifications . . . [and] all work shall be done under the direct supervision of the [engineer]. . . ." HELD: The contractual duty to supervise the project did not impose a legal duty by contract on the engineer to exercise reasonable care for the safety of the worker.

---

[243] Mears Park Holding Corp v Morse/Diesel, Inc, 427 NW2d 281 (Minn Ct App 1988).

[244] Lottman v Barnett, 62 Mo 159 (1876). *See also* Potter v Gilbert, 130 AD 632, 115 NYS 425, *affd*, 196 NY 576, 90 NE 1165 (1909) (collapse of building under construction; court held that mere nonfeasance was insufficient to fasten liability for negligence on the architect).

[245] Swarthout v Beard, 33 Mich App 395, 190 NW2d 373 (1971), *revd as to damages*, Smith v City of Detroit, 388 Mich 637, 202 NW2d 300 (1972).

[246] 575 NE2d 1058 (Ind Ct App 1991).

In a similar holding, a steel worker was killed by falling steel when a concrete pier failed. The architect had ordered the pier to be poured when it was discovered that some steel beams were too short. Plaintiff alleged that the beams should have been refabricated. The concrete was poured in freezing weather and was not properly cured, and the steel was erected without safety cables. The architect denied that it had any duty to avoid injury to the steel worker. HELD: the supervisory authority of an architect coupled with inspection duties are sufficient to impose a duty of care to the decedent.[247]

An architect is not, however, an insurer of the safety of construction workers. Negligence must be proved. In a Utah case, a worker was injured when a tunnel collapsed while the Salt Lake City Metropolitan Hall of Justice was under construction. Plaintiff alleged that the architect should have discovered the dangerous condition and shut down the job. However, the job site contained 11 acres and 58 workers, and all of the on-site workers, including the plaintiff, testified that they thought the excavation was safe. Since there was no expert testimony that the defendant was negligent, the trial court judgment for the plaintiff was REVERSED.[248]

Some courts have held that an architect is not liable to an injured worker if the architect's authority is limited to inspection for the purpose of assuring the owner that the end product complies with the requirements of the contract documents. Plaintiff, working on the ceiling of a church, fell from scaffolding erected by the contractor. The scaffolding was not designed by the architect. Summary judgment for the architect was AFFIRMED. The architect would have been liable only if the architect had the duty to supervise the "method and manner of actually doing the work," and not if the supervisory controls were limited to those necessary to ensure that the contractor's work complied with the plans and specifications prepared by the architect.[249]

In *Duncan v Pennington City Housing Authority*,[250] the plaintiff was injured when a temporary guardrail failed to support his weight. The contract between the architect and the housing authority provided that 10 per cent of the architect's fee was for supervision of the work. Furthermore, the contract referred to Occupational Safety and Health Administration (OSHA) safety requirements. HELD: although the OSHA regulations do not establish a statutory right of action, they are admissible in evidence for a jury to consider in determining the standard of care.

---

[247] Cutlip v Lucky Stores, Inc, 22 Md App 673, 325 A2d 432 (1974).

[248] Nauman v Harold K. Beecher & Assocs, 19 Utah 2d 101, 426 P2d 621 (1967).

[249] Parks v Atkinson, 19 Ariz App 111, 505 P2d 279 (1973). *See also* Reber v Chandler High School Dist No 202, 13 Ariz App 133, 474 P2d 852 (1970) (workers injured when roof, supported by six steel arches, collapsed during construction; architect had no contractual or statutory obligation to control the contractor or the method and manner of the work).

[250] 283 NW2d 546 (SD 1979).

This case and others have held that an architect has no duty to guard workers against job site injury unless the duty is assumed by contract.[251] However, two cases have pointed out that an architect, by its conduct, may assume a degree of control over the job site that will create a duty to guard workers against injury.[252]

In *Belgum v Mitsuo Kawamoto & Associates*,[253] an injured worker's claim against an architect failed because the worker did not show that the actions of the architect were the proximate cause of the injury. The worker, a subcontractor's employee, was injured in a fall from a scaffold. The "architectural technician" who was employed by the owner for the work was told that the scaffold was shaky and substandard and without "safety ends."[254] The architectural representative took no action, since it did not consider itself qualified to advise on safety matters. HELD: under the contract, the architectural representative had no control over subcontractors. The contractor had full control of the situation and, thus, the negligent conduct of the contractor was an efficient intervening cause. Therefore, even if the architectural representative was negligent, that negligence was not the proximate cause of the injury.

In *Davis v Lenox School*,[255] the contract between the architect and the owner provided that the architect was not responsible for construction means, methods, safety precautions, or acts or omissions of the contractor or subcontractor. HELD: the architect was not liable for a job site worker injury.

Worker versus Engineer

In *Parent v Stone & Webster Engineering Corp*,[256] an electrocution claim of an injured worker was defeated by a six-year statute of repose. Although the defendant engineer had performed some construction management services during a period that was not barred by the statute of limitations, the electrician failed to demonstrate that the engineer owed a duty of care to the electrician.

Workers to be employed at a toxic chemical site may be within a class of persons foreseeably at risk to negligent conduct by an engineer who was employed to make recommendations for toxic cleanup. In *Henshaw v Edward E. Clark Engineers-Scientists*,[257] the owner was a company which salvaged electrical transformers containing highly toxic chemicals. The owner employed an engineer to sample the property for contamination of groundwater and to make

---

[251] *See* §4.03.

[252] Walters v Kellam & Foley, 172 Ind App 207, 360 NE2d 199 (1977); Clyde E. Williams & Assocs v Boatman, 176 Ind App 430, 375 NE2d 1138 (1978).

[253] 236 Neb 127, 459 NW2d 226 (1990).

[254] *Id* at 129, 459 NW2d at 228.

[255] 151 AD2d 230, 541 NYS2d 814 (1989).

[256] 408 Mass 108, 556 NE2d 1009 (1990).

[257] 490 So 2d 161 (Fla Dist Ct App 1986).

recommendations for cleanup. By a report dated February 26, 1979, the engineer represented that all remedial actions had been taken and that only traces of oil containing toxic substances remained on the owner's property. Approximately four years later, the site was found to be heavily contaminated. HELD: it was improper for the trial court to grant summary judgment in favor of the engineer because material questions of fact remained as to whether plaintiff workers were within the class of persons who could be harmed by the engineer's negligent performance.

Owner Not Liable

An owner is not generally liable for the negligence of an architect which causes injury to a construction worker. Where the owner employed a competent architect to design an eight-story building, the architect was required to examine the foundations before concrete was poured. The architect failed to inspect the foundations, and as a result, a steel support column was partially implanted in an old cistern. The architect also authorized a foundation slab to be reduced from its design thickness of 18 inches to an actual thickness of 12 inches. During construction the building collapsed, killing the decedent worker among others, and an action was brought against the building owner for negligence.

The accident would not have occurred if the building had been constructed as designed. The owner knew nothing of the design change authorized by the architect, and the owner was not competent to design and construct the building. It was the owner's duty to employ a competent architect, which it did. The owner also employed a competent builder and did not interfere with the design or construction of the project. Therefore, the owner removed itself from liability for the negligence of the builder and architect. Their negligence cannot be imputed to the owner; to adopt such a rule would effectively block all building, since real estate owners would be subjected to enormous hazards and potential losses.[258]

§1.23 —Invitees, Patrons, and Occupants

A number of cases have used a negligence theory to hold an architect liable for injuries to invitees, patrons, or occupants of buildings. In a California case, the plaintiff, an 80-year-old, overweight female patron of a bus station was injured when she fell on a stairway. She alleged that the handrail did not extend all the way to the bottom of the stairway, and that tile was installed at such an

---

[258] Burke v Ireland, 166 NY 305, 59 NE 914 (1910). *See also* United Gas Improvement Co v Larsen, 182 F 620 (CC Pa 1910).

angle as to make it appear that the stairs actually ended one step before they did. A judgment for the defendant was REVERSED. An architect who plans and supervises construction has a duty to any person who foreseeably and with reasonable certainty may be injured, even though the injury may occur after the work has been accepted by the owner.[259]

In *Hiatt v Brown*,[260] the patron of an airport was blown from a pedestrian ramp by the blast from a jet aircraft and sued the architect. Summary judgment for defendant was REVERSED. If the architect's negligent design created a condition where the jet blast reached the pedestrian ramp, a dangerous condition was created and lack of privity between the architect and the injured patron would not bar an action for negligence.

One court used the doctrine of *res ipsa loquitur* to find that the designer of warehouse tile storage racks was guilty of negligence and liable for damages when the racks collapsed, destroying the tile. However, the designer of the *floating slab* foundation for the warehouse met the burden of proving that it was not negligent. Although some differential settlement occurred (the elevation of the floor at its edges was higher than at center), it was so small (only 1-9/16 inches at the greatest point) that this was not a significant factor in the collapse.[261]

Where decedents were killed when their car rammed a bridge pier on a highway, plaintiff alleged that careful practice would require the installation of

---

[259] Montijo v Swift, 219 Cal App 2d 351, 33 Cal Rptr 133 (1963). *See also* **Coffey v Dormitory Auth**, 26 AD2d 1, 270 NYS2d 255 (1966) (student injured by glass panel adjacent to door in dormitory); Schipper v Levitt & Sons, 44 NJ 70, 207 A2d 314 (1965) (infant scalded by water from hot water tap; designer failed to specify mixing valve which would have cost $3.60 (dictum)); Mlynarski v St Rita's Congregation, 31 Wis 2d 54, 142 NW2d 207 (1966) (school girl who was walking fence, fell against window of school house four feet away); Hommel v Badger State Inv Co, 166 Wis 235, 165 NW 20 (1917) (plaintiff tripped on step allegedly located too close to the entrance door and in building lobby); Sherman v Miller Constr Co, 90 Ind App 462, 158 NE 255 (1927) (school boy pushed by friend, tripped over three-inch curb and fell into basement entry way at school ground); Totten v Gruzen, 52 NJ 202, 245 A2d 1 (1968) (three-year-old plaintiff burned attempting to climb hot piping system which resembled a ladder); Johnson v Salem Title Co, 246 Or 409, 425 P2d 519 (1967) (high wind blew down masonry wall, injuring pedestrian); Russell v Community Hosp Assn, 199 Kan 251, 428 P2d 783 (1967) (trip and fall on hospital steps); Laukkanen v Jewel Tea Co, 78 Ill App 2d 153, 222 NE2d 584 (1966) (wind blew piling on plaintiff as entering building); Cubito v Kreisberg, 94 Misc 2d 56, 404 NYS2d 69 (1978), *aff'd*, 51 NY2d 900, 415 NE2d 979, 434 NYS2d 991 (1980) (tenant fell in laundry room of apartment house); Quail Hollow East Condominium Assn v Donald J. Scholz Co, 47 NC App 518, 268 SE2d 12 (1975), *review denied*, 301 NC 527, 273 SE2d 454 (1980) (condominium association versus architect, privity of contract absent).

[260] 422 NE2d 736 (Ind Ct App 1981).

[261] Home Ins Co v A.J. Warehouse, Inc, 210 So 2d 544 (La Ct App 1968). *See also* **Mai Kai, Inc v Colucci**, 205 So 2d 291 (Fla 1967) (patron injured as counterweight wheel fell from ceiling fan); Greenberg v City of Yonkers, 45 AD2d 314, 358 NYS2d 453 (1974), *aff'd*, 37 NY2d 907, 340 NE2d 744, 378 NYS2d 382 (1975) (fire of incendiary origin which was fed by plastic members designed by architect).

a guardrail. The defense contended that criteria adopted by the Kentucky Department of Highways did not require guardrails, and deviation from the criteria was prohibited. HELD: since recommendation of guardrails would have been futile and contrary to law, a failure to employ them could not have been negligence.[262]

An owner sold a building under a contract assigning the owner's right, title, and interest to all leases and contracts, including warranties, guarantees, and bonds. The buyer found fault with the building and filed an action against the design architect based on the contractual assignment. The architect asserted that the assignment was invalid based on a provision in the contract between the architect and the original owner that prohibited assignment of the agreement for architectural services. The trial court granted the architect's motion for summary judgment, and the court of appeal REVERSED. The owner assigned every right and interest that it had in the property to the buyer. The *nonassignability clause* merely prohibited the transfer of an interest in the performance of the executory contract and did not apply, as here, to prevent an action for damages for breach of a fully executed contract.[263]

In *Stephens v Sterns*,[264] a tenant sued an architect for injuries sustained when she fell down a stairwell without a handrail. HELD: the question of whether the architect had breached a duty of care and whether the absence of a handrail was the proximate cause of the injury should have gone to the jury.

California's Attorney General has opined that a registered engineer, retained to investigate the integrity of a building, who determines that there is an imminent risk of serious injury to the occupants and who is advised by the owner that no disclosure should be made and the determinations should remain confidential, nevertheless has a duty to warn identifiable occupants of the building of danger.[265]

§1.24 —Sureties and Indemnitors

An architect owes a duty of care to a contractor's performance bond surety, notwithstanding absence of privity.[266]

---

[262] Rigsby v Brighton Engg Co, 464 SW2d 279 (Ky 1970).

[263] Ford v Robertson, 739 SW2d 3 (Tenn Ct App 1987).

[264] 106 Idaho 249, 678 P2d 41 (1984).

[265] Ca Atty Gen Op, Op 208 (1985). (For further discussion of parties potentially entitled to recover in a negligence action against an architect or engineer, see Williams, *Cause of Action Against Architect or Engineer for Negligence in the Preparation of Plans or Specifications*, 5 Causes of Action §§12, 13 (Shepard's/McGraw-Hill 1983-84).)

[266] *See* Designed Ventures, Inc v Housing Auth, 132 BR 677 (Bankr DRI 1991) (surety alleged architect negligently authorized release of retention knowing that contractor was behind schedule and had not been paying its subcontractors and suppliers).

§1.24 SURETIES & INDEMNITORS   63

In *Westerhold v Carroll*,[267] the Supreme Court of Missouri, reversing the trial court which had sustained a demurrer, held that an architect can be liable to the indemnitor of a contractor's surety for certifying payments for $23,000 in excess of the value of work performed on a $325,000 church job. The architect was under a legal duty to the surety to exercise ordinary care so that the contractor would not be overpaid, since the stipulation for periodic payments is as much for the benefit of the surety as for the owner. To justify the imposition of liability to the surety (a liability not previously found in Missouri law) the court quoted from Chief Justice Fortesque. "Sir, the law is as I say it is, and so it has been laid down ever since the law began; and we have several set forms which are held as law, and so held and used for good reason, though we cannot at present remember that reason."[268]

In construction of a courthouse, an architect certified monthly payments totaling $314,000 to the prime contractor. The contractor defaulted, and the contractor's surety was required to finish the job. The surety filed an action against the architect on the theory that the architect was negligent in certifying the contractor's bills for payment. HELD: the surety was subrogated to any claim the owner would have had against the architect for negligent certification of progress payments.[269]

In *URS Co v Gulfport-Biloxi Regional Airport Authority*,[270] an airport authority filed an action for damages for breach of contract against its architect, its prime contractor, and the prime contractor's surety. The surety filed a cross-claim against the architect for indemnity. Under the terms of its agreement, the architect provided a full-time resident inspector. Despite warnings from a roofing expert, the inspector approved the roofing system and certified the construction as compliant with the requirements of the plans and specifications. Thus, the architect was found responsible for its failure to protect the owner against defective construction of the roof system. The architect was also held liable to indemnify the surety for a loss sustained by the surety when it was unable to avail itself of the equitable right of subrogation against construction funds in the hands of the owner. The construction funds were no longer in the hands of the owner: the architect had prematurely approved the release of the retention to the contractor.

---

[267] 419 SW2d 73 (Mo 1967).

[268] 3 W. Holdsworth, A History of English Law (1903). *See also* City of Durham v Reidsville Engg Co, 255 NC 98, 120 SE2d 564 (1961) (architect certified defective work, city filed suit against surety when defects were discovered; and surety cross-complained against engineer for negligence. HELD: in view of exculpatory language in contract, there was no cause of action, and engineer's demurrer was sustained).

[269] Peerless Ins Co v Cerny & Assocs, 199 F Supp 951 (D Minn 1961).

[270] 544 So 2d 824 (Miss 1989).

§1.25 —Other Remote Parties

Subsequent Purchasers

In *Southeast Consultants, Inc v O'Pry*,[271] an engineer was employed by a developer to perform percolation tests. After the developer finished construction, the owner purchased the home. Three months thereafter the noxious condition of the septic tank manifested itself. A verdict of $125,000 for the owner against the engineer was AFFIRMED. The owner had standing. It was foreseeable that the person directly injured as the result of the engineer's negligence would have been the purchaser of the house. Therefore, the engineer owed a clear duty to the future homeowner in that regard.

In a Louisiana case,[272] builder employed the House of Plans, an unlicensed architect, to prepare drawings for condominium units. Learning that it needed approval of the fire marshall in order to obtain a building permit, builder employed architect to design interior fire walls. Architect removed the House of Plans logo and applied its seal to the drawings. When brick veneer walls began to separate from wood frames, condominium owners filed an action against the architect who sealed the plans. The trial court dismissed the complaint against the architect. AFFIRMED. (1) An architect does not guaranty perfect plans. (2) The architect did not design the defective parts of the project, and there was no evidence that the builder relied on the architect's seal.

Sub-Subcontractor

In *Seattle Western Industries v David A. Mowat Co*,[273] a sub-subcontractor assigned its claims against the architect to a subcontractor. HELD: the claim was defeated by the statute of limitations.

Bondholder

In *Haberman v Washington Public Power Supply System*,[274] it was held that purchasers of bonds used to finance nuclear power plants stated a good cause of action against engineers, based on the allegation that the engineers negligently misrepresented the structural feasibility of the project knowing that this misrepresentation would be used in the prospectus for the bond issue.

For summaries of cases in which third parties who are not in privity with the architect have made claims, see Appendix A. Cases are collected under the following headings: Owner, Remote Owner, Tenant, Neighbor, Patron,

---

[271] 199 Ga App 125, 404 SE2d 299 (1991), *cert denied* (May 15, 1991).
[272] McKeen Homeowners Assn v Oliver, 586 So 2d 679 (La Ct App 1991).
[273] 110 Wash 2d 1, 750 P2d 245 (1988).
[274] 109 Wash 2d 107, 744 P2d 1032 (1987).

Lender, Third Party, Vehicle Occupant, Infant, Worker, Contractor, Subcontractor, Surety, and Architect.

§1.26 Liability Arising from Real Estate Law

An adjoining landowner's action against a surveyor for *continuing trespass* was dismissed after demurrer was sustained. AFFIRMED. A surveyor of a disputed boundary line does not owe a duty of care to an adjoining landowner who does not rely on the survey.[275]

A nuisance complaint against an engineer was dismissed after demurrer was sustained. REVERSED. The complaint alleged that the engineer, employed by the upper owner, negligently designed a landslide fix so as to obstruct the free use of the plaintiff's (the lower owner's) property. California Civ Code §3479 defines *nuisance* as an obstruction to the free use of property. Therefore, the plaintiff stated a cause of action that would support recovery.[276]

---

[275] Carlotta v T.R. Stark & Assocs, 57 Md App 467, 470 A2d 838 (1984).
[276] Shurpin v Elmhirst, 148 Cal App 3d 94, 195 Cal Rptr 737 (1983).

Liability for Intentional Torts

2

§2.01 Fraud
Fraudulent Misrepresentation
False Payment Certificate
Fraudulent Concealment
§2.02 Conspiracy
§2.03 Conflict of Interest
§2.04 Slander
Qualified Privilege
Innocent Construction Rule
Libel Per Se
Qualified Immunity
Litigation Privilege
§2.05 Interference with Contract
Requirement of Malice
Agency Defense
Immunity of Arbitrator
Tortious Interference
Litigation Privilege
Privilege Not Shown
Statute of Limitations
Privity of Contract Defense
§2.06 Trespass
§2.07 Bad Faith
§2.08 Conversion

§2.01 Fraud

Few cases can be found in which an architect or engineer is accused of fraud, and even fewer where the allegation has been proved. Naturally, since an architect or engineer is liable for negligent performance of its duties, liability is also imposed for fraudulent performance.

Fraudulent Misrepresentation

In *Strouth v Wilkison*,[1] an owner accused a designer/contractor of fraudulent misrepresentation of fact. The designer/contractor submitted plans for a country home, promised to build it for $38,000, and falsely claimed 17 years of experience in the building business (temporarily suspended because of ill health). The designer/contractor claimed the status of an engineer with bonding capacity and a net worth of $75,000. The facts were that the defendant left the construction business after becoming bankrupt, was not an engineer, had a net worth was $45,000, and because of defendant's bankruptcy, was not bondable.

After spending $25,000, the defendant abandoned the project when it had a value of $12,000. The owner employed another contractor to finish the job. The total expense was $79,300 for a house with a reasonable value of $48,000. The court held that the evidence was sufficient to support the judgment that the misrepresentations made by the defendant were intentional, were of material facts, and were the proximate cause of the plaintiff's injuries.

Where it was shown that the defendant architect, who also acted as a contractor, fraudulently underestimated the project cost at less than $12,000, whereas the actual cost was $22,000, the owners recovered $1,000 damages for the misrepresentation.[2]

An owner who is induced to commission an architect through fraudulent misrepresentations may rescind the commission even after drawing and contract documents have been prepared.[3] The county alleged that the board of supervisors was induced to give the commission to Hall by one Holcomb, who represented himself to be an unbiased expert but was, in fact, the agent of Hall.

In an Indiana case, an architect advised the owner to reject a $26,000 bid, but to award the work to plaintiff contractor on a cost-plus basis. The owner took the advice, and the project cost $47,000. The owner refused to pay the contract price, alleging that the contractor and the architect entered into a conspiracy to increase the cost of the building for their own profit.

---

[1] 302 Minn 297, 224 NW2d 511 (1974).
[2] Goldberg v Underhill, 95 Cal App 2d 700, 213 P2d 516 (1950).
[3] Hall v City of Los Angeles, 74 Cal 502, 16 P 131 (1888).

AFFIRMED. The alleged fraud constituted a good defense. The owner was not required to make any further payment to the contractor.[4]

In *Manning Engineering, Inc v Hudson County Park Commission*,[5] the plaintiff architect, having received $138,365 for engineering services, recovered judgment for an additional $134,522.37. REVERSED. Testimony at trial showed that the contract had been awarded to Manning by the Park Commission as a reward for faithful services in providing "the channel through which contractors made their payoffs on all their contracts"[6] to Mayor John V. Kenny. The trial judge concluded that Manning played a role as the "conduit between extorters and extortees."[7] The contract was illegal and corrupt. Plaintiff was not entitled to an award of damages for the breach of such a contract.

An architect was exonerated from a charge of fraud where contract documents called for structural steel flooring but included reinforced concrete as "alternate seven." Members of the school board were present when bids were opened, and it was explained that it was customary to bid alternates. The school district accused the architect of fraudulently switching from steel to concrete flooring, but the jury verdict was for the defendant.[8]

In another fraud action by a contractor, it was alleged that engineers employed by a city had dug several test trenches to determine ground water conditions but disclosed to bidders only the favorable data and concealed the unfavorable part. The court held that the allegations were sufficient to withstand a motion for judgment on the pleadings.[9]

It has been held that an architect is not liable to a contractor for failure to issue a payment certificate, since the architect, in issuing certificates, acts in the capacity of an arbitrator and has an arbitrator's immunity from suit.[10] However, a fraudulent refusal to issue a certificate is actionable.[11]

A plaintiff cannot avoid the operation of the statute of limitations by casting a malpractice complaint in the language of fraud.[12]

---

[4] Rice v Caldwell, 87 Ind App 616, 161 NE 651 (1928).

[5] 74 NJ 113, 376 A2d 1194 (1977).

[6] *Id* at 126, 376 A2d at 1200.

[7] *Id* at 119, 376 A2d at 1197.

[8] School Dist No 5 v Ferrier, 122 Kan 15, 251 P 425 (1926). *See also* Forte v Tripp & Skrip, 339 So 2d 698 (Fla Dist Ct App 1976) (summary judgment for defendant reversed because the record showed an issue of fact as to whether or not the architect misrepresented zoning requirements).

[9] Salem Sand & Gravel Co v City of Salem, 260 Or 630, 492 P2d 271 (1971).

[10] *See* §9.09.

[11] Unity Sheet Metal Works v Farrell Lines, 101 NYS2d 1000 (Sup Ct 1950) (subcontractor alleged that engineer maliciously, fraudulently, and with intent to injure refused to issue payment certificate).

[12] Lewis v Axinn, 100 AD2d 617, 473 NYS2d 575 (1984) (brick facing had pulled away from the underlying cement wall of a building).

The cause of action for fraud belongs to the party to whom misrepresentations were made and not to the party's neighbor.[13]

False Payment Certificate

In *Corey v Eastman*,[14] Justice Holmes considered the appeal of an architect from a verdict for the plaintiff on the second count of a complaint, which alleged that the defendant falsely, negligently, and in collusion with a builder gave a payment certificate which represented the value of labor and materials to be in excess of the actual value.

> This, we think, in spite of the word "negligently," is raised by the allegation of collusion to a somewhat timid charge of fraud [citation]; and whatever may be the view of an architect's position in giving a certificate, no one, we suppose, would doubt that a fraudulent combination with the builder to give a false certificate, if followed by payment on the faith of the representation, would be a good cause of action.

Probably under the English law the defendant would not have been liable for negligence in making its certificate upon a matter which the plaintiff and builder had agreed by their contract to leave to the defendant. (Apparently this was a reference to the rule that an architect may have the immunity of an arbitrator.)

A different principle applies to oral advice, since the architect, in giving such advice, may be rendering a purely partisan service under the contract:

> [T]hen he is bound to show reasonable care and reasonable professional judgment. As a consequence of his contract of employment the law throws the risk of his statements upon him at an earlier point than it would do otherwise. But for the contract he would not be liable for statements unless fraudulent, or for advice unless dishonest. Under the contract negligently erroneous statements and imprudent advice become torts, on the same principle that under a warranty an erroneous statement was a deceit by the old common law, without even negligence.

It may be impertinent to disagree with the great jurist, but if an architect is bound by a contract to employ reasonable care and reasonable professional judgment, then a negligently erroneous statement is a breach of contract. The same negligently erroneous statement may also be a tort, but it seems that the existence of the contract is just another factor to be considered in determining whether the conduct was negligent, rather than the ingredient which transmutes lawful conduct into tortious conduct.

---

[13] Shurpin v Elmhirst, 148 Cal App 3d 94, 195 Cal Rptr 737 (1983) (allegations that engineer issued a fraudulent report to the plaintiff's neighbor).

[14] 166 Mass 279, 44 NE 217 (1896).

In *Mercy Hospital v Hansen, Lind & Meyer PC*,[15] additions to a hospital were complete in 1974; in 1979 and 1981, cracks appeared in the exterior brick; water, bats, and wasps entered the building; rust appeared on the exterior brick; bricks began to crumble and chip. The engineer recommended recaulking, and represented that this would solve the problem. It did not. The Iowa Supreme Court AFFIRMED the verdict of $3,185,367 that assigned 55 per cent fault to the architect and 45 per cent to other defendants. HELD: the hospital was entitled to recover the costs of recaulking, since the architect had fraudulently misrepresented that recaulking would cure the problems.

An award of punitive damages to an owner against an architect was REVERSED in *William Dorsky Associates v Highlands County Title & Guaranty Land Co.*[16] An architect filed an action against a property owner to foreclose a mechanics lien for architectural services in connection with the construction of a hotel. The owner counterclaimed, alleging that the architect had recorded a fraudulent lien. The trial court awarded punitive damages to the owner. REVERSED. The owner contended that the architect was only entitled to payment of $30,000 since the contract was terminated during the schematic design phase. The architect contended that the contract had been terminated at the end of the design development phase, and claimed payment of an additional $53,532.87. HELD: the architect's contention was made in good faith and, therefore, punitive damages should not have been awarded. "Wrongful acts committed by mistake in the good faith assertion of a supposed right will not support a punitive award."[17]

Bond purchasers who had invested in nuclear power projects alleged that project engineers had fraudulently misrepresented the structural feasibility of the project and that these misrepresentations found their way into the bond prospectus that was relied upon by the bond purchasers when they made their investments. The court held that the bond purchasers had stated a good cause of action, since the engineers gave information to the power company knowing that the company would pass the information along to prospective investors.[18]

Fraudulent Concealment

Silence may constitute fraud if one has a duty to disclose. In *Holy Cross Parish v Huether*,[19] Holy Cross alleged fraud against the architect who designed and supervised the construction of an auditorium on unsuitable fill. The court concluded that a fiduciary relationship existed between the architect and Holy

---

[15] 456 NW2d 666 (Iowa 1990).

[16] 528 So 2d 411 (Fla Dist Ct App 1988).

[17] *Id* 412.

[18] Haberman v Washington Pub Power Supply Sys, 109 Wash 2d 107, 744 P2d 1032 (1987).

[19] 308 NW2d 575 (SD 1981).

Cross when the architect performed supervisory functions. When a fiduciary relationship exists between the parties, mere silence may constitute fraudulent concealment. The facts suggest that the architect knowingly misrepresented the actual condition of the fill when the building was completed by issuing the final certificate which assured the acceptability of the building.

A registered professional engineer was guilty of fraud in preparing a "subsoil exploration report" that was used in connection with a sale of land by the engineer's family corporation.[20] The report indicated that the water table was at a depth of seven feet when the actual water table was only one and one-half feet below the surface. The engineer failed to disclose to the purchaser the Health Department's requirement that the sewer system be located in the front yard. As a result, the plaintiff was required to redesign the sewer system, which also became more costly. HELD: the engineer made false representations to the buyer which were intended to, and did, induce the buyer to purchase the property.

In *Nei v Boston Survey Consultants, Inc*,[21] the defendant surveyors prepared a high water and percolation report for the sellers. The sellers then sold lots to plaintiff buyers. The surveyors had no contract with the buyers. HELD: mere nondisclosure does not amount to fraud where there is no duty to speak. The surveyors had no contractual or business relationship with the purchasers. However, where a registered surveyor falsely represented to the Board of Professional Engineers and Land Surveyors that the monumentation of a survey was complete, the board was authorized to suspend the surveyor's certificate of registration for misrepresentation.[22]

§2.02 Conspiracy

It may well be doubted that *conspiracy* is a separate tort. Conspiracy is fraud committed by persons acting in concert. For example, in a New York case, a consulting engineer was named as an unindicted conspirator for specifying a particular brand of pre-cast lock joint sewer pipe which was available from only one dealer, who monopolistically doubled the price.[23]

When taxpayers filed suit against an architect and others, claiming that they conspired to give an unfair advantage to a particular bidder on a botanical conservatory project, the court held that the architect's errors and omissions

---

[20] Greco v Mancini, 476 A2d 522 (RI 1984).

[21] 388 Mass 320, 446 NE2d 681 (1983). *Accord* Waterford Condominium Assn v Dunbar Corp, 104 Ill App 3d 371, 432 NE2d 1009 (1982).

[22] *In re* Shaw, 189 Mont 310, 615 P2d 910 (1980).

[23] People v Connolly, 253 NY 330, 171 NE 393 (1930). *See also* Rice v Caldwell, 87 Ind App 616, 161 NE 651 (1928) (owner alleged a conspiracy between architect and contractor to inflate the costs of a building project).

policy did not cover the risk. The policy excluded liability for intentional, dishonest, wrongful, or malicious acts.[24]

§2.03 Conflict of Interest

A striking feature of construction projects, and of construction litigation, is multiple parties. A building project is a yeasty mixture of contractors, subcontractors, material manufacturers, distributors, lenders, sureties, owners, architects, and engineers. The very position of an architect who supervises a project creates a conflict of interest with the owner, because the architect must deal fairly with the contractor even though this might damage the client's economic interests.

> [T]he high point in the architect's practice of his profession lies in those instances when, in order to do justice to the contractor, he has to oppose the desire of his employer. He occupies a position of trust and confidence. When he acts under a contract as the official interpreter of its conditions and the judge of its performance, he should favor neither side, but exercise impartial judgment.[25]

Thus, an architect needs the fortitude to rule in favor of a contractor and against a client and risk retaliation at the time for payment of fees.

The standard *percentage of cost* architectural fee contract creates a conflict of interest with the owner: The higher the cost of the project, the higher the architect's fee. The lower the cost, the lower the fee.[26]

One court has held that evidence of conflict of interest was sufficient to go to the jury on the issue of fraud where an owner employed an architect without knowing that the architect was also employed, at the same time, by the project contractor on another job. Therefore, both the owner and the contractor occupied the position of client. The architect issued payment certificates without demanding mechanics lien releases from subcontractors and material suppliers. The contractor became insolvent. The cost of the project was increased by $15,000. The court noted the suspicious circumstance that the architect had demanded releases from the same contractor on a previous job, but, after the contractor became the architect's client, certified payment without demanding releases.[27]

---

[24] Grieb v Citizens Casualty, 33 Wis 2d 552, 148 NW2d 103 (1967). *See also* State v Campbell, 217 Kan 756, 539 P2d 329, *cert denied*, 423 US 1017 (1975) (18 individuals indicted for conspiracy to bribe a public employee to award an architectural contract for a medical center).

[25] Macomber v State, 250 Cal App 2d 391, 397, 58 Cal Rptr 393, 398 (1967).

[26] *See* Rice v Caldwell, 87 Ind App 616, 161 NE 651 (1928).

[27] Palmer v Brown, 127 Cal App 2d 44, 273 P2d 306 (1954).

§2.04 Slander

Occasionally an architect, as adviser to an owner, will recommend that a contractor be ejected from the job or will advise against the employment of a contractor or subcontractor because of perceived incompetence or financial irresponsibility. This sets the stage for a claim of *slander*. *Lundgren v Freeman*,[28] is an example. An architect advised a school district to terminate its construction contract. HELD: (1) If the architect was acting as an agent of the owner, it would not be liable except for intentional misconduct. (2) If the architect was acting as a quasi-arbitrator it would be immune. (3) Sufficient evidence of intentional misconduct was present to avoid summary judgment.

A consulting engineer recommended, in a public hearing, that a public contract not be awarded to the low bidder because of the low bidder's inexperience with the system contemplated for the construction of a triple chairlift. The low-bidding contractor filed an action against the consultant to recover damages for slander and tortious interference with prospective business relations. The consultant's motion for summary judgment was GRANTED. Such statements of opinion were not defamatory under New Hampshire law. The consultant's remarks at the hearing were within the scope of the purpose of the hearing and the bidder's level of experience was not misrepresented.[29]

Plaintiff engineer submitted plans and specifications for the upgrading and expansion of a private sewer treatment plant and water supply facility. Problems were encountered in the operation of the plant and defendant engineers were employed to prepare a report regarding the design and operational characteristics of the facility. Plaintiff filed an action alleging that the statements in the report were false and defamatory. Summary judgment dismissing the complaint was AFFIRMED. The conclusions of the report were mere expressions of the defendants' engineering opinion and were adequately supported by the statement of underlying facts. There was no showing that the facts were false.[30]

Qualified Privilege

In *Alfred A. Altimont, Inc v Chatelain, Samperton & Nolan*,[31] the general contractor on a church project fell far behind schedule. The architect wrote to the contractor's bonding company, expressing distress at the slow progress and reporting that on many days no workers appeared on the job site. A few days later, the architect again wrote to the surety, concluding that the contractor was "extremely negligent in his duties." The contractor brought an action for libel

---

[28] 307 F2d 104 (9th Cir 1962).
[29] Riblet Tramway Co v Ericksen Assocs, 665 F Supp 81 (DNH 1987).
[30] Lapar v Morris, 119 AD2d 635, 501 NYS2d 82 (1986).
[31] 374 A2d 284 (DC 1977).

and interference with business relations, alleging that the acts of the architect caused the contractor to be driven out of business because of a loss of bonding capacity. The directed verdict for the defendant was AFFIRMED. Letters from the architect to the bonding company fall under the qualified privilege that exists when a party who has a common interest with another shares facts it reasonably believes the other is entitled to know. The privilege is lost only if the writer acts with malice. Here, the architect was the church's agent during construction and had a duty to protect the interest of its principal. The evidence showed that it was customary for an architect to keep a surety apprised of job status, especially when the surety might be called upon to take over performance of the project. Since the architect acted to protect the client, the evidence was insufficient to establish malice and the directed verdict for the architect was proper.

In *Twelker v Shannon & Wilson, Inc*,[32] the plaintiff soil engineer prepared a soil report that was used in the construction of a building. The structure was damaged by a landslide two months after completion. The general contractor's insurance company employed the defendant soil engineering firm to investigate and report the cause of the landslide. After inspecting the site and reviewing the plaintiff's soil report, the defendant prepared a report criticizing the soil investigation by the plaintiff. The trial court granted summary judgment for the defendant on the ground that the statements were made within the context of a judicial proceeding. REVERSED. The report to the insurance company was made before the initiation of a lawsuit; therefore, the absolute privilege for statements made in judicial proceedings was not available. However, the defendant did have a qualified privilege. The privilege could be overcome by evidence that the statements were made without a fair and impartial investigation, that the statements were not based on reasonable grounds, or that the statements were made without belief in their veracity. Since an issue of fact existed, the plaintiff was entitled to a full trial on the merits and summary judgment was improper.

In *Kecko Piping Co v Town of Monroe*,[33] an architect's claim of qualified privilege was upheld. The architect was employed by the town to examine the plans and specifications for a school remodeling project. The architect had authority to reject unacceptable subcontractors. Upon learning that the successful prime contractor had listed the plaintiff as a subcontractor, the architect requested written data from the plaintiff. The plaintiff did not respond, and the architect finally advised the town that it would be in its best interests to have the prime contractor employ a different subcontractor. HELD: when an architect is retained by a town to assist in obtaining bids and evaluating them, the

---

[32] 88 Wash 2d 473, 564 P2d 1131 (1977).
[33] 172 Conn 197, 374 A2d 179 (1977).

architect enjoys a qualified privilege, which, on the basis of the facts of this case, the architect did not exceed.

In a Texas case, *Victor M. Solis Underground Utility & Paving Co v City of Laredo*,[34] it was held that an engineer has a privilege to make reasonable recommendations to the owner with reference to a contractor's performance. The engineers on a storm sewer project, after continuing delays and disputes concerning the quality of work, recommended that the city order the contractor to suspend work. The contractor filed action against the engineers for interference with contractual relations. HELD: "Interference with contractual relations is privileged where it results from a bona fide exercise of a party's own rights or where the party possesses an equal or superior interest to that of the plaintiff in the subject matter."[35] Here, the engineer was required by contract to oversee the project and had the absolute right to reject work that did not meet contract specifications. The engineer exercised its "superior legitimate interest by recommending termination."[36]

In *Gherardi v Board of Education*,[37] a general contractor experienced a delay of 11 months on a school job which, by contract, was supposed to be finished in 400 days. The specifications provided that the architects would coordinate the work of all contractors, and that the contractor would be entitled to an extension of time, but not damages, for unavoidable delay.

A year after accepting final payment without protest, the contractor filed suit against the architect, alleging interference with the contractor's performance by failure to properly coordinate and supervise the work. The court held that the contractor failed to state a cause of action against the architect, since there was no allegation of any intent on the architect's part to injure the contractor in the business, nor did the contractor allege that the architect acted maliciously. Furthermore, the exculpatory clause in the contract clearly barred an action for damages unless it was shown that one of the parties acted in bad faith.

In *Edward B. Fitzpatrick Jr Construction Corp v County of Suffolk*,[38] a contractor employed by a county for construction of a sewer line under the Great South Bay filed an action against the engineer after the county terminated the contract when it became apparent that the contractor would not be able to finish the project on time. HELD: the evidence did not show intentional interference with contractual obligations.

It seems that the Ninth Circuit decision is correct in principle. An architect should be free, in the exercise of good faith, to require the contractor to replace

---

[34] 751 SW2d 532 (Tex Ct App 1988), *error denied* (June 28, 1989).
[35] *Id* 535.
[36] *Id* 535.
[37] 53 NJ Super 349, 147 A2d 535 (1958).
[38] 138 AD2d 446, 525 NYS2d 863 (1988).

defective work, or to withhold payment certificates, or even to recommend that the contractor be ejected from the job. Indeed, the architect, in the discharge of the fiduciary obligations to the client, on proper occasion must take action detrimental to the interests of the contractor and should be protected in doing so as long as it acts in good faith. The *qualified privilege* defense is available if the contractor sues for slander; the same privilege should exist if the suit is for intentional interference with contractual relations.

Innocent Construction Rule

In *Vee See Construction Co v Jensen & Halstead, Ltd*,[39] an architect wrote a letter to a general contractor directing the contractor to comply with the contract documents in painting a project. The contractor sued the architect, alleging libel in that the letter falsely implied that the plaintiff was cheating by applying only two, instead of the required three, coats of paint. The court applied the *innocent construction rule*, which requires that words allegedly libelous that are capable of being read innocently "must be read and declared nonactionable as a matter of law."[40] The letter was not defamatory because it reasonably could be interpreted as an attempt to resolve a misunderstanding, rather than an imputation of dishonesty.

Libel Per Se

In *Vojak v Jensen*,[41] a 10-year feud between an architect and a roofing subcontractor began on a school job in 1957, when each blamed the other for a defective roof. In 1963, the subcontractor bid another school job and was rejected by the architect who wrote two letters, one to the subcontractor with a copy to the school district and the general contractor, another to the general contractor. The letters implied that the plaintiff was incompetent:

September 5, 1963

United Roofing Company
P.O. Box 956
Fort Dodge, Iowa

Attention: Leo Campbell

    Re: Humboldt High School

    M. E. Jensen writing—

---

[39] 79 Ill App 3d 1084, 399 NE2d 278 (1979).
[40] *Id* at 1086, 399 NE2d at 280.
[41] 161 NW2d 100 (Iowa 1968).

Leo, as a result of yours and Hugo's telephone conversation of yesterday, Smitty, Hugo and myself have visited at some length regarding this matter. In view of the experience which we have had at Manson, I am sure you can understand our not being able to give you approval as the roofing sub-contractor on this project. This is harsh action Leo, but we feel that recent experience demands it.

In order to prevent future embarrassing situations such as we have here at Humboldt, we are asking Leo, that you in the future refrain from bidding work out of our office. When you can prove to our satisfaction that we may again consider you as a reliable roofing contractor, we shall give all consideration to your again bidding on our work. Your cooperation in this regard with us will be appreciated and will be of benefit to the construction industry and our clients.

Smith—Voorhees—Jensen
ARCHITECTS ASSOCIATED
/s/ M. E. Jensen
M. E. Jensen, A.I.A.

cc: Clyde Mease, Supt. Humboldt Community School District
    Sande Construction Company

(Handwritten postscript) Leo—It will not be necessary that you come into our office Monday as discussed. Will be happy, however, to visit with you any time we might get together.

September 5, 1963

Sande Construction Company
P.O. Box 368
Humboldt, Iowa

Attention: Gunnie Sande

    Re: Humboldt High School Roofing Contract

M. E. Jensen writing—

Gunnie, the attached letter to United Roofing Company I believe you will find self-explanatory. Fortunately we have not had too many instances wherein we were forced to take such action as we have here. However, when it is necessary we are prepared to do so and in the interests of General Contractors as well as our clients. We do not feel that we can afford to run the risk of involving the Humboldt School District and yourself in a situation such as has developed at Manson. We regret the necessity for having to take this action, but can see no alternative.

We are fully aware that Leo has performed considerable work in the Humboldt area and for the Humboldt School District and that his services have apparently been highly satisfactory. We are also aware that you yourself apparently have some confidence in his organization. We are reluctant to disturb these apparent good relationships but nevertheless cannot disregard our own experience.

We would consider going along with United Roofing Company on this project if you would give us a letter stating that your firm would assume complete responsibility for this work. Upon receipt of such a letter, Gunnie, we will consider the matter closed and anticipate that you would give the Humboldt School District complete protection as to the satisfactory fulfillment of the roofing contract. We trust that some such arrangement can be worked out to the satisfaction and protection of all parties, we, however, cannot ignore our responsibilities in the matter.

Smith—Voorhees—Jensen
ARCHITECTS ASSOCIATED
/s/ M. E. Jensen
M. E. Jensen, A.I.A.

cc: Clyde Mease

The general contractor canceled the subcontract. The jury awarded $60,000 actual and $15,000 punitive damages. The trial court granted a new trial on grounds of excessive verdict and injustice. The appellate court held that a new trial was necessary because of erroneous instructions. The plaintiff had a good cause of action, since a charge of business incompetence is *libel per se*. There is a qualified privilege where a communication is made in good faith by a party with a recognized interest to protect. The qualified privilege, however, is no defense if the derogatory statements are made with actual malice. Here, the relationship of architect to owner establishes the qualified privilege, and the burden was on the plaintiff to defeat the privilege by proof of actual malice.

Qualified Immunity

A city's director of design informed local newspapers that a soils engineer performed incompetent and substandard work. HELD: the director may be entitled to qualified immunity depending on whether a reasonable person in its situation could have formed a reasonable belief that plaintiff's soils analysis was primarily to blame.[42]

---

[42] Western Technologies, Inc v Neal, 159 Ariz 433, 768 P2d 165 (1988).

Litigation Privilege

The owner of a stadium retained an engineer to review geotechnical engineering work performed by the design engineer. In its report, the second engineer criticized the design engineer's work. The owner sued the design engineer, who settled. The design engineer then filed an action against the review engineer who had prepared the defamatory report. The review engineer's motion for judgment on the pleadings was granted. The Supreme Court of Arizona AFFIRMED.[43] (1) No cause of action was stated for negligent misrepresentation, since the plaintiff did not rely on the allegedly false information supplied by the review engineer. (2) Since the review engineer made its report to the owner at a time when the owner was seriously contemplating litigation, the report was a necessary step in taking legal action and, therefore, absolutely privileged. (3) Likewise, the absolute privilege protected the review engineer against the design engineer's cause of action for interference with the design engineer's continued business relationship with the owner.

§2.05 Interference with Contract

In protecting the interests of an owner, an architect may require a contractor to change its methods of construction, remove faulty work, and discharge incompetent workers, and may even recommend that a contractor be ejected from the job. Such action may expose an architect to liability for interference with contractual relationships.

In *Alfred A. Altimont, Inc v Chaterlain, Samperton & Nolan*,[44] an architect wrote letters to a general contractor's bonding company, alleging that the contractor was guilty of delay and negligence in performing a church job. Plaintiff filed an action against the architect for interference with business relations. A directed verdict for defendant was AFFIRMED. To establish a *prima facie* case, it would be necessary to show intentional interference and resulting damage. The record showed that, while the letters from the architect to the bonding company may have been a factor, the real cause for the inability to make bond was the contractor's financial condition and business history prior to the time the architect wrote the letters.

In one case, a contractor alleged that architects became enraged because the contractor pointed out defects in plans, and, thereafter, the architects delayed inspections, substituted materials, stepped out of channels by giving orders directly to subcontractors, required the contractor to cover up blunders made by the architects, vilified the contractor to its bonding company, tried to stop

---

[43] Western Technologies, Inc v Sverdrup & Parcel, Inc, 154 Ariz 1, 739 P2d 1318 (1986).
[44] 374 A2d 284 (DC 1977).

payments to the contractor, and otherwise intentionally interfered with contract relations. The architects argued immunity from suit on the theory that they were acting as quasi-arbitrators. The court held that the architects could not have been so acting, because there was no dispute between the owner and the contractor, just between the contractor and the architects. An architect is not immune just because it is an architect.[45] At a later trial, the architects moved for a directed verdict of $1 in favor of the plaintiffs, thus admitting liability, but contending that no actual damages had been proved. The Arizona Supreme Court REVERSED again, holding that the issue of damages should have gone to the jury.[46]

Requirement of Malice

An architect that acts within the scope of its contractual obligations to the owner cannot be liable for advising the owner to terminate a relationship with a contractor, unless the architect acts in bad faith or maliciously.[47]

Agency Defense

In *Commercial Industrial Construction, Inc v Anderson*,[48] an architect was retained by an owner to supervise a construction contract and issued *invitations to bid* to five contractors. Just before bids were opened, one of the contractors informed the architect that its bid contained an error. When the bids were opened, it appeared that the plaintiff was the low bidder. The architect, however, allowed the other contractor to revise its bid to correct further errors and, as revised, the other contractor's bid was lower. The plaintiff protested and the architect was directed to reject all bids and inform all contractors that negotiations would be in order. The contract was finally awarded to the contractor whose original bid had contained errors. The invitation to bid included the statement: "reserves the right to reject all bids, to waive informalities, and to accept any bid deemed desirable."[49] HELD: since the invitation to bid was so qualified, the low bidder was not assured that it would be awarded the contract. Moreover, the architect was acting as the agent of the owner. Since the agent's acts are those of the owner and an owner cannot be liable for interference with its own contractual relations, it is legally impossible for the plaintiff to maintain the action for tortious interference with contractual relations. (Industry practice does not override the owner's prerogative to reject all bids.)

---

[45] Craviolini v Scholer & Fuller Associated Architects, 89 Ariz 24, 357 P2d 611 (1960).
[46] Craviolini v Scholer & Fuller Associated Architects, 101 Ariz 33, 415 P2d 456 (1966).
[47] Dehnert v Arrow Sprinklers, Inc, 705 P2d 846 (Wyo 1985).
[48] 683 P2d 378 (Colo Ct App 1984).
[49] *Id* 379.

Immunity of Arbitrator

A contractor filed suit against an architect for wrongful interference with contractual relations and inducing breach of contract where a school district followed the architect's recommendation that the contractor be ejected from the job. The Ninth Circuit held that the architect would enjoy the immunity of a quasi-arbitrator if, in the particular case, it was acting in that capacity.[50]

It seems that the words *immunity of a quasi-arbitrator* describe a special form of privilege, and the law should recognize that the architect does indeed have a qualified privilege to interfere in the contractual relationship between a contractor and an owner whom the architect represents. The burden should rest upon the contractor to overcome the privilege by proving malice or bad faith. The *privilege* analysis fits the typical fact pattern better than the *quasi-arbitrator* analysis, because, in condemning unsatisfactory materials, in requiring improper work to be corrected, in recommending that the contractor be ejected from the job site, or in demanding the discharge of incompetent employees, the architect is acting *on behalf* of the owner, and not as an impartial quasi-arbitrator of a *dispute* between the contractor and the owner.

Tortious Interference

> Louisiana is now the only American state that does not recognize the action for tortious interference with contractual relations. . . . [A] rather broad and undefined tort in which no specific conduct is proscribed and in which liability turns on the purpose for which the defendant acts, with the indistinct notion that the purposes must be considered improper in some undefined way.[51]

In *Northrup Contracting, Inc v Village of Bergen*,[52] it was held that an engineer was guilty of tortious interference with contract. A contractor was employed by a village to construct the Bergen Waste Water Collection project. The contractor relied on plans, specifications, and tests conducted by the engineer. The contractor encountered excessive subsurface water and made a claim for additional compensation; the engineer delayed processing the claim and advised the contractor to move to another part of the job. The contractor stopped work and filed suit based on the engineer's delay in dealing with the water problem. HELD: the engineer's contractual responsibilities to the village established a relationship between the contractor and the engineer. The engineer's negligence

---

[50] Lundgren v Freeman, 307 F2d 104 (9th Cir 1962).

[51] *See* Colbert v B.F. Carvin Constr Co, 600 So 2d 719 (La Ct App 1992), *rehg denied* (May 21, 1992).

[52] 139 Misc 2d 435, 527 NYS2d 670 (Sup Ct 1986).

and the tortious interference with the contractor's contract caused damages to the contractor which entitled the contractor to recover from the engineer.

Litigation Privilege

An owner retained a review engineer to check geotechnical engineering work that had been done by a design engineer for the expansion of a stadium. The review engineer prepared a report that criticized the design engineer's work. The design engineer filed an action for intentional interference with business relations. Judgment on the pleadings for the review engineer was AFFIRMED. Since the report was made at a time when the owner was seriously contemplating litigation, it was absolutely privileged.[53]

Privilege Not Shown

A contractor alleged intentional interference with contract and intentional interference with prospective economic advantage against an engineer who was employed by a village to supervise construction of sewer and water facilities. The contractor alleged that the engineer caused inefficiencies in the contractor's work and also interfered with the contractor's relationships with material suppliers by communicating directly with them. The engineer allegedly encouraged material suppliers to file liens, and recommended that the village terminate the contractor's right to continue with the work. The engineer filed a motion to dismiss on the ground that its conduct was privileged. The court held that, although an engineer may have a conditional privilege to protect the interests of the owner, and such a conditional privilege might justify certain interferences that would otherwise be improper, the privilege was not shown. (1) An engineer may bring about a breach of a construction contract if acting to protect a conflicting interest that is considered under the law to be of a value equal to or greater than the contractor's contractual rights. (2) The engineer's acts must be legal and not unreasonable in the circumstances. Here, there was insufficient evidence to support the motion to dismiss.[54]

Statute of Limitations

In *Piracci Construction Co v Skidmore, Owings, & Merrill*,[55] the plaintiff construction company and defendant architectural company had separate contracts with the United States government for construction at the Smithsonian Institution. The construction company had a model produced according to

---

[53] Western Technologies, Inc v Sverdrup & Parcel, Inc, 154 Ariz 1, 739 P2d 1318 (1986).

[54] Santucci Constr Co v Baxter & Woodman, Inc, 151 Ill App 3d 547, 502 NE2d 1134 (1986), *appeal denied*, 115 Ill 2d 550, 511 NE2d 437 (1987).

[55] 490 F Supp 314 (SDNY), *affd*, 646 F2d 562 (2d Cir 1980).

specifications and drawings prepared by the architectural firm. The construction company was forced to correct and resubmit a second model at additional expense and delay when the architectural firm rejected the first model, claiming that it did not comply with specifications.

In 1971, the construction company made a formal claim against the United States for the cost of delay and was granted an equitable adjustment because rejection of the model constituted a *constructive change* within the meaning of the contract. In 1976, the construction company filed suit against the architectural firm for intentional interference with the contract, alleging that the architectural firm had persuaded the United States wrongfully to reject the scale model. The architectural firm moved for summary judgment on the ground that the cause of action for tortious interference with contractual relations is barred by a New York three-year statute of limitations.[56] The construction company argued that the accrual date was not until the later of the completion of the Smithsonian Institution project in September 1974, or the termination of administrative proceedings on August 29, 1974. Asserting that the claim sounds in professional malpractice, the plaintiff contended that the statute of limitations did not begin to run until the completion of construction. To require the contractor to file suit during the progress of the job would be unfair to the contractor, who must work with and is dependent on the architect. Such a policy would encourage multiple lawsuits and would fail to recognize that the full extent of damages remains unknown until construction is completed.

The general rule in malpractice cases is that the cause of action accrues at the time of wrongful conduct by the professional. The one relevant exception to this general rule, the *continuing treatment* exception, provides that when wrongful conduct is part of a course of treatment, the cause of action accrues when treatment is completed. The court concluded that even if the tortious interference cause of action were construed as one sounding in malpractice, the cause of action accrued, at the latest, in the spring of 1971.

Privity of Contract Defense

In *McKinney Drilling Co v Nello Teer Co*,[57] the plaintiff was a caisson drilling subcontractor on a university project. The defendant engineering company was responsible for the inspection of the foundation. The defendant advised the general contractor to require the plaintiff to continue drilling when the plaintiff believed that it had already complied with the requirements of the contract documents. The plaintiff requested additional compensation from the university, but the request was denied. The plaintiff brought an action for wrongful interference with the performance of the contract between plaintiff and the

---

[56] NY Civ Prac Law §214(4) (1978).
[57] 38 NC App 472, 248 SE2d 444 (1978).

general contractor, arguing that the defendant had advised the general contractor to require additional drilling beyond the limits required by the contract. Summary judgment for the defendant was AFFIRMED. There was no privity of contract between the plaintiff and the defendant, although each was in privity with the general contractor. North Carolina continues to require privity to establish a duty of care in various contexts, specifically, where the injury is economic loss rather than personal injury or property damage. The requirement of privity of contract could have been avoided by proof of bad faith; since the plaintiff did not allege bad faith, summary judgment was proper.

§2.06 Trespass

In *Johnson v Martin*,[58] a surveyor, in establishing a boundary, ran the line onto property owned by the plaintiff. There were no visible markers to establish the boundary, and there was no evidence that the trespass was attended with rudeness, wantonness, recklessness, or an insulting manner. The plaintiff filed suit for negligence and sought to recover damages for mental and emotional distress and attorneys fees. Judgment for the plaintiff in the amount of $713 was REVERSED. Only nominal damages may be awarded for simple trespass, and the court erred in charging the jury that consequential damages could be recovered.

Landowners adjoining a construction site brought a trespass action against an architect, claiming that the architect prepared erosion control plans that were inadequate and that, as a result, their property was damaged by mud and silt. An award of compensatory and punitive damages and litigation expenses was AFFIRMED. A trespasser can be liable for punitive damages if it does not act in good faith.[59]

§2.07 Bad Faith

In recent years, various courts have recognized a new tort described as *bad faith* failure to perform contractual obligations. In *City of Mound Bayou v Roy Collins Construction Co*,[60] an engineer was employed by a city to determine whether or not a contractor had properly performed its work and was entitled to payment. A contractor filed an action against the engineer, alleging that the engineer acted in bad faith in advising the city against making payment.

---

[58] 423 So 2d 868 (Ala Civ App 1982).

[59] Tomberlin Assocs Architects v Free, 174 Ga App 167, 329 SE2d 296 (1985), *cert denied* (May 1, 1985). *See also* Ragland v Clarson, 259 So 2d 757 (Fla Dist Ct App 1972) (surveyor exercised statutory right to enter upon plaintiff's land and was liable under the statute for damages to plants and trees).

[60] 499 So 2d 1354 (Miss 1986).

Judgment for the contractor was AFFIRMED. The engineer made numerous omissions and errors in dealing with the contractor. These bad faith omissions and errors were imputed to the city, which had employed the engineer to act as its agent. The engineer failed to act in good faith in the following ways: (1) it altered the contractor's pay requests without proof that the contractor had not completed the work indicated in the requests; (2) it failed to provide an on-site engineer to check the contractor's progress; (3) it failed to prepare *as-builts* to properly audit the project after its completion; (4) it ignored, without justification, a compromise agreement between the city and the contractor for payment; and (5) it refused to adequately explain its failure to authorize progress payments. The court stated:

> Our holding mirrors what every first year law student learns is necessary for a finding of breach of duty of good faith on the part of an engineer/architect. To conclude otherwise would allow an architect/engineer and an owner to act with impunity regardless of the consequences to the contractors. The contractors should recover in the instant case because Barrett and Mound Bayou by a persistent pattern of conduct waived the contractual provision requiring changes to be executed in writing, and moreover Barrett and Mound Bayou failed to act in good faith in performing their contractual obligations.[61]

§2.08 Conversion

In *Hastings & Civetta Architects v Burch*,[62] an architect and an owner fell into a dispute about payment for architectural work performed in connection with the construction of an office building. The owner delivered a set of schematics to the architect. The schematics had been prepared by another architect. When the controversy arose, the architect refused to return the schematics to the owner. The jury returned a verdict of $33,000 in favor of the architect for unpaid fees. The jury found that the architect had indeed converted the schematics, but awarded no damages. HELD: the jury acted properly in awarding no damages for the conversion. The schematics could not be reused; therefore, they had no market value.

---

[61] *Id* 1360.
[62] 794 SW2d 294 (Mo Ct App 1990).

Liability Arising from Statute

3

§3.01 Inspection and Supervision
§3.02 Licensing Statutes
 Surveyors
 Limitations
 Expert Witness
 Collapse
 Nonlicensure Prevents Recovery of Fee
 Design-Build Contract
§3.03 Failure to Comply with Building Code
 Negligence Per Se
 Illegality
 Negligence
 Compliance Defense
 Nondelegable Duty
 Trade Practice
 Workers Injured
§3.04 Safe Place Statutes
§3.05 "Scaffold Acts"
§3.06 Safety Regulations
 Evidence of Standard of Care
 Workers Injured
§3.07 Intentional Diversion of Water
§3.08 Copyright
§3.09 Seals

§3.01 Inspection and Supervision

The liability of an architect for malpractice may be created or affected by a statute, a code, or an ordinance. A statute may create a duty running from the architect to the injured party; in other cases, courts refer to a statute to determine whether the conduct of an architect was negligent or otherwise unlawful.

In one case, the Little Rock building code[1] required every owner performing certain construction operations to employ a registered architect or engineer to perform full inspection and supervision, with authority to stop the work. The code harmonized with article 38 of the contract with the owner, which also gave the architect general supervision with authority to stop the work. Workers were killed when a 17-foot vertical basement excavation collapsed. HELD: the architect was more than a mere agent of the owner and had a duty to stop the work in order to protect workers endangered by inadequate shoring.[2]

In an Arizona case, the roof of a school gymnasium was designed to be supported by six steel arches which collapsed during construction, injuring workers. The plaintiffs alleged that a statute[3] which required that the erection of public works be accomplished under the "direct supervision of a registered architect-engineer" imposed upon the architect a duty to supervise the construction techniques of the general contractor. The court held that the purpose of the statute was to ensure that the school district would receive a completed project built in accordance with the contract documents. The plaintiffs failed to establish that the architect had any duty to the plaintiffs to control the contractor's methods of construction, and the judgment for the defendant was AFFIRMED.[4]

In another case, a church was damaged when a boiler exploded four and one-half years after construction. The boiler was installed by a plumbing subcontractor. The state boiler inspector was not called to the project. The church asked for an instruction that it was the duty of the architect to have the boiler checked by the state inspector. The instruction was refused. The decision was AFFIRMED. The rules and regulations of the state boiler board did not require the architect to obtain an inspection. That responsibility could have been placed on the architect by an express or implied agreement, but the evidence supported the jury's conclusion that there was no such contractual obligation.[5]

---

[1] Little Rock Building Code Ordinance §204g.
[2] Fidelity & Casualty Co v J.A. Jones Constr Co, 325 F2d 605 (8th Cir 1963).
[3] Ariz Rev Stat Ann §32-142 (1980).
[4] Reber v Chandler High Sch Dist No 202, 13 Ariz App 133, 474 P2d 852 (1970).
[5] Wheeler v Fred Wright Constr Co, 57 Tenn App 77, 415 SW2d 156 (1966).

In *Lisbon Contractors, Inc v Miami-Dade Water & Sewer Authority*,[6] the contractor on a sewer project sued the water and sewer authority (WASA) to recover the increased costs of working in more difficult subsurface conditions than those described in WASA's bid request. WASA then brought a third-party action against the engineering firm that conducted the soil test relied on by the contractor. WASA asserted a contractual right of recovery based on the United States Environmental Protection Agency-assisted contract provision entitled "Responsibility of the Engineer," which was incorporated in the contract between the parties. The court concluded that WASA, as an assisted governmental entity, had stated a good cause of action under the Code of Federal Regulations.

§3.02 Licensing Statutes

Architecture, engineering, and surveying are generally licensed professions. Malpractice can cause a revocation of the license. In one case, an engineer was retained to test a ventilating system in a new apartment building, but made only a cursory examination and failed to discover numerous serious defects, including a concrete slab which interrupted all air flow to the basement. The engineer certified that the system complied with the building code; later it was informed that the system did not comply, but it failed to inform the authorities. The engineer was found guilty of gross negligence and unprofessional conduct. Its license was suspended for six months.[7]

The Wisconsin Supreme Court was more charitable where an engineer designed a garage addition and supervised construction. The roof collapsed. The examining board found that the design was inadequate to support a reasonable live load and that the engineer was incompetent and grossly negligent. The board also held that the engineer was guilty of misconduct because it performed welding on the project but was not a certified welder. The board recommended revocation of the license. The court upheld the finding that welding without a certificate constituted misconduct, but decided that a single instance of failure to use ordinary care is not of itself incompetence, especially since the state engineer testified that the error was not an obvious one. However, the reviewing court stated that the trial court should not find that the failure to detect the error was not gross negligence as a matter of law. The identification of gross negligence is a fact-finding process and should be determined by the board.[8]

In 1979, the Board of Architectural Examiners obtained a permanent injunction preventing a draftsman from practicing architecture or holding itself

---

[6] 537 F Supp 175 (SD Fla 1982).
[7] Shapiro v Board of Regents, 29 AD2d 801, 286 NYS2d 1001 (1968).
[8] Vivian v Examining Bd of Architects, 61 Wis 2d 627, 213 NW2d 359 (1974).

out to be an architect. In February of 1982, the board filed a contempt petition, alleging that the draftsman continued to practice architecture in violation of the permanent injunction. A judgment dismissing the action was REVERSED. (1) The trial court erroneously treated the action as one for criminal, rather than civil, contempt and (2) evidence clearly established that the draftsman willfully disobeyed the court order by hiring architects who were mere puppets in the draftsman's hands and were hired for the exclusive purpose of signing architectural plans prepared and supervised by the defendant draftsman.[9]

In a Pennsylvania case, an engineer failed to obtain a surveyor's license within the two-year *grandfather* period. It was required to meet newly established qualifications to obtain a surveyor's license.[10]

In *State ex rel Love v Howell*,[11] the defendant, without an architect's license, prepared plans and specifications, consulted with clients, signed change orders, and prepared punch lists. The defendant contended that its business was *architectural design*, not the practice of architecture. HELD: there is no legal distinction between architectural design and the practice of architecture. The defendant was, therefore, in violation of the licensing statute.

It was held in *EIS, Inc v Connecticut Board of Registration for Professional Engineers & Land Surveyors*,[12] that preparation of an environmental impact statement did not require registration by the State of Connecticut as a professional engineer. The reports prepared by EIS did not require special knowledge of mathematics, the physical sciences, or the principles of engineering acquired by professional education and practical experience.

In *Carden v Board of Registration for Professional Engineers*,[13] a decision of the California Board of Registration for Professional Engineers was upheld after the board denied registration as a professional engineer to an applicant who showed more than 15 years of experience as a fire sprinkler contractor, beginning as an apprentice and ending as president of a fire sprinkler company. HELD: the experience was in the narrow phase of fire sprinklers within the broad spectrum of fire protection engineering, and much of the experience was as an apprentice, or in the fields of sales and administration, rather than practical engineering.

Surveyors

A Montana registered surveyor filed a certificate with the Flathead County Clerk and Recorder which indicated that monumentation for a boundary survey

---

[9] State *ex rel* Love v Howell, 285 SC 53, 328 SE2d 77 (1985).

[10] Heckert v Commonwealth, Dept of State, Bureau of Professional & Occupational Affairs, 82 Pa Commw 636, 476 A2d 481 (1984).

[11] 281 SC 463, 316 SE2d 381 (1984).

[12] 200 Conn 145, 509 A2d 1056 (1986).

[13] 174 Cal App 3d 736, 220 Cal Rptr 416 (1985).

was complete. When the owner found that the monumentation was incomplete, it filed a complaint with the Board of Professional Engineers and Land Surveyors. The surveyor appeared before the board and testified that the monumentation was now complete. Thereafter, the board determined that the surveyor's testimony was false; the monumentation was still incomplete. The surveyor's certificate of registration was suspended.[14]

Revocation of the petitioner's license as a land surveyor and suspension of its license as a professional engineer were warranted where evidence indicated that the petitioner had incorrectly calculated a boundary line, permitted traverse closure errors, incorrectly described square footage of a certain land parcel, improperly depicted the outline of a structure, incorrectly included a nonexistent ravine, and made incorrect descriptions on a topographic survey. The revocation and suspension were also justified by the petitioner's false advertisements indicating that it was associated with other licensed professional engineers or land surveyors in its firm.[15]

The procedures for suspension or revocation of a license must be carefully followed to protect the rights of an engineer or surveyor. In *In re Trulove*,[16] the court concluded that since the board failed to hear the charges against the engineer within three months from the time when they were filed, the state Board of Registration for Professional Engineers and Land Surveyors acted without subject matter jurisdiction when it ruled on the claim. The statute providing that the board *shall* conduct a hearing within three months after charges are referred is mandatory and must be strictly followed. The board's failure to give the engineer a short and plain statement of the factual allegations also provided sufficient basis to vacate the board's order of suspension. The notice that the charges against the engineer involved gross negligence, incompetence, or misconduct resulting from noncompliance with statutes and regulations was not sufficient to adequately apprise the engineer of the charges against it.

Limitations

The licensing status of an architect does not affect the application of the statute of limitations in Colorado. In *Yarbo v Hilton Hotels Corp*,[17] the court ruled that the statute of limitations that restricts suits against architects for loss

---

[14] *In re* Shaw, 189 Mont 310, 615 P2d 910 (1980).

[15] Brew v State Educ Dept, 73 AD2d 743, 423 NYS2d 271 (1979). *See also* Hambleton v Board of Engg Examiners, 40 Or App 9, 594 P2d 416 (1979) (surveyor grossly negligent by failing to survey subdivisions in conformity with the regulations of General Land Office (now the Bureau of Land Management) of the United States); Voelz v Board of Engg Examiners, 37 Or App 113, 586 P2d 807 (1978), *review denied*, 285 Or 479 (1979).

[16] 54 NC App 218, 282 SE2d 544 (1981), *review denied*, 304 NC 727, 288 SE2d 808 (1982).

[17] 655 P2d 822 (Colo 1982).

sustained as a result of design defects applies to architects who are unlicensed at the time of the performance of the services.

Expert Witness

The Iowa Supreme Court has held that a license is not required in order for an engineer to testify as an expert professional safety engineer. The Board of Engineering Examiners brought a proceeding against the defendant alleging that its business cards implied status as a licensed professional engineer and alleging that the defendant was engaged in the practice of professional engineering without a license. The business card designated the defendant as: "Registered Professional Safety Engineer — State of California." HELD: the designation was not a misleading use of credentials; it was a truthful, nondeceptive recitation of the defendant's bona fide credentials. The intent of the legislature in enacting the licensing statute was to regulate activities directly related to the design and construction of projects. Evaluating facts and information for the purpose of testifying as an expert witness does not affect the public that the statute was designed to protect.[18]

Collapse

State Board of Architects, Engineers and Land Surveyors brought disciplinary proceedings arising out of the collapse of the second- and fourth-floor walkways of the Hyatt Regency House in Kansas City; 114 people were killed and 186 injured as a result of the collapse. The board concluded that this was the most devastating structural collapse ever to take place in the United States. Certificates were revoked. AFFIRMED. The engineers were guilty of gross negligence in preparation of structural drawings and failure to review shop drawings. The engineers contended that *custom* permitted engineers to rely on steel fabricators to design certain structural steel connections and the reliance on such custom was not negligence. HELD: design of the connections was a matter requiring engineering expertise, and custom, practice, or *bottom line necessity* cannot alter that responsibility. *Gross negligence* is defined as an act or course of conduct which demonstrates a conscious indifference to professional duty. Here, the structural engineer's duty was to determine that the structural plans provided safety to prevent a strong probability of harm. Indifference to the probability of harm was an indifference to the engineer's duty, therefore constituting gross negligence.[19]

Nonlicensure Prevents Recovery of Fee

In *Ransburg v Haase*, architect and homeowner, residents of Illinois, contracted for design and construction management of a residence in Colorado.

---

[18] Iowa State Bd of Engg Examiners v Olson, 421 NW2d 523 (Iowa 1988).
[19] Duncan v Missouri Bd of Architects, 744 SW2d 524 (Mo Ct App 1988).

Architect was unlicensed in Illinois or Colorado. HELD: a person practicing a profession without a license cannot recover for services provided. Moreover, to allow architect to keep the fees already paid would have allowed it to reap rewards against public policy.[20]

A Georgia architectural corporation entered into a contract to perform architectural services for a project in Florida. In the contract, the architect warranted it was properly licensed to carry out the terms of the agreement. HELD: architect's lien was invalid since architect was not registered or licensed in Florida.[21]

An unregistered engineer sued to recover compensation for industrial engineering services. The defendant moved for a directed verdict because the plaintiff was not registered as an engineer. A jury verdict in favor of the plaintiff was REVERSED. The Professional Engineer Registration Act (PERA) is designed to protect the public against the dangers of incompetent engineers. The law provides thorough regulation of the profession to maintain the necessary standards of competent and ethical behavior. The statute prohibits precisely those acts which the plaintiff performed and for which it sought payment. The legislature did not intend that a contract entered into in violation of the statute would be enforceable. Although the statute did not expressly prohibit the plaintiff's suit, the legislative prohibition against unregistered engineering services necessarily made the contract unenforceable.[22]

Design-Build Contract

A contractor entered into a design-build contract under which it was to design a project and utilize the services of a licensed engineer. The owners attempted to cancel the contract on the ground that the contractor was not licensed to practice engineering. HELD: since the contractor employed a licensed engineer, the contractor was not guilty of the unauthorized practice of engineering.[23]

§3.03 Failure to Comply with Building Code

Negligence Per Se

An architect is naturally under an obligation to be familiar with the requirements of building codes in jurisdictions of practice. The codes are for the

---

[20] 224 Ill App 3d 681, 586 NE2d 1295 (1992), *rehg denied* (Mar 10, 1992).

[21] O'Kon & Co v Riedel, 588 So 2d 1025 (Fla Dist Ct App 1991).

[22] Wheeler v Bucksteel Co, 73 Or App 495, 698 P2d 995, *review denied*, 299 Or 583, 704 P2d 513 (1985).

[23] Charlebois v J.M. Weller Assocs, 72 NY2d 587, 531 NE2d 1288, 535 NYS2d 356 (1988).

protection of the owner, job site employees, and the public. Failure to comply with a building code is *negligence per se*, and if it causes an injury to a person within the class protected by the code, it follows that the architect is liable for the damages caused by the malpractice. By the same token, it is argued, an architect by definition is not negligent if it complies with the mandatory provisions of the law.

The standards in the Handbook of the American Institute of Architects may be considered as evidence of a duty on the part of an architect, but violation of the standards does not constitute negligence per se.[24]

Illegality

It sometimes occurs that an owner intentionally induces an architect to prepare drawings that violate code requirements. In such a case, can the owner utilize the architect's failure to comply with building codes as a defense to the architect's action to recover fees? The answer is *no*, according to *Greenhaven Corp v Hutchcraft & Associates*.[25] Under an oral contract, the architect prepared plans to renovate a building. The original plan provided for the required two fire exits from the top floor; the owners requested that the architect revise the plans to provide only one exit. The owner knew that the plans might conflict with fire regulations, but nevertheless commenced construction and terminated the architect's services after the architect had performed 95-99 per cent of the work agreed to be done. The owner refused to pay the balance of the architect's fee. The architect obtained a judgment for $4,000. AFFIRMED AS MODIFIED. An architect must provide plans that comply with the requirements of building codes, standards, and restrictions *unless otherwise directed by the owner*. Here, the owner knew that the fire regulation required two exits and nevertheless asked the architect to revise the plans. Judgment, reduced to $3,550, AFFIRMED.

In contrast, the Supreme Court of Pennsylvania took a harsh view. A statute provided that no building used for the exhibition of motion pictures could be occupied or used as a dwelling, a tenement house, an apartment house, a hotel, or a department store. An architect, nevertheless, at the request of the client, prepared drawings for a building to contain a moving picture theater, turkish baths, stores, and dwellings. When the owner refused to pay the fee, the architect argued that the illegality was immaterial, since the owner got what it asked for. The court held that the architect could not enforce its fee contract. It was conspiring with the owners to commit an illegal act, and no illegal contract will be enforced by law.[26]

---

[24] Taylor, Thon, Thompson & Peterson v Cannaday, 230 Mont 151, 749 P2d 63 (1988).
[25] 463 NE2d 283 (Ind Ct App 1984).
[26] Medoff v Fisher, 257 Pa 126, 101 A 471 (1917).

In a similar case, an architect designed an eight-story building which could not be built because it would have violated building codes. The architect sued for its fee and failed to recover. The court held that if the architect knew or should have known that the contract documents violated the building ordinance, then it was negligent and could not recover a fee.[27]

Negligence

In *Chaplis v Monterey County*,[28] a building designer prepared plans for construction of a laundromat. After construction began, it was discovered that a laundromat could not legally be constructed without a special use permit. The use permit was denied. HELD: the designer was liable for its negligent failure to alert the owner to the use permit requirement.

In *Straus v Buchman*,[29] the court made the architect something of an insurer that the building would comply with the code. The supervising architect failed to catch the contractor, who, in order to make way for a new stairwell, shortened beams and supported them by attachment to a stud partition. The contractor then floored over the work, concealing it from view. The architect visited the job once every day, but by the time it arrived, the flooring had been completed. HELD: the concealment did not exonerate the architect. It was the architect's duty under the contract to see that the beams complied with the statute.

In a Massachusetts case, the trial court awarded $1,000 compensatory damages and $4,000 for mental anguish to homeowners whose lot became flooded with sewage. The designer of the septic system failed to comply with the state sanitary code. The Supreme Court of Massachusetts confirmed the award of compensatory damages but reversed as to the damages for mental anguish.[30]

An architect recovered damages from a consulting engineer for negligence and failure to design structures in accordance with the requirements of the building code. The architect was employed to design a dormitory and student union for a university, and subcontracted with a structural engineer. The engineer designed 12 steel and concrete structures known as umbrellas but failed to follow the building code. One collapsed. The architect filed an action against the structural engineer on a theory of negligent design. HELD: violation of the statute is negligence per se. The code was enacted to protect

---

[27] Bebb v Jordan, 111 Wash 73, 189 P 553 (1920). *See also* St Joseph Hosp v Corbetta Constr Co, 21 Ill App 3d 925, 316 NE2d 51 (1974) (architect was held liable to client for specifying a wooden wall panel which would not meet the Chicago fire rating code).
[28] 97 Cal App 3d 249, 158 Cal Rptr 395 (1979)
[29] 96 AD 270, 89 NYS 226 (1904), *aff'd*, 184 NY 545, 76 NE 1109 (1906).
[30] McDonough v Whalen, 365 Mass 506, 313 NE2d 435 (1974).

persons such as the architect; therefore, judgment against the structural engineer was AFFIRMED.[31]

In *Foxfire Village, Inc v Black & Veatch, Inc*,[32] the engineer obtained a city permit, but failed to obtain a permit from the Department of Health and Environmental Control for development of a mobile home park. The engineer concealed from the developer problems voiced by the department. Ultimately, the developer was required to bring the project into compliance with the department's permit requirements. A judgment in favor of the developer against the engineer was AFFIRMED. Had it not been for the engineer's numerous breaches of contract, the department would have issued a permit and would have approved the project after final inspection of the construction.

In *State v Wilco Construction Co*,[33] walls were defectively designed and failed to meet wind-load requirements of the Municipal Code. A judgment in favor of the owner and against the architect for $153,754 was AFFIRMED.

In a California case, it was held that failure to comply with the state building code was negligence per se and that it was, therefore, erroneous for the trial court to grant a nonsuit for failure to introduce expert testimony regarding the standard of care in the community.[34]

Compliance Defense

Compliance with the building code can be a defense, just as failure to comply is a basis of liability. In *Rigsby v Brighton Engineering Co*,[35] decedents were killed when their car collided with a bridge pier. The plaintiff argued that the engineer should have required guardrails around the pier and introduced expert testimony to the effect that guardrails were reasonably necessary and that, had they been present, the deaths probably would have been averted. The pier was erected according to criteria adopted by the Kentucky Department of Highways; these criteria not only failed to require guardrails but even prohibited them. Therefore, it would have been futile for the engineer to design guardrails, and the failure to recommend them was not negligence. A strong concurring opinion criticizes the majority's reliance on the design criteria determined by the state to exonerate the engineering consultant, since the state itself was protected by sovereign immunity and thus the plaintiff was deprived of any remedy.[36]

In another automobile death case, the court held that there was an issue for the jury where the district chief maintenance engineer and the district traffic

---

[31] Burran v Dambold, 422 F2d 133 (10th Cir 1970).
[32] 304 SC 366, 404 SE2d 912 (Ct App 1991), *cert denied* (Aug 15, 1991).
[33] 393 So 2d 885 (La Ct App), *writ denied*, 400 So 2d 905 (La 1981).
[34] Huang v Garner, 157 Cal App 3d 404, 203 Cal Rptr 800 (1984).
[35] 464 SW2d 279 (Ky 1970).
[36] *Id* 281.

supervisor permitted installation of a "curve-20 miles per hour" sign 708 feet from the beginning of a curve, when a directive adopted by the state highway commission required that it be 750 feet from the "hazard to be warned of." It was a question of fact whether the *hazard* was the curve or an intersection within the curve which was 794-1/2 feet from the sign.[37]

Noncompliance with the building code cannot be defended on the ground that the code was not properly adopted. In *Himmel Corp v Stade*,[38] the architect and the architect's consulting engineer advised installation of telephone wires in open cable trays in the plenum above the ceiling, even though the city building code required the lines to be enclosed to avoid fire hazard. The plaintiff replaced the trays with conduit and filed an action against the architect and the engineer for breach of contract and negligence. Summary judgment for defendants on the ground that the city building code was not properly adopted was REVERSED. It would be inequitable to foreclose inquiry into the standard of care employed by the defendants because of a possible technical flaw in the adoption of the code.

Nondelegable Duty

If an architect fails to comply with a building code and injury results, it will find little favor by arguing that the injury may have occurred even had the code been followed. In *Johnson v Salem Title Co*,[39] a pedestrian was injured when a hurricane collapsed a masonry wall. The wall had been approved by the building department, yet the design did not comply with the code. The City of Salem Uniform Building Code provided that "buildings and structures . . . shall be designed . . . to resist the wind pressure as specified."[40] This imposed a duty on the architect, as well as its consulting structural engineer. The architect was paid for the design and was responsible for the failure to comply with the code. The jury could find that a properly designed wall, designed in accordance with the code, would have withstood the hurricane force wind.

The architect argued that it did everything that a reasonable architect could do, since it employed a competent structural engineer to design the wall. However, the court held that the uniform building code was adopted by the city for the protection and safety of the public; therefore, the architect was liable for the errors committed by the structural engineer, even though the engineer was an independent contractor. *When a statute is adopted for public safety, it creates a nondelegable duty.*

---

[37] Chart v Dvorak, 57 Wis 2d 92, 203 NW2d 673 (1973).
[38] 52 Ill App 3d 294, 367 NE2d 411 (1977).
[39] 246 Or 409, 425 P2d 519 (1967).
[40] 1 Uniform Bldg Code §2307.

Trade Practice

If there is a conflict, architects and engineers are held to the standard contained in applicable statutes rather than to the standard established by local custom and practice. In *Henry v Britt*,[41] an 11-year-old boy drowned in a motel swimming pool when his arm became lodged in the main drain outlet at the deep end of the pool. Evidence showed that the boy was an excellent swimmer, but the suction of the pump was such that the parents could not have freed him, even had they known he was caught, until the pump motor was shut down. The pool drain grate was observed on the bottom of the pool several feet from the drain opening.

Pursuant to statutory authority, the state board of health had adopted rules and regulations governing the construction of swimming pools, providing in part that the main drain opening "must be covered with the proper grating which is not readily removable by bathers." The trial court admitted expert testimony to show that defendant engineers had employed ordinary skill and training in the design of the pool and then instructed the jury that the engineers were required to utilize only that degree of skill, diligence, and care ordinarily used by engineers of ordinary skill and training in the community. The holding was REVERSED. "The effect of a violation of a statute or ordinance constituting negligence cannot be avoided by the fact that the act complained of was done in accordance with the custom or practice of other persons engaged in the same type of work in the community."

In a New York case, a worker was killed when an overloaded wall collapsed. The building code permitted 11-1/2 tons, while the actual load was 60 to 90 tons. The mere fact that the owner had employed an architect to prepare the design did not protect the owner from liability.[42]

Workers Injured

An architect was held liable when a 17-foot-deep basement excavation collapsed because it was not shored in accordance with code requirements. The architect had general supervision with authority to stop the work and had a duty to do so rather than permit workers to be exposed to danger.[43]

In a similar case, forms broke, spilling workers into the Columbia River along with 200 tons of wet concrete. A statute provided that concrete forms should be checked during pour to prevent collapse. The Washington Supreme Court decided that the jury could find that the project architect was negligent in

---

[41] 220 So 2d 917 (Fla Dist Ct App), *cert denied*, 229 So 2d 867 (Fla 1969).
[42] Pitcher v Lennon, 12 AD 356, 42 NYS 156 (1896).
[43] Erhart v Hummonds, 232 Ark 133, 334 SW2d 869 (1960).

failing to exercise sufficient supervision. In reaching its decision the court referred to a statute defining architecture, engineering, and its practice.[44]

§3.04 Safe Place Statutes

A Wisconsin safe place statute[45] imposes a duty to keep public buildings as reasonably safe as the nature of the premises will permit for the benefit of frequenters and employees. A nine-year-old schoolgirl, walking on a four-foot-high railing, fell and collided with the window of a parochial school building approximately four feet distant. In a suit against school and architect, the court found no violation of the safe place statute. The purpose of the law was to impose a high standard of care upon owners of public buildings in order to protect persons who are either within, entering, or leaving the building. This plaintiff was not in the building. Therefore, no cause of action was stated under the safe place statute. The court noted, however, that a pleading of common law negligence would have been sufficient to overcome a demurrer by the architect.[46]

Another section of the Wisconsin safe place statute[47] requires every employer to furnish a place of employment that is safe for employees and frequenters. In *Hortman v Becker Construction Co*,[48] an employee of a general contractor was injured when struck by a piece of lumber that apparently blew off the top of the building. In an action against the project architect based on the safe place statute, the architect's motion for summary judgment was granted. AFFIRMED. The duty under the safe place statute was nondelegable. An employee of the general contractor was a *frequenter*. However, a party has a duty under the safe place statute "only if he has the right of supervision and control." Thus, it was necessary to look to the contract between the owner and the architect to determine application of the statute.

The contract required the architect to perform on-site inspection but provided that the architect was not responsible for construction means, methods, techniques, sequences, or procedures, or for safety precautions. The architect had authority to stop the work when necessary for proper performance of the contract. The contract also required the architect to provide a full-time project representative but limited the project representative's authority as follows:

---

[44] Loyland v Stone & Webster Engg Corp, 9 Wash App 682, 514 P2d 184 (1973), *review denied*, 83 Wash 2d 1007 (1974).
[45] Wis Stat §101.11 (1973).
[46] Mlynarski v St Rita's Congregation, 31 Wis 2d 54, 142 NW2d 207 (1966).
[47] Wis Stat §101.11(1) (1973).
[48] 92 Wis 2d 210, 284 NW2d 621 (1979).

§3.04 SAFE PLACE STATUTES   99

> Do not enter into the area of responsibility of the contractor's superintendent. . . . Do not advise on, or issue instructions relative to, any aspect of construction means, methods, techniques, sequences or procedures, or for safety precautions and programs in connection with the Work. . . . Do not stop or reject the work except on explicit instructions. . . .

HELD: the architect did not have sufficient control of the job site to give rise to liability under the safe place statute.

Another section of the Wisconsin safe place statute obligated a property owner to "construct, repair, or maintain such place of employment . . . as to render the same safe." HELD: the architect was not an "owner," and therefore was not liable. Moreover, an architect has no common law duty that requires it to ensure construction site safety.[49]

A New York court found that an owner's duty to ensure safe conditions at a construction site was nondelegable. In *Conti v Pettibone Cos*,[50] a construction worker was injured on a job site when a bucket filled with sand bags fell on the worker's head. The plaintiff charged that the inspecting engineer negligently undertook to supervise and ensure the safety of the construction site. The plaintiff also alleged that the engineer was acting as the agent of the owner City of New York, within the scope of the Labor Code,[51] and was therefore chargeable with the owner's nondelegable duty to ensure safe conditions.

The court granted the inspecting engineer's motion for summary judgment on the ground that liability is imposed under these circumstances only if there is active malfeasance on the engineer's part. Under §241 of the Labor Code, an owner and the owner's agent are chargeable with the nondelegable duty to provide for safe conditions at the job site. The court rejected the assertion that by assuming a supervisory role at the project site, the engineer acquired the status of an agent of the owner within the meaning of the Labor Code:

> [T]he term [agent] must be deemed to apply to one who acts for the owner or general contractor in the sense of one who actually stands in their shoes and performs their duties and obligations, and not one who alone or with others acts for them for specified limited purposes. . . . To impose such liability upon a resident inspecting engineer who was not an agent with the over-all authority envisioned by the statute, and whose sole contractual duty was to perform limited specified inspectional functions

---

[49] Kaltenbrun v City of Port Wash, 156 Wis 2d 634, 457 NW2d 527 (1990).
[50] 111 Misc 2d 772, 445 NYS2d 943 (1981).
[51] NY Lab Code §§240, 241 (1983).

for the owner (even if some were quasi-supervisory), would be wholly violative of the legislative intent.[52]

In a New York case, a worker was electrocuted while trouble-shooting a problem in a parking lot lighting system. The plaintiff widow contended that the architects were liable under NY Lab Law §241 for breach of a duty to provide a safe place to work. HELD: the architects were not liable since the accident occurred after completion of the construction.[53]

§3.05 "Scaffold Acts"

"Scaffold acts" have been adopted in Illinois, Missouri, and Oregon. They impose on parties deemed *in charge* of a construction project a duty to exercise care for the protection of persons on the project site.[54] Scaffold acts do not impose strict liability; negligence must be shown.

In a classic opinion, *Miller v DeWitt*,[55] the Illinois Supreme Court held that an architect *was* "in charge" of work under the scaffold act. Workers were injured when a proscenium truss was being removed during a gymnasium remodel contract and the roof collapsed. The contractor had not provided adequate support for the roof and did not calculate a safety factor in designing the steel scaffolding used to shore the truss. The architect had the power to condemn defective work and the power to stop work; therefore, the architect had the right to insist on a safe job even though there was no duty to specify the method of construction to be used by the contractor.

It has been held that an architect was not a person "in charge of the work, and therefore not liable to a worker, where there was no showing that the architect actually contracted for, or assumed, direct supervision of the particular operations that caused injury."[56] On the other hand, in *Emberton v State Farm Mutual Auto Insurance Co*,[57] the owner employed the architect to prepare plans and specifications, and to serve as a supervising architect to ensure that the work complied with the plans. The contract gave the architect the authority "to

---

[52] 111 Misc 2d at 780, 445 NYS at 948-49.

[53] Jaroszewicz v Facilities Dev Corp, 115 AD2d 159, 495 NYS2d 498 (1985).

[54] Comment, *The Supervising Architect: His Liabilities and His Remedies When a Worker Is Injured*, 64 Nw UL Rev 535 (1969).

[55] 37 Ill 2d 273, 226 NE2d 630 (1967).

[56] Getz v Del E. Webb Corp, 38 Ill App 3d 880, 349 NE2d 682 (1976) (distinguishing Miller v DeWitt, 37 Ill 2d 273, 226 NE2d 630 (1967)); McGovern v Standish, 65 Ill 2d 54, 357 NE2d 1134 (1976) (architect had the power to stop the work only in order to reject defective materials and workmanship); Meek v Spinney, Coady & Parker Architects, Inc, 50 Ill App 3d 919, 365 NE2d 1378 (1977) (architect had no general supervisory duties and no right to stop the work).

[57] 71 Ill 2d 111, 373 NE2d 1348 (1978).

require the contractor to stop the work whenever in his reasonable opinion it may be necessary for the proper performance of the contract." HELD: the architect had charge of the work within the meaning of the statute.

In *Kirk v Walter E. Deuchler Associates*,[58] an engineer failed to require the use of a complete and adequate signaling system during an operation which required a backhoe to function as a hoisting apparatus to install a concrete cone section on a partially completed manhole assembly. Judgment in favor of the injured worker was AFFIRMED. The engineer had authority to suspend the work, to make or approve variations in plans, and to require the removal of a contractor's employee from the project for carelessness or incompetence. Therefore the engineer was *in charge* under the Structural Work Act.[59]

The Illinois Structural Work Act was interpreted in *Bisset v Joseph A. Schudt & Associates*.[60] A worker sustained a knee injury when a sewer trench collapsed. A verdict for the plaintiff against the architect was AFFIRMED. (1) Evidence supported the jury's finding that the architect was in charge of construction. It had a supervisor on the job site daily, was authorized to stop work, and prepared the plans for the job. (2) Damages of $200,000 were improperly awarded. The jury awarded too much for medical expense, and too little for lost wages.

In another Illinois case, a worker was injured when scaffolding collapsed at a sewage disposal plant project. Under contract with the city, the engineer was to provide inspection to assure compliance with the contract documents. The defendant engineering company employed a resident engineer who had power to stop the work. Evidence indicated that the engineer knew that one of the vertical supports for the scaffolding had been removed on the day of injury. The trial court directed a verdict for the engineer. REVERSED. There was sufficient evidence to present a jury question on the issue of whether the defendant was "in charge of the work" as contemplated by the Structural Work Act.[61]

---

[58] 79 Ill App 3d 416, 398 NE2d 603 (1979).

[59] Ill Rev Stat ch 48 (1977). Several cases serve to define the term *in charge* as used in the structural work act: Kelley v Northwest Community Hosp, 66 Ill App 3d 679, 384 NE2d 102 (1978) (general duty to supervise the work merely creates a duty to see that the building when constructed meets the plans and specifications; no authority to control the methods or techniques of construction and no authority to stop work); Fruzyna v Walter C. Carlson Assocs, 78 Ill App 3d 1050, 398 NE2d 60 (1979) (whether or not an architect has charge is determined not only from the contract, but also from the totality of the surrounding circumstances, including the role which is in fact assumed); Diomar v Landmark Assocs, 81 Ill App 3d 1135, 401 NE2d 1287 (1980) (no power to stop the work; architect not responsible for methods of construction; architect not responsible for safety precautions and programs; architect not responsible for contractor's failure to carry out the work in accordance with the contract documents).

[60] 133 Ill App 3d 356, 478 NE2d 911 (1985).

[61] Voss v Kingdon & Naven, Inc, 60 Ill 2d 520, 328 NE2d 297 (1975).

§3.06 Safety Regulations

Evidence of Standard of Care

Safety regulations adopted by the government or by unofficial organizations are sometimes offered as evidence of the standard of care. In *Telak v Maszczenski*,[62] the plaintiff was injured after diving into a fiberglass swimming pool that was seven feet deep. The architect had no control over the design of the pool but had been employed to approve drawings prepared by a pool manufacturer in order to obtain a county permit. The manufacturer testified:

> Well, I told them that we needed the approval of a registered Maryland architect, that was what [was] asked for by the County, and I asked them to do what was necessary to give me that approval. Not being an architect, I didn't know exactly what was required. I had to leave it up to them.[63]

Drawings submitted to the county showed a profile view and transverse sections of the pool. The drawings bore the legend "Bacharach and Bacharach Architects and Engineers," and displayed the stamp of "Abram F. Bacharach Professional Engineer and Land Surveyor." Nine months after the drawings were submitted, the county adopted a building code which provided that swimming pools should be designed according to the American Public Health Association Criteria, 1949 Edition. That document recommended that "in order to be on the safe side the committee recommends that a minimum safe water depth of 8 feet be provided for diving"[64] from a diving board.

The court held that the architect was not liable because it had no control over the design. That reasoning seems questionable. Presumably, the county required approval by an architect in order to assure, among other things, the safety of the installation.

In an action by surviving parents of a 10-year-old boy, who fell to his death from a diving board, against an architect who designed a swimming facility for a high school, the trial court permitted an expert witness to read from safety standards promulgated by a private, national organization concerned with aquatics safety. The witness was the chairman of the organization's committee which drafted the regulations. HELD: safety publications drafted by private organizations are treated for evidence purposes as learned treatises and are

---

[62] 248 Md 476, 237 A2d 434 (1968).

[63] *Id* at 490, 237 A2d at 441.

[64] American Public Health Assn, Recommended Practice for Design Equipment & Operating of Swimming Pools & Other Public Bathing Places 19d (1949).

admissible as long as their probative value is not substantially outweighed by their prejudicial effect.[65]

In a questionable decision, the Supreme Court of Arkansas found that an engineer has no duty to enforce a safety code as a matter of law and cannot be charged with negligence for a contractor's failure to comply with the code. The engineer was employed to supervise construction and to make certain that the contractor complied with the requirements of the contract documents. A hook-up person was injured when a crane cable was energized by coming in contact with 13,000-volt power lines. The jury returned a verdict for the plaintiff. The trial judge granted a judgment notwithstanding the verdict. AFFIRMED. The engineer's contract created no duty to supervise the plaintiff or fellow employees in the performance of their work. If the contractor violated the provisions of safety codes, the contractor should have been made to answer to the proper authorities.[66]

Similarly, the Montana Supreme Court, with a strong dissent, has held that an engineer's only duty is to see that the end result complies with the contract documents, and that an engineer has no duty to require independent contractors to comply with minimum safety standards.[67]

A restaurant patron pushed a glass door which broke and lacerated the patron's arm. The patron filed an action that sought to impose strict tort liability on an architect based on violation of the Safety Glazing Materials Act. HELD: the Illinois act, Ill Rev Stat ch 111-1/2 et seq (1981), is prohibitory in nature and not remedial. The statute did not specifically provide for a private right of action but imposed only criminal penalties. It was not necessary to imply a private right of action in order to provide an adequate remedy for the violation of the statute.[68]

Workers Injured

In a Florida case, safety regulations required guardrails on concrete form work. A contract required that an architect supervise the work and ensure that it be done in accordance with the requirements of regulatory agencies. HELD: the architect was liable for injuries to a worker who fell from a form where the architect had instructed the contractor to install guardrails, the contractor failed to do so, and the architect took no further action.[69]

---

[65] Francisco v Manson, Jackson & Kane, Inc, 145 Mich App 255, 377 NW2d 313 (1985), *appeal denied* (Jan 28, 1986).

[66] Heslep v Forrest & Cotton, Inc, 247 Ark 1066, 449 SW2d 181 (1970).

[67] Wells v Stanley J. Thill & Assocs, 153 Mont 28, 452 P2d 1015 (1969) (employer failed to shore trench causing cave-in).

[68] Rhodes v Mill Race Inn, Inc, 126 Ill App 3d 1024, 467 NE2d 915 (1984).

[69] Geer v Bennett, 237 So 2d 311 (Fla Dist Ct App 1970).

In a Utah case, a worker was injured while digging a trench for a service tunnel. A side of the trench collapsed. The worker alleged that the trenching procedure did not comply with state regulations. The trial court dismissed the action. REVERSED. The architect had the authority to shut down the job, and if the architect should have known that conditions were unsafe to workers, the architect was under a duty to do so.[70]

Affirming a judgment for the defendant architect in a personal injury action by a worker, the court in *Vorndran v Wright*,[71] stated:

> It was the prime responsibility of the architect to determine that construction was completed in accordance with the plans and specifications.... [T]he architect, therefore, would not normally be liable for the failure of the employer (subcontractor) to comply with safety regulations, unless his contract of employment for supervision imposes upon him a duty and responsibility to supervise and/or control the actual method of construction utilized by the contractor.... [H]owever, in the instant case, the architect's contract for employment of supervision only obligates the architect to visit the construction site periodically to verify that the construction is in accordance with drawings and specifications.... [B]ased on these undisputed facts, the architect cannot be held liable for any failure of the contractor to comply with required safety regulations.[72]

In *Caldwell v Bechtel, Inc*,[73] the plaintiff worker sustained injuries from inhalation of silica dust. The district court held that the engineer had no contractual duty to the plaintiff. REVERSED. Bechtel had the power to compel compliance with safety procedures because it had the right to stop the job if unsafe conditions existed. Since Bechtel had superior skills and knowledge of the dangerous condition, Bechtel owed plaintiff a duty of care to take reasonable steps against the foreseeable risk of harm created by the unsafe levels of silica dust.

§3.07 Intentional Diversion of Water

In *Kraft v Langford*,[74] the defendant engineer designed and supervised the construction of a subdivision, including a storm sewer system. As a result of construction, surface water was diverted onto the neighboring plaintiff's property. The plaintiff sued for damage caused by intentional wrongful

---

[70] Nauman v Harold K. Beecher & Assocs, 19 Utah 2d 101, 426 P2d 621 (1967).
[71] 367 So 2d 1070 (Fla Dist Ct App), *cert denied*, 378 So 2d 350 (Fla 1979).
[72] *Id* 1071.
[73] 203 US App DC 407, 631 F2d 989 (1980).
[74] 565 SW2d 223 (Tex 1978).

diversion of water in violation of the Texas Water Code.[75] A jury verdict for compensatory and punitive damages was REVERSED. The Texas statute creates a rule of property establishing easements and limiting their use; therefore, the statute has no application to a defendant who is not a landowner. As a result, if the plaintiff is to recover at all it must be under the common law remedy for interference with an interest in real property, not under the statute.

§3.08 Copyright

A builder purchased another builder's plans from an architect and copied them to build seven houses.[76] The builder who owned the plans recovered $212,550 in profits lost on the seven houses plus $86,320 profits disgorged by the builder who stole the plans. HELD: (1) although it is possible to construct a house identical to another house depicted on copyrighted architectural plans, it is illegal to directly copy plans and use the infringing copy to construct a home; (2) the award of profits earned by the second builder, when added to the award of profits lost on the seven houses, amounted to awarding the same thing twice.

Stealing plans may constitute unfair competition under the Lanham Act, 15 USC §1125(a). The defendants trespassed on the plaintiff's property and took photographs of building interiors so as to be able to accurately copy those details of construction not shown on the plans. HELD: the wrongful appropriation of such design features is a form of commercial immorality.[77]

Although an owner of copyrighted drawings for a home does not obtain a protectable interest in the useful article depicted by those plans, the copyright owner may recover damages for infringement of copyrighted plans and may enjoin their further use.[78] The plaintiff was a homebuilder engaged in the business of building luxury homes selling for more than $1 million. The plaintiff built a home in 1986 that sold for over $2 million. The defendant, a competitor, commenced construction of a substantially identical home on another lot on the same street. The court found this, "to say the least, a bit puzzling."[79] The competitor had come into unauthorized possession of the plans. HELD: (1) the copyright owner may recover damages for infringement; (2) the copyright owner was entitled to an injunction to prevent further unauthorized use of the plans; (3) a preliminary injunction enjoining further construction of the house was inappropriate. Even with copyrighted plans, a

---

[75] Tex Water Code Ann §5.086 (Vernon 1972).

[76] Robert R. Jones Assocs v Nino Homes, 858 F2d 274 (6th Cir 1988), *rehg denied* (Nov 7, 1988).

[77] Demetriades v Kaufmann, 698 F Supp 521 (SDNY 1988).

[78] Demetriades v Kaufmann, 680 F Supp 658 (SDNY 1988).

[79] *Id* 660 n 2.

general right does not exist to prevent construction of a home of imitative design, since a competitor could take photographs or draw sketches and reproduce the structure.

In *Acorn Structure, Inc v Swant*,[80] the Copyright Act of 1976, 17 USC §301, was used by an owner as a defense to a breach of contract claim by an architect. The owner and the architect had signed a *design agreement* that provided that the drawings were copyrighted and that the owner was not authorized to use or copy the drawings. The owner took the drawings to another architect that filed the drawings under its seal. The house was then constructed. The trial court held that the design architect's breach of contract claim against the owner was preempted by the Copyright Act. REVERSED. The architect's breach of contract claim was not within the subject matter of the Copyright Act.

§3.09 Seals

In *Wynner v Buxton*,[81] an engineer signed and sealed drawings for the construction of a self-service gas station. The drawings showed the general arrangement of the project and included a framing plan for a canopy and an equipment building. The developer claimed that the plans were deficient because they did not include electrical, mechanical, or piping details and did not provide for grading and drainage.

The engineer argued that it had signed and stamped the plans merely to signify that it had made calculations to determine the structural integrity of the canopy. HELD: failure of the plans to include all details governing every aspect of the project did not render them defective. The engineer was not necessarily responsible for plans covering all aspects of the project, in spite of §6735 of the California Business and Professions Code, which provides that a licensed engineer's signature and seal indicate its responsibility for plans.[82]

In *Hutchinson v DuBeau*,[83] surveyor DuBeau prepared a plat for a purchaser's predecessor in title. DuBeau used a preexisting plat furnished by the owner as a reference for determining the boundary line. DuBeau's limited survey was in error because the boundaries depicted in the preexisting plat were incorrect. The purchaser filed an action to recover damages sustained when it bought the property in reliance on the inaccurate plat which bore DuBeau's certification that it was a true representation of the property. The court concluded that whether the purchaser's reliance upon the plat was reasonable and whether the plat adequately reflected the limited nature of the survey were issues to be

---

[80] 846 F2d 923 (4th Cir 1988) (per curiam).
[81] 97 Cal App 3d 166, 158 Cal Rptr 587 (1979).
[82] Cal Bus & Prof Code §6735 (West 1975).
[83] 161 Ga App 65, 289 SE2d 4 (1982).

determined by a jury. The statute required that plats and reports issued by a registered professional engineer or land surveyor be stamped and countersigned only if the survey work is personally performed or reviewed and found to be accurate. Under the statute, DuBeau was responsible to the public for the accuracy of the surveying work reflected and may have been liable to the purchaser who was damaged by reasonable reliance on the plat.

Liability Arising from Contract

4

§4.01 Breach of Contract and Negligence
Duties Imposed by Contract
Implied Conditions
Lack of Privity Defense
Duty Arises from Contract, Lack of Privity No Defense
Exculpatory Clause
Specific Performance
Contract Duty versus Contributory Negligence
§4.02 Design Compliance Defense of the Designer-Builder
§4.03 Contract as Creating Duty
Third-Party Beneficiary versus Duty Created by Contract
Subrogation
Active Negligence
Economic Loss
Privity
Surety's Indemnitee Protected
Contractor versus Engineer
Exculpatory Clause Is Defense to Third-Party Action
Workers Injured
No Duty to Worker
No Contractual Duty
Joint Venture
§4.04 The Duty to Supervise
No Duty to Workers
Patron
Duty Is Found
§4.05 Third-Party Beneficiary
Owner Is Third-Party Beneficiary

Owner Not Third-Party Beneficiary
Contractor Is Third-Party Beneficiary
Contractor Not Third-Party Beneficiary
Remote Owner Is Third-Party Beneficiary
Remote Owner Not Third-Party Beneficiary
Workers Not Third-Party Beneficiaries
Lenders Not Third-Party Beneficiaries

§4.06 Safety Engineering
Voluntary Safety Inspections
Insurance Carrier Not Liable

§4.07 The Power to Stop the Work
Common Law Obligation
Agency
Architect's Lack of Authority

§4.01 Breach of Contract and Negligence

A moment of reflection confirms that the same act can be, and very often is, both negligent and a breach of contract.[1] In fact, negligence in the nature of malpractice alleged by an owner against an architect almost by definition constitutes a breach of contract as well as negligence, since the architect ordinarily, by contract with the owner, undertakes to comply with the standard of practice employed by average local architects. If the condition is not express, it is implied by the courts.

Causes of action sounding in tort and contract are frequently and properly joined in the same complaint.[2]

In a Pennsylvania case, the plaintiff school district alleged two causes of action against an architect, one for breach of contract and the other for negligence. The architect had designed an earth embankment for a school project, which collapsed, damaging the project. The same act was alleged to be both a breach of contract and an act of negligence.[3]

The courts are more prone to use tort language than contract language, even when a contract exists between the plaintiff and the defendant architect. However, the legal theory employed may have important ramifications: (1) tort damages may be computed differently from contract damages; (2) the statute of limitations for breach of contract may be longer than the statute for tort; (3) the defense that a breach on one side excuses performance on the other side is good

---

[1] See §1.16.

[2] Friendship Heights Assocs v Vlastimil Koubek, AIA, 573 F Supp 100 (D Md 1983), revd, 785 F2d 1154 (4th Cir 1986); see §1.19.

[3] Trinity Area Sch Dist v Dickson, 223 Pa Super 546, 302 A2d 481 (1973).

in contract, but not in tort; (4) the defense of contributory negligence (or comparative fault) is good in tort, but in an action for breach of contract it may be invalid; (5) finally, the architect by the contract may assume a degree of liability which approaches strict liability, whereas the courts have usually refused to hold architects strictly liable in tort.

A crucial distinction between an action for breach of contract and an action founded on negligence is the measure of damages; many cases have held, and numerous commentators agree, that economic loss should not be recoverable in a negligence action.[4]

An owner may allege both negligence and a breach of contract but may recover only once for a single injury. In *Hotel Utica, Inc v Armstrong*,[5] the owner sued the architects on two counts: breach of contract and professional negligence. HELD: it was proper to allege both counts, but the owner could recover only once for damages arising out of the same facts.

Duties Imposed by Contract

In *Town of Winnsboro v Barnard & Burke, Inc*,[6] the court specifically founded its decision on contractual requirements in a situation where the conduct of the engineer was also obviously negligent. There were hundreds of defects, many of them serious, on a city street job. Because of improper backfill and compaction, there were substantial failures in the base material and many defects in curbs and gutters. The cost of repair would have been about $175,000. Judgment was entered against the contractor, the contractor's bonding company, the engineer, and the testing laboratory *in solido*.

The contract required the engineer to supervise the project. The engineer employed a high school graduate with two years of higher education in the field of veterinary medicine and some correspondence courses to act as project supervisor. The supervisor was not a licensed engineer and had been with the company only six months. Due to lack of experience, the supervisor accepted incomplete testing reports, relied on the information supplied by employees of the contractor, and permitted the use of a multipass stabilizer in direct violation of the specifications. The court concluded that the supervisor was incompetent to handle the project, relying on the contractor and the testing laboratory to the detriment of the owner.

The *skill usually exercised by others of its profession in the same general area* standard was held not to apply. Rather, the duties imposed by the terms of the contract defined the standard of performance.

---

[4] Moorman Mfg Co v National Tank Co, 91 Ill 2d 69, 435 NE2d 443 (1982). *See* §10.10.
[5] 62 AD2d 1147, 404 NYS2d 455 (1978).
[6] 294 So 2d 867 (La Ct App 1974).

In *Hambleton v Board of Engineering Examiners*,[7] a breach of contract resulted in suspension of a surveyor's license. The contract required the surveyor to perform a survey in accordance with procedures established in the Bureau of Land Management Manual. It failed to do so. The Board of Engineering Examiners suspended the surveyor's license on the ground that it was presumptively aware of its contractual duty and its persistence in following a different system constituted gross negligence and incompetence.

Implied Conditions

The court found a breach of an *implied* condition to the contract in *Graulich v Frederic H. Berlowe & Associates*.[8] The architect prepared contract documents without checking zoning and later discovered that the proposed building would be prohibited without a zoning variance. HELD: since expert testimony showed that the professional standard in the community required an architect to check zoning before preparing contract documents, failure to investigate zoning was a breach of contract relieving the owner of the financial responsibility for the architect's fee.[9]

In *Ossining Union Free School District v Anderson, LaRocca, Anderson*,[10] the district contended that the engineer failed to live up to an implied condition of its contract by failing to perform in a workmanlike manner. HELD: the party who raises breach of an implied duty as an affirmative defense has the burden of proving the claim.

Lack of Privity Defense

In a Mississippi case, a contractor filed an action against an engineering firm on the ground that it had misrepresented the amount of excavation to be performed on an airport job. One cause of action was framed on a breach of contract theory, the other on a negligence theory. The court held that there was no privity of contract, and this defense destroyed both causes of action.[11]

Duty Arises from Contract, Lack of Privity No Defense

The duty owed by an architect to a condominium association and a condominium owner may spring from a contractual promise made to the

---

[7] 40 Or App 9, 594 P2d 416 (1979).

[8] 338 So 2d 1109 (Fla Dist Ct App 1976).

[9] *See also* Comptroller *ex rel* Va Military Inst v King, 217 Va 751, 232 SE2d 895 (1977) (negligence of architect in failing to detect deterioration of stone work due to water in limestone and thermal expansion and contraction HELD to be negligence, therefore a breach of contract); Board of Educ v Del Biano & Assocs, 57 Ill App 3d 302, 372 NE2d 953 (1978) (the contract between the owner and the architect included an implied obligation to specify the use of reasonably good material; architect specified defective mortar which caused efflorescence).

[10] 73 NY2d 417, 539 NE2d 91, 541 NYS2d 335 (1989).

[11] Delta Constr Co v City of Jackson, 198 So 2d 592 (Miss 1967).

original developer; however, the duty sued on in a negligence action is not the contractual promise, but the duty to use reasonable care in affirmatively performing that promise. This duty exists independent of the contract. The terms of the contract are not the exclusive test of the existence of the duty. Whether the architect has a duty to use reasonable care to protect the interests of a plaintiff who is not a party to the contract is determined by whether the plaintiff and the architect are in a relationship in which the architect has a duty imposed by law to avoid harm to the plaintiff. Where it is foreseeable that the plaintiff will suffer injuries, the architect has a legal duty to use reasonable care to avoid unreasonable risks, and privity of contract is not required.[12]

In *Keel v Titan Construction Corp*,[13] lack of privity did not defeat a cause of action for negligence. Owners brought an action against a contractor and an architect, alleging improper design of an auxiliary solar heating system for a home. The Supreme Court of Oklahoma reversed the lower court's order sustaining the architect's demurrer. The owner's petition was sufficient to state a cause of action against the architect for negligent breach of contract. Because negligence is a tort, the architect's liability depends upon proximate cause rather than privity. The privity relationship is not required, since accompanying every contract is a common law duty to perform the contract with care, skill, reasonable experience, and faithfulness. The negligent failure to observe any of these conditions is a tort, as well as a breach of contract.

Although the duty owed by a defendant to a plaintiff may spring from a contractual promise made to another, the duty sued on in a negligence action is not the contractual promise but the duty to use reasonable care in affirmatively performing that promise. The court in *Navajo Circle, Inc v Development Concepts Corp*[14] stated: "The duty exists independent of the contract."

Exculpatory Clause

A design engineer is liable for delay in preparing facility plans. In *W. William Graham, Inc v City of Cave City*,[15] an engineer was employed by a city to prepare plans for a wastewater treatment facility. The contract provided that the plans would be completed in 135 days. Both parties understood that delay would result in a reduction of the city's funding entitlement from 75 per cent to 55 per cent. By failing to perform on time, the engineer caused a funding reduction of $338,935. Judgment for the city was AFFIRMED. A clause in the contract limited the engineer's liability to damages based on "professional

---

[12] Navajo Circle, Inc v Development Concepts Corp, 373 So 2d 689 (Fla Dist Ct App 1979).
[13] 639 P2d 1228 (Okla 1981).
[14] 373 So 2d 689, 691 (Fla Dist Ct App 1979).
[15] 289 Ark 105, 709 SW2d 94 (1986).

negligent acts, errors or omissions."[16] This clause did not limit the engineer's liability for the damage that resulted from the breach of contract.

Specific Performance

A court may not require specific performance of a contract to design a building. Such a contract calls for services that are largely intellectual, involving the powers of the mind. An action for damages, not specific performance, is the appropriate remedy.[17]

A judicial habit of mixing tort and contract language emanates from exalted regions. In *Corey v Eastman*,[18] a homeowner alleged that an architect misrepresented the value of work done by a builder, causing the owner to make a partial payment to the builder, who then became insolvent and abandoned the project. Justice Holmes, speaking for the court, held that as a consequence of the employment *contract*, the architect was tortiously liable for *negligent* statements and imprudent advice on the same principle that, under a *warranty*, an erroneous statement was a *deceit* even without negligence.

That a breach of contract can occur without negligence is shown by a case in which architects were employed to supervise construction. They visited the job site every day, as was customary, but it was impossible for them to perceive a defective cross beam structure because the contractor had floored over the area between inspections. The court held that the concealment of the defect by the contractor did not exonerate the architects, since it was their duty under the contract to see that the beams complied with the statute.[19]

Contract Duty versus Contributory Negligence

The distinction between contract and tort may have been important in *Pierson v Tyndall*.[20] In defending against a fee suit, an owner accused an architect of negligent supervision. The architect introduced evidence that the owner had made payments to the contractor with full knowledge of faulty work. The court held that the trial court should nevertheless have instructed the jury that payments with knowledge of defective work would not excuse the architect's breach, although it might be considered in determining damages. If payment to the contractor were contributory negligence, it would be a good defense against a negligence cause of action; but if the cause of action sounded

---

[16] *Id* at 107, 709 SW2d at 96.

[17] Ashworth v Cunningham/MSE, 252 Ga 569, 315 SE2d 419 (1984).

[18] 166 Mass 279, 44 NE 217 (1896).

[19] Straus v Buchman, 96 AD 270, 89 NYS 226 (1904), *affd*, 184 NY 545, 76 NE 1109 (1906). *See also* Maritime Constr Co v Benda, 262 So 2d 20 (Fla Dist Ct App 1972) (architect denied recovery of fee because unable to design parking layout to comply with city code requirements).

[20] 28 SW 232 (Tex Civ App 1894).

in contract, payment to the contractor would not excuse a breach, although it might constitute a breach of the owner's obligation to mitigate damages.

Courts often solve owner-architect cases according to principles of tort law rather than contract law.[21] However, in *Follansbee Brothers v Garrett-Cromwell Engineering Co*,[22] the distinction between an action for breach of contract and one for negligence was clearly drawn. The complaint alleged that engineers had contracted with the owner to "furnish all necessary working drawings for a pair of 25 ton basic open hearth furnaces similar to those we constructed for the C. Pardee Works at Perth Amboy, N.J." The plans as prepared differed in important respects from the New Jersey plans. The trial court required the owner to prove that the plans were not in accordance with ordinary engineering skill, in other words, negligent. REVERSED. Dissimilarity in the plans would create a prima facie case of breach of contract, whether the engineers were negligent or not.

This is a unique case. An owner usually employs an architect because the owner does not know exactly what it wants. It is up to the architect to decide how the project should be built. Therefore, the only way that the owner can prove that the contract of employment was breached is to show malpractice, that is, lack of ordinary competence. This blurring of legal theory has led the courts generally to ignore breach of contract and concentrate on tort theories in deciding malpractice cases. But as *Follansbee* shows, the distinction can be critical. Although malpractice of an architect is usually not only a tort, but also a breach of contract, an act which is a breach of contract is not necessarily also the tort of malpractice.

§4.02 Design Compliance Defense of the Designer-Builder

In a line of defense that must be considered "bizarre," builders who also designed their projects have contended that they were not responsible for flaws in the projects because they complied with the requirements of their own drawings and specifications. Where an architect designed and partially built a brick, five-story warehouse and the walls cracked because it failed to design iron lintels over the arches to support the brick work, the owner sought to recover the cost of repair on the ground that the building was negligently built or designed,

---

[21] *See, e.g.*, Roberts v Karr, 178 Cal App 2d 535, 3 Cal Rptr 98 (1960) (negligent survey); Uinta Pipeline Corp v White Superior Co, 546 P2d 885 (Utah 1976) (conflicting expert testimony as to whether it was good engineering practice to support a heavy valve on a two-inch swage fitting; an explosion followed); Surf Realty Corp v Standing, 195 Va 431, 78 SE2d 901 (1953) (sliding roof did not operate properly).

[22] 48 Pa Super 183 (1911).

and the defense was that the *architect and builder* followed the plans and specifications. The court rejected the argument. An architect-builder cannot argue that once the plans are completed it is responsible only to faithfully follow those plans; both the architect-builder and the surety were liable for the defective design.[23]

In a Louisiana case, a contractor designed and built a building and specified *super-rock*, a composition of cement and cinder which was so porous that it developed cracks and leaks from expansion and contraction of the material. The contract required the contractor to *re-execute* any work that failed to conform to the requirements of the contract, and to "remedy any defects due to faulty materials or workmanship which appear within a period of one year from the date of completion of the contract."

The contractor urged the defense that it fulfilled the contract since it complied with the requirements of the plans and specifications. HELD: one who both prepares plans and specifications for a building and then agrees to erect the building according to these plans and specifications cannot escape liability for defects in the work by taking the ground that the defects were in the specifications. That individual is responsible for both.[24]

In a similar holding, there were many defects in the house designed and built by the defendant: cracks, leaks, uneven floors, settlement, and nonfunctioning doors. The designer-builder argued that it was not responsible, since it had constructed the house according to the plans and specifications (its own). The court said that the fact that the house was built according to plans and specifications is no defense when the builder prepared the plans and specifications.[25]

In another case, the defendant designed and built a 30-foot fence as a light screen at a drive-in movie which fell down within a week after it was completed. The defendant contended that it was not responsible, since it followed the specifications which it had prepared. The court said that the defendant was responsible for both the construction and the design, and a fence that does not stand for a week does not comply with the implied promise that the structure, when completed, will serve the intended purpose.[26]

Reflecting upon these and similar cases, many practitioners, including the author of this work, advise owners who plan construction projects to consider employing a "design-build" contractor, so that, in the event construction is defective, there can be no question as to whether the defect is the fault of the

---

[23] Louisiana Molasses Co v Le Sassier, 52 La Ann 2070, 28 So 217, *affd*, 52 La Ann 1768, 28 So 223 (1900).
[24] Barraque v Neff, 202 La 360, 11 So 2d 697 (1942).
[25] Lincoln Stone & Supply Co v Ludwig, 94 Neb 722, 144 NW 782 (1913).
[26] Rosell v Silver Crest Enters, 7 Ariz App 137, 436 P2d 915 (1968).

contractor or of the design professional. Thus, the owner may avoid the burden, which is a heavy one in many cases, of proving whether a particular construction defect was caused by faults in the design or faults in the execution of the design.

§4.03 Contract as Creating Duty

Third-Party Beneficiary versus Duty Created by Contract

It is only rarely that the courts consider the possibility, let alone find, that a contract between an architect and an owner may be a third-party beneficiary contract. Yet a number of cases have defined the duty of care to a third party by reference to the contract between the architect and the owner. In *Navajo Circle, Inc v Development Concepts Corp*,[27] a condominium association filed suit against architects, alleging negligent supervision of the construction and repairs to a condominium roof. The court looked to the contract between the architect and the developer to find that the architect had a legal duty to the association.

> The duty owed by a defendant to a plaintiff may have sprung from a contractual promise made to another; however, the duty sued on in a negligence action is not the contractual promise but the duty to use reasonable care and affirmatively perform the promise. The duty exists independent of the contract. . . . Whether a defendant's duty to use reasonable care extends to a plaintiff not a party to the contract is determined by whether that plaintiff and defendant are in a relationship in which the defendant has a duty imposed by law to avoid harm to the plaintiff.[28]

Subrogation

In *URS Co v Gulfport-Biloxi Regional Airport Authority*,[29] an architect provided design and other services under a contract for construction of an airport terminal building and, for an additional fee, provided a full-time resident inspector. The resident inspector spurned the advice of a roofing expert who warned that the roof was not being built according to specifications. The architect certified that the construction was proper. Six months later, the roof began to leak. During the progress of the work, the architect approved progress

---

[27] 373 So 2d 689 (Fla Dist Ct App 1979).
[28] *Id* 691.
[29] 544 So 2d 824 (Miss 1989).

payment requests submitted by the roofing subcontractor, a result of which was that retainage funds were released by the airport authority to the contractor.

The contractor's surety was called upon to finish the job, and therefore would have been entitled to recoup its expenses by asserting a right against the retainage under the equitable doctrine of subrogation. HELD: since the authority was damaged by the act of the architect in approving the release of retainage, the surety was entitled to recover damages from the architect.

A contract between a civil engineer and a developer for preparation of surface water drainage plans did not create an obligation to subsequent owners of individual lots to establish foundation grade elevations for those lots, absent a specific contractual commitment. The homeowners built or purchased custom-built homes. The architect or builder of the individual homes, not the engineer who designed the original surface drainage system, should have established the foundation grade levels.[30]

Active Negligence

Where an engineering firm was employed to inspect the installation of a pipeline and the weight of the new line ruptured an older gas line, which caused an explosion in a nearby building, injuring the plaintiff, the court held that the engineer was liable since the inspection contract created a high degree of duty, the breach of which constituted active negligence as a matter of law.[31]

Economic Loss

In *Robinson Redevelopment Co v Anderson*,[32] a developer filed an action against an architect for breach of contract and malpractice. The architect filed cross-actions seeking contribution and indemnity against the structural engineer, mechanical engineer, and landscape architect whom the architect employed for the project. Motion for dismissal of cross-action was denied. AFFIRMED. The third-party defendants argued that there was no viable tort claim, since there was no legal duty independent of the contracts between the parties. They also argued that the architect was seeking economic damages that are not recoverable in a tort action. HELD: (1) the contractual and professional relationship between the architect and the third-party defendants gave rise to two distinct wrongs: one contractual, and one for professional negligence; (2) since the malpractice claim was the result of a contractual relationship between the parties, damages for purely economic loss were recoverable.

---

[30] Ferentchak v Village of Frankfort, 105 Ill 2d 474, 475 NE2d 822 (1985).
[31] Becker v Black & Veatch Consulting Engrs, 509 F2d 42 (8th Cir 1974).
[32] 155 AD2d 755, 547 NYS2d 458 (1989).

Privity

In *Aetna Insurance Co v Helmuth, Obata & Kassabaum, Inc*,[33] the contract provided that an architect would perform supervision of construction and "general supervisory services." The general contractor's surety became liable for breach of the construction contract with the city. There was no privity of contract between the surety and the architect. The architect had observed that some concrete forms had not been installed properly but failed to follow up and see to it that the defect was corrected. As a result, the wall bulged. The architect also failed to inspect backfill tests as called for by the contract; therefore, it was necessary to replace pavement. The court held that where the architect is obligated by contract to supervise construction, this obligation creates a duty to supervise with due care, and the duty protects the general contractor's surety, as well as the other party to the contract. The lack of privity of contract was no defense.

In reflecting upon this case, it is interesting to consider the relationship between the parties. A supervising architect should be liable to an injured worker for failure to require adequate safety precautions on a job, since the owner is likely to relax its vigilance after entrusting the enforcement of safety standards to the architect.[34] Here, however, the surety, after collecting a premium to guarantee that the contractor would not breach the contract, was permitted to recover from the architect for that very breach. Moreover, the surety had the power to either accept or reject the particular contractor, while the architect had little, perhaps no, voice in that selection.

Surety's Indemnitee Protected

The decision in *Westerhold v Carroll*,[35] is more in harmony with the attitude of modern courts. The indemnitor of a surety on a contractor's performance bond filed suit against the architect, alleging that the architect certified payments which were $23,000 in excess of the value of work performed on a $325,000 church job. The contractor defaulted, and the surety called on the indemnitor to make good the default. Looking to the contract between the owner and the contractor, the court commented that the stipulation that payments would be made periodically was as much for the protection of the surety as it was for the owner. An obligation may be assumed by contract out of which may arise a duty to others than the parties to the contract.

---

[33] 392 F2d 472 (8th Cir 1968).
[34] Restatement (Second) Agency §354 (1967).
[35] 419 SW2d 73 (Mo 1967).

Contractor versus Engineer

In *Magnolia Construction Co v Mississippi Gulf South Engineers, Inc*,[36] a contractor on a sewer project claimed that the engineer negligently prepared plans and specifications and negligently supervised and inspected the project, thereby breaching its duty of care to the contractor. The engineer acted as an on-site resident field representative during construction and approved 18 periodic partial payment requests, but disapproved the final payment request, determining that some grades were not in accordance with the plans. The contractor claimed that it had relied on the negligent approvals of previous payment requests. HELD: genuine issues of material fact existed as to the duty the engineer owed the contractor as defined by the engineer's contract with the city.

In *Farrell Construction Co v Jefferson Parrish*,[37] it was held that Louisiana law permits an action by a contractor against an engineer despite lack of privity. A contractor on two drainage pump station projects sued the city and the city's engineer claiming that defective drawings, plans, and specifications impeded the progress of construction. HELD: privity is not essential to tort claims against an engineer. An exculpatory clause did not cover claims that arose before the formation of the contract containing exculpatory language, for example, negligent delay of approval of shop drawings and change orders.

Exculpatory Clause Is Defense to Third-Party Action

In *City of Durham v Reidsville Engineering Co*,[38] the situation was similar to that in *Helmuth*, but the result was the opposite. The prime contractor's surety alleged that the supervising engineer negligently certified work which thereafter proved defective, as a result of which the city (the owner) filed an action against the surety on the prime contractor's performance bond. The surety filed a cross-complaint against the engineer, alleging that the engineer should not have certified performance if it was incorrect, and therefore, the negligence of the engineers caused the surety's loss. The engineers demurred, the demurrer was overruled, and an appeal followed. The Supreme Court of North Carolina REVERSED and in doing so relied upon exculpatory provisions in the contract between the prime contractor and the city. First, the contract did not require the engineer to make any particular inspection prior to issuance of certificates for progress payments. The engineer was only required to estimate the amount of work done during the period. Second, the contract provided that inspection of the work would not relieve the contractor of its duty to perform properly and "that any omission to disapprove any work by the Engineer ... shall not be

---

[36] 518 So 2d 1194 (Miss 1988).
[37] 693 F Supp 490 (ED La 1988).
[38] 255 NC 98, 120 SE2d 564 (1961).

construed to be an acceptance of any imperfect, unsightly or defective work." Third, the engineer was given the final determination of all matters of dispute between the city and the contractor involving the quality of the work and compensation. Therefore, the engineer was in the capacity of arbitrator and as such could not be liable to either party to the contract in the absence of bad faith. The conclusion was that even if the engineer was negligent in failing to properly supervise the work, and even if this negligence caused the surety's loss, the engineer would not have been liable in the absence of bad faith, and therefore, the demurrer should have been sustained.

At first glance it seems anomalous that a surety would be affected by exculpatory contractual provisions in the contract between the prime contractor and the owner. If the surety's theory of liability is negligence, then how could a contractual provision between strangers affect the outcome? However, upon reflection, it is clear that the surety is not really a stranger to the contract. The contract containing the exculpatory provisions is the very contract that the surety guaranteed that the contractor would perform. Therefore, the contract is the essence of the surety's obligation, the surety has notice of its provisions, and the surety is bound by its terms.

To hold otherwise would lead to its own anomalies. Courts frequently, and with justice, consider the duties imposed on an engineer by contract in finding the presence or absence of negligence. The exculpatory provisions of the contract are no less worthy of consideration.

Workers Injured

The courts have frequently looked to the provisions of the contract between an architect and an owner in determining liability to an injured worker. In *Erhart v Hummunds*,[39] the contract provided that the architect "shall have general supervision and direction of the work. He has authority to stop the work whenever such stoppage may be necessary to insure the proper execution of the contract."

An inspector employed by the architect threatened to stop the job unless the contractor employed a new superintendent to properly shore a 17-foot excavation. The next working day, however, before the shoring could be revised, the excavation collapsed, killing three workers and injuring a fourth. Since the contract gave the architect general supervision and authority to stop the work, the architect owed a duty to the workers arising out of the safety provisions of the contract and the Little Rock building code, which provided: "[A]ll excavations for buildings and excavations accessory thereto shall be protected and guarded against danger to life and property."[40]

---

[39] 232 Ark 133, 334 SW2d 869 (1960).
[40] Little Rock Bldg Code §2801.

In a Florida case, a worker was injured after falling from a form that had no guardrails. Safety regulations required guardrails. The contract required the architect to supervise the work to assure the owner that it would be done in accordance with the requirements of regulatory agencies. The architect instructed the contractor to install guardrails, but the contractor failed to do so and the architect knew it. HELD: the architect was liable. The architect was under a duty to exercise care for persons who might foreseeably be injured. Even if it was under no duty to supervise, it was liable since it did so, and did so negligently.[41]

No Duty to Worker

In *Porter v Stevens, Thompson & Runyan, Inc*,[42] a worker was injured in a cave-in. The court granted summary judgment for defendant in the worker's action against an engineer which was AFFIRMED. Liability must be founded on a duty owed to the worker. Such duty must have arisen either under the contract or by an assumption of duty. Generally, this type of duty is imposed on engineers whose contracts give them the right to stop unsafe construction practices. However, this contract exonerated the engineer, for it made it clear that the contractor, rather than the engineer, was solely and completely responsible for job safety.[43]

In *Alexander v City of Shelbyville*,[44] a worker was killed when a sewer trench caved in. The contract between the city and the engineer provided that the engineer was to "determine compliance with the plans and specifications . . . [and] all work shall be done under the direct supervision of the [engineer]. . . ." HELD: the contractual duty to supervise the project did not impose a legal duty by contract on the engineer to exercise reasonable care for the safety of the worker.

No Contractual Duty

In a case that seems against the tide of decision, *Ramos v Shumavon*,[45] the appellate division decided that an engineering company was not liable for the

---

[41] Geer v Bennett, 237 So 2d 311 (Fla Dist Ct App 1970). *See also* Loyland v Stone & Webster Engg Corp, 9 Wash App 682, 514 P2d 184 (1973), *review denied*, 83 Wash 2d 1007 (1974) (contract required supervision; contractor designed forms which collapsed; HELD: the extent of the architect's duty of supervision is for the jury to determine).

[42] 24 Wash App 624, 602 P2d 1192 (1979), *review denied*, 93 Wash 2d 1010 (1980).

[43] *See also* Sweet, *Site Architects and Construction Workers: Brothers and Keepers or Strangers?*, 28 Emory LJ 292 (1979) and three cases arising under the Illinois Structural Work Act: Kelly v Northwest Community Hosp, 66 Ill App 3d 679, 384 NE2d 102 (1978); Fruzyna v Walter C. Carlson Assocs, 78 Ill App 3d 1050, 398 NE2d 60 (1979); Kirk v Walter E. Deuchler Assocs, 79 Ill App 3d 416, 398 NE2d 603 (1979).

[44] 575 NE2d 1058 (Ind Ct App 1991).

[45] 21 AD2d 4, 247 NYS2d 699, *affd*, 15 NY2d 610, 203 NE2d 912, 255 NYS2d 658 (1964).

death of two workers and injuries to a third when temporary forms collapsed because of improper erection and maintenance. The plaintiffs' theory was that the contract documents imposed a duty upon the engineers to engage in such supervision and inspection as would promote the safety of the people working on the job. The court stated that in order to sustain the plaintiffs' position it would be necessary to find a clear obligation to perform safety inspections and an intention that for a breach of the obligation the defendants would be liable to the workers. The contract between the engineers and the state provided that the engineers would ascertain the standard practices of the state and see to it that all work would be performed in accordance with those standard practices and the provisions of the contract documents. The contract documents, in turn, required that "the contractor shall, by working methods and orders of procedure subject to the approval of the engineer, conduct the work in the most expeditious manner possible, having due regard for the contractor's employees." The court held that the language was designed to protect members of the public at large. The court went on to say that, particularly since the defendants were not parties to the agreement, any duty intended to be created in favor of the workers should have been clearly expressed. "There being no contractual duty regarding the safety of the workmen the judgment against these defendants may not stand and the complaint must be dismissed."[46]

Joint Venture

In *Farm Fuel Products Corp v Grain Processing Corp*,[47] a contractor was employed to design and oversee the construction of a distillery for the production of corn alcohol to be used as a substitute for gasoline. The contractor had limited assets and entered into an agreement with the producer to share technology, experience, and patent rights to develop and market alternate energy systems. When the project failed, the owners sued the contractor and producer on theories of negligence and breach of warranty. Judgment for the owners was AFFIRMED. The arrangement between the contractor and producer had the characteristics of a joint venture; therefore, both were liable for the failure of the project.

§4.04 The Duty to Supervise

Many cases have considered the scope of an architect's duty to supervise a project to avoid injury to third parties. The Court of Appeals of Maryland has made an exhaustive survey of the cases on the issue of whether an architect or engineer who is responsible for the day-to-day supervision of the construction

---

[46] *Id* at 8, 247 NYS2d at 703.
[47] 429 NW2d 153 (Iowa 1988).

project is liable to a worker for unsafe working conditions or liable to others for other shortcomings of the contractor.[48] The court concluded that the weight of authority is that an architect or engineer is not liable to an injured worker for the failure of the contractor to utilize safe construction procedures, in the absence of a contractual provision imposing that duty, unless the evidence shows that the architect or engineer voluntarily assumed these responsibilities.

No Duty to Workers

Absent a contractual right to supervise and control site safety, an architect/engineer is not liable for injuries to workers caused by ordinary negligence at the site.[49]

A line of cases holds that an architect is under no duty to supervise construction so as to avoid injury to workers in the absence of a specific contractual provision. In *Brown v Gamble Construction Co*,[50] decedent fell through a hole in the roof of a building under construction while applying glue to the roof. The hole had been left in the incomplete roof to permit later installation of duct work. Directed verdict for the defendant was AFFIRMED. In the absence of an express provision in the contract, an architect is under no duty to supervise construction to ensure that safe working procedures are employed. Here, the responsibility for safe working procedures was expressly imposed on the general contractor by the provisions of the contract documents.[51]

In *Wheeler & Lewis v Slifer*,[52] the employee of a subcontractor was injured in a roof collapse and brought action against the architect. HELD: as a matter of law, the architect had no duty to supervise the precautions taken by the contractor for the safety of workers, and therefore was not liable. Judgment notwithstanding the verdict in favor of architect AFFIRMED. The court commented that Michigan and Illinois courts have held that architects contractually responsible for supervision of a construction project are liable for injuries sustained by workers as a result of unsafe working conditions. However, the

---

[48] Krieger v J.E. Greiner Co, 282 Md 50, 382 A2d 1069 (1978).

[49] Yow v Hussey, Gay, Bell & Deyoung Intl, Inc, 201 Ga App 857, 412 SE2d 565 (1991), rehg denied (Nov 19, 1991) (under the AIA "Abbreviated Form of Agreement between Owner and Architect," architect/engineer was not responsible for site safety).

[50] 537 SW2d 685 (Mo Ct App 1976).

[51] *Accord* Meek v Spinney, Coady & Parker Architects, Inc, 50 Ill App 3d 919, 365 NE2d 1378 (1977) (worker fell from ladder, architect had no right to stop work); Walters v Kellam & Foley, 172 Ind App 207, 360 NE2d 199 (1977) (worker fell when bottom panel of ventilating unit gave way; HELD: although the architect did perform some supervisory functions to ensure that the owner would receive the building called for by the contract documents, the contract documents did not impose any duty on the architect to supervise the project to prevent injury to workers. Contract specifically relieved architect from responsibility for "construction means, methods, techniques, sequences or procedures, or for safety precautions").

[52] 195 Colo 291, 577 P2d 1092 (1978), *rehg denied* (May 15, 1978).

better rule is found in those jurisdictions that have refused to impose liability absent a clear assumption of duty, including Maryland, Indiana, Missouri, Wisconsin, Delaware, Arizona, Arkansas, and Louisiana. The contract provided that the architect would supervise construction to assure the owner that the project was constructed in a workmanlike manner, but imposed the duty to protect workers' safety on the contractor. Article 36 of the American Institute of Architects (AIA) General Conditions provided that the architect was not responsible for the contractor's failure to perform in accordance with the contract documents. The architect was given authority to stop the work when necessary to ensure the proper execution of the contract. The court stated that this contract provision, considered in the context of the entire contract, merely evidenced an intention that the architect exercise such supervision as necessary to assure that the work complied with plans and specifications.

In *Porter v Stevens, Thompson & Runyon, Inc*,[53] the plaintiff was injured when a ditch caved in during installation of a sewer line. The engineers had contracted with the city to "assure that the intent of the contract was fulfilled." The contract did not delegate the duty to supervise the work or to prevent unsafe conditions but expressly imposed this responsibility on the general contractor. HELD: the evidence clearly indicated that the state and the general contractor had been entrusted with safety matters, and therefore, as a matter of law, the engineers owed no duty to the plaintiff. "Before an architect will be held to have agreed to exercise direct control over a contractor with respect to day-to-day safety precautions, the duty must clearly appear in the contract."[54]

In *Rian v Imperial Municipal Services Group, Inc*,[55] a worker who was injured after falling from an unsecured flight of prefabricated stairs alleged that the architect was guilty of negligent design, negligently failed to specify and provide guidance as to federal safety regulations, and breached its duty to supervise and inspect the premises for safety. HELD: since evidence showed that it is not customary for a licensed architect to supervise construction, in the absence of a contractual provision for it, the cause of action for negligent supervision was properly dismissed. The worker, however, was entitled to go to trial on its claim of negligent design and failure to specify and provide guidance as to federal safety regulations.

In *Hanna v Huer, Johns, Neel, Rivers & Webb*,[56] employees of subcontractor were injured when a steel tie joint fell from a building under construction. They filed an action against the project architect alleging causes of action arising from contract and from negligence. HELD: architect had no contractual responsibility for job site safety under American Institute of Architects (AIA) Document

---

[53] 24 Wash App 624, 602 P2d 1192 (1979), *review denied*, 93 Wash 2d 1010 (1980).
[54] *Id* 1095.
[55] 768 P2d 1260 (Colo Ct App 1988).
[56] 233 Kan 206, 662 P2d 243 (1983).

A201, which put the duty of enforcing safe working conditions on the contractor, not the architect. Before an architect will be held responsible for safety precautions, the duty must appear in the contract. The general duty to supervise the work does not impose a responsibility for job site safety. (According to the court, Illinois and Michigan have imposed job site safety duties on architects; Maryland, Indiana, Delaware, Arizona, Arkansas, Louisiana, Colorado, Wisconsin, and Missouri have not.)

Patron

A hotel guest was injured in a fall from a spiral staircase and filed suit against the architect, alleging negligent supervision. The court held that, in the absence of a specific contractual provision, an architect does not guarantee that the supervision will be so perfect as to prevent injury to third persons.[57]

Duty Is Found

In *Balagna v Shawnee County*,[58] a worker was killed when an unshored trench collapsed. The court held that an architect's duty to supervise is basically to ensure that plans and specifications are followed and that the owner gets a finished product which is structurally sound. Any duty of the architect to provide job site safety services must be specifically assumed by contract. Here, however, the architect had knowledge of safety standards requiring shoring and had knowledge that the safety precautions were not being followed by the contractor at the time of the accident. This knowledge created a duty for the architect to take responsible action.

In *Clyde E. Williams & Associates v Boatman*,[59] the court recognized that even though the contract documents may not make the engineer responsible for the safety of workers, the engineer may nevertheless assume control of the work to such a degree as to create that duty.

In *Moundsview Independent School District No 621 v Buetow & Associates*,[60] the contract specified that the architect would perform only general supervisory services, not the more detailed services that would be provided by a *clerk of the works*. The contract further provided that the architect was not responsible for the contractor's failure to carry out the work in accordance with the contract documents. After the building was finished, a wind storm blew the roof off, allegedly because of the contractor's failure to adequately fasten the roof to the building as called for in the contract documents. Summary judgment for

---

[57] Gravely v Providence Partnership, 549 F2d 958 (4th Cir 1977).
[58] 233 Kan 1068, 668 P2d 157 (1983).
[59] 176 Ind App 430, 375 NE2d 1138 (1978).
[60] 253 NW2d 836 (Minn 1977).

defendant was AFFIRMED. The plain language of the contract exempted the architect from liability to the owner caused by the contractor's acts or omissions.

However, in *Roland A. Wilson & Associates v Forty-O-Four Grand Corp*,[61] the architect was held liable to the owner for leaking windows on the basis that the architect negligently certified completion of defective or incomplete work. The leak problem was discovered during construction, and the architect ordered caulking but did not water test the windows. Failure to determine whether the problem had been solved by the caulking work performed by the contractor constituted a breach of the contract to adequately supervise the project.

§4.05 Third-Party Beneficiary

In most cases in which courts have explicitly considered whether an injured person might be the third-party beneficiary of a contract between an owner and an architect, the theory has either been abandoned or held inapplicable.[62]

Owner Is Third-Party Beneficiary

The third-party beneficiary theory was employed to hold an architect liable to the state of Illinois, despite the fact that the architect's contract was originally signed with the Illinois Building Authority (a public corporation rather than a state agency). Although the state, the plaintiff in the action, was not a party to the original contract, the building authority was merely a funding mechanism for construction projects where the state was to become the lessee. Therefore, the clear intention was to construct facilities for the benefit of the state, and the state was a third-party beneficiary to the contract.[63]

In *Keel v Titan Construction Corp*,[64] the Supreme Court of Oklahoma concluded that owners were third-party beneficiaries of a contract between their contractor and an architect for the design of an auxiliary solar heating system.

Economic loss cannot be recovered under a negligence claim in some states. This doctrine creates a potential for injustice. To avoid the impact of the economic loss doctrine, courts may be willing to employ third-party beneficiary principles in order to award compensation to an injured party that would otherwise be denied compensation. In *Key International Manufacturing, Inc v Morse/Diesel, Inc*,[65] the court held that, even though the owner was not a party

---

[61] 246 NW2d 922 (Iowa 1976).

[62] *See, e.g.*, C.W. Regan, Inc v Parsons, Brinckerhoff, Quade & Douglas, 411 F2d 1379 (4th Cir 1969) (theory abandoned at trial).

[63] People *ex rel* Resnik v Curtis & Davis, Architects & Planners, Inc, 78 Ill 2d 381, 400 NE2d 918 (1980).

[64] 639 P2d 1228 (Okla 1981).

[65] 142 AD2d 448, 536 NYS2d 792 (1988).

to a written contract with the architect-engineer, the owner was a third-party beneficiary of a contract between architect-engineer and the owner's wholly owned subsidiary.

An engineer acting under contract with a general contractor designed a floating slab floor foundation system as opposed to a structural slab. Because of highly compressible soil, the slab sunk six to eight inches. In an action by the owner against the engineer, summary judgment for the engineer was AFFIRMED. Although the owner, as third-party beneficiary, could enforce the contract, the owner's rights were limited by a contract provision which excluded liability for defective conditions.[66]

Owner Not Third-Party Beneficiary

In *Jones v McGuffin*,[67] the plaintiff ingeniously but unsuccessfully alleged that it was a third-party beneficiary to an implied contract between an engineer and a real estate broker. Under the implied contract, the plaintiff alleged that the engineer was required to properly and professionally inspect a residence and render an accurate report.

In *Shurpin v Elmhirst*,[68] a lower owner filed an action against an engineer employed by an upper owner on a third-party beneficiary theory. After a landslide, the upper owner employed the engineer to prescribe a fix. Plaintiff alleged that the engineer was negligent and that the value of its property was diminished because of the improper fix. HELD: the plaintiff was merely an incidental beneficiary and, therefore, the demurrer was properly sustained regarding that count.

Contractor Is Third-Party Beneficiary

In *Coac, Inc v Kennedy Engineers*,[69] a public entity and an engineer entered into a contract which required the engineer to furnish promptly an environmental impact report. The engineer did not. HELD: the contractor was a third-party beneficiary of the contract and had the right to recover damages for delay from the engineer.

An owner employed a contractor and an architect to construct a warehouse to be occupied by lessee. Lessee sued the architect for breach of contract, claiming standing as a third-party beneficiary. The architect acknowledged that the lessee was, indeed, a third-party beneficiary and on that ground moved to compel the lessee to arbitrate its claim based on the arbitration clause in the contract between the architect and the owner. HELD: the lessee was bound by

---

[66] Harman v CE&M, Inc, 493 NE2d 1319 (Ind Ct App 1986).
[67] 454 So 2d 509 (Ala 1984).
[68] 148 Cal App 3d 94, 195 Cal Rptr 737 (1983).
[69] 67 Cal App 3d 916, 136 Cal Rptr 890 (1977).

the arbitration provision. A third-party beneficiary must take the burdens of the underlying contract along with the benefits.[70]

Contractor Not Third-Party Beneficiary

The Florida Supreme Court, considering questions certified by the United States Court of Appeals (5th Circuit), held that in most cases the provisions of a contract between an owner and an architect which call for supervision by the architect are intended for the benefit of the owner, and the general contractor is only an *incidental beneficiary*. Therefore, third-party beneficiary liability is not generally imposed on the architect. There may be exceptions in some situations; for example, if the contract requires the architect to supervise the project in order to ensure compliance with safety regulations for the benefit of construction workers, the third-party beneficiary theory might be maintained. Generally, however, the architect acts as the agent of the owner, and the contractor is not a third-party beneficiary.[71]

A court reached the same conclusion in *Harbor Mechanical, Inc v Arizona Electric Power Co-op, Inc*,[72] where the contract between the owner and the engineering firm provided that the duties of the engineer "run to and are for the benefit of only the owner and the administrator." HELD: under the terms of the contract, neither the general contractor nor a subcontractor was a third-party beneficiary.

In *Edward B. Fitzpatrick Jr Construction Corp v County of Suffolk*,[73] where a contract between an engineer and a county expressly provided that no third party would have rights arising under the contract, and where it was provided that the engineer's services would run "directly to the county," no third-party beneficiary rights arose in favor of the project contractor, since the contractor was not an "intended beneficiary."

In *Santucci Construction Co v Baxter & Woodman, Inc*,[74] the contractor for construction of a sewer and water facility asserted a cause of action for breach of a third-party beneficiary contract between the village and its engineer. The contract between the village and the engineer required the engineer to provide

---

[70] District Moving & Storage Co v Gardiner & Gardiner, Inc, 63 Md App 96, 492 A2d 319 (1985). (For a discussion of the requirement of due care in preparing plans and specifications, see Williams, *Cause of Action Against Architect or Engineer for Negligence in the Preparation of Plans or Specifications*, 5 Causes of Action §17 (Shepard's/McGraw-Hill 1983-84).)

[71] A.R. Moyer, Inc v Graham, 285 So 2d 397 (Fla 1973). To the same effect, under Washington law, see Detweiler Bros v John Graham & Co, 412 F Supp 416 (ED Wash 1976) (the contract must evidence "an intent that the promisor shall assume a direct obligation to the third-party beneficiary").

[72] 496 F Supp 681 (D Ariz 1980).

[73] 138 AD2d 446, 525 NYS2d 863 (1988).

[74] 151 Ill App 3d 547, 502 NE2d 1134 (1986), *appeal denied*, 115 Ill 2d 550, 511 NE2d 437 (1987).

professional services including preparation of drawings, supervision of the work, and inspection of the work. The contract required the engineer to perform all office work necessary to process payment requests submitted by the contractor, to process change orders and review shop drawings. The engineer filed a motion to dismiss the cause of action on the ground that the contractor was not a third-party beneficiary. The court held that the contractor was merely an incidental beneficiary; the intended beneficiaries of the contract were the village and its residents.

In *Umpqua River Navigation Co v Crescent City Harbor District*,[75] a subcontractor alleged that an engineer was negligent in preparing harbor plans which included dredging work performed by the subcontractor. HELD: subcontractor could not recover as a third-party beneficiary of the engineer's design contract with the harbor district.

In *EC Goldman, Inc v A/R/C Associates*,[76] a subcontractor filed an action against roofing consultants who had been employed by the owner to evaluate the construction of a roof. The consultant advised the School Board that it should not accept the roof. As a result, the board withheld payment from the subcontractor. The subcontractor filed an arbitration proceeding against the board, which resulted in a decision that the subcontractor had performed according to contract. The subcontractor then filed its action against the consultants, alleging that they owed a duty to any party who foreseeably could have been harmed by a failure to exercise reasonable care in the performance of contractual obligations to the School Board. Judgment for the consultants was AFFIRMED. The consultants were not responsible for the design or construction of the roof, and simply gave their opinion to the board. The subcontractor was not an intended beneficiary of the consulting contract. There was no intention that the subcontractor ever rely on the report of the consultant. Therefore, the consultant owed no duty to subcontractor.

Remote Owner Is Third-Party Beneficiary

In *Vandewater & Lapp v Sacks Builders, Inc*,[77] a remote landowner was held to be a third-party beneficiary of a contract between surveyors and land developers. In 1953, the surveyors contracted with the owner of the land to prepare a plot plan and drainage plan. The map was certified by the surveyors and filed with the county clerk. Later the property was sold to a realty company which in turn conveyed to defendant landowners in 1959. They built and sold houses on the land. During construction, it was discovered that the drainage pattern would have to be changed, otherwise storm water would damage a

---

[75] 618 F2d 588 (9th Cir 1980).
[76] 543 So 2d 1268 (Fla Dist Ct App), *review denied*, 551 So 2d 461 (Fla 1989).
[77] 20 Misc 2d 677, 186 NYS2d 103 (Sup Ct 1959).

neighboring house. The village rescinded the approval of the map. The defendants then employed the same engineer to prepare corrected drawings and refused to pay the fee. The engineer filed suit to recover the fee. The landowners then filed a counterclaim for the cost of correcting the prior errors. The trial court dismissed the counterclaim on the ground that the three-year statute of limitations for negligence had expired. HELD: the counterclaim was for a cause of action arising under a third-party beneficiary contract and therefore subject to the longer contract limitations period. The court stated that in order for a person to be a third-party beneficiary, it must appear that the parties to the contract intended that the person would benefit from the contract. Even though the defendants were unknown at the time the contract between the developer and the surveyor was executed, the court concluded "that a certified map filed as a public record is intended for the benefit of subsequent purchasers of the property where it is shown that they relied thereon."[78] Therefore, the counterclaim stated facts sufficient to constitute a cause of action for breach of contract under the third-party beneficiary theory, and the six-year contract limitation applied, rather than the three-year negligence limitation.

A court may be persuaded by the third-party beneficiary theory when it is necessary to salvage a cause of action. In most cases, the same act that would be a breach of contract is also negligence, and therefore, a negligence theory will do: the imposition of a contract theory would merely be to add another string to the bow of the plaintiff. In *Vandewater*, because of the difference in the period of limitations, the victim had to prevail on the third-party beneficiary theory or lose. One suspects that it is this crucial fact, rather than the correct legal definition of the term *incidental beneficiary*, which promoted the victim to third-party beneficiary status. The true nexus between the victim and the defendant was not a surveying error, but an engineering error. The boundaries upon which the landowner depended were correct. It was the grading plan that caused the damage, and the negligence was in the improper design of drainage facilities, not in an incorrect survey. Therefore, the court's reference to the certified map should be seen in the context of its true meaning: the city had approved the drainage plan, but later withdrew its approval.

Remote Owner Not Third-Party Beneficiary

In *Waterford Condominium Assn v Dunbar Corp*,[79] the Waterford Condominium Association, both as purchaser and as representative of other purchasers, filed an action against a developer (Dunbar) and architects and engineers who were retained by Dunbar. The court concluded that, absent privity of contract, the purchaser or owner of real property has no cause of action against a

---

[78] *Id* at 679-80, 186 NYS2d at 106.
[79] 104 Ill App 3d 371, 432 NE2d 1009 (1982).

defendant for breach of contract unless the purchaser or owner can demonstrate that the contractual obligations and duties were undertaken by that defendant for the purchaser or owner's direct benefit. It is not enough that the parties to the contract know, expect, or even intend that others will benefit from the construction of the building as users of it. The contracts between Dunbar and the architects and engineers contained no language indicating that the services were for the direct benefit of the condominium owners, either individually or as a class.

A contract between a developer and an architect, who was employed by the developer for the design and construction of four buildings, did not show an intention to confer rights on the ultimate owners of the units; therefore, the owners had no right to assert a cause of action against the architect.[80]

Workers Not Third-Party Beneficiaries

In a Nebraska case, the contract provided that an architect would manage and supervise the entire construction, would perform all managerial functions and inspections of field work, and would ensure compliance with the contract documents to protect the owner's interests in safety, housekeeping, and fire prevention. A steamfitter fell through an opening in a concrete deck and was impaled on reinforcing steel below. The trial court found that the steamfitter was a third-party beneficiary of the contract between the owner and the architect. The Nebraska Supreme Court affirmed the judgment on other grounds but held that it was erroneous to construe the contract as a third-party beneficiary contract.[81]

In *Zukowski v Howard, Needles, Tammen & Bergendoff, Inc*,[82] construction workers were injured, and some were killed, in the collapse of a viaduct. They filed an action against the engineers employed by the state alleging that they were third-party beneficiaries of the contract between the engineers and the state. Motion for partial summary judgment was GRANTED. The workers were not express or implied third-party beneficiaries of the contract.

Lenders Not Third-Party Beneficiaries

In *Illinois Housing Development Authority v Sjostron & Sons*,[83] the plaintiff Illinois Housing Development Authority (IHDA) attempted to analogize its position to that of the building authority in *People ex rel Resnik v Curtis & Davis*,

---

[80] Lake Placid Club Attached Lodges v Elizabethtown Builders, Inc, 131 AD2d 159, 521 NYS2d 165 (1987).
[81] Simon v Omaha Pub Power Dist, 189 Neb 183, 202 NW2d 157 (1972).
[82] 657 F Supp 926 (D Colo 1987).
[83] 105 Ill App 3d 247, 433 NE2d 1350 (1982).

Architects & Planners, Inc,[84] to assert rights as a third-party beneficiary. IHDA provided funding to Valley View to construct a 13-floor residential building for the elderly. Valley View, as beneficial owner of the proposed development, contracted with architects, contractors, and material suppliers. IHDA, as mortgagee, sought to recover for damage to the interior and exterior of the structure caused by water leakage. The court distinguished the position of IHDA from that of the building authority in *Resnik* and refused to award damages to IHDA as a third-party beneficiary of the contract. In *Resnik*, the building authority was to be the ultimate user of the structure. In this case, however, IHDA was no more than a regulatory authority and a mortgagee. As mortgagee, IHDA had certain rights to supervise and control planning and construction. Most, if not all, of the rights granted to IHDA were exercised before or during the performance of the contract and were unrelated to the contract provisions which IHDA alleged were breached.[85]

In order to recover as an intended third-party beneficiary, it was held that a lender needed to show compliance with two tests, the *duty owed* test and the *intent to benefit* test. The developer employed an architect to prepare plans for a project, then defaulted on its loan and, in lieu of foreclosure, deeded the property to the lender along with an assignment of all of its rights arising out of the construction of the project. When the lender attempted to assert claims against the architect, the court held that the attempted assignment violated the contract and was therefore invalid. The *duty owed* test was not met because full performance of the architect's duties would not have satisfied the developer's duty to pay the mortgage. Nor was the *intent to benefit* test met, because there was no evidence that the developer intended to give the lender the benefit of the architect's design services.

§4.06 Safety Engineering

It seems that an architect who occupies the specific position of a safety engineer will be liable to anyone injured as a result of its failure to discharge that duty with due care.[86]

In *Moore v PRC Engineering, Inc,*[87] a worker was injured after falling from a beam on an expressway job. An engineering firm had been employed by the

---

[84] 78 Ill 2d 381, 400 NE2d 918 (1980).

[85] Illinois Housing Dev Auth v Sjostron & Sons, 105 Ill App 3d 247, 433 NE2d 1350 (1982).

[86] *See* Simon v Omaha Pub Power Dist, 189 Neb 183, 202 NW2d 157 (1972) (contract between architect and owner required architect to protect owner's interest in safety); Chart v Dvorak, 57 Wis 2d 92, 203 NW2d 673 (1973) (state highway commission job description required defendant to be responsible for the placement of highway warning signs).

[87] 565 So 2d 817 (Fla Dist Ct App 1990).

expressway authority to ensure that each step of the construction was completed in a safe manner. HELD: privity was not required to find liability for the injury sustained.

Voluntary Safety Inspections

It is customary for workers' compensation insurance carriers to establish and promote safety engineering programs as a means of reducing loss ratios. In a Michigan case, a worker lost a hand operating a punch press. The workers' compensation carrier had voluntarily undertaken to provide safety inspections. The plaintiff alleged that the carrier had negligently performed these inspections, resulting in the injury. The court held that the case against the workers' compensation carrier should go to the jury.[88]

Insurance Carrier Not Liable

Where a worker was injured when the boom of a crane operated by a general contractor collapsed, it was alleged that the failure was caused either by improperly constructed boom stops (telescoping pipes) or by the fact that the operator elevated the boom improperly. Plaintiff further alleged that the general contractor's liability insurer was negligent because its safety engineer failed to inspect the boom. The court acknowledged that the insurance carrier had employed a safety engineer to periodically inspect the operation, and that the purpose was to assure adherence by the contractor to sound safety practices. However, if the safety engineer did find an unsafe condition, all it could do was tell the general contractor, who would be free to accept or reject the engineer's advice. Moreover, the engineer's principal duty was to require adherence to safety regulations, rather than to inspect specific machinery. Therefore, the insurance carrier was not liable.[89]

In a Nebraska case, the plaintiff recovered workers' compensation for a job site injury and then filed an action against the workers' compensation carrier of its employer. The plaintiff contended that the carrier had negligently performed its agreement with the employer to provide safety engineering services. The lower court sustained the carrier's demurrer, and the Supreme Court of Nebraska affirmed on the ground that the Nebraska workers' compensation statute made both the employer and the workers' compensation carrier immune from liability. The court did, however, recognize that some courts have allowed

---

[88] Ray v Transamerica Ins Co, 10 Mich App 55, 158 NW2d 786 (1968). *Accord* Banner v Travelers Ins Co, 31 Mich App 608, 188 NW2d 51 (1971).

[89] Smithhart v AAA Contracting Co, 260 So 2d 8 (La Ct App), *rehg denied*, 261 La 1051, 262 So 2d 38 (1972).

an injured worker to recover from an insurance carrier on a safety engineering, third-party beneficiary theory.[90]

§4.07 The Power to Stop the Work

Common Law Obligation

The courts consistently look to the contract between the architect and owner as determining, at least to some degree, the existence of a duty on the part of the architect to protect the plaintiff from injury. This will discourage architects from undertaking contractual responsibilities to protect others from injury. On the other hand, architects and engineers who voluntarily, and for a fee, make it a part of their business to supervise work and enforce safety regulations should be responsible for failure to carefully discharge those duties.

Agency

The Restatement of Agency points out that an agent is normally liable only to the principal, and not to third parties, for the breach of the contract between the agent and the principal. As we shall see,[91] an architect is an independent contractor in the preparation of contract documents but is generally considered to be the agent of the owner when discharging the supervisory functions on the job. Normally an agent is liable only to the principal for breach of contract, but if

> he undertakes as a part of his contract to render service to his principal of a type which he should recognize as necessary for the protection of third persons, he must exercise reasonable care in the performance of the undertaking. It is not the contract which gives rise to the duty, nor is the standard of care increased or diminished by the status as agent, it is his common law obligation to do that which he undertakes so as not to injure another.[92]

Having undertaken the safety role, the architect cannot abandon its performance and leave things in a dangerous condition. When an agent is charged with a duty to protect others, the principal often relaxes its own surveillance, relying on the agent to discharge the duty.[93]

---

[90] Pettigrew v Home Ins Co, 191 Neb 312, 214 NW2d 920 (1974).
[91] *See* ch 8.
[92] Restatement (Second) Agency §354 (1967).
[93] *Id* comment A.

Architect's Lack of Authority

Unfortunately for the architect, its real power on the job site may be less than is needed to discharge this heavy responsibility. The architect has no direct authority over the contractor, much less over subcontractors or workers. The architect cannot eject a general contractor from the job, nor can it discharge a subcontractor, or fire a superintendent or an employee of a contractor or a subcontractor who refuses to comply with the architect's instruction.

Courts often refer to the presence or absence of the power to stop the work in determining the liability of an architect. It seems, however, that the power to stop the work is a relevant factor, but usually not decisive. In two cases, the court pointed out that the architect had no power to stop the work and held that an architect was not responsible for injury to a worker.[94] In four cases, the architect's power to stop the work was acknowledged, but the architect was still held not to be liable for injury to the worker.[95] Finally, in three cases, the court cited the power to stop work in holding an architect liable or potentially liable.[96]

In *Bisset v Joseph A. Schudt & Associates*,[97] an architect for a city sewer improvement project designed the plans for a job, had a supervisor on the job site daily, and had the power to stop the work. HELD: a worker, injured when a trench collapsed, was entitled to recover from the architect under the state Structural Work Act.

In *Marshall v Port Authority of Allegheny County*,[98] a laborer stepped onto a steel beam which was being dismantled; when it gave way, after falling 20 feet to the ground followed by the beam, the laborer landed on his legs, receiving severe injuries. The trial court held that the owner and engineer were jointly and severally liable. REVERSED. Although the agreement between the owner and the contractor empowered the engineer to halt construction for failure to comply with safety standards, the contract did not create a duty to the worker who was not a party to the contract. The contract between the owner and the contractor provided that the contractor would be solely responsible for all construction means, methods, and techniques. Therefore, the owner delegated to the contractor sole responsibility for compliance with safety requirements.

---

[94] Meek v Spinney, Coady & Parker Architects, Inc, 50 Ill App 3d 919, 365 NE2d 1378 (1977); Emberton v State Farm Mut Auto Ins Co, 44 Ill App 3d 839, 358 NE2d 1254 (1976), *revd*, 71 Ill 2d 111, 373 NE2d 1348 (1978).

[95] McGovern v Standish, 65 Ill 2d 54, 357 NE2d 1134 (1976); Podraza v H.H. Hall Constr Co, 50 Ill App 3d 643, 365 NE2d 944 (1977); Luterbach v Mochon, Schutte, Hackworthy, Juerisson, Inc, 84 Wis 1, 267 NW2d 13 (1978); Krieger v J.E. Greiner Co, 282 Md 50, 382 A2d 1069 (1978).

[96] Caldwell v Bechtel, Inc, 203 US App DC 407, 631 F2d 989 (1980); A.R. Moyer, Inc v Graham, 285 So 2d 397 (Fla 1973); Emberton v State Farm Mut Auto Ins Co, 71 Ill 2d 111, 373 NE2d 1348 (1978).

[97] 133 Ill App 3d 356, 478 NE2d 911 (1985).

[98] 106 Pa Commw 131, 525 A2d 857 (1987), *affd*, 524 Pa 1, 568 A2d 931 (1990).

The conclusion was reinforced by the fact that the owner and engineer had eliminated the engineer's safety review duties as they had been required in an early version of the contract.

In *Fox v Jenny Engineering Corp*,[99] a sewer district employed an architect to supervise a tunnel project and the architect, in turn, employed an engineer. Plaintiff worker was struck by a rock falling from the ceiling of the tunnel. HELD: the engineer had no authority to supervise or control the worker or to direct methods of construction. The contract between the district and the general contractor gave the engineer authority to stop work if the contractor failed to correct safety violations. This authority to stop the work was insufficient to create a duty running from the engineer to the worker.

At one time the standard American Institute of Architects contract documents gave the architect the power to stop work. In an attempt to avoid liability, the contract documents have been revised so as to delete the authority to stop work. However, the lack of power to stop the job will not necessarily protect an architect from liability for the negligent discharge of safety responsibilities. As noted, it is not just the contractual power to stop work, but building code provisions, safety regulations, scaffold acts, and the supervisory function itself that create the duty which results in liability.

The power to stop work should be retained by the architect, since it is this power, more than any other, that can enable an architect to discharge safety responsibilities and thus avoid liability. However, the power to stop work is by no means a satisfactory answer to the problem of job site safety. To stop work is extremely damaging to the interests of the owner, the contractor, and the subcontractors. It spells disruption of the job, demoralization of subcontractors, and delay in the completion of the project with all of the damages and expenses which delay imposes on these parties. The workers whom the architect is required to protect are frequently contemptuous of safety regulations adopted for their benefit. The architect should be a sturdy person, able to withstand both persuasion and contempt from all sides, and willing to ignore personal financial advantage to protect workers from the hazard inherent in their calling.

---

[99] 122 AD2d 532, 505 NYS2d 270 (1986), *affd*, 70 NY2d 761, 514 NE2d 1374, 520 NYS2d 750 (1987).

Liability for Estimates 5

§5.01 The Pervasive Problem
Substantial Accuracy
§5.02 Recoverability of Fee
Major Changes
Niggardly Damages
§5.03 Duty to Establish Budget
Budget Established by Law
Guess versus Estimate
No Budget Established
§5.04 Misrepresentation
Misrepresentation Voids Contract
Damages for Misrepresentation
Estimate of Fee
Intentional Misrepresentation
§5.05 Breach of Contract
Parol Evidence Rule
Quantum Meruit Recovery
Intentional Breach of Contract
Prevention of Performance
Measure of Damages
§5.06 Willful Overrun
§5.07 Negligence
Contributory Negligence
Expert Testimony Required
§5.08 Parol Evidence Rule
Parol Evidence Received
Parol Evidence Contradicts Contract
Uncertainty of Contract

	Oral Condition
	Parol Evidence Refused
§5.09	Substantial Accuracy
	Insubstantial Error
	Substantial Error
	Quantum Meruit Recovery
§5.10	Redesign
	No Warrantor
	Project Abandoned
§5.11	Exculpatory Clauses
§5.12	Contributory Fault of Owner
	Unjust Enrichment
	Cost Increases by Owner
§5.13	Waiver
	Purported Waiver Ambiguous
§5.14	Unjust Enrichment
§5.15	Benefit-of-the-Bargain Damages
	Fraud Theory
	Measure of Damages Criticized
	Tenant's Damages
§5.16	Out-of-Pocket Damages
§5.17	Loss-of-Fee Damages
	Effect of *Quantum Meruit* Damages

§5.01 The Pervasive Problem

One of the duties of an architect is to design a project that the client can afford to build. One case goes so far as to suggest that an architect is under a positive duty to investigate the financial capacity of the client, and to advise as to the probable cost of the proposed project.[1] For the most part, the courts seem to assume that the owner will have discussed costs with the architect, whether or not the written contract specifically calls for a cost estimate.[2]

Shakespeare spoke to the subject of estimates in *King Henry IV:*

> When we mean to build,
> We first survey the plot, then draw the model;
> And we see the figure of the house,
> Then must we weigh the cost of the erection;
> Which if we find outweighs ability,

---

[1] Durand Assocs v Guardian Inv Co, 186 Neb 349, 183 NW2d 246 (1971).
[2] *See* §5.08.

> What do we then but draw anew the model
> In fewer offices or at last desist
> To build at all?[3]

There seems to be no reported case in which an architect is alleged to have *overestimated* the cost of a building project. Indeed, no case reveals that an architect has *correctly* estimated the cost of a project, although tradition assures that this does occur.

It seems that all the elements of interest, economics, and human nature are united to defeat the probability that an architect would correctly estimate the cost of a project. It is the natural desire, even the duty of an architect, to want to please the client. A low projected cost is invariably gratifying. When an estimate is made during the preliminary stages of project planning, it is in the interest of the architect that the estimate should be low, since otherwise the project might be abandoned, the owner saying: "Farewell! Thou art too dear for my possessing, and like enough thou know'st thy estimate."[4]

Substantial Accuracy

Contractors and material suppliers to whom an architect may turn for advice also, in the preliminary stages, find it against their interests that the estimate should be too high. It is their objective to sell a service or product, and an unduly high price has a dampening effect on the overall sales effort. Even inflation rates usually seem to militate against the accuracy of estimates.

In fact, the fallibility of the architect's estimate is so well known to the public that it may well be doubted that an owner is justified in expecting anything more than *substantial accuracy*. Many courts have said that substantial accuracy is all that will be required. An annotator states that two general rules have evolved: one simply states that the architect cannot recover its fee if the actual cost exceeds the agreed maximum cost; the other states that the architect may not recover compensation if the actual cost *substantially* exceeds the agreed maximum.[5]

§5.02 Recoverability of Fee

The factors relevant to a determination of an architect's right to compensation where the cost exceeds the agreed maximum are said to be: whether the

---

[3] W. Shakespeare, The Second Part of King Henry IV act 1, sc 3.

[4] W. Shakespeare, Sonnet 87.

[5] Annotation, 20 ALR3d 778 (1968). *See also* Peteet v Fogarty, 297 SC 226, 375 SE2d 527 (1988) (owners instructed architect that the cost of a house should not exceed $150,000; the bid was for $307,000. HELD: since the agreed-upon cost of construction was substantially exceeded, the architect is not entitled to recover its fee); Getzschman v Miller Chem, Inc, 232 Neb 885, 443 NW2d 260 (1989).

figure was an approximation or a guarantee; whether the client ordered changes that would increase the cost; whether the client has waived any objection by accepting the performance of the architect; and whether the architect suggests reasonable revisions to scale down the cost of the project.[6]

An architect estimated the cost of a storehouse at $4,300. The owner submitted the plans to contractors and received bids of $7,800 and $9,000. As a result, the defendant did not purchase the property nor build the project. The jury was instructed that if the bids were from competent contractors and the building could not be built for the agreed sum, then the architect could not recover the fee. A defense verdict was AFFIRMED.[7]

Major Changes

In a Texas case, the parties entered into a standard American Institute of Architects (AIA) owner-architect contract for a proposed residence located on a ranch. After several meetings the architects presented a bill for 35 per cent of their fee, based on an estimated construction cost at that time of $250,000. The bill was paid. Thereafter, the owners requested several major changes, which increased the cost of construction. They then refused to pay the final bill, asserting that the residence as planned was too expensive and the parties had agreed on a maximum cost of $250,000. In the fee suit that followed, the verdict was for the architect. The *written contract* did not include a cost limit, and the jury did not find that the parties had any such understanding outside the written contract. HELD: the evidence supported the verdict, and, moreover, the architect should have recovered attorneys fees under the Texas doctrine that attorneys fees should be awarded along with any balance due for labor or purely personal services.[8]

Niggardly Damages

In one case, it was alleged that an architect fraudulently underestimated the cost of a medical building project. The owners, a doctor and a dentist, were only awarded $1,000 damages. The evidence indicated that the cost exceeded the estimate by $10,000, but on appeal the architect argued that the award of $1,000 was improper, since the evidence indicated a discrepancy of $10,000.

---

[6] Grizwold & Rauma Architects, Inc v Aesculapius Corp, 301 Minn 121, 221 NW2d 556 (1974).

[7] Feltham v Sharp, 99 Ga 260, 25 SE 619 (1896). *Accord* Durand Assocs v Guardian Inv Co, 186 Neb 349, 183 NW2d 246 (1971) (apartment building estimate $420,000; low bid $650,000).

[8] Brown v Cox, 459 SW2d 471 (Tex Civ App 1970).

The appellate court commented that this argument came with poor grace, since the architect, not the plaintiffs, benefited from any niggardliness in the award.[9]

In *Malo v Gilman*,[10] the written contract provided: "The preliminary estimated cost of this project is Seventy Thousand Dollars ($70,000)." The contract also contained a standard clause reciting that the architect had no control over the cost of labor, materials, equipment, or market conditions, and accordingly, the architect did not guarantee that bids would not vary from cost estimates. The lowest bid was $128,000, which was negotiated down to $105,000. The owner refused to pay the fee, and the architect filed an action. Judgment for the owner was AFFIRMED. The architect did not substantially comply with the terms of the contract and was not entitled to recover for its services, as the actual cost of the structure substantially and unreasonably exceeded the estimated cost.

§5.03 Duty to Establish Budget

Two cases have opined, in dicta, that there is an affirmative duty on the part of an architect to give some definite idea of the reasonable cost of a project.[11] However, the only case found to have specifically considered the question as a part of the reasoning that led to the decision held that where the terms of the contract do not fix the cost of construction, the architect has no duty to consider costs, nor does it have any duty to advise the owner of the probable cost of the completed project.[12] In other cases, the court seemingly assumed that an architect has no duty to offer an estimate or a budget figure to the owner.[13]

Budget Established by Law

An architect dealing with a public entity may be obliged to know the budget, even if not specifically advised. In a South Carolina case, architects contracted with a county board of commissioners to prepare plans for remodeling a courthouse. The contract was silent as to the budget. The fee was fixed at 6 per cent of cost. At the next session of the legislature, a state law was enacted authorizing the county board of commissioners to appropriate $400,000 to remodel the courthouse. The lowest bid was $863,000. The board abandoned

---

[9] Goldberg v Underhill, 95 Cal App 2d 700, 213 P2d 516 (1950).

[10] 177 Ind App 365, 379 NE2d 554 (1978).

[11] Zannoth v Booth Radio Stations, 333 Mich 233, 52 NW2d 678 (1952); Durand Assocs v Guardian Inv Co, 186 Neb 349, 183 NW2d 246 (1971).

[12] Baylor Univ v Carlander, 316 SW2d 277 (Tex Civ App 1958).

[13] Guirey, Srnka & Arnold Architects v City of Phoenix, 9 Ariz App 70, 449 P2d 306 (1969) (baseball stadium project with no cost limit; architects are entitled to their fee even though city did not use plans because project would have been too expensive). *Accord* Moore v Bolton, 480 SW2d 805 (Tex Civ App 1972).

the project and refused to pay the fee. The trial court granted the county's motion for nonsuit which was AFFIRMED. An architect cannot recover more from a governmental body than the body is permitted by law to spend for the purpose. Although the contract was silent, the architect was charged with a knowledge of the law, and the law limited the budget to $400,000. Since the design exceeded the budget, the architect was not entitled to its fee.[14]

Guess versus Estimate

An architect *guessed* that construction costs would be $312,000; thereafter, the house was enlarged from 3,900 to 4,800 square feet; the low bid was $698,000. HELD: since the architect had no express contractual obligation to design within a specified budget, it was entitled to its fee based on the lowest bona fide bid for all elements of the project designed.[15]

No Budget Established

In *Matthews v Neal, Green & Clark*,[16] owners employed an architect to prepare plans to convert a farmhouse into a weekend home. Although the arrangement was informal, the architect did send the owners a letter explaining that the fee would be 10 per cent of the cost of construction. The owners did not establish a budget. After the plans were finished, the owners abandoned the project because of the excessive cost of construction. HELD: the architect was entitled to recover fees based on the reasonable value of the work performed. The defense that the plans were very costly to implement was without merit, since the owners did not specify any construction cost limitations.

§5.04 Misrepresentation

Misrepresentation Voids Contract

Some early cases used the theory of negligent misrepresentation in holding an architect responsible for underestimation of the cost of a project. In a Maine case, a member of a city council testified that an oral agreement with the architect on a schoolhouse project called for a ceiling price of $5,000; the actual cost was $17,000. The court held that misrepresentation as to the cost would void the contract, but anomalously permitted the architect to recover a fee limited to 10 per cent of $5,000, rather than 10 per cent of the total cost.[17]

---

[14] Beacham v Greenville County, 218 SC 181, 62 SE2d 92 (1950).
[15] Getzschman v Miller Chem, Inc, 232 Neb 885, 443 NW2d 260 (1989).
[16] 177 Ga App 26, 338 SE2d 496 (1985).
[17] Lane v Inhabitants of Town of Harmony, 112 Me 25, 90 A 546 (1914).

Damages for Misrepresentation

In another case, the estimate was $300,000, but the actual costs were $700,000. Applying a dramatically different measure of damages, the court allowed the owner to recover $70,000 already paid to the architect plus general damages (amount not specified). The court reasoned that the architect's statement that the cost would not exceed $300,000 was a statement of fact, and the court was evidently of the opinion that the architect would be required to guarantee that fact.[18]

Estimate of Fee

In a later case an owner alleged that a partner of an architectural firm had represented that the firm's fees would not exceed 7.6 per cent of the total cost of a renovation project. The cost of the project was $386,000; the architect billed $118,000 and the defendant paid approximately $78,000. HELD: an architect can be liable for expressions of opinion if the architect expressly guaranteed the accuracy of the opinion, or if the architect had special knowledge or skill and knew that the owner had relied upon the architect's opinion as an expert.[19]

Intentional Misrepresentation

Strouth v Wilkison[20] is an unusual case of *intentional misrepresentation*. The defendant contractor submitted plans for the construction of a country home and agreed to build the house for $38,000. During negotiations the contractor represented that he had 17 years of experience in the building business but had to stop because of ill health (the truth was, he stopped because of bankruptcy); that the contractor was an engineer (he was not); that his net worth was $75,000 (it was $45,000); and that he would be able to obtain a performance bond (because of the bankruptcy, he could not).

When the project was 20 per cent finished and $25,000 had been spent, the contractor abandoned the project. At the time, the partially completed structure had a value of $12,000. The plaintiffs employed other contractors to finish the job according to the plans and specifications prepared by the contractor, and the total expense was $79,300 for a house with a reasonable value of only $48,000. Judgment was for the plaintiffs. The misrepresentations were of material facts, which persuaded the plaintiffs to enter into contracts and which proximately caused plaintiffs' injuries.

---

[18] Edward Barron Estate Co v Woodruff Co, 163 Cal 561, 126 P 351 (1912).

[19] Pickard & Anderson v Young Men's Christian Assn, 119 AD2d 976, 500 NYS2d 874 (1986).

[20] 302 Minn 297, 224 NW2d 511 (1974).

§5.05 Breach of Contract

Parol Evidence Rule

Some cases use breach of contract analysis to decide underestimation cases. An unreasonably low estimate may be a breach of contract.[21] In *Spurgeon v Buchter*,[22] an owner entered into an oral agreement with the architect which called for an architect to prepare plans for an apartment building that would not exceed $175,000 in cost, so the apartments could be rented for $125 per month. The architect purported to reduce the oral agreement to writing but omitted any reference to the cost limit. The architect was paid $5,000. The final plans could not be constructed for less than $225,000. Rentals of $160 per month would have been required to service the capital requirements of the project. The owner demanded a return of the $5,000, while the architect claimed an additional fee of $7,320.

The court held that the written agreement did not include all the terms of the contract and that, therefore, the owner was entitled to recoup the $5,000. The parol evidence rule did not come into play since the parties had not committed their entire agreement to writing. The oral agreement was collateral to, and not inconsistent with, the written contract. Therefore, evidence of the oral budget was admissible.[23]

Quantum Meruit Recovery

In a New York case, an architect filed suit to collect a fee of 2.5 per cent of the proposed cost of an armory ($450,000). The contract provided that the total cost would be "well within the sum of $450,000"; the lowest bid was $666,000. The architect sued for its fee. The court found that the city was not liable under the contract since the architects did not substantially perform their contract. Nevertheless, the court said that while the architects were not entitled to the contract price, they could recover the reasonable value of their services on a *quantum meruit* theory. The city had benefited by the preliminary plans and other work done by the architects, especially since it was demonstrated to be impossible to construct the armory at the amount appropriated for the purpose.[24]

---

[21] Durand Assocs v Guardian Inv Co, 186 Neb 349, 183 NW2d 246 (1971).

[22] 192 Cal App 2d 198, 13 Cal Rptr 354 (1961).

[23] *See also* Wetzel v Roberts, 296 Mich 114, 295 NW 580 (1941) (oral condition precedent); Rose v Shearrer, 431 SW2d 939 (Tex Civ App 1968) (oral contract that cost would not exceed $90,000); Zannoth v Booth Radio Stations, 333 Mich 233, 52 NW2d 678 (1952).

[24] Horgan & Slattery v City of New York, 114 AD 555, 100 NYS 68 (1906).

Intentional Breach of Contract

In *Zannoth v Booth Radio Stations*,[25] an architect signed a written contract to design a broadcasting studio and transmitter building at a fee of 8 per cent of the final cost of the project plus $6 per hour for preliminary plans. The contract disclosed no budget. An employee testified that the architect was informed orally of a $55,000 cost limit, which was denied by the architect.

A letter of September 4, 1947, from owner to architect referred to a cost limitation of $52,500. The architect maintained that no estimate of costs could be made until the plans were completed in detail. The owner eliminated all but the basic requirements in a consistent effort to cut down costs and attempted to specify more cost limitations at a time when the plans were almost complete. The architect replied that it was too late to incorporate changes, that the "scheme is based on your minimum requirements and economical construction, and not on the basis of the cost mentioned in your letter."[26]

The final bid was $142,000, the owner abandoned the project, and the architect sued for its fee.

The court held that the cost overrun was a clear and intentional breach of contract. The owner made it clear from the start that costs were important. As the party that had superior knowledge, the architect had the affirmative duty to give the client some idea of the final cost, regardless of whether the client was knowledgeable or not.

Reading between the lines, it seems that the architect became so enamored of the project that it began to consider the project its own work, rather than that of the owner. Doubtless it is a hard thing to be the creator of a design, and to see it frustrated by the penury of the owner. Nevertheless, the courts place upon the architect the duty of any other professional: that of service to the client.

Prevention of Performance

In *Parrish v Tahtaras*,[27] an architect was employed to design a home with a cost limit of $65,000, which was orally imposed after the contract between the owner and the architect had been signed. The architect prepared preliminary drawings and specifications, consulted with the owners, made changes, prepared final drawings, and received bids ranging from $73,000 to $90,000. The owner told the architect to proceed but to modify the project to observe the cost limit. After modifications, new bids were submitted which the owner rejected. The owner then abandoned the project, although the architect was ready,

---

[25] 333 Mich 233, 52 NW2d 678 (1952).
[26] *Id* 682.
[27] 7 Utah 2d 87, 318 P2d 642 (1957).

willing, and able to modify the plans to further reduce the cost. The architect filed an action to recover its fee and prevailed. The court stated that the general rule is that an architect cannot recover for services rendered when the contract states a specific cost limitation and the building it designs does not observe the limitation. However, this rule does not apply where the owner abandons the project when the architect is in the process of fulfilling the obligations by modifying the plans to reduce costs. The owner's abandonment constituted a prevention of performance of the condition (the cost limit), and therefore, the owner's refusal to pay was a breach of contract.

Measure of Damages

When an architect designs a project that exceeds an owner's budget, the measure of damages may differ significantly depending on whether the underestimation is a misrepresentation, a breach of contract, or negligence. For negligent underestimation, the rule of damages should seemingly be out-of-pocket loss, whereas the damages for breach of contract or intentional misrepresentation could include benefit-of-the-bargain damages.[28]

§5.06 Willful Overrun

An architect who is guilty of willfully preparing contract documents that impose construction costs that exceed the owner's budget is not entitled to a fee.[29]

In a Michigan case,[30] an architect was commissioned to design a broadcasting studio and transmitting building to cost $55,000. The owner continually eliminated features from the project and tried to hold the cost down to the basic requirements. However, the architect replied that it was too late to incorporate changes and that the "scheme is based on your minimum requirements and economical construction, and not on the basis of the cost mentioned in your letter."[31]

The bid was $142,000. The owner abandoned the project. The court held that the overrun was a clear breach of contract. The architect could not recover its fee since the owner received no benefit from work done contrary to its instructions.

---

[28] See discussion in §§5.15-5.17.
[29] Eberhard v Mehlman, 60 A2d 540 (DC 1948).
[30] Zannoth v Booth Radio Stations, 333 Mich 233, 52 NW2d 678 (1952).
[31] *Id* 682.

§5.07 Negligence

Underestimation of costs may give an owner a cause of action against an architect for negligence.[32]

Contributory Negligence

In *Pieri v Rosebrook*,[33] an owner accused an architect of negligence but lost because of its apparent contributory negligence. The architect was employed to design and supervise the construction of a home. Originally the parties agreed on a budget of $30,000, but the owner ordered substantial changes: larger rooms, additional rooms, and more garage space. The architect warned that the cost would increase.

When bids were too high, it was agreed that the owner would go ahead without a general contractor, and that with the help of the architect the owner would deal directly with the subcontractors. During construction, the owner made more costly changes, and the final bill came to $62,192. The owner filed suit against the architect for negligence in exceeding the cost limit, and the architect filed a cross-complaint for the balance of the fees. The court awarded the architect its fee (but offset $2,500 as the reasonable cost of repairing a defective sun deck). The owner contended that the fee should have been based on the $30,000 budget rather than the total cost of $62,192. The court concluded that the evidence supported the trial court's finding that the agreement called for a fee calculated on the total construction cost, especially since the additional costs were the result of substantial changes ordered by the owner.

An architect prepared drawings to renovate a motel complex. The projected cost for each motel unit was $12,500. Based on that, owners agreed to buy the property, made a $200,000 deposit, and signed an agreement with a clause that provided for liquidated damages of $87,500 if the contract was canceled. When the owners discovered that the cost per unit would be $24,000, they canceled the contract and recovered judgment against the architect for $287,500.[34]

Expert Testimony Required

An unexplained, substantial discrepancy between an architect's projection of costs for a building and the actual bids received, standing alone, did not prove negligence. (Bids were 33 per cent to 45 per cent above the architect's estimates.) To prove negligence, it is necessary to introduce expert testimony

---

[32] *See, e.g.*, Kaufman v Leard, 356 Mass 163, 248 NE2d 480 (1969) ($17,000 estimate; $39,953.86 cost including $5,415 in extras).

[33] 128 Cal App 2d 250, 275 P2d 67 (1954).

[34] Comstock Ins Co v Thomas A. Hanson & Assocs, 77 Md App 431, 550 A2d 731 (1988).

from a witness familiar with the drawings and the manner in which the architect prepared the estimate.[35]

§5.08 Parol Evidence Rule

Parol Evidence Received

The parol evidence rule is no favorite of the courts, and it seems that in most states a court with any desire to do so can find some exception to avoid the application of the rule. This is true in underestimation cases, where the requirement of an estimate is often oral rather than a part of a written contract. If the written agreement does not mention the estimate requirement, the client may be permitted to testify as to the oral agreement, since, if the parties discussed costs, the written agreement was incomplete.[36]

It seems, and rightly, that artful drafting (especially of form contracts) will not be accepted by the courts as permitting an architect to avoid introduction of evidence of an agreement to design a project that can be built within the financial means of the owner.

In *Malo v Gilman*,[37] an architect orally agreed that the cost of construction would be kept at $20 per square foot. The written contract incorporated an estimate of $70,000. The lowest bid was $128,000. The court permitted the oral terms to be introduced, stating that "an oral cost limitation imposed on an architectural or engineering design, where not contradictory to the express terms of the written contract, may be admitted into evidence."[38]

Parol Evidence Contradicts Contract

In *Stevens v Fanning*,[39] parol evidence directly contradicted the written contract. The owner required a 40,000-square-foot Chevrolet dealership building in a hurry. The contract provided for a "multiple purpose building . . . at an approximate estimated cost of $250,000." The contract was the American Institute of Architects (AIA) standard form. The testimony was conflicting; the owner claimed that the architect agreed that the $250,000 estimate would be a guaranteed maximum price and an absolute lid; the architect claimed that the owner knew that if it employed pre-stressed concrete instead of a steel frame, the building would cost more than $250,000. The trial court believed the owner

---

[35] Pipe Welding Supply Co v Haskell, Conner & Frost, 61 NY2d 884, 462 NE2d 1190, 474 NYS2d 472 (1984).

[36] Sweet, *Architectural Cost Predictions: A Legal and Institutional Analysis*, 56 Cal L Rev 996 (1968).

[37] 177 Ind App 365, 379 NE2d 554 (1978).

[38] *Id* at 370, 379 NE2d at 557-58 (citation omitted).

[39] 59 Ill App 2d 285, 207 NE2d 136 (1965).

and held that the $250,000 *approximate estimated cost* meant a $250,000 *guaranteed maximum cost*. In doing so the court ignored another provision of the contract that stated that the architect did not guarantee the accuracy of the estimate.

Uncertainty of Contract

If a contract is silent about the budget, the courts may hold that the entire contract is ambiguous and uncertain and may be augmented by parol evidence, or that the budget is an essential element of an architect-owner contract that may be supplied by parol evidence if it is omitted from the written agreement.

In an Illinois case, the written contract was the standard American Institute of Architects (AIA) form. The courts held that the gaps in the form contract supported the view that the architect must have received oral instructions as to the project, including the budget. In view of the uncertainty of the contract, the oral evidence was admitted.[40]

In a similar decision, a school district asserted that only $10,000 was available for construction. The low bid was $14,000. The trial court admitted parol evidence supporting the $10,000 budget. AFFIRMED. The contract between the owner and the architect was silent as to essential details of construction, including costs. It is reasonable to believe that the parties must have reached an understanding on this subject, and therefore, parol evidence was properly admitted.[41]

Oral Condition

In *Haines v Bechdolt*,[42] the court allowed parol evidence to be introduced as an *external condition precedent*. Under a written agreement, an architect was to design a motel addition to a building in Tahoe, but the owner was unable to obtain financing for the project and refused to pay the architect's fee. The written contract provided that in the event the project was abandoned, the architect would be paid for its services. When the architect attempted to enforce this provision of the contract, the owner testified that, before the contract was signed, the architect said it would help finance the project. The owner had replied: "If you can't help finance it, it's no good, that is a cinch . . . [i]f we don't use the plans, we don't pay nothing."[43] The owner also claimed that "prior to when we signed the contract, when we were considering it, Mr. Larson said we

---

[40] Spitz v Brickhouse, 3 Ill App 2d 536, 123 NE2d 117 (1954). *See also* Caldwell v United Presbyterian Church, 20 Ohio Op 2d 364, 180 NE2d 638 (1961) (standard AIA contract, insufficient detail leading to ambiguity and uncertainty; HELD: since budget was omitted from written contract, oral evidence was admissible).

[41] Bair v School Dist No 141 Smith County, 94 Kan 144, 146 P 347 (1915).

[42] 231 Cal App 2d 659, 42 Cal Rptr 53 (1965).

[43] *Id* at 662, 42 Cal Rptr at 56.

didn't have to worry about the fees until we got the complete financing. Or partial financing ... payment ... would come out of the financing if we got it."[44] The architect denied these conversations. The court admitted the evidence and held that the oral condition was an *external condition precedent* which conditioned the effectiveness of the obligation to pay the fee upon the happening of an event: financing. Since the event did not take place, the fee contract was unenforceable.

Parol Evidence Refused

In a contrary holding, an architect sought to recover a fee on an American Legion Post project. The preliminary estimate was $100,000, after which the client requested changes which increased the estimate to $122,000. A subsoil problem was later discovered which further increased the costs to $205,000. The client then canceled the contract and did not proceed with the project. The standard American Institute of Architects (AIA) contract provided that "[s]ince the architect has no control over the cost of labor and materials or competitive bidding he does not guarantee the accuracy of any statement or estimates of probable construction costs."[45] The client offered evidence that the architect had orally agreed that the cost would not exceed $150,000. HELD: where a written contract provides that the architect is not responsible for estimates, parol evidence may not be admitted to prove such an outside agreement.[46]

Parol evidence was excluded in a Louisiana case where the president of a hospital testified that the oral budget was $350,000, the low bid was $821,000, and therefore the hospital abandoned the project. HELD: the contract that allowed the architect to recover for services rendered if the hospital terminated was clear and concise, precluding admission of parol evidence of limitations on costs.[47]

§5.09 Substantial Accuracy

Insubstantial Error

The Minnesota Supreme Court has held that the probable cost of a project did not substantially exceed the estimate, where the estimated maximum was $325,000 and the probable cost of completion was between $360,000 and $370,000, a difference of only about 13 per cent. The court did not consider such a degree of cost excess substantial, particularly since the owner agreed to

---

[44] *Id* at 662, 42 Cal Rptr at 56.
[45] American Institute of Architects, Document B131, art 6.6 (1963).
[46] Kurz v Quincy Post No 37 Am Legion, 5 Ill App 3d 412, 283 NE2d 8 (1972).
[47] Moossy v Huckabay Hosp, Inc, 283 So 2d 699 (La 1973).

changes that would increase the cost and since the estimate was merely an established estimate rather than a guarantee.[48]

In a Texas case the court followed similar reasoning. The estimated cost was $70,000 and the actual cost was $75,000. HELD: this constituted substantial performance.[49]

In *Cobb v Thomas*,[50] another Texas case, an architect designed a home and the contractor estimated a cost of $550,000. The owners considered the estimate too high. The architect redesigned the home so that it could be built for $400,000, excluding architectural fees. The owners then awarded a cost-plus contract without a guaranteed maximum price. After commencement of construction, the owners were advised that the cost would exceed $400,000. In the owners' suit against the architect for breach of contract, breach of fiduciary duty, and negligence, judgment for the architect was AFFIRMED. The contract with the architect did not specify a cost limit. Where owners require plans and specifications to conform to their express wishes as to the details of construction, the failure of the construction costs to conform to the amount estimated by the architect does not constitute breach of duty. Even though the jury found that the architect underestimated the probable cost of construction, this did not establish negligence as a matter of law. *An underestimation must be substantial, not merely trivial, to be actionable.* Moreover, here, the owners themselves delayed the work and in part contributed to added costs.

Substantial Error

In an Ohio case the budget was $40,000 to $45,000 and the actual estimated cost $57,800. HELD: an architect who exceeds the cost limit by more than 20 per cent does not substantially comply with the requirements of the contract and is therefore not entitled to recover a fee.[51]

A perplexing decision was rendered in a case in which an architect mistakenly believed that a project would be serviced by municipal water and therefore failed to provide for water softeners in the design. The court held that the architect was not liable for the mistake, saying that while an architect may be liable for underestimated total costs of a project resulting from failure to include all items necessary to construct a project, it must appear that the error was substantial before the architect would be liable for increased costs. The omission of water softeners worth $8,000 on a 104-unit motel was not considered substantial. Confusingly, however, the court also held that the

---

[48] Grizwold & Rauma Architects, Inc v Aesculapius Corp, 301 Minn 121, 221 NW2d 556 (1974).

[49] Vaky v Phelps, 194 SW 601 (Tex Civ App 1917), *error refused* (Nov 21, 1917). *See also* Smith v Dickey, 74 Tex 71, 11 SW 1049 (1889).

[50] 565 SW2d 281 (Tex Civ App 1978), *error refused* (Sept 13, 1978).

[51] Caldwell v United Presbyterian Church, 20 Ohio Op 2d 364, 180 NE2d 638 (1961).

architect was negligent in failing to design the water softeners. The softeners that were ultimately installed proved to be too small. The court awarded damages of $2,471.50 as the anticipated cost of installing larger water softeners.[52]

In a Colorado case, an owner put a ceiling price of $62,000 on a project, but the actual cost of construction ran to nearly $100,000. The court awarded damages computed as the difference between the actual cost and the estimated cost, less 10 per cent (deemed a normal variation) and, further, less the architect's fee. The court indulged in a sort of judicial notice that an estimate that comes within 10 per cent of the actual cost is close enough to discharge the architect's duty of care.[53]

Quantum Meruit Recovery

A New York court held that an architect was not entitled to recover the fee specified by a written contract where the contract provided that an armory should be designed so that the cost was within the sum of $450,000, and the low bid was $666,000. The court stated that a variation of that magnitude would not qualify for the application of the contract doctrine of substantial performance; nevertheless, the architect was entitled to recover on a *quantum meruit* theory the reasonable value of services performed, since the city benefited from the preliminary plans by learning it was impossible to construct an armory for $450,000.[54]

§5.10 Redesign

Perhaps the term *underestimation* is somewhat misleading when applied to a design architect. The term might imply that an architect was presented with a set of contract documents and was requested to prepare an estimate of the cost of construction. However, the reverse is what happens in practice. The client usually gives the architect an idea of what kind of a building it wants and what the budget is, and the architect tries to prepare design and contract documents that will enable the client to realize the objectives within the budget. Human nature being what it is, many clients aspire beyond their budgets. It seems that if the contract documents result in a project that exceeds the budget, the architect, as a matter of course, has the right to redesign the project so as to fit the budget. This is nothing more than a continuation of the original commission. And the courts, indeed, have allowed the architect something like a right to redesign.

---

[52] Jim Arnott, Inc v L&E, Inc, 539 P2d 1333 (Colo Ct App 1975).
[53] Kellogg v Pizza Oven, Inc, 157 Colo 295, 402 P2d 633 (1965).
[54] Horgan & Slattery v City of New York, 114 AD 555, 100 NYS 68 (1906).

No Warrantor

In the case of *Coombs v Beede*,[55] an owner alleged a special promise that plans prepared by an architect would not call for a house exceeding a cost of $2,500. The bids, four in all, ranged from $3,300 to $4,400. The owner refused to pay the fee, and the architect filed suit.

The court, in a classic statement of the architect's standard of practice,[56] stated that the undertaking of an architect does not imply or warrant a satisfactory result, and it will be enough that any failure shall not be the fault of the architect. There is no implied promise that miscalculations may not occur, and an error of judgment is not necessarily evidence of a want of skill or care. Those who employ an architect have a right to its best judgment, skill, advice, and absolute fidelity and good faith. When the architect has contributed these things, its duty has been fulfilled.

Defendant's wife had required many changes to the plans:

> The difficulty was that the defendant's wife not only wanted the expenditure not to exceed $2,500, but she wanted at the same time a house worth much more than that sum, and the architect was trying in good faith to accomplish the desired result as best he could. . . . Was it expected that he had promised to secure a house to her liking for $2,500 irrespective of actual cost or worth, and that he was agreeing to expend his services gratuitously if he did not succeed in doing so? . . . The plaintiff certainly could have reduced the cost upon the plans, and have earned his compensation, if the wife had permitted him to do so. . . . The bids which came in after the plans were advertised were disappointing, there being but four in all and ranging in amount from $3,300 to $4,400, showing the moral impossibility of an architect being able to fix precisely the cost of any building if the cost is to be measured in any such capricious way as by the bids of contractors.

Neither the defendant nor his wife would consent to modify the plans so as to obtain a bid within the price desired:

> If the house designed by him could be built for less than $2,700, it could hardly be called a failure, especially in view of the interferences on the part of the defendant's wife; nor a failure if the plaintiff could have so altered his plans as to reduce the house in price, and it seems preposterous

---

[55] 89 Me 187, 36 A 104 (1896).
[56] *See* ch 1.

to say that he could not, and he was willing to make alterations and the defendant and his wife would not consent thereto.

An architect must deal with conflicting laws of economics and human nature: one law holds that there is no limit to the human desire for material products; the other law states that man buys goods in the cheapest market.

If the cost of constructing a project designed by an architect exceeds the budget, the owner is unhappy.

On the other hand, the owner may also be unhappy if the design is *cheapened* to comply with the budget. For example, in an Oklahoma case, an owner filed an action against an architect for breach of contract and fraud. The budget was established at $9,000 and the bid was $16,000. The architect then revised the plan, and the bid was brought down to $14,000. It was then agreed that the contractor and the architect would work together within detailed specifications to produce a house for $10,500. They did. However, the owner was dissatisfied with the quality of the house. HELD: the fact that a $10,500 house is not as good as a $14,000 house is no evidence of fraud. The architect does not guarantee satisfaction, just reasonable care and professional skill.[57]

In a Minnesota case, the estimate for the expansion of a medical clinic was $325,000 and the probable cost of construction was $360,000 to $370,000. The architect suggested methods which could have brought the price down, but it would have required the elimination of *bays* (series of medical examination rooms), at a savings of approximately $35,000 per bay. The owner was not willing to eliminate bays. The court, in holding that the architect was entitled to its fee, pointed out that barring a specifically guaranteed area, a reasonable reduction in the size of the project should have been allowed if it was necessary to meet the budget.[58]

Project Abandoned

In a Utah case, the budget was $65,000 for a residence, but the bids ranged between $73,000 and $90,000. The owners told the architect to do what was necessary to modify the plans and bring the bids within the budget, and the architect did so. The owner then abandoned the project. The trial court found that the architect was ready, willing, and able to modify the plans to bring the cost down. HELD: an architect is entitled to be paid its fee when the owners abandon the project while the architect is in the process of fulfilling the contract and is ready, willing, and able to proceed. The court pointed out that compliance with the budget limitation was a condition to the contract and the

---

[57] Smith v Goff, 325 P2d 1061 (Okla 1958).
[58] Grizwold & Rauma Architects, Inc v Aesculapius Corp, 301 Minn 121, 221 NW2d 556 (1974).

owners' abandonment of the project amounted to a prevention of the performance of the condition. Therefore, the performance of the condition was excused.[59]

§5.11 Exculpatory Clauses

The current edition of the standard American Institute of Architects (AIA) contract documents provides that the architect does not guarantee the accuracy of any statement or estimate of probable construction cost.[60]

In at least one case, such boiler-plate language seems to have been the primary factor in permitting the architect to collect its fee in spite of a substantial cost overrun.

On an American Legion Post project, the architect gave an oral estimate of $100,000 based on preliminary drawings. After some redesign at the request of the owner, the estimate was increased to $122,000. Soil problems further increased the cost. The lowest bid was $205,000, whereupon the owner abandoned the project. The owner alleged an oral agreement that construction costs would not exceed $150,000. The contract provided: "Since the architect has no control over the cost of labor and materials or competitive bidding he does not guarantee the accuracy of any statement or estimates of probable construction costs." The court held that the architect was entitled to the full fee. Where the written contract provides that the architect is not responsible for the estimate, parol evidence may not be admitted to prove a contrary oral agreement.[61]

In an Illinois case, a similar exculpatory AIA clause did not save the architect's fee. The contract provided that since the architect had no control over the cost of labor or competitive bidding, it did not guarantee the accuracy of estimates. The contract further provided that the architect would design "a multiple purpose building . . . at an approximate estimated cost of $250,000." There was a conflict in testimony. The owner testified that the architect orally agreed that the $250,000 was an absolute lid. The court held that the maximum cost was $250,000 and the architect was not entitled to its fee.[62]

§5.12 Contributory Fault of Owner

Although the courts have not been very clear in assigning a theoretical basis for the outcome, it is clear that the contributory fault of the owner may excuse

---

[59] Parrish v Tahtaras, 7 Utah 2d 87, 318 P2d 642 (1957).

[60] AIA Document B141.

[61] Kurz v Quincy Post No 37 Am Legion, 5 Ill App 3d 412, 283 NE2d 8 (1972). The exculpatory language was also considered relevant by the court in holding architects entitled to fees in: Grizwold & Rauma Architects, Inc v Aesculapius Corp, 301 Minn 121, 221 NW2d 556 (1974); Impastato v Senner, 190 So 2d 111 (La Ct App 1966).

[62] Stevens v Fanning, 59 Ill App 2d 285, 207 NE2d 136 (1965).

an architect from failure to design a project that can be constructed within the owner's budget. The characterization of the legal theory may depend on whether the architect sues the owner or the owner sues the architect. If the owner sues the architect for negligence, contributory fault of the owner is contributory negligence. On the other hand, if the architect sues the owner for its fee, then contributory fault of the owner must fit within a category that is recognized as a defense in a contract case: estoppel, prevention of performance, election of remedies, breach of implied covenant, or the like.

In a California case, the owner was the plaintiff and the legal theory was negligence. The budget was $7,000 and the cost was $16,000. The evidence showed that after the plans had been completed, the plaintiff shopped for a contractor and was unable to obtain a bid in the $7,000 category; therefore, it entered into a cost-plus contract. The court held that the architect was not liable since the negligence of the architect was not the proximate cause of the injury. An owner may not recklessly proceed to make contracts which probably will exceed the estimate and hold the architect responsible for surplus expenditures.[63]

Unjust Enrichment

In *Impastato v Senner*,[64] the legal theory of contributory negligence was not available, since the architect was the plaintiff and the theory was breach of contract. The architect sued for its fee on a motel remodeling project. The budget was $150,000 and the project was to be completed by January 1963. The plans were finished by July 1962. After plan revisions were completed on August 31, the low bid was $250,000. The contract permitted the owner to reject the contract documents without fee since the bids exceeded the budget, but instead of rejecting the contract documents, the owner indulged in several months of negotiation with a contractor and, by altering the plans, reduced the cost to $166,000. The provisions of the prime contract required completion by March 1963; actual completion was April 1963.

The owners claimed an offset for motel income lost during the period of the delay. The court held that the architect was entitled to its fee. The owner had the right to reject the plans and pay no fee; instead it chose to take advantage of the architect's work, reduce the scope of the plans, and negotiate with the contractor for an acceptable price. The delay caused by these negotiations was not to be charged against the architect.

The foundation of the decision seems to be unjust enrichment: the court did not want to allow the owner to have the benefit of the architect's plans gratis.

---

[63] Benenato v McDougall, 166 Cal 405, 137 P 8 (1913). *See also* Cobb v Thomas, 565 SW2d 281 (Tex Civ App 1978), *error refused* (Sept 13, 1978) (architect not liable where owner signed a cost-plus contract with no guaranteed maximum and owner delayed the project).

[64] 190 So 2d 111 (La Ct App 1966).

On the other hand, to require the owner to reject the plans or waive its claim for damages is to put it to a Hobson's choice, since to reject the plans is to delay the project even further while new plans are prepared. It seems the owner could argue that by reducing the scope of the project and negotiating with a contractor for a lower price, it was merely mitigating damages caused by the architect's breach of contract.

Cost Increases by Owner

In a Texas case, the budget for a residence project was $250,000. The architect submitted preliminary plans, and the owners made major changes which increased the cost. They then abandoned the project on the ground that it was too expensive and refused to pay the architect's fee. The court sustained the verdict for the architect and also awarded attorneys fees under Texas law, which stated that a contract for purely personal services supports an award of attorneys fees whether or not expressly provided for in the contract.[65]

In another Texas case, *Bueche v Eickenroht*,[66] an architect filed suit against an owner to collect a fee after the cost of the building exceeded the alleged limit of $18,000. HELD: the architect was entitled to the fee; for although the contract called for supervision by the architect, the owner did not permit the architect to supervise. Further, the owner had a specific house in mind, and the architect was required to prepare plans in accordance with the owner's wishes. Nonconformity with the estimate, when the architect must follow specific design criteria, does not bar recovery for services rendered.

In *Schwender v Schraft*,[67] an architect filed suit to recover a fee after the owner abandoned the project claiming that the architect had failed to prepare plans conforming to the contract. HELD: the architect was entitled to the fee. Where an employment contract contains a definite cost limit, the architect must design in reasonable conformity to this requirement in order to recover its fee. However, when a sum named is only an estimate, and where the owner's instructions require plans and specifications for a building "according to the expressed wishes of the owner as to size, method and details of construction," mere nonconformity of the cost with the estimated amount does not prevent recovery by the architect of a fee. Here, the owner had in mind a building costing $40,000 but also gave the architect express instructions regarding various special features. Therefore, the architect was entitled to recover a fee even though the owner abandoned the project on the ground that the building would cost more than $40,000.

---

[65] Brown v Cox, 459 SW2d 471 (Tex Civ App 1970).
[66] 220 SW2d 911 (Tex Civ App 1949).
[67] 246 Mass 149, 141 NE 511 (1923).

Similarly, in a California case, the budget was $30,000, and the owners expanded the scope of the project by changing the plans to increase garage space and add more rooms. The final cost was $62,192. The owners filed suit against the architect for negligent design and supervision. The court found for the architect on its cross-complaint for a fee of 6 per cent of the actual cost (rather than 6 per cent of the estimate). The cost escalation was caused by changes ordered by the owner.[68]

§5.13 Waiver

The owner may waive the cost limit imposed by its budget, and in such circumstances the architect will be entitled to recover its fee, even though the cost may exceed the budget. In a Florida case, an engineer provided a plan for modification of waste treatment processes at a distillery. The engineer gave a written cost estimate of $9,500, which exceeded the $5,000 budget. Nevertheless, the distillery ordered the modifications accomplished and put them in use, but refused to pay the engineer's fee. HELD: when the distillery gave written authority to proceed with the preliminary phase and the installation of the pilot plant after being informed of the increase in cost, it became indebted for services rendered by the engineer in preparing the preliminary design.[69]

Purported Waiver Ambiguous

In a Louisiana case, the budget for a residence was $12,000 and the preliminary estimate was $17,926. The architect contended that the owner waived the budget, because the owner said that it wanted the residence to conform to the preliminary drawings even if it went into bankruptcy. The owner, on the other hand, claimed that it said that it would go into bankruptcy if it had to pay as much as the preliminary estimate indicated. HELD: the architect was not entitled to recover its fee. It was unreasonable for the architect to go ahead with the final drawings because of ambiguous talk by the owner about its potential bankruptcy.[70]

§5.14 Unjust Enrichment

The courts have a predisposition to follow the biblical principle that a laborer is worthy of its hire. In at least one case, the impulse to pay an architect for services rendered, standing alone, seems to have excused a serious cost overrun.

---

[68] Pieri v Rosebrook, 128 Cal App 2d 250, 275 P2d 67 (1954).
[69] Jaquin Fla Distilling Co v Reynolds, Smith & Hills Architects-Engineers-Planners, Inc, 319 So 2d 604 (Fla Dist Ct App 1975).
[70] Andry & Feitel v Ewing, 15 La App 272, 130 So 570 (1930).

The owner was required to pay the architect a fee even though the value of the architect's services to the owner was dubious at best.

The court held that the plaintiff's obligation under the contract was to furnish plans for an armory that could be built for $450,000. A $200,000 overrun amounted to a breach of contract that could not be excused under the doctrine of substantial performance. However, the court held that the architect would be entitled to the reasonable value of its services on a *quantum meruit* theory. In the final analysis, the city did benefit from the architect's performance, since its work demonstrated that it was impossible to construct the armory for the amount appropriated for that purpose.[71]

In a Texas case, the budget was $70,000 and the original low bid was $133,000; by redesign this was reduced to $84,000. The court held that since the budget was exceeded, the architect could not recover under the contract, and the trial court was correct in refusing to instruct the jury on *quantum meruit*, since the complaint was on a contract theory.[72]

Where an owner abandons a project because the cost exceeds the budget, there is no unjust enrichment. Therefore, the architect is not entitled to recover a fee on a *quantum meruit* theory.[73]

§5.15 Benefit-of-the-Bargain Damages

The most perplexing question in the field of architects' estimates is the question of owner's damages. Damages are often measured in effect by the fee: if an architect underestimates the cost of the project, it is deprived of the fee. As a rule of damages, this is imprecise, since the amount of the fee bears no necessary relationship to the actual damages suffered by the owner.

The owner can argue that its damages include such items as interest on invested capital during a period of delay while plans are being revised; income that could otherwise have been obtained from the building during the period of the delay; reimbursement for the time and effort expended by the owner and its employees in devising plans and obtaining bids; and the difference between the estimate and the actual cost. The architect, on the other hand, may justly argue that if the building is worth the price, there are, in fact, no damages, even though the estimate may have been incorrect.

In a Massachusetts case an architect not only lost its fee, but also had to pay the difference between the estimate and the actual cost. In *Kaufman v Leard*,[74]

---

[71] Horgan & Slattery v City of New York, 114 AD 555, 100 NYS 68 (1906).
[72] Torres v Jarmon, 501 SW2d 369 (Tex Civ App 1973).
[73] Zannoth v Booth Radio Stations, 333 Mich 233, 52 NW2d 678 (1952).
[74] 356 Mass 163, 248 NE2d 480 (1969).

clients asked an architect's advice as to whether a house they wished to purchase could be converted to a home and office. Relying on the architect's judgment, the clients purchased the house. The architect said the project would cost between $12,000 and $15,000. Relying on this, the Kaufmans purchased the house. The estimate was increased to $17,000. Actual cost on a time-and-material basis was $39,953.86. The evidence showed that the Kaufmans ordered extra work, not contemplated in the original estimate, costing $5,415. The court held that the architect was liable for the difference between the actual cost (minus extras) and the estimate, plus reimbursement of the portion of the fee already received ($785) and interest. The outcome was influenced by the fact that the architect, rather than the owner, engaged the contractor. The architect was negligent when it exceeded its authority by ordering and directing work costing more than $17,000.

Nevertheless, the *Kaufman* case must give us pause. Does the outcome unjustly enrich the owner? Should the court not consider the market value of the remodeled residence, in addition to the fact that it cost more than the original budget?

Benefit-of-the-bargain damages were awarded against an engineer in *Williams Engineering, Inc v Goodyear*.[75] The engineer was employed to design and oversee construction of a water slide facility. The contract between the owner and the engineer specified that the project would cost roughly $409,300. Thereafter, the owner switched to a fast-track construction method with the understanding that costs would increase but the job would be finished in time for peak usage during the summer months. The engineer's fee was to be computed as a percentage of the final cost.

By July 15, the cost had reached $409,300 and invoices indicated that the project was 85 per cent complete. The total cost of construction was $824,934. The owner, having paid $40,311 in engineering fees, refused to pay the additional $36,000 based on excess final costs. The engineer filed suit to recover the fee and owner counterclaimed for breach of contract. The jury awarded a $25,000 fee to the engineer plus $8,725 in expert witness fees and costs and also held that the engineer had breached the contract and awarded the owner $125,000 plus $3,000 in expert witness fees and costs. HELD: damages to the owner should have been calculated by subtracting the estimated cost of $470,695 and the engineer's fee that had been paid ($40,311) from the *actual* cost of construction to determine the *excess* cost of construction. Tax losses of $119,000 should have been deducted from this amount, leaving an award in favor of the owner and against the engineer in the amount of $204,928, or $79,928 more than awarded by the jury, plus costs.

---

[75] 480 So 2d 772 (La Ct App 1985), *affd*, 496 So 2d 1012 (La 1986).

Fraud Theory

In *Edward Barron Estate Co v Woodruff Co*,[76] the complaint alleged that the defendant architect fraudulently represented that it was a skilled architect and could design a hotel that could be built for $300,000. Relying on the representations, the owner awarded the architect a contract to design and construct the building. Later, the estimate was raised to $400,000 on the basis of a cost plus 15 per cent contract. A tenant was willing to pay a rental rate that would return 8 per cent per annum on the total value of the project, land, and building. After a year of construction, when the building was more than half completed, the architect for the first time advised the owner that the project would cost $700,000. The owner went forward with the project but filed suit against the architect. The architect demurred to the complaint. REVERSED. It was contended that there were no damages, since the project was presumably worth what it cost. However, the owner was entitled to recover the $70,000 in commissions paid to the architect for services procured through fraud and of no value to the owner. The court concluded:

> So here we conceive that if plaintiff can establish that, under the circumstances charged, it suffered a loss of three hundred thousand dollars, or any part thereof, it is justly entitled to recover it, if it further established that the loss was occasioned in the matter charged.... [I]nsofar as it can be established that plaintiff was fraudulently induced to expend its moneys for a structure not, as to cost, in accordance with representations, and not capable of returning a fair interest upon the invested capital, respondents have made themselves liable.[77]

The court thus used a *market value* standard apparently to be determined by capitalizing the income at a rate of 8 per cent and determining whether the value of the project thus determined was equal to the cost of $700,000. The damages, if any, would be the difference. *Benefit-of-the-bargain* damages may be awarded where there is no unjust enrichment to the plaintiff. The argument against benefit-of-the-bargain damages is that the owner may be unjustly enriched at the expense of the architect, since although the completed project cost more than the budget, it may also be worth more than the budget.

Measure of Damages Criticized

The argument against benefit-of-the-bargain damages is presented in *Capital Hotel Co v Rittenberry*,[78] which criticized *Barron Estate*. In *Capital Hotel Co*, the

---

[76] 163 Cal 561, 126 P 351 (1912).

[77] *Id* at 578, 126 P at 358.

[78] 41 SW2d 697 (Tex Civ App 1931), *dismissed* (Mar 23, 1932).

estimated cost of a hotel was $375,000 and the actual cost $500,000. HELD: such an underestimation barred the architect from recovering its fee. However, the measure of damages utilized in the *Barron Estate* case was rejected as unfair, since it allowed the owner to retain the hotel (which was worth more than the estimates since it cost more) and also recover damages.

Tenant's Damages

In *Kellogg v Pizza Oven, Inc*,[79] the plaintiff lessee employed an architect to design a restaurant building. The property owner had agreed to pay the first $60,000 of construction costs, and any overage was to be paid by the tenant. The tenant imposed a ceiling of $62,000. Actual construction costs ran to nearly $100,000. The trial court computed the damages as the difference between the estimated cost and the actual cost, with a credit of 10 per cent of the estimate, since a 10 per cent overrun was deemed to be a normal variation. Furthermore, the trial court awarded the architect an offset for the unpaid fee. HELD: this was the proper measure of damages. There was no unjust enrichment, since the client was merely a tenant, and not the owner. Moreover, the award of architect's fees was not inconsistent with an award of damages for the underestimate. The client's claim was for negligence, not breach of contract, and since no breach of contract was alleged, the architect was entitled to a fee.

The reasoning of the *Kellogg* case is questionable in at least three respects. First, even though the tenant did not own the building, the value of the tenant's leasehold interest may have been, and probably was, increased by the additional costs of construction. The court should have offset the increased value of the leasehold interest against the overrun. Next, the award of benefit-of-the-bargain damages in a negligence action is theoretically wrong. Damages for negligence should be actual out-of-pocket damages. The only justification for awarding more than out-of-pocket damages would be the theory that the architect contracted, promised, or guaranteed (for consideration) that the project would not cost more than a given amount. Thus, benefit-of-the-bargain damages should only be recoverable in a contract action for breach of contract, not in an action for negligence. Finally, the mere fact that a plaintiff sets up a cause of action for negligence should not by itself entitle an architect to recover a fee, even if the architect is guilty of a breach of contract and even though the same act may be, and often is, both negligence and a breach of contract.[80]

§5.16 Out-of-Pocket Damages

Of the rules of damages adopted by courts in underestimate (or overbudget) cases, the *out-of-pocket rule* appears to do the most precise justice. This rule

---

[79] 157 Colo 295, 402 P2d 633 (1965).
[80] *See* ch 4.

recognizes that, even though the owner may have to pay more than it budgeted for the completed project, the completed project may be worth more than it would have been worth if the budget had been observed. In justice, the owner should not retain the benefits of the more valuable project designed by the architect at the expense of the architect.

To merely deprive an architect of its fee in an overbudget case is to make the architect's fee the measure of damages; but this has no necessary relation to the actual loss sustained by the client. The *benefit-of-the-bargain rule* may result in an unjust enrichment to the owner since the owner retains the increased value which the project usually achieves by going overbudget.[81] There is no visible reason to give the owner both the increased value of the project and a damage award against the architect. The out-of-pocket rule, however, says that the owner is entitled to recover from the architect the amount by which the cost of the project exceeds the reasonable value of the project, limited by the difference between the estimate and the ultimate cost. This rule would seem to render the most satisfactory results in most cases, and a corollary to the rule is that, once the out-of-pocket damages have been deducted, the architect should be entitled to its fee. Or, to put it another way, if the architect's fee is included in calculating the total cost, then the fee should be paid; if it is not included, it should not be paid.

A rule should be developed to dispose of cases in which, because of special factors, the project desired by the owner would not ever be worth its estimated cost. Many an owner wishes to *overbuild* a specialized residence. Suppose, for example, the owner wants to improve its home with a tennis court. Because of soil conditions, the tennis court must be supported by caissons. The owner knows this is *overbuilding* in the sense that it will never be able to get its money out of the project, but the owner wants it anyway. Now if the cost of the tennis court exceeds the budget accepted by the architect, the owner will lose more than it had bargained to lose. Therefore, the measure of damages should be the difference between the loss the owner bargained for and the loss sustained: in other words, the amount by which the actual cost exceeds the market value, reduced by the amount by which the budgeted cost would have exceeded the market value.

The court correctly stated the damage rule in a Minnesota case in which the budget for a home was $39,000. The owner acted as its own contractor, and after four years of construction the residence was only partially completed at a cost of $63,000. The owner filed a negligence action against the architect, and the jury brought in a verdict for the owner. AFFIRMED: the fact that the cost substantially exceeded the estimate is strong evidence to support the jury's finding that the architect was negligent. The measure of damages is not the

---

[81] *See* §5.15.

amount by which the cost of the project exceeds the estimate, but the difference between the total cost of the property, land, and building, and the amount of money which a prudent person would pay for the property in its present condition, but not to include any loss which the owners could have prevented by reasonable care and diligence.[82]

Some appellate courts, in affirming trial court judgments, have not specified the proper measure of damages. For example, in a California case, the evidence showed that the cost of a medical building exceeded the budget by $10,000, but the trial court awarded damages of $1,000. The court of appeal found that the architect's objection to the amount of damages came with poor grace, since the architect was the one to benefit, not the plaintiff.[83] Likewise, in an Arkansas case, the budget was $23,000 and the cost was $43,000; the jury returned a verdict of $5,000. The architect contended that it should have been credited with its 6 per cent fee. AFFIRMED. A party may not profit from its own wrong; "an architect whose cost estimate is culpably below the cost of the job is not entitled to a commission upon the excess."[84]

§5.17 Loss-of-Fee Damages

Where bids so far exceed the budget that the plans are never used, no question of unjust enrichment arises, and the courts have usually held that the architect is not entitled to its fee.[85]

---

[82] Kostohryz v McGuire, 298 Minn 513, 212 NW2d 850 (1973).

[83] Goldberg v Underhill, 95 Cal App 2d 700, 213 P2d 516 (1950).

[84] Clark v Madeira, 252 Ark 157, 477 SW2d 817, 818 (1972).

[85] *See* Rowell v Crow, 93 Cal App 2d 500, 209 P2d 149 (1949) (budget $250,000, low bid $598,819, hotel building; HELD: services were worth reasonable value alleged, $20,207, but architect could not recover because of breach of oral condition); Feltham v Sharp, 99 Ga 260, 25 SE 619 (1896) (budget $4,300, bids $7,800 and $9,000, plans not used; HELD: architect is not entitled to payment unless building can be erected at a cost reasonably close to the stated estimate); Stevens v Fanning, 59 Ill App 2d 285, 207 NE2d 136 (1965) (budget was $250,000 for a 40,000 square foot Chevrolet dealership, as planned would have cost much more; HELD: architect guaranteed a maximum cost of $250,000 and was entitled to no fee for services rendered after budget was established); Spitz v Brickhouse, 3 Ill App 2d 536, 123 NE2d 117 (1954) ($25,000 budget for residence, plans would have cost $38,000); Bair v School Dist No 141 Smith County, 94 Kan 144, 146 P 347 (1915) (schoolhouse budget $10,000, lowest bid $14,000); MacDonnell v Dreyfous, 144 La 891, 81 So 383 (1919) (budget $50,000, low bid $69,000; HELD: architect could not recover if cost materially exceeded budget); Wetzel v Roberts, 296 Mich 114, 295 NW 580 (1941) (budget $15,000, bid $28,000); Zannoth v Booth Radio Stations, 333 Mich 233, 52 NW2d 678 (1952) (architect commenced design for broadcasting studio and transmitter, owner thereafter set cost limit of $55,000, low bid was $142,000; HELD: architect may recover fees for work performed up until time when cost limit was set; thereafter, nothing); Caldwell v United Presbyterian Church, 20 Ohio Op 2d 364, 180 NE2d 638 (1961) (church budget $47,000, actual cost $57,000); Rose v Shearrer, 431 SW2d 939 (Tex Civ App 1968) (grocery store remodel budget $90,000, low bid $121,000; HELD: rule is clear that where cost substantially exceeds estimate, architect cannot recover compensation); Malo v Gilman,

Effect of *Quantum Meruit* Damages

A New York case is not consistent with any of the other decisions. The budget was $450,000 and the low bid was $666,000. The project was never built. The architect was not entitled to recover a fee in an action on the contract since there was no substantial performance. Nevertheless, the architect was entitled to recover the reasonable value of its services on a *quantum meruit* theory. The court said that the city did benefit from the preliminary plans and other work done by the architect, since it demonstrated the impossibility of constructing the project within the $450,000 budget appropriated for that purpose. Most students of the subject of damages will find it difficult to accept the proposition that a city was unjustly enriched by plans that were never used.[86]

The general rule of nonrecovery where the cost substantially exceeds the estimate should be modified if the project is built, to prevent the unjust enrichment of the owner at the expense of the architect. If the cost of the project, including the architect's fee when added to the value of the real property, is less than the market value of the project to the owner, then the architect should be entitled to recover its fee on a *quantum meruit* theory.

---

177 Ind App 365, 379 NE2d 554 (1978) (engineer may not recover for services when the actual cost of the structure substantially or unreasonably exceeds the estimate); Capital Hotel Co v Rittenberry, 41 SW2d 697 (Tex Civ App 1931), *dismissed* (Mar 23, 1932) (estimated cost of hotel project $375,000, actual cost $500,000); Torres v Jarmon, 501 SW2d 369 (Tex Civ App 1973) (veterinary hospital budget $70,000 plus 10 per cent contingency, low bid $84,000; HELD: no question that if cost limitation was exceeded, architect was precluded from recovery).

[86] Horgan & Slattery v City of New York, 114 AD 555, 100 NYS 68 (1906).

Liability Arising from Warranty Law   6

§6.01   Generally
§6.02   Express Warranty
        Warranty versus Misrepresentation
        Strict Liability versus Express Warranty
§6.03   Implied Warranty
        Warranty Implied in Favor of Owner
        Benefit-of-Bargain Damages Inapplicable
        Implied Warranty of Builder
        Statute of Limitations—Privity
        Warranty Found
        Damages
§6.04   Strict Liability
        Privity Defense
        Justification for Strict Liability
§6.05   —Mass Home Builders
§6.06   —History of the Doctrine
§6.07   —Architects
        Strict Liability Rejected
§6.08   —Engineers
        Engineer Not Strictly Liable
§6.09   —Application Criticized

§6.01   Generally

The term *warranty* does not seem to have a generally accepted meaning as it is applied in cases of the malpractice of architects. In some cases the term is used to denote an express contractual promise. In others it is used as a synonym for *misrepresentation*, intentional or negligent. In still other cases it is used in the sense developed from the law of sales, as an express or implied guarantee that a product (contract documents) will meet some specified standard. One of the leading questions in the developing law of malpractice is whether the concept of warranty growing out of the law of sales will mutate into a theory that principles of strict liability can be applied to architects.

The tort law of products liability developed from the contract cause of action for breach of warranty. This development enabled courts to hold manufacturers liable for injuries even though the consumer could not prove that the manufacturer was negligent. The requirement of privity was abandoned by most courts in implied warranty actions and, ultimately, most courts abandoned the concept of warranty in favor of strict liability in tort.[1]

§6.02 Express Warranty

Warranty versus Misrepresentation

In a Washington case, *warranty* seems to have been used in the sense of *misrepresentation*. In that case, an architect filed suit to recover its fee. The client alleged that the architect had expressly represented that the architect was competent to design a well-lighted and first-class building; the client employed the architect but the resulting building was neither well-lighted nor first-class. HELD: the representations amounted to a warranty on the part of the plaintiff that the plans would be as represented; therefore, the trial court was wrong to exclude the defendant's evidence, since the allegation would have supported a valid counterclaim.[2]

Strict Liability versus Express Warranty

In a California case, the court brushed lightly over allegations of express warranty in holding that a soil engineer was not liable to a home purchaser for settlement of fill. The court stated that a soil engineer, employed in an advisory capacity, paid by the hour, and having no interest in the property sold to the plaintiff, cannot be held strictly liable for damage: any liability must be based on negligence or intentional misconduct. Since there was no evidence of negligence, the defendant was not liable. Those who sell professional services are not strictly liable, and this holding largely disposes the claim founded on express warranty.[3]

Here, the court erroneously implied that strict liability and express warranty are kindred theories. They are not. The theory of strict liability is akin to, and

---

[1] Moorman Mfg Co v National Tank Co, 91 Ill 2d 69, 435 NE2d 443 (1982).
[2] Niver v Nash, 7 Wash 558, 35 P 380 (1893).
[3] Swett v Gribaldo Jones & Assocs, 40 Cal App 3d 573, 115 Cal Rptr 99 (1974).

to some extent developed from, the law of implied warranties in sales. The theory of express warranty, however, is kindred to the breach of an express contract and exists, indeed, at the opposite pole.

The Third Circuit has clearly distinguished between the theories of express warranty and strict liability. Plaintiff's decedent contracted cancer after loading pellets coated with vanadium into a reactor. The operation generated vanadium dust. Among other theories, the plaintiff alleged that the designing and supervising engineer breached an express warranty, pointing to contract clauses by which the engineer agreed to perform services in a workmanlike manner and to construct a facility suitable for the intended purpose. HELD: contract clauses requiring *good and workmanlike* execution only indicate that the promisor is required to perform without negligence. They do not import a guarantee of safe performance under all circumstances. Therefore, the engineer was not liable in the absence of negligence.[4]

Similarly, in *Illinois Housing Development Authority v Sjostron & Sons*,[5] language in the contract that permitted the plaintiff to rescind if the development was not built in a good and workmanlike manner did not constitute a warranty running to the plaintiff that the development would be so constructed.

§6.03 Implied Warranty

A well-written legal note states that a minority of courts have held that an architect impliedly warrants the sufficiency of its plans for their intended purpose.[6] The majority of courts, however, still hold that when the function is design, the plaintiff will have to prove negligence. The note makes the further point that as of yet architects have not been, nor should they be, held to be under the doctrine of strict liability.

The illegitimacy of the application of the doctrine of implied warranty to architects is trenchantly stated in *Audlane Lumber & Builders Supply, Inc v D.E. Britt & Associates*.[7] The court noted that Alabama had held that an architect *impliedly warrants* its design.[8] The court continued:

> With respect to the alleged "implied warranty of fitness," we see no reason for application of this theory in circumstances involving professional liability. Unlike the lower court, however, we do not base our decision on the narrow ground of privity. An engineer, or any other so called

---

[4] La Rossa v Scientific Design Co, 402 F2d 937 (3d Cir 1968).

[5] 105 Ill App 3d 247, 433 NE2d 1350 (1982).

[6] Note, *Liability of Design Professionals-The Necessity of Fault*, 5 Iowa L Rev 1221 (1973) (Alabama, South Carolina, and Washington).

[7] 168 So 2d 333 (Fla 1964), *cert denied*, 173 So 2d 146 (Fla 1965).

[8] *See* Broyles v Brown Engg Co, 275 Ala 35, 151 So 2d 767 (1963).

professional, does not "warranty" his service or the tangible evidence of his skill to be "merchantible" or "fit for an intended use." These are terms uniquely applicable to goods. Rather, in the preparation of design and specifications as the basis of construction, the engineer or architect "warrants" that he will or has exercised his skill according to a certain standard of care, that he acted reasonably and without neglect. Breach of this "warranty" occurs if he was negligent. Accordingly, the elements of an action for negligence and for breach of the "implied warranty" are the same. The use of the term "implied warranty" in these circumstances merely introduces further confusion into an area of law where confusion abounds.[9]

This view is justified. It seems that the determination of liability of an architect for malpractice can be served by reference to the ordinary tort principles of negligence, rather than by resort to the doctrine of implied warranty. Similarly, the liability of a surveyor is best addressed by actions based on negligence. A surveyor cannot be guilty of a breach of warranty under the Uniform Commercial Code (UCC). A survey plan is not *goods* within the meaning of the UCC.[10]

In *State v Gatham-Matotan Architects*,[11] the state filed an action against an architect for breach of implied warranty in the design of a bay window for a penitentiary central control area. During a prison riot, injuries and a death occurred. HELD: there is no cause of action against an architect for breach of an implied warranty to furnish plans and specifications adequate for a particular purpose.

> Traditionally, architects, along with other professionals such as doctors and lawyers, do not promise a certain result. The professional usually is employed to exercise the customary or reasonable skills of his profession for a particular job. He guarantees his work only to the extent that he will use the skill customarily demanded of his profession.[12]

In *Kemper Architects, PC v McFall, Konkel & Kimball Consulting Engineers, Inc*,[13] engineer, employed as a consultant by architect under an oral agreement, did not warrant the fitness of its design for a heating, ventilation and air conditioning system. The court held an implied warranty applies to contracts

---

[9] 168 So 2d at 335.
[10] Raffel v Perley, 14 Mass App Ct 242, 437 NE2d 1082 (1982).
[11] 98 NM 790, 653 P2d 166 (1982).
[12] *Id* at 793, 653 P2d at 169.
[13] 843 P2d 1178 (Wyo 1992).

for the sale of goods, and not to professional services. Therefore, plaintiff had the burden of proving negligent performance by the engineer.

Warranty Implied in Favor of Owner

In *Broyles v Brown Engineering Co*,[14] an engineer prepared contract documents for the drainage system on a subdivision project. The plaintiff client alleged that inadequate storm drain design resulted in periodic flooding. The plaintiff did not allege negligence, but rather breach of an implied warranty of adequate results. The trial court sustained a demurrer, and the Alabama Supreme Court REVERSED, sliding from the theory that there was a contract implied in fact between the parties to the theory that the complaint established an implied warranty that the plans were sufficient to reasonably accomplish their intended purpose. The court remarked that the engineer's knowledge that the plaintiff intended to subdivide, erect buildings, and lay out a large sum of money, and the fact that defendant held itself out as an expert, justified the conclusion "that the parties mutually intended an agreement of guarantee as to the sufficiency and adequacy of the plans and specifications to accomplish proper and adequate drainage."[15] Thus, the court seemingly did some violence to the law of contract and the law of sales in order to reach the clearly correct result that the engineer could have been liable. It was only necessary to refer to the well-established tort doctrine of negligence in order to reach the same result. Why should the court have implied from the facts the existence of *an agreement of guarantee*, when the obvious realities were that no such guarantee was made?[16]

One reason, although perhaps not a justification, for the application of the doctrine of implied warranty is that the doctrine will support an award of benefit-of-the-bargain damages,[17] whereas a negligence theory is usually held to support out-of-pocket damages. This is illustrated in *Prier v Refrigeration Engineering Co*,[18] where the architect designed an ice skating rink which froze the soil to a depth of four feet, threatening the foundations.

To correct the problem it was necessary to insert an air space between the floor and the ground and provide hot air ventilation to prevent freezing. The

---

[14] 275 Ala 35, 151 So 2d 767 (1963).

[15] *Id* at 38, 151 So 2d at 770.

[16] To the effect that an architect may be liable for breach of implied warranty, see United States Fidelity & Guar Co v Jacksonville State Univ, 357 So 2d 952 (Ala 1978) (leakage caused by defect in epoxy matrix used by subcontractor who followed the specification requirements of the architect); Federal Mogul Corp v Universal Constr Co, 376 So 2d 716 (Ala Civ App), *writ denied*, 376 So 2d 726 (Ala 1979) (recognizing implied warranty theory but holding there was no evidence that the architect's plans were defective).

[17] *See* §5.15.

[18] 74 Wash 2d 25, 442 P2d 621 (1968).

cost was $36,189.71. The trial court awarded $17,500 in general damages (cost of correction minus the estimated cost of installing the air space originally) plus $2,500 in profit loss while the rink was closed. This holding was REVERSED. The plaintiff should have recovered on a theory of implied warranty rather than tort; therefore, the proper damages were $36,189.71 (the cost of correction), rather than the $20,000 awarded by the lower court. The appellate court stated that a person that holds itself out as qualified to furnish contract documents impliedly warrants their sufficiency, and the cost of correction is what was necessary to give the *buyer* what the *seller* had promised. Damages in a contract case should put the injured party in as good a position as if it received full performance.[19]

Benefit-of-Bargain Damages Inapplicable

If the objective of awarding benefit-of-the-bargain damages is valid, then the introduction of the implied warranty contract and sales doctrines might be approved. However, benefit-of-the-bargain damages should *not* be awarded in a case of the malpractice of an architect. Why should the owner be enriched at the expense of the architect in the absence of a specific guarantee? In addition, the damage award means that the owner receives not only the increased value of the real estate occasioned by the construction of the project which the architect designed, but also an award of damages sufficient to put the owner in a better position than it would have occupied if the project had been properly designed in the first place.

The true rule is best stated by Justice Traynor in *Gagne v Bertran*.[20] The owner employed the defendant tester at $10 an hour to drill test holes and check for fill on two lots which the owner had agreed to buy subject to testing. The tester negligently reported only 12 to 16 inches of fill; the correct amount was 4 to 6 feet and the increased cost of the foundations was $3,093.65, which the trial court awarded as damages. The complaint alleged breach of warranty, as well as deceit and negligence. Justice Traynor held that there was no express warranty agreement and no implied warranty. The defendant did not guarantee that the conclusion was correct; the amount of the fee and the fact that defendant was paid by the hour showed that the defendant was selling service and not insurance. Therefore, there could have been no liability without negligence. The defendant was liable for negligence, but the measure of damages adopted by the trial court was wrong. The owner relied on information which was negligently incorrect. Therefore, if the property was worth less than the owner

---

[19] 1 Restatement (Contracts) §346 (1932).
[20] 43 Cal 2d 481, 275 P2d 15 (1954) (two justices dissenting).

paid for it, the defendant would have been liable for the difference; on the other hand, if the lots were actually worth more than the price, the plaintiff was not damaged. The cost of the foundations was not caused by misinformation, but by the physical condition of the land.

An excellent discussion of implied warranty appears in *City of Mounds View v Walijarvi*,[21] where the trial court granted partial summary judgment for the defendant architect. The architect had designed an addition to the city hall; water seepage problems occurred; the city filed suit for negligence, breach of express warranty, and breach of implied warranty of fitness for a particular purpose. HELD: the majority rule limits liability of architects to those situations in which the architect is negligent in the provision of services. Architects and other professionals are "continually called upon to exercise their skilled judgment in order to anticipate and provide for random factors which are incapable of precise measurement."[22] The indeterminate nature of these factors makes it impossible for professional service people to gauge them with complete accuracy in every instance. Therefore, the law does not and should not require perfect results, but it does demand the exercise of that skill and judgment which can reasonably be expected from similarly situated professionals. To adopt the city's implied warranty theory would have imposed strict liability on architects for latent defects in the structures they design. Until the random elements can be eliminated in the application of architectural services, liability must rest on negligence alone, not implied warranty.[23]

---

[21] 263 NW2d 420 (Minn 1978).

[22] *Id* 423.

[23] A series of cases has refused to apply the doctrine of implied warranty in cases of malpractice of architects. Bates & Rogers Constr v North Shore Sanitary Dist, 92 Ill App 3d 90, 414 NE2d 1274 (1980), *affd*, 109 Ill 2d 225, 486 NE2d 902 (1985); Union College v Kennerly, Slomanson & Smith, 167 NJ Super 311, 400 A2d 850 (1979) (no implied warranty under UCC, no indication that engineer produced plans from any stock supply or that they were mass produced); Borman's, Inc v Lake State Dev Co, 60 Mich App 175, 230 NW2d 363 (1975) (shopping center tenant versus architect, defective drainage system caused flooding damage); Jacobs v Petrino, 351 So 2d 1036 (Fla Dist Ct App 1976), *cert denied*, 349 So 2d 1231 (Fla 1977) (boundary survey); Queensbury Union Free Sch Dist v Jim Walter Corp, 91 Misc 2d 804, 398 NYS2d 832 (Sup Ct 1977) (school district versus its architect for roof leaks); Johnson, Voiland, Archuleta, Inc v Roark Assocs, 40 Colo App 269, 572 P2d 1220 (1977) (recognizing rule); Ryan v Morgan Spear Assocs, 546 SW2d 678 (Tex Civ App 1977) (foundation and soil testing caused damage to building); Gravely v Providence Partnership, 549 F2d 958 (4th Cir 1977) (hotel guest injured in fall on spiral staircase).

Other cases have also held that an architect does not impliedly warrant its work. *See, e.g.*, C.W. Regan, Inc v Parsons, Brinckerhoff, Quade & Douglas, 411 F2d 1379 (4th Cir 1969) (no warranty where no privity); La Rossa v Scientific Design Co, 402 F2d 937 (3d Cir 1968) (implied warranty means strict liability which is inapplicable against engineer); Allied Properties v John A. Blume & Assocs, 25 Cal App 3d 848, 102 Cal Rptr 259 (1972) (engineer merely sells services and there is no implied warranty of fitness, notwithstanding the minority, South Carolina, view); Staley v New, 56 NM 756, 250 P2d 893 (1952) (defense of lack of privity); Gaastra v Holmes, 36 NM 175, 10 P2d 589 (1932) (residence).

Implied Warranty of Builder

It seems that where a builder both designs and builds a structure, it may impliedly warrant that the structure will serve the intended purpose. In a Minnesota case, a lumber company agreed to design and build a *poll-type* grain storage building as opposed to a conventional steel bin. The actual work was performed by a builder employed by the lumber company. Because of inadequate cables, turnbuckles, and hooks to anchor cables, the building collapsed. Rebuilding cost $7,323.24 and cleaning the wheat cost $5,311.23. Judgment for the owner was AFFIRMED on the theory that the lumber company impliedly warranted the fitness of the building for the intended purpose. The court of appeal rejected the argument that the uniform sales act (Minn Stat Ann §512.15(1)) governed a construction contract, but, nevertheless, held that there is an implied warranty of fitness where: the builder holds itself out to be competent to design and build a project; the owner has no particular expertise; the owner furnishes no plans; and the owner relies on the experience and skill of the builder.[24]

In *Waterford Condominium Assn v Dunbar Corp*,[25] a condominium association alleged a cause of action for breach of implied warranty of habitability. The court concluded that no warranty of habitability is extended by architects and engineers who are not builders or sellers. The association's remedy for breach of warranty was against the developers rather than their employees and agents.

Statute of Limitations—Privity

An important difference between an action for negligence and an action for breach of implied warranty can be the length of the applicable statute of limitations. In *Tamarac Development Co v Delameter, Freund & Associates, PA*,[26] summary judgment for defendant based on the tort statute of limitations was REVERSED. The testimony showed an oral contract that called for a specific result and testimony supported an action for breach of implied warranty. Although there was no written contract, the architect's oral promise to ensure that the grading work would be properly performed could be construed to be either a contract for a specific result (accurate grading) or an implied warranty to inspect and supervise the work in a workmanlike manner. Although design professionals do not guarantee, or warrant, that their work will be accurate, they do warrant that they have exercised their skills with care and diligence and

---

[24] Robertson Lumber Co v Stephen Farmers Co-op Elevator Co, 274 Minn 17, 143 NW2d 622 (1966).

[25] 104 Ill App 3d 371, 432 NE2d 1009 (1982). *See also* Parliament Towers Condominium v Parliament House Realty, Inc, 377 So 2d 976 (Fla Dist Ct App 1979) (implied warranties do not extend to remote condominium purchasers).

[26] 234 Kan 618, 675 P2d 361 (1984).

in a reasonable, nonnegligent manner. A claim for breach of a common law warranty does not require privity.[27]

Warranty Found

In *White Budd Van Ness Partnership v Major-Gladys Drive Joint Venture*,[28] an architect, in order to cut costs, suggested the use of "C-Tile." Many problems arose after the tile was installed. The developer filed an action against the architect alleging negligence in its investigation of the tile, in advising as to its use, and in inspection of the installation of the tile. Judgment for the developer was AFFIRMED.

> The sale of a service carries with it the implied warranty that the service will be performed in a skillful and workmanlike manner.... During recent decades, the United States has shifted from a goods oriented to a service oriented economy.... [W]ith this basic change, there has resulted a remarked decrease in the quality of services.... The ... problems led courts and the legislatures to apply the theory of implied warranty ... to service transactions.[29]

Thus, an implied warranty of good and workmanlike performance applied to the architect's professional services.

Damages

Even though an architect or an engineer may be liable to a plaintiff both for negligence and for breach of implied warranty, the plaintiff can recover no more than a single amount of compensatory damages. To award damages for negligence and then augment the award by additional damages for breach of implied warranty would be to allow the plaintiff to obtain a windfall.[30]

§6.04 Strict Liability

The rule of strict liability in tort holds that a manufacturer is liable for personal injury and property damage caused by a defect in its product, even if the product was produced without negligence. The doctrine is said to have evolved from the law of sales, where it is not necessary for a purchaser to prove

---

[27] Donnelly Constr Co v Oberg, Hunt & Gilleland, 139 Ariz 184, 677 P2d 1292 (1984) (contractor versus architect for increased costs of construction caused by error in plans).
[28] 798 SW2d 805 (Tex Ct App 1990), *cert denied*, 112 S Ct 180 (1991).
[29] *Id* 812.
[30] Rusch v Lincoln-Devore Testing Lab, Inc, 698 P2d 832 (Colo Ct App 1984).

negligence in order to recover for a breach of warranty of fitness for the intended purpose. The vendor is liable even if the item is manufactured and sold with care.

An important difference between strict liability and negligence theories is the measure of damages. In some states an owner may not recover economic damages under a theory of strict liability, but may do so under a negligence theory.[31] Damages for economic loss cannot be recovered in an action founded on strict liability.[32]

Another form of strict liability is imposed by statute in every state: the workers' compensation system, which is said to represent a legislative compromise between business and labor; business is made liable for all bodily injury suffered in the course of employment, regardless of negligence, and in return general damages for pain and suffering are eliminated and the injured worker is restricted to recovery of medical expense and loss of earning capacity.

English law developed a doctrine of strict liability that anyone collecting a dangerous substance on its land must do so at its own peril. In an English case, *Fletcher v Rylands*,[33] water escaped from the defendant's reservoir, flooding the plaintiff's coal mines.

> We think that the true rule of law is, that the person who for his own purposes brings on his lands and collects and keeps there anything likely to do mischief if it escapes, must keep it at his peril, and, if he does not do so, he is prima facie answerable for all damage which is the natural consequence of its escape.

Privity Defense

In another English case, *Winterbottom v Wright*,[34] the defendant supplied mail coaches to the postmaster general and also contracted to keep them in good condition. The plaintiff, a coachman, was injured when

> the said mail coach being then in a frail, weak, and infirm and dangerous state and condition, to wit by and through certain latent defects in the state and condition thereof . . . gave way and broke down, whereby the plaintiff was thrown from his seat, and in consequence of injuries then received, had become lamed for life.

Since the coachman had no contractual relationship with the manufacturer, the judges held that he could not recover:

---

[31] Huang v Garner, 157 Cal App 3d 404, 203 Cal Rptr 800 (1984) (purchaser of an apartment building versus architect).
[32] Moorman Mfg Co v National Tank Co, 91 Ill 2d 69, 435 NE2d 443 (1982).
[33] 1 LR-Ex 265 (1866).
[34] 10 M&W 109, 152 Eng Rep 402 (1842).

We ought not to permit a doubt to rest upon this subject, for our doing so might be the means of letting in upon us an infinity of actions. This is an action of the first impression.... Unless we confine the operation of such contracts as this to the parties that entered in them, the most absurd and outrageous consequences, to which I can see no limit, would ensue.... It is, no doubt, a hardship upon the plaintiff to be without a remedy, but by that consideration we ought not to be influenced. Hard cases, it has been frequently observed, are apt to introduce bad law.

Lack of privity of contract was established to shield the producer of a product from liability for bodily injury suffered because of negligence in the manufacture of the product. The doctrine also extended to protect the builder of structures on real property. As the law developed, manufacturers saw two defenses disappear: first, the doctrine of *privity* and, later, the very requirement of *negligence*.

The doctrine of privity is said to have been overthrown in 1916,[35] and strict liability was first imposed in 1963.[36] Readers who believe that the law develops slowly should consider that these changes, so stark and fundamental, required far less time than did the maturation of other social changes that accompanied the Industrial Revolution.

In *MacPherson v Buick Motor Co*,[37] the plaintiff, a guest in a car, was injured when the car collapsed as one of the wheels, manufactured of defective wood, crumbled. Justice Cardozo held that the manufacturer of an instrument that is probably dangerous if defectively constructed can foresee danger to individuals other than a purchaser, and thus there is a duty to avoid that danger despite the absence of privity of contract.

Justification for Strict Liability

In *Greenman v Yuba Power Products, Inc*,[38] the plaintiff was injured by a defectively designed power tool. Justice Traynor held that the manufacturer was liable for the injury, even though the plaintiff could not prove negligence. The burden of the loss should be placed on the manufacturer, who may pass the burden along to all consumers of the product in the form of price increases. Thus, all who benefit from the production of a product will equitably share the risk associated with its benefits.

---

[35] MacPherson v Buick Motor Co, 217 NY 382, 111 NE 1050 (1916).
[36] Greenman v Yuba Power Prods, Inc, 59 Cal 2d 57, 377 P2d 897, 27 Cal Rptr 697 (1963).
[37] 217 NY 382, 111 NE 1050 (1916).
[38] 59 Cal 2d 57, 377 P2d 897, 27 Cal Rptr 697 (1963).

The question now pending is whether (if not when) the doctrine of strict liability will be applied to architects. Two law review articles that treat the subject reach opposite conclusions. One commentator advocates that "architects should be held strictly liable for such injuries caused by their nonnegligent errors inevitable in the course of their business."[39] It is argued that architects can spread the risk by increasing their fees. They can purchase malpractice insurance and they are more likely to do so than are their clients.

On the other hand, in a diligently researched and flawlessly reasoned article, the editors review the three justifications for strict liability: (1) the difficulty of proving negligence in the setting of industrial mass production; (2) the social policy that risk should be assumed by those who can bear it and redistribute it; and (3) the deterrence of carelessness in design and manufacture. As applied to architects, the first point is invalid, since the architect usually designs a unique product rather than a mass-produced commodity. The second point suggests that the owner of the building rather than the designer should bear the risk, since the owner gets the economic benefit of the building and can spread the risk by purchasing insurance or increasing rent. Finally, the third point must take into account the fact that the practicing architect does not have much control over methods of construction except, in some circumstances, the power to stop the work (a power so damaging that it is compared with the power to use a nuclear weapon).[40]

In *Del Mar Beach Club Owners Assn v Imperial Contracting Co*,[41] the court rejected the application of the doctrine of strict liability to architects, soil engineers, or structural engineers. The plaintiff association alleged erosion damage to real property and injury to certain structures. The court rejected the strict liability cause of action, stating: "[I]t is settled that those who sell their services for the guidance of others in their economic financial and personal affairs are not liable in the absence of negligence or intentional misconduct."[42]

In *K-Mart Corp v Midcon Realty Group, Ltd*,[43] a store owner filed suit against an architect for property damage sustained when the roof of the store collapsed.

---

[39] Comment, *Architect Tort Liability in Preparation of Plans and Specifications*, 55 Cal L Rev 1361 (1967).

[40] Note, *Liability of Design Professionals The Necessity of Fault*, 5 Iowa L Rev 1221 (1973).

[41] 123 Cal App 3d 898, 176 Cal Rptr 886 (1981).

[42] *Id* at 913, 176 Cal Rptr at 894 (citing Gagne v Bertran, 43 Cal 2d 481, 487, 275 P2d 15 (1954)). Three other cases which have refused to apply the doctrine of strict liability to architects, designers, or engineers are: McClanahan v American Gilsonite Co, 494 F Supp 1334 (D Colo 1980) (delayed coking unit and surge tank not a product under Restatement (Second) Torts §402(a) (1965)); Union College v Kennerly, Slomanson & Smith, 167 NJ Super 311, 400 A2d 850 (1979) (quoting City of Mounds View v Walijarvi, 263 NW2d 420 (Minn 1978)); Polycon Indus v Hercules, Inc, 471 F Supp 1316 (ED Wis 1979) (doctrine of strict liability does not apply to the sale of a machine between businesses in the same industry where the engineers of both parties negotiated specifications and supervised construction and testing).

[43] 489 F Supp 813 (D Conn 1980).

The owner alleged strict liability. The court commented, in dictum, that since the doctrine of strict liability was intended to impose liability on those who market products in mass distribution, it would be inappropriate to extend the doctrine to an architect who designed a single project.

§6.05 —Mass Home Builders

The doctrine of strict liability *has* been applied against mass home builders. In a New Jersey case, a subdivider provided hot water from a radiant heating system at 190 degrees Fahrenheit. A mixing valve that would have reduced the water temperature was available for $3.60 wholesale, but not specified. An infant was scalded. HELD: a mass producer of homes is strictly liable in tort for injury caused by a defect in the home, regardless of negligence.[44]

Similarly, in *Kriegler v Eichler Homes, Inc*,[45] a mass producer of homes constructed a home in a subdivision in Palo Alto, California in 1951, which was sold to Mr. and Mrs. Resing. The Resings sold the house to Kriegler. After several years, the radiant heating system failed. The home builder had employed a system of tubing in the concrete floor slab for the construction of the radiant heating system. Copper was not available at the time (during the Korean War), so steel tubing was used. Over the years the steel tubing corroded, diminishing the value of the home by $5,073.18.

The court applied the doctrine of strict liability, reasoning that when a consumer purchases a house the consumer has no real ability to evaluate the details of construction. The consumer must necessarily rely on the skill of the developer and on the implied representation that the house will be erected in a reasonably workmanlike manner and will be reasonably fit for habitation. If construction is improper, injury to a consumer is foreseeable. Therefore, public interest dictates that if such injury does result from defective construction, the cost of the injury should be borne by the developer who created the danger and who is in a better economic position to bear the loss. This case was cited with approval by the California Supreme Court in *Miller v Los Angeles County Flood Control District*.[46] (It should be noted that the home builder ultimately obtained indemnity from the pipe manufacturers.[47])

---

[44] Schipper v Levitt & Sons, 44 NJ 70, 207 A2d 314 (1965).

[45] 269 Cal App 2d 224, 74 Cal Rptr 749 (1969).

[46] 8 Cal 3d 689, 505 P2d 193, 106 Cal Rptr 1 (1973). *See also* Avner v Longridge Estates, 272 Cal App 2d 607, 77 Cal Rptr 633 (1969) (subdivider was held strictly liable for damage to a home resulting from settlement of fill; the subdivider was a mass producer and the home buyer was not qualified to judge the soil conditions).

[47] Eichler Homes, Inc v Anderson, 9 Cal App 3d 224, 87 Cal Rptr 893 (1970).

§6.06 —History of the Doctrine

An examination of the applicability of the doctrine of strict liability to architects can begin with Babylonian law.[48] Babylonians applied the doctrine of strict liability to all professionals:

> Section 218: If the surgeon has made a deep incision in the body of a free man with a lancet of bronze and causes the man's death or has opened the carbuncle in the eye of a man and so destroys the man's eye, they shall cut off his forehand.

> Section 235: If a shipman has caulked a ship for a man and has not made his work secure and so that ship springs a leak in that very year or reveals a defect, the shipman shall break up that ship and shall make the ship sound out of his own property and give back a sound ship to the owner of the ship.

The element of privity was required, but not negligence. As in the modern doctrine of strict liability, a *defect* was all that was required.

In Babylonian law, judges were not accorded the doctrine of immunity. They were expected to stick by their guns:

> Section 5: If a judge has tried a suit, given a decision, caused a sealed tablet to be executed, and thereafter varies his judgment, they shall convict that judge of varying his judgment and he shall pay twelve fold the claim in that suit; then they shall remove him from his place on the bench of judges and assembly, and he shall not again sit in judgment with the judges.

The code treated builders even less mercifully:

> Section 229: If a builder has built a house for a man and has not made his work sound, and the house which he has built has fallen down and so caused the death of the householder, that builder shall be put to death. If it causes the death of the householder's son, they shall put that builder's son to death. If it causes the death of the householder's slave, he shall give slave for slave to the householder. If it destroys property, he shall replace anything that it has destroyed; and, because he has not made sound the house which he has built and it has fallen down, he shall rebuild the house which has fallen down from his own property. If a builder has built a house for a man and does not make his work perfect and a wall bulges, that builder shall put that wall into sound condition at his own cost.

---

[48] II Eriver and Miles, Babylonian Laws of Hammurabi (1955).

Here the outlines of the requirement of privity can be discerned: the code is silent as to the penalty for killing a guest or a bystander; only the family of the householder seems to be protected. Moreover, the code does not require proof of negligence, merely proof of defective construction.

Thus, although the ancient law required privity of contract, it did not require negligence; no more if the offending party were builder, shipwright, physician, or judge. It is the part of legal scholarship now to debate whether society is headed toward adopting, for twentieth century society, the ancient principle of Hammurabi.

§6.07 —Architects

Strict Liability Rejected

In cases that have given explicit consideration to the subject, courts have held that the doctrine of strict liability will not be applied to architects. So said the very judge who created the doctrine. In *Gagne v Bertran*,[49] a prospective owner had agreed to buy two lots for $8,500, subject to fill tests. The prospective owner employed the defendant at $10 per hour to drill test holes. The defendant reported that the fill required was only 12 to 16 inches deep. The total fee was $25. A drill rig operator had observed 4 to 5 feet of fill. Evidence showed that the lots actually contained 3 to 6 feet of fill. Plaintiff paid $3,093.65 more for foundations than would have been required had the defendant's report been accurate.

The complaint alleged breach of warranty, deceit, and negligence. Justice Traynor held that plaintiff had a good negligence case and a good deceit case, but no warranty case. The cause of action for breach of warranty was invalid. There was no *strict liability of a warranty*, because there was no express warranty agreement and nothing to indicate that the defendant assumed responsibility for the accuracy of the reports. The amount of the fee and the fact that the defendant was paid by the hour supported the conclusion that the defendant was selling services and not insurance. Therefore, there could have been no liability unless negligence was proved.[50]

---

[49] 43 Cal 2d 481, 275 P2d 15 (1954).

[50] *Accord* Swett v Gribaldo, Jones & Assocs, 40 Cal App 3d 573, 115 Cal Rptr 99 (1974) (home purchaser versus soil engineer, jury instructed on strict liability; REVERSED: although a home builder may be strictly liable, those who sell professional services are not); Allied Properties v John A. Blume & Assocs, 25 Cal App 3d 848, 102 Cal Rptr 259 (1972). *See also* Huang v Garner, 157 Cal App 3d 404, 203 Cal Rptr 800 (1984) (trial court properly granted nonsuit in a strict liability action against a building designer); Rhodes v Mill Race Inn, Inc, 126 Ill App 3d 1024, 467 NE2d 915 (1984), *appeal denied* (Jan Term 1985) (no strict tort liability cause of action against an architect for failure to comply with the requirements of the Safety Glazing Materials Act, Ill Rev Stat ch 111 1/2, §3101 *et seq* (1972)).

In *Looker v Gulf Coast Fair*,[51] an employee of a subcontractor was injured in the collapse of a grandstand. Plaintiff filed suit against the owner, alleging that the plans and specifications prepared by an architect employed by the owner were defective in that no proper permanent bracing was provided. Plaintiff argued that even though the architect was an independent contractor, defective plans would necessarily create an inherently dangerous condition which would be the responsibility of the owner. The court held that the owner was not liable for the negligent acts of a competent independent contractor. The owner reserved no control over the design. An owner may rely upon an architect's skill and ability unless the owner knows, or should know, that the plans are defective.[52] "A competent architect, pursuing an independent profession, is not an insurer of the accuracy or perfection of his work."

In *Queensbury Union Free School District v Jim Walter Corp*,[53] a school district employed architects to perform services in the planning and construction of a school building. The roof leaked. The plaintiff alleged strict products liability and breach of warranty against the architects. A motion to dismiss was granted. AFFIRMED. Although the architects may have been liable for negligent performance of their professional duties, no cause of action existed for breach of an implied warranty. Warranties under the Uniform Commercial Code were not applicable, since the contract was for professional services and not for the sale of goods. Since strict products liability developed from warranty theory, no cause of action existed on an implied warranty; likewise, no cause of action existed for strict products liability.

Although commentators have agreed that no case has applied the doctrine of strict liability to architects,[54] some cases portend the application of the doctrine if they do not, in fact, apply it. Indeed it appears that the doctrine of strict liability was applied to the designer of a home in *Hyman v Gordon*.[55]

In *Hyman*, a nine-year-old boy, the plaintiff, was painting model airplanes in his neighbor's garage. He found some paint brushes soaking in gasoline in an open coffee can on the garage floor and was using the gasoline to clean his

---

[51] 203 Ala 42, 81 So 832 (1919).

[52] *Accord* Stuart v Crestview Mut Water Co, 34 Cal App 3d 802, 110 Cal Rptr 543 (1973) (water system allegedly inadequate to fight fire; engineers rendered a professional service and are not in best position to spread cost of injuries resulting from defective products); Van Ornum v Otter Tail Power Co, 210 NW2d 188 (ND 1973).

[53] 91 Misc 2d 804, 398 NYS2d 832 (Sup Ct 1977).

[54] *See* Annot, 29 ALR3d 1425 (1970); Comment, *Architect Tort Liability in Preparation of Plans & Specifications*, 55 Cal L Rev 1361 (1967); Note, *Liability of Design Professionals: The Necessity of Fault*, 58 Iowa L Rev 1221 (1973). See also City of Mounds View v Walijarvi, 263 NW2d 420 (Minn 1978) for an excellent statement of the arguments against imposing strict liability on architects.

[55] 35 Cal App 3d 769, 111 Cal Rptr 262 (1973).

hands. The gasoline spilled, flowed toward a water heater, and ignited. The water heater was gas fired. The pilot light was only four to six inches above the garage floor.

Plaintiff alleged strict liability against the contractor who designed and built the house. The trial court granted a nonsuit. REVERSED. The plaintiff argued not that the water heater was defective, but that the location of the water heater was defective. The court accepted that argument, holding that the "determination of whether the presence of the water heater in the garage location constituted a defective design . . . should have been left to the jury."[56]

The court portentously commented that a defect may emerge from the mind of the designer as well as from the hand of the worker.

It is important to note two things about the *Hyman* case which seem to indicate the application of the doctrine of strict liability to a designer: the opinion does not say that the house was mass produced (evidently it was not); and the court specified that the defect might emerge from the mind of the designer. Thus, although the designer was also the builder, the conclusion of liability was founded upon the design function rather than the building function. Therefore, *Hyman* sweeps away one of the factors which has protected the architect from strict liability: the lack of mass production. Still, the designer was also the builder; therefore, it did in fact profit from the sale of the product, and was not engaged exclusively in rendering professional services for a fee.

In this respect the case is similar to *Schipper v Levitt & Sons*,[57] where the opinion alludes to the fact that a hot-water system was designed by an employee of the defendant subdivider. Thus, the court at least deemed relevant the fact that the defendant designed the product that injured the plaintiff.

§6.08 —Engineers

A Pennsylvania court has held that the doctrine of strict liability may be applied against an engineer. In *Abdul Warith v Arthur G. McKee & Co*,[58] a worker's hand was pinned between the rails of a skip bridge and the wheel of a car. The skip bridge was a component of a blast furnace in a steel plant. The defendant designed and constructed the skip bridge. HELD: a party who supplies a defective product while rendering a service may be held accountable for injuries attributable to the defective product. The skip bridge was a hybrid of both services and a product supplied by defendant. The fact that the skip bridge was constructed in place was irrelevant to its classification as a product.

---

[56] *Id* at 773, 111 Cal Rptr at 264.
[57] 44 NJ 70, 207 A2d 314 (1965). *See* §6.05.
[58] 488 F Supp 306 (ED Pa 1980).

The skip bridge was analogous to a large piece of industrial equipment for which the supplier may be held strictly liable.

The court acknowledged, however, that where an engineer simply provides the design, or merely supervises without participating in the construction of the product, strict liability might not apply (summary judgment for defendant was granted on the ground that there was no evidence indicating that the skip bridge was defective at the time of construction).

Engineer Not Strictly Liable

In a California case, a mortgage holder sued a soil engineer for impairment of its security interest in real estate resulting from defectively manufactured lots that settled, causing damage to houses. The court saw no reason not to extend liability for negligence to damages incurred by a real estate lender, but as to strict liability, held that even assuming that an engineer may be classified as a mass producer of homes, and therefore be subject to strict liability, such liability did not extend to the lender whose money made the marketing of the homes possible. The lender was a link in the marketing system rather than a consumer of mass-produced housing.[59]

In *La Rossa v Scientific Design Co*,[60] the court emphasized a lack of mass production in holding that an engineer was not strictly liable for injuries to a worker. The defendant designed and supervised the construction and initial operation of a chemical manufacturing plant. One of the final steps was to load a catalyst in the form of pellets coated with vanadium into a reactor. The engineer supplied the pellets and was responsible for supervising the operation. Vanadium dust was generated, which penetrated respirator masks supplied to the decedent, who a month later was found to have throat cancer. The trial court dismissed a cause of action for breach of implied warranty, and the jury brought in a defense verdict on the negligence counts. AFFIRMED. Plaintiff argued that the engineer impliedly warranted that it would insure the safety of all workers who might be affected by the furnishing of services. However, the professional services should not have been subject to the strict liability analysis, since there was no mass production of goods. Therefore, there was no large body of distant consumers and no unfair burden upon the plaintiff to trace liability back through a chain of production. Moreover, the services rendered by the engineer were highly specialized and affected only a few employees of the manufacturer. There was no impact on the public at large. Therefore, if the process of loading the pellets exposed the decedent to danger, any liability must

---

[59] United States Fin v Sullivan, 37 Cal App 3d 5, 112 Cal Rptr 18 (1974).
[60] 402 F2d 937 (3d Cir 1968).

rest on a failure to act with due care. Since the jury rejected the claim of negligence, the defense verdict was affirmed.[61]

§6.09 —Application Criticized

The conclusion from the foregoing line of cases is that an architect may be strictly liable for designing a building with a defect that injures a plaintiff, but only if the architect participates in the selling process or shares in the profits of the sale of the building. If a lack of participation in the sales process is the only thing that separates the architect from strict liability, it will be argued with justice that the mere form in which the architect takes compensation from the project (whether in fees or profits) should not determine the issue.

The social policy served by the strict liability doctrine is the notion that a mass producer can and should distribute the risk of injury among hundreds or thousands or millions of consumers of its product, so that those who ultimately benefit from the product itself will share the responsibility for defects that occur without negligence. The architect's final defense, which should be a good one, is that it cannot pass the risk to a large constituency of consumers, since the architect is paid by only one consumer: its client.

---

[61] *See also* Cincinnati Gas & Elec Co v General Elec Co, 656 F Supp 49 (SD Ohio 1986) (strict liability is a theory applied primarily to require parties who market defective products to compensate consumers of those products for unexpected injury. The theory may not be applied under Ohio law to compensate a utility for defective design by an architect/engineer); Huang v Garner, 157 Cal App 3d 404, 203 Cal Rptr 800 (1984) (nonsuit was properly granted in a strict liability action against an engineer).

No Damage Cases 7

§7.01 Generally
§7.02 Mental Anguish
§7.03 Economic Damage

§7.01 Generally

In some cases, the courts seem to concede that a defendant may be guilty of negligence, and the negligence may cause foreseeable injury to the plaintiff, yet that injury is not legally recognized damage. These are cases of *damnum absque injuria*; that is, injury without legally cognizable damage.

At first it seems anomalous that law would permit one person to injure another without legal responsibility for damage. Yet on further consideration, not every wrong can be rectified by law. A practical view reveals that a remedy may be more damaging than a wrong; a cure may be worse than a disease. The law is inclined, however, to provide a remedy for every wrong.

Winterbottom v Wright[1] relied on the doctrine of *damnum absque injuria*: "[I]t is, no doubt, a hardship upon the plaintiff to be without a remedy, but by that consideration we ought not to be influenced." It seems that the proposition that a defendant may escape liability because of the peculiar nature of the damage suffered by the plaintiff will gradually erode. How far the erosion will carry is not predictable, but some further erosion is almost certain to occur.

§7.02 Mental Anguish

It has generally been held that the law will not compensate mental anguish in the absence of physical injury, at least not unless the defendant is guilty of

---

[1] 10 M&W 109, 152 Eng Rep 402 (1842).

outrageous conduct. In a Massachusetts case, the plaintiffs bought a house for $22,500. Shortly after they took occupancy, their lot became flooded with effluent from the septic system. The jury brought in a verdict of $4,000 for mental anguish against the designer of the system. REVERSED. The type of mental injury alleged was insufficient to support a verdict as a matter of law, especially since it was not accompanied by physical injury.[2]

In a Michigan case, the plaintiff alleged anxiety flowing from an inaccurate survey that caused multiple lawsuits. The court did not dispose of the question of whether such injury is legally compensable.[3]

§7.03 Economic Damage

It has been argued that in the absence of privity, a negligent architect should not be liable for intangible economic loss, as opposed to bodily injury or property damage. This argument was rejected in a California case.[4] In this case, condominium purchasers alleged that their project was not constructed in a substantial manner, violated the requirements of building codes, was hazardous to safety, and was a fire trap, causing loss of use of and income on their property. The defendant architect argued that it should not be liable for economic loss. The court rejected the argument, holding that an architect, physician, or lawyer who is guilty of malpractice that causes foreseeable economic damage to a third party is liable for the damage.

A federal district court reached the same conclusion in *United States v Rogers & Rogers*.[5] The contractor filed suit against an architect for negligent interpretation of concrete test results, so that the contractor ultimately was required to remove defective concrete from the project. The court declared: "California courts no longer follow the old common law rule that privity of contract must exist in order for negligent performance of a contractual duty to give rise to liability for damage to an economic interest."[6]

In accord is a Michigan case in which the law seems to afford greater protection to economic interest than to freedom from bodily injury or property damage, at least where the statute of limitations is concerned. The limitation period for injury to financial expectations and economic benefit in the context of an express or implied contract was six years; the malpractice period was two years; and the negligence period was three years.[7]

---

[2] McDonough v Whalen, 364 Mass 506, 313 NE2d 435 (1974).
[3] Schenburn v Lehner Assocs, 22 Mich App 534, 177 NW2d 699 (1970).
[4] Cooper v Jevne, 56 Cal App 3d 860, 128 Cal Rptr 724 (1976).
[5] 161 F Supp 132 (SD Cal 1958).
[6] *Id* 135.
[7] Schenburn v Lehner Assocs, 22 Mich App 534, 177 NW2d 699 (1970).

The proposition that a cause of action for negligence against a design professional will not support recovery of economic damage is much disputed. In *Huang v Garner*,[8] third-hand purchasers of an apartment building filed an action against the original developer and its designer and engineer for physical and economic harm to the building resulting from negligent design and construction. HELD: damages for economic harm are recoverable in a negligence case.[9] But in *Moorman Manufacturing Co v National Tank Co*,[10] the court held that the designer and manufacturer of a tank were not responsible, under a strict liability theory, for the cost of repairing a split in the tank. The court went on to say that the policy considerations against allowing recovery for solely economic loss in strict liability cases apply also to negligence actions.[11]

The Illinois Supreme Court held that the *Moorman* doctrine applied to prevent recovery of damages for economic loss in an architectural malpractice case.[12] A condominium association brought an action against a design architect to recover the cost of repairing a condominium building. The building had loose windows and doors, a leaky roof, inadequate utilities, and a settling garage. HELD: absent privity, damages for economic loss may not be recovered in an architectural malpractice case. However, such damages may be recovered in cases of breach of contract, intentional misrepresentation, negligent misrepresentation, intentional interference with contract, or intentional interference with prospective business advantage. The distinction is that the right to recover damages for such torts is based on a duty imposed on the defendant to prevent the precise type of loss suffered by the plaintiff—economic loss.

In 1987, the Virginia Supreme Court held that a contractor could not recover tort damages from an architect for economic loss arising from the architect's alleged breach of contract with the owner where there was no provision in the contract that specified that such liability would be imposed upon the architect.[13] The court held that Va Code Ann §8.01-223 eliminated lack of privity as a defense in actions for damages for injury to person or property resulting from negligence, but did not eliminate the requirement of privity in negligence actions seeking only recovery for economic loss.

---

[8] 157 Cal App 3d 404, 203 Cal Rptr 800 (1984).

[9] *Accord* Rosos Litho Supply Corp v Hansen, 123 Ill App 3d 290, 462 NE2d 566 (1984).

[10] 9 Ill 2d 69, 435 NE2d 443 (1982).

[11] *But see* Donnelly Constr Co v Oberg, Hunt & Gilleland, 139 Ariz 184, 677 P2d 1292 (1984) (contractor recovered economic harm suffered because the owner's architect negligently prepared drawings and specifications). *See also* §10.10.

[12] 2314 Lincoln Park W Condo Assn v Mann, Gin, Ebel & Frazier Ltd, 136 Ill 2d 302, 555 NE2d 346 (1990).

[13] Blake Constr Co v Alley, 233 Va 31, 353 SE2d 724 (1987) (contractor claimed that, because of the architect's negligence in carrying out its duties under the contract, the contractor suffered economic loss of $3.8 million).

Liability Arising from Agency   8

§8.01   Generally
        Delegation of Duties of Agent
        Agent versus Independent Contractor
        Design-Build
        Liability for Acts of Agent
        Agency Relationship
§8.02   Owner Bound by Acts or Knowledge of Agent
        Knowledge of Architect Attributed to Owner
        Torts of Agent
        Actual Knowledge
        Estoppel
        Extra Work
        Collusion with Owner
        Negligent Approval of Estimates Exonerates Bond
        Agent for Design
        Limitation on Authority of Agent
§8.03   Owner Not Bound by Acts of Architect
        Independent Contractor
        No Right of Control
        Agent for Transaction
        Arbitrator, Not Agent
§8.04   Agency Relationship as a Defense to the Architect
§8.05   Liability for Acts of Consultant
        Nondelegable Duty
§8.06   Liability of Partnerships and Corporations

§8.01 Generally

It is said that in preparing plans and specifications an architect acts as an independent contractor, but in performing supervisory functions on a project, the architect ordinarily acts as an *agent* of the owner. The question of agency arises in several contexts: if the architect is the agent of the owner, then the owner is liable for the torts of the architect; an architect who is merely acting as the agent of the owner may escape liability under the *safe place* statute; an architect acting as the agent of the owner is entitled to take advantage of the defenses available to the owner; notice to an agent is notice to the principal; and an owner is not liable for the acts of an architect if the architect is acting in the capacity of an independent contractor. The question of agency also comes into play in defining the legal responsibilities that exist between architects, their consultants, and third parties.

Delegation of Duties of Agent

The relationship between owner and architect is one of trust and confidence. Cases have held that an architect, selected for personal qualities, may not delegate duties to another. In *Huggins v Atlanta Tile & Marble Co*,[1] the contract between an owner and an architect designated the architect as "A. Thomas Bradbury." However, Bradbury employed an associate to perform inspection. HELD: "[a]n architect is selected and agreed upon to exercise his personal skill, discretion and judgment, and his duty to exercise [these skills] cannot be delegated."[2]

Agent versus Independent Contractor

Courts seem to agree that, in preparing plans and specifications, an architect acts as an independent contractor. However, in performing supervisory functions, the architect ordinarily acts as an agent of the owner.[3] Moreover, employees and consultants of the architect are sub-agents, and their knowledge is therefore attributable to the owner.[4]

Design-Build

When an owner entrusts a contractor both to design and to build a structure, then that contractor is an independent contractor both in the design function and in the construction function.[5]

---

[1] 98 Ga App 597, 106 SE2d 191 (1958).
[2] *Id* 193.
[3] Trane Co v Gilbert, 267 Cal App 2d 720, 73 Cal Rptr 279 (1968).
[4] *Id* (knowledge of mechanical engineer employed by architect imputed to owner).
[5] Boswell v Laird, 8 Cal 469 (1857) (architect-contractor designed and built a dam); Bruemmer v Clark Equip Co, 341 F2d 23 (7th Cir 1965) (owner merely specified the number

Even though an architect or engineer may be an independent contractor, its negligence may be attributable to the owner if the activity is "inherently or intrinsically dangerous."[6]

Liability for Acts of Agent

In performing the function of supervision and inspection of construction, an architect acts as the agent of the owner. Therefore, the owner is liable for the negligence of the architect acting in this capacity.[7] Additionally, the owner is bound by a certificate of payment issued by the agent, the architect. A certificate of payment can be introduced against the owner as evidence that the contractor has complied with the requirements of the contract.[8] A consulting mechanical engineer is the agent of the architect, with the result that the architect is liable for negligent conduct by the engineer.[9]

Agency Relationship

In one case, the agency relationship between the owner and the developer established privity between the owner and the architects. The architects intended by their performance to benefit the owner.[10]

Existence of agency may depend on whether an architect is working *on its own* or as an employee of an architectural firm. For example, in *Harmon v Christy Lumber, Inc*,[11] an owner met with a contractor to discuss plans for a new home. The contractor called an architectural firm to see if it could prepare drawings. The president of the firm informed the contractor that the firm did not ordinarily do small residential jobs, but that an employee architect might want to do the job on its own time.

The contractor later gave the architect a rough sketch and then delivered drawings to the owner. Many problems ensued and the owner filed an action against the contractor and the architect, after which the architect filed a cross-claim against its employer, claiming the architect had prepared the drawings as an employee. Summary judgment for the employer firm was

---

of square feet for an industrial building, contractor had complete possession of the construction site and designed and built the project).

[6] Vannoy v City of Warren, 15 Mich App 158, 166 NW2d 486, 489 (1968) (methane gas in manhole).

[7] Manton v H.L. Stevens & Co, 170 Iowa 495, 153 NW 87 (1915); S. Blickman, Inc v Chilton, 114 SW2d 646 (Tex Civ App 1938).

[8] Fuchs v Parsons Constr Co, 172 Neb 719, 111 NW2d 727 (1961).

[9] Scott v Potomac Ins Co, 217 Or 323, 341 P2d 1083 (1959).

[10] R.H. Sanbar Projects, Inc v Gruzen Partnership, 148 AD2d 316, 538 NYS2d 532 (1989) (architects entered into a contract with developer for design of a public plaza. Because of failure to meet statutory requirements, a certificate of occupancy was rejected. HELD: the owner established a cause of action against the architects).

[11] 402 NW2d 690 (SD 1987).

AFFIRMED. There were no facts in the record to support the contention that the architect was working as an employee of the firm rather than *on its own*.

§8.02 Owner Bound by Acts or Knowledge of Agent

Knowledge of Architect Attributed to Owner

In *S. Blickman, Inc v Chilton*,[12] a hotel employed an architect to supervise remodeling work according to plans and specifications. Plaintiff, a customer at the hotel lunch counter, was injured when the back of a chair installed at the counter broke, causing the customer to fall to the floor. The remodeling work was still in progress at the time. The customer filed an action against the contractor. The contractor alleged that the injury was attributable to the negligence of the hotel. The court of appeal held that the architect was the agent of the hotel, and if the architect had prior knowledge of the defective condition of the chairs, the knowledge would be attributable to the employer. Therefore, the issue of the knowledge should have been submitted to the jury. In *Trane Co v Gilbert*,[13] the court held that an owner was bound by an architect's knowledge of the details of the equipment manufacturer's express warranty. The principal (the owner) was bound by the agent's (architect's) knowledge.

Torts of Agent

In *Watt v United States*,[14] plaintiff was injured in a fall from steps surrounding the fountain area of the Museum of History and Technology of the Smithsonian Institution. In a suit under the Federal Tort Claims Act,[15] the court found that the negligence of the government architect proximately caused the injuries to plaintiff, and this negligence was imputed to the government.

In *Caldwell v Cleveland-Cliffs Co*,[16] Cleveland-Cliffs Iron Company employed Bechtel as manager of engineering and construction for a project. Plaintiff, an employee of Bechtel, was seriously injured when a crate fell from a forklift truck owned by Bechtel and driven by a Bechtel employee. The employee alleged that the crate fell because the forks were bent downward. Cleveland-Cliffs was held liable because Bechtel was acting as Cleveland-Cliffs's agent. The agency relationship was demonstrated by the facts that Bechtel was subject to the general direction and control of Cleveland-Cliffs; Cleveland-Cliffs's

---

[12] 114 SW2d 646 (Tex Civ App 1938).

[13] 267 Cal App 2d 720, 73 Cal Rptr 279 (1968).

[14] 444 F Supp 1191 (DDC 1978).

[15] 28 USC §1346(b).

[16] 111 Mich App 721, 315 NW2d 186 (1981), *appeal denied*, 417 Mich 914, 330 NW2d 854 (1983).

project engineer was responsible for the design of the project and for monitoring construction; and Cleveland-Cliffs had the right to approve any subcontractors employed by Bechtel.

In *United States v Peachy*,[17] the court assumed that a landowner could be held to account for negligence on the part of the landowner's architect. However, the architect, in designing a retaining wall which collapsed, was not negligent; therefore, the landowner was not liable for damage to adjoining government property.

Actual Knowledge

In *South Union Ltd v George Parker & Associates AIA*,[18] an architect employed by a general partner of the owner prepared drawings for a 70-unit, government-subsidized apartment complex. The drawings and specifications for the paving were defective. A second architect, employed for the purpose of inspecting the project, failed to detect the problems. The owner filed suit against the inspecting architect, alleging negligence and breach of contract. The defendant architect asserted that the owner was not entitled to recover damages for defects that were caused by the design architect, who was the agent of a partner of the owner. The court held that the owner was entitled to assert its claim against the inspecting architect despite the fact that the deficient plans and specifications were prepared by the owner's agent, since there was no evidence to show that the owner had actual knowledge of the deficiencies.

Estoppel

An owner may be estopped by the conduct of an architect. In *Fuchs v Parsons Construction Co*,[19] an architect prepared contract documents and supervised construction of the building. The contract provided that final payment would be construed as an acceptance of the project by the owner. The architect did indeed certify final payment. Months later, the building began to settle and eventually severe damage occurred, primarily because of the settlement of piles supporting the exterior walls and interior columns. The owner filed suit against the contractor for breach of contract in failing to construct the building in accordance with the contract documents. The court of appeal AFFIRMED a directed verdict for the defendant. "An architect employed by the owner is the agent of such owner in supervising construction work and in the interpretation of plans and specifications relating thereto."[20] A contractor is required to follow plans and specifications even if it thinks they are wrong; consequently, a

---

[17] 36 F 160 (D Ohio 1888).
[18] 29 Ohio App 3d 197, 504 NE2d 1131 (1985).
[19] 172 Neb 719, 111 NW2d 727 (1961).
[20] *Id* 733.

contractor is not liable for defects in a building unless it deviated from the plans. Here, the architect's certificate established that the contractor complied with the contract documents in the absence of fraud or bad faith.

Extra Work

An owner is liable to a contractor for the cost of extra work ordered by the architect. In *Erskine v Johnson*,[21] extra grading work was required due to the architect's error. The owner orally agreed to pay the contractor extra compensation for the additional work, which the contractor performed under the direction of the architect. The owner then refused to pay for the work on the ground that no written change order was issued as required by the specifications. HELD: the supervising architect directed changes because of its own errors, and it did so as an agent for the owner. Therefore, the owner was liable to the contractor for the cost of the extra work.

Scribante v Edwards[22] illustrates the same rule. An owner ordered a contractor to install an extra inch of concrete in a slab. Later, the architect, on its own, ordered additional concrete to fill low spots. The owner refused to pay for the extra concrete ordered by the architect. HELD: the contract required the contractor to work under the direction of the architect; the principal authorized the agent to order the work and did not notify the contractor of any limitation on the architect's power. Therefore, the principal was bound by the agent's promise. This would have been true even if the architect had ordered more concrete than the owner had authorized.

In *Vandervoort v Levy*,[23] an architect ordered extra work on behalf of an owner. HELD: the work was reasonably required in furtherance of the contemplated renovation, and the owner would have been unjustly enriched if it did not pay for the work. Therefore, the owner was required to pay the contractor for the work even though the owner did not expressly authorize the architect to order the work.

Collusion with Owner

In *Batterbury v Vyse*,[24] a contractor agreed to perform specified works under the superintendence and to the satisfaction of the owner and the architect. Final payment was to be made after the architect issued a certificate of completion. The architect ordered extra work, which the contractor performed to the architect's satisfaction, but the architect neglected to issue the certificate of completion. The contractor alleged that the architect "had so neglected in

---

[21] 23 Neb 261, 36 NW 510 (1888).
[22] 40 Cal App 561, 181 P 75 (1919).
[23] 396 So 2d 480 (La Ct App 1981).
[24] 2 Hurl C 42, 46 Ex (1863).

collusion with defendant and by his procurement." HELD: if the certificate was withheld by fraud, the contractor had a good cause of action against the owner.

Negligent Approval of Estimates Exonerates Bond

Negligent conduct by an architect can deprive an owner of the benefit of a contractor's performance bond. In *Hall v Union Indemnity Co*,[25] the owner employed a contractor to construct a theater building. Payments were to be made upon invoices presented by the contractor and approved by the architect, in the sum of 85 per cent of all materials delivered and paid for and work incorporated into the building. The contractor submitted monthly *estimates*, unsupported by invoices, and the architect approved the estimates, which were paid by the owner. Before the job was completed, the contractor defaulted, and the owner paid $13,000 more than the contract price to complete the building and pay off mechanics liens. The owner then filed an action against the contractor's surety. The defense was that the architect had negligently issued payment certificates without calling for invoices or determining whether the contractor had paid for labor and materials incorporated in the job. The contract required the architect to review *invoices*; instead, the architect merely approved *estimates*. This allowed the contractor to be overpaid and encouraged the default. The contract provision was created as much for the benefit of the surety as for the owner; as a result, the owner created a different risk than the one insured against by the surety. Therefore, the bond was exonerated.

The outcome of this decision causes one to pause. An owner, presumably unsophisticated in the ways of the construction industry, paid architect's fees and performance bond premiums on the assumption that these expenditures would buy full protection. The surety company was in the business of collecting premiums to guarantee performance by its principal, the contractor. Upon the contractor's default, the obligee, who presumably paid the premium on the bond, found that the bond was exonerated because of the negligence of the architect. Thus, the obligee was expected to recover damages from the impecunious architect, rather than from the bonding company which collected a premium to guarantee the solvency of the contractor.

Agent for Design

It is said that an architect acts as the agent of the owner in supervising or inspecting the progress of a project but is an independent contractor when it prepares plans and specifications. However, one case made the owner responsible to a contractor for negligence of the architect in preparing plans and specifications.

---

[25] 61 F2d 85 (8th Cir), *cert denied*, 287 US 663 (1932).

In *Hammaker v Schleigh*,[26] a contract called for the remodeling of a fire protection system to be installed in accordance with underwriter's rules and in accordance with plans and specifications prepared by an architect. The contractor undertook to rearrange existing pipe to meet the requirements of the remodeled building. However, the pipes were rusty and unacceptable to the underwriter. The owner did not offer to purchase new pipes. The contractor completed the rest of the project and omitted the sprinkler system. The owner refused to pay the contractor's fee, and the contractor sued. HELD: the owner employed the architect to prepare contract documents that called for the reuse of the original pipe. It was reasonable for the contractor to believe the architect had investigated the fitness of the pipe for its intended purpose and had exercised professional skill in doing so. The owner had more opportunity to gain knowledge of the history of the pipe. The contractor was entitled to rely upon the architect's judgment without further investigation. The circumstances created an implied warranty by the owner that the pipes were fit for the intended purpose. The unfitness of the pipes constituted a breach of the implied warranty and made it impossible for the contractor to complete this portion of the contract.

Limitation on Authority of Agent

If a plaintiff is aware of limitations on the architect's authority, then the principal is not liable for acts which exceed that limitation. In *Delta Construction Co v City of Jackson*,[27] the contract between the a city and a contractor provided that the engineer could order extra work as long as it did not increase the cost of the project by more than 25 per cent of the cost of a major item, in which event a supplemental agreement signed by the city would be required. The engineer directed a letter to the contractor ordering it to perform additional excavation. HELD: the contractor was entitled to additional compensation up to the 25 per cent figure, but no more. The engineer's letter did not constitute the required supplemental agreement with the city.

The authority of an architect or engineer may be limited in other ways. In *CCC Builders, Inc v City Council*,[28] the court held that a city was not bound by the city engineer's submission of a dispute to arbitration. The dispute was between a contractor and the city as to the application of a liquidated damages clause. HELD: the arbitration clause did not apply to the determination of disputes that arose out of the liquidated damages clause, and although the city engineer may have been an agent of the city, the engineer was not empowered

---

[26] 157 Md 652, 147 A 790 (1929).
[27] 198 So 2d 592 (Miss 1967).
[28] 237 Ga 589, 229 SE2d 349 (1976).

to "waive the city's right to object to the submission of matters which were not contemplated by the arbitration clause."[29]

§8.03 Owner Not Bound by Acts of Architect

It seems that courts are likely to find that an architect is an independent contractor if such a finding will exonerate an owner from liability for the acts of the architect. In *Edwin J. Dobson, Jr, Inc v Rutgers State University*,[30] the court held that an owner was not liable for the acts of a critical path method consultant; nor was the owner liable for the acts of the architect in discharging its functions relative to extensions of time and delay. The architect had acted in the capacity of an independent umpire or arbitrator. Thus, it was not the agent of either party. In *Boswell v Laird*,[31] an owner employed an architect/contractor to construct a dam on Deer Creek above the city of Nevada. The dam broke while under construction, damaging the downstream plaintiff. Justice Field pointed out that the architect was reputed to be experienced and skillful and had exclusive control of the project. Responsibility is placed where power exists. The owner exercised no control; therefore, the owner was not liable. The architect was liable.

The case of *American Surety Co v San Antonio Loan & Trust Co*[32] goes to unusual lengths in protecting an owner against the consequences of dereliction by an architect. When the owner's building was almost finished, it collapsed because of defects in the plans and specifications prepared by the owner's architect. The owner then filed suit against the contractor for failure to complete construction. HELD: the contractor was not excused from performance by the defective contract documents. The contractor voluntarily agreed to perform the contract after studying the plans. "He should not be allowed to relieve himself from the consequences of his failure to do what he voluntarily agreed to do by shifting the burden of his nonperformance to the other party, who was no more to blame for entering into the contract than was he." This case was wrongly decided according to modern legal thinking. Modern cases hold that an owner impliedly warrants the sufficiency of contractor documents supplied to a contractor.[33] In *Norair Engineering Corp v St Joseph's Hospital, Inc*,[34] a hospital sued a general contractor for defects in construction of the hospital. The general

---

[29] *Id* 353.

[30] 157 NJ Super 357, 384 A2d 1121 (1978), *affd sub nom* Broadway Maintenance Corp v Rutgers State Univ, 90 NJ 253, 447 A2d 906 (1982).

[31] 8 Cal 469 (1857).

[32] 44 Tex Civ App 367, 98 SW 387 (1906).

[33] *See* J. Acret, Construction Litigation Handbook §14.04 (Shepard's/McGraw-Hill 1986 & Supp 1992).

[34] 147 Ga App 595, 249 SE2d 642 (1978).

contractor defended by asserting that the architect employed by the owner failed to properly inspect and supervise the work and, as a result, did not detect deviations from the contract documents. HELD: the architect had no power to modify the contract between the owner and the contractor. Even though the architect may have certified that the work had been completed according to contract, the certification did not bind the owner. The owner had the right to insist on the terms of the contract even though the architect may have accepted inferior work or materials.

Independent Contractor

In *Collins Co v City of Decatur*,[35] it was held that an engineer was an independent contractor in its relationship with a city and, therefore, the construction contractor could not establish a cause of action against the city for breach of contract.

In *M.J. Womack, Inc v House of Representatives of State*,[36] a contractor sued an owner (the State House of Representatives) and its architect for delay that prevented the contractor from earning a bonus for early completion of a contract for renovation of the state capitol. The drawings prepared by the architect failed to disclose a metal X-brace which could have been discovered by an examination of old drawings available to the architect. The court held that, although the architect was negligent, the state was not responsible for that negligence because the architect acted as an independent contractor in the preparation of the drawings.

A contractor who bid $105,705 to an owner for construction of a theater was the low bidder. The architect modified the drawings to further reduce the cost to $95,000. One modification reduced the air conditioning system from 20.43 tons to 8 tons; the theater was then too warm. The owner sued the contractor for damages and recovered $11,180. AFFIRMED. The architect may have consented to the modification to the contract, but the owner did not.[37]

No Right of Control

In *Burke v Ireland*,[38] an owner was found not to be liable to the administratrix of a deceased worker who was killed when a building under construction collapsed, because the owner employed a competent contractor and architect. The architect had authorized a reduction of the foundation slab from 18 inches to 12 inches and failed to detect that a cast-iron column designed to support the

---

[35] 533 So 2d 1127 (Ala 1988).
[36] 509 So 2d 62 (La Ct App), *writ denied*, 513 So 2d 1211 (La 1987).
[37] Chapple v Big Bear Supermarket No 3, 108 Cal App 3d 867, 167 Cal Rptr 103 (1980).
[38] 166 NY 305, 59 NE 914 (1901).

beams and girders of the building was partially installed in an old cistern. The column collapsed, leading to the demise of the plaintiff's intestate.

If the building had been built according to the plans and specifications, the accident would not have occurred. The owner did not know that the architect and contractor had changed the plan and could not have been liable for the negligence of the builder or the architect. The owner has the right to build upon its property, and as long as it is not guilty of personal negligence, the owner will not be responsible for accidents during the course of construction. Here, the owner was not competent to personally build the building. It was the owner's duty to employ competent parties, and the owner did so without reserving or exercising any right of control. The owner was thereby removed from liability for the negligent acts or omissions of the architect. (A contrary rule would block all building since real estate owners would be subjected to enormous hazards.)[39]

Agent for Transaction

In *Birch v Hale*,[40] a contractor sued an owner for the balance of the contract price. The owner defended on the ground that the contractor had connected pipes from a water pump in the basement to a water tank on the roof in such a crooked manner that, when the pump was operated, the building shook from the resulting noise. The contractor offered testimony that the pipes were installed in accordance with the specific orders of the architect. The court acknowledged that this evidence would be relevant if the architect were the agent of the owner; however, declarations of an agent, to be admissible, must be related to a transaction pending at the very time. It did not appear that the architect was still the agent of the owner when the admission sought to be proved was made, nor did it appear that it related to a transaction then pending. Therefore, the owner was not bound by the orders of the architect.

In *White v Green*,[41] a building owned by the defendant collapsed, destroying a neighbor's property. The building was constructed according to plans and specifications prepared by an architect. The plans were defective, which caused the collapse. The court held that the defendant was not liable, since an owner is not an insurer against accidents from defects in construction. If an owner employs a skilled and competent architect to prepare plans and specifications, the owner is exonerated from liability. Here, the owner was not liable for the negligence of the architect, since the architect was an independent contractor. The owner's only duty was to use reasonable care in the selection of an

---

[39] *See also* Smith v Milwaukee Builders & Traders Exch, 91 Wis 360, 64 NW 1041 (1895) (plaintiff, injured by falling brick, sued the owner and the contractor; HELD: the architect had no control over the manner of the work, and in the absence of any other ground of liability, the owner was not responsible).

[40] 99 Cal 299, 33 P 1088 (1893).

[41] 82 SW 329 (Tex Civ App 1904).

architect. The erection of an ordinary building is not an intrinsically dangerous activity. Therefore, the owner was not liable for the negligence of the architect.

In *Moloso v State*,[42] the state contracted with several construction and engineering firms to reroute an existing road. A rock slide killed two employees. A wrongful death action alleged that the state failed to ensure job safety, a duty derived from the state's status as the owner of the premises and the employer of the excavation contractor. The trial court directed a verdict in favor of the state on the ground that plaintiffs failed to prove that the state owed an affirmative duty to assure job safety to the employees of an independent contractor. HELD: reasonable minds could differ as to whether the state obtained sufficient control over the construction operations so that it owed a duty of care to the plaintiffs. This determination should have been left to the jury.

A structural engineer of a construction project brought suit against a general contractor to recover attorneys fees spent defending an action brought by two workers injured on the project. The court concluded that the structural engineer was not protected by a provision in the contract between the owner and the prime contractor which promised to indemnify the owner, architect, and subcontractor from all expenses arising out of the performance of the work. The engineer did not have a direct relationship with the contractor and never acted for the architect in those areas which are normally within the architect's area of responsibility. The court of appeal AFFIRMED the lower court's ruling that the engineer was an independent contractor and not an *agent* protected under the language of the indemnity clause in the agreement. Any discussions in which the engineer represented the architect were restricted to explanations of structural design, with the engineer acting on its own behalf.[43]

In *MacKay v Benjamin Franklin Realty & Holding Co*,[44] the administrator of the estate of a deceased architect filed an action against a hotel owner, alleging that the owner had converted hotel plans prepared by the decedent. The defense was that the owner's architect, and not the owner, had converted the plans. HELD: in preparing the plans, the architect was acting as an independent contractor and not as the owner's agent. Although the architect might have been liable for conversion of the decedent's plans, the owner was not liable.

In *Bruemmer v Clark Equipment Co*,[45] an owner entered into a contract with a "package" builder that designed and built a manufacturing plant containing the number of square feet specified by the owner. A worker fell through the roof while construction was in progress and filed suit against the owner under the Indiana Dangerous Occupations Act of 1911.[46] HELD: the owner was not

---

[42] 644 P2d 205 (Alaska 1982).
[43] Lagerstrom v Beers Constr Co, 157 Ga App 396, 277 SE2d 765 (1981).
[44] 288 Pa 207, 135 A 613 (1927).
[45] 341 F2d 23 (7th Cir 1965).
[46] Ind Code Ann §§20-301 through -307 (Burns 1950).

in charge of the project, and the job site was in the possession and control of an independent contractor. Therefore, the owner was not liable.

Arbitrator, Not Agent

In *Prichard Brothers v Grady Co*,[47] based on an American Institute of Architects (AIA) form of contract, the court held that the architect was not the agent of a school district but rather acted as an *arbiter* or *umpire* during the construction phase of the project.

Not all summarized cases reviewed in this section can be reconciled with those collected in the preceding section. The generally accepted rule seems to be that an architect *usually* acts as an independent contractor in the preparation of plans and specifications, but as an agent of the owner in supervising and inspecting the work.

§8.04 Agency Relationship as a Defense to the Architect

In some circumstances an architect is protected from liability by the existence of an agency relationship. In *Cox v City of Freeman*,[48] a contractor filed suit against a city engineer for damages for delay, alleging that the engineer was tardy in locating the site, did not produce necessary engineering documents on time, and inserted discrepancies in the contract documents. The city, also a defendant, asserted the defense of accord and satisfaction on the ground that the contractor had accepted a check tendered with a letter certifying *final payment*. HELD: accord and satisfaction between the principal and the claimant also protects the agent.

In *Manton v H.L. Stevens & Co*,[49] a bricklayer received a skull fracture after a wrecking gang on the sixth floor dislodged a piece of concrete. The plaintiff filed an action against the owner and the architect on the ground that they had failed to supply a reasonably safe place to work. The court dismissed the action against the architect. Since the architect was merely an agent of the owner, the architect had no independent duty to supply a reasonably safe place to work.

The evidence supporting the court's finding of an agency relationship was: although the architect entered into many contracts, the contracts were formed on behalf of the owner, and the architect assumed no personal responsibility; the

---

[47] 436 NW2d 460 (Minn Ct App 1989), *review denied* (May 2, 1989).
[48] 321 F2d 887 (8th Cir 1963).
[49] 170 Iowa 495, 153 NW 87 (1915).

architect approved deliveries of materials; the architect made many changes in the original contract documents with no objection from the owner; and the owner kept a daily itemized statement of expenditures for labor and materials.

In *Hill v McDonald*,[50] a child fell five stories after slipping in a puddle and sliding under a handrail. Suit was filed against the landlord and the design architect. The suit against the landlord was settled for $75,000 in exchange for a release. The guardian then filed a separate suit against the architect, who moved for dismissal on the ground that a release of the principal also acts as a release of the agent. The trial court dismissed the complaint but was REVERSED. Although most courts agree that the release of an agent necessarily releases the principal, the converse is not necessarily true, and the more modern decisions indicate that a release of a principal does not release the agent unless it is expressly intended to do so. Here, the proper rule is that a release of one joint tortfeasor does not release the other joint tortfeasor. The landlord was guilty of allowing a puddle to accumulate; the architect was guilty of improper design. Each of these two causes contributed to the accident. Therefore, the release of the landlord did not constitute a release of the architect.

In *Tri-City Construction Co v A.C. Kirkwood & Associates*,[51] a contractor for improvement of a wastewater system settled a lawsuit against the owner/city for $975,000, then filed suit against the engineer who had been employed by the city, alleging negligence in the administration of the contract and breach of an implied warranty of fitness of the contract drawings. Summary judgment for the engineer was AFFIRMED. A settlement agreement provided that the contractor fully, finally, and forever released the city and its officers and employees from all claims arising out of the project. Since the engineer was an agent of the city in its dealings with the contractor, the release was effective to protect the engineer against the claim. The contract between the city and the contractor specified that the engineer was the agent of the city.[52]

In *Hogan v Postin*,[53] a millwork subcontractor brought action against an architect for $2,413 in expenses incurred restoring a historical building. The expenses were the result of alleged errors in the drawings of the storefront window layout. The architect directed the subcontractor to build according to blueprints, which were subsequently found to be too large. HELD: the architect supervised the restoration of the building as an agent of the city and an agent

---

[50] 422 A2d 133 (DC 1982).

[51] 738 SW2d 925 (Mo Ct App 1987).

[52] *See also* Cook v Oklahoma Bd of Pub Affairs, 736 P2d 140 (Okla 1987) (engineer was exonerated from liability for damages suffered by a contractor in renovation of a fish hatchery on the ground that the engineer was an agent of the state).

[53] 695 P2d 1042 (Wyo 1985).

is not personally liable absent agreement to assume liability for nonperformance of the contract. As the city's agent, the architect had power to bind the city to pay for its professional mistakes in preparing drawings.[54]

In *Commercial Industrial Construction, Inc v Anderson*,[55] a disappointed bidder filed an action against an architect for tortious interference with contractual relations. The architect had presided over a bid opening at which all bids were rejected. Negotiations ensued and a contract was awarded to a contractor other than the original low bidder. The court held that the architect was the agent of the owner for the purpose of opening bids and negotiating contracts and that it would have been legally impossible for the owner to be liable for interfering with its own contractual relations. Since the principal could not be liable, neither could the agent.

§8.05 Liability for Acts of Consultant

An architect may be liable for the acts of its consultants under the doctrine of *respondeat superior*. In other cases, the consultants may be independent contractors, but nevertheless architects may be liable for their activities if the activities are *inherently dangerous*. Finally, an architect may assume contractual responsibility to an owner for the acts of its consultant.

In *Scott v Potomac Insurance Co*,[56] an architect was employed to design a hospital and in turn employed a heating engineer to design the heating system. The engineer specified steel tubing, since copper was not available at the time (during the Korean War). Within a few months after completion of the hospital, the steel tubing began to leak because of extensive corrosion. The hospital claimed damages from the architect. The architect's malpractice insurance carrier refused to adjust the claim, and the architect settled directly with the hospital. The architect then filed suit against the insurance carrier, and the carrier defended on the grounds that the settlement paid by the architect was voluntary and the architect was not liable for the defect, since the design was actually performed by the heating engineer, an independent contractor.

The court held that the heating engineer was acting as the agent of the architect. Therefore, the architect was liable for the malpractice of the engineer. The insurance carrier argued that the architect could not be expected to be

---

[54] See also Huber, Hunt & Nichols, Inc v Moore, 67 Cal App 3d 278, 136 Cal Rptr 603 (1977), where a similar result was reached. (In its capacity as agent of the owner, an architect supervising construction was not liable for simple negligence.)

[55] 683 P2d 378 (Colo Ct App 1984).

[56] 217 Or 323, 341 P2d 1083 (1959).

aware of all the characteristics of steel tubing and was justified in relying on the consulting engineers. The court stated: "It ill behooves a man professing professional skill to say I know nothing of an article which I am called upon to use in the practice of my profession."[57]

In *Bayuk v Edson*,[58] plaintiff homeowners obtained a judgment of $18,500 against Edson, an architect, and Bosworth, an associate not licensed to practice architecture but who was an assistant professor at the University of Oregon and had considerable training as an architect. Edson agreed to divide the fee with Bosworth according to the amount of work done by each, and Bosworth thus received $1,700 of the $2,000 fee.

The contract between Edson and the owners provided that the architects would not supervise the project; however, Bosworth did. The plans were defective: the closets were only 18 inches wide, the floor was designed poorly, and the doors were too elaborate for the local artisans to fabricate. The supervision was also deficient: the floor did not conform to the specifications, the kitchen tile was sloppy, the sliding doors stuck, and the fireplace cracked.

The court held that the relationship between Edson and Bosworth was that of principal and agent, since that is what they represented themselves to be. Edson was thus liable to the owner for Bosworth's mistakes.

An architect's claim against its structural engineer consultant was disallowed with exotic reasoning in *Soriano v Hunton, Shivers, Brady & Associates*.[59] When the architect presented its designs to the builder, the builder protested that the structural design was defective. The architect obtained opinions of two other structural engineers who said the design was defective. The consultant engineer, however, disagreed and refused to remedy the design. The architect then obtained a new design that required modification of a portion of the building that was already built. The architect sought damages for breach of contract and indemnity from the consultant. HELD: even though the modifications to the building may have been necessary for the protection of the owner, the modifications were not authorized by the owner, nor was the architect authorized to act as the owner's agent. The architect assumed the financial responsibility for the modifications as a volunteer. To have permitted the architects to recover from the engineer would encourage acts of volunteerism under a guise of mitigating an owner's damages without the owner's consent.

The reasoning of this case should be criticized. Architects should be encouraged to voluntarily protect the interests of the owner and the public in structurally safe construction, rather than be discouraged from doing so.

---

[57] *Id* at 334, 341 P2d at 1088.

[58] 236 Cal App 2d 309, 46 Cal Rptr 49 (1965).

[59] 524 So 2d 488 (Fla Dist Ct App), *review denied*, 534 So 2d 399 (Fla 1988).

Nondelegable Duty

Although a consulting engineer may be an independent contractor, an architect may still liable for the engineer's acts in an *inherently dangerous* activity.

For example, in *Johnson v Salem Title Co*,[60] a pedestrian was injured when a hurricane-force wind collapsed a masonry wall. The wall was designed by a consulting engineer, but the design plan was signed by the architect. The court acknowledged that it is the general rule that a party is not liable for the negligence of an independent contractor, but in this case the engineer had failed to design the wall to comply with the requirements of the building code. The City of Salem building code required structures to be designed to resist wind pressure as specified. Thus, the case was covered by the Restatement (Second) Torts §424 (1965), which lays down the rule that one who by statute is under a duty to provide safeguards or precautions is liable for the failure of its independent contractor to do so. The architect was paid for the design and assumed responsibility for the structural engineering that went into the contract documents. The duty to safeguard the public was nondelegable.

To the same effect is *Vannoy v City of Warren*.[61] The decedent was overcome by methane gas in a manhole, fell into water, and drowned. Engineers employed by the city had failed to make reasonable inspections of the job site to protect the decedent from injury. The court held that the city was liable for the negligence of the engineer in spite of the fact that the engineer was an independent contractor. Where the work to be done is inherently or intrinsically dangerous, the owner of a project is liable even if it delegates the supervision of the work to an independent contractor. This doctrine is based on a theory that imposes a nondelegable duty upon a party who undertakes a dangerous activity. Therefore, the jury should have determined the question of whether the activity was intrinsically dangerous.

The court wrongly compared the doctrine of nondelegable duty to the theory of strict liability. The theory of strict liability holds that a party can be liable for damages caused by a defective product, without negligence. The theory of nondelegable duty does not do away with the need for negligence; it merely makes one party responsible for the negligence of another.

An architect may assume the risk of loss caused by a mechanical designer who operates without a license. In *State Board of Registration v Rogers*,[62] the respondent called itself a *mechanical designer* but had no license. It prepared mechanical drawings for heating, ventilating, air conditioning, plumbing, and similar work. All its clients were architects, and it never solicited work from, or

---

[60] 246 Or 409, 425 P2d 519 (1967).
[61] 15 Mich App 158, 166 NW2d 486 (1968).
[62] 239 Miss 35, 120 So 2d 772 (1960).

performed work for, members of the public. The court held that the respondent did not violate the license law, since an architect may delegate any part of its duty to a helper or an employee. However, the court remarked that the architect does so at its own peril, since the architect remains responsible for the quality of the work performed by the helpers and employees.

In *Financial Building Consultant, Inc v Guillebau, Britt & Waldrop*,[63] FBC, a design-and-build firm, employed Paul, an architect, as vice president. In 1978, the roof collapsed at a building that Paul and others on behalf of FBC had designed for a Tennessee bank. The employment contract between Paul and FBC obligated FBC to provide insurance for Paul, and FBC did so. Seven months after the accident, Paul's employment was terminated. For some reason, neither Paul nor FBC notified the errors and omissions insurer of the roof collapse until after policy coverage lapsed. As a result, neither Paul nor FBC was covered by the policy. A year later, FBC sued Paul, contending negligence in the design of the roof. Summary judgment in favor of Paul was AFFIRMED. The action was simply unconscionable. FBC had a duty to notify the insurance company of the claim, which would have protected both FBC and Paul. Paul had the right to rely on FBC to give such notice. Since FBC failed to do so, it would have been unconscionable to allow it to recoup its loss from Paul.

In *Graulich v Frederic Berlowe & Associates*,[64] an architect indirectly became liable for the fees of its consultants. The architect failed to investigate zoning before preparing drawings, and, as a result, the owners abandoned the project. The consulting mechanical and electrical engineers recorded mechanics liens against the owners' property. In the mechanics lien foreclosure action, the owners brought a third-party action against the architect. HELD: the architect was negligent in failing to investigate the zoning. A judgment foreclosing the mechanics lien in favor of the consultants against the owners' property was rendered, and judgment in favor of the owners against the architect was AFFIRMED.

Although the doctrine that an architect is responsible for errors committed by its consulting engineer, an independent contractor, seems harsh, it is a harshness that can be eliminated if the architect can alter the conventional relationship with consulting engineers. If the owner directly employs a consulting engineer, then, under the doctrine of the cases reviewed herein, the architect would not be responsible for the engineer's errors. Since it is customary for the architect to employ consulting engineers, the architect ends up carrying the responsibility not just to pay the consulting engineer's fee, but also to pay for any damages occasioned by a defect inserted into the contract documents by the consultant.

---

[63] 163 Ga App 607, 295 SE2d 355 (1982).
[64] 338 So 2d 1109 (Fla Dist Ct App 1976).

Where the architect prefers to retain control over the engineer, the responsibility follows the control. Such considerations have had their effect. It is now customary for architects to recommend (or insist) that owners directly employ soil engineers.

§8.06 Liability of Partnerships and Corporations

In *Marszalk v Van Volkenburg*,[65] architect partners restricted their partnership business to former clients and public works. Plaintiff, a new client, filed suit against both partners on a project where only one partner had actually rendered services. HELD: the existence of the partnership did not make a partner who did not participate in the project liable where the project was outside the scope of the partnership business.

In *Commonwealth Department of Transportation v Upper Providence Township Municipal Authority*,[66] the court held that an incorporation of civil engineers results in an entity with all the attributes of any other business corporation, including limited liability for its principals. As a corollary, an engineering firm is liable for the negligence of its president and its lay employees.[67]

---

[65] 24 Wash App 646, 604 P2d 501 (1979).
[66] 55 Pa Commw 398, 423 A2d 769 (1980).
[67] American Fidelity Fire Ins Co v Pavia-Byrne Engg Corp, 393 So 2d 830 (La), *writ denied*, 397 So 2d 1362 (La Ct App 1981).

Defenses 9

§9.01 Generally
§9.02 Privity of Contract
Foreseeability
Doctrine of Invitation
§9.03 —Rejection
Warranty
§9.04 Economic Loss
§9.05 —Continuing Application of Privity Defense
§9.06 Completion and Acceptance
§9.07 Patent Defect
§9.08 Immunity—Architect as Arbitrator
§9.09 —Application
§9.10 —Criticism
§9.11 No Duty
Defense Rejected
§9.12 Architect No Insurer
§9.13 No Causation
§9.14 Assumption of the Risk
§9.15 Contributory Negligence
§9.16 Comparative Negligence
Apportionment and Comparative Negligence
§9.17 —Application
§9.18 Reliance on Information Furnished by Others
§9.19 Approval by Building Department
§9.20 Waiver and Estoppel
Failure to Complain
Estoppel Rejected
Waiver and Estoppel Accepted

§9.21	Approval by Owner
	Approval Accepted as a Defense
§9.22	No Supervision
	Duty to Supervise
§9.23	No Control
	Reverse Application
§9.24	—Methods of Construction
§9.25	—Application
	Vitality of the Defense
	Assumption of Responsibility by Conduct
	Details of Construction
§9.26	—Rejection
	Supervisory Power
	Positive Protective Duty
	Summary
§9.27	Defective Work Concealed
§9.28	Deviation from Plans
§9.29	Exculpatory Clauses
	Architect as Drafter of Contract Documents
	Contract Documents
	Public Contracts
	Standard Forms
§9.30	—Application
	Claims by Sureties
	Claims by Contractors
	Claims by Owners
	Claims by Workers
	Defense Rejected
§9.31	—Criticism
§9.32	Exclusive Remedy
§9.33	Privilege
§9.34	Sovereign Immunity
§9.35	—Application
§9.36	—Rejection
§9.37	Release
	Release of Joint Tortfeasor
	Release of Principal Releases Agent
§9.38	Accord and Satisfaction
§9.39	No License
§9.40	Other Forms of Illegality
§9.41	Res Judicata and Collateral Estoppel

§9.42   Other Defenses
        Nonfeasance versus Misfeasance
        Compliance with Statute
        Act of God
        Lack of Federal Jurisdiction
        Percolating Waters
        Superseding Cause
        Riparian Law
        Compliance with Contract
        Duplicate Recovery
        Statute of Frauds

§9.01   Generally

The most frequently reported defense to an action for the malpractice of an architect is *lack of privity*. Beginning in 1950, this defense was *discredited* in almost every jurisdiction that considered it. As may have been expected, architects learned to assert a variety of other defenses. The most important of these seems to be the assertion that the architect had no control over the activity or device that caused the injury. The architect often asserts that it is not responsible for the methods of construction employed by the contractor. The architect may also enjoy sovereign immunity. It may assert that the injury was caused by a deviation from plans that were properly prepared. The defenses of contributory and comparative negligence are asserted with relative infrequency. A welter of rare but sometimes potent defenses has developed, among which are: approval by the building department, reliance on information furnished by others, payment as acceptance, exculpatory contract provisions, the parol evidence rule, privilege, release, accord and satisfaction, and illegality. An important and controversial new line of cases resurrects, in some states, the "privity" defense in cases of *economic loss*.

The review of defenses starts with an examination of the now discarded rule which held that an architect was not liable to a third party for damage suffered because of a defect in a structure designed or supervised by the architect, in the absence of privity of contract.

§9.02   Privity of Contract

For more than a century, architects were protected by a doctrine that held that they would not be liable for bodily injury or property damage caused by a defect in a structure which they designed or supervised, in the absence of privity of contract. The rise and fall of this defense has been a favorite subject of commentators on the liability of architects for malpractice.[1]

The doctrine was frequently criticized, especially after it was seen to conflict with Justice Cardozo's holding in *MacPherson v Buick Motor Co.*[2] In that case, a guest in an automobile was injured when a defectively manufactured wooden wheel on the automobile collapsed. The court held that when a manufacturer should know that the product will endanger another if defective, the manufacturer has a duty to protect that person from harm.

The privity of contract defense is said to have originated in *Winterbottom v Wright*,[3] where the plaintiff, a coachman, was injured when his coach, "through certain latent defects in the state and condition thereof . . . gave way and broke down, whereby the plaintiff was thrown from his seat, and in consequence of injuries then received, had become lamed for life." The defendant was under a contract to the postmaster general to supply and maintain the mailcoach. The judges held that since the plaintiff had no contract with the defendant, it could not recover.

> We ought not to permit a doubt to rest upon this subject, for our doing so might be the means of letting in upon us an infinity of actions . . . unless we confine the operation of such contracts as this to the parties who entered into them, the most absurd and outrageous consequences, to which I can see no limit, would ensue . . . it is no doubt a hardship upon the plaintiff to be without a remedy, but by that consideration we ought not to be influenced. Hard cases, it has been frequently observed, are apt to introduce bad law.

Thus the practical justification for the decision in *Winterbottom* was a perverse economy of judicial time. However, the mere fact that large numbers of damaged persons seek justice is no good reason to deny justice. Thus, the doctrine of *Winterbottom v Wright* was doomed to be overthrown by future legal thinking.

Until *MacPherson*, the doctrine of *Winterbottom v Wright* protected the manufacturers of chattels. After *MacPherson* it continued to protect contractors and architects. As applied to contractors, the doctrine found expression in the defense that a contractor would not be liable for injuries caused by latent defects in a building after completion and acceptance by the owner.

---

[1] *See, e.g.*, Annotation, 59 ALR3d 869 (1974); Arness, *Architects and Engineers: A Consideration of Basic Liability Principles & Legal Trends in Foundation Engineering*, 34 Ins Counsel J 334 (1967); Gouldin, *Liability of Architects & Contractors to Third Persons: Inman v Binghamton Housing Authority Revisited*, 33 Ins Counsel J 361 (1966).

[2] 217 NY 382, 111 NE 1050 (1916).

[3] 10 M&W 109, 152 Eng Rep 402 (1842).

The rationale for the doctrine that completion and acceptance was a defense was that the true proximate cause of the plaintiff's injury was the fact that the owner maintained the building in a defective condition, rather than the original negligence of the contractor which created that condition. This doctrine is said to have been overthrown by *Dow v Holly Manufacturing Co.*[4]

The Restatement of Torts[5] now holds that a contractor is liable for physical harm caused by the dangerous character of a structure after its work has been accepted by the owner under the same rules as those determining the liability of one who manufactures a chattel for the use of others.

The *completion and acceptance* defense for contractors became known as the *privity of contract* defense to architects, and it has been said that the courts have adhered to that doctrine because of the large number of potential plaintiffs and the potential lifelong liability of the architect since the statute of limitations does not start until the injury occurs. This justification has been criticized by noting that the length of potential liability should be corrected by amending the statute of limitations, rather than by eliminating possible claimants.[6]

Foreseeability

In *Ferentchak v Village of Frankfort*,[7] homeowners filed an action against a developer's architect to recover for damages resulting from improper surface drainage. HELD: the architect may have been liable to the homeowners despite lack of privity. The proper analysis focuses on *foreseeability of injury* rather than on the concept of privity.

Lack of foreseeability served as a defense to an architect in a 1988 Minnesota case.[8] The court held that an architect is not liable for negligent damage caused to a third party unless the damage to the party was foreseeable at the time the negligent act occurred. A developer defaulted on its loan and assigned its rights arising out of the construction of the project to the lender along with a deed in lieu of foreclosure. The lender then attempted to assert claims of negligence against the architect who had been employed by the developer. The assignment was invalid since it was prohibited by the contract. On the negligence cause of action, the court stated that design professionals are liable in negligence to those who foreseeably rely upon their professional services, but the possibility of

---

[4] 49 Cal 2d 720, 321 P2d 736 (1958).

[5] Restatement (Second) of Torts §385 (1965).

[6] Bell, *Professional Negligence of Architect and Engineers*, 12 Vand L Rev 711 (1959).

[7] 121 Ill App 3d 599, 459 NE2d 1085 (1984), *aff'd in part, rev'd in part*, 105 Ill 2d 474, 475 NE2d 822 (1985). *See* **ch 4**.

[8] 427 NW2d 281 (Minn Ct App 1988).

damage to the lender following foreclosure of a mortgage after the developer's default was *too remote to be foreseeable*.

Illustrative of the early application of the privity defense is *Geare v Sturgis*, a 1926 case overruled in 1956.[9] A theater patron was killed in the collapse of the Knickerbocker Theatre in Washington on January 28, 1922. The heirs complained that the collapse was caused by the negligence of the architect in designing and supervising the project. The court of appeal held that the demurrer to the complaint should have been sustained, pointing out that both architects and contractors are immune from suit after completion and acceptance by the owner, otherwise there would be no end to suits. The true proximate cause was the negligence of the owner in maintaining the defective building.

In *Mayor & City of Albany v Cunliff*,[10] the plaintiff was crossing a bridge that was defectively designed and was injured when the bridge collapsed. The court stated that an architect or a builder of a public work would be liable only to the employer for a breach of duty. There is no liability to third persons for accidents or injuries that might occur after the work is completed.

In *Bilich v Barnett*,[11] the complaint alleged that a sewer contractor followed grade sheets prepared by an engineer for the property owner; the grade sheets were inaccurate, and as a result, the contractor incurred additional expense to complete the contract according to specifications. The trial court sustained a general demurrer. The appellate department of the superior court AFFIRMED, holding that there is no liability for negligent misrepresentation in the absence of privity of contract.

In *Gherardi v Board of Education*,[12] a contract required the contractor to complete a school job in 400 days, but the job was completed 11 months late. The contractor accepted final payment without making any claim for damages for the delay and, one year later, filed suit for damages against the architect. The contractor alleged that the architect failed to coordinate and properly supervise the work and contended that this was a breach of contract. The court held that there was no contractual relationship between the contractor and the architect; therefore, the breach of contract claim was invalid. Moreover, the contractor failed to allege malice or any intentional wrongdoing by the architect. Therefore, summary judgment was properly granted. Interference with contractual relations is an intentional tort.

---

[9] 56 App DC 364, 14 F2d 256 (1926), *overruled*, Hannah v Fletcher, 97 US App DC 310, 231 F2d 469 (1956).

[10] 2 NY 165 (1849).

[11] 103 Cal App 2d Supp 921, 229 P2d 492 (1951).

[12] 53 NJ Super 349, 147 A2d 535 (1958).

The privity doctrine was even applied to deprive a homeowner of a right of action against the architect who designed the radiant heating system for thehome. The homeowner employed a construction contractor to build the home; the contractor paid for the plans and added them to the cost of the house. Therefore, it was held that the architect who designed the defective system could not be liable to the homeowner for the defects in the radiant heating system which it designed, since the architect was in privity of contract with the contractor and not the homeowner. This was held to be the case even though the owner's agent had been the one who originally asked the architect to prepare the design.[13]

The opposite conclusion was reached in *Robitscher v United Clay Products Co*,[14] where the plaintiff homeowner employed a builder to remodel a home. The builder purchased a heating and air conditioning unit from a material dealer who also provided a schematic layout for the necessary ducts and registers. The system malfunctioned, and the homeowner filed suit against the dealer. The lower court dismissed the complaint on the ground that there was no privity of contract between the homeowner and the dealer, but the court of appeal held that the dealer could be liable to the homeowner since the dealer voluntarily undertook to perform a service, and it is a rule of long standing that one who performs a service for another voluntarily, even though gratuitously, has the duty to exercise care and is liable for failure to do so.

To fully express the doctrine of privity of contract as a defense would be to say: the architect is not under a common law duty to exercise due care in the practice of its profession for the protection of those who might foreseeably be injured by a defect in the project; therefore, any liability must arise from a contractual relationship with the plaintiff, and not from the law of torts. However, to express fully the concept is to show its absurdity. Thus, the term *privity of contract* is seen to be a rubric which obscured the true (and unjust) rule that an architect had no duty to protect anyone but the client from design defects. Such a bald statement of the rule would have endangered its existence.

In *Peyronnin Construction Co v Weiss*,[15] a subcontractor employed an engineer to estimate dirt quantity, the engineer underestimated, and the subcontractor defaulted to the damage of the prime contractor, who filed suit against the engineer for negligence. The trial court sustained the defendant's demurrer, and the court of appeal AFFIRMED, pointing out that the complaint did not allege any fact that indicated a relationship between the plaintiff and the engineer which would create a duty of care, and the complaint included no allegation of privity of contract.

---

[13] Staley v New, 56 NM 756, 250 P2d 893 (1952).

[14] 143 A2d 99 (DC 1958).

[15] 137 Ind App 417, 208 NE2d 489 (1965).

In a similar case, *Delta Construction Co v City of Jackson*,[16] the contractor alleged that the engineer negligently misrepresented the amount of excavation necessary to complete an airport job. The contractor alleged two causes of action, one for breach of contract and the other for negligence. The court held that the lack of privity of contract destroyed both causes of action.

In *Wood Brothers Construction Co v Simons-Eastern Co*,[17] a contractor sued a project designer-supervisor for delay damages on a project for construction of a wood energy system plant. Numerous change orders and other delays caused the work to be extended six months beyond the scheduled completion date. The designer/supervisor was employed by the owner. HELD: the claim for negligent supervision arose out of the contract between the owner and the designer/supervisor. The contractor's claim was defeated by lack of privity between contractor and designer/supervisor.

In *Harbor Mechanical, Inc v Arizona Electric Power Co-op, Inc*,[18] the court held that an engineering firm employed by the owner to prepare contract documents for the construction of a power plant owed no duty to the contractor hired to perform certain phases of construction. The contractor could not state a cause of action in negligence. However, the court found that the lack of privity of contract did not destroy a cause of action against the engineer for negligent misrepresentation.

In *Edward B. Fitzpatrick Jr Construction Corp v County of Suffolk*,[19] a contractor on a sewer pipe line project filed an action against the engineering firm employed by the public agency, alleging construction delays caused by professional negligence and corruption. Judgment for the engineer was AFFIRMED. Since the contractor lacked privity of contract with the engineer, the engineer had no duty to disclose subsurface conditions that were different from those stated in the specifications.

The lack of privity of contract was successfully asserted as a defense by an architect in *R.H. Macy & Co v Williams Tile & Terrazzo Co*.[20] An architect designed tiles to be installed in a store. When the tile proved to be defective, the owner filed suit against the contractor and the supplier. The contractor and the supplier, in turn, filed third-party claims against the architect. The contractor alleged that the architect negligently selected the tiles; the supplier contended that the architect negligently failed to have the tile tested. Summary judgment

---

[16] 198 So 2d 592 (Miss 1967).

[17] 193 Ga App 874, 389 SE2d 382 (1989), *cert denied* (Jan 25, 1990). *See also* Morse/Diesel, Inc v Trinity Indus, 859 F2d 242 (2d Cir 1988) (subcontractors had no privity with architect/engineer. Under New York law, privity of contract was required to hold a professional responsible for economic loss for negligent performance of professional duties).

[18] 496 F Supp 681 (D Ariz 1980).

[19] 138 AD2d 446, 525 NYS2d 863 (1988).

[20] 585 F Supp 175 (ND Ga 1984).

in favor of the architect was AFFIRMED. Any duty owed by the architect to the contractor or the supplier could only have been the result of the architect's contract with the owner. Under a Georgia statute,[21] however, an action in tort for breach of a duty arising from contract is limited to those parties in privity with the defendant, except where the plaintiff would have a right of action independent of contract. Here, the cause of action was dependent on the contract, since the architect had no duty of care either to the contractor or the supplier.

Doctrine of Invitation

In *Colbert v Holland Furnace Co*,[22] the plaintiff was seriously injured after falling through a floor grating of a heating system which was supported by old, weak, brittle, and unsafe cleats. The grating had been installed a year earlier under contract with the plaintiff's husband, and the defendant guaranteed material and workmanship for five years. The court sustained a jury verdict for plaintiff. The court acknowledged the lack of privity of contract between the injured wife and the furnace company and recognized the general rule that privity is a defense to an independent contractor where the plaintiff is injured after the item has been accepted by the employer (here, the husband). However, there is an exception to the rule where the item is such that it is obvious any defect is likely to result in injury to the user and a person, properly using the item, suffers such an injury from the defective condition. The court stated: "The doctrine of invitation has been invoked as a ground of liability in such cases, proceeding upon the theory that he who furnishes a thing for a certain use by others invites others to use it, and is therefore bound to make it safe for such purpose."[23]

The emergence of the rubric *privity of contract* as a label for a defense in cases of the malpractice of architects is an example of an unfortunate disposition to substitute words for thought. The lack of privity of contract, standing alone, is really no defense to anything. If a child is run down in the street, the law does not pause to ask whether the driver had entered into a contract with the child to avoid the mishap. Instead, the law asks whether the driver was under a duty to avoid injury to the child, and whether the driver negligently failed to discharge that duty. It is true that a contractual relationship can impose or eliminate liability, but it does not follow that the contractual relationship is *necessary* to liability.

---

[21] Ga Code Ann §51-1-11 (Harrison 1981).

[22] 333 Ill 78, 164 NE 162 (1928).

[23] *Id* at 81, 164 NE at 164.

§9.03 —Rejection

It has been said that the defense of privity was destroyed by *Inman v Binghamton Housing Authority*,[24] where the *MacPherson*[25] doctrine was applied to architects. However, the court in *Inman* required that the defect causing injury be *latent*. Since the defect was the absence of a protective railing around a stoop and other *patently* obvious features which allowed a two-year-old plaintiff to fall, the architect was not liable.[26]

In *Detweiler Brothers v John Graham & Co*,[27] a mechanical subcontractor sued an architect, alleging that the architect first approved a submittal for grooved piping rather than welded piping and thereafter ordered the grooved piping to be replaced by welded piping. HELD: the absence of privity did not preclude a claim by the subcontractor against the architect if the subcontractor can establish the existence of a duty between the parties, the architect's breach of such a duty, and the proximate cause of the damage.[28]

In Massachusetts, the defense of privity was specifically rejected in *McDonough v Whalen*.[29] The doctrine was clearly repudiated in California in *Montijo v Swift*,[30] where the court stated that the architect who plans and supervises a project as an independent contractor has a duty to any person who foreseeably and with reasonable certainty may be injured, even though the injury may not occur until after the work has been completed and accepted. Likewise, Louisiana law recognizes the existence of a duty of care owed by architects to persons with whom the architect has no privity of contract.[31]

In *Laukkanen v Jewel Tea Co*,[32] a piling fell on the plaintiff during a windstorm, after plaintiff entered a building, rendering plaintiff paraplegic. The engineer had prepared plans and specifications for the building which

---

[24] 3 NY2d 137, 143 NE2d 895, 164 NYS2d 699 (1957).

[25] MacPherson v Buick, 217 NY 382, 111 NE 1050 (1916). *See* §9.02.

[26] In M. Miller Co v Central Contra Costa Sanitary Dist, 198 Cal App 2d 305, 18 Cal Rptr 13 (1961), it was held that the lack of privity does not necessarily indicate no liability (contractor versus soil test engineer employed by sanitary district). *Accord* Owen v Dodd, 431 F Supp 1239 (ND Miss 1977) (general contractor versus architect); Oakes v McCarthy Co, 267 Cal App 2d 231, 73 Cal Rptr 127 (1968) (home buyer versus soil engineer); Craig v Everett M. Brooks Co, 351 Mass 497, 22 NE2d 752 (1967) (contractor versus engineer who negligently located offset stakes).

[27] 412 F Supp 416 (ED Wash 1976).

[28] *Accord* Normoyle-Berg & Assocs v Village of Deer Creek, 39 Ill App 3d 744, 350 NE2d 559 (1976) (general contractor versus supervising engineer).

[29] 365 Mass 506, 313 NE2d 435 (1974) (lot flooded by septic system).

[30] 219 Cal App 2d 351, 33 Cal Rptr 133 (1963) (bus station patron fell, handrail improperly designed).

[31] Farrell Constr Co v Jefferson Parish, 693 F Supp 490 (ED La 1988) (contractor filed suit against engineer claiming inadequate and defective drawings impeded the progress of drainage and pump station projects).

[32] 78 Ill App 2d 153, 222 NE2d 584 (1966).

were ambiguous as to the type of concrete block to be used on the piling. The builder used a lightweight aggregate block which failed to withstand the rigors of the windstorm. The engineer argued that it had no duty to plaintiff who was a member of the general public. HELD: lack of privity does not absolve liability where negligence proximately causes a foreseeable injury.[33]

The court in *A.E. Investment Corp v Link Builders, Inc*[34] held that lack of privity does not prevent liability of an architect to a remote supermarket tenant in the absence of public policy considerations. Although it reserved the determination of whether such policy considerations existed or not to the trial court, the Supreme Court of Wisconsin strongly indicated that if the architect were negligent and the tenant harmed, the architect would be liable. "Professionalism is the very antithesis to irresponsibility to all interests other than those of an immediate employer."[35]

Warranty

Architects implicitly warrant not that their plans will be accurate and adequate, but that they will exercise reasonable skill, care, and diligence in preparing them. In an Arizona case, the contractor properly stated a cause of action against an architect under common law warranty, despite lack of privity.[36]

By contrast, it has been held that privity of contract is still necessary to the allegation of a good cause of action against an architect for breach of warranty.[37]

§9.04 Economic Loss

It is still an open question in some states whether the lack of privity of contract can be a defense to an action against an architect for economic loss, as opposed to bodily injury or property damage. Economic loss may be recoverable by parties not in privity upon a showing of negligence, misrepresentation, and justifiable reliance. States in which an action may be maintained against an

---

[33] *See also* Hiatt v Brown, 422 NE2d 736 (Ind Ct App 1981) (Indiana court rejected lack of privity as a defense where an airport patron was blown from a pedestrian ramp by the blast of a jet aircraft).

[34] 62 Wis 2d 479, 214 NW2d 764 (1974).

[35] *Id* 769.

[36] Donnelly Constr Co v Oberg, Hunt & Gilleland, 139 Ariz 184, 677 P2d 1292 (1984).

[37] C.W. Regan, Inc v Parsons, Brinckerhoff, Quade & Douglas, 411 F2d 1379 (4th Cir 1969).

engineer, architect, contractor, or other design professional despite lack of contractual privity: AL, AZ, AR, CA, CO, DE, FL, IL, LA, MA, MI, MS, MN, NJ, NY, NC, RI, TX, WA, WI. States where purely economic loss cannot be recovered in tort absent privity: OH, PA, GA, VA.[38]

The Supreme Court of Wisconsin, in *A.E. Investment Corp v Link Builders, Inc,*[39] stated that the question of whether intangible economic loss should be recoverable is a policy question to be determined by the trial court. However, the California Court of Appeal, in *Cooper v Jevne,*[40] has determined that an architect out of privity is liable to a remote condominium buyer for economic loss and, by dictum, extended that rule to cover physicians and lawyers too, if they are guilty of malpractice causing economic damage to a third party out of privity.

In the absence of privity, a contractor was not permitted under Virginia law to recover economic loss damages (for delay) caused by the negligence of the architect. Economic losses may be recovered for negligence of a design professional only by parties who are in privity of contract with the design professional.[41]

One New York case does not permit a negligence action for economic loss against an architect, a professional, absent a contractual relationship or a relationship approaching that of privity.[42] A subcontractor appealed an order granting an architect's motion for summary judgment in a case where the subcontractor alleged that the architect, under contract with the county, prepared a site plan with incorrect elevations, thus causing the subcontractor to perform more work than anticipated in installing fill.

In rejecting privity as a defense, the court in *Rozny v Marnul*[43] named the factors to be considered in determining whether a surveyor should be liable to a remote homebuyer who relied on its survey. The relevant factors were deemed to be: the fact that the plat of survey was inscribed with a written guarantee; the fact that the defendant knew the plat would probably be relied upon by others; the fact that potential liability would be restricted to a relatively small group; the consideration that the innocent purchaser should not carry the burden of the surveyor's professional mistakes; and that a holding of liability would promote cautionary techniques among surveyors.

An architect-engineer may be liable to a general contractor for negligent misrepresentation and failure to disclose subsurface debris, despite lack of

---

[38] John Martin Co v Morse/Diesel, Inc, 819 SW2d 428 (Tenn 1991).
[39] 62 Wis 2d 479, 214 NW2d 764 (1974).
[40] 56 Cal App 3d 860, 128 Cal Rptr 724 (1976).
[41] Bryant Elec Co v City of Fredericksburg, 762 F2d 1192 (4th Cir 1985).
[42] Widett v United States Fidelity & Guar Co, 815 F2d 885 (2d Cir 1987).
[43] 43 Ill 2d 54, 250 NE2d 656 (1969).

privity. A general contractor relied on the plans and specifications prepared by the architect-engineer, which failed to disclose the existence of underground obstructions.[44]

In *Council of Co-Owners Atlantis Condo, Inc v Whiting-Turner Contracting Co*,[45] owners of 198 separate condominium units in a 21-story building brought an action against architects contending that utility shafts and related electrical work were not installed properly, thus causing a fire hazard. The court held that privity was not an absolute prerequisite to the existence of a duty to prevent injury to the owners. The duty of an architect to use due care in the design and inspection of condominium units extends to those persons foreseeably subjected to the risk of injury created by latent and unreasonable conditions resulting from their negligence.

Similarly, in *Forte Brothers v National Amusement, Inc*,[46] the court held that a third-party general contractor, who may be foreseeably injured or suffer an economic loss proximately caused by the negligent performance of a contractual duty by an architect, had a cause of action in negligence against the architect notwithstanding the absence of privity.

With perhaps excessive enthusiasm, the Supreme Court of Missouri, in *Westerhold v Carroll*,[47] rejected the defense of privity in finding that an architect, in preparing certificates of payment on a church job, owed a duty of care to the indemnitor or the surety on the contractor's performance bond. It was alleged that the architect had certified payments for $23,000 in excess of the value of work performed on a $325,000 job so that the contractor, overpaid, lost economic motivation to complete all of the obligations under the contract. The court stated that the stipulation for periodic payments was as much for the protection of the surety (and indemnitor) as the owner.

In another case involving an architect's certification, a partnership had standing to bring suit against a bank's architect despite lack of privity. The bank loaned the partnership money to finance the cost of a building and employed an architect to supervise the construction. The court concluded that it was reasonably foreseeable that the partnership, as owner of the property, might have relied on the architect's certification that the project was complete. An architect that contracts to perform services is liable for damages proximately caused by its negligence to anyone who can foreseeably rely on the architect's performance, regardless of privity.[48]

---

[44] Gulf Contracting v Bibb County, 795 F2d 980 (11th Cir 1986).

[45] 308 Md 18, 517 A2d 336 (1986).

[46] 525 A2d 1301 (RI 1987).

[47] 419 SW2d 73 (Mo 1967).

[48] Browning v Maurice B. Levien & Co, 44 NC App 701, 262 SE2d 355, *review denied*, 300 NC 371, 267 SE2d 673 (1980). Privity has also specifically been rejected as a defense in the following cases: Kent v Bartlett, 49 Cal App 3d 724, 122 Cal Rptr 615 (1975) (survey);

In a New York decision,[49] a school district employed an architect which, in turn, employed consulting engineers to evaluate buildings belonging to the school district. Both consulting engineers reported structural weaknesses in concrete. Based on the reports the school was closed. The school district later learned from an independent expert that both consultants had made erroneous findings because they used incorrect materials information in making their calculations. The district filed an action against the consultants. HELD: a professional has no liability for negligent representations that cause pecuniary loss to a party with whom the professional has no contractual relationship. Here, however, the relationship between the consultants and the school district was so close it *approached that privity*. The consultants undertook their work knowing that it was for the school district.

In another New York case, a subcontractor filed an action against an architect and a supplier to recover damages incurred when it was required to replace pipe. The supplier filed a cross-claim against the architect, alleging faulty design and failure to properly advise the supplier of contract requirements. HELD: the lack of privity of contract between the supplier and the architect did not defeat its cross-claim.[50]

North Carolina upholds the requirement of privity for liability of an architect except where products liability, bodily injury, or property damage is involved. In *McKinney Drilling Co v Nello Teer Co*,[51] a caisson subcontractor alleged that it suffered economic loss because the supervising engineer required the subcontractor to drill deeper than called for by the contract documents. Defendant's motion for summary judgment was granted and AFFIRMED. Plaintiff could not recover in the absence of an allegation of bad faith.

Lack of privity of contract is also an effective defense in Illinois. In *Waterford Condominium Assn v Dunbar Corp*,[52] the association filed an action against the developer, the architect, and the structural engineer. The trial court, noting the absence of privity, granted a motion to dismiss for failure to state a cause of action for breach of contract. The dismissal was AFFIRMED. It is not enough that the parties to the contract know, expect, or even intend that others will

---

Swarthout v Beard, 33 Mich App 395, 190 NW2d 373 (1971), *revd as to damages by*; Smith v City of Detroit, 388 Mich 637, 202 NW2d 300 (1972) (excavation collapsed, worker killed); Simon v Omaha Pub Power Dist, 189 Neb 183, 202 NW2d 157 (1972) (worker stepped through hole in deck, impaled on reinforcing steel); Cooper v Cordova Sand & Gravel Co, 485 SW2d 261 (Tenn Ct App 1971) (settlement damage to brick house). *See also* A.R. Moyer, Inc v Graham, 285 So 2d 397 (Fla 1973) (architect may be liable to a contractor for damage resulting from negligent preparation of plans and specifications, despite lack of privity of contract).

[49] Ossining Union Free Sch Dist v Anderson La Roca Anderson, 73 NY2d 417, 539 NE2d 91, 541 NYS2d 335 (1989).

[50] Haseley Trucking Co v Great Lakes Pipe Co, 101 AD2d 1019, 476 NYS2d 702 (1984).

[51] 38 NC App 472, 248 SE2d 444 (1978).

[52] 104 Ill App 3d 371, 432 NE2d 1009 (1982).

benefit from the construction of the building. The contracts between the developer and the architects and engineers did not indicate that the architects or engineers were acting for the direct benefit of the condominium owners, either individually or as a class.[53]

But many cases hold architects liable for economic loss absent privity.

§9.05 —Continuing Application of Privity Defense

The doctrine that lack of privity can operate as a defense in a case of architect malpractice, though moribund, may not be utterly deceased in at least some jurisdictions. The Georgia Court of Appeals, in *Hunt v Star Photo Finishing Co*,[54] held it to be the general rule that an architect is not liable to a third party for negligent performance of a contract except if the work is a nuisance per se, intrinsically dangerous, or so negligently defective as to be imminently dangerous to third persons.

In *Engle Acoustic & Tile, Inc v Grenfell*,[55] subcontractors had alleged that the architect negligently certified dishonest progress payment applications of the prime contractor. The Supreme Court of Mississippi, in dictum, stated that on private construction projects no duty arises between an architect and a subcontractor by implication of law; therefore, liability must be found within the express terms of the contract.

In a case which draws a questionable distinction between active and passive negligence, the New York appellate division in 1973 held that a supervising engineer was not liable for damages sustained by a worker who was injured on the job in the absence of privity, unless the engineer was guilty of active negligence.[56]

---

[53] Three Florida cases rejected lack of privity of contract as a defense. Navajo Circle, Inc v Development Concepts, 373 So 2d 689 (Fla Dist Ct App 1979) (condominium association and unit owners versus architects, for a defective roof); Parliament Towers Condominium v Parliament House Realty, Inc, 377 So 2d 976, 978 (Fla Dist Ct App 1979) (condominium association versus architects; "Since the damages are foreseeable, both the builder and the architect have a legal duty to use reasonable care to protect secondary purchasers from the type of damage alleged"); Luciani v High, 372 So 2d 530 (Fla Dist Ct App 1979) (homeowners versus engineer for negligent soil testing). *See also* Conklin v Cohen, 287 So 2d 56 (Fla Dist Ct App 1973) (plaintiff worker contracted silicosis from inhalation of silica dust while mucking for the Washington Metro Subway System and filed an action against the supervising engineer, Bechtel, Inc.; the courts stated that the issue of contractual liability between Bechtel and the owner was irrelevant; a contract entered into with a third party may impose an obligation sounding in tort (not contract) to act in such a way that a noncontracting party will not be injured).

[54] 115 Ga App 1, 153 SE2d 602 (1967).

[55] 223 So 2d 613 (Miss 1969).

[56] Hamill v Foster-Lipkins Corp, 41 AD2d 361, 342 NYS2d 539 (1973). An Indiana court has shown sympathy to the predicament of professionals. Quoting Justice Cardozo, in Ultramares Corp v Touche, 255 NY 170, 179, 174 NE 441, 444 (1931):

In *Hortman v Becker Construction Co*,[57] the architect was held to have no duty to a worker under the Wisconsin Safe Place Statute[58] where the contract provided that the architect would not be responsible for construction means, methods, techniques, or procedures, or for safety precautions related to the work. Likewise, in *Fruzyna v Walter C. Carlson & Associates*,[59] an architect was held blameless for a job site injury under the Illinois Structural Work Act[60] where the contract contained the same provision.

Lack of privity may serve as a defense in Louisiana. In *C.H. Leavell & Co v Glantz Contracting Corp*,[61] the general contractor alleged that it suffered damage because the architect prepared plans improperly, delayed the issuance of change orders, and was tardy in the delivery of plans. HELD: the contract between the owner and the architect did not include a stipulation pour autrui, since the contract was primarily for the benefit of the owner and not the general contractor. The architect owed no contractual duties to the plaintiff, and summary judgment was AFFIRMED.

In a Georgia case, an engineer negligently performed percolation tests for a developer. The developer sold a home to the plaintiff homeowner. After the noxious condition of the septic tank manifested itself, the homeowner filed an action against the engineer. The engineer defended on the ground that it possessed no privity with the homeowner. HELD: it was foreseeable to the engineer that the person directly injured as a result of its negligence would have been the purchaser of the house; therefore, a clear duty was owed.[62]

> If liability for negligence exists, a thoughtless slip or blunder . . . may expose professionals to a liability in an indeterminate amount for an indeterminate time to an indeterminate class. The hazards of a business conducted on these terms are so extreme as to enkindle doubt whether a flaw may exist to the implication of a duty that exposes to these consequences. . . .

Justice Cardozo's caution is particularly relevant today given the increasing litigiousness of our society and the rising cost of malpractice insurance. Section 522 does not, in our view, sufficiently guard against imposing unwieldy duties upon providers of professional opinions—professionals would be like the bowman in Longfellow's poem, *The Arrow and the Song*, "I shot an arrow into the air, it fell to earth I know not where." Lest the courts drive professionals from their chosen vocations, we believe the privity requirement, subject to an actual knowledge exception, properly balances the competing interests of consumer and professional in a case such as the one before us. *See also* Essex v Ryan, 446 NE2d 368 (Ind Ct App 1983) (inaccurate survey of residential lot in 1955 led to an action for quiet title in 1976—referring to Restatement (Second) of Torts §552 (1965)).

[57] 92 Wis 2d 210, 284 NW2d 621 (1979).
[58] Wis Stat Ann §101.01(2)(b)-(d) (West).
[59] 78 Ill App 3d 1050, 398 NE2d 60 (1979).
[60] Ill Rev Stat ch 48 (1977).
[61] 322 F Supp 779 (ED La 1971).
[62] Southeast Consultants, Inc v O'Pry, 199 Ga App 125, 404 SE2d 299 (1991), *cert denied* (May 15, 1991). *See* Edward B. Fitzpatrick Jr Constr Corp v County of Suffolk, 138 AD2d 446, 525 NYS2d 863 (1988) *and* §9.03.

A claimant against an engineer must establish either contractual privity or a relationship equated with contractual privity.[63]

In *R.H. Macy & Co v Williams Tile & Terrazzo Co*,[64] an owner filed an action against a tile manufacturer and a contractor for damages arising from defective tile. The contractor and manufacturer filed cross-claims against the architect. HELD: the architect had no independent duty to the contractor or the manufacturer. Neither was in privity with the architect. Therefore, any liability depended on the existence of a contract between the architect and the owner. A Georgia statute,[65] however, limits an action in tort for breach of a duty arising from contract to those parties in privity with the defendant. Therefore, summary judgment was properly GRANTED in favor of the architect.

§9.06 Completion and Acceptance

As noted previously,[66] there is a close relationship between the architect's defense that it is not liable to parties out of privity of contract and the rule that a contractor is not liable to third persons for damage resulting from defects in the work after the completion and acceptance of the project.

In *Sherman v Miller Construction Co*,[67] the *completion and acceptance* defense was applied in favor of an architect. The architect prepared plans for a schoolhouse which were approved and accepted by the school trustees. Plaintiff, a schoolboy, was injured several months later when he was pushed by another child, tripped over a three-inch curb, and fell into a basement opening. He alleged that the architect negligently failed to provide a guardrail. The demurrer was sustained. Since the plans were approved and accepted by the trustees who had the statutory duty to decide whether they were *suitable*, the architect was not liable.

However, in *Totten v Gruzen*,[68] the court rejected the completion and acceptance rule as archaic. An architect had designed hot water pipes in a ladderlike arrangement in the late 1940s, and in 1961 the three-year-old plaintiff, a tenant in the project, was burned on the leg after touching the exposed piping which was less than a foot from the floor. Plaintiffs sued the architect for negligence, alleging that the design was hazardous. The trial court dismissed the action on the ground that the project had been completed and

---

[63] Northrup Contracting, Inc v Village of Bergen, 139 Misc 2d 435, 527 NYS2d 670 (Sup Ct 1986) (such a relationship was established where it was alleged that negligent supervision by engineers delayed the work, causing the contractor to terminate its contract).

[64] 585 F Supp 175 (ND Ga 1984).

[65] Ga Code Ann §51-1-11 (Harrison 1981).

[66] *See* §9.02.

[67] 90 Ind App 462, 158 NE 255 (1927).

[68] 52 NJ 202, 245 A2d 1 (1968).

accepted. REVERSED. Architects and engineers may be liable for improper design even if the work has been completed and accepted. Moreover, there is no hard-and-fast rule that only a latent defect will support a cause of action against an architect.

> [T]he obviousness of a danger does not necessarily preclude a jury finding of unreasonable risk and negligence; however, it will so preclude if the obviousness to the claimant justifies the conclusion that the condition is not unreasonably dangerous; otherwise it is simply a factor to consider on the issue of the negligence of the contractor.[69]

In *Elliott v Nordlof*,[70] the completion and acceptance defense was rejected when a grading plan designed by an engineer resulted in the diversion of surface water onto neighboring property. However, completion and acceptance can be a defense for an architect in a suit for mandatory injunction. In *Bodin v Gill*,[71] the plaintiff sought a mandatory injunction to require the architect to modify the grading plan for a church to prevent the diversion of storm water. The court pointed out that the job was finished; therefore, the architect had no right to enter the church property. An interlocutory injunction against the church would have been proper, but not against the architect.

One case shows that a nineteenth century architect could be liable for damage occurring to a third party out of privity of contract, if the architect were in full charge of the job and the damage occurred before completion and acceptance by the owner. In *Boswell v Laird*,[72] in the early mining days of California, an architect-contractor was employed to build a dam to accumulate water for mining operations. The 40-foot high dam was on Deer Creek, above the city of Nevada. The dam burst while under construction, damaging the plaintiff's store downstream. The owner had made some progress payments during construction. Justice Field of the California Supreme Court REVERSED the $5,000 verdict for plaintiff against the owner on the ground that it was the architect-contractor who was liable. The architect was reputed to be experienced and skillful, and the owner exercised no control over the project. Responsibility is placed where power exists. However, if the dam had burst after completion and acceptance, it would have been the owner who would have been liable. It was the responsibility of the owner to see to it that the work was safe and tested for the protection of third parties. By acceptance, owners assumed to the world their responsibility, and the liability of the architect ceased.

---

[69] *Id* at 210, 245 A2d at 6.
[70] 83 Ill App 279, 227 NE2d 547 (1967).
[71] 216 Ga 467, 117 SE2d 325 (1960).
[72] 8 Cal 469 (1857).

This opinion, though it would be considered wrong under modern legal thinking, still has the virtue of avoiding the *privity of contract* analysis, and it does advance a plausible reason for imposing liability on the owner, although that reason would not justify the removal of liability from the architect.

Although the *completion and acceptance defense* is generally rejected by modern courts, it may still have proper effect as a defense to a *safe place case*. In *Jaroszewicz v Facilities Development Corp*,[73] a worker was electrocuted when troubleshooting a parking lot lighting system. HELD: the architect was not liable under the safe place statute[74] because the accident occurred after completion of construction and after a certificate of acceptance had been issued.

§9.07 Patent Defect

The very opinion that is said to have overthrown the doctrine of lack of privity of contract as a defense for architects announced the dubious proposition that *an architect is not liable to remote users for a patent defect in a structure.* *Inman v Binghamton Housing Authority*,[75] held that the two-year-old plaintiff who fell off a stoop could not recover damages from the architect because the court determined, as a matter of law on a motion to dismiss, that the defect, if any, was *patent*. Plaintiff had alleged that the stoop was defective because it had no protective railing, because the arc made by the door when opened might force a person close to the edge of the stoop, and because the step did not extend the full length of the stoop. The court stated that the architect was under no duty to make the property foolproof or accident proof, and that in order to recover, a plaintiff must allege a latent or hidden defect. The owner, however, would have been liable since it was actively negligent under the allegations of the complaint in maintaining a known defective condition of the premises.

The latent/patent distinction was much criticized and was rejected in *Schipper v Levitt & Sons*.[76] However the defense has been successfully asserted. In *Hackley v Waldorf-Hoerner Paper Products Co*,[77] the defect was in the design of an access ladder permanently attached to a turbine pit in a paper mill. The trial court directed a verdict for the architect and refused to admit evidence of safety regulations; however, numerous witnesses testified that the ladder was nonstandard, not approved, and unsafe. The court of appeals AFFIRMED. The excluded evidence would have been cumulative, and therefore the trial court had the discretion to exclude it. Since the ladder did not collapse or fail to

---

[73] 115 AD2d 159, 495 NYS2d 498 (1985).
[74] NY Lab Law §241.
[75] 3 NY2d 137, 143 NE2d 895, 164 NYS2d 699 (1957).
[76] 44 NJ 70, 207 A2d 314 (1965).
[77] 149 Mont 286, 425 P2d 712 (1967).

function for the purpose designed, any alleged defect must have been open, obvious, and without concealment. Because there was no showing that the architect had designed a latent defect or concealed danger, the court properly directed a verdict in favor of the architect.

In *DiPerna v Roman Catholic Diocese*,[78] the *patent defect* defense stood up again. An infant plaintiff was injured while attending a basketball game when pushed against a metal railing protruding from the bleachers designed by the defendant. The court dismissed the complaint. AFFIRMED. Plaintiff alleged negligence on the part of the defendant but failed to allege that the complained of danger or defect was hidden or concealed. Such an allegation is necessary where a remote user, such as the infant plaintiff here, is involved. Similarly, in *Hutchings v Harry*,[79] the court held that lack of privity can only be overcome by pleading the existence of a latent defect which the architect negligently failed to discover.

The patent defect defense is justly criticized, not only in theory, but in its application to the facts of the cases where it has been employed. The lack of a handrailing on a stoop might be a defect patent to an adult, but it creates a danger that is not obvious to a two-year-old girl. Likewise, if a handrail attached to bleachers in a gymnasium might be considered an obvious danger to an adult, the fact that the danger is obvious should hardly excuse liability for it when an infant is shoved against the railing and injured during the excitement of a basketball game. It seems that the obviousness of the danger should not relieve the defendant of liability except under the doctrines of contributory or comparative negligence.

The doctrine can only be explained as a vestige of the now discredited legal thinking which held that an owner, by accepting a structure, assumed liability for its defects and thereby relieved the architect of any duty to remote users. At least in this context, the latent/patent distinction does make some sense, since the owner should justly be held responsible for obvious, although not for concealed, defects.

The latent/patent distinction was rejected in *Totten v Gruzen*.[80] An engineer had designed a hot-water piping system for a housing project in the late 1940s. In 1961, the three-year-old plaintiff, a tenant, was injured by hot, exposed bedroom piping that was designed in a ladderlike arrangement less than a foot from the floor. The child tried to climb the piping and was burned.

The engineer urged that the defect was patent, and therefore there was no liability. The court stated that the fact that the defect was patent did not preclude recovery, it was just one more factor for the jury to consider.

---

[78] 30 AD2d 249, 292 NYS2d 177 (1968).
[79] 242 So 2d 153 (Fla Dist Ct App 1970).
[80] 52 NJ 202, 245 A2d 1 (1968).

[T]he obviousness of a danger does not necessarily preclude a jury finding of unreasonable risk and negligence; however, it will so preclude if the obviousness to the claimant justifies the conclusion that the condition is not unreasonably dangerous; otherwise it is simply a factor to consider on the issue of negligence of the contractor.[81]

Courts that have held architects liable for patent defects have done so without a discussion of that defense. In *Montijo v Swift*,[82] the plaintiff was injured while descending a stairway in a Greyhound bus depot. The handrail was a few inches short of extending all the way to a point directly above the end of the last step, and a tile wainscot along the wall tended to create an illusion that the stair landing was on a plane actually occupied by the last step. These were patent defects. The court held:

Under the existing status of the law, an architect who plans and supervises construction work, as an independent contractor, is under a duty to exercise ordinary care in the course thereof for the protection of any person who foreseeably and with reasonable certainty may be injured by his failure to do so, even though such injury may occur after his work has been accepted by the person engaging his services.[83]

§9.08 Immunity—Architect as Arbitrator

To American lawyers the doctrine that judges are immune from liability for their decisions is a necessary ingredient in any system of jurisprudence. However, the Babylonians were not so protective of their judges:

If a judge has tried a suit, given a decision, caused a sealed tablet to be executed, and thereafter varies his judgment, they shall convict that judge of varying his judgment and he shall pay twelve fold the claim in that suit; then they shall remove him from his place on the bench of judges in assembly, and he shall not again sit in judgment with the judges.[84]

Immunity of judges is dictated by sound policy considerations. There should be an end to litigation. To allow a disappointed litigant to sue the judge, and

---

[81] *Id* at 210, 245 A2d at 6.

[82] 219 Cal App 2d 351, 33 Cal Rptr 133 (1963).

[83] *Id* at 353, 33 Cal Rptr at 134-35. In various cases the patent defect defense, though seemingly indicated by the facts, is not discussed by the court. Natal v Phoenix Assurance Co, 305 So 2d 438 (La 1974) (glass door); O'Connor v Altus, 123 NJ Super 379, 303 A2d 329 (1973), *affd in part, revd in part*, 67 NJ 106, 335 A2d 545 (1975) (glass door); Coffey v Dormitory Auth, 26 AD2d 1, 270 NYS2d 255 (1966) (glass door).

[84] II Eriver & Miles, The Babylonian Laws (1955).

then appellate justices would truly make litigation endless. The courts would presumably produce more litigation than they settled. Who would aspire to the office of a judge who could be sued for wrong decisions? The very threat of such litigation would tend to distort the judgment of even the hardiest magistrate.

Architects are often called upon to perform functions which, to one degree or another, resemble arbitration. They are called upon to interpret contract documents and to determine whether the performance tendered by the contractor, in effect, amounts to a breach of contract. This is a function judicial in character. The parties to the dispute are the contractor and the owner.

The contractor contends that its performance meets the requirements of the contract documents, and the owner alleges that the performance constitutes a breach of contract. Under the contract documents, it is up to the architect to determine the dispute. The architect's decision may be made final by the contract documents. Or, the decision may be final in the absence of gross error, bad faith, or obvious mistake. In the issuance of payment certificates, the architect is called upon to determine the percentage of project completion, and in connection with certifying final payment, to determine whether the building has been completed in accordance with the contract documents. These are heavy responsibilities; they call for mature judgment; they are at least superficially similar to the duties imposed on a judge or an arbitrator, and the question is whether an architect should receive the same immunity in performing those functions as would a judge or an arbitrator in deciding cases.

§9.09 —Application

One case concerning architect arbitrator immunity has gone so far as to hold that an architect would not be liable for fraud or corruption when exercising functions *judicial in nature*. A contractor filed suit against a city and an engineer, alleging that the engineer improperly interpreted the provisions of the contract and required the contractor to perform work not required by the contract documents. The court noted that by the terms of the contract, the engineer was placed in a position "somewhat analogous to that of an umpire or arbitrator" and that its decisions were "accordingly judicial in nature." In such a situation, the engineer could not be held liable in damages for failure to exercise care or skill in the performance of its functions, and it would not even be liable if the decision were the result of fraud or corruption.[85]

However, in *City of Durham v Reidsville Engineering Co*,[86] the court held that a supervising engineer could be liable for bad faith in the refusal to certify work completed by a contractor, even though the engineer would not be liable for ordinary negligence.

---

[85] Wilder v Crook, 250 Ala 424, 34 So 2d 832 (1948).
[86] 255 NC 98, 120 SE2d 564 (1961).

In *Lundgren v Freeman*,[87] an architect employed by a school district advised the district to terminate the employment of the contractor on a swimming pool job. The contractor filed suit against the architect for wrongful interference with contractual relations, inducing breach of contract, and damage to reputation. The trial court granted summary judgment in favor of the architect. REVERSED. The court pointed out that the architect might have been acting as a quasi-arbitrator, in which case the architect would be immune from suit. On the other hand, the architect might have been acting as the agent of the owner and if so, would be liable only for intentional misconduct.

In *Blecick v School District No 18*,[88] a contractor alleged that the architect refused to issue a final certificate of payment, contending that there were defects in the roof, walls, flooring, and painting. The contractor contended that the school had been built in accordance with the contract documents and alleged that the architect's plans were defective and that the architect wrongfully and arbitrarily refused to issue the final payment certificate.

The trial court granted the architect's motion for dismissal. AFFIRMED. An architect is not liable to a contractor for defects in plans. The architect's duty is to the owner, and the contractor must look to the owner for recovery. Architects are immune from suit for failure to issue payment certificates, since they act in a quasi-judicial capacity or as arbitrators.[89]

In *E.C. Ernst v Manhattan Construction Co*,[90] an electrical subcontractor alleged that the architect refused to approve proper submittals and prepared faulty specifications for an emergency generator system. The architect claimed immunity in performing the duties under the contract since the architect was acting in an arbitral or quasi-judicial function. HELD: the immunity only applies to the limited extent that, in discharging functions under the contract, the architect resembles a judge. When serving in the role of an interpretor of the contract, the architect has a duty to make reasonably expeditious decisions. When action or inaction can be "characterized as delay or failure to decide rather than timely decision making, he loses claim to immunity because he loses his resemblance to a judge."[91]

In *Craviolini v Scholer & Fuller Associated Architects*,[92] the Supreme Court of Arizona REVERSED a trial court dismissal of a contractor's action against an architect. The complaint alleged that the contractor had called the architect's attention to defects in the contract documents, which enraged the architect who

---

[87] 307 F2d 104 (9th Cir 1962).
[88] 2 Ariz App 115, 406 P2d 750 (1965).
[89] *Accord* Chambers v Goldthorpe, 1 KB 624 (1901).
[90] 551 F2d 1026, *opinion modified*, 559 F2d 268 (5th Cir 1977).
[91] *Id* 1032.
[92] 89 Ariz 24, 357 P2d 611 (1960).

thereafter required the contractor to cover up blunders of the architect, delayed inspections, substituted materials, interfered with subcontractors, withheld funds, vilified the contractor to the bonding company, and intentionally interfered with the contractual relations between the contractor and the owner. The court stated that the dispute here was between the contractor and the architect, not the contractor and the owner. Therefore, the architect could not have been acting as an arbitrator. The architect was not immune from suit merely because it was an architect.

Although architects are sometimes protected by the immunity of an arbitrator, their decisions cannot be enforced as if they were arbitration awards. In *Harry Skolnick & Sons v Heyman*,[93] the architect decided that the contractor was entitled to be paid $247,500 by the owner on two shopping center projects. The contractor sought to confirm the architect's decision as if it were an arbitration award under Conn Gen Stats §52-417. HELD: although no particular form of words is required to form an agreement to arbitrate disputes, the intent of the parties that arbitration be the exclusive method for settling disputes must be clearly manifested. Here, the trial court found that the parties merely intended for the architect's determination to constitute a condition precedent to the contractor's right of payment. However, the final resolution of the contractor's claim for payment was in the jurisdiction of the courts.

In *Donnelly Construction Co v Oberg, Hunt & Gilleland*,[94] a contractor alleged that the architect negligently prepared plans and specifications for an owner, causing foreseeable economic damage to the contractor. The architect asserted its status of a quasi-judge as a defense. HELD: the architect's status as a judge or an arbitrator does not protect against claims relating to design.

§9.10 —Criticism

In an early case, *Corey v Eastman*,[95] Justice Holmes showed some discomfort with the concept of English common law that an architect enjoyed the immunity of an arbitrator. He commented that although the immunity might still prevail where the architect is called upon to issue a payment certificate, an architect might still be liable for false statements made to an owner that might wrongfully prevent the contractor from receiving payment for the work. The thinking of Justice Holmes seemed to be that the quasi-immunity of an arbitrator should be restricted to the actual issuance, or nonissuance, of payment certificates.

---

[93] 7 Conn App 175, 508 A2d 64, *cert denied*, 200 Conn 803, 510 A2d 191 (1986).
[94] 139 Ariz 184, 677 P2d 1292 (1984).
[95] 166 Mass 279, 44 NE 217 (1896).

It is often difficult to distinguish between arbitral actions and those actions taken by an architect as an advocate of the owner, or for the protection of the architect. The dictum of *Wilder v Crook*[96] is clearly incorrect: there is no sound policy to support the proposition that an architect should be immune from liability for fraud in the issuance of a payment certificate. The social policy behind the doctrine of judicial immunity is to promote courageous impartiality, not to shield corruption.

It also seems doubtful that the social policy that there must be an end to litigation, which argues for the immunity of judges, applies with equal force to the situation of the architect. To grant an architect immunity from liability is not just to deny a party its second day in court, and then its third, fourth, fifth, and sixth; it is to close the doors on the first day, since the effect is to make the architect's decision final—not subject to review by any court.

The final policy supporting the doctrine of judicial immunity serves the need for judicial manpower. Who would want to be a judge if he or she could be sued by every dissatisfied litigant? However, it can never be admitted that a party should be placed beyond the law merely to avoid the possibility of suit. This denies justice to the injured party for the convenience of the wrongdoer.

The doctrine of judicial immunity is at least ameliorated by the availability of appeal: if the trial judge is not induced to be careful by the fear of litigation, control is nevertheless asserted by the prospect of reversal on appeal. The appellate court can do justice to a party who is injured by a wrong decision.

To extend the doctrine of immunity to an architect is not only to prevent the possibility of appeal, but also to frustrate the application of law in the first instance. Society has no trouble producing enough physicians, lawyers, and architects despite the threat of malpractice suits. It would seem that malpractice in the issuance of a payment certificate, or in the interpretation of contract documents, should be as justiciable as any other kind of malpractice.[97]

An architect should not be immune from liability for either negligently or willfully issuing or refusing to issue a payment certificate, or for negligent or intentional misinterpretation of contract documents. The doctrine of immunity has been ignored in many cases, without visible detrimental social results. The architect is more likely to make courageously correct decisions if those decisions can be reviewed by a court than if they are sanctified by the doctrine of immunity.

---

[96] 250 Ala 424, 34 So 2d 832 (1948).

[97] Indeed, many cases have held that an architect can be liable for negligent issuance of a payment certificate. *See, e.g.*, Bump v McGrannahan, 61 Ind App 136, 111 NE 640 (1916); Westerhold v Carroll, 419 SW2d 73 (Mo 1967) (contractor's surety alleged architect negligently certified payments for $23,000 in excess of the value of work performed); Unity Sheet Metal Works v Farrell Lines, 101 NYS2d 1000 (Sup Ct 1950) (engineers "maliciously, fraudulently and with intent to injure subcontractor" refused to certify payment); Pierson v Tyndall, 28 SW 232 (Tex Civ App 1894).

§9.11 No Duty

As previously noted,[98] the doctrine that an architect is not liable to the remote user of a structure designed and supervised by the architect unless the user is in privity of contract with the architect is, in essence, a rule that the architect simply has no duty to remote users. The rubric *privity of contract* developed, seemingly, as a screen to the assertion of *no duty*. Likewise, the defense that an architect is not liable for injury caused by a defect in a structure after its completion and acceptance by the owner is simply another way of saying that the architect is under no duty to a remote user.

In *Blecick v School District No 18*,[99] an architect refused to issue a final payment certificate, claiming that the flooring, walls, painting, and roof were defective. The contractor alleged that if the building was defective, the defect was in the plans, not in the construction. The court held that an architect's obligation is to the owner, and the architect is under no duty to the contractor to supply plans without defects. The bald statement that an architect is under no duty to a contractor is contradicted by many cases.[100]

The effect of the *no duty* analysis is to absolve an architect from liability. In *Olsen v Chase Manhattan Bank*,[101] the court held that an architect was under no duty to protect a job site worker. The worker was injured when struck by a heavy drill that fell from the vicinity of a platform supporting vibrating air compressors. Evidence indicated that the architect's sole function as a supervisor was to insure that the project would be performed in accordance with the contract and that the permanent structure would meet applicable safety standards. HELD: the architect was under no duty to see to it that temporary platforms used by the contractor during construction would be free from danger.

Similarly, in *Reber v Chandler High School District No 202*,[102] the court held that an architect is under no duty to control the operations of a contractor so as to protect workers from injury. The architect was given general supervision of the erection of a school gymnasium. The contract documents did not specify any method or sequence for the erection of steel components. The method was left to the discretion of the contractor. The roof was designed to be supported by six steel arches, which collapsed during construction, injuring employees of the general contractor.

The court held that an architect is liable only if the contract reserves in the architect a right to control the manner in which the details of the work are

---

[98] *See* §9.02.
[99] 2 Ariz App 115, 406 P2d 750 (1965).
[100] *See* **app A**.
[101] 9 NY2d 829, 175 NE2d 350, 215 NYS2d 773 (1961).
[102] 13 Ariz App 133, 474 P2d 852 (1970).

performed. The architect's contract with the school district provided for "general supervision to guard the Owner against defects and deficiencies in the work." This was not sufficient to support a finding that the architect was under any duty to control the manner or method of the contractor's work. An Arizona statute,[103] required the erection of public works under "direct supervision of a registered architect, engineer." The statute did not impose on the architect a duty to supervise the procedures and techniques used by the contractor. The purpose of the statute was to insure that the plans and specifications were followed, not to require the architect to supervise the methods of construction. Since no duty was imposed on the architect either by contract or by statute, judgment for defendant was AFFIRMED.

In *Kaltenbrun v City of Port Washington*,[104] a subcontractor's employee was injured when a cliff on a construction site gave away. A contract between the city and the general contractor provided that the contractor was responsible for the methods used to complete the work, and for implementing all safety precautions associated with the work. The employee sued the architect, asserting a duty to research and design safety measures for the project. (The employee also filed suit against the city and general contractor.) HELD: the court was not satisfied that there existed any common law duty that required a supervising architect to ensure construction site safety, or that there was any reason to create such a duty.

In *Parent v Stone & Webster Engineering Corp*,[105] an electrician was injured while testing voltage drops in a panel. Unknown to the electrician, the panel was energized by 2,300 volts. An arc-over caused severe burns. The electrician sued the company that had installed the electrical distribution panel and, also, later served as project manager. HELD: (1) Alleged negligence in failing to label the panel was barred by the six-year statute of repose. (2) The electrician failed to demonstrate that the project manager owed a duty of care to the electrician.

An architect has no duty to notify workers employed by contractor or subcontractors on a job site of hazardous conditions.[106] Here, the architect's only duty was to make periodic visits to the site to ensure that work was proceeding in accordance with the contract documents. The contract imposed no safety responsibilities on the architect.

---

[103] Ariz Rev Stat Ann §32-142 (1976).

[104] 156 Wis 2d 634, 457 NW2d 527 (1990). *See also* Waggoner v W&W Steel Co, 657 P2d 147 (Okla 1982) (construction contracts required the contractor to supervise the project and employ reasonable safety procedures. Workers were injured as a result of unsafe procedures. HELD: the architect was not liable).

[105] 408 Mass 108, 556 NE2d 1009 (1990).

[106] Young v Eastern Engg & Elevator Co, 381 Pa Super 428, 554 A2d 77, *appeal denied*, 524 Pa 611, 569 A2d 1369 (1989).

In *Tittle v Giattina, Fisher & Co Architects, Inc*, the estate of a prisoner who had committed suicide alleged the architect negligently designed jail facilities, proximately causing death. HELD: an architect has no duty to design a jail in such a manner as to prevent an inmate from committing suicide.[107]

In *MacIntyre v Green's Pool Service, Inc*,[108] the general contractor on a residential construction project left the job incomplete, leaving the owner to cope with mechanics lien claims of subcontractors and suppliers. The owner filed a third-party claim against the architect, alleging negligence in the selection of the general contractor and failure to advise as to procedures for making progress payments. Plaintiff also alleged that the architect should have advised it as to filing a notice of commencement of the project. (Filing this notice would have helped protect the owner's title against mechanics lien claims.) Judgment for defendant was AFFIRMED. The owner failed to establish a duty on the part of the architect with respect to any of the alleged negligent omissions. There was no evidence that any of these functions "fall within the duties ordinarily assumed or placed upon an architect by custom and practice."[109]

The *no duty* defense was successfully employed by an engineer in *Alexander v State Through Department of Highways*.[110] A worker was burned when the bulldozer he was operating to clear a right-of-way for road construction struck a submerged butane tank. Under contract with the state, the defendant engineer had agreed to prepare plans and specifications and locate all *existing utilities*. The butane tank was not shown on the profile sheets of the area prepared by the engineer. Judgment for the engineer was AFFIRMED. A single butane tank does not qualify as a *utility*. Moreover, the tank was not discernible by ordinary visual observation. Therefore, there was no breach of any duty owed by the engineer to the worker.

An engineer was similarly absolved of liability in *Conti v Pettibone Cos*,[111] when a construction worker was hit on the head by a bucket filled with sand bags being lifted by a crane. Summary judgment in favor of the inspecting engineer was AFFIRMED.

> It is well established that the law of New York does not impose liability upon an engineer who is engaged to assure compliance with construction plans and specifications for an injury sustained by a worker at a construction site unless active malfeasance exists or such liability is

---

[107] 597 So 2d 679 (Ala 1992).
[108] 347 So 2d 1081 (Fla Dist Ct App 1977).
[109] *Id* 1083.
[110] 347 So 2d 1249 (La Ct App), *writ denied*, 350 So 2d 1224 (La 1977).
[111] 111 Misc 2d 772, 445 NYS2d 943 (Sup Ct 1981).

imposed by clear contractual provisions, creating an obligation explicitly running to and for the benefit of workers.[112]

The contract imposed on the inspecting engineer only the duty of insuring that the project was built in compliance with construction plans and documents; the engineer did not assume the duty of assuring worker safety at the site.

In *Harbor Mechanical, Inc v Arizona Electrical Power Co-op, Inc*,[113] the court stated that an engineering firm that designed an electrical generating station had no duty to the contractor employed to perform certain phases of the work absent specific contract language. Therefore, alleged negligent performance of the contract with the owner did not provide the contractor with a cause of action for *negligence*. However, the contractor could have stated a cause of action for *negligent misrepresentation*.

In *Barnes v Rakow*,[114] plaintiff employed a surveyor to survey three separate, 3-acre parcels from a larger parcel that contained approximately 30 acres. Relying on an earlier survey, the surveyor stated that the remainder of the main parcel, after subtracting the 9 acres, was approximately 21 acres. The surveyor failed to discover an error in the previous survey. In fact, the entire parcel was approximately 27 acres instead of 30 acres. The surveyor's fee was about $200 for each survey rather than the $2,000 that a complete survey of the entire parcel would have cost. Plaintiff did not warn the surveyor of any suspected defects in the earlier survey, and plaintiff did not employ the surveyor specifically to verify the earlier survey. HELD: defendant had no duty to verify the accuracy of the master survey.

In *Reiman Construction Co v Jerry Hiller Co*,[115] an engineer prepared a soil report disclosing that the soil possessed a high swell potential and suggested in the report that the building be designed to accommodate this condition, including drains to carry water away from the building. The final specifications, however, were not prepared by the soil engineer. Those specifications permitted drains to deposit water near the building. The trial court dismissed the claim against the soil engineer. AFFIRMED. The engineer's report was accurate. It was under no duty to specify how the building should be designed in order to accommodate the soil problems: that was the job of the architect and the structural engineer.

In *Jewish Board of Guardians v Grumman Allied Instruments, Inc*,[116] a subcontractor delivered modular school building units to a job site on Friday. The units were to be assembled the following Monday. The subcontractor

---

[112] *Id* at 774-75, 445 NYS2d at 945.
[113] 496 F Supp 681 (D Ariz 1980).
[114] 78 Ill App 3d 404, 396 NE2d 1168 (1979).
[115] 709 P2d 1271 (Wyo 1985).
[116] 62 NY2d 684, 465 NE2d 42, 476 NYS2d 535 (1984).

covered the units with Visqueen. A weekend storm nevertheless damaged the modules. The owner alleged that the architect was negligent for not instructing the subcontractor to properly protect the units. HELD: there was a clear division of duties among the parties; the architect had no duty to see that the subcontractor properly protected the units.

In *Travelers Indemnity Co v Ewing, Cole, Erdman & Eubank*,[117] a contractor was employed to prefabricate modular units in its factory. The units were to be delivered to Rutgers University and fabricated into buildings. The contractor commenced work and completed much of the fabrication within its own factory. Before the modules were delivered to the job site, the contractor filed a petition in bankruptcy and the trustee in bankruptcy successfully laid claim to possession of the modules at the plant. The contractor's surety, Travelers, employed another contractor to complete the project and, as subrogee of the owner, filed an action against the architect. Travelers contended that the architect should have warned the university of the danger that the contractor would become bankrupt and should have recommended field warehousing or bonded warehousing as desirable procedures. HELD: the university was not a helpless and unsophisticated consumer. An architect has no duty to warn a sophisticated owner and its legal counsel about matters that are beyond the scope of its professional responsibilities.

Defense Rejected

The *no duty* defense was rejected in *Cutlip v Lucky Stores, Inc*,[118] where a steel worker was killed when a concrete pier supporting steel beams collapsed. The architect had ordered the pier when it was discovered that the beams were short. The collapse may have been because the concrete was poured in freezing weather or because the steel was erected without safety cables. The architect denied that it had any duty to the steel worker. However, the court held that the supervisory authority of the architect imposed a duty to perceive the danger to the worker caused by negligent construction.

Likewise, in *Laukkanen v Jewel Tea Co*,[119] an engineer contended that it had no duty to members of the general public. The plaintiff, upon entering a building, was injured when a piling designed by defendant fell during a windstorm. The engineer had failed to specify the type of concrete block to be used. The builder had selected a lightweight aggregate block which failed to withstand the rigors of the windstorm. HELD: an engineer is liable for negligent conduct that proximately causes foreseeable injury to a member of the public.

---

[117] 711 F2d 14 (3d Cir 1983), *cert denied*, 464 US 1041 (1984).
[118] 22 Md App 673, 325 A2d 432 (1974).
[119] 78 Ill App 2d 153, 222 NE2d 584 (1966).

§9.12 Architect No Insurer

It is sometimes said that an architect is no insurer; it does not guarantee satisfactory results. This conception is not particularly helpful in determining whether an architect should be liable in a given situation; it is a makeweight, a judicial flourish, an embellishment to lend an appearance of symmetry to an opinion that might otherwise seem to stand on one leg.

> The law provides that absent a special agreement an architect does not imply or guarantee a perfect plan.... This court has held that the responsibility of an architect does not differ from that of a lawyer or a physician. When he possesses the requisite skill and knowledge, and in the exercise thereof has used his best judgment, he has done all the law requires. The architect is not a warrantor of his plans and specifications. The result may show a mistake or defect, although he may have exercised the reasonable skill required.[120]

In *Surf Realty Corp v Standing*,[121] an architect devised a complicated sliding roof panel for a ballroom. The steel roof was designed to slide in cantilevered beam tracks 120 feet above the floor. The court held that the architect was not responsible, even though the roof did not work. An architect must possess and exercise the care and skill of those of ordinary competence in the profession but, in the absence of a special agreement, does not guarantee a perfect result.[122]

In *Ressler v Nielsen*,[123] the specifications called for water pipes to be installed in the ventilating system. This design caused the pipes to freeze and burst. Steam pipes laid under a cement floor in the basement became leaky and required replacement. Radiators were placed near a plate glass window, causing it to break. HELD: the architect is not a guarantor of its plans and specifications. The architect is liable only for failure to exercise reasonable care and skill.[124]

In *Three Affiliated Tribes of the Fort Berthold Reservation v Wold Engineering PC*,[125] an engineer designed a *wet* water system which froze. The engineer then redesigned the system as *dry*, but it froze again. HELD: the engineer did not guarantee a perfect plan or that satisfactory results would occur, but only

---

[120] Lukowski v Vecta Educ Corp, 401 NE2d 781, 786 (Ind Ct App 1980).

[121] 195 Va 431, 78 SE2d 901 (1953).

[122] *Accord* Maloney v Oak Builders, Inc, 224 So 2d 161 (La Ct App 1969), *revd in part*, 256 La 85, 235 So 2d 386 (1970).

[123] 76 NW2d 157 (ND 1956).

[124] *See also* 530 East 89 Corp v Unger, 54 AD2d 848, 388 NYS2d 284 (1976), *affd*, 43 NY2d 776, 373 NE2d 276, 402 NYS2d 382 (1977) (architects did not guarantee that their plans would receive approval of the city building department).

[125] 419 NW2d 920 (ND 1988).

238 DEFENSES

promised that it would exercise that degree of skill and care exercised according to the standards of the profession. The design of the system met professional standards (there was evidence that the damage was caused by vandalism and negligent maintenance by the owner).

In *Cowles v City of Minneapolis*,[126] the architect failed to detect that the general contractor neglected to drive pilings deep enough to support a bridge abutment. Each pile was designed to carry 15 tons, but some were driven that would support only 7 to 13 tons. The architect was required by the contract documents to supervise and inspect the work. It visited the job two or three times a day and requested that records be kept of the driving of all of the piles. Although it was not present when the piles in question were driven, it asked the workers how they had been driven and was assured by them that they had been driven to the required depth. These same workers had been found reliable by the architect in the past. HELD: the architect's duty was to exercise ordinary care, skill, and diligence under the circumstances, but it was not an insurer that the contractor would perform properly in all respects. The evidence indicated that the architect performed the duties with due care.

In *White v Pallay*,[127] a building began to settle after it was constructed, and it was necessary to shore up the walls using jack screws at an expense of $1,700. Judgment on a verdict for the architect was AFFIRMED. The architect must act with reasonable diligence to perform its duties. The jury found that the architect met the standard of care and, therefore, was not liable even though the results of the work were unsatisfactory.

In *Gagne v Bertran*,[128] a soil tester was employed on an hourly basis to drill test holes and advise whether two lots which the client intended to purchase contained any significant amount of fill. The driller made the tests and reported no significant amount of fill, but when construction commenced, it was determined that the lots contained four to six feet of fill. As a result, additional expense was incurred to install the foundations. Justice Traynor stated that the defendant was supplying services, not insurance. Therefore, the measure of damages was not the additional cost of the foundations, but the difference between the amount paid for the lots in reliance on the report, and their market value at that time.[129]

In *United States v Peachy*,[130] an architect designed a retaining wall to support an excavation next to a stone sidewalk owned by the federal government. The retaining wall collapsed, damaging a sidewalk. HELD: the architect's employer was not liable because the architect was not negligent. Even though the decision

---

[126] 128 Minn 452, 151 NW 184 (1915).
[127] 119 Or 97, 247 P 316 (1926).
[128] 43 Cal 2d 481, 275 P2d 15 (1954).
[129] *Accord* Swett v Gribaldo, Jones & Assocs, 40 Cal App 3d 573, 115 Cal Rptr 99 (1974).
[130] 36 F 160 (D Ohio 1888).

as to the type and size of wall might have been defective, the architect had consulted with other architects and examined similar projects in other parts of the city, and its conduct was not negligent.[131]

The *no insurer* defense is more apposite to the question of damages than it is to the issue of liability. On the issue of liability, the question is not whether the architect was an insurer, it is whether it exercised sufficient professional skill.

§9.13 No Causation

The malpractice of an architect, of course, does not spell liability in the absence of causation. This principle was misapplied in *Hutchings v Harry*,[132] where the minor plaintiff, a social guest, was injured after running into a sliding glass door. The plaintiff filed an action against the architect who designed the home, alleging that the defendant held itself out as skilled and knowledgeable; that it designed the home and specified the materials for the home; that it was careless in that the design did not provide for any decals or markings on the sliding door; and furthermore, that it did not specify the use of tempered or breakaway glass. The trial court dismissed the complaint. AFFIRMED. The complaint was fatally defective: "there was no causal connection between the duty owed the public and the injury."[133] The court also asserted that lack of privity was a defense to the action, since the plaintiff had failed to allege a latent defect which the architect negligently failed to discover.

In *Mai Kai, Inc v Colucci*,[134] a patron in a restaurant was injured when a metal counterweight fell from a ceiling fan. The counterweight became dislodged because of defective welding on the by the metal fabricator who installed the device. The imperfection was not apparent to inspection. The plaintiff filed an action against the architect who had designed the restaurant, including the fan. HELD: the defective weld was not discoverable by a reasonable inspection. If the weld had been proper, the counterweight would not have fallen. Since the architect had no reason to know of the defective weld, the architect's conduct was not the proximate cause of the plaintiff's injuries.

---

[131] "An engineer is not an insurer of a project against defects nor does he guarantee that he will be able to complete it to perfection. He is required to exercise the care . . . expected of a member of his profession." Morrison-Maierle, Inc v Selsco, 186 Mont 180, 606 P2d 1085, 1088 (1980) (because of time constraints imposed by the owner, the engineers were forced to purchase substandard valves). *Accord* Breiner v C&P Home Builders, Inc, 536 F2d 27 (3d Cir 1976) (engineer no insurer that subdivision plan would not cause diversion of surface waters to property of neighboring strawberry groves).

[132] 242 So 2d 153 (Fla Dist Ct App 1970).

[133] *Id* 154.

[134] 205 So 2d 291 (Fla 1967).

In *Minor v Zidell Trust*,[135] a motorist lapsed into unconsciousness while parking on the second level of a garage. The car surged forward over a curb, broke through a three-foot brick wall, and landed on the street below. The court held that summary judgment was properly awarded to the architect defendants because plaintiff had failed to prove that the alleged negligence of defendants was the proximate cause of the plaintiff's injury. The three requirements for a *supervening cause* were met: (1) independence from the original act, (2) adequacy in and of itself to bring about the result, and (3) not a reasonably foreseeable event. The motorist's lapse into unconsciousness, coupled with the ensuing loss of control, was so "unusual and extraordinary an event as to merit recognition as unforeseeable in law."[136]

In a North Carolina case, the plaintiff owner of a shopping center complex under construction became concerned about the financial stability of a contractor. Beginning in June, defendant architects were required to submit progress reports whenever a disbursement was made to the contractor. These reports were issued until the construction company abandoned the project in October 1970. All of the progress reports concluded that the work was proceeding in a satisfactory manner and on schedule. The owner sued the architect for increased costs caused by the contractor's default. The architect's motion for a directed verdict was granted. AFFIRMED. Even assuming that the architects were negligent in making the progress reports, it was not shown that this negligence was the proximate cause of any damage sustained by the plaintiff. Even if the owner had been fully and accurately informed of the status of the project, there was no evidence that the owner could have taken action to decrease the eventual total cost of the project or to advance the ultimate opening date of the shopping center. Thus, the damage was caused by the default of the contractor, not by the allegedly negligent preparation of the progress reports.[137]

In *Podraza v H.H. Hall Construction Co*,[138] a worker was injured while pulling an electrical wire from under the ground. As the worker strained at the wire, it came loose, causing the worker to fall backwards onto a piece of conduit. Judgment on a verdict for plaintiff was REVERSED. The fact that the underground wire may have run through the construction site in an unsafe manner did not produce the injury. At best, it furnished no more than a condition upon which the plaintiff's independent negligent actions resulted in injury. Therefore, the defendant architect's conduct was not the proximate cause of the plaintiff's injury.

---

[135] 618 P2d 392 (Okla 1980).

[136] *Id* 394.

[137] People's Center, Inc v Anderson, 32 NC App 746, 233 SE2d 694 (1977). *See also* 530 East 89 Corp v Unger, 43 NY2d 776, 373 NE2d 276, 402 NYS2d 382 (1977) (expert testimony failed to establish that delay by the architect was proximate cause of plaintiff's injury).

[138] 50 Ill App 3d 643, 365 NE2d 944 (1977).

In *Belgum v Mitsuo Kawamoto & Associates*,[139] a worker filed an action against an architect for damages sustained in a fall from a scaffold. The court held that the worker failed to establish proximate cause. The contract provided that the architect had no control over subcontractors or persons performing the work and was not responsible for the failure of any of them to carry out the work in accordance with the contract documents. The "architectural technician," who had been informed by job site personnel that the scaffold was shaky, substandard, deficient, and without "safety ends," did not inquire as to whether the scaffold violated safety standards, since it did not consider itself qualified to advise on safety matters.[140] HELD: if the architect was negligent, that negligence was not the proximate cause of the injury. The others had full control of the job site, and such control was an *efficient intervening cause*.

In *Hansen v Ruby Construction Co*,[141] a worker recanted deposition testimony of tripping on rubber bumper strips and falling from a loading dock. After revisiting the accident site, the worker claimed to have actually tripped on metal plates. Summary judgment for the architect was AFFIRMED on the ground that the architect had no role in the design or construction of the rubber bumper strips. Since there were no eyewitnesses to the accident, the worker was bound by the original unequivocal testimony.[142]

An engineer defended on the ground of a lack of causation in *Hutcheson v Eastern Engineering Co*.[143] The engineer had prepared contract documents that called for removable guardrails around open hatches to be used as elevator shafts. Decedent worker, while attempting to pull loose a heavy load of asbestos siding, walked between the load and the elevator shaft from which the guardrail had been removed. A signal from a worker on another floor caused the load to swing and knock the decedent into the shaft. The engineer had no control over the method of construction employed by the subcontractor, and the engineer did not remove the guardrails. Summary judgment for the defendant was AFFIRMED. The defendant had no control over the methods of construction.

In *Montgomery Industries International, Inc v Southern Baptist Hospital, Inc*,[144] the court found the essential ingredient of proximate cause lacking where a subcontractor deviated from the plans and specifications and fire ensued. "There is nothing in *Moyer*, or for that matter any of the cases relied upon by appellant, which holds that a subcontractor may unilaterally alter the architect's plans and sue the architect when the resulting construction becomes deficient."

---

[139] 236 Neb 127, 459 NW2d 226 (1990).

[140] *Id* at 129, 459 NW2d at 228.

[141] 155 Ill App 3d 475, 508 NE2d 301 (1987).

[142] *See* Three Affiliated Tribes of the Fort Berthold Reservation v Wold Engg PC, 419 NW2d 920 (ND 1988) *and* §9.12.

[143] 132 Ga App 885, 209 SE2d 680 (1974).

[144] 362 So 2d 145, 146 (Fla Dist Ct App 1978).

A judgment of $713 was entered against a surveyor for trespass.[145] The evidence showed that the surveyor, running a boundary line, probably stepped on the plaintiff's property. There were no markers to show where the boundary might be located, and no actual damage was done. The judgement was REVERSED. When a trespass is without rudeness, wantoness, or recklessness, and is not accomplished in an insulting manner, only nominal damages may be awarded against a surveyor.

§9.14 Assumption of the Risk

The owner of a construction project makes many decisions in the analysis of cost-benefit ratio analysis. Sometimes an owner trades quality for cost. In doing so, the owner may *assume the risk* of a defective end product. In *Pittman Construction Co v City of New Orleans*,[146] an engineer designed a floating slab foundation despite warnings from the contractor that there was a serious danger of settlement. The city chose to take the chance of using floating slabs, rather than supported slabs, in order to save money. HELD: the city assumed the risk of settlement. Neither the contractor nor the engineer was liable for damage.

In *Henry v Britt*,[147] the court rejected the affirmative defense of assumption of the risk asserted against an 11-year-old boy who was drowned when his arm became lodged in a swimming pool drain. This defense required proof that the decedent had actual knowledge of the condition that created the peril. There was no evidence that the child knew of the dangerous suction created by an uncovered swimming pool drain. There was also a lack of evidence that the decedent, with knowledge and appreciation of the danger, voluntarily assumed it.

Under the Colorado Comparative Negligence Statute,[148] it is improper to instruct a jury on assumption of the risk, since the fact that a plaintiff knowingly encountered a risk is merely a factor for the jury to consider in apportioning the negligence of the parties. Assumption of the risk is not a complete bar to a plaintiff's recovery.[149]

§9.15 Contributory Negligence

The courts of appeal do not often consider the subject of contributory negligence in connection with determining cases of the malpractice of architects.

---

[145] Johnson v Martin, 423 So 2d 868 (Ala Civ App 1982).

[146] 178 So 2d 312 (La Ct App), *appeal denied* 248 La 434, 179 So 2d 274 (1965).

[147] 220 So 2d 917 (Fla Dist Ct App), *cert denied*, 229 So 2d 867 (Fla 1969).

[148] Colo Rev Stat §13-21-111 (1973).

[149] Loup-Miller v Brauer & Assocs Rocky Mountain, Inc, 40 Colo App 67, 572 P2d 845 (1977).

There is no doubt of the availability of the defense in a proper case, but it is rarely the subject of judicial exposition, for several reasons. An architect is by definition an expert. Since an architect is employed for special skill and knowledge, the argument that the client should detect errors comes with very poor grace.

An architect's liability may be founded upon failure to comply with a safety regulation designed to protect workers from the consequences of their own carelessness. However, an Illinois court concluded that where both a safe way and a dangerous way are available to perform a job, and a worker selects the dangerous way, contributory negligence bars recovery as a matter of law.[150]

In *Benenato v McDougall*,[151] the court asserted that an owner was barred by contributory negligence, and it seemed that the owner also failed to discharge the duty to minimize damages. The budget for a remodeling project was $7,000; the cost exceeded $16,000. However, the owner entered into a cost-plus contract under circumstances that made it obvious that the cost would probably exceed the budget. The court stated that the negligence of the architects was not the proximate cause of the injury, since the owner had recklessly proceeded with the project after the owner knew it would probably cost more than the budgeted amount.[152]

In *Peyronnin Construction Co v Weiss*,[153] a prime contractor filed suit against engineers employed by a subcontractor to estimate the quantity of excavation required. The engineer underestimated, as a result of which the subcontractor defaulted. However, the court pointed out that the prime contractor was contributorily negligent, since it accepted the low subcontractor bid of $16,100 when the next low bid was $68,000. Such a wide discrepancy in the bids should have put the contractor on notice that something was wrong with the low bid.

In *New Orleans Unity Society of Practical Christianity v Standard Roofing Co*,[154] a roofing subcontractor claimed that an architect had negligently specified unsuitable material (butyl rubber) as a result of which the roof leaked, and the owner called upon the subcontractor for repairs. The court stated that although the owner might have had a good case against the architect, the subcontractor did not, since the subcontractor participated in inducing the architect to specify the faulty material in the first place.

In *Schiltz v Cullen-Schiltz & Associates*,[155] the court recognized contributory negligence as a defense, but a jury verdict in favor of the plaintiff was,

---

[150] Podraza v H.H. Hall Constr Co, 50 Ill App 3d 643, 365 NE2d 944 (1977).

[151] 166 Cal 405, 137 P 8 (1913).

[152] *See also* Paxton v Alameda County, 119 Cal App 2d 393, 259 P2d 934 (1953) (contributory negligence as a defense to an architect malpractice case recognized).

[153] 137 Ind App 417, 208 NE2d 489 (1965).

[154] 224 So 2d 60 (La Ct App), *rehg denied*, 254 La 811, 227 So 2d 146 (1969).

[155] 228 NW2d 10 (Iowa 1975).

nevertheless, AFFIRMED. An engineer designed a sewer project including aeration tanks. During construction a severe cloudburst caused water to enter the project site, floating the tanks. The contractor filed suit against the engineer, alleging that the engineer failed to design a sufficient dike to protect the tanks. The engineer alleged that the contractor was contributorily negligent in failing to properly investigate the site, delaying completion of the project, and failing to properly inspect and supervise the project. Judgment on a verdict for plaintiff was AFFIRMED. It was supported by substantial evidence.[156] Without evidence to support it, however, contributory negligence should be stricken as an affirmative defense.[157]

In *Bell v Jones*,[158] the court found a surveyor negligent for failing to ascertain the use to which an architect intended to put a survey, and negligent in certifying that it had carefully surveyed the property when it had not actually done so. The architect, however, was contributorily negligent in failing to advise the surveyor of the intended use of the survey.

§9.16 Comparative Negligence

An examination of the doctrine of comparative negligence occasions a consideration of the multiparty quality so characteristic of construction litigation. The fundamental problem in many construction liability cases is: how should the liability be divided among the project participants? The discussion of strict liability[159] suggests that an emerging social policy is to compensate the injured by spreading the risk among those defendants who in turn can spread the risk among consumers. Although the doctrine of strict liability may not, indeed, be applied to architects, the social policy that led to its application to manufacturers and builders does not disappear just because the defendant is an architect. The social policy served by the doctrine of strict liability is also served by the doctrine of comparative negligence.

Comparative negligence is usually viewed as a doctrine that allocates fault between a plaintiff and a defendant with more precision than the doctrine of contributory negligence. Damages are assessed in the same proportion as fault. One may ask why damages should be proportional to fault. Is there a rational connection between the two elements?

It has been recognized, forever it seems, that damages are related to fault. Zero fault spells zero damages except in cases of nondelegable duty, ultrahazardous activity, and strict liability. Ordinary fault spells compensatory damages.

---

[156] *See also* Pacific Form Corp v Burgstahler, 263 Or 266, 501 P2d 308 (1972).
[157] *See* Henry v Britt, 220 So 2d 917 (Fla Dist Ct App), *cert denied*, 229 So 2d 867 (Fla 1969).
[158] 523 A2d 982 (DC 1986).
[159] *See* ch 6.

Egregious fault spells compensatory damages plus punitive damages. The concept that damages should be graded according to degree of fault is not confined ot the doctrine of comparative negligence. (The doctrine of comparative negligence has been applied by admiralty courts for centuries.) If a comparison to the principles of criminal law is admissible, it is immediately apparent that the severity of the penalty is directly proportional to the gravity of the crime. It seems to be universally accepted, at all times and places, that the punishment should fit the crime.

The doctrine of contributory negligence violates the principle that the punishment should fit the crime. It will be answered that the office of tort law is to render compensatory damages, not punish wrongdoing. However, the doctrine of contributory negligence can be seen as an exception to the general rule of compensatory damages, since the effect seems to be to deny to a contributorily negligent plaintiff any compensation, no matter how mild its fault. A denial of compensation proportionate to fault would be compensatory in nature, and the margin between proportionate denial and total loss of damages partakes of the nature of punishment.

The doctrine of comparative negligence is especially well suited to the disposition of multiple party tort cases because the doctrine is available to render precise justice not just between the plaintiff and the defendant, but also between all defendants whose negligence contributed to the injury. Early judges employed draconian, although perhaps commendable, simplicity. The doctrine of contributory negligence stated that it would be too complicated to try to allocate fault; therefore, the slightest fault destroyed the plaintiff's case. Likewise, *Winterbottom v Wright*[160] held that if a remote consumer had the right to recover damages from a manufacturer, it would produce too many lawsuits for the judges to handle. The rule that there could be no contribution among joint tortfeasors is also a rule of simplicity: if the defendants were negligent and therefore liable to the plaintiff, why should the judges concern themselves with the allocation of damages among those who contributed to the loss?

The history of jurisprudence shows that every parent doctrine of simplicity engenders generations of complexities. Thus, the doctrine that the courts would not allocate damages among joint tortfeasors was the parent of the intricate doctrines of implied indemnity under which a passively negligent tortfeasor could obtain common law indemnity from one who was actively negligent. Meanwhile, those in a position to do so avoided the rule against contribution between joint tortfeasors by contractual indemnity agreements.

The doctrine of contributory negligence played its part in the adoption of the workers' compensation laws and the evolution of the rule that contributory

---

[160] 10 M&W 109, 152 Eng Rep 402 (1842).

negligence is no defense to willful misconduct. In law, simplicity is the parent of complexity.

The doctrine of comparative negligence, discarded by the early judges as too complicated, turns out to be a simpler and perhaps more precisely just method for allocation of fault among multiple defendants than the application of principles of common law indemnity or the application of the contribution statutes in those states where they have been adopted. For one thing, indemnity and contribution may nourish two lawsuits, while the comparative negligence doctrine can be applied in the original liability action.

Apportionment and Comparative Negligence

In states which have adopted the doctrine of comparative negligence, it seems that implied indemnity will remain in effect, although it will be less important. In order to respect the common law rule against contribution between joint tortfeasors, some courts developed a rule which states that any active, primary negligence, even though slight, prevents a party from obtaining indemnity from a joint tortfeasor.

The rule that the indemnitee could not be negligent has led courts to strain against a finding of negligence when the proposed indemnitor is far more culpable than the proposed indemnitee. This is not necessary when the doctrine of comparative negligence is extended to apply between defendants, since the damages may be apportioned according to fault.

§9.17 —Application

The multiple party, construction job site injury dispute requires courts to allocate liability among owner, contractor, engineer, and architect. "These appeals present rather intricate questions of negligence and indemnity."[161] In the *Associated* case, a worker injured by electrical shock in a job site mishap obtained workers' compensation from the employer. The worker then filed an action against the owner and the engineer; the owner filed a third-party complaint for indemnity against the construction company and the engineer; the engineer in turn filed a cross-claim against the owner and the construction company; and the construction company filed a counterclaim for workers' compensation payments previously made to the worker. The trial court found all three defendants equally negligent and entered judgment of $200,000, one-third to be paid by each. Thus, the trial court solved the case based on the application of principles of *comparative negligence*. The court of appeal held that the owner, under the written indemnity agreement, was entitled to 100 per cent

---

[161] Associated Engrs, Inc v Job, 370 F2d 633, 635 (8th Cir 1966), *cert denied*, 389 US 823 (1967).

indemnification by the contractor, since the owner's fault was passive (failure to control the contractor's negligent conduct), while the contractor's fault was active.

In *Greenberg v City of Yonkers*,[162] a fire of incendiary origin killed 11 people and injured others trapped on the fourth floor. The plaintiffs filed an action against the owner, the architect, and the supplier who had provided flammable plastic panels specified by the architect. The jury found that the owner was 30 per cent at fault and the architect 70 per cent. In turn the material supplier was responsible for 60 per cent of the owner's portion and 70 per cent of the architect's portion.

In *Coons v Washington Mirror Works, Inc*,[163] a truck driver was injured when a load fell from a hoist. The trial court allocated liability equally between owner (*res ipsa loquitur*) and designer. The court of appeal awarded indemnity to the owner on the ground that there was no credible evidence of negligence by the owner, but ample evidence of improper design.

In *Wheat Street Two, Inc v James C. Wise, Simpson, Aiken & Associate*,[164] the court of appeal approved a comparative negligence instruction. The owners of an apartment building claimed that the architects were guilty of negligence in designing a water system that was subject to freezing. The evidence of comparative negligence showed that the apartment manager asked the owner to supply blueprints showing the location of cut-off valves. Although the owner had the prints, they were not given to the manager, and as a result, the cut-off valves were not used and the damage occurred.

Under the Colorado Comparative Negligence Statute,[165] it is improper to instruct the jury on assumption of the risk. The fact that a plaintiff knowingly encountered a risk is merely one factor for the jury to consider in apportioning negligence.[166] The doctrine of comparative negligence has no application to an analysis of proximate cause.

"The concept of comparative negligence affects not causation inquiries, but breach of duty inquiries, issues of assumption of the risk and contributory negligence."[167]

In *Hunt v Ellisor & Tanner, Inc*,[168] an owner filed suit against an architect claiming negligent design of a parking deck and breach of contract. The jury

---

[162] 45 AD2d 314, 358 NYS2d 453 (1974), *affd*, 37 NY2d 907, 340 NE2d 744, 378 NYS2d 382 (1975).

[163] 477 F2d 864 (2d Cir 1973).

[164] 132 Ga App 548, 208 SE2d 359 (1974).

[165] Colo Rev Stat §13-21-111 (1973).

[166] Loup-Miller v Brauer & Assocs Rocky Mountain, Inc, 40 Colo App 67, 572 P2d 845 (1977).

[167] Minor v Zidell Trust, 618 P2d 392, 395 (Okla 1980).

[168] 739 SW2d 933 (Tex Ct App 1987), *error denied* (Mar 23, 1988).

found no negligence, but did find that the architect had breached its contractual obligations, causing defects in construction that diminished the value of the project by $41,500. The general contractor was held 95 per cent liable, the architect 5 per cent, and judgment was against the architect for $2,075. REVERSED. The trial court erred in asking the jury to compare the architect's nonconstruction breach against the general contractor's construction breach. The owner was not required to show proportionate fault of each wrongdoer, only that the architect was a producing cause of the damages.

In *Mercy Hospital v Hansen, Lind & Meyer PC*,[169] fault for cracking, chipping, and crumbling of exterior brick was assigned 55 per cent to the architect and 45 per cent to other defendants who settled on the first day of trial.

In *Jack Frost, Inc v Engineered Building Components Co*,[170] an owner sued a manufacturer and retailer of building supplies used in a chicken barn that collapsed. The retailer and manufacturer impleaded the designer. HELD: evidence of design error was sufficient to justify apportionment of 55 per cent of the negligence to the designer and 15 per cent to the manufacturer. (Plaintiff owner was itself 30 per cent contributorily negligent.) Nevertheless, the plaintiff was entitled to recover a full 70 per cent of its damages from the designer, even though the designer was only 55 per cent negligent, since the design was found to be the direct cause of the loss.

§9.18 Reliance on Information Furnished by Others

An architect is responsible for defects in the contract documents that are caused by a surveyor or a consulting engineer employed by the architect. Where the plaintiff is the architect's client, the liability seems to be based upon the architect's contractual obligation to furnish plans which are carefully prepared. Since the architect is employed to produce a finished product, is paid for the engineer's work, and incorporates that work in contract documents signed by the architect, the architect is under a duty to see that the engineer's work product does not contain defects. Liability may be imposed even though the architect may show that it has done everything that a reasonable architect would do under the circumstances.

Where the plaintiff is a worker or a third party injured by a defect created by the consultant, it seems that liability is imposed on the architect on the theory of nondelegable duty.[171] In *Hubert v Aitken*,[172] the architect relied on the

---

[169] 456 NW2d 666 (Iowa 1990).
[170] 304 NW2d 346 (Minn 1981).
[171] *See* ch 8.
[172] 15 Daly 237, 2 NYS 711 (CP 1888), *affd*, 123 NY 655, 25 NE 954 (1890).

contractor to designate the size of a chimney flue to be installed in an apartment house. It proved inadequate, causing incomplete combustion in the heating system. The court held that the architect was responsible for the error: "No one would contend at this day an architect could shelter himself behind the plumber.... It is not enough for him to say, 'I asked the steamfitter,' and then throw the consequences of any error that may be made upon the employer who engages him."

However, when the information which the architect relies upon is furnished not by a consultant or contractor, but by the owner or by some person on behalf of the owner, then the architect may be excused for a defect in plans which results from the incorrect information.

For example, in *Marine Colloids, Inc v M.D. Hardy, Inc*,[173] the architect prepared drawings and submitted a bid to construct a fire wall according to the owner's specifications. The superior court concluded that the architect erected the metal-clad building and constructed the fire wall in a workmanlike manner and in compliance with the *owner's specifications*. The holding was AFFIRMED. The architect was not liable to the owner for damages caused by the fire wall's collapse, since it was designed by the owner, and any defects in the plans resulted from inappropriate use of the wall after construction was completed.

In *Segall Co v W.D. Glassell Co*,[174] a mechanical engineer designed a heating and cooling system based upon the size and placement of the unit selected by the owner's general contractor. The court denied the general contractor's claim for the cost of corrective work required by the allegedly faulty design of the system, because the engineer merely installed the system and was not charged with the full responsibility of designing it.

In a Florida case, an architect relied on information supplied by the owner's lawyer in preparing plans and specifications. The verdict for defendant was AFFIRMED. Although an architect normally owes to its client a duty of due care in preparing drawings that conform to the zoning and building codes, the duty is discharged where the architect reasonably relies on the legal advice of the client's lawyer.[175]

In preparing a survey for a subdivision, a surveyor relied on information supplied by the seller of the property to the effect that the town's main water line ran along the length of the frontage. Relying on this and also on information supplied by another engineer for the town, the surveyor established a boundary indicating direct access to the water supply. HELD: the master did

---

[173] 433 A2d 402 (Me 1981).
[174] 401 So 2d 483 (La Ct App 1981).
[175] Krestow v Wooster, 360 So 2d 32 (Fla Dist Ct App 1978).

not abuse any discretion in determining that the surveyor was justified in relying upon this information, and therefore was not guilty of malpractice.[176]

A different result was reached in *Hutchinson v Dubeau*.[177] The owner provided a surveyor with a preexisting plat from which a limited survey of a disputed boundary was prepared. A subsequent purchaser of the property filed an action against the surveyor to recover damages sustained when the purchaser relied upon the inaccurate plat which bore the surveyor's certification that the plat was a true representation of the property. The court relied on a Georgia code,[178] which provided that plans, specifications, plats, and reports shall be stamped or countersigned only if the registered engineer or surveyor has personally performed the work involved or reviewed the work of another and is completely satisfied that it is accurate. Under the statute, the surveyor is responsible to the public for the accuracy of the surveying work and may be liable to purchasers damaged by reasonable reliance on the plat, even if the survey information is provided by the previous owner.

In *Ohio River Pipeline Corp v Landrum*,[179] the court stated that a contractor "is not relieved from liability because it acted in accordance with the plans and specifications and at the directions of the owner and architect."[180]

In *Jacka v Ouachita Parish School Board*,[181] the school board employed an architect to prepare contract documents including "all engineering services necessary to complete the work." However, the architect relied on a topographical survey provided by a member of the school board. The survey was erroneous, and the school board charged the cost of correction against the architect's fee. The architect sued for the fee and recovered. The court held that the provisions of the contract, in view of custom in the industry and in view of the actual conduct of the parties, indicated that the parties did not contemplate that the architect would be responsible for the topographical survey.

In a confusing opinion which evidently does not disclose all of the relevant facts, an engineer utilized information supplied by the port authority in preparing plans and specifications. In an action against the port authority by the contractor, who alleged that the plans were defective, the trial court dismissed the port authority's cross-claim against the engineers, holding that the

---

[176] Rabe v Carnaby, 120 NH 809, 423 A2d 610 (1980).

[177] 161 Ga App 65, 289 SE2d 4 (1982).

[178] Ga Code Ann §84-2121 (1976).

[179] 580 SW2d 713, 721 (Ky Ct App 1979).

[180] *Id* 721. *See also* Barnes v Rakow, 78 Ill App 3d 404, 396 NE2d 1168 (1979) (surveyor relied on master survey).

[181] 249 La 223, 186 So 2d 571 (1966).

port authority was equally responsible for any design errors. Therefore, there was no damage for which the engineering firm was solely responsible.[182]

§9.19 Approval by Building Department

It has occasionally been asserted as a defense that a building department approved plans negligently prepared by an architect. However, the failure of the building department to discover defects in plans prepared by the architect does not absolve the architect from responsibility; nor does approval by the building department foreclose the issue of whether the plans complied with the requirements of the building code.[183]

In *Thomas E. Hoar, Inc v Jobco, Inc*,[184] a memorandum decision, the appellate division upheld the trial court's refusal to dismiss an affirmative defense to the effect that prior governmental approval of plans absolved the architect from responsibility in a case where the plaintiff's inventory was damaged by flooding. The dissenting opinion argued that prior governmental approval is no defense to an action for negligent design.

In *Patin v Industrial Enterprises, Inc*,[185] decedent worker was electrocuted while holding a 20-foot gutter section that came into contact with an uninsulated electric line near a metal building that was under construction. The plan met with every requirement of the building code. HELD: the engineer was responsible only for the plans and not for the construction. The engineer was not negligent in failing to warn of the close proximity of the offsite electrical wires.

§9.20 Waiver and Estoppel

Waiver and estoppel are occasionally raised, as the facts may warrant, as defenses to claims of malpractice.

Failure to Complain

In *Major v Leary*,[186] an architect was employed to prepare a pretentious residence. It prepared contract documents and also acted as builder. Many changes were ordered by the owner, who made a few complaints during the progress of the job. When the job was practically finished, the owner ejected the

---

[182] V.C. Edwards Contracting Co v Port of Tacoma, 7 Wash App 883, 503 P2d 1133 (1972), *affd*, 83 Wash 2d 7, 514 P2d 1381 (1973).

[183] Johnson v Salem Title Co, 246 Or 409, 425 P2d 519 (1967).

[184] 30 AD2d 541, 291 NYS2d 380 (1968).

[185] 421 So 2d 362 (La Ct App), *writ denied*, 423 So 2d 1166 (La 1982).

[186] 241 AD 606, 268 NYS 413 (1934).

architect from the job and refused to pay the architect's fee. The owner offered extensive expert testimony criticizing the contract documents.

The court stated that the alleged errors were to a large extent trivial, captious, and artificial, depending on the testimony of experts and not on actual complaints made during the progress of construction; therefore, the architect was entitled to its fee.

It seems that the basis of the court's decision was the theory that if the owner had been dissatisfied with the architect's performance, the owner should have said so during the job, instead of waiting until the project was finished to raise complaints. The owner's failure to protest deprived the architect of the opportunity to make corrections, and tended to promote the unjust enrichment of the owner at the expense of the architect. Failure to complain undermined the credibility of the owner's claim of dissatisfaction, and may have amounted to a waiver of the owner's right to complain.

Estoppel Rejected

In *Pierson v Tyndall*,[187] an architect prepared contract documents, supervised construction, and issued certificates for payment. The owner paid the contractor according to the certificates issued by the architect, even though the owner was aware that the work did not comply with the requirements of the contract documents.

The architect filed an action to recover its fee. The owner's defense was negligent preparation of contract documents and supervision of construction. The owner offered an instruction that payment to the contractor with knowledge of faulty work would not preclude the owner from recovering damages from the architect as an offset against the architect's commission. HELD: the instruction should have been given. An architect is under a duty of care and skill, and payment to a contractor does not estop an owner from recovering damages for a breach of this duty. The payments may, however, be considered on the general issue of the amount of damages.

Waiver and Estoppel Accepted

In *Newton Investment Co v Barnard & Burk, Inc*,[188] the court held that an owner waived a cause of action against an architect for allegedly improper issuance of payment certificates. The contract called for installation of a pipeline but was ambiguous as to compensation. The contract called for a unit price of $1.50 per foot, but the extension of the price on the same line indicated that the contractor had intended to bid the sum of $15 per foot. The contractor threatened to abandon the project unless the owner authorized payment of $15

---

[187] 28 SW 232 (Tex Civ App 1894).
[188] 220 So 2d 822 (Miss 1969).

per foot, and thereafter the owner instructed the engineer to certify payments at that figure. In doing so the owner ignored the engineer's advice to pay at the rate of $1.50 per foot. When the owner filed a suit against the engineer for the issuance of erroneous payment certificates, the court held that the owner was estopped from asserting noncompliance with the terms of the contract, and that the owner's actions constituted a waiver of the lower unit price.

In *Huber, Hunt & Nichols, Inc v Moore*,[189] a contractor alleged that the architect had caused damages by delaying the approval of change orders. Nevertheless, the contractor signed the change orders which provided that the compensation stated in the change order was full compensation for all costs and expenses incurred in connection with the changes. HELD: signing the change orders constituted a waiver of claims of damages resulting from the change order work.

§9.21 Approval by Owner

If an architect produces a defective design and it is approved by the owner, the approval is not conclusive. The owner is still entitled to compensation for the negligent design. To hold otherwise would be absurd. It is the very acceptance (or approval) of the architect's defective plan that results from the negligence of the architect.

In *Simpson Brothers Corp v Merrimac Chemical Co*,[190] a contractor agreed to design and build an underground concrete storage tank for fuel oil. The architect submitted plans and specifications for the project to the owner, who approved them. The owner also employed a consulting engineer to examine the plans, specifically to determine whether the tank would be secure against flotation. In an arbitration proceeding, arbitrators ruled that the contractor was not entitled to recover its fee because the tank was negligently designed. AFFIRMED. The general approval of plans by the owner does not excuse the designer from the obligation to use ordinary and reasonable skill. Even if the owner's consulting engineer approved the plan for flotation, this is not binding upon the owner if the design was in fact negligent.

The fact that an owner accepts and uses plans belatedly delivered by an architect does not deprive the owner of its claim of damages for delay.[191]

It is occasionally asserted, apparently upon reasoning analogous to waiver, that an owner who pays a contractor in full for defective work is not entitled thereafter to assert that the supervision by the architect was negligent. This

---

[189] 67 Cal App 3d 278, 136 Cal Rptr 603 (1977).
[190] 248 Mass 346, 142 NE 922 (1924).
[191] Edwards v Hall, 293 Pa 97, 141 A 638 (1928).

defense was rejected in *Schwartz v Kuhn*,[192] where the owner had paid the contractor the full amount of the contract price, even though the trial court found as a matter of law that the buildings as constructed were defective because of the architect's negligence in supervising the work. The fact that the contractor was paid in full did not affect the case; failure to seek remedy against the negligent contractor did not excuse the negligence of the architect.

Approval Accepted as a Defense

In *Bailey v Jones*,[193] the court found a form of approval where the owner renewed a note given to an architect for its fee and thereafter claimed damages against the architect because of defects in workmanship and delay in completion. The court held that, by renewing the note after discovering the defects, the owner waived any right to recover damages.

Knowing approval of a specific defective design is to be distinguished from acceptance of contract documents. In *Greenhaven Corp v Hutchcraft & Associates*,[194] an architect designed two exits from the top floor to comply with fire regulations. The owner, knowing that the fire regulations probably required two exits, nevertheless requested the architect to redesign so as to require only one exit. The building, as designed, violated the fire regulations and the owner discharged the architect and refused to pay the fee. HELD: the owner knew of the fire regulation and requested the alteration; this justified what would otherwise have been negligent performance.

§9.22 No Supervision

An architect is not responsible for damage to a project caused by improper workmanship, unless it has contracted to be responsible for the supervision of the project.[195]

In *Walker v Wittenberg, Delony & Davidson, Inc*,[196] a worker who was standing on a wall was injured when it collapsed during construction because of inadequate shoring. Directed verdict for defendant architects was AFFIRMED, based primarily on contract provisions. The standard American Institute of Architects (AIA) contract between owner and architect did not

---

[192] 71 Misc 149, 125 NYS 568 (Sup Ct 1911).

[193] 243 Mich 159, 219 NW 629 (1928).

[194] 463 NE2d 283 (Ind Ct App 1984).

[195] Duggan v Arnold N. May Builders, Inc, 33 Wis 2d 49, 146 NW2d 410 (1966) (poor workmanship during excavation caused shearing of drainage tile; furnace flooded).

[196] 241 Ark 525, 412 SW2d 621 (1966).

require the architect to be present continuously during construction or to prescribe safety precautions or enforce the safety provisions of the contract.[197]

The contract only required supervision to the extent necessary to insure compliance of the final building with the plans and specifications. Moreover, the contract between the owner and the contractor called for the contractor to designate an individual in the contractor's organization to be responsible for accident prevention. This was a further indication that the owner did not expect the architect to supervise day-to-day safety precautions.[198]

In *St John Public School District v Engineers-Architects PC*,[199] an owner employed a contractor to install a new boiler and the contractor employed an engineer to prepare shop drawings only. The contractor failed to install the boiler according to the plans and specifications. The trial court held that the engineer had failed to properly supervise the work. REVERSED. The engineer did not agree to provide inspection and the wording of the contract did not mislead the owner.

In *Pugh v Butler Telephone Co*,[200] a construction company agreed to lay 18 miles of telephone cable under contract with an owner. An employee was killed when the excavation caved in. Summary judgment for the engineer was AFFIRMED. The responsibility of the engineer was to insure compliance with plans and specifications; the engineer had no responsibility under the contract documents to supervise the contractor.

In *Jewish Board of Guardians v Grumman Allied Instruments, Inc*,[201] a subcontractor delivered modular units to a school building site and covered them with Visqueen. However, a weekend storm damaged the units. The owner filed an action against the architect, the prime contractor, and the subcontractor. HELD: there was a clear division of duties among the parties and the architect was not retained to supervise performance of the job.

Duty to Supervise

However, in *Dickerson Construction Co v Process Engineering Co*,[202] the contract documents required the architect to be present at certain stages of

---

[197] AIA Document B141, 3.4.3. (1963).

[198] *Accord* Walters v Kellam & Foley, 172 Ind App 207, 360 NE2d 199 (1977) (by contract the architect declined to "guarantee the contractor's performance" or to take responsibility for "construction means, methods, techniques, sequences or procedures, or for safety precautions").

[199] 414 NW2d 285 (ND 1987).

[200] 512 So 2d 1317 (Ala 1987).

[201] 62 NY2d 684, 465 NE2d 42, 476 NYS2d 535 (1984).

[202] 341 So 2d 646 (Miss 1977).

construction, certify progress payments, and make final inspection. This implied that the architect would use reasonable care to see that the contractor constructed the building in substantial compliance with the plans and specifications. The court found that it was proper to instruct the jury that it was the duty of the architect "to exercise reasonable care and skill in supervision of construction to the extent necessary to attain the purposes intended."[203]

§9.23 No Control

It is axiomatic that legal responsibility follows the power to control. In the nature of things, an architect's power to effectively control job site activities is somewhat limited. The architect usually does not have the power to hire and fire. Job site employees are employed by the owner, the contractor, or the subcontractors. When contract documents give the architect the power to stop the job, it is a bold architect who exercises that power, since its exercise is so destructive to the economic interests of the owner, the contractor, the subcontractors, and even the architect. At a minimum, stopping the job provokes delay. It means that the owner will be curtailed in the enjoyment of the property, that the contractor and subcontractors will lose money because they remain responsible for payroll and equipment rental during a period of nonproductivity, and that the final payment on the architect's fee will be delayed while the architect devotes more time than anticipated to solving job site problems.

In *Vorndran v Wright*,[204] a worker was injured in a job site accident. The contract provided that the architect would visit the job site at least weekly and advise the owner of any omissions, substitutions, defects, or deficiencies in the work. "Supervision of Architect is to be distinguished from the continuous personal supervision to be obtained by a resident inspector." HELD: the architect was not responsible for job safety. It was the architect's prime responsibility to determine that the construction was completed in accordance with the plans and specifications. An architect is not liable for the failure of an employer to comply with safety regulations unless the contract imposes upon the architect a duty to supervise or control the actual methods of construction. Here, the architect had no control over methods of construction and accordingly could not have been held responsible for the failure of the contractor to comply with safety regulations.

In *Sherwood v Omega Construction Co*,[205] a worker fell from a 15-foot-high concrete platform after crawling through an unfinished window. The worker

---

[203] *Id* 650.
[204] 367 So 2d 1070 (Fla Dist Ct App), *cert denied*, 378 So 2d 350 (Fla 1979).
[205] 657 F Supp 345 (SDNY 1987).

filed a complaint against the prime contractor. HELD: engineers who did not directly control the work activities of the contractor were not liable to injured workers.

In *Hamby v High Steel Structures, Inc*,[206] a steel beam collapsed causing injury and death; the estate of the deceased filed an action against the project engineer. HELD: the engineer had no power to supervise or control the work site or to establish construction methods or safety procedures. Therefore, the engineer was entitled to summary judgment. Control over the work is a precondition to liability under a common law duty to provide a safe work place.

In *Bisset v Joseph A. Schudt & Associates*,[207] the architect provided a supervisor on the job site daily and had the power to stop the work. HELD: the architect was in charge of the construction and, therefore, liable to a worker under the State Structural Work Act[208] for a knee injury sustained when a sewer trench collapsed.

In *Jaroszewicz v Facilities Development Corp*,[209] architects were employed to provide supervision and inspection of a building project to assure compliance with contract specifications. The architects had neither the duty nor the right to control the methods by which construction work was performed. A worker was electrocuted troubleshooting the parking lot lighting system after completion and acceptance of the project. Summary judgment for the architects was AFFIRMED. The architects had no right to control the manner in which the work was performed nor was there proof of any malfeasance that caused or contributed to the accident.

In *Kerr v Rochester Gas & Electric Corp*,[210] an injured construction worker was denied recovery from an engineer on the ground that the engineer had neither authority over the worker nor authority to direct construction procedures and safety measures employed by the contractor.

Also in accord is *Kelly v Northwest Community Hospital*,[211] an action under the Illinois Structural Work Act.[212] A general duty to supervise work merely creates a duty to see that the building constructed meets the plans and specifications. Absent a contractual provision charging the architect with control of methods or techniques of construction, and absent the authority to stop work, an architect cannot be charged with a duty to provide safety precautions for programs at the construction site.

---

[206] 134 AD2d 884, 521 NYS2d 926 (1987).
[207] 133 Ill App 3d 356, 478 NE2d 911 (1985).
[208] Ill Rev State ch 48, para 60 (1979).
[209] 115 AD2d 159, 495 NYS2d 498 (1985).
[210] 113 AD2d 412, 496 NYS2d 880 (1985).
[211] 66 Ill App 3d 679, 384 NE2d 102 (1978).
[212] Ill Rev Stat chs 48, 69 (1971).

One commentator has discussed the "emergence of the great split" in worker versus architect cases and noted that most cases find that the architect has no duty to safeguard workers from job site injuries in the absence of specific contractual provisions imposing such a duty.[213]

In a Wisconsin case, an architect who had no "control . . . of . . . place of employment" was exempt from liability under the Wisconsin Safe Place Statute,[214] where the contract provided that the architect would not be responsible for construction means, methods, techniques, sequences, or procedures, or for safety precautions and programs in connection with the work.[215]

The question of control was crucial to affirmance of a summary judgment for the defendant architect in *Parks v Atkinson*.[216] The architect was employed under an oral contract to design and supervise the remodeling of a church. The project required ceiling work. The contractor installed scaffolding and trusses to facilitate the work. Plaintiff fell from the scaffolding and filed an action against the architect for failure to properly supervise the project. The court held that a supervising architect is liable to an injured worker only if the architect had a duty to supervise the method and manner employed by the contractor in actually doing the work.

The plaintiff pointed out that the architect had intervened in the conduct of the work in two instances: once to disallow the use of improper concrete, and again to prevent pouring concrete into wet footings. However, the court held that it was incumbent upon the plaintiff, in order to avoid summary judgment, to produce evidence showing control by the architect of means and methods of construction. The two stoppages of work referred to were not sufficient to show control over the method of performing the work. They merely indicated that the architect was insuring that the final product would conform to the requirements of the contract documents. Therefore, there was not sufficient evidence to raise a jury question as to the degree of control retained by the architect.

In *Wheeler & Lewis v Slifer*,[217] a worker was injured while working on a roof that collapsed because of insufficient shoring. HELD: the better rule is to hold an architect responsible for unsafe working conditions only when the contract documents impose a clear duty of care on the architect.

---

[213] Sweet, *Site Architects and Construction Workers: Brothers and Keepers or Strangers?*, 28 Emory LJ 290 (1980). *Accord* Fruzyna v Walter C. Carlson Assocs, 78 Ill App 3d 1050, 398 NE2d 60 (1979).

[214] Wis Stat §101.11(1).

[215] Hortman v Becker Constr Co, 92 Wis 2d 210, 284 NW2d 621 (1979). *Accord* Porter v Stevens, Thompson & Runyan, Inc, 24 Wash App 624, 602 P2d 1192 (1979), *review denied*, 93 Wash 2d 1010 (1980) (contract placed responsibility for jobsite safety on the contractor).

[216] 19 Ariz App 111, 505 P2d 279 (1973).

[217] 195 Colo 291, 577 P2d 1092 (1978).

In *Persichilli v Triborough Bridge & Tunnel Authority*,[218] the court opined that an engineer who merely supervises a project is not to be responsible for nonfeasance alone; but an engineer in control of a project on behalf of the owner has a duty of reasonable care to protect job site employees from injury. The plaintiff's decedent had been smothered on an underground job. The court charged the jury that the engineer had the authority to control the project as a matter of law. REVERSED. The jury would have to determine as a question of fact whether the engineer was merely the supervising engineer or was in charge of the project.[219]

In *Thomas v Fromherz Engineers*,[220] the court held that there is no general duty on the part of an engineer to supervise a contractor's method of performing a contract. Therefore, in the absence of some contractual provision, defendant engineers (employed by the state) were not liable for injury to plaintiff workers sustained when a piling fell from the lead line of a pile driver, allegedly because the lead line was not equipped with an end unit.[221]

Similarly, in *Seeney v Dover Country Club Apartments, Inc*,[222] a worker was injured when a ditch collapsed. The court stated that liability must be founded on the breach of some duty imposed by law on an architect with respect to employees of an independent contractor; such a duty is imposed only where active control of the methods of construction employed by the contractor is exercised by the architect. This kind of control does not exist where the architect merely exercises supervisory authority so as to assure the owner that the final result of the contractor's work conforms to the requirements of the contract documents. Since the architect did not possess or voluntarily exercise control over the contractor's methods of construction, the architect did not owe any duty to the employees of the contractor.[223]

In *Natal v Phoenix Assurance Co*,[224] an engineer was found to be responsible only for the "soundness of the foundation and the framing of the house"; thus,

---

[218] 21 AD2d 819, 251 NYS2d 733 (1964), *modified*, 16 NY2d 136, 209 NE2d 802, 262 NYS2d 476 (1965).

[219] *See also* Clyde E. Williams & Assocs v Boatman, 176 Ind App 430, 375 NE2d 1138 (1978), in which the court held that the jury should be instructed to make a factual determination as to the engineer's assumption of control of the job site.

[220] 159 So 2d 612 (La Ct App), *writ refused*, 245 La 799, 161 So 2d 276 (1964).

[221] *Accord* McGovern v Standish, 65 Ill 2d 54, 357 NE2d 1134 (1976) (Illinois Structural Work Act); *see also* Caine v New Castle County, 379 A2d 1112 (Super Ct 1977) (11-year-old boy killed in sledding accident when he struck a metal post erected as part of an incomplete chain link fence).

[222] 318 A2d 619 (Del Super Ct 1974).

[223] *Accord* Scavone v State Univ Constr Fund, 46 AD2d 895, 362 NYS2d 22 (1974) (memorandum decision).

[224] 286 So 2d 738 (La Ct App 1973), *revd as to other parties*, 305 So 2d 438 (La 1974).

the engineer could not be liable to a 14-year-old guest of a homeowner who was injured after walking through a sliding glass door.

Reverse Application

The question of control was used in a reverse application to exonerate a municipality from liability for the acts of its independent contractor and engineer. In *Vannoy v City of Warren*,[225] a worker drowned after being overcome by methane gas in a manhole. The jury was instructed that the city was vicariously liable for negligence of the engineer. The court stated that there can be no such vicarious liability in the absence of an inherently or intrinsically dangerous activity, since the engineer was an independent contractor. The question of whether the activity was inherently or intrinsically dangerous, and therefore whether the municipality was under a nondelegable duty to protect the plaintiff, was held properly submitted to the jury, since there was a conflict in testimony as to the presence of gas and other circumstances surrounding the employment.

§9.24 —Methods of Construction

The defense most often used by architects is the simple denial of the allegation of negligence. Next to that, the most frequently cited defense has been *privity of contract*—more precisely *lack of privity of contract*—in reality, the assertion that the architect is responsible only to protect the interests of the owner, and not third parties. Of the many other defenses available, a favorite now is *methods of construction*.

This defense asserts that, by the terms of the contract, the architect does not assume responsibility for the contractor's methods of construction. The architect is responsible to insure that the completed project complies with the requirements of the contract documents. The purpose of the supervisory or inspection function furnished by the architect is to assure the owner that the completed project is what the owner bargained for—that it complies with the requirements of the plans and specifications.

Typical contract documents are voluminous. The specifications may run to several hundred pages, and they incorporate national codes and standards which in turn add thousands of pages. Nevertheless, the physical nature of construction is such that the specifications, with all of their incorporated documents, do not attempt to designate every detail of construction. Many of the details are in fact furnished by subcontractors or by the contractor in the form of shop drawings, which in turn incorporate specifications that may be supplied by an equipment manufacturer.

---

[225] 15 Mich App 158, 166 NW2d 486 (1968).

Nails must be driven. The specifications may, and frequently do, detail the size, quality, design, composition, and quantity of the nails. But how are they to be driven? With a hammer or a nailing machine? Where will the worker be standing who drives the nail? Will the worker be on a ladder, platform, scaffold, rafter, or nail keg? Such details are determined by the contractor or the worker.

If the building is masonry, how will the scaffolding be designed? If it is concrete, how will the forms be built? How will the concrete be supported while it cures? The design and placement of scaffolding and false work may be left to the contractor or a subcontractor.

If a detail of construction is omitted from the contract documents and the contractor selects a method that the architect disapproves, how will the architect enforce the objection? The contractor's bid was based upon the assumption that, unless otherwise specified, the contractor could select its own method to accomplish the finished result desired by the owner. If the architect, after the contract has been signed, requires a more expensive method or detail of construction, will the owner not be required to pay the extra cost occasioned by the method belatedly specified? If the architect does, nevertheless, specify a more expensive method of construction and the contractor refuses to comply with the method specified, how can the architect enforce the demand? Acting alone, an architect cannot eject a contractor from the job site. If the contract documents *do* give the architect the power to stop work, is the architect justified in doing so against the wishes of the owner (whose project will be delayed) and the contractor (whose costs will be increased)?

As applied to a case where the plaintiff is not the owner, the defense that the architect has no control over methods of construction employed by the contractor is, in fact, a special instance of the proposition that an architect has no duty to protect persons with whom it is not in privity of contract. The essence of the defense is that the architect's only duty is to the owner; that duty is to insure that the completed project complies with the contract documents. The duty does not extend to protect third parties from danger caused by the methods of construction employed by the contractor.

§9.25 —Application

The proposition that an architect is not responsible for methods of construction reaches its limit when it is applied to excuse an architect's failure to correct direct violations of the contract documents on the ground that the architect is responsible only for the completed project, and not for violations that occur during the progress of the job. This view appears to have been accepted in only one case.[226] There, the specifications required a thermostat and a pressure relief

---

[226] Day v National United States Radiator Corp, 241 La 288, 128 So 2d 660 (1961).

valve for a boiler. The contract required that the architect check shop drawings, furnish adequate supervision to reasonably insure strict conformity with the contract documents, and make frequent visits to the work site.

The plumbing subcontractor submitted two brochures showing boiler design, each of which was submitted by the architect to the consulting mechanical engineer and each of which was rejected. A third brochure submitted to the architect was not referred to the engineers but was endorsed by the architect, *approved as noted.* The contract provided: "Shop drawings marked 'Approved as Noted,' are assumed to be approved for fabrication or placing orders." The approved brochure did not include all the details of construction and apparently did not specifically display a thermostat or pressure relief valve on the boiler.

The subcontractor mistakenly installed the valve and the thermostat on the hot-water storage tank rather than the boiler. When the subcontractor fired the boiler it exploded, as expert testimony showed it was bound to do. This explosion caused the scalding death of the plaintiff's decedent. The architect had not inspected the boiler; neither it nor the engineer was present when the explosion occurred. The trial court entered judgment for the plaintiff which was REVERSED by the Louisiana Supreme Court on the ground that the architect had no duty to supervise the installation of the hot-water system or inspect it during its installation. The architect's only duty was to see to it that the overall job complied with the requirements of the contract documents before the owner accepted the building.

Implicit in this opinion is the proposition that the architect would have complied with all of the duties under the contract documents if the architect had discovered the defect at any time before the issuance of the certificate for final payment.

The methods of construction defense has been applied even against a claim by an owner. In *Clinton v Boehm*,[227] a construction employee was killed during construction; his survivors recovered judgment against the owner. The owner refused to pay the architect's fee on the ground that negligent supervision by the architect had contributed to the death. The appellate division approved the trial court's action sustaining the architect's demurrer. The *very utmost obligation* assumed by the architect under the contract was to insure that the building was properly constructed, and not to examine or inspect the contractor's means of construction.[228]

In *Swartz v Ford, Bacon & Davis Construction Corp*,[229] a worker, injured in a high fall, sued the project architect. No temporary flooring or safety nets had been provided, as required by safety regulations. The architect had agreed with

---

[227] 139 AD 73, 124 NYS 789 (1910).

[228] Criticized in Associated Engrs, Inc v Job, 370 F2d 633 (8th Cir 1966), *cert denied*, 389 US 823 (1967), as an exemplification of the "old" rule.

[229] 469 So 2d 232 (Fla Dist Ct App 1985).

the owner to comply with all applicable codes, ordinances, rules and regulations. Summary judgment in favor of the architect was AFFIRMED. The contract did not explicitly impose on the architect the duty to supervise and control the contractor's methods of construction; therefore, the architect was not liable for the contractor's failure to comply with safety regulations.

In *Olsen v Chase Manhattan Bank*,[230] the *methods of construction* defense protected an owner from liability for injury to a worker. The employee was injured by an object that fell from a temporary platform constructed by the contractor. The platform was not a part of the architect's overall plans. The plaintiff, in an action against the architect, the consulting engineer, and the owner, alleged that the defendants had control and supervision over the platform and failed to exercise reasonable care to protect the plaintiff. The court held that since the accident arose from the accomplishment of details of construction furnished by the contractor, the owner could not be liable for a breach of the nondelegable duty to furnish a safe place to work. The court also held that the architects and engineers, even though they may have had a duty of general supervision, could only be charged with *nonfeasance*, and therefore, although they might be liable to the owner, they could not be held responsible to the injured worker.

Vitality of the Defense

One commentator has concluded that the architect's attempt to restrict responsibility to a determination that work be performed in accordance with the contract documents is a lost cause.[231] However, the *methods of construction* defense has retained great vitality.

In *Fox v Jenny Engineering Corp*,[232] a worker was injured while working on a tunnel project when a rock became dislodged from the roof of the tunnel. HELD: neither the architect nor the engineer had authority to supervise or control the injured worker, or to direct construction procedures or safety measures employed by the general contractor. Therefore, neither was liable to the worker.

In *Peterson v Fowler*,[233] a worker was injured in a fall from a floating scaffolding utilized to clean beams in the dome of a sports arena. The contractor had requested that the architect issue a change order authorizing the erection of floating scaffolding for the cleaning operation. The architect refused and

---

[230] 10 AD2d 539, 205 NYS2d 60 (1960), *affd*, 9 NY2d 829, 175 NE2d 350, 215 NYS2d 773 (1961).

[231] 1 J. Arthur Miller, *The Liability of the Architect in His Supervisory Function*, No 2 Forum 28 (1966).

[232] 122 AD2d 532, 505 NYS2d 270 (1986), *affd*, 70 NY2d 761, 514 NE2d 1374, 520 NYS2d 750 (1987).

[233] 27 Utah 2d 159, 493 P2d 997 (1972).

instructed the contractor to proceed as the contractor saw fit. The contractor then employed a subcontractor to furnish the scaffolding. HELD: the architect had neither designed nor constructed the scaffolding, it did not designate the materials for it, nor did it have anything to do with renting or maintaining it. The architect had no duty to the employees of subcontractors with respect to scaffolding. Its sole responsibility was to the client, "to see that the sports arena was properly erected so that it would be safe for the uses to which it would be put when finished." Summary judgment for architect AFFIRMED.

In *Parks v Atkinson*,[234] a carpenter fell from temporary scaffolding while participating in the repair of a church ceiling. The architect had been retained under an oral contract to design and supervise the project. HELD: the supervising architect was not liable to the injured employee unless the architect had the duty to supervise the *method and manner of actually doing the work*. There can be no liability if supervisory controls are limited to those necessary to assure that the contractor's work complies with the plans and specifications. The burden was on the plaintiff to show that the architect retained control over methods of construction.

The plaintiff argued that the architect retained such control, as demonstrated by evidence of two incidents: the architect condemned improper concrete and stopped the pouring of concrete into wet footings. However, the court took the view that, by those activities, the architect was merely assuring compliance of the final product with the requirements of the contract documents. The plaintiff did not introduce sufficient evidence to go to the jury.

In *Reber v Chandler High School District No 202*,[235] an architect designed and supervised the erection of a school gymnasium. The roof was to be supported by six steel arches, which collapsed during construction, injuring workers. The contract documents did not include any method or sequence for the erection of the steel arches. This was left to the discretion of the contractor.

Plaintiffs contended that the architect was under a duty to supervise the work of the contractor so as to prevent injury to job site employees. The court opined that liability for negligent supervision occurs only when a duty has been created by the reservation of a contractual right to exercise day-to-day control over the details of the work. This must be over and above the supervision and inspection rights generally reserved to insure that the final work product complies with the requirements of the contract documents.

The court examined the contract between the architect and the school district, and the contract between the contractor and the school district, to determine the amount of control reserved by the architect. The contract between the school

---

[234] 19 Ariz App 111, 505 P2d 279 (1973).
[235] 13 Ariz App 133, 474 P2d 852 (1970).

district and the architect provided for "general supervision to guard the Owner against defects and deficiencies in the work of the contractors, but he [the architect] does not guarantee the performance of their contracts." This provision was found to be insufficient to support a finding that the architect had a duty to control the method and manner of the contractor's work.

Furthermore, Arizona law requires the erection of public works to be done under "direct supervision of, a registered architect, engineer" but does not impose duty on the architect to protect job site employees from dangerous practices employed by the contractor.[236] The purpose of the statute is to insure that public contractors produce a finished product that complies with the requirements of the contract documents.

The *methods of construction* defense overcame a vigorous dissent in *Wells v Stanley J. Thill & Associates*.[237] A worker was injured in a cave-in. The employer failed to shore the trench with timber and violated state safety laws. The court stated that the engineer's only duty was to the city: to see that the end result envisioned by the contract documents was accomplished. The engineer had no duty to require the contractor to comply with minimum safety standards, and therefore was not liable for the plaintiff's injuries.

The dissenting justice agreed that the majority opinion reflected the current state of law but argued that precedent should be abandoned. The contract required shoring the trench. The design was inherently dangerous. The contractor could not have been relied upon to comply with safety standards, since the employee's only remedy was workers' compensation. From an economic point of view, it might be cheaper to endanger the safety of an employee than to provide protective devices.

In *United Gas Improvement Co v Larsen*,[238] a contract between a lessee and a prime contractor provided that the architect would act as the agent of the lessee and would have the final determination as to the interpretation of the contract documents. Plaintiff's decedent was killed when the building collapsed during remodeling. Plaintiff filed an action against the lessee, alleging that the architect was negligent. The court held that the contractor was entitled to select the methods of construction, and the architect merely had the right to inspect the work so that the end product would comply with the requirements of the contract documents. If the architect had undertaken to direct the details of the work, it would have been acting outside the scope of its contractual duty, and such unauthorized acts would not have been attributable to the employer/lessee. No affirmative action taken by the architect was shown to have any

---

[236] Ariz Rev Stat §32-142 (1976).
[237] 153 Mont 28, 452 P2d 1015 (1969).
[238] 182 F 620 (CCA Pa 1910).

causal connection with the accident. Therefore, there was no proof of negligence on the part of the lessee. The trial court judgment in favor of plaintiff was REVERSED.[239]

In *Seeney v Dover Country Club Apartments, Inc*,[240] a worker was injured when a trench collapsed. Under the contract documents, the architect had authority to supervise the work in order to assure conformity to the contract documents. The details of the excavation were not specified. HELD: since the architect performed only *architectural* services and did not retain *active control* over the methods used by the contractor in performing the work, the architect was not liable. It is only where the architect retains control over the methods of construction, or voluntarily exercises such control, that a duty arises to protect the employees of contractor.[241]

In *Vonasek v Hirsch & Stevens, Inc*,[242] the plaintiff was a contractor who suffered damage when steel joists for a gymnasium roof collapsed during construction. The contractor claimed that the architect was responsible for the loss, alleging defective design and supervision.

The gymnasium roof was to be supported by 26 steel joists. The contract documents did not designate a method to tie the joists down during erection. Testimony showed that all experienced steel erectors know that the first joist should be tied down before proceeding to the next, and so on. The steel erection subcontractor only partially tied down the first joist before proceeding, causing the collapse. The court held that an architect is under no duty to warn against hazards commonly known to the trade. The contract required only periodic inspections to insure that the end product would comply with the requirements of the contract documents. There was no requirement to prescribe the methods of construction to be followed by the contractor. The architect was not a general safety supervisor on the job site.

In *Heslep v Forrest & Cotton, Inc*,[243] the plaintiff was injured when the boom of a crane was energized by contact with 13,000-volt power lines. The plaintiff contended that the engineer was under a duty to require the contractor to provide safety devices on the mobile crane. The jury brought in a verdict of

---

[239] *See also* Olsen v Chase Manhattan Bank, 9 NY2d 829, 175 NE2d 350, 215 NYS2d 773 (1961) (employee injured by falling object; HELD: architect was under no duty to see to the safety of temporary platforms used in the accomplishment of the work).

[240] 318 A2d 619 (Del Super Ct 1974).

[241] *See also* Walters v Kellam & Foley, 172 Ind App 207, 360 NE2d 199 (1977) (worker was installing duct work above a heating and ventilating unit and fell after stepping on the bottom panel of a unit which gave way; contract between the owner and the architect specifically provided that the architect did not take responsibility for "construction means, methods, techniques, sequences or procedures, or for safety precautions"). *Accord* Thomas v Fromherz Engrs, 159 So 2d 612 (La Ct App), *writ refused*, 245 La 799, 161 So 2d 276 (1964) (worker injured in trench collapse).

[242] 6 Wis 2d 1, 221 NW2d 815 (1974).

[243] 247 Ark 1066, 449 SW2d 181 (1970).

$7,500. The trial court granted judgment n.o.v. The court of appeal AFFIRMED. The contract imposed no duty on the engineer to supervise the plaintiff or its fellow employees in the performance of their duties, nor was the engineer responsible for the enforcement of safety codes. If the contractor violated the code, it should have been made to answer to the proper authorities, not to the engineer.

Assumption of Responsibility by Conduct

In *Krieger v J.E. Greiner Co*,[244] an engineer was responsible for the design of a bridge and overall supervision of its construction. Plaintiff, an injured worker, appealed from judgment entered after demurrer sustained. The Maryland Supreme Court granted certiorari because of the public importance of the issue. The complaint alleged that the engineer, under its contract with the owner, was required to plan, direct, and coordinate construction layout surveys; perform detailed field inspections; and observe and comply with all federal, state, and local laws affecting those working on the project. The contract provided that the engineer would be responsible for all damage to life and property due to its activities or those of its agents. The engineer was to supply resident inspection of workmanship and materials incorporated into the project.

The general contractor in *Kreiger* was engaged in the placement of iron reinforcement bars and allegedly performed this work in an ultradangerous manner by erecting the bars into a vertical position without properly securing them. The bars toppled over, causing injury. The complaint alleged that the engineer had exercised the right to stop the work on numerous occasions when the work was being performed in a negligent and dangerous manner.

The Maryland Supreme Court AFFIRMED the defense judgment. Cases imposing liability fall into one of two categories: (1) cases where contractual provisions impose terms by which the engineer might be said to be liable, or (2) cases in which courts "have disregarded fundamental contractual principles in attempting to parlay general inspection or supervision clauses which give the owner or architect a right to stop observed unsafe construction processes into a *duty* which is neither consistent with generally accepted usage nor contemplated by the contract of the parties."[245] The court pointed out that the provisions of the contract in this case did not attempt to impose upon the engineer a duty to see that the contractor obeyed all the laws; the contract was simply an agreement entered into by the engineer that it would perform the work in compliance with laws, and that the engineer would be responsible for damage to life and property that it might cause. There was no provision imposing any duty on the engineer to supervise the methods of construction.

---

[244] 282 Md 50, 382 A2d 1069 (1978).
[245] *Id* at 59, 382 A2d at 1074.

Some mathematics instructors have been heard to observe that there is more than one solution to a given problem and thus they are unable to say that any given method of solving a problem is the only correct solution, being able only to determine that the correct answer is produced. The same reasoning would apply to methods of construction. One skilled contractor may prefer one method for performing a given task while another contractor may choose what seems to him a simpler, less expensive way of reaching the same end result, either of which procedures would be a proper method. It could well be, however, that one method might not have occurred to an engineer or another contractor.[246]

The court acknowledged that the engineer might have *assumed*, by its conduct, responsibility for the safety of the workers on the job. The case was sent back to the trial court with instruction that the plaintiff should be given an opportunity to amend the complaint to strengthen the allegations that the engineer assumed responsibility for job safety even though that responsibility was not imposed by the contract documents.

As a matter of contract interpretation, the court in *Garden City Floral Co v Hunt*,[247] rejected the contractor's surety's contention that the owner was guilty of a breach of contract in failing to provide an architect with full supervisory authority. The owner provided an architect who had no authority over the methods or manner of construction used; this complied with the requirements of the contract.

Details of Construction

In *C.W. Regan, Inc v Parsons, Brinckerhoff Quade & Douglas*,[248] a tunnel contractor filed suit against an engineer when portions of the work were destroyed by water which entered the tunnel with an unanticipated spring tide, more than three feet above the previous record. Part of the water entered through a bulkhead with inadequate caulking. The court stated that there was no evidence of any duty on the part of the engineer to specify how the bulkhead should be caulked. This was a construction detail for the contractor to determine.

§9.26 —Rejection

A commentator points out that a number of cases have held that an architect is responsible for construction methods and suggests that this is at least arguably

---

[246] *Id* at 68, 382 A2d at 1079.
[247] 126 Mont 537, 255 P2d 352 (1953).
[248] 411 F2d 1379 (4th Cir 1969).

a form of strict liability, since typically the architect does not reasonably assume responsibility for the methods of construction employed by the contractor.[249]

Supervisory Power

The first case that held an architect responsible for the methods of construction employed by the contractor is said to be *Erhart v Hummonds*,[250] where an excavation collapsed because of inadequate shoring. It was shown that the architect's field supervisor had condemned the shoring installed by the contractor, stating that "it wasn't worth a damn" and it was like "whitewash." The architect demanded that the contractor employ a new superintendent, threatening otherwise that it would stop the work. The new superintendent arrived Friday and promised to rebuild the shoring first thing Monday morning, but it rained over the weekend and three employees were killed in the Monday morning collapse. The majority opinion pointed out that the contract gave the architect general supervision along with the authority to stop work. Therefore, the architect owed a duty to workers who might be injured because of the contractor's violation of the safety provisions of the contract and of safety ordinances.

The architect's power to stop work was also a factor in the decision in *Miller v De Witt*.[251] A roof collapsed during a gymnasium remodeling project because the steel scaffolding used to shore proscenium trusses would not support the load. The architects did not design the scaffolding, since this was within the province of the contractor. However, the court held the architect liable to injured workers, since the architect had the power to condemn defective work and the power to stop the job. Even though the architect may have had no duty to specify the method to be used in supporting the trusses, the architect did have the right to insist on adequate safety precautions.

Positive Protective Duty

A sensitive Iowa Supreme Court in *McCarthy v J.P. Cullen & Son Corp*[252] characterized the *methods of construction* defense as *startling*. The court was understandably irritated with an architect who displayed crass insensitivity to the problems of an innocent homeowner. The plaintiffs lived next to a high school site with their seven children. While the high school was under construction, storm water was diverted in such a manner as to enter their house, ruining all their furniture and possessions. Eventually the plaintiffs abandoned the first story of their house and moved into the second story, putting five girls

---

[249] Note, *Liability of Design Professionals—The Necessity of Fault*, 5 Iowa L Rev 1221 (1973).
[250] 232 Ark 133, 334 SW2d 869 (1960).
[251] 37 Ill 2d 273, 226 NE2d 630 (1967).
[252] 199 NW2d 362 (Iowa 1972).

in one bedroom and two boys in the other. They complained to the architect and the contractor, who proceeded with the project as though they had no connection with the situation. The jury awarded $5,500 in compensatory damages against the contractor and the architect, and $15,000 punitive damages against the contractor. The Iowa Supreme Court AFFIRMED. The architect has a duty to provide a design which would have protected the neighbor's property from storm water. The architect contended that the plans were designed to accommodate storm water after the completion of the project, but the contractor was responsible to restrain storm waters while the project was under construction. The court stated:

> We cannot agree defendant architect can so easily wish off his duty to the public generally for harm resulting from negligence in furnishing plans and specifications which cause damage during the work itself. We reject the ingenious and startling theory that a person can, by contract with a third party, lay down its own rules as to when it will be liable to those whom its negligence injures.[253]

Thus, the Iowa court held that an architect is under a positive duty to design a project so that third parties will not be injured during construction, and it is prevented by law from allowing the owner to leave these construction details in the hands of the contractor. Whether such a formulation of the rule would be applied in a case lacking the egregious disregard of public safety that characterizes the *McCarthy* case may well be doubted.

In *Loyland v Stone & Webster Engineering Corp*,[254] the Washington Court of Appeals held that failure to control methods of construction does not automatically cause liability. The question is to be resolved by the jury. The contract between an architect and an owner called for design, supervision, and administration of construction. The contractor was required by the contract documents to provide concrete forms subject to the approval of the architect. The forms broke, spilling wet concrete and workers into the Columbia River. Judgment on the verdict against the architect was AFFIRMED. The jury could have found the architect negligent, since a statute existed that required constant supervision and checking of forms during the installation of concrete; and the jury could have found that the architect was responsible for checking the adequacy of the forms even though they were designed by the contractor. Thus, it was the province of the jury to reject the architect's contention that it was responsible only for the finished product, and the jury did so.

---

[253] *Id* 370.
[254] 9 Wash App 682, 514 P2d 184 (1973), *review denied*, 83 Wash 2d 1007 (1974).

Summary

The assertion that the architect is not responsible for the methods of construction employed by the contractor has been accepted by some courts and rejected by others and has been both accepted and rejected in cases where the plaintiff is a contractor (or the surety of a contractor) and in cases where the plaintiff is an injured worker (or his survivor).

The courts that have rejected the defense hold an architect responsible for design and supervision of the details of construction, even though the owner does not require the architect to assume this responsibility and, presumably, is not willing to pay the architect to do so. But, it is not for the courts to say that an architect is responsible for the methods of construction merely because of its title or license: it is for the jury to determine whether, under all circumstances, including the terms of the contract between architect and owner, the architect breached a duty to protect third parties from injury from dangerous conditions that may occur during the progress of a job.

§9.27 Defective Work Concealed

An architect who accepts responsibility for the conformity of a project to the requirements of the contract documents undertakes a job that cannot be done to perfection. To insure conformity to the contract documents would require the continuous inspection of every operation. It may be possible for this to occur on some types of projects; for example, small pipeline projects. However, when the project is a building, it is impossible, without unlimited manpower, to inspect everything. This being the case, imperfections may occur despite vigilant inspection.

Imperfections occur even in manufactured products that are subject to searching inspection. The manufactured product is replicated many times from the same design, with the same personnel, at the same place. A manufacturer has the power to establish inspection procedures that should, in theory, be foolproof.

A construction project is a very different thing. It is built only once, and from a specially prepared design that contains thousands of elements. It is not unusual to find dozens of subcontractors employed on a project at the same time, performing different operations in different places. In many cases an architect relies on the manufacturer of an item of equipment to have performed its own inspections. Although an architect may specify a particular mixture for mortar or concrete block, it is not usually in a position to determine whether that specification has been followed. In view of all the circumstances, it may be taken as axiomatic that some imperfections always occur in any substantial project.

Yet, by the contract the architect may make itself responsible to the owner for project compliance with the requirements of the contract documents. It seems to be the customary procedure for the architect to visit a job but once daily, and then only for part of the day. As a result, much work is done when the architect is not present and may contain undiscovered imperfections.

It is elemental to the definition of malpractice that an architect does not guarantee a perfect result.[255] This concept is applied chiefly in cases of imperfection in plans. If it is the supervision or inspection process that has been imperfect, courts do not apply the doctrine so readily. Although an architect does not guarantee the perfect plan, seemingly it may guarantee perfect realization of the plan.

Perfection is a high standard. An architect could, as a matter of contract law, guarantee perfection. It could sell insurance rather than services. Yet, in cases which have considered strict liability, courts have held the opposite.[256]

An architect may be liable for damages caused by concealed defects. In *Straus v Buchman*,[257] the plaintiff purchased a partially completed building in New York City and employed architects to supervise the completion of construction undertaken by the vendor. In order to make way for a new stairwell, portions of the floor beams were shortened. Unbeknownst to the architect, they were improperly attached to a crossbeam and floored over. This procedure violated the building code, which provided that "in no case shall either end of a beam or beams rest on stud partitions."[258]

The architect visited the site once daily, as customary, but the improper work was performed and concealed between visits. It was discovered when the floor began to settle, causing great damage.

The court held that the architect was liable to the owner and that the concealment by the construction company was no defense, since it was the duty of the architect, under the contract, to see to it that construction conformed to the requirements of the building code.

The architect here was not the design architect, but the supervising (or inspecting) architect. Therefore, its liability was founded only on its failure to discover an improper technique employed by the contractor. It may be to the economic interest of a contractor to deceive an architect and owner by employing less expensive construction techniques. The supervising architect may therefore become responsible not just for detecting human error, but human venality. As elsewhere in life, venality may be accompanied by ingenuity.

---

[255] *See* §1.04.
[256] *See* ch 6.
[257] 96 AD 270, 89 NYS 226 (1904), *affd*, 184 NY 545, 76 NE 1109 (1906).
[258] NY Laws 1892, ch 275, 476, at 547.

Paxton v Alameda County[259] was decided on a theory of negligence rather than contract. An architect specified a roof composed of 16-inch sheathing over rafters on 32-inch centers: thus a span of approximately 30 inches. The specifications called for Douglas fir select merchantable seasoned lumber laid solid horizontally across the rafters. This specification was permitted by the building codes and was customary. A roofer, carrying hot tar, fell through the roof when the sheathing gave way.

At one inspection, the architect condemned sheathing that had been delivered but not installed, and instructed that it be removed from the job site. By the time of the architect's next visit, the roof had been installed and covered over with tar and gravel. The court AFFIRMED judgment on a verdict for the plaintiff against the owner on the ground that the owner's agent, the architect, failed to prevent the employment of defective, dangerous materials. The jury could have found that the architect was put upon inquiry and negligently failed to make another inspection until after the sheathing had been concealed from view.

By contrast, in *Cowles v City of Minneapolis*,[260] the court held that an engineer was not liable to an owner for failure to discover improperly driven piling. The engineer was employed "to inspect and supervise the materials and work during the course of construction so as to secure the best results, mechanically and architecturally." The project required that the contractor drive piling that would carry a load of 15 tons. After the project was completed, cracks appeared. It was then discovered that some of the piling would only support a load of 7 to 13 tons, rather than the designed 15 tons. The owner refused to pay the engineer's fee, and the engineer filed suit. Judgment for plaintiff AFFIRMED. The engineer had a duty to exercise ordinary care, skill, and diligence. It was not an insurer that the contractor would perform properly in all respects, and it had exercised reasonable care. The engineer inspected the project two or three times daily and tried to obtain proper records. Although it was not present when the defective piles were driven, it checked with employees of the contractor as to how the work had been performed and was assured that the piles had been driven to the required extent. These same workers had been reliable in the past. This evidence was sufficient to support the judgment of the trial court.

§9.28 Deviation from Plans

Many cases have asserted the self-evident proposition that, where the plaintiff complains that plans furnished by the architect were defective, it is part

---

[259] 119 Cal App 2d 393, 259 P2d 934 (1953).
[260] 128 Minn 452, 151 NW 184 (1915).

of the plaintiff's case to prove that the plans were followed.[261] In *McGuire v United Brotherhood of Carpenters & Joiners of America*,[262] the architect designed a retaining wall that was expected to deflect about three-fourths of an inch from the pressure of backfill. The wall was not built according to the contract documents: it protruded three and one-half inches over neighboring property, and rested against an adjoining building at one end. At the other end a designated joint was omitted. As a result, the deflection was uneven. The wall bowed in the middle with a deflection of as much as four inches there, but with no deflection at the ends since they were restrained by adjoining buildings. The court held that the architect was not responsible for the bowing and cracking, since it was caused by a failure to comply with the contract documents.[263]

In *Balcom Industries v Nelson*,[264] a grain storage bin was not built in accordance with the design: only 11 walers were used instead of 12; the walers were lapped instead of continuous; rebar was not directly tied; and roof rafters were not lapped to the studs. The bin collapsed. The court held that when a plaintiff alleges that an architect is negligent in preparing plans, it is essential that the plaintiff prove that the construction was in accordance with the plans.

In *Covil v Robert & Co*,[265] the plaintiff was injured when a T-joint dislodged from a 24-inch pipe in a pump station, releasing millions of gallons of water. The complaint alleged that the construction was "begun according to the plans and specifications." The architect moved for dismissal. HELD: the trial court should have dismissed the complaint. It is essential not merely to allege that the project was begun according to plans and specifications, but that at least the allegedly defective portion was actually constructed in accordance with the requirements of the plans and specifications.[266]

---

[261] Bayne v Everham, 197 Mich 181, 163 NW 1002 (1917) (building collapsed while under construction; the builder had omitted some steel called for by the plans and had lengthened the building without notifying the architect); Gaastra v Holmes, 36 NM 175, 10 P2d 589 (1932) (architect warned against defective construction); Lake v McElfatrick, 139 NY 349, 34 NE 922 (1893) (archway in opera house collapsed; plan required stone; arch was constructed of brick).

[262] 50 Wash 699, 314 P2d 439 (1957).

[263] *See also* Frank M. Dorsey & Sons v Frishman, 291 F Supp 794 (DDC 1968) (air conditioning system did not comply with the contract documents); Wheat Street Two, Inc v James C. Wise, Simpson, Aiken & Assocs, 132 Ga App 548, 208 SE2d 359 (1974) (an architect cannot be held liable for negligent design if the negligent design is not a part of the proximate cause of the damages).

[264] 169 Colo 128, 454 P2d 599 (1969).

[265] 112 Ga App 163, 144 SE2d 450 (1965).

[266] *See also* Ressler v Nielsen, 76 NW2d 157 (ND 1956) (plate glass cracked because of proximity to radiator; evidence that plaintiff did not use the quality of glass specified); Frank M. Dorsey & Sons v Frishman, 291 F Supp 794 (DDC 1968) (air conditioning plans were not installed in accordance with engineer's design).

In *Montgomery Industries International, Inc v Southern Baptist Hospital, Inc*,[267] a subcontractor deviated from the contract documents, and a resulting fire destroyed portions of the subcontractor's work. HELD: "A subcontractor may not unilaterally alter an architect's plans and then sue the architect when the resulting construction is deficient."[268]

In *Lukowski v Vecta Educational Corp*,[269] decedent fell from a set of bleachers while attending a basketball game. His widow alleged that the architect negligently failed to require compliance with drawings that called for installation of guardrails. Furthermore, the project was incomplete at the time of the accident. HELD: the evidence was insufficient to establish that the architect had assumed responsibility for the safety of persons on the construction site.

In *Goette v Press Bar & Cafe, Inc*,[270] the owner employed an architect to provide conceptual drawings at hourly rates. It was assumed that the walls would be constructed of masonry. When the architect noticed that the building was brick veneer over wood frame, it prepared a plan calling for *through bolting*. The contractor, after consulting with owner, employed *lag bolting*, and removed 8-inch brick across the front of the building, thus removing support. The parapet collapsed, causing property damage and personal injury. HELD: the architect's motion for summary judgment was properly granted. The architect had no duty to inspect or supervise the work and the trenching was a deviation from the architect's plans.

In *Cincinnati Riverfront Coliseum, Inc v McNulty Co*,[271] an architect was employed to design the Cincinnati Riverfront Coliseum. The architect employed an engineer to perform *all structural engineering services*. The construction of an elevated outdoor walkway designed by the engineer deviated from the plans and specifications. HELD: the contractor's deviations from the plans and specifications prepared by the engineer should have been regarded as material only if the deviations served independently to break the causal relation between the design and the plaintiff's damages by completely removing the effects of any negligence of the engineer in preparing the design.

An architect is not responsible, either to an owner or to a contractor, for damages and defects resulting from the contractor's failure to construct the project in accordance with the plans prepared by the architect.[272]

---

[267] 362 So 2d 145 (Fla Dist Ct App 1978).

[268] *Id* 146. *See also* Weston v New Bethel Missionary Baptist Church, 23 Wash App 747, 598 P2d 411 (1978) (collapse of a *rockery* designed to be 16 feet high and actually raised to a height of 22 feet).

[269] 401 NE2d 781 (Ind Ct App 1980).

[270] 413 NW2d 854 (Minn Ct App 1987).

[271] 28 Ohio St 3d 333, 504 NE2d 415 (1986).

[272] Keel v Titan Constr Corp, 721 P2d 828 (Okla Ct App 1986); Town of Urania v M.P. Dumesnil Constr Co, 492 So 2d 888 (La Ct App 1986).

An engineer designed a saltwater intake structure that called for a 30-inch pipe to be covered to a depth of 17 feet. Judgment for the engineer was AFFIRMED. The contractor did not comply with the engineer's design requiring 100 psi pipe with a minimum thickness of .310 inches. The contractor installed pipe that was .184 inches thick. Since the contractor did not comply with the engineer's design, it was not shown that the failure of the intake was caused by erroneous design.[273]

A contractor's deviation from plans and specifications does not necessarily exonerate an architect from liability. In *Corbetta Construction v Lake City Public Building Commission*,[274] the exterior walls of a courthouse complex separated and tilted outward, and the interior concrete walls tilted and pulled away from the ceilings. Independent engineers testified that the contractor had deviated from the plans and specifications. The architect claimed exoneration because of the contractor's deviation from the contract documents. HELD: the architect was responsible for the damage since the evidence showed that the building would have leaked and deteriorated even if constructed in strict accordance with the plans. Moreover, the architect was required by the contract to provide field supervision for not less than one-half of the working day; therefore, it was the architect's duty to discover the defects that caused the damage.

§9.29 Exculpatory Clauses

Modern legal thinking disdains exculpatory clauses. This is a departure from conventional common law thinking. The common law regarded the freedom to contract as a sanctified right. Courts would strictly enforce promises voluntarily undertaken by contracting parties. The more modern thinking is to limit the defendant's ability to gain advance consent to damaging conduct, particularly if consent is in boilerplate clauses buried in a barely coherent document, which is palmed off on a consumer of unequal bargaining power.

Architect as Drafter of Contract Documents

Part of the architect's professional function is to prepare contract documents. Although it may be suggested that this function is the practice of law, no case has been found that considers this point. It would seem that practicalities demand that architects, not just lawyers, prepare contract documents. Lawyers are not qualified to prepare technical specifications and plans. On the other hand, some elements of contract documents are really not within the architect's area of expertise: for example, indemnity clauses, insurance provisions,

---

[273] Ralph M. Parsons Co v Combustion Equip Assocs, 172 Cal App 3d 211, 218 Cal Rptr 170 (1985).

[274] 64 Ill App 3d 313, 381 NE2d 758 (1978).

arbitration clauses, and provisions relating to mechanics liens and substantial performance. It seems that lawyers should be employed in the preparation of standard forms of contract documents customarily used by architects. Lawyers should be consulted before legally sensitive clauses are omitted or changed.

Contract Documents

Contract documents are usually divided into five categories. The *agreement* may consist of only one or two pages. It is the document signed by the contractor and the owner, and incorporates the rest of the contract documents.

The *general conditions* may be 2 to 30 pages in length. They concern payment procedures, insurance, indemnity, subcontracts, delay, liquidated damages, arbitration, and other elements of the legal relationship among the contractor, subcontractors, architect, and owner.

The *special conditions* augment or modify the general conditions to reflect special characteristics of the job. The general conditions are designed to be used in a boilerplate fashion on all jobs. The special conditions contain necessary modifications because of the special characteristics of a particular job.

Drawings include the familiar roll of "plans" containing lines, figures, dimensions, measurements, and notes by which the architect depicts the physical characteristics of the project. Drawings contain considerable verbiage, sometimes of a contractual nature.

Specifications, sometimes in hundreds of pages, describe construction equipment, materials, and procedures. They are usually divided into sections that roughly correspond to conventional divisions of work among subcontractors: for example, excavation and grading, plumbing, heating-ventilation-air conditioning, electrical, paving, concrete, carpentry, and the like. Specifications in turn refer to published standards and codes produced by various agencies which furnish greater detail as to methods of installation, components, testing procedures, and the like. National codes and standards fill thousands of pages. They are incorporated into the contract documents, with sometimes unanticipated results. For example, the uniform building code contains language that is contractual in nature, yet it may not harmonize with the contractual provisions of the general conditions or the specifications.

In addition to the contract documents between the contractor and the owner, the architect usually furnishes a form of contract between the owner and the architect. Most often this document employs a form published by the American Institute of Architects (AIA). The provisions, thus, naturally provide full contractual protection of the interests of the architect.

Public Contracts

Contract documents for public projects include bidding documents. The *invitation to bid*, often incorporated into the contract, gives the nature of the job and appoints the time and place for the opening bids. It usually specifies the bonding requirements imposed on the contractor.

The *bid form* is, in public contract procedure, part of the contract documents. It is usually one or two pages long and constitutes the contractor's offer to perform work. When a public agency awards a contract, it accepts the bid. A contract is then formed which in its turn incorporates general conditions, special conditions, drawings, and specifications.

Standard Forms

Often, contract documents are prepared with a bias favoring the party who employed the drafter. Contract documents for public projects are carefully prepared for the protection of the public entity.

Contract documents for private projects may be prepared by the contractor, the architect, or the owner. The architect may be biased in favor of its client (the owner). Standard contract documents furnished by the AIA are in great currency. Although they take into consideration the contractor's point of view, such documents, for the most part, carefully protect the interests of the owner and, not incidentally, the architect. National contractors organizations play a considerable role in drafting the AIA contract documents. The Associated General Contractors (AGC) markets an extensive series of forms that give sensitive consideration to the interests of contractors.

§9.30 —Application

Exculpatory clauses inserted into contract documents for the protection of the architect may appear in the general contract documents or in the owner-architect contract. In recent years architects have shown concern about decisions that have held them liable to injured third parties for failure to properly supervise a project. As a result, the American Institute of Architects (AIA) general conditions reject the word *supervise*, and provide that the architect "will not be required to make exhaustive or continuous on-site inspections to check the quality or quantity of the work and he will not be responsible for the contractor's failure to carry out the construction work in accordance with the contract documents."[275]

Claims by Sureties

This provision served to protect an architect from liability in *J&J Electric, Inc v Gilbert H. Moen Co.*[276] An electrical subcontractor who was guilty of

---

[275] AIA Document B141, art 1.5.4 (1977).
[276] 9 Wash App 954, 516 P2d 217 (1973), *writ denied*, 83 Wash 2d 1088 (1974).

grossly deficient performance was finally ejected from the job and replaced by another subcontractor. The prime contractor then filed an action against the surety on the subcontractor's performance bond, claiming damages for improper performance. The surety, in turn, filed suit against the project architect and electrical engineer. The court referred to the AIA language that appeared in the provisions of the contract between the architect and the owner. This language was held to specifically absolve the architect and the consulting engineer from liability for the subcontractor's failure to properly perform work.

In *City of Durham v Reidsville Engineering Co*,[277] a surety of a defaulting contractor filed an action against supervising engineers, alleging that their failure to properly supervise contributed to default by the contractor. The court held that, under the terms of the contract between the owner and the contractor, the supervising engineer acted in the capacity of an arbitrator rather than a supervisor, and as a result, the engineer could not be liable in the absence of bad faith.

Claims by Contractors

In *C.W. Regan, Inc v Parsons, Brinckerhoff, Quade & Douglas*,[278] the contract between a general contractor and an owner provided:

> approval by the engineer merely means that at the time the engineer grants approval he knows of no good reason for objecting; approval does not relieve the contractor of any of his responsibilities; the engineer will instruct the contractor to replace unsatisfactory work; the contractor will indemnify the engineer and the owner from all claims arising out of operations of the contractor; and the engineer will have no personal liability.

The contractor filed an action against the engineer on three theories: third-party beneficiary (this was abandoned at trial); breach of warranty; and the negligent performance of a duty of inspection. Water had entered the contractor's tunnel during an unanticipated spring tide, causing damage. The contractor alleged that the water entered the job site because of inadequate design of bulkheads and caulking devices. In holding that the engineer was not guilty of any breach of implied warranty, the court referred to the provisions of the contract and held that the possibility of an implied warranty was excluded by the contract provisions: there can be no implied warranty where the contractor agrees to indemnify the engineer and where approval is said to merely designate that the engineer knows of no reason to object.

---

[277] 255 NC 98, 120 SE2d 564 (1961).
[278] 411 F2d 1379 (4th Cir 1969).

In *J&J Electric*, the exculpatory clause that precluded liability was found in the contract between the owner and the architect; in *C.W. Regan*, the exculpatory clause was in the contract between the contractor and the owner.

In *Harbor Mechanical, Inc v Arizona Electric Power Co-op, Inc*,[279] the contract between a design engineer and an owner provided that the obligations of the engineer "run to and are for the benefit of only the owner and the administrator." HELD: the engineer owed no duty to contractors or subcontractors. Therefore, summary judgment was granted in favor of the engineer on the negligence cause of action.

In *Gherardi v Board of Education*,[280] a contractor was required to construct a school project in 400 days. Completion was delayed by 11 months. The contractor filed suit against the architect, claiming that the architect interfered with performance of the contract by failing to properly coordinate and supervise the work. The exculpatory clause in the contract provided that the contractor would be entitled to an extension of time for unavoidable delays, and: "[a]part from extension of time for unavoidable delays, no payment or allowance of any kind shall be made to the Contractor as compensation for damages on account of hindrance or delay from any cause in the progress of the work, whether such delay be avoidable or unavoidable." HELD: the exculpatory clause clearly barred an action for damages unless the architect acted in bad faith.

Claims by Owners

In *Shepherd v City of Palatka*,[281] a city sued its architect for negligent preparation of plans and specifications and charged that the architect failed to make timely and proper inspection of the contractor's work. The city also sued the contractor and the contractor's surety for negligent failure to follow plans and specifications. The architect cross-complained against the contractor for indemnification. Summary judgment for the city against all three defendants was REVERSED. The exculpatory clause in the contract provided that, while the architect was required to make inspections, the architect was not under a duty to discover the contractor's omissions. This language absolved the architect of liability for errors by the contractor.

In *Moundsview Independent School District No 621 v Buetow & Associates*,[282] the contract stated that the architect was not "responsible for the contractor's failure to carry out the work in accordance with the contract documents." A windstorm blew the roof off the completed building, allegedly because of the

---

[279] 496 F Supp 681 (D Ariz 1980).
[280] 53 NJ Super 349, 147 A2d 535 (1958).
[281] 399 So 2d 1044 (Fla Dist Ct App 1981).
[282] 253 NW2d 836 (Minn 1977).

contractor's failure to properly fasten the roof to the building. Summary judgment for defendant was AFFIRMED. The architect contracted and was paid only for general supervisory services, and not for the more detailed checking that was to be performed by a *clerk of the works*. The plain language of the contract exculpated the architect from liability caused by acts or omissions of the contractor.

In *530 East 89 Corp v Unger*,[283] architects were under time pressure to file plans with the city building department before adoption of a new, more restrictive ordinance. The contract with the owner provided: "We will make every effort to satisfy all requirements. Under no circumstances do we imply a guarantee." Despite seven amendments, the city building department never approved the plans. The trial court dismissed the complaint and was AFFIRMED. The contract specifically negated any guarantee that the plans would be accepted.

In *Harman v CE&M, Inc*,[284] an exculpatory clause in an oral contract between an engineer and a contractor was effective to prevent liability of the engineer to the owner. The contractor employed the engineer to design a floating slab as opposed to a structural slab. Because of the compressive nature of the soil, the slab sunk six to eight inches. The oral contract specifically excluded any responsibility for the slab, the foundation, or the drawings for each. HELD: although the owners were third-party beneficiaries to the oral contract, they were bound by the contract provisions. Here, the contract specifically excluded liability for the defective condition of the slab.

In *M. Miller Co v Central Contra Costa Sanitary District*,[285] the defendant was a soil consultant employed by the district engineer of a sanitary district. The contractor alleged that the soil consultant negligently failed to disclose unstable materials in its reports, which were furnished to builders and relied upon by the contractor in submitting its bid. The contract between the contractor and the sanitary district provided that the bidder would carefully examine the site, that the district did not guarantee the accuracy of soil information, and that the engineer would not be personally responsible for any deficiencies. The court held that these exculpatory provisions would not serve to protect the soil consultant since it was an independent contractor.

In *McCarthy v J.P. Cullen & Son Corp*,[286] the plaintiff's house was flooded by storm waters from a high school construction site. The architect argued that the contractor was responsible for drainage during construction and pointed out

---

[283] 54 AD2d 848, 388 NYS2d 284 (1976), *affd*, 43 NY2d 776, 373 NE2d 276, 402 NYS2d 382 (1977).
[284] 493 NE2d 1319 (Ind Ct App 1986).
[285] 198 Cal App 2d 305, 18 Cal Rptr 13 (1961).
[286] 199 NW2d 362 (Iowa 1972).

provisions in the contract between the contractor and the owner which held the contractor responsible for safety precautions during the construction process. In rejecting the architect's contention that it was absolved from responsibility for drainage during construction by the provisions of the contract documents, the Iowa Supreme Court stated:

> We cannot agree defendant architect can so easily wish off his duty to the public generally for harm resulting from negligence in furnishing plans and specifications which caused the damage during the work itself. We reject the ingenious and startling theory that a person can, by contract with a third party, lay down his own rules as to when he will be liable to those whom his negligence injures.[287]

The effect of an exculpatory clause may be limited by an agency's contracting power. In *White Construction Co v Commonwealth*,[288] White Construction brought an action against the commonwealth demanding compensation for extra construction costs allegedly due to defective and inadequate plans and specifications. The commonwealth, in turn, brought a third-party complaint against the architectural firm that prepared the plans and specifications. The summary judgment for the architectural firm was REVERSED. The exculpatory clause drafted by the commonwealth conferred upon the architect an unconditional release of all liability before construction of the project even began. Architects are bound by the general rule that persons who deal with governmental agencies must take notice of limitations on their contracting power and cannot rely on contract provisions which overstep these limitations. The exculpatory clause did not relieve the architectural firm of its professional responsibilities under the contract.

An architect required a pile driving subcontractor on an airport project to stop work, to then perform load tests, and to use additional materials that were not called for in the contract documents. The subcontractor filed an action against the architect in order to recover compensation for the extra costs incurred. The architect alleged that it was not liable because of exculpatory language in the subcontract. HELD: the exculpatory clause did not apply to pre-construction negligence. "Claims for pre-construction negligence necessarily did not fall within the proscription of the exculpatory clause since the contract did not exist at that time."[289]

---

[287] *Id* 370.
[288] 81 Mass App 640, 418 NE2d 357 (1981).
[289] S.K. Whitty & Co v Laurence L. Lambert & Assocs, 576 So 2d 599, 601 (La Ct App), *writ denied*, 580 So 2d 928 (La 1991).

Claims by Workers

In *Luterbach v Mochon, Schutte, Hackworthy, Juerisson, Inc*,[290] a worker was injured in a cave-in at a construction site. Plaintiff alleged that the excavation was improperly shored and braced, and that the architect had failed to supervise the project. Defendant's motion for summary judgment was granted and AFFIRMED. Under the contract documents, the architect was responsible for the *general supervision* and *direction of the work*. However, the contract provided that the architect was *not* responsible for the methods of construction or for safety precautions. HELD: the contract was unambiguous, and the architect had no duties with regard to the safety of the construction site.

The exculpatory clause found in an inspecting engineer's contract in *Conti v Pettibone Cos*[291] precluded liability to third parties. A bucket filled with sandbags dropped on the head of a construction worker. As one theory of liability, the plaintiff charged that the inspecting engineer failed in the duty to insure the safety of the area. Summary judgment for defendant was AFFIRMED. The engineer was not chargeable with the duty of insuring a safe construction site. The sole purpose of the engineer's inspection of the site was to assure that the project was built in compliance with the contract documents. Further, the contract specifically stated that the "Agreement shall not create or give third parties any claim or right of action against the engineer or the city."[292]

In *Harman v CE&M, Inc*,[293] an exculpatory clause in an oral contract between an engineer and a contractor was effective to prevent liability of the engineer to the owner. The contractor employed the engineer to design a floating slab as opposed to a structural slab. Because of the compressive nature of the soil, the slab sunk six to eight inches. The oral contract specifically excluded any responsibility for the slab, foundation, or the drawings for each. HELD: although the owners were third-party beneficiaries to the oral contract, they were bound by the contract provisions. Here, the contract specifically excluded liability for the defective condition of the slab.

Defense Rejected

In *Farrell Construction Co v Jefferson Parrish*,[294] a contract between the engineer and the city contained exculpatory clauses. HELD: the exculpatory

---

[290] 84 Wis 2d 1, 267 NW2d 13 (1978).

[291] 111 Misc 2d 772, 445 NYS2d 943 (Sup Ct 1981).

[292] *See also* Brown v Gamble Constr Co, 537 SW2d 685 (Mo Ct App 1976) (worker fell through hole in roof during construction; directed verdict for defendant architect was AFFIRMED; the contract provided that the architect was not responsible for job site safety; the contractor had assumed that duty).

[293] 493 NE2d 1319 (Ind Ct App 1986).

[294] 693 F Supp 490 (ED La 1988).

clauses did not protect the engineer, since the acts that caused damage to the contractor (negligent delay in approval of shop drawings and change orders) occurred before the contract containing the exculpatory clause was signed.

In a contract between a design engineer and a city under which the engineer was to prepare plans for a wastewater treatment facility in 135 days, a clause limited the engineer's liability to the city for damages to loss caused by "professional negligent acts, errors or omissions." HELD: limitation of liability clauses are not favored, and will be strictly construed and limited to their exact language. Here, it was clearly understood by both parties that failure to have the plans ready within the specified time frame would result in a reduction of the city's funding entitlement from 75 per cent funding to 55 per cent funding. Judgment against the engineer in the amount of $338,935 was AFFIRMED.[295]

Among cases that give strict construction to exculpatory clauses is *Lincoln Pulp & Paper Co v Dravo Corp*.[296] Dravo contracted to design and construct a new heat and chemical recovery boiler at a fixed fee of $5.2 million. The exculpatory clause provided: "Dravo shall not be liable for any liability or special or consequential damages resulting from loss of time in putting the unit in operation, or resulting from delays or loss of time affecting other plants or property of Lincoln or for loss of profits or products." HELD: this clause shielded Dravo from liability for breaches of contract, but not from liability for consequential damages resulting from negligence. It is valid for parties to contract to relieve themselves from the results of their own negligence, but such contracts are not favored by the law and will be construed strictly, with every doubt resolved against the party seeking their protection, particularly when that same party drafted the contract. In this case, the language chosen lacked an expression of clear and unequivocal intent to relieve Dravo from liability for damages caused by its own negligence.

In *Kleb v Wendling*,[297] the architect claimed exoneration because, in an oral contract with the owner, the architect agreed to *administer the contract* rather than *supervise the work*. The architect testified that it used the jargon *administer* rather than *supervise* in order to avoid liability under the Structural Work Act. However, it also testified that its role did not change whether it was supervising or administering a contract. The court held that the term *administer the contract* as used in the conversations between the architect and the owner was the functional equivalent of *supervise the contract*. "It is the architect's duty, when superintending or overseeing the construction of a building, to prevent gross

---

[295] W. William Graham, Inc v City of Cave City, 289 Ark 105, 709 SW2d 94, 96 (1986).
[296] 436 F Supp 262 (D Me 1977).
[297] 67 Ill App 3d 1016, 385 NE2d 346 (1978).

carelessness or imperfect construction. Mere detection of defective workmanship does not relieve him of a duty to prevent it."[298]

In *Della Corte v Incorporated Village of Williston Park*,[299] owners employed the defendant engineer to inspect a home before they purchased it. The report included a disclaimer stating that it covered only portions of the premises which could be examined visually. After plaintiffs purchased the house, they discovered drainage and seepage problems occurred after every rainfall. Summary judgment for defendant was REVERSED. Exculpatory clauses should be given a strict construction. The engineer was only liable for negligence in the inspection and reporting of *visually* perceptible features.

§9.31 —Criticism

There is a sharp contrast between the judicial attitude of *J&J Electric, Inc v Gilbert H. Moen Co*,[300] and that in *McCarthy v J.P. Cullen & Son Corp*.[301] One court blandly held that the architect's duty to the contractor's surety was measured by the provisions of the contract between the owner and the architect; the other found such a theory to be ingenious and startling. The cases are indeed distinguishable: in one case the plaintiff was a neighbor; in another it was the surety standing in the shoes of a subcontractor. In one case the exculpatory clause appeared in the contract between the architect and the owner; in the other it appeared in the contract between the owner and the prime contractor. Yet, in each case, the architect urged the court to give effect to exculpatory language in a contract between strangers to the plaintiff. One court enforced the clause; the other was startled by the concept.

This divergence of attitude is explained by the failure of the courts to enunciate consistent theories (or sometimes any theory) of malpractice liability to third parties. Few court employ third-party beneficiary contract theory to impose liability. The third-party beneficiary theory will not usually work in malpractice cases, because the contract between the architect and the owner is seldom expressly for the benefit of a third party. If it were found so, the next edition of the contract form would expressly negate any such intention. Yet, the courts do frequently refer to the provisions of the contract documents between owner and contractor to determine the extent of an architect's responsibility to third parties. It seems that the responsibility of an architect is not founded just on its status as architect, but also on contract provisions that relate to that status.

---

[298] *Id* at 1020, 385 NE2d at 349.
[299] 60 AD2d 639, 400 NYS2d 357 (1977).
[300] 9 Wash App 954, 516 P2d 217 (1973), *writ denied*, 83 Wash 2d 1088 (1974).
[301] 199 NW2d 362 (Iowa 1972).

Where the theory of liability is contract, third-party beneficiary contract, express warranty, or implied warranty, then it seems that the courts should give effect to exculpatory clauses, unless policy considerations forbid their enforcement. Theories of liability that developed from the law of contract expressly depend upon the provisions of the contract to impose liability.

If the theory of liability is negligence, then the court should instruct the jury to consider the provisions of the contract as an element in determining whether the architect exercised ordinary professional care to avoid injury to the plaintiff. Referral to an exculpatory clause is not ingenious or startling; nor do its provisions conclusively exonerate the architect from liability. The clause is one of many elements to be considered in determining whether the conduct of the architect has satisfied the standard of professional care.

§9.32 Exclusive Remedy

The exclusive remedy defense is generally asserted against, rather than by, an architect. It is, however, occasionally asserted by an architect against a contractor or an owner.

As pointed out in an excellent law review comment,[302] the defense arises in indemnity cases where the asserted indemnitor is the employer of the injured worker. A typical case arises when an employee of a general contractor is injured on the job and recovers workers' compensation from the contractor's insurance carrier. The worker (or the workers' compensation carrier by subrogation) then files an action against the architect for malpractice. The architect in turn alleges that it is entitled to indemnity from the general contractor on the theory that the contractor's negligence caused the injury, and the architect's only fault was its failure to discover and prevent the negligent activity of the contractor. At this point, the contractor may assert the exclusive remedy defense: the workers' compensation statutes were enacted as a legislative compromise between workers and employers under which the worker exchanged damages for liability; the amount of damages was limited, but the employer's liability was made certain. Thus, workers' compensation damages are computed according to schedule. They do not include compensation for pain and suffering. However, the employer is liable whether it is negligent or not. One of the elements of this compromise was the provision that the claimant's right to recover workers' compensation would be its exclusive remedy against the employer. If the employer is required to pay workers' compensation, and

---

[302] Comment, *The Supervising Architect: His Liabilities and His Remedies When a Worker Is Injured*, 64 NWL Rev 535 (1969).

thereafter general damages in an indemnity action, it is deprived of the benefit of the legislative bargain: a limitation of damages to those scheduled under the workers' compensation laws.

The exclusive remedy defense operated to protect the manager of engineering and construction in *Caldwell v Cleveland-Cliffs Co.*[303] An employee of Bechtel Corporation was seriously injured when a crate fell from a forklift truck. The forklift was owned by Bechtel and driven by a Bechtel employee. Bechtel was described in a written contract as the manager of engineering and construction and acted subject to the general direction and control of the owner, Cleveland-Cliffs. The court of appeals AFFIRMED the lower court's ruling that the workers' compensation statute limited the plaintiff's remedy against Bechtel. However, because Bechtel was found to be Cleveland-Cliffs' agent, Cleveland-Cliffs was liable to the plaintiff for the entire amount of the damage award.[304]

The exclusive remedy defense was denied in *Miller v DeWitt*. The court suggested the solution should have been statutory. This would seem to be the correct approach. However, one commentator has criticized the *judicial fiat* of *Miller*.[305] In justice to the architect, it should be afforded indemnity by the contractor in a case where the contractor was negligent and the architect merely failed to detect that negligence. On the other hand, the employer who "traded" liability for damages should be accorded the benefit of the legislative bargain.

The exclusive remedy defense found an unusual application in *Pettigrew v Home Insurance Co.*[306] A worker was injured on the job and recovered workers' compensation. Then it sued the employer's workers' compensation carrier, alleging that the carrier had agreed to perform safety engineering inspections and had negligently failed to protect the plaintiff against injury. HELD: the Nebraska statute rendered both the employer and the workers' compensation insurance carrier immune from liability after workers' compensation has been paid.

The exclusive remedy defense was held available to an engineer who was employed by a general contractor when the claimant was a worker employed by that same general contractor.[307]

---

[303] 111 Mich App 721, 315 NW2d 186 (1981), *appeal denied*, 417 Mich 914, 330 NW2d 854 (1983).

[304] The exclusive remedy defense, under facts similar to those hypothesized above, was rejected in Miller v DeWitt, 37 Ill 2d 273, 226 NE2d 630 (1967), accepted in Fidelity & Casualty Co v J.A. Jones Constr Co, 325 F2d 605 (8th Cir 1963), and Howard, Needles, Tammen & Bergendoff v Stears, Perini & Pomeroy, 312 A2d 621 (Del Super Ct 1973), and ignored in White v Morris Handler Co, 7 Ill App 3d 199, 287 NE2d 203 (1972).

[305] Comment, *The Supervising Architect: His Liabilities and His Remedies When a Worker Is Injured*, 64 NWL Rev 535 (1969).

[306] 191 Neb 312, 214 NW2d 920 (1974).

[307] Conklin v Cohen, 287 So 2d 56 (Fla 1973).

§9.33 Privilege

In performing its duties, an architect may advise the owner as to the qualifications of contractors and subcontractors. Courts have held that an architect is liable for a failure to warn a client against incompetent contractors. The duty, apparently, is one that is implied from the architect's status as a fiduciary to the owner. It need not be expressly imposed by the terms of the contract between the architect and the owner.

Accordingly, an architect must have a qualified privilege to communicate to the owner derogatory information about a contractor. In *Vojak v Jensen*,[308] the architect did so and became a defendant in a libel suit. A feud between the subcontractor and the architect began on a school job in 1957. The roof was defective. Each blamed the other: the architect claimed the workmanship was wrong; the subcontractor claimed the design was wrong.

When the general contractor on a subsequent job awarded roofing work to the same delinquent subcontractor, the architect wrote two letters, one to the subcontractor with a copy to the owner and the general contractor, another to the general contractor with copies to the owner and subcontractor. The architect stated that it could not approve the subcontractor for the roofing project and requested that the subcontractor refrain from bidding further work from the architect's office until it proved itself reliable. The letters induced the general contractor to cancel the subcontract. A jury brought in a verdict of $60,000 in actual damages and $15,000 in punitive damages. REVERSED on cross-appeal.

The court acknowledged that a charge of business incompetence is libel per se. Nevertheless, an architect has a qualified privilege to communicate derogatory information in good faith to a party with an interest in the subject matter. The privilege does not excuse actual malice. The evidence established the qualified privilege, and therefore the burden was on the plaintiff to establish malice. The instruction of the trial court was erroneous, since it failed to put this burden on the plaintiff.

In *Dehnert v Arrow Sprinklers, Inc*,[309] a contractor submitted a bid to a school district based on use of a nonconforming, non-specified plastic sprinkler head. The engineer and the architect approved shop drawings that were not specific regarding the sprinkler head to be used. After they had been installed, the architect objected, but the contractor refused to change the sprinkler heads, alleging that the architect had approved the change. The architect then recommended, and the school board effected, termination of the contract. The contractor obtained a verdict against the architect for intentional interference with contractual relations. REVERSED. An architect acting within the scope

---

[308] 161 NW2d 100 (Iowa 1968).
[309] 705 P2d 846 (Wyo 1985).

of its contractual obligations to the owner cannot be liable for advising the owner to terminate a relationship with a contractor, unless the architect has acted in bad faith or maliciously. The architect's preliminary approval of the substituted sprinkler heads did not waive the requirement that the contractor obtain a change order. Therefore, the architect's recommendation that the school board terminate the contract was justified.

§9.34 Sovereign Immunity

The doctrine of sovereign immunity follows from the doctrine of the infallibility of the king: "The King, moreover, is not only incapable of doing wrong, but even of thinking wrong; he can never mean to do an improper thing; in him is no folly or weakness."[310]

However, an even earlier principle announced that "the prince is not above the laws, but the laws above the prince."[311] Chief Justice Jay, in *Chisholm v Georgia*, could "wish the state of society was so far improved, and the science of government advanced to such a degree of perfection, as that the whole nation could in the peaceable course of law, be compelled to do justice, and be sued by individual citizens."[312]

Courts are uncomfortable with the doctrine of sovereign immunity. In many states the doctrine has been restricted or abolished. In states where the doctrine merely has been restricted, courts have striven to find exceptions to the rule of immunity. Why, after all, should the state, which derives its power from the people, and which exists only for the benefit of the citizenry, not be called to justice when it commits injuries against the population it was created to protect?

Under modern legal thinking, it is no answer to say that damage judgments against the state will have to be paid by the taxpayers. An objective of modern tort law is to distribute risk, and the risk of injury to a citizen should be spread among the population that benefits from the activity that causes the injury.

It may be argued that fear of liability would impregnate the bureaucracy with unseemly caution. Yet, an objective of modern tort law is to discourage recklessness that injures. Under the weight of such arguments, the doctrine of sovereign immunity may be destined for extinction.

As courts have sought to excise the doctrine of governmental immunity, the legislative response has confused the issue. Year after year, lawyers and courts blunder through a miasma of irrational, ambiguous, and unfair distinctions among proprietary functions, governmental functions, ministerial duties, discretionary functions, special statutes of limitations, and lethal claims requirements. Meanwhile, the legislatures, hurried by lobbyists of municipalities

---

[310] 1 W. Blackstone, Commentaries 246.
[311] G.C. Pliny, Panegyricus 65.
[312] 2 US (2 Dall) 419, 478 (1793).

verging on bankruptcy, hurriedly erect barriers to exempt society from responsibility for injuries perpetrated by its ministers.

An axiom of modern tort thinking holds that risk should be spread among those who benefit from the activity that causes injury, especially among those of heavy purse. The most perfect engine that human ingenuity has devised to spread cost among those who can afford to pay is taxation. It follows that government is an ideal agency to absorb risk. Indeed, a primary function of government is to absorb risks. This is shown by programs of disaster relief—universally accepted as an ordinary and proper function of government. A distinctive feature of the welfare state is acceptance by government of responsibility for risks that it does not create. However, let it be suggested that government should be responsible for risks that it *does* create, and it is argued that civilization would be shaken to its foundations by disregard of the ancient and venerable doctrine of sovereign immunity. It is a strange reflection of the common law's inconsistency that while wind and rain, yet not the king, could enter the most humble cottage, a citizen could not sue the king without permission. In modern times this same doctrine is applied to shelter negligent architects who are minions of the state.

§9.35 —Application

Although courts in Arizona have abrogated the judicial doctrine of sovereign immunity, a statute provides that no action shall be brought against the state, the state engineer, or any employee of the state for damages sustained through the partial or total failure of any dam.[313]

The statute figured in a case in which a builder proposed dam plans, which were approved by the state engineer. The dam failed. Plaintiff was injured. Plaintiff argued that the state must not exercise absolute control over design and construction and at the same time avoid any responsibility for failure of the dam. The court held that the specific legislative pronouncement of immunity in a special case must be observed, even though the judicial doctrine of governmental immunity had been abrogated. Rejecting the argument that enforcement of the statute in this case would constitute a taking of private property without due process, the court refused to inquire into the wisdom, justice, or expedience of the enactment of the legislature.[314]

In *Snell v Stein*,[315] plaintiff's husband and father were killed in a traffic accident, allegedly because the parish and its engineer had negligently designed an *entrapping traffic control system* at an intersection. The court dismissed the

---

[313] Ariz Rev Stat Ann §45-715 (1956).
[314] Turner v Superior Court (Pima County), 3 Ariz App 414, 415 P2d 129 (1966).
[315] 201 So 2d 876 (La Ct App), *writ refused*, 251 La 35, 202 So 2d 652 (La 1967).

complaint on the ground that the Louisiana cases clearly establish that the erection and maintenance of traffic signals is a governmental rather than a proprietary function. Therefore, the government and its officers were immune from liability unless the legislature specifically waived immunity in the particular case. The engineer partakes of governmental immunity unless acting "without the scope of his authority or in bad faith in the performance of his duties."[316]

In *Panepinto v Edmart, Inc*,[317] a city engineer negligently approved sewer plans for a subdivision. Plaintiffs' basements were flooded with sewage. The trial court held that the engineer was liable for *affirmative negligent conduct*. REVERSED. The engineer approved the plans in good faith. Its acts involved the exercise of "discretionary quasi-judicial functions and duties, and so afford no basis for imposing liability in damages either on the engineer or his employer, the city."[318]

The owners of a single-family dwelling sought compensatory and punitive damages against a municipality, its elected officials, certain municipal employees, and the municipal engineer for losses resulting from the construction of two municipal wells. The water supply was interrupted as a result of the construction, and the owners were forced to abandon their dwelling, which was subsequently robbed. Summary judgment for defendants was AFFIRMED. The complaint failed to state a cause of action based on negligence and on alleged civil rights violations because discretionary judgments affecting the design and construction of public works or improvements are protected by the doctrine of municipal immunity.[319]

The Tennessee Attorney General opines that a licensed architect, who as an employee of the state stamps all plans and specifications prepared in-house, is not personally liable to injured private individuals where the action involved was discretionary; where the architect acted within the scope of the discretion granted; and where neither malice, corruption, nor willful misconduct could be imputed.[320]

In *Ogle v Billick*,[321] the court found that a trial would be necessary to determine whether a county engineer was protected by the doctrine of sovereign immunity. The county lowered the grade of a road at the bottom of a stairway leading from the plaintiff's house, which undermined the handrail. Plaintiff fell

---

[316] *Id* 879.

[317] 129 NJ Super 319, 323 A2d 533, *cert denied*, 66 NJ 333, 331 A2d 33 (1974).

[318] *Id* at 324, 323 A2d at 536. *Accord* McDonough v Whalen, 365 Mass 506, 313 NE2d 435 (1974) (*dictum*).

[319] Woodsum v Pemberton Township, 177 NJ Super 639, 427 A2d 615 (1981).

[320] Op Tenn Atty Gen 82-161 (Mar 31, 1982).

[321] 253 Or 92, 453 P2d 677 (1969).

when the handrail gave way. The trial court dismissed the complaint, on the ground that the engineer was immune from liability. REVERSED.

The complaint alleged that the engineer was personally negligent in not properly supervising construction. Plaintiff was entitled to a jury determination as to whether the functions of the engineer were *discretionary* (in which case it would be immune) or *ministerial* (in which case it might be liable).

The United States is not liable under the Federal Tort Claims Act[322] for any claim based upon the exercise or performance of, or failure to exercise or perform, discretionary functions by a federal agency or government employee, whether or not the discretion is abused.[323]

In *McDermott v TENDUM Constructors*,[324] the plaintiff brought a wrongful death action against a joint venture consisting of contractor, subcontractor, and architectural firms. (The decedent was a mail handler at the New York Bulk and Foreign Mail Center.) HELD: the contractor and subcontractor were protected by the doctrine of governmental immunity, since they performed their work in strict compliance with plans and specifications provided by the United States Post Office Department. The architect, on the other hand, was fully responsible for planning and designing all aspects of the facility and, thus, would not be protected by the doctrine of governmental immunity.

§9.36 —Rejection

In a series of cases, courts have found public engineers and inspectors liable for damage caused by negligent activity. In *Cox v City of Freeman*,[325] a contractor sued a city engineer, claiming that the engineer delayed completion of a job by failure to have engineering work ready on time, and alleging delay in locating the site, and other discrepancies. The court held that if the engineer were negligent, it would be liable, and the city would also be liable under the doctrine of *respondeat superior*, but both were protected by an accord and satisfaction: the contractor had released all claims in order to obtain *final payment*.

Although it is usually held that a governmental agency's performance of building inspections does not give rise to a duty of care to any individual, the Minnesota Supreme Court has held that a county can be liable for negligently requiring an owner to build a defective septic tank system.[326] A county health

---

[322] 28 USC §2680(a).

[323] Patton v United States, 549 F Supp 36 (WD Mont 1982) (alleged negligent roadway design).

[324] 211 NJ Super 196, 511 A2d 690 (1986).

[325] 321 F2d 887 (8th Cir 1963).

[326] Gilbert v Billman Constr, Inc, 371 NW2d 542 (Minn 1985).

inspector examined the owners' land and instructed them to build a *mound* septic system. The owner used plans provided by the county, but the system overflowed and it was necessary to construct a new pressurized system. HELD: the *public duty* immunity did not protect the county from liability since the county acted negligently by requiring the owner to build a particular system which the county should have known created an unreasonable risk of injury.

In *Chart v Dvorak*,[327] the Supreme Court of Wisconsin held that a state engineer did not share the governmental immunity of the state highway commission. Plaintiff alleged that the engineer had failed to post a *curve 20 mile per hour* sign as required by state regulations. The court examined the state highway commission job description of the district chief maintenance engineer and district traffic supervisor and found that they had "official nondelegable authority and responsibility for the placement of such highway warning signs."[328] Therefore, without discussion, the court held that they were not immune from liability.

Similarly, the state was found liable for faulty design resulting in a dangerous condition causing injury to a driver in *Erfurt v State*.[329] When plaintiff reached the crest of an uphill climb, the sun suddenly shown in plaintiff's eyes. The highway lacked guiding markings and had no noise buttons in the surface of the road. Judgment for plaintiff was AFFIRMED. Expert testimony indicated that the combination of the design of the highway with an absence of warning devices constituted a pattern of traffic control that was part of a dangerous condition.

In *Blackburn v State*,[330] it was held that the state is not immune from liability for alleged negligence in failing to provide proper highway signs and markings. If such negligence created a *dangerous condition*, the defense of sovereign immunity would not be available.

In *Japan Airlines Co v State*,[331] Japan Airlines sued the state of Alaska after one of its airplanes slid off a taxi-way designed by state-employed engineers. The trial court granted partial summary judgment for the state on the basis that design decisions are within the shield of immunity provided by the *discretionary function* exemption from state tort liability. Summary judgment for the state was REVERSED: A state may be liable for injuries which result from negligent design. The design decisions made by the state's engineers concerning the taxi-way plans were operational decisions that merely implemented the basic policy to build a taxi-way suitable for wide-bodied jets. Once the basic policy

---

[327] 57 Wis 2d 92, 203 NW2d 673 (1973).
[328] *Id* 676.
[329] 141 Cal App 3d 837, 190 Cal Rptr 569 (1983).
[330] 98 NM 34, 644 P2d 548 (1982).
[331] 628 P2d 934 (Alaska 1981).

decision was made, the state was obligated to use due care to assure that the taxi-way was reasonably safe.

In *McDonough v Whalen*,[332] the defendant was a private septic system designer who was also an official of the North Attelboro Board of Health. It designed a septic system and performed a percolation test. In designing the system it acted in a private capacity; in performing the percolation test it acted as an official of the Board of Health, but was paid by the builder. HELD: the designer was acting in a private capacity; therefore, it was not protected by the doctrine of sovereign immunity.

The sovereign immunity doctrine did not protect the United States Army Corps of Engineers from a malpractice indemnity claim filed under the Federal Tort Claims Act.[333] A contractor alleged that the Corps negligently performed both its duty to review, approve, and reject designs and its function of redesigning an anchor rod. As a result of this alleged negligence, grout supplied by the claimant failed, and the claimant suffered economic damage. Summary judgment for the resident engineer was REVERSED. The defense of sovereign immunity depends upon evidence of the specific functions performed by the employees of the government.[334]

In *Cooper v Jevne*,[335] the court went out of its way to give some sophisticated legal advice to the plaintiff's counsel as to how to avoid the application of the California doctrine of sovereign immunity. Condominium purchasers filed suit against local building inspectors, alleging that the project violated the building code and that it was hazardous to personal safety, subject to structural failure, and a fire trap. The inspectors set up the doctrine of sovereign immunity as a defense. The court held that the doctrine in California does not protect a public employee from liability for fraud. Fraud is a misrepresentation of fact. The inspectors misrepresented the facts in at least three respects: they issued a building permit which falsely represented that the plans complied with the building code; they posted an inspection record on the job site and, by signing off various phases of the work, represented that the work complied with the requirements of the building code; and, they issued a certificate of occupancy, which represented that the building complied with the code. If the plaintiff proved the representations were false, then the inspectors would be liable.

In two cases, though not specifically discussing the doctrine of governmental immunity, the courts seem to have assumed that a public engineer can be liable for negligence.[336]

---

[332] 365 Mass 506, 313 NE2d 435 (1974).

[333] 28 USC §2680(a).

[334] Green Constr Co v Williams Form Engg Corp, 506 F Supp 173 (WD Mich 1980).

[335] 56 Cal App 3d 860, 128 Cal Rptr 724 (1976).

[336] Rigsby v Brighton Engg Co, 464 SW2d 279 (Ky 1970); Salem Sand & Gravel Co v City of Salem, 260 Or 630, 492 P2d 271 (1971).

§9.37 Release

The effectiveness of the defense of *release* depends on contract interpretation and the status of the defendant as agent, independent contractor, or joint tortfeasor.

In *Jefferson Mills, Inc v Gregson*,[337] an architect sued for its fee, and the owner filed a counterclaim for negligent performance. To defeat the counterclaim, the architect introduced a document signed by the owner releasing the architect from any further damages for the cost of repair and correction. The release specifically did not bar future fee claims. It was given by the corporation in exchange for a cash settlement paid by the architect's insurance carrier.

Interpreting Georgia law,[338] the court concluded that "[t]he legislature could not have intended to give one party the right to sue and simultaneously bar the other party from defending."[339] Therefore, the owner was allowed to use the malpractice claim defensively, even though the release might have prohibited the owner from seeking to recover further damages for the malpractice.

In *Duncan v Pennington City Housing Authority*,[340] the court enforced a settlement agreement between an insured worker and defendants, which provided that the amount paid plaintiff in settlement of the claim was to be deducted from any judgment obtained against the architect. Since the architect's proportional liability amounted to $16,000 and the amount paid under the settlement agreement exceeded $16,000, the architect was not required to pay monetary damages to the plaintiff.

Release of Joint Tortfeasor

In *Hill v McDonald*,[341] an eight-year-old boy fell five floors from an apartment stairway. He slipped in a puddle and fell under the handrail. The plaintiff gave a release to the apartment owner in exchange for $75,000. In a suit against the architect alleging negligent design of the handrail, the architect asserted the release of the principal, the apartment owner, as a defense. HELD: the release of a principal does not necessarily afford a defense to the agent. However, this case should not have been decided under the law of principal and agent, but under the law of joint tortfeasors. A release of one joint tortfeasor does not constitute a release of the other joint tortfeasor.

---

[337] 124 Ga App 96, 183 SE2d 529 (1971).
[338] Ga Code Ann §56-408-1 (1963).
[339] *Id* 531.
[340] 283 NW2d 546 (SD 1979).
[341] 442 A2d 133 (DC 1982).

Release of Principal Releases Agent

In *Seattle Western Industries v David A. Mowat Co*,[342] a subcontractor sued owner, architect, contractor, and contractor's surety for breach of contract, misrepresentation, and negligence. A sub-subcontractor settled its claim with other defendants, and assigned its claim against the architect to the subcontractor. The subcontractor, in turn, settled with all the defendants except the architect. HELD: the subcontractor's settlement with other defendants did not exonerate the architect: such a release does not discharge liability of third parties unless the release so provides. A release of a principal generally operates to also release liabilities of the agent arising from the same act. The subcontractor sued the Georgia Department of Transportation and its engineer for losses arising out of construction of post-tensioned bridges and settled with the Department of Transportation for $2,650,000. The court stated that, since the release did not identify the engineer as one of the parties to be released from liability, the issue of whether the engineer was an agent of the Department of Transportation was a material question of fact. The contract between the engineer and the Department of Transportation provided for *consultant services* and it did not define the relationship as one of principal and agent.

In *Tri-City Construction Co v A.C. Kirkwood & Associates*,[343] a contractor settled litigation with a city and signed a settlement agreement releasing the city and "its officers, officials and employees" from all further claims. The contractor then prosecuted an action against an engineer who had been hired by the city to prepare improvement plans. The contractor argued that the engineer was not protected by the release because it was an independent contractor rather than an officer, official or employee. HELD: the acts of the engineer were subject to the direction and control of the city. Therefore, the engineer was an agent of the city. In reaching its conclusion, the court considered the fact that the contract between the contractor and the city provided, in part, that the "engineer acts as engineering representative of the owner."[344]

§9.38 Accord and Satisfaction

In *Cox v City of Freeman*,[345] a contractor and a city negotiated a final settlement of disputes surrounding a construction project and signed an

---

[342] 110 Wash 2d 1, 750 P2d 245 (1988).

[343] 738 SW2d 925 (Mo Ct App 1987).

[344] *See also* Associated Constr Co v Camp, Dresser & McKee, Inc, 646 F Supp 1574 (D Conn 1986) (release entered into between contractors and the city operated to release claims against the engineer).

[345] 321 F2d 887 (8th Cir 1963). *See also* Associated Constr Co v Camp, Dresser & McKee, Inc, 646 F Supp 1574 (D Conn 1986) (contractor's agreement with a city to settle claims resolved claims against the engineer by the doctrine of accord and satisfaction).

agreement which liquidated the balance due on the contract. The agreed sum was then tendered to the contractor with a letter signed by the city engineer certifying *final payment*. The contractor cashed the check. Then the contractor filed suit against the city and the city engineer for breach of contract and tort, alleging, as against the engineer, failure to have necessary engineering work done on time, delay in locating the site, overpressuring the water line, and discrepancies in the contract documents. The court held that the acceptance of the final payment constituted an accord and satisfaction, and that by the great weight of authority, an accord and satisfaction between the principal and the claimant also protects the agent.

§9.39 No License

The *doctrine of illegality* holds that an architect who is not licensed to practice the profession may not resort to the courts to collect an unpaid fee. The courts may not be used for the enforcement of an illegal contract.

In *Marshall-Schule Associates v Goldman*,[346] it was held that an unlicensed architect could not recover compensation for work performed pursuant to an illegal contract to prepare floor plans, elevations, and architectural drawings for a new kitchen and two new bathrooms. The work went far beyond the practice of interior design. The contract was, therefore, based upon an illegal bargain which was contrary to public policy and invalid. Nor was the firm entitled to recover for nonarchitectural services rendered, since the contract was *entire and indivisible*.

The doctrine also applies to an architect is licensed but violates the licensing statute. This was the case in *Palmer v Brown*,[347] where the architect did business in the partnership name of "Dan Saxon Palmer, Architect, William Cricell, Associate." The court held that this was proper, since it showed that Cricell was not licensed although Palmer was. However, in the specific case, Cricell prepared most of the drawings, which were thereafter checked by Palmer. Cricell also signed a payment certificate over the word *architect*, thus holding himself out to be an architect. Therefore, the court held that although the contract was valid, the performance was illegal, and a verdict of $1,497.03 in favor of the architect and against the owner for fees was REVERSED.

In *Medak v Cox*,[348] the court interpreted a California statute that allows an unlicensed architect to prepare plans for "single family dwellings of wood frame construction not more than two stories high."[349] An architect sued for fees for

---

[346] 137 Misc 2d 1024, 523 NYS2d 16 (Civ Ct 1987).
[347] 127 Cal App 2d 44, 273 P2d 306 (1954).
[348] 12 Cal App 3d 70, 90 Cal Rptr 452 (1970).
[349] Cal Bus & Prof Code §5537 (West 1974).

the design of houses in a subdivision. The court allowed plaintiff to recover the fee, even though the architect designed the entire subdivision, since there was no limit to the number of dwellings that were exempted from the licensing requirement. The unlicensed architect had also designed an industrial building which was not exempted from the operation of the statute. Here, the court held that the architect was entitled to recover despite illegality. The owner should not have been permitted to obtain unjust enrichment, at the expense of the architect, when the owner knew at the time of hiring that the architect was unlicensed.

In *State Board of Registration v Rogers*,[350] the defendant listed itself as a *mechanical designer*. All of its customers were architects or engineers. The court enjoined the defendant from continuing to use the title *mechanical designer* and from doing mechanical work for private individuals or members of the public, but refused to prohibit it from working under the supervision and control of registered architects or engineers. AFFIRMED. An architect or engineer may delegate any part of its duties. Not every line must be drawn by a licensed practitioner; such work may be entrusted to competent employees.

§9.40 Other Forms of Illegality

A public agency may not properly make payment to an engineer under a contract improperly awarded.[351] In an Illinois case, the president of a park district entered into an oral contract with an engineer for preparation of a building integrity report. HELD: "When an employee of a municipal corporation purports to bind the corporation by contract without prior approval, in violation of an applicable statute, such a contract is utterly void. . . . Such a contract cannot be validated by principles of ratification or estoppel."[352]

In *McKee v City of Cohoes Board of Education*,[353] a Board of Education contracted with an engineer for design services, but funds for the project had not been appropriated. HELD: the engineer was not entitled to recover its fee because the applicable statute prohibited the Board of Education from entering into contracts for which funds were not appropriated. The execution of the contract by the superintendent of schools was *ultra vires* and void.

The doctrine of illegality was applied against an architect in another context in *Medoff v Fisher*,[354] where the owner asked the architect to prepare drawings for a building that was to contain a moving picture theater, turkish baths, stores, and dwellings. The zoning code provided that no building used for the

---

[350] 239 Miss 35, 120 So 2d 772 (1960).

[351] D.C. Consulting Engrs, Inc v Batavia Park Dist, 143 Ill App 3d 60, 492 NE2d 1000 (1986).

[352] *Id* at 63, 492 NE2d at 1002.

[353] 99 AD2d 923, 473 NYS2d 269 (1984).

[354] 257 Pa 126, 101 A 471 (1917).

exhibition of motion pictures could be occupied or used as a dwelling, tenement house, apartment house, hotel, or department store. The court held that since the plaintiff and the defendant conspired to commit an illegal act (construction of an illegal building), the architect was denied access to court to recover its fee.[355]

In *Manning Engineering, Inc v Hudson County Park Commission*,[356] plaintiff was awarded an engineering contract by the park commission as a reward for serving as a bag man and extortionist for Mayor John V. Kenny. HELD: the contract was infected with illegality and, despite the fact that plaintiff performed the contract, the plaintiff was not to be entitled to recover its fee.

In *City of Marlborough v Cybulski Ohnemus & Associates*,[357] the city awarded an architect a contract to design and supervise the renovation of a post office. The contract contained an arbitration clause. The arbitrator's award of $17,800 in favor of the architect was VACATED. The city had only appropriated $5,000 for the project, and it is well settled that persons dealing with municipalities must take notice of, and are bound by, limits placed upon the contracting power of the city. The mere fact that the controversy was submitted to arbitration did not eliminate the prohibition against a city spending more than its appropriations.[358]

It may be possible for an architect to recover for services provided to a municipal corporation in the absence of a valid contract if the architect can prove the services were rendered for the corporation with the full knowledge of the municipal corporation's governing body, that the governing body knowingly accepted the benefits of this service, and that the contract for services was not wholly beyond the scope of the municipal corporation's powers.[359]

In *Mardirosian v American Institute of Architects*,[360] an architect violated Standard 9 of the American Institute of Architects (AIA) Code of Ethics (1989), which, as the court stated, provides:

> An architect shall not attempt to obtain, offer or undertake or accept a commission for which the architect knows another legally qualified individual or firm has been selected or employed until the architect has evidence that the latter's agreement has been terminated and the architect gives the latter written notice that the architect is so doing.

---

[355] *Accord* Burger v Roelsch, 77 Hun 44, 28 NYS 460 (1894).

[356] 74 NJ 113, 376 A2d 1194 (1977).

[357] 370 Mass 157, 346 NE2d 716 (1976).

[358] *Accord* Murphy v City of Brockton, 364 Mass 377, 305 NE2d 103 (1973) (appropriation of $40,000 was paid to architect; balance of $101,317 could not be paid because "plaintiff was obliged to proceed no further with its work under the contract than was covered by an appropriation").

[359] Board of Pub Works v L. Cosby Bernard & Co, 435 NE2d 575 (Ind Ct App 1982).

[360] 474 F Supp 628 (DDC 1979).

The AIA imposed sanctions against the architect for taking over architectural services in connection with refurbishing the historic Union Station without the consent of the prior architect. HELD: Standard 9 violated the Sherman Act[361] by preventing competition.

§9.41 Res Judicata and Collateral Estoppel

The *doctrine of res judicata* allows courts to protect themselves and litigants from repetitious litigation.

In *Associated Construction Co v Camp, Dresser & McKee, Inc*,[362] a contractor arbitrated construction claims against a city and an arbitration award was rendered. Then the contractor sued the engineer, seeking compensation for extra expense incurred because of improper plans and specifications. HELD: an arbitration award, whether or not sustained by a court judgment, constitutes a final decision for purposes of the doctrine of *res judicata*.

The doctrines of *res judicata* and collateral estoppel do not arise from the entry of a stipulated dismissal with prejudice. Actual litigation of issues on the merits is required to invoke these doctrines.[363]

A contractor arbitrated a claim against an owner for damages because of delay. After the award was rendered in the first proceeding, the contractor, not satisfied, filed suit against the architect for the same damages. The trial court GRANTED summary judgment. REVERSED. The doctrine of collateral estoppel must be applied only after a clear determination that the issues litigated in the first proceeding are the same as those to be litigated in the second proceeding. Though the claims were similar, the record is not sufficient to show whether all of the claims against the architect were decided previously in the arbitration against the owner.[364]

In *Idaho State University v Mitchell*,[365] an architect vainly relied on the doctrine *res judicata* as a defense. A new university sports arena had been heavily damaged by flood water. The university filed suit against the contractor and the architect. The trial court granted summary judgment in favor of the architect but also granted summary judgment in favor of the university against the contractor. Summary judgment for the university against the contractor was REVERSED.

The court then considered whether the summary judgment in favor of the architect against the university was binding on the contractor. The contractor

---

[361] 15 USC §1.
[362] 646 F Supp 1574 (D Conn 1986).
[363] Chaney Bldg Co v City of Tucson, 148 Ariz 571, 716 P2d 28 (1986).
[364] French v Jinright & Ryan, PC Architects, 735 F2d 433 (11th Cir 1984).
[365] 97 Idaho 724, 552 P2d 776 (1976).

alleged that the negligence of the architect was a defense to the university's claim of negligence against the contractor. However, did the summary judgment in favor of the architect and against the university preclude the contractor from relying on this defense? HELD: the contractor was not bound by the prior judgment. The contractor was not a party to that action, nor should the contractor be bound under the principle of collateral estoppel because the university asserting the estoppel was using it offensively, rather than defensively, and the contractor had no opportunity to litigate the issue of the architect's negligence.

In *Kingsbury v Tevco, Inc*,[366] adjoining landowners became involved in a boundary dispute. The court ordered a survey and entered final judgment establishing the boundary in accordance with that survey. In this action, the landowner sought damages against the surveyor for fraud and negligence, contending that the survey was inaccurate. HELD: the plaintiff was collaterally estopped under the doctrine of *res judicata* from challenging the accuracy of the survey. The prior judgment was the final judgment on the merits. Plaintiff had the opportunity to challenge the survey at the time of the earlier action.

In *Teachers Credit Union v Horner*,[367] in the first suit the credit union sued the contractor, alleging that the contractor had not installed the heating and air conditioning systems and the roof in accordance with the contract documents, and that the contractor failed to grade and drain the property in accordance with the plans and specifications. The jury found in favor of the contractor.

In the second suit the credit union sued the architects, alleging that the architects failed to inspect and observe construction deficiencies which resulted in the failure of the heating and air conditioning systems and improper drainage. HELD: the owner lost these issues in the trial against the contractor and would not be permitted to relitigate them in the trial against the architects. However, the credit union could have litigated the issues of *faulty design* (as opposed to *improper inspection and observation*), since that issue was not decided in the previous action.

§9.42 Other Defenses

Nonfeasance versus Misfeasance

Courts formerly drew a distinction between nonfeasance and misfeasance in cases of third-party liability. An architect was not liable for injury a worker suffered on the job if the architect was merely guilty of nonfeasance.[368]

---

[366] 79 Cal App 3d 314, 144 Cal Rptr 773 (1978).
[367] 487 F Supp 246 (WD Mo 1980).
[368] Lottman v Barnett, 62 Mo 159 (1876) (court accepted the rule but held architect was guilty of malfeasance in approving use of jack screws to raise pillars supporting girders);

Compliance with Statute

In *Rigsby v Brighton Engineering Co*,[369] plaintiff's decedent was killed when a car struck a bridge abutment. Plaintiff introduced testimony that good design practice would have required the architect to specify a guardrail. However, the Kentucky Department of Highways criteria did not require guardrails, and furthermore, the criteria did not permit deviation. The court held that since the architect complied with the statute and was prohibited from departing from the statute, the architect could not be found negligent.

Act of God

In *Northwestern Mutual Insurance Co v Peterson*,[370] defendant building contractor and a church member prepared drawings and specifications for, and commenced construction of, a new church building. The building collapsed during a windstorm. The defendant asked for an instruction to the effect that if the collapse were due to an act of God, the defendant should be free of liability. The trial court refused the instruction but was REVERSED. The defendant's evidence was to the effect that the wind was the strongest encountered in the country in the memory of man. One witness testified that the wind had blown down a concrete block wall that was seven inches thick. This raised a jury question as to whether the severity of the weather was at the level of an act of God. In order for the act of God defense to apply, a natural event must be the sole proximate cause of the injury. The jury should have been allowed to decide whether the building would have stood had it been properly constructed or whether even a properly constructed building would have fallen in such a wind.

Lack of Federal Jurisdiction

In *Jaillet v Hill & Hill*,[371] the owner alleged that the architect negligently designed a sewer system and misrepresented the availability of federal grant money under the Water Pollution Prevention and Control Act.[372] HELD: the plaintiff had no private cause of action under the Water Pollution Prevention and Control Act because the action sounded in professional malpractice and tortious misrepresentation.

Potter v Gilbert, 130 AD 632, 115 NYS 425, *affd*, 196 NY 576, 90 NE 1165 (1909) (wall collapsed injuring worker; plaintiff failed to allege specific defect in plan, or that architect was aware of improper construction methods used by contractor).

[369] 464 SW2d 279 (Ky 1970).
[370] 281 Or 773, 572 P2d 1023 (1977).
[371] 460 F Supp 1075 (WD Pa 1978).
[372] §§202(a), 505; 33 USC §§1282(a), 1365.

Percolating Waters

In *Lee v City of Pontiac*,[373] plaintiff owned and operated a business which used a well fed by percolating waters. The city widened and deepened an existing drainage ditch located east of plaintiff's property, thus restricting the supply of water to the well. Plaintiff sued the city, its engineering consultant, and the excavating company, alleging negligence. Following the *common law*, or *English*, rule regarding percolating waters, the court of appeal AFFIRMED the trial court's order to dismiss the complaint for failure to state a cause of action. In reaching its decision, the court relied on *Edwards v Haeger*,[374] wherein the court stated:

> Water which is the result of natural and ordinary percolating through the soil is part of the land itself and belongs absolutely to the owner of the land, and, in the absence of any grant, he may intercept or impede such underground percolations, though the result be to interfere with the source of supply of springs or wells on adjoining premises.[375]

Superseding Cause

An architect designed swimming facilities with a diving board that did not comply with safety standards promulgated by a private organization. A 10-year-old boy was killed by a fall from the diving board. HELD: the architect was not relieved of responsibility by the school district's intervening negligence, since the district did nothing more than accept the architect's suggestions for a diving board.[376]

Riparian Law

In *Irwin v Michelin Tire Corp*,[377] a lower owner brought action against an upper owner and its engineer for damages caused by the design, construction, and maintenance of a manufacturing plant. The upper owner, in preparing a site for construction of a plant, graded land and installed drainage systems which directed water into preexisting culverts through which water and silt entered the lower owner's lake. Judgment for defendants was AFFIRMED. The action was governed by the Virginia Rule, which holds that upper riparian owners are not liable to lower riparian owners merely because of the presence of an artificial drainage system, where there has been no increase in surface

---

[373] 99 Ill App 3d 982, 426 NE2d 300 (1981).
[374] 180 Ill 99, 54 NE 176 (1899).
[375] *Id* at 106, 54 NE at 177.
[376] Francisco v Manson, Jackson & Kane, Inc, 145 Mich App 255, 377 NW2d 313 (1985), *appeal denied* (Jan 28, 1986).
[377] 288 SC 221, 341 SE2d 783 (1986).

water drainage. The court declined to follow the New Jersey Rule, which holds that an upper owner who increases the volume of flow to a lower owner by decreasing soil absorption on the upper property is liable for damages caused by the increased flow. The court held that such a rule would have a traumatic effect on the orderly development of the state, since

> every construction project of any magnitude could decrease the absorption, seepage and percolation rate of the land, and potentially allow every lower riparian or adjoining landowner to institute a cause of action. If there is to be such a fundamental change in the law, we believe that it should be by legislative action and not be judicial decision.[378]

Compliance with Contract

In *Brown v McBro Planning & Development Co*,[379] the plaintiff slipped in the emergency room of a hospital that had been flooded by heavy rain. The plaintiff claimed that the floor was improperly sloped toward the interior of the building, which exacerbated the flooding. HELD: the mere fact that the architect may have met its contractual obligations did not absolve the architect from being held negligent in such a way as to have caused injury to the plaintiff.

Duplicate Recovery

In *City of Bismark v Toltz, King, Duvall, Anderson & Associates*,[380] a city in an arbitration proceeding against a contractor arising out of the construction of a sewer project filed a brief arguing that the contractor was liable for the cost of total replacement of the sewer system. The arbitrators awarded $612,463 in favor of the city and against the contractor, but also awarded $885,058 in favor of the contractor against the city. The city then prosecuted an action against the engineer, seeking compensation for defects in the sewer system. HELD: this would be a duplicate recovery. The city presented the same claims against the engineer for which it was fully compensated in the arbitration proceedings.

Statute of Frauds

In *Biller v Zeigler*,[381] a masonry subcontractor continued work on a project despite news that the contractor was about to declare bankruptcy, induced by a promise by the architect that it would be paid some $9,000 owed to the subcontractor by the contractor on other jobs. When payment was not forthcoming, the subcontractor stopped work. Judgment for the subcontractor

---

[378] *Id* at 225, 341 SE2d at 785.
[379] 660 F Supp 1333 (DVI 1987).
[380] 855 F2d 580 (8th Cir 1988).
[381] 406 Pa Super 1, 593 A2d 436 (1991).

against the architect was AFFIRMED. It is true that the guarantee for payment was oral and would have been unenforceable under the Pennsylvania statute of frauds as a promise to answer for the debt or default of another. However, the Statute of Frauds does not apply if the main object of the promisor is to serve its own pecuniary or business purpose. Here, the architect had an interest in completing the work as soon as possible, since payments to the architect were based on completed phases of the work. In addition, the reputation of an architect depends on timely completed work.

Damages 10

§10.01 Generally
   Approaches to Damages
   Consequential Damages
   Market Value
§10.02 Cost of Correction of Public Project
§10.03 —Private Project
   Cost Saving or Value
   Betterment
   Cost of Correction
   Cost of Repair
   Moorman Doctrine
§10.04 Negligent Survey
   Difference Minus Fee
   Lost Profit Denied
§10.05 Convenience, Comfort, and Enjoyment
§10.06 Development of Out-of-Pocket Damages
§10.07 —Application
§10.08 Cost of Correction Uneconomic
§10.09 Rental Value
   Rent versus Interest
   Rent Plus Interest
§10.10 Economic Loss
   Economic Loss Awarded
   Flawed Jury Instruction
   Moorman Doctrine
   Doctrine Rejected
   Conflicting Decisions

§10.11   Mental Anguish
§10.12   Punitive Damages

§10.01   Generally

Cases in which an owner or a tenant alleges that the malpractice of an architect caused a defect in a building present perplexing questions of damages. The fact that courts frequently fail to consider the issue of the rule of damages to be applied should not mask the fact that the issue is present in almost every such case. The resolution of the issue is of primary practical importance, since it can mean the difference between a nominal and a substantial award.

Approaches to Damages

Two fundamental approaches control the amount of damages. They cannot be reconciled and lead to very different mathematical conclusions. Each approach has variants, and each passes under different names. Assume that the expectations of an owner have been frustrated by the malpractice of an architect. The one rule proposes that the architect should pay as damages a sum of money sufficient to enable the owner to realize its expectations. The other proposes that the sum should equal the actual out-of-pocket loss caused by the malpractice.

The first approach developed in the law of contracts and holds that the promisee is entitled to the benefit of its bargain. The second rule developed from the law of torts and prescribes that the amount of damages should be such as to compensate the plaintiff for its actual out-of-pocket loss. Under the first rule the architect is in effect made to guarantee or insure monetary value of the work; under the second, the architect has merely sold a service, and not insurance. Well-reasoned cases that have specifically considered the rule of damages to be applied have adopted the out-of-pocket rule as the one calculated to render the most precise justice.

In many cases the application of the out-of-pocket rule yields smaller damages. It is not surprising, then, that the courts are more likely to award benefit-of-the-bargain damages if the plaintiff's theory of liability is fraud or intentional misrepresentation. Likewise, the benefit-of-the-bargain rule is more appropriate if the theory of liability is contract, rather than tort.

The philosophy of benefit-of-the-bargain damages may be resolved to an award measured by the cost of correction[1] or the replacement value.[2] The out-of-pocket approach usually dictates an award based on the diminution in market value of the property.

---

[1] See §10.02.
[2] See §10.03.

In cases where the architect underestimates the cost of a project, benefit-of-the-bargain reasoning yields an award measured by the difference between the estimate and the cost, while out-of-pocket reasoning yields the difference between market value and the cost.

Consequential Damages

Consequential damages may be recovered for breach of contract if such damages are within the contemplation of the parties at the time they entered into the contract.[3]

In a Virginia case, an engineer had prepared plans and specifications for replacement of air conditioning units in an apartment project. The units that were specified were too large to fit in the mechanical rooms. The trial court ruled that the cost of constructing a storage area for storage of the air conditioning units was inadmissible on the ground that such consequential damages were so remote that they were not anticipated by the parties. HELD: whether such consequential expenses—cost of repairing old units and cost of storing unused new units—were within the contemplation of the parties was an issue of fact for the jury.

Market Value

It may be stated with confidence that the *market value* of the project is always at least one element used in the computation of out-of-pocket damages, and that market value is never used to compute benefit-of-the-bargain damages. There is no logical connection between market value and the value of an owner's bargain. But it is impossible to compute out-of-pocket damages without taking market value into consideration.

One method used to ascertain damages is a combination of benefit-of-the-bargain and out-of-pocket theories. It comes into play if cost of correction is uneconomic. Then the measure of damages is the difference between the value of the building as constructed and its value if designed or constructed without malpractice.

In some cases, damages sustained by an owner are in practical effect, and illogically, measured by the architect's fee. Thus, in *Roland A. Wilson & Associates v Forty-O-Four Grand Corp*,[4] an architect filed suit to recover a fee. The owner defended on the ground that the architect failed to require the contractor to properly caulk leaks discovered during construction. Judgment: plaintiff was to take nothing.

---

[3] Fairfax County Redevelopment & Hous Auth v Hurst & Assocs Consulting Engrs, Inc, 231 Va 164, 343 SE2d 294 (1986).

[4] 246 NW2d 922 (Iowa 1976).

It would seem that the architect's fee was an undependable measure of damages. The cost of caulking the windows properly may have been more or less than the fee.

In *School District No 11 v Sverdrup, Parcel & Associate*,[5] a school district filed an action against the architect for failure of a re-roofing system. HELD: a jury verdict of $956,010 was not to be overturned as *excessive* unless there was *plain injustice* or a *monstrous* or *shocking* result. The district court correctly concluded that the total award was fully supported by the evidence.

§10.02 Cost of Correction of Public Project

The market value analysis breaks down when the project under consideration is a public building. Public buildings are not often up for sale. Their market value cannot be established. It therefore seems that cost of correction (or benefit-of-the-bargain) theory is most appropriate to the computation of damages for malpractice affecting a public building.

In *Larrimore v Comanche County*,[6] an architect filed suit against a county for fees in the amount of $1,401.60. The county filed a cross-complaint for $1,500 in damages for defective stove flues. Evidence showed that the flues did not draw smoke, and smoke was injected into the rooms of the county courthouse. Various experts testified as to damages: one witness recommended that the smoke tower be pulled down at an expense of $1,600, and another gave the opinion that the installation of a $40 climax ventilator would solve the problem. No testimony was offered as to the market value of the building.

The jury brought in a verdict for the county in the amount of $423, and the court of appeal AFFIRMED. The jury was not bound by the opinions of the experts in fixing either the value of professional services or the amount of damages.

In *School District No 172 v Josenhans*,[7] the roof of a school building collapsed under a heavy load of snow. The architect knew that the roof was not supported as required by the plans but certified final payment and did not advise the owner of the defects.

On appeal the architect contended that the proper measure of damages should have been the difference in the value of the building if constructed in accordance with the plans and the value as actually constructed; or, alternatively, the measure of damages should have been the cost of installing supporting beams. The court held that the damages were those actually caused by the breach of the architect's duty, that is, the cost of reconstruction according to the contract documents.

---

[5] 797 F2d 651 (8th Cir 1986).
[6] 32 SW 367 (Tex Civ App 1895).
[7] 88 Wash 624, 153 P 326 (1915).

The architect also argued that the owner was guilty of a breach of its duty to mitigate damages. There had been some sign of potential collapse, and the ultimate disaster might have been averted if the school district had timely removed the snow or installed additional supports. It seems that the architect was really arguing that the amount of damages should have been computed as of some moment before the collapse, rather than afterwards.[8]

This case reminds us that the market value analysis and the cost of correction analysis may yield the same numerical result. Presumably the difference between the market value of a building with a collapsed roof and the market value of the same building with a sound roof is equal to the cost of correction, augmented by the value of the use of the capital invested in the building during the period of correction.

§10.03 —Private Project

Some courts employ a rule that if the cost of repairing the injury and restoring the premises to their original condition is less than the diminution in value of the property, such cost is the proper measure of damages. If the cost of restoration exceeds the diminution in value, the diminution in value is the proper measure.

In a California case, testimony showed that the diminution in value was $50,000 and the repair cost would have been $15,000 plus $44,700 for remedial steps. HELD: it was error for the trial court to instruct the jury in such a manner as to allow it to award damages for diminution in value of the property, plus costs of repair.[9]

Absent evidence of economic waste, damages may be measured by either cost of repair or diminution-in-value and are awarded at the court's discretion. In a Florida case a repair cost of $198,000 for a $4.9 million building was clearly not economic waste. Therefore, the damages were properly measured by the cost of repair rather than by diminution-in-value. (An architect had failed to design flashings, which caused leaks in a medical office complex.)[10]

In *Schwartz v Kuhn*,[11] the owner alleged multiple defects in a project caused by the architect's negligence in supervising the builders. The court held that the measure of damages would be the cost of putting the building into the condition it would have been in had the architect performed with the standard of ordinary

---

[8] *See also* Kevin Roche-John Dinkelo & Assocs v City of New Haven, 205 Conn 741, 535 A2d 1287 (1988) (damages for defective design of a public arena, an exhibition hall, and a parking garage were to be computed according to the cost of repair at the time of the breach, rather than according to the cost of repair at the time of trial).

[9] Mozzetti v City of Brisbane, 67 Cal App 3d 565, 136 Cal Rptr 751 (1977).

[10] Pearce & Pearce, Inc v Kroh Bros Dev Co, 474 So 2d 369 (Fla Dist Ct App 1985).

[11] 71 Misc 149, 126 NYS 568 (Sup Ct 1911).

care required by the contract. This amount could be offset against any fee remaining unpaid to the architect and, if greater, the owner would have been entitled to recover the excess.

In *South Union Ltd v George Parker & Associates AIA*,[12] it was held that the proper measure of damages was the reasonable cost of material and labor necessary to place electrical work in the condition contemplated by the parties at the time when they entered into the contract, where to do so would not result in economic waste.

In *Prier v Refrigeration Engineering Co*,[13] an engineering company designed the ice arena for a skating rink. The design caused the soil under the arena to freeze to a depth of four feet. This threatened the structural integrity of the building. The remedy was to install the rink on two-foot piers and provide hot air ventilation in the space between the floor and the earth. The cost of correction was $36,189.71.

The trial court computed the damages by taking the cost of the original project plus the cost of repairs and subtracting the cost of the project if it had originally been properly constructed. (This yielded general damages of $17,500, to which the trial court added $2,500 in profits lost during the period when the rink was closed.)

The court of appeal held that the proper measure of damages was the cost of correction, $36,189.71, rather than the $20,000 awarded by the trial court. The error of the trial court was said to be in awarding damages on a tort theory rather than on the theory of implied warranty. If a person holds itself out as qualified to furnish a design, that person impliedly warrants the sufficiency of the design, and the corrections were necessary to give the *buyer* the benefit of what the *seller* had promised. The damages in a contract case should put the injured party in as good a position as it would have occupied if it had received the benefit of full performance.[14] In addition, the plaintiff should receive $2,500 in lost profits, and interest on the cost of correction.

For a plaintiff to recover both lost profits and interest is clearly wrong. A plaintiff has a certain amount of capital and is entitled to a return on that capital. Net profit and interest are just two different ways of measuring the return on capital. The award of the one should exclude the award of the other.

The method of computing damages adopted by the trial court was closer to the mark. The decision of the Washington Supreme Court allowed the plaintiff a clear a windfall because it did not take into consideration the amount it would have cost the owner to build a nondefective building in the first place. If the defendant had designed the building properly, the owner would have incurred an additional cost. Default of the engineering company resulted in an initial

---

[12] 29 Ohio App 3d 197, 504 NE2d 1131 (1985).
[13] 74 Wash 2d 25, 442 P2d 621 (1968).
[14] Restatement (Second) of Contracts §346 (1981).

saving to the owner. In fact, part of the motivation for the original defective design probably was to achieve the savings. This initial saving, caused by the defective design, should have been taken into account in computing the owner's ultimate damages. Otherwise, the owner retained the benefit of the cost saving achieved by the very defect of which it complained. This put the owner in a better position than it would have occupied if the building had been properly designed and constructed in the first instance.

Cost Saving or Value

The measure of damages flows from the liability theory adopted by the Washington Supreme Court: implied warranty rather than negligence. This highlights the issue actually at stake. Should the law protect the expectations of the owner which are nurtured optimistically, but negligently, by the architect? Or should it only protect the owner against expense which exceeds the amount which a project, in the physical nature of things, should actually cost? The architect is called upon to exercise professional judgment in balancing cost against value. If the architect omits an element of design, in an attempt to reduce the cost, and it turns out that the project as designed will not serve the purpose, should the owner retain the benefit of both the erroneous cost saving and the value of the project as ultimately constructed? On balance, it seems the owner should not receive both. Since the owner would be the one to benefit from a skimpy, though economical, design that works, the owner should also share part of the risk that it will not work. The malpracticing architect, on the other hand, should be responsible for the loss of return on the owner's capital during the period of repair and the cost of correction.

The measure of damages adopted by the trial court in effect gave both parties the benefit of their bargain. The owner received the cost to make the project that was bargained for; the architect was awarded the saving achieved by the original, defective design.[15]

Betterment

In *Grossman v Sea Air Towers Ltd*,[16] a concrete deck in a highrise apartment building collapsed. A jury returned a verdict of $540,000, assessing 80 per cent against the engineer and 20 per cent against the architect. HELD: the proper measure of damages was the amount necessary to restore the deck to its original condition, not to a condition that would have increased the load-bearing capacity of the deck.

---

[15] *See also* Seiler v Levitz Furniture Co, 367 A2d 999 (Del Super Ct 1976) (architect mistakenly certified that the electrical work had been completed in accordance with the design. Damages based on the cost of correction were approved).

[16] 513 So 2d 686 (Fla Dist Ct App 1987), *review denied*, 520 So 2d 584 (Fla 1988).

If repair work does not suffice to restore the total value of a project, an owner is entitled both to recover the cost of the repair and, in addition, to recover an amount to compensate for the resultant diminution in the value of the building subsequent to the repair.[17]

Cost of Correction

Many cases, without discussion, use cost of correction as the measure of damages. In *General Trading Corp v Burnup & Sims, Inc*,[18] the cost of installing a Danish hip roof was ordered after a flat roof had erroneously been specified by the architect and disapproved by the planning commission. In *Jim Arnott, Inc v L&E, Inc*,[19] the architect mistakenly believed that the project was to be serviced by the municipal water system and therefore failed to provide water softeners. The owner then installed softeners which proved to be too small. The court held that the architect was negligent both in originally failing to call for water softeners and in failing to assist in the design of proper softeners. The court awarded $2,471.50 in damages for the cost of installing larger softeners, but nothing for the original omission. In the view of the court, the original error was not *substantial* ($8,000 on a 104-unit motel).

It seems that the measure of damages adopted in these two cases affords an element of *unjust enrichment* to the owner. Because of the architect's negligence, should the owner receive a free roof or free water softeners? It may have been negligent to omit the hip roof at the outset, but had it been specified at the outset, the original cost would have included the cost of the hip roof. Thus, the owner's true damages should have been the difference between the cost (or market value) as properly designed and the cost (or market value) as actually designed.

Cost of Repair

In *Schlitz v Cullen-Schlitz & Associates*,[20] the court stated that the measure of damages should be equal to the reasonable cost of correction, not to exceed the value of the improvements immediately prior to damage. This measure of damages is not surprising until it is revealed that the plaintiff was the contractor, not the owner.

In *Schlitz* the engineer had prepared plans for a sewage system which included aeration tanks. During a cloudburst, water from a nearby creek entered the job site, floating the tanks. They were so badly damaged that it was necessary for the contractor to remove and reconstruct them. The contractor

---

[17] Italian Economic Corp v Community Engrs, Inc, 135 Misc 2d 209, 514 NYS2d 630 (Sup Ct 1987).

[18] 523 F2d 98 (3d Cir 1975).

[19] 539 P2d 1333 (Colo Ct App 1975) (not officially published).

[20] 228 NW2d 10 (Iowa 1975).

filed suit against the engineer on the ground that the engineer had negligently failed to design a sufficient dike to prevent water from entering the project. Judgment on verdict for the plaintiff. AFFIRMED.

The standard of practice required the engineer to design a dike sufficiently high to prevent flood water from entering the project. Therefore, the contractor was able to recover the reasonable cost of repair, not to exceed the value of the improvements immediately prior to the damage, plus the actual amount spent in cleanup operations.

Aside from the difficulty of determining the market value of aeration tanks for a sewer project, it seems that the application of a market value rule in determining damages suffered by a contractor is anomalous. The negligence of the engineer created a risk to the owner and a risk to the contractor. The risk to the owner was the loss of the value of an existing facility. The risk to the contractor was the cost of replacing a damaged facility. Therefore, if the cost of correction exceeds the market value, that should not prevent the contractor from recovering the full amount of the loss.

Moorman Doctrine

In *Moorman Manufacturing Co v National Tank Co*,[21] the plaintiff purchased a grain storage tank from the defendant. A crack developed in one of the steel plates. The plaintiff filed an action under theories of: (1) strict liability; (2) misrepresentation; (3) negligence; and (4) breach of warranty. The court held that the cost of correction was *economic loss* that was not recoverable in an action founded on principals of strict liability or negligence. According to the Illinois Supreme Court, "the vast majority of commentators and cases support the view against allowing recovery in negligence for economic losses."[22]

Although many courts opine that economic loss is not recoverable in a negligence cause of action, some of the same courts routinely award damages for economic loss in actions by third parties against architects and engineers.[23] There appears to be a distinction between the liability of a manufacturer and that of a design professional. The liability of a manufacturer for economic loss may more properly be determined under the provisions of the Uniform Commercial Code, rather than under negligence or strict liability theory.

The Illinois Court of Appeal, distinguishing *Moorman*, has held that economic loss caused by an architect's negligent performance of professional duties is recoverable under tort law.[24] In *Rosos Litho Supply*, an architect approved a fill before the concrete slab was poured; because of frost, the slab

---

[21] 91 Ill 2d 69, 435 NE2d 443 (1982).
[22] *Id* at 87, 435 NE2d at 456.
[23] *See* ch 1.
[24] Rosos Litho Supply Corp v Hansen, 123 Ill App 3d 290, 462 NE2d 566 (1984).

settled and cracked. HELD: the proper measure of damages was the cost of correcting the defective structure. If, however, the defect was so fundamental that it could not have been corrected without extensive repairs and expense, the proper measure of damages should have been the difference in value between the building as it stood, and its value had the architectural services been rendered properly.

§10.04 Negligent Survey

What should the measure of damage be when a surveyor mistakenly computes the acreage of a parcel of land which the plaintiff then buys on a *price per acre* basis?

Benefit-of-the-bargain reasoning yields the result that the purchaser should recover the difference between the price paid and the amount yielded by multiplying the true acreage by the price per acre. Out-of-pocket reasoning would say that if the property was worth what the buyer paid, it suffered no actual damage.

Both approaches have their difficulties. If it turns out that the buyer received full value for its investment, the out-of-pocket analysis frustrates the buyer's expectation of making a good bargain. On the other hand, benefit-of-the-bargain reasoning seems to give the buyer a windfall. Would not the same reasoning require that the seller reimburse to the surveyor the unintended profit?

Difference Minus Fee

In *Jenkins v J.J. Krebs & Sons*,[25] the plaintiff employed a surveyor to *confirm* an earlier survey. It did so but failed to correct an overstatement of the acreage. A note on the survey recorded that the tract contained 13.16 acres, but after the sale it was determined that the correct computation was 11.26 acres. Plaintiff purchased the property for $3,600 per acre and filed an action against the surveyor for $6,840, the amount of the putative overpayment. The court held that the plaintiff's loss resulted directly from the failure of the surveyor to exercise professional skill, but that the surveyor was still entitled to a fee, since the plaintiff derived some benefit from the services. Plaintiff was awarded the price difference, reduced by the amount of the fee.

Lost Profit Denied

In *Reighard v Downs*,[26] a real estate broker employed a surveyor to survey a tract the broker intended to sell on behalf of a client. The survey determined the

---

[25] 322 So 2d 426 (La Ct App 1975), *writ denied*, 325 So 2d 611 (La 1976).
[26] 261 Md 26, 273 A2d 109 (1971), *appeal after remand*, 265 Md 344, 289 A2d 299 (1972).

area to be 22.075 acres. Later the broker became personally interested in purchasing the tract, and, after negotiations, bought the property. An error was discovered; the actual size of the tract was 19.58 acres.

The trial court granted the surveyor's motion to dismiss on the ground that the plaintiff failed to produce sufficient evidence to show a breach of duty. REVERSED. An overstatement of the acreage by 10 per cent (caused by inverting coordinates) was clearly negligent. The plaintiff offered evidence that it purchased the property on a *per acre* basis, and that it mentioned several times to the surveyor that it wanted to be able to fit a certain number of lots into the tract. The trial court was directed to determine damages, with the injunction that *lost profits* (for the nonexistent lots) were not recoverable, since subdivision lots often remain unsold for many years. On remand, the court of appeal approved the award on the basis of benefit of the bargain. The purchaser had expected approximately 2.5 additional acres, and the trial court awarded it the value of this loss.

§10.05 Convenience, Comfort, and Enjoyment

Although it is factually removed from the main line of architect malpractice cases, *Ragland v Clarson*,[27] states a unique rule of damages that apparently has not been applied in any other case.

A Florida statute[28] gives a surveyor the right to enter the land of another, but not to destroy, injure, damage, or move anything on the land without the written permission of the owner. In *Ragland*, the plaintiff who owned a private park alleged that the surveyor violated the statute. Plaintiff's lawyer had written to the surveyor, warning that the surveyor was expected to strictly comply with the requirements of the statute. In order to conduct its survey, however, the surveyor found it necessary to remove plant material. The trial court entered a defense judgment, evidently on the theory that the surveyor was as careful as possible. The court of appeal held that the statute was unequivocal and since the actions of the surveyor violated the statute there should have been a directed verdict for the plaintiff. As to damages, the plaintiff argued that it should have been entitled to prove the *replacement value* of each plant, tree, and shrub that was damaged. But the court, without citing authority, held that the plaintiff was entitled to damages for the loss of convenience, comfort, and enjoyment of the park. The court did not indicate how such damages were to be calculated. On retrial, the plaintiff would also be entitled to claim punitive damages.

---

[27] 259 So 2d 757 (Fla Dist Ct App 1972).
[28] Fla Stat Ann §472.14 (West).

In this case, the replacement value rule of damages advanced by plaintiff is analogous to the *cost of correction* rule which has been adopted by many courts.[29] This principle was rejected in favor of a *convenience, comfort, and enjoyment* theory. However, it would seem that the two theories should not be mutually exclusive: presumably the plaintiff was entitled to recover for loss of convenience, comfort, and enjoyment only during the period of correction, but it was also entitled to recover for the cost of correction in addition to the loss of convenience, comfort, and enjoyment.

The same element of loss is present in other cases. A plaintiff householder may suffer a period of inconvenience and discomfort during a period of correction. Indeed, the very motive for employment of an architect, at least by a householder, is to obtain, for a fee, comfort, convenience, and enjoyment. The goal of damages is to compensate the plaintiff for all detriment proximately caused by the wrongful act. So why should the loss of convenience, comfort, and enjoyment be excluded?

If the project is a commercial one, the value of *enjoyment* is readily ascertainable and routinely awarded: it is either the difference in rental value or the loss of profits during that period of correction. Should a householder be denied damages which it could have recovered if the householder operated a commercial enterprise? Difficulty of calculation alone should not spell denial.

§10.06 Development of Out-of-Pocket Damages

The two great contending rules of damages in cases of malpractice are *benefit-of-the-bargain* versus *out-of-pocket*.

Benefit-of-the-bargain damages are rooted in contract law; they partake of the nature of a guarantee; their measure begins with the cost of correction.

Out-of-pocket damages are rooted in tort law; their purpose is to compensate the injured party for pecuniary loss rather than to protect its contractual expectations against disappointment; their measure begins with the ascertainment of market value.

A foundation case in the field is *Bayshore Development Co v Bonfoey*,[30] which in formulating a classic definition of the architect's duty of care rejected the idea that an architect guarantees a satisfactory result. It seemingly follows from this definition that the measure of damages in the ordinary case would not be such as to guarantee the client its anticipated satisfaction, but rather to compensate the client's out-of-pocket loss.

The court detailed the architect's duty:

---

[29] *See* §10.02.
[30] 75 Fla 455, 78 So 507 (1918).

The responsibility resting on an architect is essentially the same as that which rests upon the lawyer to his client or upon the physician to his patient, or which rests upon anyone to another where such person pretends to possess some skill and ability in some special employment, and offers his services to the public on account of his fitness to act in the line of business for which he may be employed. The undertaking of an architect implies that he possesses skill and ability, including taste, sufficient to enable him to perform the required services at least ordinarily and reasonably well, and that he will exercise in the given case his skill and ability, his judgment and taste, reasonably and without neglect. But the undertaking does not imply to warrant a satisfactory result. It will be enough that any failure shall not be the fault of the architect.[31]

In *Bayshore*, the plaintiff employed an architect to prepare contract documents for residence buildings. There was evidence that the buildings were not rainproof, the stucco was faulty, and the chimneys were defective. The trial court directed a verdict for the defendant. REVERSED. There was sufficient evidence to go to the jury. There was no evidence of faulty supervision, since the building was constructed as specified. The measure of damages should have been the difference between the value of the building as designed and the value the building would have had if it had been properly designed, but the plaintiff was not entitled to recover loss of rentals during the period of delay. The loss of rentals was too remote and speculative.

Bayshore illustrates that the concept of *guarantee* may come into play at two stages in the resolution of a malpractice case: stage one is the determination of liability; stage two is the calculation of damages.

If *guarantee* is the theory of liability, then it follows logically that it should likewise control the measure of damages. A guarantee is a promise, and if it is to be enforced, this means that the expectations of the promisee should be protected. The only way to do that is to give the plaintiff what it would have received if the promise had been kept and the project had been satisfactory. This means that the defendant must pay the cost of making the project conform to the expectations of the client.

On the other hand, if *guarantee* is not the theory of liability, it might or might not be the measure of damages. If it is determined on a negligence theory that a defendant is liable, it still remains necessary to select between guarantee (benefit-of-the-bargain) damages and compensatory (out-of-pocket) damages.

Although the selection of negligence as the theory of liability does not logically dictate the selection of *out-of-pocket* as the theory of damages, the history of tort law shows that courts have usually applied the out-of-pocket rule

---

[31] *Id* at 459, 78 So at 509.

to negligence cases. Indeed, the converse of this proposition is recognized in *Prier v Refrigeration Engineering Co*,[32] where it was held that since the proper theory of liability was implied warranty (rather than negligence), the proper measure of damages was benefit-of-the-bargain (rather than out-of-pocket).

Thus, the *Bayshore* court's definition of malpractice, by excluding the element of guarantee, foreshadowed that the plaintiff's damages would be the out-of-pocket damages measured by the difference in market value.

The *Bayshore* decision is flawed by the statement that loss of rental is too remote and speculative to be considered in calculating damages. The loss in rental value is not remote; it is the immediate effect of malpractice in design. Nor is it speculative. Modern courts have no more difficulty in determining rental value than they do in determining market value. Indeed, the one is a recognized reciprocal of the other.

§10.07 —Application

That out-of-pocket (diminution-in-value) and benefit-of-bargain (cost-of-correction) damages are not mutually exclusive is shown by a sensible Minnesota decision.[33]

In this case, the construction defects were of such a nature that they could not economically be fully corrected. The court awarded damages consisting of the cost-of-correction plus the diminution-in-value. A manufacturing and warehouse building designed by the defendant began to collapse because of inadequate foundations. It was partially repaired, but it was uneconomic to restore the building to its intended new condition. The building as partially repaired still had cracks, bowed walls, and pillars out of plumb. HELD: the measure of damages was the cost of reconstruction or, if this was impossible without economic waste, the difference in value between the building as contracted for and as actually built. Here, where total reconstruction would have been wasteful, the owner should have recovered the cost of correction plus the diminution in value of the building as partially corrected.

Perhaps the most intriguing proposition in the field of malpractice damages is illustrated by *Edward Barron Estate Co v Woodruff Co*.[34] Here, a landowner was seeking an investment that would return 8 per cent per annum. It found a tenant who guaranteed a return of 8 per cent computed on the value of the land plus a $400,000 building. The architect falsely and maliciously represented that it could design and build a suitable structure for $400,000. After the

---

[32] 74 Wash 2d 25, 442 P2d 621 (1968).

[33] Northern Petrochemical Co v Thorsen & Thorshov, Inc, 297 Minn 118, 211 NW2d 159 (1973).

[34] 163 Cal 561, 126 P 351 (1912).

building was more than half completed, the architect advised the owner that the building would cost $700,000. By then the owner had paid the architect $70,000 in commissions. The completed project would have returned 8 per cent on a $400,000 investment, but not on a $700,000 investment. The defendant argued that there were no damages.

If the architect were to be held to the standard of guarantee, it would have been accomplished by an award of $300,000. The California Supreme Court in *Barron Estate* was willing to make such an award. "If, in truth, plaintiff has been so damaged, we think it clear that the law affords it redress."[35]

The court continued:

> So here we conceive that if plaintiff can establish that, under the circumstances charged, it suffered a loss of $300,000, or any part thereof, it is justly entitled to recover it, if it further establishes that the loss was occasioned in the manner charged. Respondent's objection, therefore, we think, goes rather to evidentiary matters than to the rule of damages. A large and growing city is not the Sahara Desert, and the burden of proof cast upon plaintiff will necessarily be a heavier one than that which a plaintiff would have to carry in the illustration given. Nevertheless, as we have said, insofar as it can be established that the plaintiff was fraudulently induced to expend its moneys for a structure not, as to cost, in accordance with representations, and not capable of returning a fair interest upon the invested capital, respondents have made themselves liable.[36]

Gagne v Bertran,[37] is most frequently cited for the proposition that architects, engineers, and surveyors are not subject to strict liability. However, Justice Traynor's opinion also deals with the rule of damages to be applied in cases of malpractice.

In *Gagne*, the defendant was employed at a rate of $10 per hour to test for the presence of fill on two lots which the plaintiff intended to purchase. After drilling test holes, the defendant reported 12 to 16 inches of fill; the reality was 4 to 6 feet of fill. Relying on the report, the plaintiff bought the lots for $8,500. The cost of the additional footings occasioned by the presence of the fill was $3,093.65, which was the amount awarded by the trial court. REVERSED. There was no express warranty agreement and nothing to indicate that the defendant assumed responsibility for the accuracy of its statements. The amount of the fee (total $25) and the fact that the defendant was paid by the hour indicated that it was selling services and not insurance. The defendant was

---

[35] *Id* at 578, 126 P at 358.
[36] *Id* at 578, 125 P at 358.
[37] 43 Cal 2d 481, 275 P2d 15 (1954).

liable for innocent misrepresentation (deceit) and negligence. The trial court applied the wrong measure of damages. The cause for the increased cost of the footings was not the defendant's false report, it was the very existence of the fill, the physical condition of the land. Once given the decision to build, the costs were inevitable. The defendant did not undertake to insure against this loss. Therefore, the damages should have been the out-of-pocket damages measured by the difference between the market value of the lots and the price plaintiff paid. If the lots were worth what plaintiff paid, then plaintiff was not damaged; if the defendant's false report induced the plaintiff to pay more than their value, the difference would be attributable to the negligence of the defendant. Therefore, the plaintiff was not damaged unless it proved that the reasonable cost of the improved lots exceeded their value. The trial court committed error by excluding evidence offered by defendant to show that the value of the property as improved exceeded the amount of the plaintiff's investment.

Even though plaintiff might have proven that it would not have undertaken to build had it known the truth, it had yet to prove a loss flowing from that decision.

This opinion focuses attention on the fact that, in many cases, the true cause of plaintiff's expense is not malpractice committed by the architect, but rather physical characteristics of the property as governed by the laws of nature.

In *Gagne*, the expense was caused by the physical condition of the land and not by any act of the soils tester. This is also an element of the *underestimate* cases: the expense is caused by the physical fact that a building as designed by the defendant requires a determinable number of cubic yards of concrete, board feet of lumber, feet of electrical conduit, and man-hours of labor.

In another class of cases, it is the malpractice which directly, naturally, and physically causes expense: wrong design may cause a beam to deflect or a chimney to smoke; but wrong design does not change building costs, nor does it introduce fill.

Another case in which a loss was caused by the laws of nature rather than malpractice is *Bonadiman-McCain, Inc v Snow*,[38] where an engineer prepared a grading plan for hillside property showing 33 lots. The physical dimensions of the property were such that the amount of the fill created by grading was greater than anticipated. Therefore, the lots had to be erected at a higher level. This reduced the number of level square feet in an area planned for three lots to an amount that would only accommodate two lots. Thus, the subdivision contained 32 lots rather than 33. Neither the trial court nor the court of appeal could see that the plaintiff was entitled to recover damages. The physical characteristics of the earth when worked caused it to expand rather than

---

[38] 183 Cal App 2d 58, 6 Cal Rptr 52 (1960).

contract. Given those physical properties, the subdivision could only accommodate 32 lots. Given the state of the art of soil mechanics as it was known at that time, the engineer was not negligent. The engineer expected the earth to shrink, but it expanded. An engineer's client purchases services, not insurance. Here, since there was no evidence of negligence, there were no damages.

Similarly, in *Roberts v Karr*,[39] the court held that the plaintiff's loss was caused by physical conditions rather than the negligence of a surveyor. The surveyor reported that there would be at least 51,000 cubic yards of excess dirt in a project. In fact, there were only 15,802 cubic yards. The plaintiff alleged that the reasonable value of the dirt was $0.15 per cubic yard, and relying on the report, the plaintiff sold the land for $100,000 plus the amount by which the value of the excess dirt exceeded the cost of leveling.

The court held the plaintiff had a good cause of action for negligence and deceit (negligent misrepresentation), but the surveyor did not guarantee the accuracy of its findings; therefore, the plaintiff could recover only out-of-pocket damages. The misrepresentation did not cause the loss; the physical fact that the dirt did not exist on the property caused the loss. Plaintiffs argued that they sold their property for less than its market value because of the misrepresentation, but the court of appeal held that there was an implied finding that this allegation was false. Therefore, since the plaintiffs sold their property for its market value, there was no loss except $300, which was the cost of additional survey work. Therefore, the proper amount of damages was $300.

An erroneous survey made it appear that a parcel of land contained more acreage than it actually did contain. Plaintiff, the purchaser of the land, paid for the land in a lump sum. HELD: since the plaintiff bought the land on a lump sum rather than a per acre basis, it could not be determined with certainty that the lump sum paid would have been any smaller had the plaintiff known that the tract contained less acreage than that stated on the surveyor's map. Plaintiff failed to prove that the surveyor's error caused it to pay too much for the tract.[40]

The out-of-pocket rule was applied in an overbudget case in *Strouth v Wilkison*.[41] The defendant contractor made numerous willfully false representations to induce the plaintiff to contract with it to build a country house, including a representation that the house could be built for $38,000. The ultimate cost was $79,300 for a house which had a reasonable value of $48,000. The trial court awarded the difference between the contract price and the cost. REVERSED. The proper measure of damages was the difference between the market value of the property received and the price paid, not the difference between the contract price and cost. The court held to the out-of-pocket rule

---

[39] 178 Cal App 2d 535, 3 Cal Rptr 98 (1960).
[40] Broussard v Continental Casualty Co, 421 So 2d 341 (La Ct App), *writ denied*, 423 So 2d 1165 (1982).
[41] 302 Minn 297, 224 NW2d 511 (1974).

even though it may have been tempted to punish the engineer for willfully made false statements: the engineer claimed that 17 years of experience in building stopped because of ill health, and a net worth of $75,000. In reality, the engineer left the construction business because of bankruptcy, was not a licensed engineer, and had a net worth of $45,000.[42]

In *Bayuk v Edson*,[43] numerous flaws in a residence were created by negligence of the architect, both in design and supervision: the closets were only 18 inches wide; the floors were not level; the fireplace was cracked; and the doors were too elaborate to be properly constructed by local artisans.

The court received expert testimony as to the reasonable value of the house had it been properly designed and built and its reasonable value as actually designed and built. The court held that the proper measure of damages was the difference between the two figures.

§10.08 Cost of Correction Uneconomic

Courts will seldom award damages measured by the cost of corrective work which, in its nature, would be uneconomic. The rule of damages is related to the contract doctrine of substantial performance. If a contractor constructs a building that does not comply with the requirements of the contract documents, the contractor is guilty of a breach of contract which under ordinary contract law would excuse counterperformance by the owner. If the breach is not intentional, however, the contractor is still entitled to recover the contract price if the contract has been substantially performed. The amount of the recovery is reduced, however, by what it would cost to correct the inadequate performance.[44]

Suppose the cost of correction would be uneconomic. For example, if the specifications require steel pipe, but the contractor has installed copper pipe, there is a breach of contract. Yet, to remove and replace the pipe would be uneconomic. The owner is therefore entitled not to offset the cost of correction but merely to offset the amount by which the market value of the project has been reduced by the breach of contract.

In *Trunk & Gordon v Clark*,[45] the plaintiff architect filed an action to recover its fee for the design of an opera house. The owner alleged design defects: the private boxes had no view of the stage, and the arch was improperly designed, causing the sustaining walls to bulge. The Iowa Supreme Court held that the question of the defendant's offset should go to the jury, and if the jury found that

---

[42] *See also* Sard v Berman, 47 AD2d 892, 367 NYS2d 266 (1975).
[43] 236 Cal App 2d 309, 46 Cal Rptr 49 (1965).
[44] *See* Thomas Haverty Co v Jones, 185 Cal 285, 197 P 105 (1921).
[45] 163 Iowa 620, 145 NW 277 (1914).

the architect had failed to prepare the contract documents with reasonable technical skill, the measure of damages would be the cost of correction. However, if a defect could not be corrected without unreasonable expense, then the measure of damages would be the difference between the value of the building as designed and the value it would have had if properly designed.

In *Rosos Litho Supply Corp v Hansen*,[46] the owner alleged that the architect negligently approved a fill that was frozen, which caused the slab to settle and crack. HELD: the measure of damages is the cost of repair; if, however, the defect is so fundamental or widespread that it cannot be ameliorated without extensive repairs and expense, the proper measure of damages is the difference in value between the building as it stands and its value had the architectural services been rendered properly.[47]

The reason for the rule is sound, and a consideration of the reasoning raises an inference that the market value rule is superior: it is more likely to do precise justice. The courts should not allow a rule of damages to be applied so as to unjustly enrich the plaintiff at the expense of the defendant. Suppose copper pipe is just as good as steel pipe. The cost of removing the copper pipe and replacing it with steel pipe would be $100,000. The value of the building is $500,000. If the defendant pays the plaintiff $100,000, will the plaintiff really use those funds to repair the broken promise? Presumably not. Therefore, the plaintiff would get both the building and the $100,000 and would be unjustly enriched. Thus, the enforcement of the defendant's promise becomes punitive rather than compensatory. In plain fact the cost of correction is not necessarily logically related to the damages actually sustained by the plaintiff.

The logical connection exists only if the preponderance of the evidence suggests that the plaintiff indeed would use the damages to make the correction. Where this is true, the difference in market value is, in fact, the same as the cost of correction.

If an owner can increase the value of a building by correcting a defective skylight, it will do so, but only if the increase in value will exceed the cost of correction. If the cost of correction exceeds the increase in value, it becomes uneconomic to make the correction. Therefore, in cases of ordinary negligence if the cost of correction exceeds the difference in market value, then the market value difference should be the measure. If the cost of correction equals or is less than the difference in market value, then the cost of correction should be the measure. A willing buyer would presumably deduct the cost of correction from the computation of market value, but nothing more, since by incurring the cost of correction, the buyer can realize the full market value.

---

[46] 123 Ill App 3d 290, 462 NE2d 566 (1984).

[47] *See also* Greco v Mancini, 476 A2d 522 (RI 1984) (when damage is temporary, the proper measure is cost of repairs; when damage is permanent, the proper measure is diminution in value).

The term *cost of correction* should properly be understood to include all of the costs, including loss of use, rent, or income during the period of correction.

Thus, it would appear that in cases of ordinary negligence the difference in market value should normally be the measure of damages. The difference in market value can never be more than the cost of correction although it can be measured by the cost of correction. In cases where the difference in market value is less than the cost of correction, to give the owner the cost of correction, when according to the laws of economics the owner will not use the fund to fulfill the defendant's promise, is to unjustly enrich the plaintiff at the expense of the defendant.

§10.09 Rental Value

If malpractice delays the progress of the work, the owner sustains a loss. The owner's capital is invested but yields no income. The owner should be compensated in damages for the delay. Damages for delay may be measured either by interest or by rent, but not both.

In order to recover damages for delay, it is necessary to establish a projected completion date for the project. In a Nevada case, an engineer improperly surveyed the location of caissons, causing delay in the completion of a hotel building. HELD: it could not be said that the loss of profits caused by the delayed opening of the hotel was a direct and natural result of the surveyor's breach as there was no evidence that the parties contemplated a particular completion date at the time the contract was formed.[48]

Rent versus Interest

It seems that the most precise measure of damages is rent, rather than interest, if the owner's objective was to rent rather than occupy the project. Since the owner's purpose in constructing the building is to obtain rent and the architect's malpractice has frustrated the purpose, the most precise compensation is rent rather than interest.

If a project is for use rather than for rent, an appropriate measure of damages for delay is interest. The owner's capital is invested in an uncompleted project during a period when the project cannot be used. If the owner had saved the capital rather than expending it, it would have received interest. Presumably the owner was willing to forego the interest for the occupancy, but if the architect's malpractice prevents the occupancy, then the owner should have the interest.

---

[48] Daniel, Mann, Johnson & Mendenhall v Hilton Hotels, 98 Nev 113, 642 P2d 1086 (1982).

Rent Plus Interest

The appearances of the situation can be confused by the fact that an owner may be paying interest while it is losing rent. Since most construction is done with borrowed capital, the owner can introduce evidence that it paid interest on a construction loan during the period of the delay and was at the same time deprived of rent which it could otherwise have obtained. Since the owner has both paid the interest and lost the rent, it seems plausible that it should recover both. However, this would be a double recovery. Interest, profits, and rent are really just three embodiments of the same thing: a return on capital. To award more than one is to give a double return to the same capital.

If a plaintiff has a sum of money in a bank account at interest and converts that money into an equity in a rental building, it exchanges interest for rent.

If the same plaintiff had borrowed the same sum to invest in a rental building, it would likewise exchange interest for rent, but in the second example, the plaintiff has made a decision to pay interest in order to obtain rent. Thus, the interest is a cost of producing the rent, and the damage award should recognize that cost by denying a recovery of interest if the rent is awarded, and vice versa.

As has been seen,[49] interest, rent, or profit is a component of the cost of correction in determining damages for defective design or supervision when the plaintiff's ability to use premises is curtailed or destroyed during the period of correction.

As was illustrated in *Bayshore Development Co v Bonfoey*,[50] the rental value of a project may be a factor in determining its market value. In *Bayshore*, the court held that an award of rent lost to delay in the completion of a project would be too remote and speculative, but such damages are routinely awarded in other cases and should clearly be recoverable in a case of project delay due to the malpractice of an architect.

§10.10 Economic Loss

A question is sometimes raised as to whether a court will award damages for pecuniary or *economic loss* in a case of malpractice. This question may properly be one of duty rather than damages: it may be argued that the architect is under no duty to protect a third party against economic or pecuniary loss. The same proposition may be framed as a rule of damages by asserting that the plaintiff is not entitled to recover damages for pecuniary or economic loss.

---

[49] *See* §10.08.
[50] 75 Fla 455, 78 So 507 (1918). *See* §10.06.

Economic Loss Awarded

Economic loss is a damage to the pecuniary interests of the plaintiff, as distinguished from bodily injury or physical damage to property. In *A.E. Investment Corp v Link Builders, Inc*,[51] a supermarket occupied by a tenant became useless when the floor broke up because of subsoil conditions. The tenant filed an action against the project architect for economic loss, alleging a negligent failure to diagnose the condition of the subsoil. The Wisconsin Supreme Court held that a cause of action may exist in favor of a tenant and against an architect not in privity if public policy considerations do not intervene. Whether *economic loss* is recoverable is a policy decision that must be resolved by the trial court rather than on demurrer.

In *Davidson & Jones, Inc v New Hanover County*,[52] a general contractor filed a third-party complaint against an architect and an engineer on a public project, and the court ordered summary judgment for these defendants. REVERSED. Even in the absence of privity of contract, an architect, surveyor, or civil engineer may be liable to a general contractor for economic loss for breach of a common law duty of care. Where breach of the contract results in a foreseeable injury, economic or otherwise, to persons so situated by their economic relations and community of interests as to impose a duty of due care, liability will arise from the breach of that duty flowing from the parties' working relationship.

Flawed Jury Instruction

In *Dickerson Construction Co v Process Engineering Co*,[53] the owner's metal-plating operation was interrupted because of damage to the building caused by the expansion of Yazoo clay when it became saturated with water. The court instructed the jury to determine "all damages, if any, which will be caused as a result of business interruption during permanent repairs made to the building." REVERSED. The instruction was fatally defective. It was so vague and general that it allowed the jury to determine the measure of damages without furnishing any guide as to the proper computation.

Other cases have held that economic loss is recoverable.[54] In most states the defense that an architect is not liable to a third party for economic loss expired

---

[51] 62 Wis 2d 479, 214 NW2d 764 (1974).

[52] 41 NC App 661, 255 SE2d 580, *review denied*, 298 NC 295, 255 SE2d 780 (1979).

[53] 341 So 2d 646 (Miss 1977).

[54] Craig v Everett M. Brooks Co, 351 Mass 497, 222 NE2d 752 (1967) (general contractor versus engineer for additional construction costs incurred because of negligently located offset stakes); Rozny v Marnal, 43 Ill 2d 54, 250 NE2d 656 (1969) (remote buyer versus surveyor for encroachment); Cooper v Jevne, 56 Cal App 3d 860, 128 Cal Rptr 724 (1976) (condominium buyers versus architect for loss of use and income of condominium property).

along with the defense that an architect is not liable for malpractice causing physical injury to a third party in the absence of privity of contract.

Moorman Doctrine

The Illinois Supreme Court has affirmed that the Moorman doctrine[55] applies to cases of architectural malpractice.[56] A condominium association sued an architect to recover the cost of repairing windows, glass doors, roof, utilities, and a garage (which was settling). The question certified to the supreme court was whether an exception to the Moorman rule should be recognized for actions alleging architectural malpractice. HELD: a plaintiff may not recover economic loss in a tort action for architectural malpractice. There are four exceptions: (1) intentional misrepresentation; (2) negligent misrepresentation; (3) intentional interference with contract; and (4) intentional interference with prospective business advantage. Plaintiffs who can establish these four torts in architectural malpractice claims may recover for economic loss, because these four torts are based on the premise that a defendant owes a duty to the plaintiff to prevent the very type of economic harm that occurs. However, a plaintiff may not recover for economic loss in an architectural malpractice claim founded on allegations of ordinary negligence.

New York law holds that damages for economic losses may be recovered only in contract, and Illinois courts have frequently held that an architect, out of privity with the claimant, is not liable for economic loss. Responsibility for such economic loss is a matter of contract rather than tort law.[57]

As an example, in *Oldenburg v Hagemann*,[58] a subcontractor filed a third-party complaint against an architect alleging negligence in approving incorrect ceiling tile and failure to detect that the subcontractor's bid did not conform to specifications, followed by a failure to see that the subcontractor installed improper ceiling tile. The court held that the subcontractor's tort claim against the architect was barred by the economic loss doctrine, and that the remedy for economic loss lies in contract and not in tort law. The court pointed

---

[55] *See* §10.03.

[56] 2314 Lincoln Park West Condominium Assn v Mann, Gin, Ebel & Frazier Ltd, 136 Ill 2d 302, 555 NE2d 346 (1990).

[57] Carmania Corp v Hambrecht Terrell Intl, 705 F Supp 936 (SDNY 1989) (allegation of $8.5 million loss because of delay in completion of building; negligence cause of action against architect dismissed). *See also* Lake Placid Club Attached Lodges v Elizabethtown Builders, Inc, 131 AD2d 159, 521 NYS2d 165 (1987) (there is no recovery in negligence of damages for physical deterioration resulting in consequential economic loss); Long Island Lighting Co v IMO Delaval, Inc, 668 F Supp 237 (SDNY 1987) (HELD: engineer was free of liability for economic loss due to operation or nonoperation of a nuclear power station).

[58] 159 Ill App 3d 631, 512 NE2d 718 (1987), *appeal denied*, 188 Ill 2d 546, 520 NE2d 387 (1988).

out that there are exceptions to the economic loss doctrine which allow recovery for false representations, both intentional and negligent. Furthermore, the doctrine does not prevent consumers from recovering economic loss where their reasonable expectations are frustrated by a negligent architect. Here, however, the subcontractor was not without a remedy, because a contractual relationship did exist between the subcontractor and the prime contractor. Therefore, under that contract, there was an adequate remedy available to the subcontractor for economic damages.[59]

In *City of East Moline v Bracke Hayes & Miller*,[60] an Illinois architect employed a New York engineer who in turn employed a New Jersey engineer for design of a municipal swimming pool project in Illinois. HELD: since the damages claimed against the engineer were economic only, they could not be recovered in a negligence action, but only in an action for breach of contract.

In *Bates & Rogers Construction Corp v North Shore Sanitation District*,[61] a contractor and subcontractor sued an architect/engineer for damages sustained because of the negligence of defendants in the design and supervision of a sewage treatment plant, which resulted in cost overruns and additional expenses sustained by the contractors. Summary judgment for defendants was AFFIRMED. Purely economic loss arising from disappointed commercial expectation is recoverable only in a contract action. Plaintiffs could not recover for economic loss arising from the negligence of the architect/engineer, since there was no privity of contract.

The Ohio Supreme Court has also adopted (four to three) the view that a contractor may not sue an architect for economic loss in the absence of privity. In *Floor Craft Floor Covering, Inc v Parma Community General Hospital Assn*,[62] a contractor alleged that an architect negligently prepared specifications, which resulted in damage to flooring that the contractor had installed. The court held that the Restatement (Second) Torts §552 (1977), which imposes liability on one who supplies false information for the guidance of others in their business transactions, should not apply in the case of design professionals.[63]

---

[59] *See also* Santucci Constr Co v Baxter & Woodman, Inc, 151 Ill App 3d 547, 502 NE2d 1134 (1986), *appeal denied*, 115 Ill 2d 550, 511 NE2d 437 (1987) (doctrine of economic loss bars tort claims arising from negligence where negligence of an engineer in failing to obtain easement agreements from property owners along a right-of-way for a sewer and water project allegedly caused delay and inefficiency to the contractor).

[60] 133 Ill App 3d 136, 478 NE2d 637 (1985).

[61] 128 Ill App 3d 962, 471 NE2d 915 (1984), *affd*, 109 Ill 2d 225, 486 NE2d 902 (1985).

[62] 54 Ohio St 3d 1, 560 NE2d 206 (1990).

[63] Dissenting justices objected to the resurrection of the doctrine of privity of contract as providing a defense to architects and engineers in economic loss cases. According to the dissent, at least 21 state courts have held that the absence of contractual privity *does not* shield design professionals from liability for malpractice which causes economic loss.

In *Blake Construction Co v Alley*,[64] the Supreme Court of Virginia held that a general contractor with no privity of contract with the architect had no right to recover, in a common law tort action, for economic loss arising from the architect's alleged breach of contract with the owner.[65]

In *Cincinnati Gas & Electric Co v General Electric Co*,[66] a utility alleged that an architect failed to properly design portions of a nuclear power plant. The utility filed contract and negligence causes of action against the architect. HELD: the tort claims for negligent misrepresentation and professional malpractice were variations of the contract claims for economic loss; the tort claims were, therefore, dismissed. Recovery, if any, was to be under contract theory.

In *Bryant Electric Co v City of Fredericksburg*,[67] plaintiff contractor claimed economic loss in the form of delay damages against an architect. HELD: a contractor may not recover for purely economic loss caused by the negligence of a design professional in the absence of privity of contract with the design professional.

Doctrine Rejected

In *Beachwalk Villas Condominium Associates v Martin*,[68] the trial court held that condominium owners lacking privity of contract with an architect were barred by the economic loss rule from asserting a cause of action against the architect for negligence in failing to properly design a condominium project. REVERSED. It has been held that a builder may be responsible in negligence and implied warranty to new home purchasers even though there is no privity and damages suffered were only of an economic nature. It is logical to expand this principal to provide protection to homebuyers against negligent architects.[69]

In *Seattle Western Industries v David A. Mowat Co*,[70] a subcontractor filed an action against an architect alleging contractual losses sustained because of an architect's negligent performance of its functions on a public project. The court awarded damages based on the *modified total cost* method of computing contract losses in which the subcontractor proved that its estimate was reasonable and

---

[64] 233 Va 31, 353 SE2d 724 (1987).

[65] *See also* Sensenbrenner v Rust, Orling & Neals Architects, Inc, 236 Va 419, 424, 374 SE2d 55, 57 (1988): "When a product 'injures itself' because one of its component parts is defective, a purely economic loss results to the owner for which no action in tort will lie." (Homeowners purchased a package including land, design services, and construction. A component part of the package was defective, causing damage to other parts. Therefore, the homeowner had no cause of action against the design architect absent privity of contract.)

[66] 656 F Supp 49 (SD Ohio 1986).

[67] 762 F2d 1192 (4th Cir 1985).

[68] 305 SC 144, 406 SE2d 372 (1991).

[69] Citing Kennedy v Columbia Lumber & Mfg Co, 299 SC 335, 384 SE2d 730 (1989).

[70] 110 Wash 2d 1, 750 P2d 245 (1988).

that the total cost of performing the contract work exceeded the estimate because of the fault of the architect, and claimed the difference as damages after subtracting cost overruns suffered because of the contractor's own erroneous performance.

In *Malta Construction Co v Henningson, Durham & Richardson, Inc*,[71] a contractor on a bridge project sued an engineer that was employed by the Department of Transportation alleging damages sustained because of inadequate plans and specifications which caused delays. HELD: the claim was not barred by the economic loss rule. The contractor was a foreseeable third party with a pecuniary interest in information supplied by the engineer.

In *Forte Brothers v National Amusement, Inc*,[72] it was held that a supervising architect's duty of care to exercise the abilities, skills, and care customarily exercised by architects in similar circumstances extends to contractors who share an economic relationship and community of interest with the architect on a construction project. Therefore, a "third party general contractor who may be foreseeably injured or suffer an economic loss proximately caused by the negligent performance of a contractual duty by an architect/site engineer has a cause of action in negligence against the architect/site engineer notwithstanding the absence of privity."[73]

In *Council of Co-Owners Atlantis Condominium, Inc v Whiting-Turner Contracting Co*,[74] an architect argued that owners of 198 condominium units suffered only economic loss and not personal injury or property damage and were, therefore, precluded from recovering judgment for diminution in property value resulting from latent defects in the design of a 21-story condominium project. HELD: the duty of architects and builders to use due care in the design, inspection, and construction of condominium units extends to those persons foreseeably subjected to the risk of injury created by a latent and unreasonable condition resulting from their negligence. Here, a defective electrical system created a risk of personal injury and an action could be maintained to recover the reasonable cost of correcting the dangerous condition.

In *Doran-Maine, Inc v American Engineering & Testing, Inc*,[75] the defendant was a testing laboratory which negligently condemned concrete pipe manufactured by plaintiff as failing to comply with specifications. Applying Maine law, the court permitted the manufacturer in a negligence action against the testing laboratory to recover damages for lost profits, costs of procuring independent tests, and carrying charges on rejected pipe.

---

[71] 694 F Supp 902 (ND Ga 1988).

[72] 525 A2d 1301 (RI 1987).

[73] *Id* 1302. (Negligent failure to measure removal of mass rock and boulders, failure to approve payments to contractor in cinema construction project.)

[74] 308 Md 18, 517 A2d 336 (1986).

[75] 608 F Supp 609 (D Me 1985).

In *Bay Garden Manor Condominium Assn v James D. Marks Associates*,[76] engineers were employed to inspect an apartment project before it was converted to condominiums. The condition of the building was misrepresented. HELD: the economic loss rule did not apply, since engineers were hired to prepare reports to guide owners in making a business decision. Florida follows the Restatement view provided in Restatement (Second) Torts §552 (1976):

> One who, in the course of his business, profession or employment, or in any transaction in which he has a pecuniary interest, supplies false information for the guidance of others in their business transactions, is subject to liability for pecuniary loss caused to them by their justifiable reliance on the information, if he fails to exercise reasonable care or competence in obtaining or communicating the information.

Conflicting Decisions

Conflicting decisions by courts of appeal in Illinois as to the vitality of the economic loss doctrine in cases of architectural malpractice presaged clarification of the doctrine by the Illinois Supreme Court.[77] In *Skinner v FGM, Inc*,[78] the state filed action against the architect, contractor, subcontractors, manufacturers, and surety on an elementary school job. The main issues in the case revolved around the statute of limitations, but the state did allege economic loss damages resulting from roof leaks. The court held that economic losses were not recoverable in tort; therefore, the negligence claims were properly dismissed *except against the architect*, since to have dismissed the negligence claim against the architect would have eliminated and conflicted with law defining the scope of an architect's liability for professional negligence. In addition, dismissal would have set aside earlier cases where damages were awarded in architectural malpractice cases.

In *Skinner v Graham*,[79] the court of appeal again considered the "ill-fated Capitol Area Vocational Center" which was closed because of serious structural defects. Judgment for the architects was AFFIRMED. The court held that economic loss alone cannot be a basis for recovery in tort. "[W]here the construction defects do not cause physical injuries or damage to other property, [courts] are unwilling to impose tort liability on a builder for breach of his

---

[76] 576 So 2d 744 (Fla Dist Ct App 1991).

[77] 2314 Lincoln Park West Condominium Assn v Mann, Gin, Ebel & Frazier Ltd, 136 Ill 2d 302, 555 NE2d 346 (1990).

[78] 166 Ill App 3d 802, 502 NE2d 1024, *appeal denied*, 122 Ill 2d 593, 530 NE2d 263 (1988).

[79] 170 Ill App 3d 417, 524 NE2d 642 (1988).

contract with the purchaser, even if the breach was willful and wanton."[80] The state could not recover economic loss arising from negligent performance of professional services.

§10.11 Mental Anguish

It is sometimes stated that a plaintiff cannot recover damages from an architect for mental anguish and emotional suffering. Although it is thus formulated in the guise of a rule of damages, the principle should really be classified as a substantive question of tort law: whether an architect is under a duty to avoid conduct that will cause mental anguish and emotional suffering to its client or a third party.[81]

Allegations of negligent conduct will not sustain a claim of relief for intentional infliction of emotional distress. Such damages must be supported by outrageous or intentional conduct.[82]

In *Johnson v Martin*,[83] the court stated that a landowner could not recover for mental suffering since the surveyor's trespass was not committed under circumstances of insult. In *Guthrie v Rudy Brown Builders, Inc*,[84] the court stated that the purchaser was not entitled to mental anguish damages since the object of a contract for the sale of the house was primarily physical gratification, while under the Louisiana code,[85] nonpecuniary damages are recoverable only if the contract has as its exclusive object intellectual enjoyment, rather than physical gratification. Although some aesthetic enjoyment may be anticipated, the main object of a contract for the purchase of a house is physical gratification.[86]

§10.12 Punitive Damages

In rare cases, *punitive damages* may be awarded against an architect. In *Muehlstedt v City of Lino Lakes*,[87] an engineer who acted in a managerial

---

[80] *Id* at 434, 524 NE2d at 652.

[81] *See* ch 7.

[82] Zukowski v Howard, Needles, Tammen & Bergendoff, Inc, 657 F Supp 926 (D Colo 1987) (construction workers killed or injured in collapse of viaduct; negligence suit against design engineers).

[83] 423 So 2d 868 (Ala Civ App 1982). *See also* Hogan Exploration, Inc v Monroe Engg Assocs, 430 So 2d 696 (La Ct App 1983); Guthrie v Rudy Brown Builders, Inc, 416 So 2d 590 (La Ct App), *writ denied*, 420 So 2d 455 (La 1982) where courts denied recovery for mental anguish where surveyors made incorrect surveys.

[84] 416 So 2d 590 (La Ct App), *writ denied*, 420 So 2d 455 (La 1982).

[85] LSA-CC arts 1926, 1934, subd 3.

[86] *See also* Hogan Exploration, Inc v Monroe Engg Assocs, 430 So 2d 696 (La Ct App 1983) (corporation cannot suffer mental anguish).

[87] 473 NW2d 892 (Minn Ct App 1991), *review denied* (Sept 25, 1991).

capacity authorized a tree removal subcontractor to remove trees and bury them on the owner's property, without authority from the owner. When the owner later attempted to build a house on the property, it was necessary to remove the buried trees and backfill the hole. A jury awarded $500,000 in *punitive damages* against the engineer, which the trial court reduced to $100,000. AFFIRMED: (1) Punitive damages may be allowed in cases that do not involve personal injury. (2) The engineer improperly concealed the information that it had not consulted with the owner about burying trees on its property.

In a Georgia case, the landowners sued an architect for trespass, alleging that the architect's design of an adjoining construction site was negligent, causing property damage from mud and silt that escaped from the construction site. The jury awarded punitive damages in addition to compensatory damages. HELD: punitive damages were properly awarded. The jury was properly instructed that punitive damages are available in cases of willful misconduct, malice, fraud, and oppression.[88]

---

[88] Tomberlin Assocs Architects v Free, 174 Ga App 167, 329 SE2d 296 (1985), *cert denied* (May 1, 1985).

Limitations 11

§11.01 Generally
Estoppel
Compendium
Criticism
§11.02 Applicable Period
Damage to Project
Contract
Contract Statute Applied
Contract versus Malpractice
Malpractice
Design versus Malpractice
Contract and Tort
Tort
Tort versus Contract
Tort versus Contract versus Property Damage
Third-Party Beneficiary
Economic Loss
Negligence Statute Applied
Bodily Injury
Professional Service
Statute of Repose versus Negligence
Indemnity
§11.03 Accrual—Negligent Act
New York Rule
§11.04 —Time of Completion
§11.05 —When Damage Occurs
Payment as Damage
Criminal Prosecution

§11.06 —Discovery Rule
§11.07 —Statutes of Repose
Bodily Injury
Discovery Extension
Fraud Claim
Auto Accident
Completion of Services
Contract Action
Latent Defect
Retrospective Effect
Statute of Repose Does Not Extend Time to Sue
§11.08 —Constitutional Considerations
A Box Score
Constitutionality of Statute Upheld
Statute of Repose Held Unconstitutional
§11.09 —Statute of Repose Applied
Indemnity Action
Completion of Construction
Improvement to Real Property
§11.10 —Application of Statute Rejected
§11.11 Continuous Services
Attempted Repairs
Continuing Inspections
Assurances of Repair
Professional Assurances
Contractor Does Not Rely on Architect
Gap in Services
§11.12 Arbitration
§11.13 Remedial Efforts

§11.01 Generally

Questions of the limitation of actions are peculiar to the language of statutes. The outcome of any particular case depends upon the statutory pattern of the jurisdiction. Therefore, a rule valid and sensible in one state may not pertain in another, and a nationwide view of the cases that consider limitation of actions as it applies to the malpractice of architects shows that the states have adopted many conflicting views.

Moreover, courts display discordant attitudes toward the statute of limitations. It is viewed by some as a technical and unfavored defense which may operate so as to unjustly deprive a plaintiff of its action. Other courts view the statute of limitations as beneficial and deserving of liberal construction, since it protects a defendant against unjust cases where the plaintiff, by delaying the assertion of its rights, deprives the defendant of evidence necessary to an adequate defense.

The first step in applying a statute of limitations is to determine whether the malpractice action is for bodily injury or property damage and whether it is framed in tort, contract, warranty, or misrepresentation. The next step is to determine the time when the cause of action accrues: whether when the negligent act occurs, or at the date of completion of the project, or when the damage occurs, or when the plaintiff discovers the injury.

Problems of accrual are especially critical in construction cases because of the long lifetime of a construction project. Damage may occur many years after a project is completed.

Estoppel

In *Senior Housing, Inc v Nakawatase, Rutkowski, Wyns & Yi, Inc*,[1] an architect was estopped to assert the statute of limitations. A residential building leaked. The architect advised the owner that it had instructed the contractor to re-caulk. The fix did not work. Three years after completion, the owner employed a contractor to correct the problems at a cost of $11,120, then demanded reimbursement from the architect. When the architect failed to accept responsibility, the owner filed suit for breach of contract. The architect alleged that a two-year statute of limitation applied, which began to run when the building was substantially complete. HELD: the architect apparently took direct responsibility for repair work, and never denied responsibility until September 1986 when the owner demanded restitution. The architect acted as an intermediary between the owner and the contractor and acted in apparent acknowledgement of its responsibility under the contract. It was, therefore, reasonable for the owner to refrain from filing suit in reliance on the architect's representations that the problem would be monitored and corrected.

Compendium

The American Institute of Architects (AIA) publishes the *Compendium: State Statutes of Limitations for Design Professionals* in which the statute of limitation for each state is both summarized and stated in its entirety. The publication, a useful working tool, can be obtained by writing the AIA, 1735 New York Avenue, N.W., Washington, D.C. 20006.

---

[1] 192 Ill App 3d 766, 549 NE2d 604 (1989). *See also* 65th Center, Inc v Copeland, 825 SW2d 574 (Ark 1992) (engineer designed a roadway in 1967; accident occurred in 1990. HELD: four-year statute of limitations barred action against architect. The absence of a guardrail was not a "concealed defect").

Criticism

The statute of limitations should be a favorite target for reformers. It is difficult to understand why a plaintiff with a negligence action should be held to a higher standard of diligence in filing suit than one with a contract action. Conversely, why should a contract defendant be exposed to suit longer than a negligence defendant? The division of actions into categories with various periods of time attached is inconsistent, arbitrary, and irrational. Add to this the difficulty of classification, especially since the plaintiff's case will stand or fall on the category assigned. The same act may be malpractice, negligence, and a breach of contract; that act may engender bodily injury, property damage, economic loss, and mental anguish. All the statutory periods are logically applicable to the same act, but the court must choose one, and upon that choice depends the question of whether or not the plaintiff will be compensated for its injuries. This absurd state of affairs which prevails in most states would invite instant criticism from any person of discretion not trained in law. The problem is created by statute and thus must be solved by statute. However, the solution does not have much political glamour, and presumably reform will come through the organized bar if it comes at all.

§11.02 Applicable Period

The pattern of statutes of limitation is to establish different periods for different causes of action. Thus, the statute of limitations may include periods for negligence, breach of contract, breach of warranty, malpractice, bodily injury, property damage, fraud, deceit, misrepresentation, and other categories, two or more of which might arguably apply to the same case. For example, a single act of negligence may be both malpractice and a breach of contract; that act may cause both personal injury and damage to property. The classification of the act determines the period of limitations.

Damage to Project

In a Colorado case,[2] a homeowner brought an action against an engineer for damages from extensive cracking in a basement floor. The trial court granted summary judgment on the ground that the two-year statute of limitations applicable to the architects had expired. REVERSED. The two-year statute of limitations was inapplicable to claims for damages for deficiencies in the structure itself. It applies only to claims for personal injury or damages to property other than the defective improvement itself; therefore, in the situation

---

[2] Tamblyn v Mickey & Fox, Inc, 195 Colo 354, 578 P2d 641 (1978).

the six-year statute applied.[3] The nature of the injury, not whether the claim was for negligence or breach of contract, determined the applicable period.

In *City of Aurora v Bechtel Corp*,[4] the trial court erroneously applied Colorado's two-year statute of limitations[5] which applied to architects and engineers. The Colorado Supreme Court held that the two-year statute of limitations did not apply to claims for damages for deficiencies in the structure itself. Instead, the six-year statute for actions of assumpsit, contract, or express or implied liability applied.[6]

Contract

In a New York case,[7] an owner charged an architect with negligent design and supervision of a residence project. The architect was awarded summary judgment on the ground that the action was barred by the statute of limitations. Summary judgment was REVERSED: the complaint stated a good cause of action in contract as well as in tort, and the complaint sought no greater recovery than would be permitted under the law of damages applicable to contract actions. Therefore, the three-year tort statute of limitations was inapplicable.

In another New York case,[8] an owner brought suit against an architect, alleging faulty design of a parking ramp system. The complaint alleged negligent design, breach of implied warranty, and breach of contract arising from the lack of professional care in performing services. The trial court dismissed the action on the ground that the three-year statute of limitations for actions based on negligence had expired. REVERSED. A statute of limitations is selected according to the remedy sought rather than theory of liability. Here, the applicable statute was the six-year contract statute rather than the three-year negligence statute. The obligations of the architect, whether verbalized in tort, professional malpractice, or contract language, arose out of the contractual relationship between the parties. "Absent the contract between them, no services would have been performed and thus there would have been no claim."[9] Since all liability arose from the contractual relationship, the six-year contract statute rather than the three-year tort statute applied.

---

[3] Colo Rev Stat §13-80-110 (1973).

[4] 599 F2d 382 (10th Cir 1979).

[5] Colo Rev Stat §13-80-127 (1973).

[6] *Id* §13-80-110.

[7] Steiner v Wenning, 43 NY2d 831, 373 NE2d 366, 402 NYS2d 567 (1977).

[8] Sears Roebuck & Co v Enco Assocs, 43 NY2d 389, 372 NE2d 555, 401 NYS2d 767 (1977).

[9] *Id* at 395, 372 NE2d at 558, 401 NYS2d at 770-71.

However, since the action was not brought within the three-year period, plaintiff was restricted to the recovery of damages allowable under contract law and could not recover tort damages (for example, lost profits).

In *Paver & Wildfoerster v Catholic High School Assn*,[10] the owner sued the architect to enforce a demand for arbitration, alleging that improper design caused leaks in a building. HELD: the owner alleged a breach of contract by improper design and also alleged that the architect failed to use reasonable care. The claim could have been classified as either a contract claim or a tort claim. Here, the six-year contract period rather than the three-year tort period governed. The arbitration statute permits the assertion of the statute of limitations in order to bar stale claims "not to fragmentize claims into legal theories, the very categories from which arbitration frees those who choose arbitration as their mode of dispute determination." Therefore, "if the claim sought to be arbitrated is substantially related to the subject matter of the substantive agreement, as in this case, it will not be barred merely because it would prevent recovery in a tort action."

Contract Statute Applied

The Oregon court distinguished *Bales for Food* in *Securities-Intermountain, Inc v Sunset Fuel Co.*[11] The assignee of a general contractor filed suit against an architect, alleging economic loss caused by defective design of a heating system in an apartment complex. The plaintiff alleged redesign costs, costs of reaccomplishing certain work, and damages for delay caused by the architect's breach of contract in failing to supervise properly the work of the heating contractor by: failing to review drawings, authorizing disbursements for uncompleted work, and failing to make proper inspections. Summary judgment for defendants was REVERSED. The sole issue was which statute of limitations should apply: the statute for injuries to persons or property arising from construction, alteration, or repair of improvements to real property; the six-year breach of contract statute; or the residual statute for actions not arising on contract and not especially enumerated otherwise. HELD: the six-year breach of contract statute applied.

(1) The statute for damages for injuries to person or property arising out of the construction, alteration or repair or improvements to real property (ORS §12.125) does not apply to an action to recover damages for "financial losses." "Injuries to a person or to property" means bodily injury or physical damage to tangible property.

---

[10] 38 NY2d 669, 345 NE2d 565, 382 NYS2d 22 (1976).

[11] 289 Or 243, 611 P2d 1158 (1980). See Bales for Food, Inc v Poole, 246 Or 253, 424 P2d 892 (1967) further in this section.

(2) The residual statute for actions not arising from contract not covered by other statutes of limitations (ORS §12.110(1)) is not applicable, since the complaint does allege breaches of contract.

(3) The applicable section is in ORS §12.080(1) which allows six years to bring an action "upon a contract or liability either express or implied."

The contract statute was also applied in *Skidmore, Owings & Merrill v Connecticut General Life Insurance Co.*[12] The owner complained that copper pipes used in the heating, ventilating, and air conditioning system corroded because of the chemical content of water drawn from wells and specified by the architect for use as a cooling agent. The statute of limitations for negligence was one year from the date of the injury or three years from the date of the negligent act; the limitation period for breach of contract was six years. The court held that the six-year contract period rather than the shorter negligence period was applicable since the gravamen of the complaint was the architect's breach of a contractual obligation to design, supervise, and inspect.

In *State v Robert E. McKee, Inc*,[13] the state contracted with an architect for construction of an addition to the LSU Medical Center. The architect in turn contracted with an engineer to design and construct the HVAC system. The project was completed in February 1986; on March 1, 1989 the state filed an action against the engineer, alleging HVAC problems relating to air balance and design. HELD: since there was no contractual relationship with the engineer, the one-year statute of limitations (and not the ten-year statute for construction defects) applied.

Contract versus Malpractice

In *Kittson County v Wells, Denbrook & Associates*,[14] the county charged its architect with breach of warranty and negligence in design of a courthouse (marble chip exterior finish began to crack and fall from the walls). HELD: the six-year statute governing actions for breach of contract governed rather than the two-year statute for "injury to property arising out of defective condition of improvement to real property brought against any person performing or furnishing the design, planning, supervision or observation of construction." The court concluded that the statute was to be strictly construed because of the shortness of the two-year discovery provision and absolute nature of the 10-year nullification provision also included within the statute. The statute was to be construed to apply to actions sounding in tort brought by third parties. Supporting this interpretation was the fact that the statute referred to *injury* to

---

[12] 25 Conn Supp 76, 197 A2d 83 (1963).
[13] 584 So 2d 1205 (La Ct App 1991).
[14] 308 Minn 237, 241 NW2d 799 (1976).

person or property, and to injuries arising out of *the defective and unsafe condition of the improvement*, and that this condition was one *constituting the proximate cause of the injury*. All this is tort-type language peculiarly applicable to claims by third parties against architects and engineers.

Malpractice

In *Nicholson-Brown, Inc v City of San Jose*,[15] a contractor alleged numerous errors and omissions in contract documents prepared by an architect. The architect relied on a California Code of Civil Procedure section which provides a two-year limitation on actions for obligations or liabilities not based upon instruments in writing.[16] Plaintiff contended that professional malpractice was governed by the California Code of Civil Procedure section which deals more specifically with architectural malpractice and provides a four-year statute of limitations for actions arising out of patent deficiencies in the design or planning of real estate.[17] HELD: the four-year statute applied. The provision, "nothing in this section shall be construed as extending the period prescribed by the laws of this state for the bringing of any action," was simply intended to prevent the statute from being given retroactive application.

In *City of Omaha v Hellmuth, Obata & Kassabaum Inc*,[18] architects designed a library and a perimeter retaining wall which rapidly deteriorated. The city employed an engineer who investigated the problem and reported that the design was probably deficient. Four years after receiving the engineer's report and eight years after the wall was constructed, the city filed suit. HELD: the action was barred by the professional negligence statute of limitations which requires that an action be commenced within two years after the alleged act or omission or within one year from discovery of facts which would reasonably lead to the discovery of the cause of action.

In *Baskerville-Donovan Engineers, Inc v Pensacola Executive House Condominium Assn*,[19] a condominium homeowners association filed suit against an engineer. Recovery was governed by the four-year tort statute of limitations rather than the two-year period for suits for professional malpractice.

In a Michigan case, *City of Midland v Helger Construction Co*,[20] the city filed an action against an architect to recover damages for defective construction of a roof of an ice arena. The architect rendered services pursuant to written agreement. HELD: the action, subject to the two-year general professional malpractice statute of limitations, was time-barred.

---

[15] 62 Cal App 3d 526, 113 Cal Rptr 159 (1976).
[16] Cal Civ Proc Code §330(1) (West 1982).
[17] *Id* §337(1)(a) (a *completion statute*).
[18] 767 F2d 457 (8th Cir 1985).
[19] 581 So 2d 1301 (Fla 1991).
[20] 157 Mich App 736, 403 NW2d 218 (1987).

In *Horn v Burns & Roe*,[21] an injured steamfitter alleged that it was the engineer's negligent design that caused its fall. HELD: the two-year statute covering actions for *professional negligence* was applicable.

Design versus Malpractice

In Idaho, an action for injuries was sustained when a tenant fell on a stairway without a handrail. HELD: the claim against the architect fell under the six-year statutory period for an action arising out of the design and construction of a building, rather than the two-year period for professional malpractice. The complaint alleged failure of proper inspection.[22]

In Massachusetts, a truck driver, injured when his truck struck a stone wall at the end of a dead-end road, sued the engineer nine years after the road was completed. HELD: the action was barred by the six-year statute of limitations, Mass Gen L ch 260, §2 B amended 1973 Stat ch 777, §2.[23]

Contract and Tort

A community college board sued its engineer alleging breach of contract and negligence. HELD: either the six-year breach of contract or the two-year tort period applied. The action was DISMISSED. The board waited more than seven and one-half years after completion of the work to file the action and six years after notice of the alleged negligence.[24]

Tort

In *Merchants National Bank & Trust Co v Smith, Hinchman & Grylls Associates*,[25] a subcontractor sought to recover economic loss incurred as a result of defective plans and specifications prepared by the architect. At least 800 drawings were revised, resulting in increased costs. HELD: the one-year tort statute of limitations, not the 10-year statute of repose, applied to bar subcontractor's claim.

Tort versus Contract

In *Bales for Food, Inc v Poole*,[26] an owner and an architect had signed a standard American Institute of Architects contract form for professional

---

[21] 536 F2d 251 (8th Cir 1976).

[22] Stephens v Sterns, 106 Idaho 249, 678 P2d 41 (1984).

[23] Milligan v Tibbitts Engg Corp, 391 Mass 364, 461 NE2d 808 (1984).

[24] State *ex rel* State Community College Bd v Sergent, Hauskins & Beckwith, Inc, 27 Ariz App 469, 556 P2d 23 (1976). *See also* South Burlington Sch Dist v Goodrich, 135 Vt 601, 382 A2d 220 (1977) (school district sued an architect for the cost of replacing a leaking roof. HELD: the claim was recognized either in tort or contract, and each had a six-year statute of limitations).

[25] 876 F2d 1202 (5th Cir 1989).

[26] 246 Or 253, 424 P2d 892 (1967).

services. The plaintiff alleged that the building was misplaced, so the parking lot was insufficient. The complaint alleged a breach of contract (six-year statute) rather than negligence (two-year statute). The court cited medical malpractice cases in holding that the failure to exercise due care is tortious, not contractual:

> From our analysis of the problem we have concluded that there is a need for change in the law relating to the limitation of actions, but we think that the change should come through legislation rather than by a judicial effort to make refinements such as plaintiff suggests in this case.[27]

In *Gomes v Pan American Associates*,[28] a Massachusetts six-year statute of repose applied only to actions in tort. Therefore, the statute did not bar the action of an owner against an architect that was founded on contract.

Tort versus Contract versus Property Damage

An architect designed a defective heating system for a hospital in a Wisconsin case.[29] Here, the court pointed out that malpractice can be either a tort or a breach of contract, but under Wisconsin law the six-year limit on actions for damages for injury to property would apply.

Third-Party Beneficiary

In *Vandewater & Lapp v Sacks Builders, Inc*,[30] an engineer prepared a grading plan in 1953. It was certified by the engineer and filed by the county clerk. The defendant purchased the land in 1959. During construction, it was discovered that the drainage plan prepared by the plaintiff engineer would have caused storm water to damage a preexisting neighboring house. The defendant employed the engineer to prepare a new plan, then refused to pay the fee. The engineer filed suit for the value of its work. Defendant filed a counterclaim for the cost of correcting the engineer's original error.

The lower court dismissed the counterclaim on the ground that the three-year negligence statute of limitations had expired. REVERSED: the defendant was a third-party beneficiary of the original contract between the landowner and the engineer. Therefore, the six-year contract period, rather than the three-year negligence period, was applicable. This seems to be a clear case of a court stretching a point to find a theory of liability which would avoid the application of the statute of limitations.

---

[27] *Id* at 256-57, 424 P2d at 893.
[28] 406 Mass 647, 549 NE2d 1134 (1990).
[29] Milwaukee County v Schmidt, Garden & Erikson, 43 Wis 2d 445, 168 NW2d 559 (1969).
[30] 20 Misc 2d 677, 186 NYS2d 103 (Sup Ct 1959).

Economic Loss

In *Schenburn v Lehner Associates*,[31] the plaintiff avoided the application of the statute of limitations by *theory shopping*. The plaintiff employed the defendant to survey land and then sold the land. The survey was inaccurate, and the vendee filed suit against the plaintiff. The parties agreed that the cause of action accrued on December 19, 1961, and the action was filed on March 20, 1967. The plaintiff sought to recover damages to compensate for the legal fees in defending the prior suit, the time and effort expended in the defense, damage to its reputation, loss of friends, anxiety, and damage to its future career. The trial court granted a motion for summary judgment, theorizing that either the two-year malpractice or three-year negligence statute of limitations applied rather than the six-year contract statute. The court of appeal held that an action for injury to person or property must be brought within three years regardless of whether the injury arises out of a contractual relationship. Here, however, the plaintiff did not claim personal injury or property damage, but economic loss (litigation costs, damage to future career) and the case law established that where such an inquiry occurs in the context of an express of implied contract, the six-year statute applied.

Negligence Statute Applied

In *Naetzker v Brocton Central School District*,[32] a school district sought arbitration against an architect for defective design causing a roof leak. The architect moved to stay the arbitration proceedings on the ground that the statute of limitations had expired. The project was completed in 1968. In September 1970, the architect had instructed the contractor to correct leaks, and after they were corrected, authorized final payment. In February 1974, the district complained about continuing leaks, and it was discovered that the roof was defective. In June 1974 the school district demanded arbitration.

The school district alleged three theories: malpractice, breach of contract, and constructive fraud. The court held that the true basis of the claim was malpractice, since it was alleged that the planning, construction, and supervision of the architect were responsible for the leaking roof. Where, as here, a claim of breach of contract is based on negligent performance of contractual duties, the three-year negligence statute applied rather than the contract statute, unless the contract guaranteed a specific result beyond the normal professional standard of performance. Since the cause of action accrued when the building was completed, the motion to stay arbitration was properly granted.

---

[31] 22 Mich App 534, 177 NW2d 699 (1970).
[32] 50 AD2d 142, 376 NYS2d 300 (1975), *revd*, 41 NY2d 929, 363 NE2d 351, 394 NYS2d 627 (1977).

In *Lisbon Contractors, Inc v Miami-Dade Water & Sewer Authority*,[33] the sewer authority charged its engineer with the performance of defective soil tests. HELD: the one-year statute of limitations for specific performance of a contract did not apply. Either the four-year statute for negligence actions or the two-year statute for actions based on professional malpractice was applicable.

Bodily Injury

In *City of Utica v Holt*,[34] a fireman sued the city for injuries sustained when a ladder collapsed. The city sued the architect, alleging that the negligence of the architect caused the fire. HELD: the applicable statute was the same one that would have applied if the fireman had sued the architect directly. Here, since the claims were based on personal injuries arising from an accident occurring within three years of the time the suit was filed, and since the cause of action accrued on the date of the injury, the motion to dismiss was DENIED.

Professional Service

In *Board of Regents v Wilscam Mullins Birge, Inc*, the University alleged design deficiencies and negligent supervision that resulted in cracks in walls. HELD: the two-year statute of limitations for professional negligence applied. "A professional act or service is one arising out of a vocation, calling, occupation, or employment involving specialized knowledge, labor, or skill, and the labor or skill involved is predominantly mental or intellectual, rather than physical or manual."[35]

Statute of Repose versus Negligence

In most states, statutes of repose have been adopted to limit the period of time within which actions may be brought for construction defects to a period of time after the substantial completion of the project. A particular construction defect may also appear to fall within one or more other periods of limitation; for example, limitations applicable to negligence actions or limitations applicable to contract actions.

In such a case[36] a city filed actions against an architect, a structural engineer, and a mechanical engineer for breach of contract and negligence. Summary judgment that the negligence claims were barred by the three-year statute applicable to negligence claims, Connecticut General Statute §52-584, was AFFIRMED. The statute that barred actions brought against architects and

---

[33] 537 F Supp 175 (SD Fla 1982).
[34] 88 Misc 2d 206, 387 NYS2d 377 (Sup Ct 1976).
[35] 230 Neb 675, 682, 433 NW2d 478, 479 (1988).
[36] R.A. Civitello Co v City of New Haven, 6 Conn App 212, 504 A2d 542 (1986).

engineers more than seven years after completion of an improvement did not extend the three-year period applicable to negligence actions or the six-year period applicable to contract actions. The seven-year statute of repose established an absolute maximum on such actions based on the substantial completion of the project, regardless of the date of the act or omission complained of or the date that the right of action accrued.

In *Anderson v Brouwer*,[37] an owner sued an architect for breach of contract, negligence, and breach of warranty resulting in construction defects in the second-story addition to a dental office. Within four months after substantial completion, the owner discovered a rut at the head of the staircase. Two years later, additional ruts began to appear and they were still appearing seven years after completion of construction. The architect contended that the owner's action was barred by California Code of Civil Procedure §337, which created a four-year statute of limitations for an action on a contract, obligation or liability founded on an instrument in writing. HELD: California Civ Proc Code §337 (four years) and California Civ Proc Code §337.15 (ten years, latent construction defects) create a two-step procedure requiring that suit be filed within the shorter of two periods, either four years from discovery or ten years from substantial completion of the project, whichever is shorter.

North Carolina has a four-year statute of repose for professional malpractice claims and a six-year statute of repose for claims against persons who design, construct, and supervise the construction of buildings. The four-year statute could arguably apply to all persons who might be called *professionals*, including architects and engineers as well as health care professionals. However, the six-year statute, which deals more directly and specifically with the architectural profession, was held to apply in *Trustees of Rowan Technical College v J. Hyatt Hammond Associates*.[38] The six-year statute applies whether the damages sought are for correction of defects or as a result of some further injury caused by the defect.

Indemnity

A sewer line was constructed across a canal which interfered with navigation. The United States government filed an action against the county drain commissioner, who filed a cross-claim against the architect for indemnity. DISMISSED. The six-year statute of limitations applicable to torts by architects had elapsed. The statute expressly applied to claims for indemnity.[39]

---

[37] 99 Cal App 3d 176, 160 Cal Rptr 65 (1979).
[38] 313 NC 230, 328 SE2d 274 (1985).
[39] United States v Burton, 580 F Supp 660 (ED Mich 1984).

§11.03 Accrual—Negligent Act

Conventional legal reasoning has it that the statute of limitations begins to run when the cause of action accrues, and the cause of action accrues when the plaintiff has the right to sue the defendant. Since the plaintiff has the right to sue, its failure to do so for the applicable statutory period bars the cause of action.

In many cases the negligent act and the damage to the plaintiff occur simultaneously. The rule therefore developed that the plaintiff has a cause of action when the defendant commits the wrongful act, and the statute of limitations starts to run upon the occurrence of the wrongful act. This thinking is obviously flawed, however, when it is applied to a situation where there has been negligence, but no damage. A plaintiff's cause of action must contain at least two elements: negligence and damage. Where there is no damage, there is probably no right, and certainly no motive to sue. Yet, an architect may commit a negligent design in 1970, which could be incorporated into a building in 1972, and which could cause damage to the plaintiff in 1976. For example, suppose an architect designs a wall with insufficient strength to withstand wind. It may be argued that the owner of the wall had a cause of action when it was built (since it could theoretically fall down), but the bystander injured by the collapse of the wall had no damage and certainly no cause of action until 1976. Yet, this could be well beyond the statutory period if measured from the time of the negligent act. Nevertheless, some courts still apply the rule that a cause of action for malpractice accrues against an architect when the negligent act occurs.

In *Nelson v Commonwealth*,[40] a judgment awarding the state $1,286,750 against an architect was REVERSED on the ground that the statute of limitations had elapsed. The state asserted damages against the architect arising out of alleged breach of contract on a 550-bed teaching hospital at the Virginia Commonwealth University campus. HELD: once the plans were accepted, the architects had completed their duties under the working drawings phase of the contract and were entitled to full payment of fees for that phase. At that time, the statute of limitations began to run for that phase and the applicable period was five years. Therefore, claims for design defects were time-barred. (Plans were accepted in July 1977 and a counterclaim was filed in February 1983.)

In *Farash Construction Corp v Stanndco Developers, Inc*,[41] a building was completed in 1971; the building was damaged by fire in 1981; the owners filed suit against the architects in 1983 alleging negligent design. HELD: the cause of action accrued in 1971. Claims against architects arising out of negligent

---

[40] 235 Va 228, 368 SE2d 239 (1988).
[41] 139 AD2d 899, 527 NYS2d 940 (1988).

design and construction accrue for purposes of the statute of limitations upon the completion of construction.

New York Rule

In *Seger v Cornwell*,[42] the plaintiff engaged the professional services of a surveyor, who laid out the lines for a proposed building in April 1958. Later, encroachments were discovered which plaintiff corrected at its own expense. The owner filed suit against the surveyor for malpractice, governed in New York by a three-year statute of limitations. The action was dismissed. The dismissal was AFFIRMED: the statute of limitations in a malpractice action begins to run upon the commission of the negligent act and not the discovery of the malpractice. The court stated that the rule would be applied until changed by the legislature. The decision was subsequently followed in *Sosnow v Paul*.[43]

Piracci Construction Co v Skidmore, Owings & Merrill is in accord.[44] Here, the plaintiff, a construction company, and the defendant, an architectural company, each had a separate contract with the United States government for the construction of the Smithsonian Institution. The plaintiff prepared a model according to the specifications and drawings prepared by the architectural firm. The defendant rejected the model because it did not comply with the contract documents; therefore, the contractor rebuilt and resubmitted a second model. The construction company made a formal claim against the United States for the cost of delays and was granted an equitable adjustment because rejection of the model constituted a *constructive change* within the meaning of the contract. Five to six years later, the contractor filed suit against the architect for intentional interference with contractual relations. HELD: the cause of action for interference with contractual relations accrued in 1971 at the time of the contractor's action against the government. Therefore, the cause of action against the architectural firm was barred by the three-year statute of limitations.[45]

The general rule in malpractice cases is that the cause of action accrues at the time of the original conduct by the professional. An exception is the *continuing treatment* situation where the cause of action accrues when treatment is completed. However, unlike an owner, the contractor does not have to depend on the architect to discover the contractor's claim. Here, the basis for the claim

---

[42] 44 Misc 2d 994, 255 NYS2d 744 (Sup Ct 1964).

[43] 43 AD2d 978, 352 NYS2d 502 (1974), *affd*, 36 NY2d 780, 330 NE2d 643, 369 NYS2d 693 (1975) (building completed 1965; cracks and bulges, suit commenced 1971. "The rule in cases where the gravamen of the suit is professional malpractice is now and has always been that the cause of action accrues upon the performance of the work by the professional").

[44] 490 F Supp 314 (SDNY), *affd*, 646 F2d 562 (2d Cir 1980).

[45] NY Civ Prac Law §214(4).

was apparent and complete in 1971, and the accural date did not change because of continuing consequential damages.

In *McCloskey & Co v Wright*,[46] the United States government employed architects to design a post office. The plans and specifications were assigned to plaintiff builder in February 1968. In March 1973, the builder filed suit against the architect, alleging breach of warranty of the sufficiency of the plans. The Virginia statutory period of five years was held to have commenced at the time the defective plans were delivered to the government. The builder, as assignee, stepped into the shoes of the assignor. Thus, the cause of action was barred. However, in the same case, the court held that the builder's cause of action for negligent supervision (a three-year statute) was not barred. That cause of action did not accrue until the builder paid for the damage.[47]

In *Lembert v Gilmore*,[48] a registered, professional surveyor, employed by plaintiff property owner, installed survey stakes at the property line of plaintiff's property in 1965. The plaintiffs thereafter erected a concrete structure and posts on the property line as indicated by the stakes. In 1970 they discovered the survey was inaccurate and filed suit on June 3, 1971.

The Delaware limitations statute provides:

> No action to recover damages for trespass . . . no action based on a promise, . . . and no action to recover damages caused by an injury unaccompanied with force or resulting indirectly from the act of the defendant shall be brought after the expiration of three years from the accuring of such cause of action.[49]

The court acknowledged that in *Layton v Allen*,[50] a medical malpractice case, the Delaware Supreme Court had held that "when an inherently unknowable injury . . . has been suffered by one blamelessly ignorant of the act or omission and injury complained of, and the harmful effect thereof developed gradually over a period of time, the injury is 'sustained' . . . when the harmful effect first manifests itself and becomes physically ascertainable."[51]

However, in *Layton* the court also stated: "we do not intend any broad relaxation of the rule of ignorance"[52] (ignorance of the existence of a cause of action does not toll the running of the statute of limitations).

---

[46] 363 F Supp 223 (ED Va 1973).

[47] See also Board of Educ v Perkins & Will Partnership, 119 Ill App 2d 196, 255 NE2d 496 (1970), applying the former Illinois rule (Illinois has adopted the discovery rule).

[48] 312 A2d 335 (Del Super Ct 1973).

[49] Del Code Ann tit 10, §8106 (1975).

[50] 246 A2d 794 (Del Super Ct 1969).

[51] *Id* 797.

[52] *Id* 799.

The professional services were completed in 1965. The stakes were presumably in plain view. Nothing was concealed from the plaintiff. The general rule that the statute begins to run from the date of the injury caused by the defendant, rather than from the date when the plaintiffs became aware of or discovered the injury, applied here. Accordingly, defendant's motion to dismiss was granted.

In *Commonwealth Land Title Insurance Co v Conklin & Associates*,[53] surveyors erroneously located the New York-New Jersey boundary line in 1963 and, after 1963, relied on their own negligently located boundary in laying out individual subdivision lots. HELD: the 10-year statute of limitations applied;[54] however, the cause of action accrued when each individual act of negligence occurred after 1963. In each individual survey, the state line was determined by reference to the original survey, and in repeating the error by relying on the original mistaken survey, defendant engaged in a new, independent course of conduct. Defendant was estopped from asserting that reliance on its own negligence was reasonable. (Defendant's original negligence lay in locating only one, rather than several, of the available field markers delineating the state boundary.)

In *Wellston Co v Sam N. Hodges Jr & Co*,[55] the plaintiff first became aware that it had a problem when its roof partially collapsed on February 19, 1961. Plaintiff filed suit against the architect on February 18, 1965, precisely four years after the collapse. The trial court sustained the architect's demurrer on the ground that the action was barred by the four-year statute of limitations applicable to injuries to real property and was AFFIRMED. The construction contract was executed on February 12, 1957, and the building was completed late that same year. Soon thereafter, the slab began to sag and shift.

A cause of action accrues at the time when a plaintiff could first successfully maintain an action against the defendant. This is the time when there has been such a breach of duty that the plaintiff could sue for the breach. Here, the alleged negligent design and construction of the building in and of itself constituted a legal injury to the plaintiff, even though it was not aware of the wrong at the time it occurred.

Mere ignorance of facts constituting a cause of action does not prevent the running of the statute of limitations. When the roof began to sag a few months after completion of the project, there was sufficient damage, even though it was slight and unknown to the plaintiff, to make the legal injury complete and give the owner the right to sue. The cause of action therefore accrued in 1957, and the action filed in 1965 was too late.

---

[53] 152 NJ Super 1, 377 A2d 740 (1977), *affd*, 167 NJ Super 392, 400 AD2d 1208 (1979).
[54] NJ Stat Ann §2A:14-11 (West 1952).
[55] 114 Ga App 424, 151 SE2d 481 (1966).

In a Georgia case,[56] the plaintiff purchased a building in 1976, which had been constructed in 1949, with floors added in 1954. Severe cracks were discovered in the building in 1979. Plaintiff sued the architects for defective design. The architect's motion for summary judgment was granted on the ground that the claim was barred by the statute of limitations. The holding was AFFIRMED: the claim was barred because an action for damage to real property must be brought within four years after a negligent act is coupled with a proximately resulting injury. The cause of action arose in both 1949 and 1954, at the time of the defective construction. The fact that the building was sold to the present plaintiff did not revive a cause of action which was barred as to the original owner.

In a Vermont case,[57] a school district brought suit, claiming damages for a defective roof designed by an architect, who certified the construction to be in accordance with the terms of the contract documents on August 3, 1962. The suit was filed February 29, 1972. Summary judgment for defendant was AFFIRMED. Vermont follows the rule that a cause of action accrues when the act upon which the claim is founded took place. Therefore, the six-year statute of limitations commenced to run, at the latest, when the architect certified that the project was completed in conformity with the contract documents. The discovery rule does not apply in Vermont.[58]

In *Milwaukee County v Schmidt, Garden & Erikson*,[59] the statute of limitations for injury to property was six years.[60] Plaintiff filed suit against the architect on a hospital job for negligent design and supervision which caused the hospital to be inadequately heated. The contract was signed in April 1949, the hospital opened in August 1957, and the final payment certificate (for $2,000 withheld pending completion of improper work) was issued in March 1959. At the same time, the architect issued the final bill.

Analogizing to the rule for physician and banker malpractice, the court held that the cause of action accrued when the injury occurred, rather than when it was discovered. Regardless of whether the malpractice constituted tort or a breach of contract, the cause of action accrued at the moment when the breach of duty occurred. Both the defective design and the defective supervision, if any, occurred long before March 18, 1959.

In *Regency Wood Condominium, Inc v Dessent, Hammach & Ruckman, Inc*,[61] the condominium association brought suit against the developer and contractors responsible for the design, construction, engineering, and maintenance of a

---

[56] U-Haul Co v Abrea & Robeson, Inc, 247 Ga 565, 277 SE2d 497 (1981).
[57] South Burlington Sch Dist v Goodrich, 135 Vt 601, 382 A2d 220 (1977).
[58] See §11.06 for a discussion of the discovery rule.
[59] 43 Wis 2d 445, 168 NW2d 559 (1969).
[60] Wis Stat Ann §893.19(5).
[61] 405 So 2d 440 (Fla Dist Ct App 1981).

common driveway which sank and cracked. The association claimed it was a third-party beneficiary of the developer's contracts with the engineer, the contractor, and others. The court concluded that the statute of limitations did not begin to run until the unit owners elected a majority of members to the board of administration. Otherwise a developer could retain control over an association long enough to bar a potential cause of action. The complaint was timely filed within four years of the date when the majority control over the condominium association passed to the owners.

The rule of these cases is clearly unsatisfactory. The fact that it may be difficult to render perfect justice in stale cases does not excuse ignoring those cases by depriving a plaintiff of its rights before it knows of the defendant's wrong.

§11.04 —Time of Completion

The cases previously summarized held that a cause of action accrues, and therefore the statute of limitations commences, when the breach of duty to the plaintiff occurs.[62] However, some courts have held that the breach occurs not when the negligent act takes place, but when the construction project is completed.

The rule that the breach occurs when the project is completed and accepted by the owner is supported by the consideration that the architect had the power, at any time during the progress of the project, to correct any defect in the work; so it is only when the architect turns a completed project over to the owner that there is an actual breach of the architect's duty of care.

A more trenchant argument to support the rule would be that the owner has the right to rely on the architect to properly discharge its duties during the period of construction, including the duty to find and correct any flaw. However, when the architect certifies the project to be complete, the professional-client relationship terminates, and the owner should search the project for defects.

In *Hilliard & Bartko Joint Venture v Fedco Systems, Inc*,[63] the owner filed a demand for arbitration against an architect within three years after the final inspection to determine completion and the issuance of the final certificate for payment. The owner relied on the *continuation of events* theory to permit recovery for negligent acts that occurred during the construction of the project more than three years before the suit was filed. HELD: the statute of repose did not permit use of the continuation of events theory and, therefore, the only

---

[62] *See* §11.03.
[63] 309 Md 147, 522 A2d 961 (1987).

claims recognized were those that actually arose within three years of the date when the arbitration demand was filed.

In *Board of Managers of Yardarm Beach Condominium v Vector Yardarm Corp*,[64] an owner sued an architect for damages arising out of structural defects to condominiums designed by the architect. The contract was dated January of 1974, the project was completed in November of 1976, the owners discovered defects in September of 1979, and action was filed in June of 1982 for negligence and breach of implied and express warranties. HELD: the cause of action accrued when the architect "wrongfully put into motion forces which caused the injury and when his liability for the injury arose, *i.e.*, upon his completion of the building."[65] The cause of action, therefore, arose when the certificate of occupancy was issued and the three-year statute of limitations barred the suit.

In *Wills v Black & West Architects*,[66] the project was completed and accepted by the owner in 1946. Soon thereafter the roof began to leak, and over the years numerous repairs were made as the leaking became worse. Suit was filed in 1955 (nine years after the completion of the project), and the court held that the architect's demurrer should have been sustained on the ground that the two-year statute of limitations had expired. A malpractice cause of action accrues at the time the building is completed and accepted by the owner since this is when the breach of duty occurs, if at all. In the absence of false or fraudulent representations which would have tolled the statute, it expired in 1948, and the suit in 1955 was too late.[67]

A cause of action for negligent design by an architect against the consulting engineer arises when the plans are paid for, completed, and accepted.[68] A shopping center fire in 1972 destroyed several stores. The owner filed an action against the architect, alleging negligence in failing to install a sprinkler system as required by the building code. The architect filed a third-party complaint against the consulting engineer who had prepared the mechanical plans. The consulting engineer's work was completed and accepted in 1967. The action against the architect was filed in 1976, and the third-party complaint against the consulting engineer was also filed in 1976. Summary judgment for the consulting engineer was AFFIRMED. The action was one for breach of an

---

[64] 109 AD2d 684, 487 NYS2d 17 (1985).

[65] *Id* at 686, 487 NYS2d at 19.

[66] 344 P2d 581 (Okla 1959).

[67] See also Naetzker v Brocton Cent Sch Dist, 50 AD2d 142, 376 NYS2d 300 (1975), *revd*, 41 NY2d 929, 363 NE2d 351, 394 NYS2d 627 (1977) where the court stated that the general rule in cases of architectural malpractice is that the cause of action accrues when the building is completed (citing Sosnow v Paul, 43 AD2d 978, 352 NYS2d 502 (1974), *affd*, 36 NYS2d 780, 330 NE2d 643, 369 NYS2d 693 (1975)). *See also* Sears Roebuck & Co v Enco Assocs, 43 NY2d 389, 372 NE2d 555, 401 NYS2d 767 (1977).

[68] Waddey v Davis, 149 Ga App 308, 254 SE2d 465 (1979).

oral contract, and the statute of limitations was four years from the time of breach.[69] The time began to run when the breach occurred. The breach occurred only when the plans were completed, accepted, and payment for the plans was made.

In *Comptroller of Virginia ex rel Virginia Military Institute v King*,[70] the architect had no right to contribution from the engineer as a joint tortfeasor.

The cause of action for negligent design accrues when the plans are finally approved, since at that time the architect has the right to demand payment for services. However, where the architect has a duty to supervise and inspect the construction of the project, it also has a duty to report to the owner any serious problems with the design that become known before the completion of construction. Here, the architect failed to notify the owner of errors in design, and since the action was filed within five years after substantial completion of the project, the statute of limitations was not available as a defense.

§11.05 —When Damage Occurs

Some cases hold that the statute of limitations begins to run, and the cause of action accrues, when significant damage occurs. For example, in *Oakes v McCarthy Co*,[71] a homeowner in a subdivision filed an action against a soil engineer for damage caused by soil settlement. The court held that the applicable statute of limitation was a three-year statute for negligent damage to real property. The statute commenced to run when appreciable damage resulted, rather than when the first hairline cracks in the soil appeared.

In *Crawford v Shepherd*,[72] the statute of limitations on negligent construction of a dwelling began to run from the time of injury and not from the time of the negligent act or commission. Here, an apartment complex was completed in 1970. In 1977, the plaintiff sued the architect, alleging negligent construction, because the roof began to rot and leak "within the last four years." The trial court denied the architect's motion for summary judgment based on a six-year statute of limitations and the contention that the statute began to run on the date when the negligence occurred. This holding was AFFIRMED.

In *MBA Commercial Construction, Inc v Roy J. Hannaford Co*,[73] engineers were found to be negligent in their design of a project. (Subcontractors had discovered that negligence.) The subcontractors filed suit more than two years

---

[69] Ga Code Ann §3-706.
[70] 217 Va 751, 232 SE2d 895 (1977).
[71] 267 Cal App 2d 231, 73 Cal Rptr 127 (1968).
[72] 86 Wis 2d 362, 272 NW2d 401 (1978).
[73] 818 P2d 469 (Okla 1991), *rehg denied* (Oct 29, 1991).

after the discovery of the negligence, but within two years after they suffered actual damages. HELD: injury became certain and known only when the subcontractors knew or should have known they were not going to be paid for the extra costs incurred because of the defective plans.

In *Linn Reorganized School District No 2 v Butler Manufacturing Co*,[74] a school district filed an action to recover for damages arising from faulty design of a roof system which "leaked from day one." Summary judgment was granted for defendants on the ground that the statute of limitations had expired. REVERSED. Further evidence was required to determine whether the statute of limitations elapsed.

> If the wrong done is of such character that it may be said that all of the damages, past and future, are capable of ascertainment in a single action . . . the statute of limitations begins to run from that time. If . . . the wrong may be said to continue from day to day, and create a fresh injury from day to day, and the wrong is capable of being terminated, a right of action exists for the damages suffered within the statutory period immediately preceding the suit.[75]

Payment as Damage

Applying Virginia law in *McCloskey & Co v Wright*,[76] the federal district court held that the statute of limitations commenced to run when the damage not only occurred, but when payment was made. The federal government employed architects to design a post office building and supervise its construction. The government assigned the plans and specifications to the plaintiff builder, who proceeded with construction. The roof was defective, and the builder filed an action against the architect, alleging negligent supervision. HELD: the applicable three-year statute of limitations on negligent supervision commences when a builder pays or discharges an obligation. Since the builder would allegedly suffer further damage and pay additional expense after the suit was filed, the claim was not barred by the statute of limitation (plans and specifications were assigned to the builder in 1968, suit was filed in 1973).

In *Doyle v Linn*,[77] the surveyor delivered a certified plan in 1960. In 1964, the government discovered that the plaintiff had built a house on government land and notified the plaintiff of its contention in 1965. In 1968, the government filed an action for trespass which was AFFIRMED on appeal in

---

[74] 672 SW2d 340 (Mo 1984).
[75] *Id* 343.
[76] 363 F Supp 223 (ED Va 1973).
[77] 37 Colo App 214, 547 P2d 257 (1975).

1972. The owners removed their house at a cost of $14,721.66 and filed suit against the surveyor for damages. The trial court held that the six-year statute began to run in 1965 when the government notified the plaintiff of its claim. The trial court was REVERSED. The mere assertion of adverse title does not constitute damage. The plaintiff was not actually injured or damaged until 1972 when the court of appeal upheld the government's claim. Since the statute did not begin to run until damage occurred, the plaintiff's action was timely filed.

In *Kashmir Corp v Barnes*,[78] the plaintiff bargained and paid for a lot which was 330 feet, but knowingly accepted only 320 feet (May 1973). The 10-foot shortage in the lot was the result of a surveying error made by defendant in 1965. Plaintiff discovered the source of the error in June 1974 and filed suit for negligence in June 1975. HELD: the cause of action accrued when the plaintiff knowingly acquired less property than expected. The fact that the plaintiff did not discover the identity of the wrongdoer within the two-year statutory period did not affect the date when the injury occurred.[79]

In a New York case, a tenant fell and was injured in the laundry room of an apartment house in 1974. The tenant brought action against the architect in 1977. HELD: the cause of action for damages due to negligence accrues when the invasion of the plaintiff's personal rights occurs. In this case, plaintiff's cause of action accrued when it fell. The malpractice statute of limitation did not apply, since malpractice applies to negligence of a professional person in the relationship with the client. In this case, plaintiff was a third party with no professional relationship to the architect.[80]

Criminal Prosecution

In *State v Ireland*,[81] a criminal action, an architect prepared plans for a bathhouse in 1927, and a citizen was killed when the building collapsed in 1940. The architect was indicted for manslaughter. The code provided that an architect who, through neglect or violation of a building code, designs a building which collapses is subject to indictment for manslaughter. The design of a defective building creates a public nuisance which is a continuous offense. The nuisance continued until the collapse occurred.

---

[78] 278 Or 433, 564 P2d 693 (1977).

[79] *See also* City of Utica v Holt, 88 Misc 2d 206, 387 NYS2d 377 (Sup Ct 1976) (a cause of action for personal injury arising from the allegedly negligent inspection of a construction project by the architect accrues at the date of the injury where the alleged wrong is tortious and there was no prior professional relationship between the injured party and the defendant architect).

[80] Cubito v Kreisberg, 94 Misc 2d 56, 404 NYS2d 69 (Sup Ct 1978), *affd*, 51 NY2d 900, 415 NE2d 979, 434 NYS2d 991 (1980).

[81] 126 NJL 444, 20 A2d 69 (1941).

§11.06 —Discovery Rule

The moment for the accrual of the cause of action, and thus for the commencement of the running of the statute of limitations, can be selected mechanically or according to policy considerations.

The mechanical test, and the one easiest to apply, is that the statute starts to run when the cause of action accrues, the cause of action accrues when the plaintiff could sue the defendant, and thus the statute begins to run upon the commission of the wrongful act. As noted, this rule works well enough when the wrongful act is simultaneous with the damage and with the plaintiff's knowledge of the damage. However, when the wrongful act is separated by years from the damage, application of the rule produces an unwanted result: as far as the plaintiff is concerned, its rights are barred before they arise. The modern solution is to balance the difficulty of the defendant's proof as time passes against the hardship to a plaintiff whose cause of action might be barred before being discovered. This has led many states to adopt the *discovery rule*.

For example, in *Watson, Watson & Rutland, Architects, Inc v Montgomery County Board of Education*,[82] the court stated that negligence claims accrue as soon as a plaintiff is entitled to maintain a cause of action, *i.e.*, at the time of the first legal injury regardless of whether the full amount of the damages is apparent. (Action was filed well beyond either the two-year or the one-year statute of limitations.)

In *Georgetowne Ltd Partnership v Geotechnical Services, Inc*,[83] the court held that an action was barred by the statute of limitations because the owner had discovered sufficient facts to start the running of the statute of limitations by April 27, 1983. The engineer submitted a soils report on October 4, 1978 and the building was complete in April 1979. In February of 1982, the owner's representative notified the engineer that a crack had appeared in the floor. The crack was grouted but reappeared. On April 27, 1983, the owner delivered a letter to the engineer advising of its reliance on the soils report and requesting additional tests at the expense of the engineer. A new engineer made findings dated June 8, 1983 determining the cause of cracking to be soils settlement. Summary judgment for the engineer was AFFIRMED.

In *Skinner v Graham*,[84] it was held that the state, as a *body politic*, was bound by Ill Rev Stat ch 110, par 13-214. The statute provides that actions alleging defective design, planning, or supervision of an improvement to real property shall be commenced within two years from the time the person knew or reasonably should have known of the act or omission. The state alleged that it

---

[82] 559 So 2d 168 (Ala 1990).
[83] 230 Neb 22, 430 NW2d 34 (1988).
[84] 170 Ill App 3d 417, 524 NE2d 642 (1988).

discovered the cause of action when it received an independent engineering report detailing structural failure. HELD: significant structural defects were identified early in the project and the statute began to run no later than 1979, when the state threatened the engineers with legal action if design defects were not remedied.

In *Freeport Memorial Hospital v Lankton, Ziegele, Terry & Associates*,[85] the owner of a hospital filed an action against architects alleging that it was not aware of defects until an inspection was conducted in September of 1983. In a letter dated April of 1981, an employee of the architect had recommended that the owner consult a masonry contractor to determine causes of masonry cracks. HELD: the two-year statute of limitations was triggered by the letter that was sent in April, 1981. At that time, the owner possessed sufficient knowledge of its injury to determine whether there was an actionable wrong and promptly filed suit.

In *City of Aurora v Bechtel Corp*,[86] the city contracted with the defendant in 1962 for the design and construction of a water tunnel. Construction occurred between 1963 and 1966. Six cave-ins were discovered in 1974, and in 1976, the city sued for negligence and breach of implied warranty in the design and supervision of the project. Colorado's six-year statute for actions of assumpsit, contract, and express or implied warranty was applied.[87] HELD: the cause of action did not accrue until the plaintiff knew, or should have known in the exercise of reasonable diligence, all material facts essential to show the elements of the cause of action.

In *City of Aurora*, the court discussed four approaches that have been used by the courts: (1) the traditional concept that the cause of action accrues upon completion and acceptance of the project; (2) the approach that the statute begins to run when the cause of action accrues; and (3) that the cause of action accrues when *significant damage occurs*; and (4) the concept that the statute begins to run when the injured party discovers, or should have discovered, that damage has occurred and that it has probably resulted from malpractice. Here, in adopting the third approach, the court reasoned that: all professionals owe a special duty to perform their services with skill—the layman may not be able to recognize even patent design defects; design defects may be latent; although the passage of time may have inhibited the defendant's ability to defend, plaintiff still bore the burden of proof; and the discovery rule did not frustrate the policies underlying the statute of limitations.[88]

---

[85] 170 Ill App 3d 531, 525 NE2d 194 (1988).

[86] 599 F2d 382 (10th Cir 1979).

[87] Colo Rev Stat §13-80-110 (1973).

[88] The court pointed out that Washington, Wyoming, Maryland, New Jersey, and Iowa have applied the discovery rule to actions against architects and engineers.

In *Knox College v Celotex Corp*,[89] the roofing materials used on a newly constructed math-science building differed from those originally specified by the architects. The material supplier assured the college that the roofing materials used were the functional equivalent of those specified in the plans. For three years the leaks in the roof were repaired by the roofing contractor pursuant to its guarantee, and the college shared in the repair costs for two years thereafter. The college eventually replaced the roof at the recommendation of an independent roofing consultant who believed that the leaks were caused by the use of alternate materials. HELD: the trial court was to determine when Knox College had sufficient information to put a reasonable person on inquiry as to the nature of the defect in the roof. The court could not rule, as a matter of law, which roof leak or repair constituted a *discovery* of the defect by Knox College and triggered commencement of the running of the statute of limitations.

In *Society of Mt Carmel v Fox*,[90] a school project was completed in 1963. Cracks soon appeared in the plaster. The architect assured the defendant that this was merely a maintenance problem. Costly repairs were made, but the cracks reoccurred. In 1969, a contractors association was called in for inspection and issued an opinion that the problem was faulty design: lack of expansion joints. In February 1970, the school district filed an action against the architect, alleging negligence. The architect raised the five-year statute of limitation and obtained summary judgment. The court of appeal REVERSED. Balancing the difficulty of proof against the hardship to the plaintiff, the court concluded that the *time of discovery* rule should be applied in cases of architect malpractice, rather than the *completion of construction* rule. In cases of architect malpractice, the passage of time does not cast an unbearable burden on the defendant. The building was a physical reality which was available for inspection, and the plans and specifications were available for review.[91]

In *Waterford Condominium Assn v Dunbar Corp*,[92] the association, both as purchaser and representative for other purchasers, filed an action against the developer and the companies involved in the construction of the condominium in 1977. The complaint alleged causes of action in breach of contract, breach of implied warranty of habitability, and misrepresentation, or fraud. The association alleged that during negotiations for purchase of the units, the defendants

---

[89] 88 Ill 2d 407, 430 NE 976 (1981).

[90] 31 Ill App 3d 1060, 335 NE2d 588 (1975).

[91] For similar holdings, see Rozny v Marnul, 43 Ill 2d 54, 250 NE2d 656 (1969) (encroachment caused by survey); Orleans Parish Sch Bd v Pittman Constr, 261 La 665, 260 So 2d 661 (1972) (school completed in 1960, structural defects discovered in 1968 required the building to be demolished and replaced); Kundahl v Barnett, 5 Wash App 227, 486 P2d 1164, *review denied*, 80 Wash 2d 1001 (1971) (encroachment-surveyor case; opinion analogizes medical malpractice cases and lawyer malpractice cases).

[92] 104 Ill App 3d 371, 432 NE2d 1009 (1982).

routinely misrepresented, by way of advertising, brochures, and plans, the nature and quality of the construction of the condominium and materials used. The trial court granted defendants' motion to dismiss the claim in fraud as barred by the five-year statute of limitations. This holding was AFFIRMED: The representations were allegedly made before 1973, but the suit was not brought until the spring of 1980, more than seven years after they were made. Plaintiff contended there was a question of fact as to when the purchasers discovered the fraud. However, the discovery rule was not applicable here because the association failed to plead that the fraud remained undiscovered.[93]

In *Mattingly v Hopkins*,[94] plaintiff, a lawyer, employed surveyors to subdivide his land. The corners were erroneously staked, which involved plaintiff in many lawsuits. A statute provided: "All actions of account, actions of assumpsit, or on the case . . . shall be commenced . . . within three years from the time the cause of action accrued."[95] The court adopted the discovery rule, as in medical, legal, and accounting malpractice. However, the suit was not filed until 1964, while the subdivision took place in 1952. The plaintiff argued that the damage did not occur until the plaintiff lost his cases in court, but the court held that the plaintiff knew about the error sooner, and could then have filed an action to recoup survey costs.

The plaintiff was prejudiced by circumstances. When he elected to stand on the survey and defend the lawsuits, he must have believed, and therefore argued, that the survey was correct. The plaintiff did not know for sure that the survey was incorrect until he lost. However, under the court's decision, the plaintiff would have been required to undercut his own position by filing an action against the surveyor at the very time when he was defending himself on the ground that the survey was correct.

It seems that the discovery rule is superior to the other rules concerning limitation statutes.[96] Its application deters plaintiffs from sleeping on their rights, without putting them to the injustice of being without a remedy for damage caused by the malpractice of an architect.

---

[93] *See also* Salem Sand & Gravel Co v City of Salem, 260 Or 630, 492 P2d 271 (1971) (court pointed out that the two-year statute of limitations for fraud (Or Rev Stat §12.110(1) runs from the time of discovery. Therefore, judgment on the pleadings was REVERSED where the complaint did not affirmatively show that the cause of action was barred); Holy Cross Parish v Huether, 308 NW2d 575 (SD 1981) (plaintiff alleged that the contractor and architect knowingly misrepresented the actual condition of the fill over which an auditorium was constructed. The court concluded that plaintiff's claim was not barred, as the fraudulent concealment of the cause of action tolled the statute of limitations until the cause of action was discovered).

[94] 254 Md 88, 253 A2d 904 (1969).

[95] Md Ann Code art 57, 1 (1957).

[96] *See* §§11.03–11.05.

Some of the agony suffered by courts in their attempts to adopt the discovery rule are displayed in *Auster v Keck*.[97] The complaint alleged that architects designed a house in 1960, the plaintiffs bought it in 1969, and between January 1971 and March 1972, the ceilings of various rooms collapsed. Suit was filed in May 1972, alleging that the architects were guilty of malpractice because they failed to design a vapor barrier. The complaint alleged that the defect was latent and plaintiffs had no means of learning of it until after they purchased the premises and the ceiling collapsed.

The architect moved to dismiss the action on the ground that the plans and specifications were prepared in August 1960, and that the five-year statute of limitations had therefore expired.

The statute provided:

> 16. On oral contracts, damages, etc. 15. Actions . . . to recover damages for an injury done to property, real or personal, . . . and all civil actions not otherwise provided for, shall be commenced within five years next after the cause of action accrued.[98]

The court stated that the question so posed was not an easy one to answer and had long troubled, and still troubled, legislators, lawyers, and the courts: "Unless the Illinois cases on this issue are read in strict chronological sequence and with proper deference to Supreme Court rather than Appellate Court decisions, they appear to be in hopeless confusion."[99]

The court quoted Prosser to the effect that the application of the rule that the statute of limitations commences to run when the negligent act occurs often brings "obvious and flagrant injustice."[100] The court concluded: "In the light of the foregoing, we now apply the emerging 'discovery' or 'knew or should have known' rule . . . to the facts of this case and hold that the statute did not start to run until the ceiling fell." This decision was reversed by the Illinois Supreme Court.[101]

In *Pollock v Hafner*,[102] a building settled and cracked. HELD: the discovery rule applies in actions of architect malpractice, and a cause of action accrues

---

[97] 31 Ill App 61, 333 NE2d 65, *revd*, 63 Ill 2d 485, 349 NE2d 20 (1975).

[98] Ill Rev Stat ch 83, 16 (1959).

[99] 31 Ill App at 62, 333 NE2d at 66. The court reviewed a number of cases including Rozny v Marnul, 43 Ill 2d 34, 250 NE2d 656 (1969) (survey error, discovery rule applied); Board of Educ v Perkins & Will Partnership, 119 Ill App 2d 196, 255 NE2d 496 (1970) (architect malpractice, discovery rule not applied); Board of Educ v Joseph J. Duffy Co, 97 Ill App 2d 158, 240 NE2d 5 (1968) (architect malpractice, discovery rule not applied); Simoniz v J. Emil Anderson & Sons, Inc, 81 Ill App 2d 428, 225 NE2d 161 (1967) (roof collapse, discovery rule not applied).

[100] W. Prosser, Law of Torts §30 (3d ed 1964).

[101] Auster v Keck, 63 Ill 2d 485, 349 NE2d 20 (1975).

[102] 108 Ill App 3d 410, 439 NE2d 85 (1982).

when "a person knows or reasonably should know of its injury and also knows or reasonably should know that it was wrongfully caused." Here, subsidence began and structural damage became visible in 1957. The owners argued, however, that while some defects were noticeable in 1957, additional subsidence occurred in 1962 and in 1976. They sought damages for the subsidence that occurred in 1976, which, they asserted, gave rise to a new cause of action. HELD: the rubble under the foundation which caused the subsidence was under the building since its construction. This defect, the one that caused the damage, was discovered more than five years before the lawsuit was filed; therefore, judgment for architect/engineer was AFFIRMED.[103]

In *Society of Mt Carmel v Fox*,[104] the architects designed a high school which was completed in 1963. In 1966, leaks and breaks were noted in various parts of the building, which the architect insisted were due to building maintenance problems. Suit was filed in 1969 after the plaintiff received a report from the Lake County Contractors' Association which concluded that cracks were caused by the architect's failure to include expansion joints in the building design. The verdict for the plaintiff was AFFIRMED. The suit was not barred by the statute of limitations because the discovery rule applied. Thus, the statute of limitations period began to run when the plaintiff knew or should have known of the defective design, rather than when the first crack appeared in the building.

In *Union School District No 20 v Lench*,[105] the plaintiff school district discovered a leaking roof in September 1966. The school district discovered that the roof leaked because of negligent design in January 1972. HELD: the cause of action accrues when the plaintiff discovers the facts constituting the basis of the cause of action or the existence of facts sufficient to put a prudent person on inquiry which would lead to the discovery. Therefore, the cause of action accrued when the leaks occurred in 1966, rather than in 1972 when the plaintiff discovered that the defendant might be responsible for those leaks.

In *Lisbon Contractors, Inc v Miami-Dade Water & Sewer Authority*,[106] the contractor on a sewer project sued to recover the increased costs of working in more difficult subsurface conditions than those described in the Water and Sewer Authority (WASA) bid request. WASA then brought a third-party action against the engineering firm that conducted the soil tests relied upon by the contractor. The court denied the engineer's motion to dismiss. The one-year statute of limitations for specific performance of a contract was not applicable here. Instead, the four-year statute (negligence actions) and the two-year statute (professional malpractice) applied. WASA's third-party complaint was timely

---

[103] *See* Annotation, 12 ALR4th 866 (1982).
[104] 90 Ill App 3d 537, 413 NE2d 480 (1980).
[105] 134 Vt 424, 365 A2d 508 (1976).
[106] 537 F Supp 175 (SD Fla 1982).

filed, since the limitations period began running either when the work was performed in May 1980, or when the cause of action was discovered.

In *Golden Grain Macaroni Co v Klefstad Engineering Co*,[107] the structure was completed in 1963, a portion of the roof collapsed in 1972, and plaintiff filed suit within four months thereafter. HELD: the statute of limitations began to run when the plaintiff discovered it had been injured. In determining whether the statute should run from the time of the breach or the time of the discovery, the court should balance the hardship of the plaintiff (who neither knew nor should have known of the existence of the right to sue) against the detriment to the defendant that arises from the difficulty of asserting an adequate defense many years after the occurrence of the disputed facts. Here, where the cause of action was rooted in drawings, plans, specifications, and material, the passage of time did little to harm the defendant. Nor, in this case, had the passage of time increased the danger of a false, frivolous, fraudulent, or speculative claim. Therefore, the balance favors the plaintiff, and the discovery rule was properly applied.[108]

In *Mutual Service Life Insurance Co v Galaxy Builders, Inc*,[109] the purchaser of a warehouse sued an architect for damages sustained because of a cracked slab. The building was completed in 1982, the owner obtained test reports in 1983 and filed suit in 1985, two years and two months after the test reports were received. Summary judgment based on the two-year statute of limitations was AFFIRMED. It is true that the statute did not run against actions for fraud until the fraud was discovered. Here, however, suit was filed more than two years after the discovery of the fraud.

§11.07 —Statutes of Repose

Since buildings have a long life, the potential liability of architects, engineers, surveyors, designers, builders, contractors, and subcontractors is of equal longevity. It is not unusual for a defect in a building to suddenly appear after a decade or more. Likewise, survey mistakes may not be revealed until a neighbor starts to build, years after the survey.

Many personal liability insurance policies, including architect malpractice policies, are written on a "claims made" basis rather than on an occurrence

---

[107] 45 Ill App 3d 77, 358 NE2d 1295 (1976).

[108] *See also* Ciancio v Serafini, 40 Colo App 168, 574 P2d 876 (1977) (allegedly negligent survey was completed in 1960, and the action was filed in 1973. Plaintiffs (subsequent owners of the property) discovered the error in 1972 when their improvement plans were thwarted by the inaccurate survey. HELD: the cause of action accrued when the error was discovered in 1972).

[109] 435 NW2d 136 (Minn Ct App 1989), *review denied* (Apr 19, 1989).

basis. Thus, if an architect retires and cancels insurance, and thereafter a claim is made, personal financial disaster may ensue.

These are some considerations which have persuaded builders and architects to lobby for liability cut-off dates, and most state legislatures have adopted statutes that may terminate a plaintiff's cause of action before either damage or discovery of the damage. The statutory pattern is to prohibit actions commenced more than a specified period after the completion of the project.

It is pointed out in an excellent article by one commentator that limitations statutes implement two basic policies: they promote stability in business relationships, and they avoid the uncertainties and burdens in defending against stale claims. The primary concern is fairness to the defendant. However, these considerations should be relevant only when there is an actionable claim to assert. Thus, if the statutory period closes before the plaintiff is aware of its right of action, the traditional justification of plaintiff's delay is not applicable. Therefore, a growing number of cases in physician, lawyer, and architect malpractice actions have adopted the discovery rule.[110] The author also points out that for a statute of limitations to bar an action which has not accrued is anomalous: such a statute does not limit the remedy but bars the right from ever coming into existence. Therefore, statutes which bar an action before it accrues are statutes of limitations in form only. In essence, they define substantive legal rights. They lay down the rule that, in some circumstances, there is no right of action at all.

The author points out that it would not be unconstitutional to bar a right of action: such has been approved, for example, in heartbalm actions and guest statute cases. The legislature, therefore, has power to abolish rights of action. However, this should not obscure the fact that statutes of limitations in this category are really limitations only in form: in reality, they prevent a right of action from ever coming into existence.

States have considered the applicability and constitutionality of statutes of repose. In *Perkis v Northeastern Log Homes*,[111] the Kentucky Supreme Court stated:

> Recognizing that a majority of the states have upheld the construction industry's statute of repose against attack on constitutional grounds, our obligation is to comply with the letter and spirit of the Kentucky Constitution. If that places us in a statistical minority, we can only commiserate with the citizens of other states who do not enjoy similar protection.[112]

---

[110] Comment, *Limitation of Action Statutes for Architects and Builders—Blueprint for Non-Action*, 18 Cath UL Rev 361 (1969).
[111] 808 SW2d 809 (Ky 1991).
[112] *Id* 818.

So said the Kentucky Supreme Court, considering a five-year statute of repose as it applied to plaintiff who contracted lymphoma from exposure to Pentachlorophenol used as a preservative in a log home.

Bodily Injury

In *Parent v Stone & Webster Engineering Corp*,[113] it was held that a six-year statute of repose barred an injured worker from maintaining a negligence claim against a company that provided engineering and architectural services. The plaintiff claimed that the defendant negligently failed to install a *Danger—High Voltage* label on an electrical panel.

Discovery Extension

In *Hartford Fire Insurance Co v Architectural Management, Inc*,[114] an insurance company sued architects for damages resulting from a school fire and, after a delay, the architects filed a third-party complaint for contribution against mechanical and electrical engineers. The original suit was filed in 1981, the counterclaim in December of 1985. HELD: the action was barred by the two-year *discovery* extension of the statute.

Fraud Claim

A contractor completed a building in 1968; in 1981, the owner discovered that the brick face had pulled away from the cement wall. HELD: the statute of limitations for the architect and the contractor began to run on completion of construction. The owner's claim of fraud was nothing more than an attempt to invoke a later accrual date.[115]

Auto Accident

The Rhode Island statute of repose was applied to a personal injury action against an architectural firm arising out of a head-on collision on the Newport Bridge, which was designed by defendant architects. This statute was enacted in response to the demise of privity of contract as a defense, which resulted in subjecting architects and engineers to unlimited potential liability to third parties. The statute applies to all architects and engineers, contractors, and

---

[113] 408 Mass 108, 556 NE2d 1009 (1990).
[114] 158 Ill App 3d 515, 511 NE2d 706, *appeal denied*, 117 Ill 2d 543, 517 NE2d 1086 (1987).
[115] Lewis v Axinn, 100 AD2d 617, 473 NYS2d 574 (1984).

subcontractors, not just those who build houses or commercial buildings. Here, the Newport Bridge was an *improvement to real property* covered by the statute.[116]

Completion of Services

The Nebraska Supreme Court has upheld the Nebraska statute of repose in an action by a homeowner against an architect.[117] The 10-year statute runs from the date of rendering professional services. Where, as here, the architect had a duty to inspect the construction as it progressed, its duty ended with the completion of the house. Therefore, the action against the architect was not barred. However, the engineer completed *its* services when it prepared the specifications. This occurred more than 10 years before the action was filed, so the action against the engineer was barred.

> We recognize in so holding, the result may at times be that one whose design is alleged to have caused or contributed to the failure of a structure becomes, by the passage of time, insulated from liability, while others involved in the construction process may remain subject to liability. Such, however, is the nature of periods of repose.[118]

Contract Action

In *Moseley v Abrams*,[119] an apartment house purchaser filed an action against an architect, alleging breach of the contract between the owner and the architect. Substantial completion of the project was 11 years before plaintiffs learned of the defects (dry rot, decay, and disintegration of wood framing). A demurrer based on the 10-year statute of repose was sustained. AFFIRMED. The 10-year statute applies to actions for breach of contract as well as to tort actions.

Latent Defect

The California statute of repose establishes a four-year period of limitation with respect to patent defects and a 10-year period for latent defects. A woman contracted pneumonia and died because of faulty air conditioning units in a

---

[116] Walsh v Gowing, 494 A2d 543 (RI 1985).

[117] Witherspoon v Sides Constr Co, 219 Neb 117, 362 NW2d 35 (1985).

[118] *Id* at 157, 362 NW2d at 43 (subcontractor installed cast iron pipe instead of ductile iron pipe; the pipe broke, causing a foundation wall to collapse and $353,753 in damage). *See also* Akins v Parish of Jefferson, 591 So 2d 800 (La Ct App 1991), *writ denied*, 592 So 2d 1288 (La 1992) (10-year statute protected an engineer from liability to property owners for damage caused in 1985 by Hurricane Juan. Engineer had designed a levee and drainage culverts).

[119] 170 Cal App 3d 355, 216 Cal Rptr 40 (1985), *review denied* (Oct 23, 1985).

10-year-old building where she was employed. In the son's wrongful death action against the architect, it was contended that the defect was patent and the four-year statute should apply. HELD: the statute of repose does not apply to manufacturers who supply products that are installed in an improvement. Moreover, the heating and cooling deficiencies were latent, rather than patent and, thus, would not have been subject to the four-year limitation.[120]

Retrospective Effect

In *Durring v Reynolds Smith & Hills*,[121] plaintiffs were injured in a car accident on a highway constructed more than 15 years earlier. A month before the accident, the Florida Supreme Court had ruled that the 12-year statute of repose was unconstitutional. Plaintiffs filed an action against the highway engineer, claiming negligent design. The following month, a new 15-year statute of repose became effective. HELD: the new statute applied prospectively only. Litigants have a constitutional right to a reasonable time for filing suit before a new statute of limitations becomes effective.

Statute of Repose Does Not Extend Time to Sue

In *Coon v Blaney*,[122] the plaintiff attempted to use the 10-year statute to avoid the application of the normal period of limitations. Plaintiff alleged that it fell from a ladder which was negligently designed. The one-year personal injury statute had elapsed before the suit was filed. Plaintiff pointed to the 10-year statute.[123] HELD: the statute did not apply to plaintiff. It was intended only to cover actions by an owner against a contractor.

§11.08 —Constitutional Considerations

A Box Score

In *Blaske v Smith & Entzeroth, Inc*,[124] the Supreme Court of Missouri has upheld its statute of repose:

> Presently, thiry-five states have statutes that impose time limitations upon actions against architects and builders for injuries or deaths caused by defective or unsafe conditions of improvements on real property. Generally, these statutes provide for a period of four to twenty years following

---

[120] Baker v Walker & Walker, Inc, 133 Cal App 3d 746, 184 Cal Rptr 245 (1982).
[121] 471 So 2d 603 (Fla Dist Ct App 1985).
[122] 311 So 2d 622 (La Ct App 1975).
[123] La Civ Code Ann art 3545 (West 1972).
[124] 821 SW2d 822 (Mo 1991).

the substantial completion of an improvement in which action may be brought against design professionals: AZ, AR, CA, CO, CT, DE, DC, GA, ID, IL, IN, LA, ME, MD, MA, MI, MN, MS, MT, NE, NV, NJ, NM, NC, ND, OH, OK, OR, PA, RI, TN, TX, VA, WA, WV. Thirty-two of these states have held these statutes constitutional; the remaining three states have not yet considered this issue (AZ, ME, WV). Eleven other jurisdictions have enacted similar statutes, which have been declared unconstitutional: ALL, AK, FL, HI, KY, NH, SC, SD, UT, WI, WY. Kansas and New York have statutes of repose, but they are not specifically for architects and builders for improvements to real property. Iowa and Vermont do not appear to have similar statutes.

Constitutionality of Statute Upheld

It is rational that the legislature might conclude that after 10 years, the liability potential of designers and builders should be foreclosed, but the responsibility of owners and occupiers should continue contemporaneously with their continuing control of the property.[125]

In *Zapata v Burns*, three people were killed and three injured when a span of a bridge over the Mianus River, Connecticut Turnpike I95, collapsed. HELD: the seven-year statute of repose rests on a rational basis. Rational distinctions exist between architects and engineers and others involved in the construction process and such classifications bear relationships to legitimate state ends. "One of the purposes of a statute of limitations is to protect the defendant from finding himself in a situation where, because of the lapse of time, it is unable to gather facts, evidence and witnesses necessary to afford him a fair defense."[126]

In *In re San Juan Dupont Plaza Hotel Fire Litigation*,[127] a fire in the San Juan Dupont Plaza Hotel in Puerto Rico killed 97 persons and injured over 100. A motion to dismiss based on the 10-year statute of repose was granted. HELD: the injured plaintiffs were not left without a remedy: liability for damages, after 10 years, shifted exclusively to the owner who, over time, was in a better position to discover and repair defective construction.

In *American Liberty Insurance Co v West & Conyers, Architects & Engineers*,[128] an insurer brought a subrogation action against an architect for damages caused by fire to the insured's building. Summary judgment for defendant was AFFIRMED. The building was completed in 1960. Florida Stat Ann §95.11 (West 1980) provided that actions founded on design or construction of

---

[125] *See* Freezer Storage, Inc v Armstrong Cork Co, 476 Pa 270, 382 A2d 715 (1978).
[126] 207 Conn 496, 509, 542 A2d 700, 707 (1988).
[127] 687 F Supp 716 (DPR 1988).
[128] 491 So 2d 573 (Fla Dist Ct App 1986).

improvements to real property were to be brought no later than 15 years after the date of actual possession. The preamble to the statute showed "overpowering public necessity." Therefore, the statute properly abolished causes of action for injuries occurring more than 15 years after completion of the improvement to real property.

The Montana statute establishing 10 years from completion as the period for action has survived attack on constitutional grounds. The statute does not cut off a vested right of plaintiff but merely eliminates accrual of the right to sue after 10 years. The statute does not violate equal protection. Although it does not extend to owners and material suppliers, there is a reasonable basis for the classification.[129]

The court in *McMacken v State*,[130] ruled that the South Dakota statute of limitations does not violate equal protection requirements. A student at the University of South Dakota sustained serious personal injuries after falling down a dormitory stairwell. The student sought damages from the state, as owner of the dormitory, and from the architectural design firm. The trial court granted the architect's motion to dismiss the action on the ground that it was not commenced within six years of the dormitory's completion, as required by South Dakota law.[131] The Supreme Court of South Dakota AFFIRMED. The six-year statute of limitations did not violate the equal protection provisions of the South Dakota and United States Constitutions by arbitrarily singling out one class of persons potentially liable for building defects. The limitation on builders' liability rests on real distinctions between builders and landowners. There is a larger class to whom builders may be liable, and builders lack control over the product after relinquishing it to the landowner. The landowner, however, can ordinarily avoid liability by taking adequate care of the land and structures. Nor did the statute violate rights under the due process clause.

Anderson v Fred Wagner[132] found a valid distinction between persons furnishing the design and planning of construction and persons in possession or control of the property at the time of an injury. A child's arm went through a glass door as the child was leaving school. The minor alleged that the architect and contractor failed to specify safety glass. More than 10 years had elapsed from the date of completion and acceptance of the school building. HELD: the 10-year limitation period did not violate the state's constitutional provision guaranteeing access to court.

---

[129] Reeves v Ille Elec Co, 170 Mont 104, 551 P2d 647 (1976). *Accord* Howell v Burk, 90 NM 688, 568 P2d 214, *cert denied*, 91 NM 3, 569 P2d 413 (1977).

[130] 320 NW2d 131 (SD 1982).

[131] SD Comp Laws Ann §15-2-9 (1967).

[132] 402 So 2d 320 (Miss 1981).

A 10-year statute of repose was upheld by the Mississippi Supreme Court in *Reich v Jesco, Inc.*[133] A chicken house was built in 1973; 12 years later, the roof collapsed after an accumulation of ice and snow. The owners filed suit in 1985 alleging negligence and breach of express and implied warranties. Summary judgment for the designer and contractor was AFFIRMED. The owners failed to establish the existence of fraudulent concealment.

The Michigan Supreme Court, in *O'Brien v Hazlet & Erdal*,[134] found a statute constitutional even though it applied only to state-licensed architects and professional engineers and not to contractors. "The legislature may have concluded that the different education, training, experience, licensing and professional stature of architects and engineers make it more likely that a limitation on tort liability would not reduce the care with which they performed their tasks than would be the case with contractors." Therefore, the fact that the statute applied only to architects and engineers and not to building contractors who also design and supervise construction of improvements to real property did not violate the equal protection or due process clause.

A Michigan court has upheld the constitutionality of Michigan's statute of repose.[135] Six years after a mill was completed, its roof collapsed. The owner filed an action against the Oregon supplier, who filed a third-party complaint against an Oregon architect who had prepared shop drawings. Dismissal based on the Michigan six-year statute of limitations applicable to licensed architects was AFFIRMED. The statute of limitations was constitutional. It did not violate due process even though it deprived parties of a cause of action unless the cause accrued within six years after completion of the project. The statute did not violate equal protection by protecting architects but not contractors. The statute applied to architects licensed in states other than Michigan. Moreover, the statute of repose applied to transactions that occurred entirely outside of Michigan. The Oregon supplier's action for indemnity from the Oregon architect was derivative: it existed only if the supplier itself was found primarily liable under Michigan law.

The Michigan courts have held that the statute does not violate due process by unreasonably restricting the right to sue. The legislature may abolish a common law right of action before it vests. "The present statute is better termed a statute of abrogation rather than a statute of limitations."[136]

---

[133] 526 So 2d 550 (Miss 1988).

[134] 84 Mich App 764, 270 NW2d 690 (1978), *affd*, 410 Mich 1, 299 NW2d 336 (1980).

[135] Cliffs Forest Prods Co v Al Disdero Lumber Co, 144 Mich App 215, 375 NW2d 397 (1985), *appeal denied*, 424 Mich 896, 384 NW2d 8 (1986).

[136] O'Brien v Hazelet & Erdal, 84 Mich App 764, 270 NW2d 690, 691 (1978). *See also* Bouser v Lincoln Park, 83 Mich App 167, 268 NW2d 332 (1978). Both cases *affd by*, 410 Mich 1, 299 NW2d 336 (1980).

In *Burmaster v Gravity Drainage District No 2*,[137] plaintiff's decedent was drowned on a job site after tripping on a protruding guardrail brace. His widow alleged that the engineer negligently designed the guardrail. The trial court, denying the engineer's motion for summary judgment based on the 10-year statute, ruled that the statute was unconstitutional. REVERSED. The statute provides that no action, whether ex contractu, ex delicto, or otherwise, shall be brought against any person furnishing the design, planning, supervision, inspection, or observation of construction more than 10 years after the date of registry in the mortgage office or acceptance of the work by the owner.[138]

The statute does not create an impermissible special law. There is a valid distinction between a person furnishing the design and construction of improvements to property and a person in possession or control of property. The architect cannot guard against neglect, abuse, mishandling, poor maintenance, or improper modification after completion of the project. Manufacturers need not be included in the statute, they produce components in large quantities, and can maintain high quality standards in the controlled environment of the factory.

The statute does not *destroy* a plaintiff's cause of action. It prevents what otherwise would be a cause of action from ever arising. Therefore, "[t]he harm that has been done . . . is *damnum absque injuria*—a loss that does not give rise to an action for damages against the person causing it."[139]

A student brought an action against an architect for injuries sustained when the outer door of a building at a student center struck plaintiff, causing plate glass panels in the door to shatter. HELD: the six-year statute of repose did not violate principles of due process or equal protection, nor did it violate the right to remedy by recourse of laws guaranteed by the state constitution. Unlike a manufacturer, an architect does not implicitly guarantee that its work is fit for its intended purposes.[140]

A widower charged that an architect's defective design of a hotel caused his wife to fall over a radiator and through the hotel window. Summary judgment for the architect was AFFIRMED. The 10-year statute did not deny due process of law, violate the equal protection clause, or violate the constitutional prohibition against special legislation. There is a reasonable relationship between the legislative objective of limiting liability for architects, contractors, and engineers, and the exclusion of material suppliers, owners, and occupiers of real property who do not come within the protection of the statute. The fact that

---

[137] 366 So 2d 1381 (La 1978).
[138] La Rev Stat Ann §9:2772 (West 1964).
[139] *Id* 1387.
[140] Klein v Catalono, 386 Mass 701, 437 NE2d 514 (1982).

the architect was not licensed in the state at the time the design services were rendered did not prevent the application of the statute.[141]

A student sued an architect after falling through a glass wall between entrance doors, and the school corporation sued the architect for indemnity against loss arising out of the same claim. Summary judgment for defendants was AFFIRMED. The Indiana 10-year statute did not deny equal protection or violate the privileges and immunities clause or the special laws provision of the state constitution. A reasonable basis exists for the distinction between owners and builders. The statute did not violate the due process clause of the United States Constitution or the open court clause of the state constitution. The legislature has power to alter or abolish a common law action which is not vested.[142]

Statute of Repose Held Unconstitutional

A statute of repose barring actions against planners, designers, and builders of improvements to real property for injuries occurring within a seven-year period after completion of construction, if no action is filed within that time, violates the Utah open courts constitutional provision which guarantees a remedy by due course of law for injuries to person, property, or reputation.[143]

The Supreme Court of Wisconsin has held that the state's six-year statute of repose violates the Wisconsin and United States Constitutional guarantees of equal protection. ("As of 1978, 43 states, plus the District of Columbia, had enacted statutes giving special treatment to suits against builders.")[144]

The Supreme Court of Alaska has held a six-year statute of repose applicable to design professionals unconstitutional in that it does not protect all defendants similarly situated since the statute applies to design professionals but not owners, tenants, or material suppliers.[145] "It follows that whenever an unprotected owner is 50 per cent at fault and a protected contractor is 50 per

---

[141] Yarbro v Hilton Hotels Corp, 655 P2d 822 (Colo 1982). *See* Twin Falls Clinic & Hosp Bldg v Hamill, 103 Idaho 19, 644 P2d 341 (1982).

[142] Beecher v White, 447 NE2d 622 (Ind Ct App 1983). However, to the contrary, see McClanahan v American Gilsonite Co, 494 F Supp 1334 (D Colo 1980); and Overland Constr Co v Sirmons, 369 So 2d 572 (Fla 1979). For a further discussion of the constitutional issues related to the statutes of limitations for building professionals, see Sisson & Kelly, *Statutes of Limitations for the Design and Building Professional—Will They Survive Constitutional Attack?*, 49 Ins Couns J 243 (1982).

[143] Horton v Goldminer's Daughter, 785 P2d 1087 (Utah 1989).

[144] Collins, *Limitations of Action Statutes for Architects and Builders—An Examination of Constitutionality*, FIC Quarterly (Fall 1978); Funk v Wollin Silo & Equip, Inc, 148 Wis 2d 59, 435 NW2d 244 (1989).

[145] Turner Constr Co v Scales, 752 P2d 467 (Alaska 1988).

cent at fault, the unprotected owner would be 100 per cent liable for all damages, without a remedy for contribution."[146]

In *Phillips v ABC Builders, Inc*,[147] homeowners filed an action against a builder alleging negligence and breach of the implied warranty of fitness. The home was completed in May of 1969; in May of 1978, after heavy rains, the basement and foundation walls began to collapse. The complaint was filed in September of 1979. Judgment for the builder was REVERSED. The statute of repose applied to persons performing or furnishing the design, planning, supervision, construction, or supervision of construction, of buildings. It was not a statute of limitations, but an immunity from suit granted to a narrow class of defendants: architects, engineers, and builders. There is no justification for the granting of such immunity. The statute was "a special law at least to the extent that no special law can be enacted where a general one can be made applicable." The Wyoming Constitution prohibits special laws; therefore, the statute was unconstitutional.[148]

§11.09 —Statute of Repose Applied

In *Rosenberg v Town of North Bergen*,[149] the court noted that some 30 states adopted *statutes of repose* during the period 1964 through 1969. Plaintiff sustained injuries in a fall on June 6, 1968, after catching a heel in a crack in the pavement of a highway which had been repaved in about 1935. An action was filed against the paving company and the township.

The court pointed out that New Jersey had adopted the discovery rule and also had rejected the rule that an architect or contractor's liability for negligent planning and construction terminates upon completion and acceptance by the owner. The court characterized these two developments as enlightened advances; nevertheless, their adoption increased the exposure which architects and contractors suffer. Therefore, the legislature thought to provide a reasonable measure of protection against this greater hazard, and the remedial intention of the legislature was to be given a liberal construction.

The court then pointed out that the negligence of the paving company alone did not give plaintiff a cause of action; its cause of action did not arise until the plaintiff fell and sustained an injury. Since this was many years after the period fixed by the statute, the effect was to prevent the plaintiff's right from ever arising. Plaintiff argued that such a statute is unconstitutional since it flouts due process. However, the court found this to be a misconception. The real function

---

[146] *Id* 471.

[147] 611 P2d 821 (Wyo 1980), *affd*, 632 P2d 925 (Wyo 1981).

[148] To the same effect, see Broome v Truluck, 270 SC 277, 241 SE2d 739 (1978) (statute of repose violates the equal protection and due process clauses of the state and federal constitutions).

[149] 61 NJ 190, 293 A2d 662 (1972).

of the statute was to define substantive rights rather than to modify a remedy. The legislature is at liberty to create new rights or abolish old ones as long as no vested right is disturbed.

In *Fennell v John J. Nesbitt, Inc*,[150] a school faculty brought an action against engineers for injuries allegedly caused by defective design, installation, operation, and maintenance of a heating, ventilating, and air conditioning system. The statute provided a six-year period from completion and occupancy of the project for suit. The faculty contended that the statute was unconstitutional as applied because it did not afford a reasonable time in which to bring suit since the causal connection between their injuries and the HVAC system was not discovered before the expiration of the statutory period. HELD: the statute of repose was valid and enforceable.

The New Jersey Constitution forbids special laws granting to any corporation, association, or individual any exclusive privilege or immunity.[151] In the statute under consideration, the favored class included not just architects and contractors, but any person furnishing design, planning, supervision of construction, or construction. This includes, for example, the designer of a sewage plant, a landscape gardener, and a well driller, as well as many other classifications. There is no such exclusion from the class as to justify a determination that it is a special law prohibited by the state constitution.

In *Josephs v Burns*,[152] the Oregon Supreme Court stated that it is proper to limit available causes of action to protect a recognized public interest. The court also noted that it is in the public interest that there be a definite end to the possibility of future litigation.

The Oregon statute provided: "[i]n no event shall any action for negligent injury to person or property of another be commenced more than ten years from the date of the act or omission complained of." The architect supervised construction in 1951, and the roof collapsed in 1969 (17 years later). The court stated that the statute started to run when the negligent act occurred, and the enactment was not contrary to the provision of the Oregon Constitution which states: "every man shall have remedy by due course of law for injury done him and his person, property, or reputation."

In *O'Connor v Altus*,[153] the plaintiff was injured in 1967 by a glass side light adjoining a glass door in a lobby. The plaintiff alleged that the architect was guilty of negligent design furnished in 1955. The court held that the action

---

[150] 154 Mich App 644, 398 NW2d 481 (1986).

[151] NJ Const arts 4, 7, 9(8).

[152] 260 Or 493, 491 P2d 203 (1971). *Accord* Mount Hood Radio & Television Broadcasting Corp v Dresser Indus, 270 Or 690, 530 P2d 72 (1974) (television tower designed and constructed by defendant in 1954, collapsed in 1971).

[153] 123 NJ Super 379, 303 A2d 329 (1973), *affd in part, revd in part*, 67 NJ 106, 335 A2d 545 (1975).

was barred by the statute of limitations which prohibits actions more than 10 years after the performance of professional services.

In *Deville Furniture Co v Jesco, Inc*,[154] an architect specified a "Barrett's 20-year type" built-up roof over a poured-in-place roof deck. The project was completed in 1972; leaking occurred in February 1974; re-roofing occurred in 1979; suit was filed by the owner against the architect in 1979. HELD: the 10-year statute of limitations applied to both latent and patent defects. The discovery rule did not apply.[155]

In *Presidents & Directors of Georgetown College v Madden*,[156] Georgetown College alleged breach of contract and negligence against architects, structural engineers, general contractors, masonry subcontractors, and the surety company involved in the construction of a dormitory. The dormitory was substantially completed in 1966. In 1976, the college discovered that the surface brick was cracking and bulging, and that the design and construction of the dormitory were otherwise defective. The court granted summary judgment for defendants on the ground that the 10-year statute of limitations had run by the time suit was filed in 1977. Congress intended to place reasonable limitations on the tort liability of those involved in the design and construction of improvements to real property. The legislative history of the statute indicated that there was no basis for the college's assertion that the statute was not intended to apply to actions brought by owners against design professionals.

In another case, a worker brought suit against the designer of an industrial electrical distribution system for injuries sustained while painting the bushing caps on the top of an air circuit breaker. HELD: the 10-year statute was constitutional. Separate classification of architects, engineers, and contractors from owners, tenants, and manufacturers is reasonable and not arbitrary. There is a valid distinction between persons performing design and persons in control of the work of improvement as owners or tenants.[157]

Indemnity Action

In *Nevada Lake Shore Co v Diamond Electric, Inc*,[158] a six-year statute of repose was applied to protect an architect against an indemnity action by an owner where the decedent was electrocuted by defective swimming pool wiring and the decedent's representative filed an action against the owner, who sought indemnity from the architect.

---

[154] 697 F2d 609 (5th Cir 1983).
[155] Miss Code Ann §15-1-41 (1972).
[156] 660 F2d 91 (4th Cir 1981).
[157] Mullis v Southern Cos Servs, Inc, 250 Ga 90, 296 SE2d 579 (1982).
[158] 89 Nev 293, 511 P2d 113 (1973).

§ 11.09 STATUTE OF REPOSE APPLIED

In *Sandy v Superior Court (Daon Corp)*,[159] architect Sandy rendered services on an apartment project in 1970; the project was completed in 1971. In 1979, Daon purchased the project and converted it to condominiums. Massive renovation and reconstruction was completed in 1981. In 1983, the homeowners association sued Daon and, in 1987, Daon filed a cross-complaint for indemnity against 40 cross-defendants, including subcontractors who participated only in the original construction. HELD: a cross-complaint for indemnity is permitted even after more than 10 years has elapsed from completion of construction, but indemnity must be sought under a transactionally related cross-complaint. Here, there was no transactional relationship because the subcontractor did not participate in the renovation and reconstruction.

In *Klein v Allen*,[160] plaintiff was injured while opening a door at a bank in April of 1981. Suit was filed against the owners of the building in July of 1981. They filed a third-party claim against the tenant in September of 1981 and the tenant filed a third-party claim against the contractor, subcontractor, designer, and manufacturer in April of 1982. The contractor filed a third-party claim against the architect in June of 1984. (As a California court once said, "Everybody sued everybody.") HELD: the third-party action by the general contractor seeking indemnity against the architect was timely filed, even though it was beyond the end of the preemptive period. The 10-year preemptive period ran on June 30, 1981, but under the statute, if injury occurred in the ninth year of the preemptive period, an action to recover damages for those injuries might be brought within one year of the injury. The injury was on April 8, 1981 and, therefore, the preemptive period was extended to April 8, 1982. The original suit was timely. The question was whether a claim for contribution or indemnity arising out of this action was covered by the one-year extension. HELD: the bank's action against the contractor was timely, because it was covered by the one-year extension. The contractor then filed an action for indemnity against the architect within 90 days. The statute provided that claims for indemnity were not barred by the preemptive period if they were filed within 90 days of the date of service of the third-party complaint. Thus, all actions were timely; none were barred by the statute of limitations.

Ten years after completion of the work of construction, if no complaint is yet on file against any of the participants, they may all assume their exposure has ended. Under the contrary interpretation, this repose could never occur; instead every subsequent renovation would raise the liability specter anew. Hardy would be the person who ventured into the

---

[159] 201 Cal App 3d 1277, 247 Cal Rptr 677 (1988).
[160] 470 So 2d 224 (La Ct App 1985).

construction industry under such conditions, assuming he could get liability insurance at all.[161]

In *Montaup Electric Co v Ohio Brass Corp*,[162] an electric company filed suit against Ohio Brass alleging that brackets supplied by Ohio Brass were understrength. Ohio Brass filed a third-party claim against engineers, seeking indemnity or contribution. Summary judgment for engineers was AFFIRMED. Ohio Brass had no right of contribution unless the engineer could be held directly liable to the owner, but the owner's claim against the engineer was barred by the six-year completion statute. The statute likewise barred an indemnity action.

In a North Carolina case, a widow sued an architect for the wrongful death of her husband, who fell through the sixth-floor window of a Hilton Hotel. The hotel company filed a cross-complaint for indemnity against the architect. HELD: first, the six-year statute of repose did not violate the Fourteenth Amendment to the United States Constitution nor §19 of Article 1 of the North Carolina Constitution (the law-of-the-land clause). A rational basis exists for the distinction between those in possession and control of the property and those who are not. Second, the statute of limitations barred a wrongful death action against the architect, since the design was completed more than 11 years before the death of plaintiff's intestate. Moreover, the indemnity claim of the hotel company against the architect was also barred. The legislature intended to prohibit all claims and cross-claims, even those asserted by persons in possession and control of the land.[163]

Completion of Construction

In *Rosenthal v Kurtz*,[164] the statute provided that no action should be brought more than six years after the furnishing of services *and* construction. The architect's services spanned a period from 1960 to December 1963, but construction of the building was not completed until 1967. In 1970, a portion of the suspended ceiling began to sag and threatened to collapse. This rendered the building untenable. Plaintiffs claimed $200,000 in damages for repairs and loss of rental income. The architects pleaded the six-year statute.[165] The trial court held that the statute ran from the date of the last architectural services; but, the Supreme Court, in a case of first impression, held that the time must be measured from the completion of construction even though the services may have been terminated earlier.

---

[161] *Id* at 1286, 247 Cal Rptr at 682.
[162] 561 F Supp 740 (DRI 1983).
[163] Lamb v Wedgewood S Corp, 308 NC 419, 302 SE2d 868 (1983).
[164] 62 Wis 2d 1, 213 NW2d 741, *rehg denied*, 62 Wis 2d 1, 216 NW2d 252 (1974).
[165] Mich Stat Ann §893.155.

In *Hooper Water Improvement District v Reeve*,[166] the court AFFIRMED the order dismissing an action against a consultant engineer who was allegedly negligent in supervising the construction of a water well. The statute required claims for damages to real property to be filed within seven years of completion of construction. The limitations period for the consultant engineer's alleged negligence commenced running at the completion of the construction and not at the time of discovery of the negligence. The court specifically rejected cases such as *City of Aurora v Bechtel Corp*.[167]

In *Pinneo v Stevens Pass, Inc*,[168] the question was whether the *substantial completion* statute (six years) applied to protect an architect against a claim of negligence in the design of a ski lift facility. The design took place in 1953; the injury was to a skier in 1973. The statute protected certain persons "having constructed, altered, or repaired any improvement upon real property." The plaintiff contended that the ski lift was a trade fixture, since it was to be removed when a government lease on the facility expired. The court, however, concluded that the purpose of the legislation was to protect architects, contractors, engineers, and others from extended potential tort liability. Therefore, the term *improvement to real property* should be given a broad construction. The ski lift added to the value of property and was therefore an *improvement*.

Improvement to Real Property

In *Keeler v Pennsylvania Department of Transportation*,[169] plaintiff sustained personal injuries and property damage on November 11, 1975, in a car accident allegedly resulting from the negligent design and construction of guardrails, lights, signs, and directional signals. Plaintiff sued the Department of Transportation, the consulting engineer, and the contractor. A motion for summary judgment was granted on the ground that the action was barred by the 12-year statute of limitations, since the highway improvements had been completed in 1958. Summary judgment was AFFIRMED. Guardrails, road signs, and highway illumination lights are not personal property; they are fixtures or improvements and therefore subject to the 12-year limitation period relating to improvements to real property. No genuine issue of fact existed. A road improvement need not be a *fixture* to fall within the term of *improvement to real property*.

In *Leeper v Hiller Group, Architects, Planners PA*,[170] a woman fell from a third-floor dormitory after stepping through a sliding glass door designed to give

---

[166] 642 P2d 745 (Utah 1982).

[167] 599 F2d 382 (10th Cir 1979) (cause of action does not accrue until plaintiff knows all material facts essential to show the elements of that cause of action).

[168] 14 Wash App 848, 545 P2d 1207, *review denied*, 87 Wash 2d 1006 (1976).

[169] 56 Pa Commw 236, 424 A2d 614 (1981).

[170] 543 A2d 258 (RI 1988) (per curiam).

access to a balcony. (Balconies were never built.) The dormitory was finished in 1971 and the fall occurred in 1982; suit followed in 1984. HELD: the action was barred under the 10-year statute of repose.

In *Barnes v J.W. Bateson Co*,[171] a worker was injured in 1984 after coming into contact with a high voltage line in a *bus duct* at an American Airlines terminal. Construction of the terminal was substantially completed in January, 1974. HELD: the statute was constitutional; it did not offend the guarantees of equal protection; and a rational relationship existed between the state's legitimate interest of relieving certain construction professionals from the burden of indefinite potential liability.

§11.10 —Application of Statute Rejected

In *Skinner v Anderson*,[172] a statute provided that architects and contractors were immune from liability for causes of action arising out of a defective condition of improvements to real estate but accuring more than four years after the negligent act.

Here, the architect designed a residence in 1956. The design failed to require that rooms provided with air conditioning be adequately ventilated, thus violating the village ordinance and national safety standards. Leaking refrigerant gas entered an adjoining boiler room and corroded the gas-fired burners, and carbon monoxide entered the residence, killing the plaintiff's husband and daughter, and injuring the plaintiff on September 19, 1965, nine years after the design.

The statute provided:

> No action . . . for any injury . . . arising out of the defective and unsafe condition of an improvement to real estate . . . shall be brought against any person performing or furnishing the design, planning, supervision of construction or construction of such improvement . . . unless such cause of action shall have accrued within four years after the performance or furnishing of such services and construction.[173]

The court opined that the statute, in effect, granted immunity to architects, contractors, and builders. Therefore, it was invalid since it violated an Illinois constitutional provision prohibiting laws which grant "to any corporation, association, or individual any special or exclusive privilege, immunity, or

---

[171] 755 SW2d 518 (Tex Ct App 1988).
[172] 38 Ill 2d 455, 231 NE2d 588 (1967).
[173] *Id* 589.

franchise."[174] Since the benefits of the immunity were not extended to all similarly situated, the classification of architects and contractors could not be sustained.

A Minnesota statute of repose did not apply to contract or tort claims by an owner who was in privity of contract with the defendant for injuries arising out of the design and construction of an improvement to real estate.[175]

A number of courts have found statutes of repose unconstitutional. In *McClanahan v American Gilsonite Co*,[176] employees were injured when hot oil erupted or overflowed from a coking unit and surge tank at an oil refinery in 1975. Survivors filed an action under the Colorado wrongful death statute in 1977, one day less than two years after the accident. An injured employee filed an action for damages for personal injuries, alleging negligent design of the refinery, negligent concealment, failure to warn, strict liability, breach of express and implied warranties, misrepresentation, fraud, and wanton and reckless disregard of plaintiff's rights. The refinery had been constructed and commenced operation in 1957, 18 years before the accident.

As to the wrongful death action, the wrongful death statute of limitations applied rather than the statute of repose. As to the injured plaintiff, Colorado's statute[177] was unconstitutional. The statute provided:

> All actions against any architect, contractor, engineer, or inspector brought to recover damages for injury to person or property caused by the design, planning, supervision, inspection, construction, or observation of construction of any improvement to real property should be brought within the two years after the claim for relief arises . . . but in no case shall such an action be brought more than ten years after the substantial completion of the improvement to the real property.

The coking unit and surge tank were improvements to real property. The year of substantial completion was 1957. The statute was unconstitutional under the equal protection guarantee of the Fourteenth Amendment and under the Colorado Constitution, because it created a classification that did not bear a reasonable relation to the object sought to be achieved. Relying heavily on *Skinner v Anderson*,[178] the court particularly objected to the fact that architects and contractors are granted special immunity, whereas the owner of the

---

[174] Ill Const art IV, 22.

[175] Caledonia Community Hosp v Liebenberg, Smiley, Glotter & Assocs, 308 Minn 255, 248 NW2d 279 (1976). *Accord* Kittson County v Wells, Denbrook & Assocs, 308 Minn 237, 241 NW2d 799 (1976).

[176] 494 F Supp 1334 (D Colo 1980).

[177] Colo Rev Stat §13-80-127.

[178] 38 Ill 2d 455, 231 NE2d 588 (1967).

property and the supplier and manufacturer of materials and equipment installed in the property are not.

> It is not at all inconceivable that the owner or person in control of such an improvement might be held liable for damage or injury that results from a defective condition for which the architect or contractor is in fact responsible. Not only is the owner or person in control given no immunity; the statute takes away his action for indemnity against the architect or contractor . . . the arbitrary quality of the statute clearly appears when we consider that the architects and contractors are not the only persons whose negligence in construction of a building or other improvement may cause damage to property or injury to person.

In *Overland Construction Co v Sirmons*,[179] a building was completed in 1961. In 1975, the plaintiff worker was injured in the building and sued the owner and the builders. HELD: Florida's statute of repose was unconstitutional.[180] It violated §21 of Article 1 of the Florida Constitution which provides: "The courts shall be open to every person for redress of any injury, and justice shall be administered without fail, deny, or delay."

In *State Farm Fire & Casualty Co v All Electric, Inc*,[181] the Supreme Court of Nevada held that the Nevada six-year statute of repose[182] violated the equal protection clause of the United States Constitution in that it improperly granted immunity from suit to a certain class of defendants without a reasonable basis of classification. Concerns about stale evidence are virtually unfounded since plans and specifications of architects and engineers become public records and normally would be easily located. The statute arbitrarily discriminated against owners and material suppliers.

A Supreme Court of New Hampshire case is in accord.[183] An owner sued a bricklayer for peeling, falling, and disintegrating bricks in a department store. The brick supplier claimed indemnity against the architect. The architect's motion to dismiss the indemnity action on the ground that the statute of limitations had elapsed was granted. REVERSED.

Shibuya v Architects Hawaii, Ltd[184] supports the same proposition. Immunity bestowed on architects because of their membership in the construction industry does not rest upon reasonable consideration of differences which have a fair and substantial relation to the object of the legislation. In *Shibuya*, a worker sued the

---

[179] 369 So 2d 572 (Fla 1979).
[180] Fla Stat §95.11(3)(c) (1975).
[181] 99 Nev 222, 660 P2d 995 (1983).
[182] Nev Rev Stat §11.205 (1979).
[183] Henderson Clay Prods, Inc v Edgar Wood & Assoc, 122 NH 800, 451 A2d 174 (1982).
[184] 65 Haw 26, 647 P2d 276 (1982).

architect, contractor, fabricator, and manufacturer for injuries sustained when a metal grating covering a culvert became dislodged.

In *Terry v New Mexico State Highway Commission*,[185] a one-car accident was the basis for a wrongful death action. Summary judgment for the engineer and contractor based on the 10-year statute of repose was REVERSED. The statute denied equal protection where the cause of action arose approximately three months before the expiration of the 10-year period. Three months is not a reasonable time for institution of an action. Fundamental considerations of due process require that the 10-year limitation not apply to actions arising within, but close to the end of, the 10-year period.

A California court has limited the application of the California statute of repose.[186] In *Sevilla v Stearns-Roger, Inc*,[187] an employee was injured while repairing a large *pan* installed by a defendant in a sugar refinery. Plaintiff sued the engineer and the manufacturer of the pan. HELD: the completion statute was not applicable to finished products. The simple process of installing the pan did not transform it into an *improvement to real property*.

In another California case, *Martinez v Traubner*,[188] the Supreme Court of California held that the 10-year statute of repose[189] does not apply to personal injury cases.[190]

In *Baker v Walker & Walker, Inc*,[191] a legal secretary died of pneumonia, caused by faulty performance of an air conditioning system in a 10-year-old building. An action against the general contractor, the air conditioning subcontractor, and the manufacturers of the air conditioning units was dismissed on the ground that the four-year-after-completion-of-construction limitation established by the California Code of Civil Procedure §337.1 had expired.[192] REVERSED. Section 337.1 does not apply to manufacturers. Moreover, the deficiencies were latent, not patent, and thus the 10-year statute rather than the four-year statute applied. Plaintiffs could not have discovered the cause of the deficiency. Therefore, the deficiency was not one which, as is required by the statute, "is apparent by reasonable inspection."

The New Jersey Supreme Court has construed the statute of repose (though constitutional) so as to apply only to errors that create a hazardous or unsafe

---

[185] 98 NM 119, 645 P2d 1375 (1982).
[186] Cal Civ Proc Code §§337.1, 337.15 (West 1982).
[187] 101 Cal App 3d 608, 161 Cal Rptr 700 (1980).
[188] 32 Cal 3d 755, 653 P2d 1046, 187 Cal Rptr 251 (1982).
[189] Cal Civ Proc Code §337.15 (West 1982).
[190] Overruling Ernest W. Hahn, Inc v Superior Court (Los Angeles County), 108 Cal App 3d 567, 166 Cal Rptr 644 (1980).
[191] 133 Cal App 3d 746, 184 Cal Rptr 245 (1982).
[192] §337.1 applies to actions arising out of patent defects.

condition. In *E.A. Williams, Inc v Russo Development Corp*,[193] an erroneous survey caused economic loss because plaintiff located a building too close to the true boundary. The suit was allowed despite the 10-year statute of limitations, since the discovery rule was held applicable in this case.

In *Canton Lutheran Church v Sovik, Mathre, Sathrum & Quanbeck*,[194] a school house cracked 14 years after it was built. Plaintiff owner alleged that the evidence was conflicting as to whether the architect knew or should have known that the contractor had inserted calcium chloride into the concrete mix. Calcium chloride, an additive used to allow concrete to set faster in cold weather, may have contributed to the cracking. HELD: if the architect knew that it had been added, it might be equitably estopped to assert the statute of limitations on the ground that it failed to disclose this knowledge to the owner. Moreover, the plaintiff should have been given an opportunity to prove that the architect breached a fiduciary duty as an agent of the church. Such proof would have also estopped the architect from asserting the statute of limitations defense.

In *Raffel v Perley*,[195] the plaintiff brought an action against a civil engineer and land surveyor who incorrectly located boundaries on a 1973 plan. The action was dismissed. REVERSED. The six-year statute of repose did not apply. A survey dividing property into lots is not the *design* or *planning* of an improvement to real property.

In *Board of Education v Celotex Corp*,[196] an elementary school building was completed in 1973, and a malpractice action commenced in October 1980 against the design architect. The final certificate of payment had not been issued by defendant until June 1976. HELD: the action was not barred by the six-year statute of repose, since the project was not *complete* until the certificate for final payment had been issued.

§11.11 Continuous Services

If an architect commits malpractice but retains its professional relationship with the owner after the negligent act occurs, then the commencement of the statute of limitations may be delayed until the professional relationship is terminated. The theory is that the client continues to repose trust and confidence in the architect and is not placed on its guard against misconduct until after the termination of the professional relationship.

---

[193] 82 NJ 160, 411 A2d 697 (1980).
[194] 507 F Supp 873 (DSD 1981).
[195] 14 Mass App 242, 437 NE2d 1082 (1982).
[196] 58 NY2d 684, 444 NE2d 1006, 458 NYS2d 542 (1982).

Attempted Repairs

In *Northern Montana Hospital v Knight*,[197] the architect designed a hospital ventilation system. When problems occurred, the architect assured the hospital that the design was not at fault. The hospital relied on the architect's advice in attempting to repair the defects in the system for three years. HELD: the *continuing relationship doctrine* extended the accrual of the cause of action until the time when the relationship ended.

Continuing Inspections

In a 1985 New York case, a school board filed an action against an architect who designed a defective roof. The architect alleged that the action was barred by a six-year statute of limitations. Evidence indicated that the architect learned of the roof problems during construction, but did not inform the owner. HELD: although the cause of action usually accrues when the certificate of completion is issued, the *continuous treatment* doctrine applied. Therefore, the statute of limitations was tolled as long as a confidential professional relationship existed between the owner and architect.[198]

The school district's contract with the architect required the architect to inspect the building annually for three years subsequent to its completion. The building was completed in 1972; suit was filed by the district against the architect in 1979. During construction, the architect carried on extensive negotiations with the contractor as to the quality of workmanship on the roof, but did not convey this information to the district: the architect made inspections after completion of the building, but did not inform the district of the defects in the roof. A confidential professional relationship existed, which tolled the statute of limitations under the *continuous treatment* doctrine.

Assurances of Repair

In *Broome County v Vincent J. Smith, Inc*,[199] the county entered into a contract with an architect in 1966. The architect received final payment for services in June 1968. One month later leaks began appearing in the roof. For the next several years there was regular communication between the architect and the owner, with the architect giving assurances that repairs would be accomplished. In September 1971, the owner filed suit for malpractice. The statutory period was three years. The court held that the action was not barred. Although a cause of action for malpractice accrues at the time of the wrongful act or omission, the *continuous treatment* exception is applicable "when a course

---

[197] 248 Mont 310, 811 P2d 1276 (1991).

[198] Board of Educ of Hudson City Sch Dist v Thompson Constr Corp, 111 AD2d 497, 488 NYS2d 880 (1985).

[199] 78 Misc 2d 889, 358 NYS2d 998 (Sup Ct 1974).

of treatment by a professional which includes wrongful acts and omissions has been continuous and is related to the original condition of complaint, [and then] the claim accrues at the end of the treatment."[200]

The reason for the exception to the general rule is the fact that the client must repose trust and confidence in the professional; the client must rely on the professional's judgment. Malpractice is usually not readily apparent to the client. The professional relationship did not terminate with the final payment to the architect, but continued while the architect met with officials of the county and contractors and offered recommendations to solve the problems.

Professional Assurances

In *School Board v GAF Corp*,[201] a school board sued to recover for alleged improper design of the roofs of three schools built 1969 through 1971. The trial court held that the four-year statute of limitations for improper design applied, and as a matter of law, the school board should have discovered the design defects more than four years before suit was filed. REVERSED. All three schools developed roof leaks during the first few years and were repaired under warranty. After the warranty period expired, the leaks became increasingly severe, and an investigation by the head of maintenance revealed that it was the architect's failure to design proper expansion joints that caused the failures. The architect had coordinated roof repairs. The school board was not told that the leaks were caused by structural problems until 1976. HELD: where a client has relied on a professional to correct a problem that lies within the ambit of the professional relationship, and where the professional continuously works on the problem and assures the client that the problem is being solved, it is a question of fact for the jury as to when the client should have known its problem was permanent and irreparable. The school board's reliance on the architect to diagnose the problem may reasonably have prevented the board from discovering the design defects more than four years prior to the suit.

Contractor Does Not Rely on Architect

In *Piracci Construction Co v Skidmore, Owings & Merrill*,[202] the court acknowledged that:

> The general rule in malpractice cases is that the cause of action accrues at the time of the wrongful conduct by the professional . . . the one relevant exception to this general rule, the "continuing treatment" exception,

---

[200] *Id* at 890, 358 NYS2d at 1000.

[201] 413 So 2d 1208 (Fla Dist Ct App 1982), *opinion quashed by*, Kelley v School Bd, 435 So 2d 804 (Fla 1983).

[202] 490 F Supp 314 (SDNY), *affd*, 646 F2d 562 (2d Cir 1980).

provides that when the wrongful conduct was part of a course of treatment, the cause of action accrues when treatment is completed. . . . This exception was applied in a malpractice action against an architect, . . . and it has been applied in actions against other professionals.[203]

However, the *continuing treatment* exception does not apply when the plaintiff is a contractor as opposed to an owner. A contractor is an expert; a contractor does not depend on the architect to discover that it may have a claim. There is no relationship of trust between a construction company and an architectural firm.

Gap in Services

In *Tool v Boutelle*,[204] the defendant performed surveying services to establish property lines and building locations in 1967. In 1972 the defendant performed further services (locating a vestibule to be added to the existing building). Other surveying services were performed in 1975. HELD: in surveyor malpractice actions, the continuous services exception applies only if the subsequent services were related to the original services. Even if the subsequent services are related, any three-year gap between the services prevents the application of the exception. Here, there was such a three-year gap between 1968 and 1972; summary judgment for defendant was AFFIRMED.

§11.12 Arbitration

Does the expiration of the statute of limitations bar arbitration proceedings, as it would an action at law? The answer appears to be *yes* and *no*. Three policies affect the question: (1) the plaintiff should not be deprived of its remedy; (2) the defendant should not be put to the defense of stale claims; and (3) if the parties by their contract have agreed to settle their dispute by arbitration, the law should enforce their agreement, and arbitrators may decide the dispute in accordance with their perceptions of justice rather than in accordance with legal rules, including the statute of limitations.

In *Skidmore, Owings & Merrill v Connecticut General Life Insurance Co*,[205] the contract between architect and owner was executed in May 1953. Plans were delivered in February 1955. The building was occupied in 1957. The owner (an insurance company) became aware of defective air conditioning in June 1960. The defect was the corrosion of copper pipes in the system caused by the chemical content of the water drawn from wells and specifically designed to be

---

[203] *Id* 317.
[204] 91 Misc 2d 464, 398 NYS2d 128 (Sup Ct 1977).
[205] 25 Conn Supp 76, 197 A2d 83 (1963).

used as a cooling agent for the system. In July 1962, the owner demanded arbitration, as provided by the 1953 contract. The architects filed an action for declaratory judgment that the arbitration proceeding was barred by the statute of limitations.

The court stated that the applicable period should have been six years (contract) rather than one or three years (negligence), since the gravamen was the architect's breach of the contractual obligation. The breach continued until 1957, when the building was completed. This was because the contract provided for continuing responsibility until the attainment of the end result. Thus, the action was within the six-year limitation period.

The court also held that arbitration is not a common law action, and the institution of arbitration proceedings does not constitute *bringing an action* under any statute of limitations. Even assuming it is, the application of the statute is to be determined by the arbitrators and not by the court, since the arbitration clause commits all disputes regarding the contract to arbitration.

In *Paver & Wildfoester v Catholic High School Assn*,[206] the court noted that a party may assert the statute of limitations as a bar to an arbitration if the claim sought to be arbitrated would also have been barred if it had been brought before a court.[207]

In *Framlau Corp v Kling*,[208] a contractor unsuccessfully argued that its malpractice action against an architect could not be filed until after the completion of arbitration proceedings between the contractor and the owner; therefore, the running of the statute of limitations was tolled until the completion of arbitration. The court rejected the argument. The contract between the contractor and the owner had provided for arbitration of all claims that arose from the neglect "of the other party or of anyone employed by him." Even assuming that the architect was an employee rather than an independent contractor, since the architect was not a party to the contract, it was not bound to arbitrate. Therefore, the contractor could have filed a lawsuit against the architect regardless of arbitration proceedings, and the action was barred by the passage of time.

§11.13 Remedial Efforts

In *Freeport Memorial Hospital v Lankton, Ziegele, Terry & Associates*,[209] the owner alleged that the statute of limitations was tolled because of the architects' unsuccessful repair efforts. HELD: architects were not estopped from raising

---

[206] 38 NY2d 669, 345 NE2d 565, 382 NYS2d 22 (1976).
[207] NY Civ Prac Law §7502(b).
[208] 233 Pa Super 175, 334 A2d 780 (1975).
[209] 170 Ill App 3d 531, 525 NE2d 194 (1988).

the statute of limitations as a defense because the owner was not lulled into a false sense of security. When a vendor has unsuccessfully attempted to repair defects, the statute of limitations tolls only where the vendor has insisted repairs will correct the problem.

In *City of Midland v Helger Construction Co*,[210] the city filed an action against an architect to recover damages for defective design and construction of a roof for an ice arena. HELD: the action was subject to the two-year general professional malpractice statute of limitations. The remedial efforts made by the architectural firm four years after completion of the project did not revive the city's action for malpractice.

---

[210] 157 Mich App 736, 403 NW2d 218 (1987).

Indemnity

12

§12.01 Generally
§12.02 Contractual Indemnity
    Subrogation to Indemnity
    No Indemnity for Architect
    Indemnity against Architect
    Joint Negligence
    Attorneys Fees
    Architect Indemnifies Owner
    Mechanics Lien
    Contractor Indemnifies Engineer
    No Indemnity for Economic Damages
    No Omission, No Indemnity
    Ambiguous Clause
§12.03 Indemnity against Own Negligence
    Narrow Construction
    Broad Construction
§12.04 Statute Annulling Indemnity Provision
§12.05 No Contribution
    No Joint Fault
§12.06 Implied Equitable Indemnity—Development
    Early Development: Active/Passive
    Active/Passive Distinction
    No Duty, No Indemnity
§12.07 —Sought from Architect or Engineer
    Active/Passive
    Indemnity Based on Implied Warranty
    Numerous Factors
    No Indemnity to Active Tortfeasor

                Disproportionate Fault
                No Indemnity Where Both Parties Negligent
                No Indemnity for Parties in pari delicto
                Indemnity for Defective Design
                Negligent Approval
                Active or Affirmative Negligence
                "Primary" Fault
                Joint Fault
                No Duty
                Indemnity Enforced
§12.08   —Sought by Architect or Engineer
                Active/Passive
                Architect Actively Negligent
                Contractor Indemnifies Architect
                Nonfeasance Is Active Negligence
                More versus Less Negligent
                Indemnity to Actively Negligent Engineer
                Architect versus Supplier
                Fault Destroys Right to Common Law Indemnity
                Vouching In
                Contribution Permitted
                Exclusive Remedy Defense
                Release Bars Indemnity
                Required Relationship
                No Duty of Contractor to Engineer
                Independent Wrongs—No Indemnity
                Common Wrong
                Contribution Statute—Economic Loss
§12.09   Limitations
                Statutes of Repose
                Other Statutes

§12.01 Generally

    The subject matter of indemnity is peculiarly important to the field of architectural malpractice because of the multiple party nature of the construction process. When a job site injury occurs, or if there is a defect in a building, the injured party is always presented with a selection of defendants: architect, engineer, contractor, subcontractor, owner, material supplier, and others. Defendants, in turn, are usually presented with a selection of third-party defendants. The allocation, apportionment, or designation of liability among those who share responsibility for the injury is the subject matter of indemnity.

Most construction is pursuant to written contract. The party with the greatest bargaining power is usually in a position to control the contents of the indemnity provisions of the contract. In modern circumstances, the contents of contractual indemnity provisions are given slight weight by bargaining parties: they may perceive that they are really bargaining for their insurance carriers anyway, and the intangible, remote circumstance that liability premiums might increase or decrease based upon the acceptance or rejection of an indemnity clause is of relatively little significance when compared to the contract price. It is a rare contractor who would forego a lucrative job because of objection in principle to the contents of an indemnity clause.

Many indemnity clauses are controlled in practice by the American Institute of Architects (AIA) and the contractor organizations that cooperate in drafting the AIA general conditions. Indemnity clauses in public contracts are, of course, controlled by the public entity. A public contractor has no opportunity to bargain about contract clauses: the contractor bids the job as presented or not at all.

Indemnity is not only contractual but may also be implied from circumstances. Most state courts have felt a need to equitably allocate damages among plaintiffs and wrongdoers. Such allocation was by the common law rule that there could be no contribution between joint tortfeasors. The doctrine of implied equitable indemnity evolved to meet the need to devise a method to allocate liability among defendants. The term *implied indemnity* is the label attached to decisions that, without benefit of contract, shift liability from one defendant to another. The doctrine is of broad application.

Indemnity, however, is not automatic. For example, one who acts as a volunteer may not be entitled to indemnity. In *Soriano v Hunton, Shivers, Brady & Associates*,[1] an architect determined that its consulting structural engineer had not properly designed a bank building. After the opinions of two other structural engineers held that the design was defective, the architect modified portions of the building that had already been constructed. The architect then sought indemnity from the engineers. HELD: even though the modifications may have been necessary for the protection of the owner, they were not authorized by the owner; therefore, the architect acted as a volunteer. "To permit [the architect] to recover from [the engineer] in this instance may encourage acts of volunteerism under a guise of mitigating an owner's damages without the owner's consent."[2] Unfortunately, this decision would discourage architects from volunteering to remedy defective building for the protection of the owners.

---

[1] 524 So 2d 488 (Fla Dist Ct App), *review denied*, 534 So 2d 399 (Fla 1988).
[2] *Id* 489-90.

An employer is not entitled to common law indemnity from an engineer where the employer's own conduct actively contributed to the cause of the accident. Furthermore, the legislature's enactment of comparative negligence does not mandate the application of comparative contribution between joint tortfeasors.[3]

§12.02 Contractual Indemnity

White v Morris Handler Co[4] illustrates several facets of *contractual indemnity clauses*. A worker employed by a subcontractor was injured after falling from a third-floor walkway without safety rails. The worker was leaving the job site and slipped on gravel on the walkway. An action was then filed against the prime contractor and the architect by the worker. The architect and the prime contractor in turn filed an action for indemnity against the subcontractor.

The first problem in a case like this is whether the subcontractor should be liable to indemnify, since this requires an employer to pay more than workers' compensation, and the employee's exclusive remedy against the employer is intended to be measured by the workers' compensation statutes. Here, the court held, without discussion, that the subcontractor could be liable for indemnity and was not protected by the *exclusive remedy* defense.

The second problem is whether it is good public policy to enforce a clause that indemnifies a party against the results of its own negligence. Might not the enforcement of such a clause encourage negligent conduct?

The clause in the contract between the prime contractor and the subcontractor required the subcontractor to indemnify and hold harmless the contractor and architect from liability for injury arising out of the performance of the subcontractor's work. Since the injured party was an employee of the subcontractor, the injury arose out of the subcontractor's work, and by its terms the subcontractor was required to indemnify the contractor and the architect. HELD: the indemnity clause required the subcontractor to hold the others harmless not only from the subcontractor's negligence, but also from their own negligence. Leaving the job site is within the activities which are a part of the performance of the subcontractor's work. Therefore, the indemnity clause was applicable and enforceable.

The court noted that the state of Illinois has adopted a statute annulling clauses that purport to indemnify a party against the results of its own negligence, but the court refused to apply that statute retroactively.

---

[3] Weston v New Bethel Missionary Baptist Church, 23 Wash App 747, 598 P2d 411 (1978).
[4] 7 Ill App 3d 199, 287 NE2d 203 (1972).

Subrogation to Indemnity

In *St Paul Fire & Marine Insurance Co v United States National Bank*,[5] the indemnity clause required the contractor to indemnify the Oregon State Highway Commission and its employees from any damage or loss sustained by any person and caused by the neglect of the contractor or its employees. During construction, an employee of the general contractor was killed when a vehicle collided with a barricade. The administratrix filed an action against the engineers and the commission, who tendered the defense to the contractor. The contractor refused to defend.

The action was successfully defended by the commission's general liability insurance carrier, which then filed suit against the contractor under the indemnity clause. HELD: the clause was enforceable. The insurer was subrogated to the rights of its insured to enforce the indemnity clause. To construe the clause to exclude claims arising from alleged negligence of the commission and its engineers (as held by the lower court) would have made the clause meaningless.

No Indemnity for Architect

In *McCarthy v J.P. Cullen & Son Corp*,[6] an indemnity clause was interpreted against an architect. The clause required the general contractor to indemnify the architect against liability arising out of the operations of the contractor but specifically provided that the indemnity obligation would not extend to liability arising out of the preparation of drawings and specifications.

The injured party was a neighbor whose home was flooded after storm waters escaped from a high school construction site. The architect contended that it was responsible only for the disposition of storm water from a completed project, and that the contractor was responsible for containing storm water which might fall during the progress of construction. The court, however, AFFIRMED judgments on verdicts against both the contractor and the architect, holding that the architect had a duty to provide a design which would have protected neighboring property from surface water during the construction process. Thus, since the liability of the architect was for a design flaw, the indemnity clause was not applicable.

A structural engineer was denied recovery under the indemnity clause in *Lagerstrom v Beers Construction Co*.[7] The owner hired a general contractor to erect a six-story office building. The architect, retained by the general contractor, hired a structural engineer who was responsible for selecting the proper size steel piping and for supervising attachment of the pipe to the roof.

---

[5] 251 Or 377, 446 P2d 103 (1968).
[6] 199 NW2d 362 (Iowa 1972).
[7] 157 Ga App 396, 277 SE2d 765 (1981).

§12.02 CONTRACTUAL INDEMNITY   395

The structural engineer was named as one of the parties responsible for the death of two workers who fell 70 feet when one of the steel pipe supports broke loose. The engineer incurred $14,000 in legal fees to successfully defend against the claim. It then sued the owner to recover the fees, relying on the indemnity clause in the agreement between the general contractor and the owner. The clause provided that the owner, architect, and subcontractors would be indemnified for all expenses (including attorneys fees) arising out of the performance of the work on the building. The trial court granted summary judgment to the owner on the ground that the engineer was an independent contractor. AFFIRMED. The engineer was neither an employee nor an agent of the owner, general contractor, or architect as defined by the terms of the indemnity clause.

Indemnity against Architect

In another case,[8] the contract provided that the contractor would indemnify the engineer against liability for damages arising out of operations performed under the contract. The engineer, under the contract, was obliged to inspect a pipeline during construction. It was laid over another line, and its weight caused a rupture in the lower line, causing gas to escape and explode, injuring a worker. The court stated that the contract with the utilities company imposed a high duty of inspection on the engineer, the breach of which constituted negligence. The indemnity clause was not enforceable by the engineer against the contractor, since the damages were not caused by work performed under the construction contract within the contemplation of the indemnity agreement.

In *Skidmore, Owings & Merrill v Volpe Construction Co*,[9] the construction contract contained an indemnity clause that provided that the contractor would indemnify the architect for claims against the architect arising out of the contractor's work. HELD: the developer's claims against the architect did not arise out of the contractor's work; therefore, the architect was not entitled to indemnity.

A South Dakota statute mandates the inclusion of a construction contract indemnity clause to the effect that the contractor's obligation to indemnify the architect does not extend to indemnity against the architect's liability arising out of the approval of shop drawings.[10] Such a provision prevented an architect

---

[8] Becker v Black & Veatch Consulting Engrs, 509 F2d 42 (8th Cir 1974). *See also* Fidelity & Casualty Co v J.A. Jones Constr Co, 325 F2d 605 (8th Cir 1963) (clause which requires the contractor to indemnify the owner was not to be interpreted to require the contractor to also indemnify the architect).

[9] 511 So 2d 642 (Fla Dist Ct App 1987), *review denied*, 520 So 2d 586 (Fla 1988).

[10] SD Codified Laws Ann §56-3-16 (1980).

from claiming indemnity from a general contractor in a case where the architect approved shop drawings for a stairway where two workers were injured.[11]

In *Nicholson-Brown, Inc v City of San Jose*,[12] an architect agreed to indemnify the city against loss arising from the failure of the architect to perform services in a skillful manner. During the progress of the job, problems occurred with the specified concrete. Experiments led to changes in the plans and specifications. Finally, work on the exterior concrete finish was suspended by the architect at the direction of the city. The general contractor filed an action against the city and the architect, claiming that additional costs were sustained because of defects in the contract documents and because of suspension of the work. Judgment in favor of the contractor against the city and the architect was AFFIRMED; judgment of indemnity in favor of the city and against the architect was also AFFIRMED: The city's liability resulted from a breach of contract between the city and the general contractor which in turn was occasioned by the negligence of the architect. "Where the injury is solely the result of the indemnitor's negligence, the indemnification provision will apply."[13]

Joint Negligence

In *Robertson v Swindell-Dressler Co*,[14] a worker employed by Ford Motor Company was injured in the process of rotating jobs with another worker and attempting to step across a moving conveyor. The worker slipped, became entrapped in the machinery, and suffered amputation of a leg. On a verdict of $931,000 in favor of the worker against the plant designer and the conveyor system designer, judgment for the worker against both defendants was AFFIRMED; judgment of indemnity in favor of the plant designer against the conveyor designer was also AFFIRMED. The negligence and breach of warranty action alleged that the designers utilized straight rather than tapered rollers; they utilized *pop-out* rollers; and they designed no means for workers to cross the assembly line. Both defendants participated in the design, but the contract between the two defendants provided that the subcontractor would indemnify and save the contractor and owner harmless from claims for injury arising under the subcontract, except claims resulting from the sole negligence or willful acts or omissions of the contractor. In Michigan,[15] an indemnity provision in a construction contract which seeks to protect the promisee from

---

[11] Henningson, Durham & Richardson, Inc v Swift Bros Constr Co, 739 F2d 1341 (8th Cir 1984).
[12] 62 Cal App 3d 526, 133 Cal Rptr 159 (1976).
[13] *Id* at 536, 133 Cal Rptr at 165.
[14] 82 Mich App 382, 267 NW2d 131 (1978).
[15] Mich Comp Laws Ann §691.991 (Mich Stat Ann §26.1146(1)).

liability for its sole negligence is void. HELD: this indemnity clause complied with the statute and was therefore enforceable.

Attorneys Fees

In *Campbell v Southern Roof Deck Applicators, Inc*,[16] church trustees sued a contractor and an architect when a new roof collapsed. The trustees alleged that the contractor had agreed to indemnify both the church and the architect against all claims and expenses, including attorneys fees, arising out of performance of the contract. HELD: the indemnification clause referred only to claims against the church or the architect by employees of the contractor. No reasonable construction of the clause permitted indemnification for attorneys fees incurred by the trustees in an action brought by them against the contractor.

Architect Indemnifies Owner

In *Jones v Boeing Co*,[17] a neighbor filed an action against the owner of a trailer park for storm water flooding. The owner brought the architect in as a third-party defendant under the *hold harmless* agreement of the contract and recovered. Since the construction was in accordance with drawings prepared by the architect, the architect was liable under the indemnity clause to the owner.

In *Fairbanks North Star Borough v Roen Design Associates*,[18] an indemnity clause in a contract between a borough and an architect provided that the architect would indemnify the borough against liability for injuries or damages to persons or property. A construction contractor employed to build roads in a subdivision pursuant to plans prepared by the architect filed suit against the architect (alleging design deficiencies and professional malpractice) and the borough (alleging breach of express and implied warranties). HELD: the indemnity clause limited the architect's obligation to indemnify claims for physical injury or damage to persons or tangible property; the contractor's claim against the borough was not such a claim; therefore, the indemnity clause did not apply. However, the borough was not precluded from maintaining a claim against the architect for common law indemnity.

Mechanics Lien

In *Graulich v Frederic H. Berlowe & Associates*,[19] the court held that an architect who employs mechanical and electrical engineers as consultants and

---

[16] 406 So 2d 910 (Ala 1981).
[17] 153 NW2d 897 (ND 1967).
[18] 727 P2d 758 (Alaska 1986), *opinion vacated in part on rehg*, 823 P2d 632 (Alaska 1991).
[19] 338 So 2d 1109 (Fla Dist Ct App 1976).

fails to pay their fees must indemnify the property owner against the mechanics lien claims from the consultants.

Contractor Indemnifies Engineer

It is possible for an architect to draft contract documents to obtain indemnity from the contractor against claims arising out of injuries caused by the acts of the contractor, even if the architect is also negligent. In *Shea v Bay State Gas Co*,[20] Camp Dresser & McKee Inc (CDM), an engineering firm, prepared the design for the construction of a sewer system on Turnpike Street. CDM also performed inspection services and prepared other contract documents. A few months after the completion of construction, a gas pipe ruptured and an explosion injured the plaintiffs (members of the public). They filed suit against the contractor, who filed a third-party complaint against the engineering firm, CDM, seeking contribution. CDM filed a motion for summary judgment in which, for purposes of argument, it admitted that it was partially at fault for the explosion.

One of the contract documents that CDM prepared was a certificate of insurance. This document, signed by an authorized insurance representative, certified that the contractor had certain liability insurance and went on to provide: "The contractor . . . shall at all times indemnify and save harmless the owner [and engineers] . . . on account of any and all claims, damages, losses . . . arising out of injuries . . . caused in whole or in part by the acts, omissions, or neglect of the contractor." Summary judgment awarding indemnity to defendant CDM was AFFIRMED. Although the language in the clause at issue was less broad and less precise than might have been desired, effect was to be given to the parties' intentions, and the language was to be construed to give it reasonable meaning.

In *Drzewinski v Atlantic Scaffold & Ladder Co*,[21] a worker was injured as a result of a fall from scaffolding; negligence was allocated 70 per cent to the scaffolding company, 20 per cent to the bank, and 10 per cent to the architect. The employer was held responsible for 20 per cent of the bank's share and the architect's share. HELD: contracts between the bank, the architect, the scaffolding company, and the injured worker's employer provided that the employer would indemnify the bank and the architect against claims arising from the work "to the fullest extent permitted by law." The bank and the architect were entitled to full contractual indemnity.

---

[20] 383 Mass 218, 418 NE2d 597 (1981).
[21] 70 NY2d 744, 515 NE2d 902, 521 NYS2d 216 (1987).

No Indemnity for Economic Damages

In *Friedman, Alschuler & Sincere v Arlington Structural Steel Co*,[22] the owner employed an architect to design and oversee the construction of an office and warehouse facility. Four years after completion, a portion of the roof collapsed because of poor workmanship. The owner sued the architect and the general contractor, and the architect settled the claim assuming responsibility for 25 per cent of the cost. The architect then demanded contribution and indemnification from the subcontractor. Judgment dismissing the claim for failure to state a cause of action was AFFIRMED. The architect claimed to be a third-party beneficiary of the indemnity agreement between the contractor and the subcontractor. However, indemnity was limited to property damage. Here, the architect sought indemnity for repair and reinforcement costs, which were economic damages, rather than property damage falling within the indemnity provision.

No Omission, No Indemnity

In *St Joseph Hospital v Corbetta Construction Co*,[23] a hospital was denied an operating license because wall paneling that had been approved by the architect failed to comply with a city code that required the paneling to have a flame-spread rating not to exceed 15. The paneling had a rating of 255, 17 times the maximum. Removal and replacement costs were $300,000. The architect claimed indemnity from the contractor under a contract provision that required the contractor to indemnify the hospital and the architect against all losses. HELD: the architect specified the paneling and the hospital approved it. Therefore, the contractor was not liable to indemnify the architect under the indemnity clause; the duty to indemnify was limited to losses arising out of acts and omissions by the contractor. Since the contractor furnished precisely what the architect and the owner had ordered, the contractor was not guilty of any *omission* and the indemnity clause did not apply.

Ambiguous Clause

In *Schiavone Construction Co v Nassau County*,[24] a prime contractor sued the county to recover costs of repair work on a sewer pipeline. The county sought indemnity from the design engineer. The indemnity clause provided:

> Further, the engineers agree that they will be responsible for and save the County harmless from all claims, damages, costs and expenses arising

---

[22] 140 Ill App 3d 556, 489 NE2d 308 (1985), *appeal denied* (June 3, 1986).
[23] 21 Ill App 3d 925, 316 NE2d 51 (1974).
[24] 717 F2d 747 (2d Cir 1983).

from the use of any patented articles in connection with the work and also arising from the performance of the work of the Engineers including damages to persons or property and the defense, settlement or satisfaction of such claims.[25]

HELD: this language was ambiguous and required parol evidence to explain its meaning.

§12.03 Indemnity against Own Negligence

Narrow Construction

Although most courts will give effect to an indemnity clause which explicitly requires the indemnitor to satisfy damages caused by the negligence of the indemnitee, the contract must be explicit. In *Crockett v Crothers*,[26] a homeowner filed an action against a contractor and an architect for property damage which occurred when the contractor hit a water line not shown on plans prepared by the engineer. The trial court found that the concurrent negligence of the contractor and the engineer caused the damage.

The engineer claimed indemnity from the contractor under a clause which provided that the contractor would indemnify the engineer from all claims arising out of the performance of the work. However, the clause did not specifically call for the contractor to indemnify the engineer from claims caused by its own negligence in the preparation of contract documents. Therefore, the court construed the clause against the engineer and denied indemnity.

In another case, a power company filed an action against its project engineer for damages arising out of the sudden collapse of a cooling water reservoir embankment. Summary judgment in favor of the engineer was AFFIRMED. The contract required the owner to indemnify the engineer against damages arising out of the engineer's own negligence. Here, the indemnity clause called for the engineer to provide liability insurance and went on to provide that the engineer would be liable to the owner only to the extent of the insurance coverages and amounts. The contract specified that the engineer would not be liable for any other damages and that the owner would indemnify and hold the engineer harmless from damages or liability caused by the negligence of the engineer. HELD: the indemnity clause satisfied Florida's strict test, which requires that an indemnity clause, if it is to protect the indemnitee against its own negligence, must be clear and explicit.[27]

---

[25] *Id* 750.
[26] 264 Md 222, 285 A2d 612 (1972).
[27] Florida Power & Light Co v Mid-Valley, Inc, 763 F2d 1316 (11th Cir 1985).

§12.03 INDEMNITY AGAINST OWN NEGLIGENCE   401

In *Facilities Development Co v Miletta*,[28] engineer was denied indemnity or contribution from project contractor and subcontractor. AFFIRMED. (1) An indemnity clause in the construction contract did not clearly connote an intent to indemnify engineer against the consequences of the engineer's own misconduct. (2) Neither contractor nor subcontractor had breached any duty independent of their obligations under their contracts.

In *Sargent v Johnson*,[29] an employee was injured after falling down an elevator shaft, and obtained a judgment against the subcontractor (55 per cent), the architect (15 per cent), and the general contractor (30 per cent). The architect filed an action against the general contractor and the subcontractor for indemnity, seeking to recover attorneys fees expended in its defense. HELD: a negligent indemnitee is not entitled to indemnity from a negligent indemnitor unless there is an express provision in the contract to allow the indemnitee to recover for liability occasioned by its own negligence. The court, quoting *Farmington Plumbing & Heating Co v Fisher Sand & Aggregate, Inc*,[30] stated: "Indemnity agreements are to be strictly construed when the indemnitee . . . seeks to be indemnified for his own negligence. There must be an express provision in the contract to indemnify the indemnitee for liability occasioned by his own negligence; such an obligation will not be found by implication."

In *Ohio River Pipeline Corp v Landrum*, the owners, architects, and contractor were all found liable for placing 18 feet of fill on a pipeline easement. The contractor sought indemnity from the architects but was DENIED. "[If] the contractor knows that his acts are wrongful, indemnity is denied because the contractor and owner are *in pari delicto*."[31]

In *St Joseph Hospital v Corbetta Construction Co*,[32] the city notified the hospital when the building was almost completed that its application for a license had been disapproved because the wall paneling used in the rooms and corridors did not comply with the Chicago fire code regarding *flame spread rating*. The rating was 17 times the maximum permitted. The hospital withheld final payment from the contractor and replaced the paneling at a cost of $300,000. Judgment was in favor of the hospital and against the architect, contractor, and manufacturer. The architect claimed indemnity against the contractor on the ground that the contract between the owner and the contractor included a *hold harmless* clause calling for the contractor to indemnify the architect against claims. The judgment refusing to enforce the indemnity clause was AFFIRMED. The architect was legally required to know, and in fact did

---

[28] 180 AD2d 97, 584 NYS2d 491 (1992).
[29] 601 F2d 964 (8th Cir 1979).
[30] 281 NW2d 838, 842 (Minn 1979).
[31] 580 SW2d 713, 721 (Ky Ct App 1979).
[32] 21 Ill App 3d 925, 316 NE2d 51 (1974).

know, that the Chicago code required paneling in such a building to have a flame spread rate not to exceed 15. Nevertheless, the architect specified the paneling without determining whether the paneling met the required standard. The contractor merely installed the paneling as ordered. Ordering indemnification would have resulted in the contractor indemnifying the architect for the architect's own carelessness.

Broad Construction

It has been held in an Oregon case that an engineer is entitled to recover the costs of defense from a contractor under an indemnity clause when the engineer successfully defends the action. To construe the clause to exclude indemnity for claims founded upon the alleged negligence of the indemnitee, as the lower court held, would make the clause meaningless.[33]

§12.04 Statute Annulling Indemnity Provision

A contractor or subcontractor in need of a job may be willing to accept harsh indemnity provisions as a part of the construction contract. A provision by which a contractor agrees to indemnify the owner against the results of the contractor's negligence is equitable and natural. Since the general contractor is at least theoretically in charge of the entire job, it is not surprising for the general contractor to also agree to indemnify the owner against liability arising from the negligent operations of subcontractors. The next step is to require the contractor to indemnify the owner when the owner's negligence contributes to the loss, or even when the loss is caused by the sole negligence of the owner.

The courts find it distasteful to require an innocent party to indemnify a guilty party; but a clearly drawn provision would seem to be enforceable. It is, in effect, a contract of insurance.

Some states have adopted statutes declaring such indemnity clauses unenforceable. The state of Delaware adopted one specifically aimed at architects and engineers. This was probably in reaction to a provision formerly contained in the American Institute of Architects (AIA) general conditions that required the contractor to indemnify the architect against liability.

The Delaware statute[34] provides that a covenant in connection with a construction contract

> purporting to indemnify or hold harmless architects, engineers, surveyors, owners or others, for damages arising from liability for bodily injury or

---

[33] St Paul Fire & Marine Ins Co v United States Natl Bank, 251 Or 377, 446 P2d 103 (1968).

[34] Del Code Ann tit 6, §2704(a).

death to persons or damage to property caused by or resulting or arising from or out of the negligence of such architect, engineer, surveyor, owner or others than the promisor or indemnitor . . . arising from or out of defects in maps, plans, designs, specifications prepared, acquired or used by such architect, engineer, surveyor, owner or others than the promisor or indemnitor . . . is against public policy and is void and unenforceable.

In *Wenke v Amoco Chemical Corp*,[35] an employee of a subcontractor was injured on the job. The indemnity clause in the subcontract provided that the subcontractor was to hold the general contractor and the owner harmless from liability for injury to or death of any person or damage to property arising out of the performance of the subcontract.

The injured worker brought an action against the general contractor and the owner, who sought indemnity under the clause. The court held that the indemnity clause was enforceable. The statute did not prevent the subcontractor from indemnifying the prime contractor, it was merely applicable to architects and others active in the preconstruction phrase to make sure that they stood behind their product.[36]

A Michigan statute[37] voids indemnity provisions in construction contracts that seek to protect the promisee from liability for the sole negligence of the promisee. In *Robertson v Swindell-Dressler Co*,[38] the indemnity provision required that the subcontractor indemnify and save harmless a contractor from claims for injury arising under the subcontract except claims resulting from the sole negligence or willful acts or omissions of the contractor. HELD: the indemnity clause was enforceable.

Florida Stat Ann §725.06 prevents an architect from seeking indemnity for its own active negligence. In *Cuhaci & Peterson Architects, Inc v Huber Construction Co*,[39] the employee of a subcontractor was killed during construction of a shopping center and the architect and the contractor were sued by the estate. The architect's insurance company paid for the architect's defense, after which the architect, on behalf of the insurance company, brought an action against the contractor seeking indemnity for the attorneys fees. The indemnity clause in the contract between the contractor and the owner provided that the contractor would indemnify *the owner and the architect* against claims, including

---

[35] 290 A2d 670 (Del Super Ct 1972).

[36] *See also* White v Morris Handler Co, 7 Ill App 3d 199, 287 NE2d 203 (1972) (similar indemnity clause enforceable; statute not applied retroactively; the subcontractor may be required to hold the contractor or architect harmless from the results of its own negligence).

[37] Mich Comp Laws Ann §691.991 (Mich Stat Ann §26.1146(1)).

[38] 82 Mich App 382, 267 NW2d 131 (1978) (indemnity action by a plant designer against the designer of a conveyor system in the plant where the original claimant was a worker who was injured when he became enmeshed in the machinery of the conveyor system).

[39] 516 So 2d 1096 (Fla Dist Ct App 1987), *review denied*, 525 So 2d 878 (Fla 1988).

attorneys fees, attributable to bodily injury and caused in whole or in part by a negligent act or omission of the contractor. HELD: the architect was entitled to indemnity, since it was not seeking indemnity for its own active negligence.

§12.05 No Contribution

The common law rule denied contribution between joint tortfeasors. Under the common law rule, a plaintiff could pick and choose between joint tortfeasors, obtain a judgment against one or all, and fully satisfy the judgment against any one. However, the one who satisfied the judgment was deemed to have no right of contribution from the other tortfeasors. This rule has been abandoned in many states,[40] and has become less important in those states which have adopted the doctrine of comparative negligence.[41]

The common law rule was enforced in *Salt River Valley Water Users Assn v Giglio*.[42] Homeowners filed an action against a water users association claiming compensation for flooding from breaches in an irrigation canal operated by the water users association. The water users association filed a cross-claim against the civil engineer who designed the housing project. The cross-claim was dismissed. The dismissal was AFFIRMED. Contribution among joint tortfeasors is not permitted in the absence of statute. Both the engineer and the water users association were primarily liable to the homeowners association. The engineers were, at most, joint tortfeasors, and the water users association had no right of contribution.

In *Wenatchee Wenoka Growers Assn v Krack Corp*,[43] plaintiff employed a designer to design additional capacity for refrigerated apple storage facilities. The new units leaked ammonia gas causing damage to stored apples. The plaintiff filed an action for damages against the designer and the manufacturer; the manufacturer claimed contribution from the designer, alleging failure to design an automatic leak detection system. Summary judgment dismissing the manufacturer's claim against the designer was AFFIRMED. There is no right of contribution between joint tortfeasors. The manufacturer urged that this rule should be abandoned because of adoption of comparative negligence by the state.[44] HELD: contribution is not necessarily inherent in a comparative negligence system. A comparative negligence system is concerned with allowing an injured party to recover from the tortfeasor despite the injured party's own negligence, while the rules respecting contribution between joint tortfeasors are

---

[40] *See* Coons v Washington Mirror Works, Inc, 477 F2d 864 (2d Cir 1973).

[41] *See* Associated Engrs, Inc v Job, 370 F2d 633 (8th Cir 1966), *cert denied*, 389 US 823 (1967).

[42] 113 Ariz 190, 549 P2d 162 (1976).

[43] 89 Wash 2d 847, 576 P2d 388 (1978).

[44] Wash Rev Code §4.22.010.

concerned with the equitable distribution of damages among tortfeasors. In the present uncertain state of the law, this was an inappropriate case to be used as a vehicle for discarding the long-standing common law rule.

No Joint Fault

In jurisdictions that permit contribution, the rule operates only when there exists a relationship between the tortious actions of wrongdoers so that one may be held legally responsible for damages caused or contributed to by the conduct of another. In *City of Utica v Holt*,[45] this relationship was missing. A fire fighter was injured at a fire when a ladder on a city fire truck collapsed. The fire fighter filed an action against the city, contending that the city negligently maintained the ladder. The city filed a third-party complaint against the architect who designed the building where the fire occurred, claiming that the negligence of the architect caused the fire. HELD: the city was not entitled to assert a right of contribution, since the defective condition of the ladder was not in any way the fault of the architect.

In *Bushnell v Sillitoe*,[46] plaintiff property owners sued their neighbors and the vendor/builder of the neighbors' property, claiming encroachment because of an improper boundary survey. The vendor/builder brought a cross-claim against the surveyor for negligence. Judgment against the surveyor was AFFIRMED. This judgment did not provide for contribution among joint tortfeasors, since the surveyor was not in privity with the plaintiff owners and therefore was not liable to them. The vendor/builder and the surveyor were not joint tortfeasors, but the surveyor was responsible to the vendor/builder for negligence in conducting the survey. Thus, although lack of privity may have constituted a defense to the surveyor in an action by the property owners, that same lack of privity became the linchpin of liability to the vendor/builder.

The rule of no contribution set the stage for the development of the doctrine of implied equitable indemnity. This protean doctrine furnishes a flexible means by which courts can allocate blame among defendants.[47]

§12.06 Implied Equitable Indemnity—Development

Claims of indemnity are a prominent feature of modern construction litigation. For example, an architect may be held liable to an injured worker for failure to prevent dangerous conduct by a contractor. Simple justice requires

---

[45] 88 Misc 2d 206, 387 NYS2d 377 (Sup Ct 1976). *See also* Facilities Dev Co v Miletta, 180 AD2d 97, 584 NYS2d 491 (1992); §12.03.

[46] 550 P2d 1284 (Utah 1976).

[47] *See* Alisal Sanitary Dist v Kennedy, 180 Cal App 2d 69, 4 Cal Rptr 379 (1960); Russell v Community Hosp Assn, 199 Kan 251, 428 P2d 783 (1967).

that if the architect is required to pay for a contractor's negligence, the contractor should reimburse the architect. In another instance, an owner is required to pay for an architect's mistakes and should likewise be able to recoup from the architect. Practitioners in comparative fault jurisdictions will be aware of the fact that, in many states, the old rule that denied indemnity to an active wrongdoer has given way to notions of comparative allocation of liability.

Early Development: Active/Passive

Alisal Sanitary District v Kennedy[48] illustrates the nature of the problem and contains a good explanation of the early development of the doctrine of implied indemnity.

In *Alisal*, a sanitary district employed engineers to design and supervise the construction of a sewage treatment and disposal installation, including an out-fall line discharging into the Salinas River. In December 1955 the water level in the river reached 47 feet above sea level, causing sewage to be discharged from manhole #12 into nearby celery fields. The farmers took judgment against the sanitary district totaling $17,800.

The sanitary district then filed an action against the engineers for indemnity. The court pointed out that since the cause of action arose before 1958, the common law rule against contribution between joint tortfeasors applied. The district and the engineers were joint tortfeasors, and therefore the question was whether the district was entitled to seek indemnity (rather than contribution) from the engineers.

At this stage, before the adoption of the doctrine of comparative negligence, implied indemnity shifted the entire loss from indemnitee to indemnitor:

> The right of indemnity rests upon a difference between the primary and secondary liability of two persons each of whom is made responsible by the law to an injured party. It is a right which inures to a person who, without active fault on his part, has been compelled, by reason of some legal obligation, to pay damages occasioned by the initial negligence of another, and for which he himself is only secondarily liable. The difference between the primary and secondary liability is not based on a difference in degrees of negligence or on any doctrine of comparative negligence.
>
> . . . It depends on a difference in the character or kind of the wrongs which cause the injury and in the nature of the legal obligation owed by each of the wrongdoers to the injured person. . . .
>
> [I]t is clear that the right of a person vicariously or secondarily liable for a tort to recover from one primarily liable has been universally recognized. But

---

[48] 180 Cal App 2d 69, 4 Cal Rptr 379 (1960).

the important point to be noted in all the cases is that secondary as distinguished from primary liability rests upon a fault that is imputed or constructive only, being based on some legal relation between the parties, or arising from some positive rule of common or statutory law or because of a failure to discover or correct a defect or remedy a dangerous condition caused by the act of the one primarily responsible.[49]

The court went on to hold that the engineers were obliged to perform their work in a skillful and expert manner, and such an obligation carried with it an implied agreement to indemnify and discharge foreseeable damages resulting to the plaintiff from the defendant's negligent performance.

Therefore, the trial court committed error by sustaining the engineer's demurrer to the district's action for indemnity. The district was liable to the farmers because of a rule of law which required them to prevent effluent from escaping from their facility to the damage of neighboring property owners. However, the active and primary negligence was that of the engineers, who allegedly designed a system which could have caused the damage. The only fault of the district was its failure to detect the negligence of the engineers.

Active/Passive Distinction

A condominium association sued an architect and an engineer for negligence and they filed third-party complaints against a construction lender. The complaints were DISMISSED. The architect and the engineer could have maintained an indemnity action only if they were passively or secondarily negligent and the construction lender was actively or primarily negligent. Here, any liability of the lender must have arisen from imputed or constructive fault. Since their negligence was necessarily active, the architect and the engineer were prohibited from asserting a cause of action for implied indemnity against the lender.[50]

In *John Grace & Co v State University Construction Fund*,[51] an engineer approved shop drawings for a hot water distribution system on a college campus. Serious leaks developed in the heat exchangers, the result of galvanic corrosion because of the use of dissimilar metals. The contractor made repairs and filed an action against the university for compensation. The university filed a third-party claim against the engineer, seeking indemnity. HELD: the

---

[49] *Id* at 75, 4 Cal Rptr at 383.

[50] Pyramid Condominium Assn v Morgan, 606 F Supp 592 (D Md 1985), *aff'd*, 823 F2d 548 (4th Cir 1987). *See also* Henningson, Durham & Richardson, Inc v Swift Bros Constr Co, 739 F2d 1341 (8th Cir 1984) (architect's active negligence, failing to properly evaluate shop drawings, barred common law recovery under an implied indemnity theory).

[51] 99 AD2d 860, 472 NYS2d 757, *aff'd*, 64 NY2d 709, 475 NE2d 105, 485 NYS2d 734 (1984).

engineer was liable. Expert testimony established that leaks were inevitable once dissimilar metals were approved for use.

In *Irondequoit Bay Pure Waters District v Nalews, Inc*,[52] an owner filed an action against a contractor for defective water pumps; the contractor brought a third-party claim for indemnity against the engineer. HELD: the contractor had the right to seek indemnity regardless of whether the engineer owed a duty of care to the contractor. The right of implied indemnity rests on a showing that a contractor might be held liable to an owner because of an engineer's negligence. Here, it was possible for the contractor to be held liable for supplying defective pumps, and the defects may have been caused by improper engineering design.

No Duty, No Indemnity

In *R.H. Macy & Co v Williams Tile & Terrazzo Co*,[53] tile work installed in a store building was defective. The owner filed an action against the contractor, who filed a third-party claim against the architect. Likewise, the supplier filed a third-party claim seeking indemnity from the architect. Summary judgment for the architect was AFFIRMED. Under Ga Code Ann §51-1-11 (Harrison 1981), a tort action for breach of a duty arising from contract is limited to parties in privity with the defendant, except where a right of action would exist independent of the contract. Since neither the supplier nor the contractor was in privity with the architect, the architect owed them no duty of care.

§12.07 —Sought from Architect or Engineer

Active/Passive

In *Russell v Community Hospital Assn*,[54] the plaintiff fell on outdoor steps leading from a hospital to a parking lot. The plaintiff filed an action against the hospital association, which filed a third-party complaint against the architect and contractor. The trial court sustained the third-party defendants' motion for dismissal. REVERSED. Although the hospital association was not entitled to seek contributions from its joint tortfeasors, here the third-party complaint alleged that the architect and the contractor were primarily or actively at fault, while the hospital association was secondarily or passively responsible. Thus, although not entitled to contribution, the hospital association had alleged a good cause of action for indemnity, and the motion for dismissal should have been denied.

---

[52] 123 Misc 2d 462, 472 NYS2d 842 (Sup Ct 1984).
[53] 585 F Supp 175 (ND Ga 1984).
[54] 199 Kan 251, 428 P2d 783 (1967).

Thus, the touchstone of the doctrine of implied indemnity was to distinguish *active, direct, actual, primary* fault from *passive, imputed, constructive, secondary* fault. In states that have adopted notions of comparative negligence, the active/passive feature is no longer required for application of the doctrine.

Indemnity Based on Implied Warranty

In *Coons v Washington Mirror Works, Inc*,[55] a wheel of a hoist slipped off the track causing a load to fall on the plaintiff. HELD: the owner was liable on a theory of *res ipsa loquitur*. The designer was guilty of negligence in the design of the hoist. The trial court apportioned damages at 50 per cent each. REVERSED. The owner was entitled to full indemnity from the designer. There was no credible evidence of negligence by the owner, but ample evidence of improper design. The designer impliedly warranted the hoist's fitness for its purpose. Therefore, the owner was entitled to full indemnity.

Numerous Factors

In *Coffey v Dormitory Authority*,[56] a student was injured in a collision with a clear glass panel in a dormitory. The student filed an action against the dormitory owner, who brought in the architect as a third-party defendant.

The plaintiff alleged that the owner failed to furnish adequate lighting, failed to warn of the danger by appropriate signs, and allowed the entrance way to be installed in a dangerous manner. The owner alleged that the architect created a defective plan, failed to follow proper architectural standards, and took no precautions to avoid injury to the plaintiff.

The trial court dismissed the third-party complaint on the ground that the owner and the architect were joint tortfeasors and there was no right of contribution between them. REVERSED. The third-party complaint set forth a potential case of passive negligence by the owner and active negligence by the architect. The right to indemnity depends upon numerous factors, such as the length of time between the completion of the project and the accident; whether the defects were readily noticeable; whether one party contracted to indemnify the other; and the active/passive classification. Here, the third-party complaint disclosed that the active/passive criterion might have been established by the owner, and therefore the complaint should not have been dismissed.

No Indemnity to Active Tortfeasor

In *Inman v Binghamton Housing Authority*,[57] the two-year-old plaintiff fell from a stoop. The complaint alleged that the stoop was defective because: it

---

[55] 477 F2d 864 (2d Cir 1973).
[56] 26 AD2d 1, 270 NYS2d 255 (1966).
[57] 3 NY2d 137, 143 NE2d 895, 164 NYS2d 699 (1957).

lacked protective railing; the arc made by the door when opened might force a person close to the edge; and the step did not extend the full length of the stoop.

The owner filed a third-party complaint against the architect for indemnity. The court held that the owner would not be entitled to indemnity from the architect, since the complaint alleged that the owner was actively negligent by maintaining premises with a known defective condition. This cast the owner in the role of an active tortfeasor, and an active tortfeasor cannot compel indemnity.

Contrast this holding with that of the previous case: to maintain a defective stoop is active negligence as a matter of law; to maintain a defective glass door is not.

Disproportionate Fault

Henneberger v Herman Schwabe, Inc[58] states a different rule. A property owner filed a third-party complaint for indemnity against an architect, alleging that the architect's improper supervision induced the property owner to wrongfully enter and damage adjoining property. The court held that the complaint stated a good cause of action. One who induces or originates a tort, or who wrongs in a disproportionately higher degree, should indemnify a joint tortfeasor.

No Indemnity Where Both Parties Negligent

In a typical trial court pattern, the architect and the contractor claimed indemnity from each other in *McCarthy v J.P. Cullen & Son Corp.*[59] The court finally held that each was negligent, and the negligence of each proximately caused the injury; therefore, neither was entitled to indemnity.

In *McCarthy*, the architect had designed, and the contractor had built, a high school. During construction, storm water damaged a neighboring residence. The architect claimed that only the contractor was responsible for drainage patterns during construction, and that the architect would be responsible for storm water after completion of the project. The court rejected this argument: "We cannot agree defendant architect can so easily wish off his duty to the public generally for harm resulting from negligence in furnishing plans and specifications which caused damage during the work itself."[60] Since both were negligent, neither was entitled to indemnity.

---

[58] 58 Misc 2d 986, 297 NYS2d 381 (Sup Ct 1968).
[59] 199 NW2d 362 (Iowa 1972).
[60] *Id* 370.

No Indemnity for Parties in pari delicto

In *Ohio River Pipeline Corp v Landrum*,[61] the owner, contractor, and architect suffered judgment against them for placing 18 feet of fill in a pipeline easement. The contractor sought indemnity from the architect. HELD: the contractor was not entitled to indemnity since it was fully aware that it was covering the gas pipeline easement with an excessive amount of fill. When a contractor knows that its acts are wrongful, indemnity is denied, based on the principle of *in pari delicto*.

Indemnity for Defective Design

In *Turner, Collie & Braden, Inc v Brookhollow, Inc*,[62] the general contractor agreed to construct an underground sewer system for the owner and hired an engineer to assist. The line was installed beneath the water table. Before final inspection, numerous leaks and cracks developed. The contractor attempted to repair the defects but eventually abandoned the project and demanded payment. The owner sued the engineer for indemnity against the claims of the contractor. The engineer counterclaimed against the owner for the unpaid engineering fees. HELD: the owner's liability to the general contractor arose solely because of the wrongful acts of the engineer hired by the owner. Therefore, the court concluded that the owner was entitled to indemnity from the engineer for the entire liability, including attorneys fees and interest. Failure of the general contractor to complete the project did not prevent entry of the judgment for indemnification since the contractor was not obligated to deliver the sewer line in operating condition if there were deficiencies in the plans and specifications.

Negligent Approval

In *Green Construction Co v Williams Form Engineering Corp*,[63] the court held that a supplier may have had an indemnity claim against the United States Army Corps of Engineers under the Federal Tort Claims Act.[64] The suit originated when a contractor brought an action against a supplier of defective grout. The supplier impleaded the Corps, alleging that the negligence of the supplier was only passive or vicarious while that of the Corps of Engineers was active and direct. The Corps had the duty to review, approve, and reject designs and materials proposed by the contractor, and to inspect the work in progress. The Corps redesigned an anchor rod so that it would be required to bear stress. When stress was applied to the grout, it cracked. Therefore, the Corps was

---

[61] 580 SW2d 713 (Ky Ct App 1979).
[62] 624 SW2d 203 (Tex Civ App 1981).
[63] 506 F Supp 173 (WD Mich 1980).
[64] 28 USC §§1346(b), 2671 *et seq.*

allegedly negligent in approving the use of the grout. HELD: the supplier stated a cause of action; summary judgment was inappropriate since material issues of fact remained in dispute.[65]

Active or Affirmative Negligence

In Nebraska, implied indemnity was not available to a tortfeasor whose conduct was "actively or affirmatively negligent." In *Danny's Construction Co v Havens Steel Co*,[66] a subcontractor filed an action against a prime contractor, alleging delay and interference with the performance of the subcontract. The prime contractor sought indemnity from the engineer. A motion to dismiss the third-party claim was granted. AFFIRMED. The prime contractor contended that it was not liable at all to the plaintiff, essentially claiming that the plaintiff was suing the wrong party. Such language states a defense, but not a recognizable claim for implied indemnity.

"Primary" Fault

In *Goulette v Babcock*,[67] parents of children who nearly drowned when they fell through the ice of a pond at a housing complex filed suit against the owner and manager, who sought indemnity from the design architect. Dismissal of the action was AFFIRMED. The owner and the manager knew that the pond was not fenced, and acquiesced in the design for approximately nine years before the accident. Therefore, the negligence of the architect in failing to provide a fence around the pond was no more *primary* than the negligence of the owner or manager, who left the pond unguarded for so many years.

Joint Fault

In *South Dakota Building Authority v Geiger-Berger Associates PC*,[68] an owner employed an architect to design and build an air-supported roof system for a physical education facility. The roof collapsed. The owner obtained a jury verdict of $325,261 for past damages and $46,920 for future damages. The architects sought indemnity from the engineer. HELD: since the architect was not free from fault, the architect was not entitled to indemnity from the engineer. The architect reviewed the engineer's plans and placed its own

---

[65] City of Elkhart v Middleton, 346 NE2d 274 (Ind Ct App 1976) (third-party claim of indemnity against an architect may be dismissed at the discretion of the trial court where the number of claims and counterclaims in issue creates confusion. Contractor versus city for balance of contract price; city versus estate of engineer for indemnity).

[66] 437 F Supp 91 (D Neb 1977).

[67] 153 Vt 650, 571 A2d 74 (1990).

[68] 414 NW2d 15 (SD 1987).

personal seal on them. The architect had the affirmative duty to review the plans and insure that they were architecturally sound.

No Duty

In *Board of Education v Fry, Inc*,[69] a school board filed an action against a contractor for damages resulting from a defective roof. The contractor filed a third-party proceeding against the architect, the manufacturer, and the roofing subcontractor for indemnity. HELD: the architect was not required to indemnify the contractor. Since the owner had adopted the specifications proposed by the architect, there were no circumstances under which the contractor's liability to the school board could have been predicated upon the negligence of the architect in designing the building.

Indemnity Enforced

In *Zontelli & Sons v City of Nashwauk*,[70] plans and specifications for a sewer construction project were discrepant from actual conditions: concrete was found under two streets in ten intersections rather than *one street under two intersections*. Specifications were prepared by an apprentice engineer who failed to take soil borings and failed to question the superintendent of streets as to subsurface conditions. The contractor sued the city and the engineer for breach of warranty, negligent preparation of plans and specifications, and as a third-party beneficiary of the contract between the city and the engineer. HELD: the contractor was entitled to rely on the owner's plans and specifications and had no independent duty to investigate. The engineer negligently and drastically underestimated the quantity of concrete and other materials to be removed, and misled bidders so as to increase the contract costs by almost $300,000. The city was entitled to indemnity from the engineer for all costs attributable to the engineer's breach of contract.

In an Oklahoma case,[71] a contractor sued a city for lost profits and delay damages; the city sought indemnity from the engineer. Judgment for the contractor against the city ($129,446), and judgment for the city against the engineer ($22,500) AFFIRMED. Shortly after starting work, the contractor encountered an unstable muddy area and asked the engineer how to proceed. The engineer issued a change order requiring the contractor to use crushed rock to stabilize the area. This solution failed. The contractor repeatedly requested advice, but was told by the engineer to "keep trying." The city then terminated the contractor's performance and obtained another contractor to finish the

---

[69] 22 Ohio App 3d 94, 489 NE2d 294 (1984).

[70] 373 NW2d 744 (Minn 1985).

[71] Miller v City of Broken Arrow Okla, 660 F2d 450 (10th Cir 1981), *cert denied*, 455 US 1020 (1982).

work. HELD: the $22,500 awarded to the city against the engineer did not adequately compensate the city. REMANDED for determination of all costs incurred by the city as a result of the engineer's persistent refusal to assist the contractor.

In *Lane v Geiger-Berger Associates*,[72] a dispute arose between the subcontractor and contractor as to the kind of fill material that could be used to bring the project to finish grade. In an action between the contractor and the subcontractor, the subcontractor sought indemnity from the engineer alleging that the increased cost that resulted from the use of clay material for fill was proximately caused by the negligence of the engineer. Judgment for the subcontractor on the indemnity claim was AFFIRMED.

In the foregoing cases, the weapon of indemnity was trained against the architect; in those that follow, the architect turned the weapon against another job site participant.

§12.08 —Sought by Architect or Engineer

Active/Passive

In *Owings v Rose*,[73] an architect obtained indemnity from a structural engineer when a large slab floor cracked because of improper design. The architect contributed $108,200 to settle the owner's damage claim and filed an indemnity action against the structural engineer. Judgment on a verdict for the architect was AFFIRMED. The Oregon court stated that indemnity will be granted only if a plaintiff can show: that it discharged a legal obligation to a third party; that the defendant was also liable to that third party; and that as between the two, the defendant ought to discharge the obligation. This means that the indemnitee must be passively or secondarily negligent, while the indemnitor must be actively or primarily at fault.

In *Crockett v Crothers*,[74] an engineer sought indemnity from a contractor when a homeowner was damaged by water escaping from a line broken by the contractor. The line was not shown on the plan prepared by the engineer. HELD: the negligence of the engineer was not secondary; therefore, it was not entitled to indemnity from the contractor.[75]

---

[72] 608 F2d 1148 (8th Cir 1979).
[73] 262 Or 247, 497 P2d 1183 (1972).
[74] 264 Md 222, 285 A2d 612 (1972).
[75] *See also* Board of Educ v Joseph J. Duffy Co, 97 Ill App 2d 158, 240 NE2d 5 (1968).

Architect Actively Neglient

In *Pyramid Condominium Assn v Morgan*,[76] an architect sought indemnity from a construction lender in a dispute surrounding defects in a condominium complex. There was no showing of any active or primary negligence by the construction lender. HELD: since the architect's negligence was active and primary and the lender's negligence, if any, was secondary and derivative, the architect had no right to indemnity from the construction lender.

In *Burns v DeWitt & Associates*,[77] an architect successfully defended against a bodily injury action brought by an employee of a roofing subcontractor who had fallen from a roof, then filed an action for indemnity against the project contractor, seeking to recover costs and attorneys fees incurred in defending the bodily injury action. The AIA "Standard Form of Agreement Between Owner and Contractor" included a provision that contractor would indemnify architect. Summary judgment in favor of architect was AFFIRMED.

Nonfeasance Is Active Negligence

An architect is not necessarily passively or secondarily liable merely because it is guilty of nonfeasance rather than misfeasance. Nonfeasance itself can be active negligence where the architect is aware of the danger but does nothing.

In *Fidelity & Casualty Co v J.A. Jones Construction Co*,[78] workers were killed in a cave-in. By special interrogatory the jury found that the contractor and architect were both negligent. The contractor failed to adequately shore the excavation, and the architect knew of the dangerous condition but failed to stop the work.

The architect sought indemnity from the contractor. The court stated that there was just as much reason to say the architect owed a duty to the contractor as the reverse. The architect knew the condition was unsafe but failed to correct the condition or stop the job. The general rule denies indemnity among parties whose only legal relationship is that of joint tortfeasor.

More versus Less Negligent

The Restatement of Restitution[79] denies indemnity where a party discovers a dangerous condition and is guilty of acquiescence. Equitable indemnity is awarded only where the liability of the indemnitee is secondary, imputed, or constructive, being based on some legal relationship between the parties or some positive rule of law, or a failure to discover or correct a defect. There is,

---

[76] 606 F Supp 592 (D Md 1985), *affd*, 823 F2d 548 (4th Cir 1987).
[77] 826 SW2d 884 (Mo Ct App 1992).
[78] 325 F2d 605 (8th Cir 1963).
[79] Restatement of Restitution §95 (1937).

however, no right to indemnity between concurrent or joint tortfeasors. This is true even though one may have been much more negligent than the other. The rule here was that the injured party may recover from all or any, in which case the latter was not entitled to indemnity from those who caused the injury.[80]

Indemnity to Actively Negligent Engineer

The protean nature of the doctrine of implied equitable indemnity is shown by *Cooper v Cordova Sand & Gravel Co.*[81] A residence was damaged by the settlement of uncontrolled fill. The homeowner filed an action against the vendor and construction lender. The lender in turn filed an action against the developer who had manufactured the lot, the home builder, and the foundation engineer. The court held that the developer, the home builder, and the engineer were all equally liable to indemnify the lender, but the engineer was in turn entitled to indemnity from the developer.

The developer had intentionally misrepresented to the engineer that the lot had been prepared according to soil engineering standards, with adequate compaction. The builder employed the engineer to inspect the foundations and paid it $25 to $30 to certify that the foundations were adequate. The certificate was delivered to the county building department with a copy to the lender. The engineer accepted assurances that the fill was properly compacted without making an independent investigation. Here, the engineer was actively negligent, but was nevertheless entitled to seek indemnity from the developer, which had intentionally misrepresented the condition of the ground.

Architect versus Supplier

In *Standhardt v Flintkote Co*,[82] an architect sought indemnity from a manufacturer of roofing materials. It appeared that the architect had used the material in a manner for which it was not intended; therefore, the manufacturer was not negligent, the architect was negligent, and there was no right to contribution or indemnity.

An architect sought indemnity or contribution from a material supplier in *Mulverhill v Mulverhill*.[83] The architect substituted materials procured from United Technology Corporation and Posi-Seal International for the materials specified in the contract documents for use in the chilled water system. Leaks developed, the University Construction Fund filed an action against the

---

[80] To the same effect, see Becker v Black & Veatch Consulting Engrs, 509 F2d 42 (8th Cir 1974) (gas escaping from broken pipeline exploded; inspecting engineer guilty of active negligence; no common law indemnity).

[81] 485 SW2d 261 (Tenn Ct App 1971).

[82] 84 NM 796, 508 P2d 1283 (1973).

[83] 78 AD2d 748, 432 NYS2d 654 (1980).

architect, and the architect filed a cross-complaint against the supplier for indemnity or contribution based on theories of warranty and negligence. HELD: the architect was entitled to contribution or indemnity from the material supplier if negligence or breach of warranty was proved.

Fault Destroys Right to Common Law Indemnity

Plaintiffs, employees of a steel fabricator, fell when a beam pulled away from a column. Plaintiffs sued the contractor, who brought third-party actions against the development company and the architect. The architect filed a claim against the other defendants and a subcontractor, seeking *common law indemnity*. HELD: the architect was not entitled to common law indemnity, since there was no theory of liability in the case under which the architect could have been held liable without some determination of fault on its behalf.[84]

Vouching In

An architect seeking indemnity from its consulting engineer for potential liability arising out of an arbitration claim by the owner against the architect should *vouch in* the consultant in the original arbitration proceeding, rather than bring separate arbitration proceedings against the consultant.[85]

Contribution Permitted

In *Salley v Charles R. Perry Construction, Inc*,[86] the architect and contractor selected and installed solar bronze glass for the windows of the building. The glass cracked and fell out during the winter because it could not withstand thermal stresses. The trial court dismissed the action against the contractor because the complaint did not specifically allege a breach of duty on its part. The architect then filed a cross-claim against the contractor for contribution. The Florida Supreme Court REVERSED the dismissal of the cross-claim by the trial court. There was a sufficient showing of common liability by the architect and contractor to establish a right of contribution. The architect and contractor were engaged in the common enterprise of designing and constructing a building. The architect negligently designed the windows, the contractor negligently altered the material specified for the design or negligently installed the glass, and the architect then negligently failed to inspect the substituted glass

---

[84] Tiffany v Christman Co, 93 Mich App 267, 287 NW2d 199 (1979).

[85] Perkins & Will Partnership v Syska & Hennessy, 41 NY2d 1045, 364 NE2d 832, 396 NYS2d 167 (1977) (the arbitration clause between the architect and the consultant provided: "any decision or determination resulting from arbitration between the architect and the owner which relates to the consultant's services shall be binding upon the consultant, provided that the consultant has been afforded the opportunity to participate in the arbitration").

[86] 403 So 2d 556 (Fla Dist Ct App 1981).

and its installation. The architect was entitled to seek contribution, since the architect's and the contractor's duties to the building owner were closely related.

Exclusive Remedy Defense

A special problem arises in cases where the injured party is a worker, and the proposed indemnitor is the employer. Here, the architect's indemnity depends upon the concurrent existence of two exceptions: (1) the exception to the common law rule against contribution among joint tortfeasors, that a passively, secondarily liable defendant may seek indemnity from an active, primarily liable defendant; and (2) an exception to the rule that the employer's sole responsibility to a worker is measured by the *exclusive remedy* of the workers' compensation statutes.[87]

The question of whether an employer should be required to indemnify a third party, such as an architect, in these circumstances is said to be "the most evenly balanced controversy in all of compensation law."[88] Why should the architect, a stranger to the compensation system, subsidize that system by assuming liabilities which it could normally shift to or share with the employer? On the other hand, why should the employer be deprived of the legislative compact under which it is responsible for a job site injury suffered by the employee, regardless of negligence, but liability is limited to the statutory amount? Either the employer will be deprived of the benefits of the legislative compact or the indemnitee will be forced to pay more than fairness would dictate.

The Illinois Supreme Court, in *Miller v DeWitt*,[89] resolved the dilemma in favor of indemnity. A proscenium truss in a gymnasium collapsed, injuring workers. The contractor had installed inadequate supports which were not designed by the architect. However, the architect did have the power to condemn defective work and the power to stop the job. The trial court held that the architect was not entitled to indemnity from the contractor, since the workers' compensation statute prohibited a direct or an indirect action against an employer by an employee. REVERSED: the architect was passively negligent in failing to prevent the contractor's active negligence, and therefore the architect was entitled to indemnity on a quasi-contractual theory.

Release Bars Indemnity

In *Carter v Deitz*,[90] passengers were injured in an automobile accident on a bridge and filed action against the bridge authority and the engineers who were

---

[87] Comment, *The Supervising Architect: His Liabilities and His Remedies When a Worker Is Injured*, 64 Nw UL Rev 535 (1969).

[88] 2 A. Larson, Workmen's Compensation §§76.10, 76.52 (1952).

[89] 37 Ill 2d 273, 226 NE2d 630 (1967).

[90] 505 So 2d 106 (La Ct App 1987).

responsible for evaluating the safety of the bridge. Engineers sought indemnity or contribution from the bridge authority. The bridge authority settled with the plaintiffs and was released from further liability. HELD: the engineers were not entitled to pursue a contribution claim against the defendant who had settled with the plaintiffs and obtained a release. The question of *active* versus *passive* negligence was irrelevant.

Required Relationship

In *Friedman, Alschuler & Sincere v Arlington Structural Steel Co*,[91] an architect sought implied indemnity from a subcontractor who erected structural steel in an office and warehouse facility. A portion of the roof collapsed and the architect settled with the owner by assuming 25 per cent of the cost of repair. The architect then sought implied indemnity from the subcontractor. HELD: a claim for implied indemnity requires a showing of a pre-tort legal relationship beyond mere involvement in a common undertaking. Here, the complaint showed no direct relationship between the architect and the subcontractor.

No Duty of Contractor to Engineer

In *Intamin, Inc v Figley-Wright Contractors, Inc*,[92] an engineer sought indemnity from a general contractor. The engineer's claim was DISMISSED on the ground that the engineer did not provide an explanation of how the contractor's improper performance could have impacted the engineer. Although there might have been a duty of care running from engineer to contractor, there was no such duty of care running from the contractor to the engineer. The contractor agreed to construct a roller coaster; the project suffered from defects both in design and construction. HELD: the contractor had no duty to indemnify the engineer.

Independent Wrongs—No Indemnity

In *Board of Education v Mars Associates*,[93] portions of exterior masonry on a school building collapsed and the city filed suit against the contractor and the architect. The contractor and subcontractor filed cross-claims against the architect for indemnity and contribution. HELD: the claim for indemnity should have been dismissed, since the city did not contend that the contractor was responsible for wrongs committed by the architect. If the contractor followed the architect's plans and specifications with reasonable care and skill, it was not responsible for defects in the architect's plans.

---

[91] 140 Ill App 3d 556, 489 NE2d 308 (1985), *appeal denied* (June 3, 1986).
[92] 608 F Supp 408 (ND Ill 1985).
[93] 133 AD2d 800, 520 NYS2d 181 (1987).

Common Wrong

In *New York Facilities Development Corp v Kallman & McKinnell, Russo & Sonder*,[94] an owner filed an action against an architect alleging negligent design and supervision of the roof and parking deck of a hospital structure. The architect brought a third-party action against the subcontractor who had contracted directly with the owner for the construction of the roof and parking deck. HELD: since the plaintiff's claim against the architect was based on the wrongdoing of the architect, not the wrongdoing of the subcontractor, the architect had no right of implied indemnity.

Contribution Statute—Economic Loss

In *Board of Education v Sargent, Webster, Crenshaw & Folley*,[95] it was held that a contribution statute, permitting two or more persons subject to liability for damages for the same injury to property to claim contribution, did not apply to a situation in which the potential liability of both the defendant contractor and the defendant architect arose out of the loss of a purely contractual benefit of the bargain or loss of value promised in the contracts, respectively, between the school board and the contractor on the one hand and the contractor and the architect on the other hand.

§12.09 Limitations

Statutes of Repose

In *Board of Education v Joseph J. Duffy Co*,[96] an owner filed an action against an architect who filed a third-party complaint against the contractor. The third-party complaint alleged that the damage complained of by the board of education was caused by the active and primary carelessness and negligence of the contractor, and that the default of the architect, if any, was passive or secondary only. The court dismissed the third-party complaint on the ground that the cause of action was barred by the five-year statute of limitations. The cause of action accrued when the negligent act occurred, and ignorance of the cause of action did not toll the running of the statutory period.

The Massachusetts legislature, when it enacted a statute of limitations which runs six years from the date of performance of design services, intended to bar both direct actions and actions for indemnity and contribution.[97]

---

[94] 121 AD2d 805, 504 NYS2d 557 (1986).

[95] 125 AD2d 27, 511 NYS2d 961, *affd*, 71 NY2d 21, 517 NE2d 1360, 523 NYS2d 475 (1987).

[96] 97 Ill App 2d 158, 240 NE2d 5 (1968).

[97] Montaup Elec Co v Ohio Brass Corp, 561 F Supp 740 (DRI 1983). *See also* United

In *Lamb v Wedgewood South Corp*,[98] a hotel guest died in a fall after being pushed through a window which allegedly lacked sufficient strength or protective devices. Suit was brought against the owner of the hotel and the franchisor. The franchisor in turn filed a cross-claim against the architect. The court of appeals held that the franchisor's claim for contribution against the architect was barred by a six-year statute of limitations. The statute provided that no action for contribution or indemnity for damages for wrongful death shall be brought against any person furnishing the design, planning, supervision of construction, or construction of such improvement to real property, more than six years after the service was performed.

Other Statutes

Many statutes of repose specifically bar indemnity actions. Absent special statutory treatment, a cause of action for indemnity does not commence until the liability has been imposed by judgment or until the judgment has been paid.

In such a case, *Owings v Rose*,[99] it was stated that the statute of limitations in an indemnity action is that applicable to an action upon an implied contract: six years.

In *Mulverhill v Mulverhill*,[100] the plaintiff filed an action against an architect and two material suppliers; the architect in turn filed an action for contribution or indemnity against the suppliers. The court held that the action by the plaintiffs against the suppliers was barred by the statute of limitations, but the indemnity action by the architect against the suppliers was not.

In *Grimmer v Harbor Towers*,[101] a mother brought suit against an apartment owner for injuries sustained by her 18-month-old daughter after she fell through a second-floor railing. The owner then filed a cross-claim against the builder/architect, seeking implied indemnity on a theory of contributory fault. The trial court granted the builder/architect's motion for summary judgment, concluding that the cross-complaint was barred by the California Code of Civil Procedure section[102] which established a 10-year period of limitations for actions to recover damages for an injury to property arising out of a latent deficiency in construction of an improvement to real property. **REVERSED.** Section 337.15 applies only to property damage and does not apply to actions for indemnity where the underlying action is based on damages for personal injuries.

States v Burton, 580 F Supp 660 (ED Mich 1984) (six-year statute of limitations applicable to torts by architects governs claims for indemnity).

[98] 55 NC App 686, 286 SE2d 876 (1982), *affd*, 308 NC 419, 302 SE2d 868 (1983).
[99] 262 Or 247, 497 P2d 1183 (1972).
[100] 78 AD2d 748, 432 NYS 654 (1980).
[101] 133 Cal App 3d 88, 183 Cal Rptr 634 (1982).
[102] Cal Civ Proc Code §337.15 (West 1982).

Insurance   13

§13.01 Generally
§13.02 Comprehensive Liability Coverage
        Comprehensive versus Professional Insurance
        Breach of Contract Enforced
        Professional Services Exclusion
        Insurance Extended by Contract
        Bad Faith
§13.03 Professional Services Exclusion
        Claim Covered
        Claim Excluded
        Duty to Defend Not Excluded
        Exclusion Applied
§13.04 Exotic Coverage
        Wrapup Policy
        Builders Risk
§13.05 Subsurface Exclusion
§13.06 Professional Liability Insurance
        Slander Claim Covered
        Duty to Notify Carrier
§13.07 Duty to Defend
        Late Presentation of Claim
        Multiple Claims
        Known Error or Omission
        Intentional Wrongdoing
§13.08 Claims Made during Policy Period
        Claim after Policy Expired
        Notice to Excess Carrier

	Tardy Notice
	Wrong Address
§13.09	—Application
	Claims Made
	Insurer's Duty of Disclosure
	Late Report
	Discovery versus Occurrence Policy
	Claim by Telephone
	Prior Knowledge of Claim
	Lack of Written Notice
	Late Report
§13.10	—Policy Arguments
	Freedom of Contract
§13.11	Settlement by Insured
§13.12	Responsibility of Carrier Where Insured Loses or Forgives Fee
§13.13	Deductible
§13.14	Waiver and Estoppel
§13.15	Excess Clause
	Excess Clause versus *Pro Rata* Clause
§13.16	Subrogation

§13.01 Generally

A crucial prerequisite to the lawyer's handling of a malpractice case is sensitivity to the insurance environment within which the dispute arose. If a defendant is insured, the claim must be recognized and reported to the insurance carrier. This is both to avoid a loss of coverage under the policy, and to engage the assistance of the carrier in the settlement of the claim.

However, the lineaments of malpractice are sometimes masked by other considerations. The architect may believe that its exercise of professional judgment did not sink to the level of malpractice, or the controversy may assume the guise of a fee conflict, a dispute with a building department, a claim for extra work by a contractor, or a claim of poor workmanship or delay against a contractor.

Many architects and engineers do not carry malpractice insurance because they deem it inordinately expensive. Indeed, loss experience has driven many carriers from the market, and the premiums exacted by those carriers remaining in the market have multiplied in recent years. The lawyer should not be satisfied with advice from the client that the client is "not insured against that." The lawyer should examine all policies, both professional responsibility and comprehensive liability, in effect at the time when the act occurred, when the damage occurred, when the architect obtained knowledge of the claim, and when the architect obtained notice of the claim. Policies with coverage intervening between the negligent act and the notice of claim should be examined.

Courts take an expansive view of policy language capable of interpretation in favor of coverage. The promise that the insurance carrier will defend the insured is an independent promise of great significance. The cost of defending an architect malpractice case is high. The carrier may be under a duty to defend even if the loss itself ultimately turns out to be beyond the coverage of the policy.

About 10 per cent of architect malpractice claims involve bodily injury, another 10 per cent are claims by the contractor against the architect, 15 or 20 per cent involve the selection of materials or equipment, 25 per cent are in connection with surveys, profiles, soil conditions, and elevations, and 20 to 25 per cent are for negligent preparation of plans and specifications. The balance are miscellaneous.[1]

A 1992 study by Schinerer Management Services, Inc. shows that 75 per cent of claims are for property damage and 25 per cent for bodily injury. Fifty-six per cent of claimants are owners, 7 per cent general contractors, and 5 per cent subcontractors.

One commentator has said that the insured frequently does not recognize that a claim has been made and will often settle a claim itself and thereafter present it to the insurance carrier.[2]

Some malpractice insurance carriers have close connections with professional architect and engineer associations, and offer extensive programs to identify and prevent malpractice.

§13.02 Comprehensive Liability Coverage

Architects may decide to drop their malpractice insurance because of premium rates, but this does not necessarily mean they are uninsured for all malpractice. If the architect drops its malpractice policy but retains the usual comprehensive liability coverage (frequently with a different carrier), the liability carrier may be under a duty to defend an action against the insured and sometimes must also pay the loss.

Comprehensive versus Professional Insurance

This is illustrated in *American Employers Insurance Co v Continental Casualty Co*,[3] an action between a professional liability carrier and a comprehensive liability carrier. Continental issued a malpractice policy. American Employers

---

[1] Truinfol, *Professional Liability of Architects & Engineers*, 499 Ins LJ 461 (1964).
[2] *Id.*
[3] 85 NM 346, 512 P2d 674 (1973).

issued a comprehensive liability policy. Both policies were issued to a single engineering firm, which became a defendant in a wrongful death suit following a gas explosion. Continental defended and settled the actions. American Employers refused to participate because its policy contained two exclusions: the policy did not apply to injury arising out of defects in maps, plans, or specifications; and the policy did not apply to the *products hazard*.

The injuries resulted from gas escaping from a city system, in connection with which the engineers had contracted to perform services.

The court held that the *maps, plans, or specifications* exclusion did not apply because the complaint contained general negligence allegations. It was also held that the *products hazard* exclusions did not apply because it was impossible to determine from the allegations of the complaint whether the actions arose out of completed operations or not. Therefore, Continental was entitled to reimbursement from American proportionate to the limits of the policies.

In a similar case, *Atlantic Mutual Insurance Co v Continental National American Insurance Co*,[4] where the liability arose when workers were injured in the collapse of a sewer trench, the court held that the comprehensive liability carrier was not required to contribute. Its policy excluded coverage for acts of professional malpractice. The plaintiffs alleged negligent supervision and the failure to detect and report safety code violations by the contractor. These were acts of professional malpractice, since they involved the exercise of mental or intellectual skills rather than physical or manual work.[5]

In *United States Fidelity & Guaranty Co v Continental Casualty Co*,[6] a person fell through an unprotected, unguarded, and inadequate skylight on a job site where an architect was in charge. The architect was covered by two insurance policies. One covered liability arising out of the performance of professional services. The other, a comprehensive general liability insurance policy, covered liability for damages for bodily injury or property damage caused by accidents. The comprehensive general liability policy included an endorsement excluding coverage for claims arising out of the rendering or failure to render of any professional services. Each carrier contended that the loss was covered by the policy issued by the other carrier. HELD: the court must look to the allegations of the underlying complaint to determine coverage. The professional liability policy covered, since it did not specifically exclude coverage for the architect's activities as a *design/build* architect.

---

[4] 123 NJ Super 241, 302 A2d 177 (1973).
[5] *See* 7A J. Appleman, Insurance Law and Practice §4504.3, at 7 (Supp 1972).
[6] 153 Ill App 3d 185, 505 NE2d 1072 (1987).

Breach of Contract Enforced

In *Bewley Furniture Co v Maryland Casualty Co*,[7] an owner filed an action against a project engineer alleging that faulty design caused the roof on its 78,000-square-foot steel building to leak. The engineer's insurance carrier asserted that the comprehensive liability policy covered only torts, not the engineer's breach of its contract to properly design the project. The court rejected that interpretation. The policy required the insurer to pay on behalf of the insured sums which the insured was legally obligated to pay because of *accident*. No provision of the policy limited its coverage to *ex delicto* conduct. The phrase *caused by accident* does not imply a limitation of coverage to damage caused by tortious conduct. The damage was unintended, the insured was *legally obligated*. Therefore, the loss was covered.

Professional Services Exclusion

In *Sheppard, Morgan & Schwaab, Inc v United States Fidelity & Guaranty Co*,[8] a worker was injured on a sewer construction project and brought an action against the engineer, alleging improper supervision. The exclusion in the engineer's comprehensive general liability policy withheld coverage for "bodily injury or property damage arising out of any professional services" including "supervisory, inspection or engineering services." REVERSED. The basis for determining whether a cause of action falls within the coverage of a policy is the language of the complaint, and here the allegations of the personal injury complaint fell squarely within the exclusion.

Insurance Extended by Contract

In *Sterns-Roger Corp v Hartford Accident & Indemnity Co*,[9] two employees of an engineering firm were injured on a construction project and filed suit against the owner. The owner claimed coverage under an engineering company's comprehensive liability policy. The carrier refused to defend the case, and the owner brought a declaratory relief action against the carrier.

The owner was not a named insured on the policy. However, the owner occupied the position of a named insured because the policy included a clause extending coverage to "an organization to which the named insured is obligated by virtue of a written contract to provide insurance." The contract between the engineering company and the owner included a provision that required the engineering company to provide insurance against personal injuries sustained in connection with the work. HELD: the owner was covered by the policy.

---

[7] 285 So 2d 216 (La 1973).
[8] 44 Ill App 3d 41, 358 NE2d 305 (1976).
[9] 117 Ariz 162, 571 P2d 659 (1977).

When there are two separate, concurrent proximate causes of a loss and only one of them is excluded from coverage, the loss is covered.[10]

Bad Faith

Insurance carriers guilty of bad faith may be liable for punitive damages. In *Trus Joist Corp v Safeco Insurance Co of America*,[11] a designer employed a non-engineering employee to design trusses which were approved by a licensed engineer, installed in an automobile showroom, and then collapsed because of a clear design defect. The designer admitted liability and informed the insurer that it felt responsible for the collapse and wanted a quick settlement, even going so far as to itemize the damages which did not exceed policy limits. The insurer refused to act. The designer then arranged a meeting directly with the claimant to attempt to effect settlement, but the insurer insisted that it would not permit the designer to enter into such negotiations unless the designer agreed to reduce the $250,000 coverage by $20,000. The insurer's representative then attended the meeting but refused to participate. The designer eventually filed suit against the insurer, which attempted to avoid liability based on exclusion (h): "(h) to contractual liability assumed by the insured, if the insured or his indemnitee is an architect, engineer or surveyor, for ... property damage arising out of the rendering of or the failure to render professional services by such an insured, or the indemnitee...."[12] HELD: exclusion (h) did not apply because it only affected liability assumed by contract; the designer was defending against a direct claim, not one assumed by contract. Under the Arizona bad faith test, an insurer is guilty of bad faith if it acts unreasonably toward the insured at a time when the insurer knows that its actions are unreasonable or if the actions are taken with a reckless disregard. The trial court's instructions to the jury on the issues were inadequate and, therefore, a new trial on the issue of punitive damages was ordered.

§13.03 Professional Services Exclusion

It is customary for most businesses, and many individuals (homeowners), to carry comprehensive liability insurance. The insurance industry recognizes that architects, because of their occupation, are susceptible to special risks of liability. Therefore, when a carrier issues a comprehensive liability policy to an

---

[10] Comstock Ins Co v Thomas A. Hanson & Assocs, 77 Md App 431, 550 A2d 731 (1988) (architect estimated cost at $12,500 and actual cost was $24,000; exclusion (f) provided that the policy did not apply to estimates of probable construction costs. The underestimate was the proximate result of design defects as well as errors in estimating).

[11] 153 Ariz 95, 735 P2d 125 (1986).

[12] *Id* at 98, 735 P2d at 128.

architect, an engineer, a surveyor, or a testing laboratory, it may exclude from the insurance afforded by the policy the risk of professional malpractice.

Sometimes the endorsement is specially written for the policy; most often it is a standard printed endorsement. An example reads:

EXCLUSION

(Engineers, Architects or Surveyors Professional Liability)

It is agreed that the insurance does not apply to bodily injury or property damage arising out of any professional services performed by or for the named insured, including

(1) the preparation or approval of maps, plans, opinions, reports, surveys, designs or specifications and
(2) supervisory, inspection or engineering services.

Claim Covered

In recent years many architectural and engineering firms have dropped professional liability coverage on the ground that the premiums are too expensive and the deductibles are too high. Yet, it may be contended that a claim against an architect falls within the coverage of a comprehensive liability policy, despite the exclusion. Such a claim was successful in *Shaw v Aetna Casualty & Surety Co.*[13] The architect was engaged by a housing authority. The plaintiff suffered a fractured skull in a hoisting accident. The complaint alleged that the architect was in charge of the erection of the structure and failed to operate and place the hoist in such a manner as to prevent injury to the plaintiff.

By its terms, the policy excluded injury arising out of defects in plans, designs, or specifications, and injury due to general supervision by the insured architect in connection with the operations of any contractor.

Relying on the exclusion, the carrier refused to defend the action. The court held that the measure of the carrier's obligation to defend was the allegations of the complaint. The language of the complaint was broad enough to indicate that the architect had *erected* the hoist, not just planned it or supervised it. Therefore, the carrier had a duty to defend.

Claim Excluded

American Employers Insurance Co v Continental Casualty Co[14] was a suit between two insurance carriers to determine apportionment of liability for a loss

---

[13] 407 F2d 813 (7th Cir 1969).
[14] 85 NM 346, 512 P2d 674 (1973).

that occurred when the insured engineering firm became a defendant in wrongful death suits resulting from gas explosions. The engineer was under contract with a city to perform services in connection with improvements and additions to the gas system. Continental Casualty Company, another insurer, had in force a professional liability policy covering the same period during which American had in force a comprehensive liability policy. The American policy excluded injuries arising out of defects in maps, plans, or specifications. HELD: the exclusion did not apply. If the allegations of the complaint brought the case within the coverage of the policy, or if the complaint failed to state facts with sufficient clarity so as to determine whether or not the exclusion applied, then there was a duty to defend.

In *Tampa Electric Co v Stone & Webster Engineering Corp*,[15] the engineer was sued by a plaintiff who alleged that the engineer prepared specifications and installed a generator negligently, causing fractures in an oil line, which in turn caused a fire. An endorsement to an engineer's liability policy excluded coverage for property damage caused by the insured's improper plans, design, or specifications. HELD: the claim of negligent design was excluded from coverage, but the claim of negligent installation was covered. Therefore, the carrier was obliged to defend the insured. The costs of the defense could not be prorated, as requested by the carrier. When some claims are covered by a policy and some are not, the insurer must defend against all claims. "The duty of Royal to defend both the covered and the non-covered claims gives rise to a correlative duty to pay the costs of defending both such claims."[16]

In *Wheeler v Aetna Casualty & Surety Co*,[17] the court rejected the plaintiff's reliance on the *Shaw* decision. An iron worker was injured when a plank on a scaffold collapsed. The worker filed suit against the architect, who tendered the defense to its comprehensive liability carrier. The carrier refused to defend, citing an endorsement that excluded coverage for professional services, including the preparation of plans, designs, or specifications, and supervisory, inspection, or engineering services.

Aetna pointed out that the architect also held a professional liability policy, issued by CNA, which provided:

> The company will pay on behalf of the insured all sums which the insured shall become legally obligated to pay as damages if legal liability arises out of the performance of professional services for others in the insured's capacity as an architect or an engineer and if such legal liability is caused by an error, omission or negligent act.

---

[15] 367 F Supp 27 (MD Fla 1973).
[16] *Id* 32.
[17] 57 Ill 2d 184, 311 NE2d 134 (1974).

Summary judgment for the architect REVERSED. While it is true that an insurance carrier can only refuse to defend when the complaint shows on its face that there is no coverage, here the complaint showed that the alleged liability of the architect arose out of the preparation of plans and specifications and supervisory and inspection services, all of which were specifically excluded.

Although the lower court construed the complaint to allege that the architect built the faulty scaffold, the court of appeal found that employees of contractors and subcontractors, not architects, built the scaffolding.

In *Womack v Traveler's Insurance Co*,[18] the insured architects advanced an ingenious argument that was rejected by the court. The decedent was killed and his wife seriously injured by an explosion which occurred when a gas line was ruptured by a bulldozer working on a road construction project. The insured engineering firm had prepared the plans and specifications for the project. Under the terms of the contract the engineers were required to prepare preliminary plans showing the locations of all utilities and transmit the plans to the utility companies for verification. The engineers noted the location of the gas pipeline, but failed to determine its depth and neglected to send the drawings to the gas company. The injured bystander alleged that this conduct was negligent.

The policy issued by Traveler's excluded coverage for professional malpractice claims against the insured, including the preparation of plans, surveys, and specifications. Summary judgment for defendant insurance carrier was AFFIRMED.

The engineer acknowledged that the policy did not insure against liability arising from professional malpractice, but asserted that the negligent act complained of was administrative rather than professional. The court rejected the argument; submission of the plans to the gas company was a step in the preparation of the contract documents; therefore, liability for that act was specifically excluded from the coverage of the policy.

Duty to Defend Not Excluded

In *United States v United States Fidelity & Guaranty Co*,[19] the court held that a professional services exclusion might protect the insurer from the duty to indemnify, but not from the duty to defend. The architecture and engineering firm had a comprehensive general liability insurance policy which obligated the insurer to defend any suit seeking damages on account of bodily injury or property damage.

> The Company will pay on behalf of the Insured all sums which the insured shall become obligated to pay as damages because of

---

[18] 251 So 2d 463 (La Ct App 1971).
[19] 601 F2d 1136 (10th Cir 1979).

(a) bodily injury or

(b) property damage to which this insurance applies, caused by an occurrence and the Company shall have the right and duty to defend any suit against the insured seeking damages on account of such bodily injury or property damage . . .

EXCLUSION (G307)

(Engineers, Architects and Surveyors Professional Liability)

It is agreed that the insurance does not apply to bodily injury or property damage arising out of any professional services performed by or for the Named Insured, including

(1) the preparation or approval of maps, plans, opinions, reports, surveys, designs or specifications and
(2) supervisory, inspection or engineering services.

HELD: even though the insurer was not liable under its policy to pay any judgment against the insured, the basic promise to defend was broad and apparently all-inclusive. The exclusions did not excuse the insurer from the promise to defend a suit of the *general nature and kind* of action covered by the policy. Under Oklahoma law, ambiguity is interpreted in favor of the insured. If an insurance company wants to protect itself from the duty to defend in this type of situation, it should clearly state that the exclusion applies to both the duty to indemnify and the duty to defend.[20]

Exclusion Applied

In *First Insurance Co v Continental Casualty Co*,[21] a comprehensive liability insurer filed a subrogation action against a professional liability insurer. The plaintiff's policy excluded coverage for any "hazard arising out of faulty design, maps, plans and specifications." The insured had contracted to provide engineering and supervisory services in the development of an industrial park. Although the original plan called for the use of excess soil to fill depressions, the insured decided on its own to spread excess soil in a swamp near the boundary line. The weight of the soil caused slippage, which bent several oil pipelines located on adjoining property. One line broke, spilling oil into a harbor. The owner of the pipeline filed an action against the engineer, and the comprehensive liability carrier defended.

---

[20] *See also* Sheppard, Morgan & Schwaab, Inc v United States Fidelity & Guar Co, 44 Ill App 3d 481, 358 NE2d 305 (1976).

[21] 466 F2d 807 (9th Cir 1972).

The court held that the fault of the engineering firm was its negligence in ignoring a soil report, furnished by its consulting soil engineer, which showed the unstable subsoil conditions which caused the loss. The intention of the exclusion was to remove from coverage claims arising from professional services. The loss was caused by negligence in the performance of professional services. While the original plan prepared by the insured may not have been negligent, the change was. Therefore, the exclusion in the comprehensive liability policy applied to the loss.

The professional liability carrier also relied on an exclusion, in this case, for claims arising out of "the making of, or absence of surveys of the subsurface condition or ground testing." The court found that this exclusion was inapplicable since the negligence was not in failing to make a survey, but in failing to follow one which had already been made. Therefore, the comprehensive liability carrier was entitled to full subrogation from the professional liability carrier.

§13.04 Exotic Coverage

Wrapup Policy

In *Hartford Accident & Indemnity Co v Case Foundation Co*,[22] the carrier issued a liability policy to the owner, the architect, the construction company, and the subcontractors participating in the construction of the John Hancock Building in Chicago. The policy excluded:

(1) liability for damages to property outside the boundary lines of the project, and
(2) liability for damages for injury to the project itself.

The policy was apparently to afford coverage against liability for bodily injury or damage to property owned by third parties if the damage occurred within the boundaries of the project. To avoid indemnity and liability wars between defendants, all job site participants were included as named insureds.

Faulty caissons were installed, which delayed the project. The owner brought an action against the architect and the contractor for $75 million, claimed as the loss of anticipated profits, loss of the return on its investment, and injury sustained when the owner found it necessary to liquidate other investments to carry the construction project.

The court held that financial interests in business ventures and anticipated profits are intangibles not included within the word *property* as that word was

---

[22] 10 Ill App 3d 115, 294 NE2d 7 (1973).

used in the policy. Moreover, the exclusion of liability for damages to the project itself would also exclude consequential economic damages. Therefore, the insurer had no duty to defend the owner's action against the defendants.

Builders Risk

An architect or engineer, although not a named insured, may be protected under a builder's risk insurance policy if so required by the contract documents.

In *Dyson & Co v Flood Engineers, Architects, Planners, Inc*[23] under a contract for construction of a sewage treatment plant, a contractor was required to maintain builder's risk insurance protecting its interests as well as the city's and the engineers' interests in the project. The contractor purchased a policy that named only the contractor and its subcontractors as insureds. During performance testing, a fire broke out and the contractor's insurer paid $231,956.66 for damages caused by the fire. The contractor and insurer then filed a complaint against the engineers alleging negligent design. The engineers moved for summary judgment on the ground that the contractor breached its obligation to insure the interests of the engineers. The contractor and insurer argued that the engineers could not be insured since they had no insurable interest in the property. HELD: the engineers had an insurable interest. In general, a builder's risk insurer may not recover from a co-insured for damages to property covered by the policy. Under the majority view, a builder's risk policy may include liability as well as property interests. "[W]here the potential risk to be insured under a builder's risk policy is one of liability for damages to the construction project, such risk will constitute an 'insurable interest.' "[24] Here, the insurable interest of the engineers was the fact that they might have become legally responsible for property loss caused by a fire resulting from their own negligence.

§13.05 Subsurface Exclusion

Some professional liability policies attempt to exclude liability for soils engineering activities. In *First Insurance Co v Continental Casualty Co*,[25] the exclusion covered claims arising out of "the making of, or absence of surveys of the subsurface condition or ground testing."

The insured engineer had employed a consulting soil engineer who gave an accurate report of unstable subsoil conditions in a swamp area. Nevertheless, the insured decided to dump excess dirt in the area, displacing unstable soil and breaking oil pipelines on adjoining property. HELD: the exclusion did not

---

[23] 523 So 2d 756 (Fla Dist Ct App 1988).
[24] *Id* 759.
[25] 466 F2d 807 (9th Cir 1972).

apply. The negligence of the insured was not in the failure to make a subsurface survey, but the failure to use one already provided by its consultant.

§13.06 Professional Liability Insurance

The comprehensive liability policy attempts to exclude liability for professional acts and omissions. Likewise, the professional liability policy (also known as malpractice insurance, errors and omissions insurance, or E & O) attempts to exclude all types of liability except those that arise from the professional practice.

Slander Claim Covered

In *First Insurance Co v Continental Casualty Co*,[26] the policy excluded coverage against claims for acts or omissions "not arising out of the customary and usual performance of professional services for others in the insured's capacity as architect and/or engineer."

The claimant was a superintendent who had been discharged by a contractor. The superintendent filed suit against the engineers, alleging that they made false accusations of incompetence, causing the superintendent to be fired. The engineers tendered the defense to the insurance carrier, which the carrier declined. The engineers then defended themselves, won, and filed suit against the carrier for the costs of defense.

The engineers had contracted to provide engineering services, including drawings, specifications, and supervision, for the construction of a county sewer project. Under the contract the engineers were required to pass judgment on the rate of work and the quality of workmanship and materials. They had power to order the contractor to discharge any employee whom they deemed to be careless or incompetent.

The court held that the policy afforded coverage for the acts alleged by the superintendent. The engineers were responsible for quality control throughout the project. They had the necessary responsibility to criticize and reject, and when they felt an employee was incompetent they were duty bound to have that employee removed from the job.

Duty to Notify Carrier

In another case, an architect was employed for five years by Financial Building Consultants, Inc (FBC), a design, build, and consult firm. The employment contract required FBC to provide liability insurance to protect the architect. A roof designed by FBC and the architect collapsed. Seven months

---

[26] 466 F2d 807 (9th Cir 1972).

later, the architect's employment with FBC was terminated. Without notifying the architect, FBC removed it as an insured under its errors and omissions policy. A year later, FBC filed suit against the architect, alleging negligent design of the building. Meanwhile, FBC had failed to notify the insurance carrier of the claim, and, as a result, insurance coverage for the claim was lost. The trial court dismissed FBC's complaint against the architect as unconscionable and was AFFIRMED. It was the employer's duty, as the principal insured, to have given proper notice to the insurance carrier in order to perfect coverage both for itself and its employees. The architect was entitled to rely on FBC to give such notice as would perfect coverage. To allow FBC, under the circumstances, to assert a claim against the architect, would have been unconscionable.[27]

§13.07 Duty to Defend

Liability insurance policies usually give the insurer the right, and the duty, to defend the insured against any claim covered by the policy. The promise to defend is an independent promise of substantial value. The insured may be entitled to a defense, even though it may ultimately be determined that the lawsuit was not caused by a loss within the coverage of the policy.

The presence or absence of the duty to defend is measured by the allegations of the complaint. Since insurance policies are written by the carrier, and since the insured usually has no influence on the phraseology employed, insurance policies have characteristics of a contract of adhesion: they are presented to a customer of unequal bargaining strength on a take-it-or-leave-it basis.

Insurance policies are notoriously hard to read and understand. Courts are inclined to place responsibility for ambiguous draftsmanship on the drafter employed by the insurance carrier, rather than on the insurance consumer.

These considerations produce opinions which surprisingly impose an obligation to defend, even though common experience would suggest that neither the carrier nor the insured intended the occurrence to be within the coverage of the policy.[28]

A lawyer examining a malpractice claim should not be satisfied with the conclusions of the insurance agent or the client as to the presence or absence of coverage.[29]

---

[27] Financial Bldg Consultants, Inc v Guillebau, Britt & Waldrop, 163 Ga App 607, 295 SE2d 355 (1982).

[28] *See* United States v United States Fidelity & Guar Co, 601 F2d 1136 (10th Cir 1979); Sheppard, Morgan & Schwaab, Inc v United States Fidelity & Guar Co, 44 Ill App 3d 481, 358 NE2d 305 (1976).

[29] A number of cases illustrate the extent of the duty to defend, for instance, Shaw v Aetna Casualty & Sur Co, 407 F2d 813 (7th Cir 1969), a case involving a job site injury.

Late Presentation of Claim

If a claim is made under a liability policy where potential coverage for the claim exists, the insurer may defend the insured under a reservation of rights while it seeks a declaratory judgment as to the issue of coverage. In *Graman v Continental Casualty Co*,[30] the court held that there was no potential coverage, thus, no obligation to provide a defense. The policy covered only *claims made* during the policy period and reported to the insurance company no later than 60 days after the expiration of the policy. The policy was in effect from February 1, 1961, to June 26, 1974. On December 18, 1967, the plaintiff architect contracted with the school district for construction of a new school building. On September 1, 1973, the school district notified the plaintiff of problems with the roof, and on October 11, 1977, the district filed suit against the architect, and it tendered the defense to the insurance carrier. HELD: there was no potential coverage since no claim was presented to the company before the expiration of the policy in 1974.

Multiple Claims

In *American Employers Insurance Co v Continental Casualty Co*,[31] a bystander was killed when a gas pipe was ruptured by a bulldozer. EXCLUSIONS: policy does not apply to injury arising out of defects in plans or specifications; does not apply to the products hazard. HELD: the pleading of uninsured grounds did not relieve the carrier of the duty to defend if the complaint also alleged grounds of liability which would have been within the coverage of the policy.

Known Error or Omission

In *Lapierre, Litchfield & Partners v Continental Casualty Co*,[32] an exclusion provided that the carrier would defend if: "no insured had any knowledge of such prior error, omission, or act at the effective date of the policy." The architect was aware of a school board's complaint; the carrier refused to defend an arbitration proceeding stemming from that complaint. HELD: the duty to defend existed: "Mere knowledge of the existence of a claimed defect does not amount to knowledge of a defect or omission when none is found to exist."[33] The architect successfully defended the claim in arbitration, and the arbitration award conclusively established that no defect existed.

EXCLUSION: policy does not apply to injury arising from defects in designs or specifications nor due to supervision by the insured.

[30] 87 Ill App 3d 896, 409 NE2d 387 (1980).
[31] 85 NM 346, 512 P2d 674 (1973).
[32] 32 AD2d 353, 302 NYS2d 370 (1969).
[33] *Id* at 355, 302 NYS2d at 372.

Intentional Wrongdoing

In *Grieb v Citizens Casualty*,[34] the policy excluded coverage for intentional torts. A taxpayer filed an action against the architect and others, alleging that they conspired to give a favored contractor an unfair advantage over other bidders on a public project. The architect successfully defended the action, then filed an action against the insurance carrier to recover the costs of defense. HELD: the complaint alleged dishonest, wrongful, and malicious acts; therefore, the insurance carrier had no duty to defend.

§13.08 Claims Made during Policy Period

Malpractice insurance may be written either on an *occurrence* or a *claims made* basis. The former covers occurrences during the policy period; the latter covers claims made during the policy period. The definition of *occurrence* or *claims made* may be ambiguous as it applies to a particular case. *Occurrence* could mean a negligent act, or damage, or the knowledge of damage. In the construction field, a negligent act may be far removed from damage, and even farther removed from discovery of damage. For example, an architect could design a building in 1960 which could begin to settle in 1970 and crack in 1980. The owner might not be aware of the damage until 1987.

The identification of the moment when a claim is made is not free from difficulty. From the point of view of an architect, the problem with claims made coverage is that the claim may be made years after the project was designed and built, and after the architect has left the employment of the insured or retired. Thus the architect must consider lifetime coverage and liability for premiums, even after retirement from active practice.

Illustrative language from a Lloyd's policy is found in *San Pedro Properties, Inc v Sayre & Toso, Inc*:[35]

> NOW THEREFORE this insurance, subject to the terms and conditions hereof, indemnifies the Assured against any claim or claims for breach of duty as Surveyors and/or Civil Engineers and/or Architects which may be made against them during the period stated in the said Schedule by reason of any negligent act, error or omission, whenever or wherever committed or alleged to have been committed, on the part of the Assured or any person who has been, is now, or may hereafter during the subsistence of this Insurance be employed by the Assured, in the conduct of any business conducted by or on behalf of the Assured in their capacity as Surveyors and/or Civil Engineers.

---

[34] 33 Wis 2d 552, 148 NW2d 103 (1967).
[35] 203 Cal App 2d 750, 21 Cal Rptr 844 (1962).

Claim after Policy Expired

In *San Pedro Properties*, the insurer issued a malpractice policy covering the period November 4, 1955, through November 4, 1956. In December of 1955, the insured contracted for architectural, engineering, and surveying work which was allegedly negligently performed during 1956 and 1957. On May 27, 1957, the client informed the engineer that it claimed damages for negligent work, and on May 28 the insured gave notice to the carrier. The client obtained a judgment against the engineer after the carrier refused to defend. HELD: even though the negligent act may have occurred during the policy period, if the claim was made after the end of the policy period, there was no coverage. The insurance carrier had the right to set the terms of the policy and was only liable for losses which fell within those terms. This was especially true since the policy included a provision permitting the assured to give written notice to the underwriters of occurrences during the policy period which the assured might apprehend could become the subject of a future claim. If such notice was given during the policy period, the policy covered the claim, even though it might not have actually been *made* until after the expiration of the policy period.

Notice to Excess Carrier

In *Charles T. Main, Inc v Fireman's Fund Insurance Co*,[36] an engineer gave notice of a claim to its primary insurer on September 20, 1984, but did not give notice of the claim to the excess insurer until March of 1987. HELD: under the terms of the policy, the engineer was required to give notice of the claim during the policy period or within 30 to 60 days after the expiration of the policy. The policy expired on May 1, 1985. Since notice was not given until March of 1987, it was untimely.

Tardy Notice

In *Stine v Continental Casualty Co*,[37] claims were made against an architect several years after the cancellation of an insurance policy. The policy was a hybrid combination of claims made and discovery policies. The policy covered only claims which occurred during the policy period (a feature of occurrence policies), and for which a claim was made during the policy period (a feature of claims made policies). HELD: the language of the policy was not ambiguous. Claims made after the expiration of the policy period were clearly excluded.

---

[36] 406 Mass 862, 551 NE2d 28 (1990).
[37] 419 Mich 89, 349 NW2d 127 (1984).

Wrong Address

In *Troy & Stalder Co v Continental Casualty Co*,[38] an architect was denied liability insurance coverage because a notice of claim was improperly addressed and was not delivered to the defendant. The policy insured the architect against liability caused by errors, omissions, or negligent acts "provided that claim therefore is first made against the insured during this policy period and reported in writing to the Company during this policy period or within 60 days after the expiration of this policy." In a dispute arising out of the construction of a pork-processing plant, the architect sued for fees, and the plant counterclaimed, alleging malpractice. The architects mailed written notice to a "Mr. Hunt" at the insurance broker's office in Washington, D.C. Mr. Hunt was indeed an agent of the defendant insurance company, who was in charge of the Omaha claims office, but had never lived or worked in Washington D.C. The district court found that the written notice was incorrectly addressed and was not delivered to the defendant. There was no presumption that the improperly addressed notice was received by the addressee. Therefore, the architect was not entitled to coverage.

§13.09 —Application

Claims Made

In *Carter v Deitz*,[39] an engineer's professional liability policy provided that claims arising from a single error, omission, or negligent act or out of related errors, omissions, or negligent acts would be treated as a single claim. Plaintiff was injured in a collision on a bridge designed by the engineer. HELD: the coverage should have been afforded by the policy in effect at the time the first claim was made.

Insurer's Duty of Disclosure

In 1964, Stein and Frank formed an architecture and engineering firm. Between 1964 and 1969, they obtained a *claims made* professional liability insurance policy with Continental Casualty Company. The claims made policy required that the insured party maintain continuous coverage in order to have protection against liability if a claim was not made in the same policy year in which the alleged negligent act occurred. Between 1969 and 1970, Stein and Frank discontinued their insurance policy. They were not specifically informed of the consequences of cancellation. When they renewed their policy in 1971,

---

[38] 206 Neb 28, 290 NW2d 809 (1980).
[39] 478 So 2d 996 (La Ct App 1985).

they were not advised that a *prior act* endorsement was available to reinstate the continuous coverage. In 1973, while their insurance was in effect, a suit was commenced against Stein and Frank alleging fraud and breach of duty in performing professional work during 1967 and 1968.

Continental refused to defend the suit, claiming that the failure to continue the insurance between 1969 and 1971 released it from responsibility. In an action brought by Stein and Frank against Continental seeking declaratory judgment, the court ruled that where a special relationship exists with an insured, an insurance agent has a duty to advise a client about adequacy of coverage. An insurance policy may be reformed by the court where, through the fault of the insurer, the policy does not cover the person or property intended. Reformation of the insurance policy to cover acts prior to 1971 was justified by the jury's special finding that the Continental agent's silence induced Stein and Frank to make a mistake.[40]

Late Report

In another case between the same architect and the same insurance company, Stein had obtained a professional liability policy that provided that any claims must be reported to the company during the policy period or within 60 days thereafter in order for coverage to be effective. Stein allowed the policy to lapse after 23 months. Two years later a claim was made against Stein alleging professional malpractice that had occurred before, during, and after the policy period. Stein notified Continental of the claim within seven days after it had been made, but Continental refused to defend on the ground that the notice was more than 60 days after the expiration of the policy. Summary judgment for Stein was AFFIRMED. Coverage is not invalidated where it is shown that it was not reasonably possible to give notice within the time specified, and the notice was given as soon as reasonably possible. Since Stein gave the notice only seven days after receiving notice of the claim, Continental was required to provide a defense.[41]

In *Graman v Continental Casualty Co*,[42] the policy was in effect from February 1, 1961, to June 26, 1974. In 1967, the insured architect entered into a contract for architectural services with a school district. The district notified the architect of roof problems in September of 1973. In October of 1977, the district filed suit against the architect, and the architect tendered the matter to the insurance carrier for defense. The policy was a claims made policy which required any claim to be made within the policy period and reported to the

---

[40] Stein, Hinkle, Dawe & Assocs v Continental Casualty Co, 110 Mich App 410, 313 NW2d 299 (1981).

[41] Stine v Continental Casualty Co, 112 Mich App 174, 315 NW2d 887 (1982).

[42] 87 Ill App 3d 896, 409 NE2d 387 (1980).

insurance company no later than 60 days after the expiration of the policy. HELD: under these facts, there was not sufficient potential coverage to impose the duty to defend on the insurance carrier.

In *VTN Consolidated, Inc v Northbrook Insurance Co*,[43] the insurer issued a malpractice policy covering claims made during the policy period. Two months after the expiration date of the policy, the plaintiff was named in a cross-complaint for damages that alleged the plaintiff had negligently performed engineering duties under a contract. The carrier refused to defend. The plaintiff filed an action for declaratory relief, claiming that the insurance policy was a hybrid mixture of a claims made policy and an occurrence policy and therefore ambiguous. The plaintiff contended that a retroactive exclusion clause (which excluded coverage for negligent acts that occurred prior to the inception date of the policy) rendered the policy ambiguous. HELD: the retroactive exclusion clause did not create an ambiguity. The case involved a claim based on wrongful conduct committed during the policy period; the retroactive exclusion clause was silent as to any mandatory date of presentation of the claim; and when the provisions were read together, the specific provision which set a definite date for presentation of the claim took precedence over the terms of the exclusion clause.

Discovery versus Occurrence Policy

In *Samuel N. Zarpas, Inc v Morrow*,[44] the policy afforded coverage for "any claim or claims for breach of duty as land surveyors which may be made against them during the period stated in the said schedule." The policy continued:

> If during the subsistence hereof the Assured shall become aware of any occurrence which may subsequently give rise to a claim against them by reason of any negligent act, error or omission, and shall during the subsistence hereof give written notice to the Underwriters of such occurrence, any claim which may subsequently be made against the Assured arising out of that negligent act, error or omission shall be deemed for the purposes of this Insurance to have been made during the subsistence hereof.

The insured performed engineering and surveying work for a NIKE Hercules missile site in New Jersey. The work was finished about March 24, 1961, which was a week before the expiration of the policy. Six months later, the contractor notified the engineer that its work was negligently performed (one of the buildings on the site was improperly located). Three days thereafter the engineer notified the insurance company.

---

[43] 92 Cal App 3d 888, 155 Cal Rptr 172 (1979).
[44] 215 F Supp 887 (DNJ 1963).

The court heard expert testimony that there are two types of errors and omissions policies: the *discovery* policy and the *occurrence* policy. In the former, the coverage is effective if the wrongful act is discovered and brought to the attention of the insurance company during the policy period, no matter when the act occurred. In the latter, coverage is effective if the wrongful act occurred during the period of the policy, regardless of the date of discovery.

The court concurred with the expert testimony that the policy was a discovery policy; therefore, the loss was not covered. Not noted by the court in its opinion is the irony of accepting expert testimony as to the meaning of an insurance policy. It would seem that an insurance policy should be given the meaning that would be understood by a reasonably prudent insured. However, here the court mutely acknowledged ambiguity by accepting expert testimony on a subject presumably within the expertise of judges: construction of language.

Claim by Telephone

In *Continental Casualty Co v Enco Associates*,[45] the owners informed a representative of the architect by telephone, during the policy period, that they claimed that the architect improperly designed parking ramps. The ramps had cracked. A year passed, and the owner gave a formal written claim to the architect. The telephone call was during the policy period; the written claim was delivered after the policy had expired. HELD: the coverage of the policy applied. A telephone call describing the damage to the architects' representative was a claim, even though not accompanied by formal written notice.

Prior Knowledge of Claim

The insurance carrier with a claims made policy will naturally attempt to avoid writing insurance for an architect who anticipates a claim, although it may not yet have been formally submitted. In *Lapierre, Litchfield & Partners v Continental Casualty Co*,[46] the carrier attempted to cover claims during the policy period provided that "no insured had any knowledge of such prior error, omission, or act at the effective date of the policy."

When the architect purchased the policy, it was aware that a school board had complained about the planning and construction of school buildings. During the policy period, the school district commenced arbitration proceedings against the architect, and the insurance carrier refused to defend. The architect successfully defended.

---

[45] 66 Mich App 46, 238 NW2d 198 (1975).
[46] 32 AD2d 353, 302 NYS2d 370 (1969).

The court turned the language of the policy against the carrier. "Mere knowledge of the existence of a claimed defect does not amount to knowledge of a defect or omission when none is found to exist."[47]

Since the architect won the arbitration, it was established that there was no defect. Therefore, the carrier was obliged to reimburse the costs of defense.

Lack of Written Notice

In *Lemmon, Freeth, Haines & Jones, Architects Ltd v Underwriters at Lloyd's*,[48] the carrier issued an *occurrence notice* policy. It afforded coverage for occurrences during the policy period; however, the architect was required to give notice of the occurrence before the expiration of the policy. Thus, two things were required for coverage: an occurrence within the policy period, plus notice to the carrier within the policy period.

At a grand opening of a building within the policy period, the architect and its insurance agent were present and observed water stains from leaks. The architect failed to give written notice to the agent before the expiration of the policy period. The agent had handled the architect's insurance for 10 years and in the past had received oral reports followed by written reports. HELD: the purpose of the written report was to facilitate investigation by the insurance agent, and since the agent already had oral notice, and where the custom had been to accept oral notification, the lack of a written report of the occurrence within the policy period did not bar coverage.

Late Report

In *Breaux v St Paul Fire & Marine Insurance Co*,[49] the policy applied to "all claims discovered during the policy period" but also provided that "the company shall not be liable . . . for any claims reported after the termination date of this policy." The occurrence (not described in the opinion) took place during or before the policy period but was not reported until after the expiration of the policy period. HELD: on summary judgment, the loss was not covered by the policy. Absent conflict with statute or public policy, an insurer may limit liability and impose reasonable conditions upon the obligations it assumes by contract. The policy here was a discovery policy, not an occurrence policy. Since there was no material fact in question, summary judgment was properly granted.

In *Livingston Parish School Board v Fireman's Fund American Insurance Co*,[50] the policy provided:

---

[47] *Id* at 355, 302 NYS2d at 372.
[48] 52 Haw 614, 484 P2d 141 (1971).
[49] 326 So 2d 891 (La Ct App 1976).
[50] 263 So 2d 356 (La Ct App 1972), *affd*, 282 So 2d 478 (La 1973).

(a) During the Policy Period

The insurance afforded by this policy applies to errors, omissions or negligent acts which occur within the United States of America, its territories or possessions, or Canada during this policy period if claim therefor is first made against the insured during this policy period.

(b) Prior to the Policy Period

The insurance afforded by this policy also applies to errors, omissions or negligent acts which occur within the United States of America, its territories or possessions, or Canada prior to the effective date of this policy if claim therefor is first made against the insured during this policy period and if all of the following requirements are present:

(1) the error, omission, or negligent act was also insured by this Company under the prior policy (as defined below) except that the period for making a claim against the insured under the prior policy (as defined below) has expired and

(2) no insured, at the effective date of the prior policy (as defined below), had any knowledge of a pending claim against any insured, had any knowledge of any claim which might be made against any insured or had any knowledge of any circumstance which may reasonably be expected to create a claim against any insured.

The policy terminated July 11, 1969, when the insured failed to send in the renewal premium despite the active efforts of the insurance broker. The trial court's summary judgment was AFFIRMED. The insurance policy clearly limited coverage to claims made during the policy period, even if the acts complained of occurred during the term of a prior policy. The engineer had adequate warning of the pending termination of the policy and did nothing about it.

§13.10 —Policy Arguments

In *Rotwein v General Accident Group*,[51] the professional liability policy covered:

> negligent acts, errors or omissions from services rendered during the policy period and then only if such cause an accident during the policy

---

[51] 103 NJ Super 406, 247 A2d 370 (1968).

period, and further provided claim, suit or other action arising therefrom is reported during the policy period and is commenced in the United States of America.

The policy was in effect from April 15, 1961, through April 15, 1964. The architect had performed services in April 1963 but was not aware that the services were defective until served with a negligence complaint in July 1966. The architect argued that the policy was ambiguous because some portions of the policy, for example the limits and conditions sections, did not reiterate the policy period. The court held that the policy language was clear.

The architect also argued that the policy inhibited freedom of contract, since the insured would be induced to renew coverage with the same carrier in order to get continuous protection. The court rejected that argument, noting that the architect had the option to either renew the policy with the same company or purchase a policy with retroactive coverage from another carrier.

Freedom of Contract

However, in a similar case,[52] the court came to an opposite conclusion. An engineer obtained a policy from the insurer in February 1965 which, with renewals, extended to April 1970. The plaintiff performed work on a sewer plant beginning in 1966. Several tanks began to settle. In March 1970, the engineer instructed the contractor to perform corrective work. In August 1971, the contractor filed an action against the engineer. The policy covered only occurrences during the policy period provided that claim was made during the policy period.

Plaintiff argued that the limitation was invalid, since the insured had to maintain continuous coverage with the same company in order to be protected. Moreover, an insured would be required to maintain coverage after retirement, or death, so as to protect against claims which might be made long after the actual loss. The policy provision, therefore, tended to destroy freedom of contract.

The court held that the stipulation that the claim must be made during the policy period was invalid. The provisions of the policy subjected the insured to hidden pitfalls. The policy did not meet reasonable expectations as to the protection which should be offered by an insurance policy.

The court distinguished *Rotwein* on the ground that in that case coverage was afforded if the insured had a prior policy issued by any company, not just the same company.

---

[52] Jones v Continental Casualty Co, 123 NJ Super 353, 303 A2d 91 (1973).

§13.11 Settlement by Insured

The obligation of the insurance carrier to defend the insured against claims arising under the policy is usually both a duty and a privilege. A material part of the consideration which an insured receives in return for the premium is the knowledge that, in the event of a claim, the insurance company will carry the costs of the defense. On the other hand, the insurance carrier has the right to insist on furnishing a defense, so as to be able to control both the cost of the defense and the ultimate loss or settlement. Since the carrier's money will pay the loss or the settlement, it is logical for the carrier to control the defense.

Some policy forms give the carrier the right, but not the duty, to defend the insured. With this type of policy, if the insured voluntarily assumes the cost of its own defense, then the insured cannot later seek reimbursement. This is true even if the policy imposes the duty, and not just the right, to defend.[53]

Many liability policies contain a provision that prohibits the insured from settling a claim without the consent of the carrier. If the insured does so, it cannot later claim reimbursement for the costs of the settlement.[54]

In *Scott v Potomac Insurance Co*,[55] the architect designed a hospital and specified copper tubing for a radiant heating system. Part way through construction, the government prohibited the use of copper tubing for this purpose because of the Korean War. The architect consulted with the mechanical engineer to determine whether the substitution of steel tubing would be acceptable. It was approved and used. The steel tubing was improperly installed, and even the portion that was not improperly installed corroded. The architect reported the claim, and the carrier refused to defend. The architect settled the claim and demanded reimbursement from the insurance carrier. The carrier refused. The architect filed suit against its carrier and prevailed. The carrier defended on the theory that the insured was not negligent (design was by the heating engineer), and that if there was any negligence, it did not occur during the policy period. As to the first defense, the court stated that the heating engineers were agents of the architect; therefore, the principal was liable for the malpractice of the agent. Furthermore, the negligent act occurred during the policy period.

§13.12 Responsibility of Carrier Where Insured Loses or Forgives Fee

If an owner has a malpractice claim against an architect, and it knows about it in time, the owner will not pay the architect's fee. Does this make the

---

[53] *See* Gribaldo, Jacobs, Jones & Assocs v Agrippina Versicherunges AG, 3 Cal 3d 434, 476 P2d 406, 91 Cal Rptr 6 (1970).
[54] *Id.*
[55] 217 Or 323, 341 P2d 1083 (1959).

insurance carrier responsible for the fee? The policy language, at least taken literally, seems to say *no*. Most policies require the insurance carrier to pay sums for which the insured shall become liable as damages. Taken literally, this language seems to say that the carrier is only responsible if the insured becomes liable to pay a sum to the claimant; where the claimant merely refuses to pay the architect's fee and makes no further claim, then the architect does not become liable to pay a sum to the claimant.

The insurance carrier can argue, with reason, that it did not undertake to guarantee that the architect's work would always satisfy the client, nor that the architect would always collect fees for its work, even though improperly done.

On the other hand, an insured can argue that a client's refusal to pay a fee comes under the legal classification of setoff and is in fact the offset of a malpractice claim against the fee which would otherwise be due and payable. When the architect purchased insurance, the architect expected to be reimbursed for all malpractice claims, not just claims which exceed the owner's fee liability to the architect.

In *Gribaldo, Jacobs, Jones & Associates v Agrippina Versicherunges AG*,[56] an engineer settled an owner's claim by forgiving fees. In a declaratory judgment action, the court held that the forgiveness of a debt as consideration for the settlement of a claim imposes an obligation on the insurance carrier to reimburse the insured for the debt forgiven along with the expenses incurred in the defense of the claim, provided the forgiveness was tendered with the express consent of the insurance carrier. Here, however, the engineer forgave the debt without the consent of the carrier, and the carrier was not liable.

A related question is whether the payment of a malpractice settlement by an insurance carrier precludes an architect from recovering its fee.

In *Jefferson Mills, Inc v Gregson*,[57] the architect's insurance carrier settled a malpractice claim with the owner and obtained a release. The document released any past, present, or future claims arising out of the architect's work on the building, but specifically did not bar any claim the architect might have chosen to assert against the owner. The architect filed suit against the owner for the balance of its fee; the owner alleged offsetting malpractice, and the architect introduced the release, claiming that the owner had been fully compensated for the malpractice and had released any further claim.

Without citation of authority, the court concluded that the release barred the owner from offensively asserting any further malpractice claim against the architect, but would not bar the owner from defensively asserting malpractice in an action for its fee. Nor was the defense affected by the Georgia statute which was enacted to change the common law rule barring an insured from asserting

---

[56] 3 Cal 3d 434, 476 P2d 406, 91 Cal Rptr 6 (1970).
[57] 124 Ga App 96, 183 SE2d 529 (1971).

a claim after the insurer has effected a settlement.[58] The court concluded that the legislature could not have intended to give one party the right to sue and simultaneously bar the other party from defending.

The result of this case is to make the loss of the architect's fee an uninsured loss rather than, as the previous case implied, an insured one.

The Georgia decision also seems to put the architect at the mercy of the carrier, in that the carrier was able to settle the claim on the most favorable basis to the carrier and disregard the interest of the insured in recovering its fee.

The terms of the release strongly implied that the owner should have anticipated a fee suit from the architect, but the release was ambiguous as to the effect of the amount paid by the insurance carrier in settlement. Was it intended to provide the owner with sufficient funds to pay the architect's fee? Or did the parties anticipate that the owner could retain both the settlement and the offset against the fee?

§13.13 Deductible

In *Gribaldo, Jacobs, Jones & Associates v Agrippina Versicherunges AG*,[59] a carrier issued a policy to indemnify "against claims . . . in excess of $2,500 deductible."

The insured, in a declaratory relief action, contended that the carrier had a duty to defend and should pay the costs of defense if the demand exceeded $2,500 no matter what the outcome. The position of the carrier was that the policy would cover costs of defense only when the amount actually paid out by the insured for settlement and defense costs exceeded $2,500.

Interpreting California law,[60] the court stated that the carrier would be under a duty to defend if the plaintiff demanded it, but was under no duty to reimburse costs of defense voluntarily assumed by the plaintiff.

California Civil Code §2778 provides that, upon an indemnity against claims, the indemnitee may recover only upon payment of the claim. Therefore, it would be necessary for the insured to actually pay a claim in excess of $2,500 to be entitled to recover from the carrier, and then the carrier would be responsible for the total of the claim plus the costs of defense, reduced by the $2,500 deductible.

The court pointed out that there had been considerable negotiation of the policy provisions, and that in this case the insured was of equal bargaining status with the carrier. Therefore, the policy was not interpreted against the carrier.

---

[58] Ga Code Ann §56-408.1 (1963).
[59] 3 Cal 3d 434, 476 P2d 406, 91 Cal Rptr 6 (1970).
[60] Cal Civ Code §2778(4) (West 1983).

In *Shaver v Continental Casualty Co*,[61] the insured had two policies: a professional liability policy issued by Continental Casualty Company, with a deductible of $7,000, and a general comprehensive liability policy issued by Employer's Liability Insurance Company, with no deductible.

A worker was killed on a construction project, and a wrongful death action was filed against the insured alleging defective design (which was covered only by the Continental policy) and improper supervision (which was covered by both policies). The action was settled for $24,500, with Employer's paying $10,500 and Continental paying $14,000. Continental then filed an action against the insured for reimbursement of the $7,000 deductible.

The policy provided:

Part III

2. Definitions

   a. Deductible

   The amount stated as the "Deductible" in item V of the definition shall first be subtracted from the amount required to satisfy a claim against the insured.

   b. Net loss

   The net loss is the amount required to satisfy a claim against the insured . . . less the amount of the deductible.

3. Computation of Amounts Payable by the Company (Per Claim)

   The company shall pay all of the net loss attributable to a claim solely for bodily injury, sickness, disease or death.

The court held that the carrier was not entitled to recover the amount of the deductible from the insured. The definitions were held to be unambiguous. The net loss was $24,500, less the $7,000 deductible, or $17,500. Since Continental actually paid only $14,000, it paid nothing in excess of the net loss.

§13.14 Waiver and Estoppel

Representations made by an insurance agent may constitute a waiver of a policy defense or estop the insurance carrier from asserting such a defense. In *Cornell, Howland, Hays & Merryfield, Inc v Continental Casualty Co*,[62] the carrier issued a policy covering errors and omissions which occurred prior to the

---

[61] 210 Kan 189, 499 P2d 513 (1972).
[62] 465 F2d 22 (9th Cir 1972).

effective date of the policy only if the insured had no knowledge of the errors, and if no other insurance was applicable.

An agent of the carrier solicited the architect for insurance business. The architect disclosed that it was possible that a contractor would make a claim on the ground that contract documents prepared by the architect lacked necessary information. The agent orally advised the architect's counsel that, if such a claim were made, there would be coverage. HELD: the insurer may have been willing to waive the policy provision in order to obtain the business, but even if there was no intentional waiver, the carrier would have been estopped from asserting the clause, since the agent represented there would be coverage in order to obtain the business.

The representation that there would be coverage may have been ambiguous. The agent may have been referring to coverage issued by another carrier for the prior period. However, the prior insurance did not cover the loss, since the prior coverage issued by the other carrier expired before the claim was made. Regardless of the ambiguity of the representation made by the agent, the insurer would have been estopped to assert the defense, since to do so would have been to falsify the representation of its agent.

§13.15 Excess Clause

The excess clause is inserted in a liability policy in recognition of the fact that the same loss may be covered by two different policies. In such an event, it is the objective of each carrier to impose the entire loss on the other. This may be attempted by the employment of an *excess clause* or *other insurance* clause, to the effect:

> This policy is in excess of all other valid and collectible insurance and shall not be called upon in contribution.

In *American Employers Insurance Co v Continental Casualty Co*,[63] the claim against the insured engineering firm was for wrongful death resulting from gas explosions. The professional liability policy was issued by Continental Casualty Company, and the insured also had a comprehensive liability policy issued by American Employers Insurance Company. Continental defended and settled the suits, and American refused to participate. Each policy contained an *other insurance-excess* clause. The court held that the clauses were mutually repugnant and should be disregarded. Since the limit of American's policy was $500,000 and the limit of the Continental policy was $200,000, Continental was entitled to recover from American 5/7ths of its outlay.

---

[63] 85 NM 346, 512 P2d 674 (1973).

Excess Clause versus *Pro Rata* Clause

In *Atlantic Mutual Insurance Co v Continental National American Insurance Co*,[64] the comprehensive liability policy contained a *pro rata* clause, and the professional liability policy contained an excess clause. The court stated *(dictum)* that if both policies covered the loss, the excess clause would govern and the policy containing the *pro rata* clause would pay the entire loss to the monetary limit of its coverage.

In *Shaver v Continental Casualty Co*,[65] a comprehensive liability carrier and a professional liability carrier joined in settlement of an action against the insured for $24,5000, $14,000 of which was paid by the professional liability carrier. The professional liability policy contained a deductible clause of $7,000, and the carrier claimed reimbursement of the $7,000 deductible from the insured. The carrier relied on the excess clause, but the court held that under the circumstances the excess clause was irrelevant. Even if its coverage were excess only, it had unequivocally obligated itself to pay all of the net loss attributable to a claim; and *net loss* was defined as the amount necessary to satisfy a claim against the insured, less the amount of the deductible. Since $24,500 was necessary to satisfy the claim, the net loss was $17,500, and Continental only paid $14,000.

§13.16 Subrogation

When an insurance carrier pays a loss on behalf of its insured, it acquires the power to enforce the rights of its insured against a third party that caused the loss. In *Fireman's Fund American Insurance Co v Phillips, Carter Reister & Associates*,[66] the defendant architectural firm prepared plans and specifications for excavation, sheet piling, and compaction. During the construction process, damage was caused to surrounding buildings and roads. The contractor, acting under its interpretation of its contract with the owner, made necessary repairs, and the contract's insurance carrier reimbursed the contract. Thereafter, the insurance carrier claimed rights of subrogation against the defendant architect.

The court of appeal REVERSED the trial court, holding that the right of subrogation did not exist here, even though the damage was caused by the negligence of the architect. The insurance carrier was attempting to step into the contractor's shoes to enforce the contractor's right against the architect. However, the contractor had no such right, because the contract between the owner and the contract or did not require the contractor to make the repairs.

---

[64] 123 NJ Super 241, 302 A2d 177 (1973).
[65] 210 Kan 189, 499 P2d 513 (1972).
[66] 89 NM 7, 546 P2d 72 *cert denied*, 89 NM 5, 546 P2d 70 (1976).

Therefore, the contractor was, without obligation, satisfying the debt of the architect. Subrogation is not available to one who intervenes to satisfy the obligation of another unless that intervention is in turn supported by legal obligation.

Arbitration   14

§14.01　Generally
　　　　Architect as Arbitrator
§14.02　Right to Compel Arbitration
　　　　Architect versus State
　　　　Limited Scope
　　　　Stay of Litigation Pending Arbitration
　　　　Broad Scope
　　　　Arbitration Agreements Unenforceable
　　　　Arbitration Agreements Enforceable
　　　　Third-Party Beneficiary
§14.03　Waiver
　　　　AAA Rule
　　　　Pursuit of Discovery
§14.04　Conditions Precedent to Arbitration
§14.05　Multiple Parties
　　　　Collateral Estoppel
　　　　Consolidation
　　　　Anti-Consolidation Clause
§14.06　—Joinder and Consolidation
　　　　Joint Arbitration Ordered
　　　　Collateral Estoppel
§14.07　—Vouching In
§14.08　Selection of Arbitrator
§14.09　Conduct of Arbitration Hearing
§14.10　Considerations in Selecting Arbitration
　　　　Time
　　　　Appeal
　　　　Expense

American Arbitration Association Fees
Postponement Fees
Additional Hearing Fee
Hearing-Room Rental
Refund Schedule
Other Cost Factors
Privacy
Discovery
Legal Error
Evidence Rules
Statute of Limitations
Provisional Remedies
Multiple Parties
Expertise
Lawyers
Pretrial and Settlement
Other Factors
§14.11 Mediation
§14.12 Enforcement of Award
§14.13 Vacation of Award

§14.01 Generally

It is possible that the majority of claims of malpractice by owners against architects are decided by arbitrators rather than judges. Arbitration has long been a favored method of settling these disputes. To determine whether an architect has been guilty of malpractice requires expert knowledge. In court, this knowledge is imparted by expert testimony. In arbitration, the expert knowledge may be a part of the equipment brought to the proceedings by the arbitrators themselves.

The standard form of agreement between owner and architect provides for arbitration in accordance with the construction industry arbitration rules of the American Arbitration Association (AAA).[1] The presence of this clause presumably represents the considered opinion of the American Institute of Architects (AIA) that the interests of the public and the profession of architecture are better served by arbitration of disputes between architects and owners than by litigation.

In some ways arbitration proceedings are very similar to judicial proceedings. In other ways, they are very different. The differences, in part, are designed. Arbitrators reject what they consider to be the undesirable features of legal proceedings.

---

[1] AIA Document B141.

Other differences are imposed by the very nature of arbitration. Judges, not arbitrators, command the sheriff. And since arbitrators are not public officials, they are not supported by public funds. Either they must act without compensation, or the compensation must be supplied by the parties.

Architect as Arbitrator

Some contracts provide that an architect or engineer will decide controversies that may arise between the owner and prime contractor. Such clauses are not necessarily arbitration clauses. A provision that the engineer will make a final and conclusive decision as to all questions relative to the execution of the work does not subject a dispute between the owner and the contractor to arbitration under the Uniform Arbitration Act.[2] The provisions in question call for the engineer to make decisions as the work progresses, without formal hearings. An arbitrator should not be the one to supervise the performance out of which the dispute arises.[3]

Many construction contracts provide that the architect, in the first instance, will be the judge of performance of the owner and the contractor. Under one such provision, an architect decided that a contractor was entitled to be paid $247,500 from the owner of two shopping centers. The contractor attempted to enforce the architect's decision as a final award under Connecticut General Statutes Ann §52-417. HELD: the decision of the architect was not an arbitration award because the parties failed to clearly indicate an intention that the architect's decision would be the exclusive method for settling disputes. Here, the trial court found that the architect's decision was a condition precedent to the contractor's right of payment, rather than the final adjudication of that right, which remained within the jurisdiction of the courts.[4]

§14.02 Right to Compel Arbitration

The American courts generally follow the rule that a contract to submit a dispute to arbitration is enforceable. Any supposed conflict of public policy between the right to have disputes decided by judges and freedom of contract has been resolved in favor of freedom of contract. Congress and most of the states have enacted statutes which define procedures to be followed by arbitrators, methods to compel arbitration, and devices for the enforcement of arbitration awards.

---

[2] Ill Rev Stat ch 10, §101 *et seq* (1981).

[3] Allied Contracting Co v Bennett, 110 Ill App 3d 310, 442 NE2d 326 (1982).

[4] Harry Skolnick & Sons v Heyman, 7 Conn App 175, 508 A2d 64, *cert denied*, 200 Conn 803, 510 A2d 191 (1986).

Architect versus State

An arbitration clause may be enforced against the state, as well as against an architect. In *Pytko v State*,[5] an architect entered into an agreement with the state for the design of a medical-dental building for a university. The agreement included an arbitration clause. The contract was executed on behalf of the state by the president of the university, under the authority of Connecticut law giving the university trustees the power to expend funds for the construction of buildings.

The contractor filed an action against the state, and the state in turn brought a third-party action against the architect.

The architect filed a motion to stay the third-party action pending arbitration, which the state opposed on the ground that the trustees did not have the specific power to enter into an arbitration agreement.

The court held that the general Connecticut policy favors arbitration, and there was no statute prohibiting the trustees from agreeing to arbitrate a dispute. Therefore, the trustees had an implied power to enter into arbitration agreements, which were enforceable.

However, *State Department of Human Resources v Williams*[6] implies that the policy of the state of Oregon is not so hospitable to arbitration. The agreement between owner and architect provided that disputes would be submitted to arbitration but also provided that upon full performance, the contract would terminate.

After the project was finished, the owner paid the architect's fee, thereafter discovered water leaks, and brought an action for negligence.

The architect contended that the lawsuit should have been abated pending arbitration under Oregon statutes.[7] The trial court ordered abatement. REVERSED. Since the dispute arose after the contract had been fully performed, the arbitration agreement was terminated along with the rest of the contract. Therefore, the architect had no right to compel arbitration. "The arbitration of a dispute . . . cannot be equated with a litigant's remedy at law for a wrong."[8]

A provision that an agreement *terminates* is always ambiguous, and its inclusion in a contract is usually ill advised. The draftsman probably intends to say that the obligation of the parties to perform terminates, or that the employment of the architect terminates. It can seldom be intended that the agreement would terminate in the sense that it be canceled, rescinded, or entirely destroyed. If an agreement does not exist, then its breach would not be

---

[5] 28 Conn Supp 173, 255 A2d 640 (1969).
[6] 12 Or App 133, 505 P2d 936 (1973).
[7] Or Rev Stat §33.240 (1976).
[8] 12 Or App at 137, 505 P2d at 938.

actionable. So the court, in interpreting the "agreement terminates" language, must pick and choose between those provisions which will still be given effect and those which will not. In *Williams*, the court selected the arbitration clause as a part of the agreement which was not given effect.

Limited Scope

In *General State Authority v Kline*,[9] the arbitration clause provided:

> All questions or disputes concerning questions of fact arising between the parties respecting any matter pertaining to this agreement shall be decided by the Executive Director of the Authority subject to written appeal by the Architect within 30 days to the Board of Authority, whose decision and award shall be final, binding and conclusive upon all parties hereto without exception or appeal; and all right or rights or any action at law or in equity under and by virtue of this Agreement and all matters connected with it and relative thereto are hereby expressly waived. Reference to questions under this arbitration provision must be presented prior to the final payment.

The General State Authority filed a complaint, naming the architect and alleging negligent design and supervision, causing leaks to school building roofs. The architect objected on the ground that the contract required arbitration. HELD: the arbitration clause dealt only with questions of fact arising under the contract and could not have reasonably been interpreted as plaintiff's exclusive remedy so as to bar an action for a defective design.

Stay of Litigation Pending Arbitration

In *American Home Assurance v Vecco Concrete Construction Co*,[10] a subcontractor filed an action against a general contractor, an architect, and a sanitary district on a waste water treatment plant project. The prime contractor demanded arbitration under an arbitration clause contained in the subcontract. HELD: the court should have stayed the entire action pending arbitration. This was true even though the arbitrator's findings were not binding on the court in the litigation between the subcontractor and the architect and the sanitation district. Since an arbitration may decide issues that must also be addressed in litigation, a court should await an arbitrator's decision to avoid inconsistency between the judgment and the award.

---

[9] 29 Pa Commw 232, 370 A2d 402 (1977).
[10] 629 F2d 961 (4th Cir 1980).

Broad Scope

In *Morton Z. Levine & Associates Chartered v Van Deree*,[11] the arbitration clause provided:

> 11.1. All claims, disputes and other matters in question arising out of, or relating to, this agreement or the breach thereof shall be decided by arbitration in accordance with the construction industry arbitration rules of the American Arbitration Association then obtaining unless the parties mutually agree otherwise. This agreement to arbitrate shall be specifically enforceable under the prevailing arbitration law.

The owner sued architects in three counts: breach of contract; misrepresentation and breach of fiduciary duty; and negligence. The trial court ordered the plaintiffs to submit the first count to arbitration, but allowed the suit to continue as to the second and third counts. REVERSED. The purpose of arbitration is to prevent litigation. Therefore, the entire controversy should have been submitted to arbitration.

In *Mercury Construction Corp v Moses H. Cone Memorial Hospital*,[12] general contractor Mercury's contract with Cone Hospital contained a comprehensive arbitration clause which provided that all claims against the owner had to be submitted to the architect before arbitration. During construction, the architect was appointed as the hospital's representative. The hospital refused to honor Mercury's claim for additional payment due to "delays and impact inefficiencies" which were submitted after the project was substantially completed. Before Mercury commenced its federal suit to compel arbitration, the hospital sought an injunction in state court barring Mercury from initiating the arbitration proceedings. Cone Hospital also brought an action against the architect in state court, claiming indemnity from the architect for any judgment in favor of Mercury. The district court stayed Mercury's arbitration proceedings pending resolution of the state court action. REVERSED. The fact that the hospital's action against the architect was "inextricably intertwined and incapable of severance" from the controversy between the hospital and Mercury was not a ground for denial of arbitration of a dispute embraced within the arbitration clause of the contract. The addition of the architect as a party defendant might prevent removal of the state action, but it certainly could not frustrate Mercury's plain, indisputable right to arbitration of *its* dispute with the hospital.

---

[11] 334 So 2d 287 (Fla Dist Ct App 1976).
[12] 656 F2d 933 (4th Cir 1981), *affd*, 460 US 1 (1983).

Arbitration Agreements Unenforceable

One or two states still cling to the view that arbitration agreements *oust* the courts of jurisdiction and are, therefore, unenforceable. In *Overland Constructors, Inc v Millard School District*,[13] a dispute arose between a contractor and a school district as to responsibility for utility charges. The contract included an arbitration clause under which the determination of the architect would be final. The architect determined that the contractor was responsible. HELD: the parties were not bound by the architect's determination. An arbitration agreement that is formed before a dispute arises denies the parties their right to seek the assistance of the courts and is contrary to public policy.

Arbitration Agreements Enforceable

In *Anderson-Parrish Associates v City of St Petersburg Beach*,[14] a contractor sued a city for breach of contract and the city filed a third-party action against the architect, alleging failure to properly design and supervise the project. The architect petitioned for an order that its dispute with the city be decided by arbitration, as required by an arbitration clause in the contract between the architect and the city. HELD: the arbitration agreement was enforceable. The city claimed that its action was merely for indemnification, but this position was not supported by an examination of the complaint, which also alleged breach of contract by the architect. Even if the city's claim was purely for indemnity, though, the architect would probably still be entitled to enforce the arbitration clause.

Third-Party Beneficiary

The trend of decision is to expand the enforceability of arbitration agreements. In *District Moving & Storage Co v Gardiner & Gardiner, Inc*,[15] the principle was expanded to cover a party who had not signed the agreement that contained the arbitration clause, but claimed to be a third-party beneficiary of it. When the owner contracted separately with the architect and the contractor, all parties knew that the building would be used by the lessee as a warehouse. The owner's contract with the architect and the owner's contract with the contractor each contained an arbitration clause. The owner and the lessee jointly filed suit against the architect and the contractor for breach of contract and negligence. The lessee contended that it was a third-party beneficiary of the contracts with the defendants. Based on the arbitration clause in the contracts, the trial court ordered the entire matter to arbitration. AFFIRMED. Whether

---

[13] 220 Neb 220, 369 NW2d 69 (1985).
[14] 468 So 2d 507 (Fla Dist Ct App 1985).
[15] 63 Md App 96, 492 A2d 319, *affd*, 306 Md 286, 508 A2d 487 (1986).

a third-party beneficiary to a contract is bound by an arbitration clause, even though it is not a signatory to the contract, presents a question of first impression. A third-party beneficiary should be benefited and burdened by the underlying contract to the same extent as the signatory. In order to obtain the benefits of the contract, the lessee was to abide by its terms, including the arbitration clause.

§14.03 Waiver

Although a party to an arbitration agreement is entitled to enforce the agreement, parties retain the ability to waive an arbitration clause, either by agreement or by conduct.

Generally speaking, conduct inconsistent with the enforcement of the right to arbitrate may constitute a waiver of that right. By filing a complaint and an answer on the merits of the lawsuit, parties may waive the right to insist on arbitration. This rule is a reflection of the necessary policy that parties must not speculate on the outcome of litigation and, if dissatisfied, reject the judgment of the court and insist on the commencement of arbitration proceedings.[16]

AAA Rule

The rules of the American Arbitration Association (AAA) provide that "no judicial proceedings by a party relating to the subject matter of the arbitration shall be deemed a waiver of the party's right to arbitrate."[17] The intent of the rule is to permit provisional and statutory remedies in court without affecting the agreement to arbitrate the underlying dispute.[18] However, the language of the rule, taken at face value, goes far beyond that. It would, in fact, permit a party to speculate on court proceedings, then demand arbitration. Although the rules do not seem to have been cited in any reported case, it is doubtful that a court would permit a party to go so far as to play fast and loose with a judgment of a court and, in effect, appeal a court judgment to an arbitration tribunal.

Pursuit of Discovery

In *Board of Education v Architects Taos*,[19] a school district sued an architect for breach of contract. The architect answered the complaint, denying allegations and asserting affirmative defenses, including the defense that the school district was contractually required to arbitrate its claim. After the architect filed numerous discovery requests, it scheduled a hearing seeking an order to compel

---

[16] Annotation, 117 ALR 308 (1938); Annotation, 161 ALR 1429 (1946).
[17] American Arbitration Association Rule 46.
[18] American Arbitration Association, Lawyers Arbitration Letter No 52, at 3 (Nov 15, 1972).
[19] 103 NM 462, 709 P2d 184 (1985).

arbitration or, in the alternative, to vacate the trial date and compel discovery. The motion to compel arbitration was granted. REVERSED. The architect waived the right to arbitrate. Waiver may be inferred when a party takes advantage of the judicial system, whether through discovery or direct invocation of the court's discretionary powers or both. Although the architect raised the issue of arbitration in its first affirmative defense, it did not press that issue but went ahead with discovery, thus realizing a benefit under litigation which it would have lost under arbitration. The school district was prejudiced by the burden of discovery, both in time and money.

In *Adams v Nelsen*,[20] the contract between owner and engineer contained an arbitration clause. Ignoring the clause, the engineer filed a court action to enforce a claim of mechanics lien. HELD: the owner failed to demand arbitration within three years of the filing of the court action as required by the contract and, therefore, waived the right to enforce the arbitration agreement.

§14.04 Conditions Precedent to Arbitration

The American Institute of Architects standard general conditions provide for submission of disputes to the architect, and also for arbitration of disputes under the rules of the American Arbitration Association.

This provision was not given the effect of a condition precedent in *Bartley, Inc v Jefferson Parish School Board*.[21] The contractor demanded arbitration against the owner and subcontractor but neglected the contract provision which required submission of disputes to the architect. The appellate court held that the demand for arbitration was premature where the architect had made no final decision. REVERSED. "[T]hese questions of procedural arbitrability should not be decided by the courts, without having been submitted to the arbitrator, when a party sues to enforce an arbitration agreement."[22]

§14.05 Multiple Parties

Construction disputes characteristically engage multiple parties. Assume that an owner is dissatisfied with some construction feature. If the contractor has built the feature as described in the contract documents, the contractor is not guilty of a breach of contract, and fault, if any, rests with the architect. On the other hand, if the feature was properly designed, and the contractor did not comply with the requirements of the contract documents, then the contractor is

---

[20] 313 NC 442, 329 SE2d 322 (1985).
[21] 302 So 2d 280 (La 1974).
[22] *Id* 283.

at fault. If the feature is both properly designed and built, then the owner has received proper performance from the contractor, and the architect is guilty of no malpractice.

In construction disputes, circumstances often make allies of the architect and the owner. The owner employs the architect, and the architect owes the owner a special responsibility. If the contractor attacks the architect's drawings, the architect will naturally defend its reputation. A successful defense of the drawings will usually result in a judgment favorable to the owner.

On the other hand, if the owner is dissatisfied with the architect's documents, the owner often finds a willing ally in the contractor. If the defect is in the drawings, then its existence cannot be the fault of the contractor.

Collateral Estoppel

An instance of multiple party problems in arbitration is provided by *French v Jinright & Ryan PC Architects*,[23] where a contractor demanded arbitration against an owner seeking damages caused by construction delays on a courthouse project. The delay was allegedly caused by acts of the architect. The arbitration clause specifically exempted the architect from being required to join in the arbitration proceedings without its written consent. After the conclusion of arbitration proceedings with the owner, the contractor filed suit against the architect for damages. The architect moved for summary judgment on the ground that the prior arbitration proceedings barred the litigation. The trial court granted the motion for summary judgment. VACATED. It was possible that the contractor's claim against the architect was settled in the arbitration proceedings. However, the trial court was not provided with a record of the claims litigated in the arbitration proceedings. Therefore, the case was remanded to determine whether the contractor's present claims against the architect were included in the arbitration proceedings.

Consolidation

Some states have adopted consolidation statutes applicable to arbitration proceedings. In other states, courts assert an inherent power to consolidate. In *Episcopal Housing Corp v Federal Insurance Co*,[24] an owner made claims against an architect and a contractor, alleging defects in design and construction. Both the architect and the contractor demanded arbitration. The owner moved for consolidation. Motion granted. AFFIRMED. The appellant builder demonstrated no convincing evidence of prejudice that would have resulted from the consolidation of the arbitration proceedings. Consolidation would have provided a logical, expeditious method by which to enforce the right to arbitration.

---

[23] 735 F2d 433 (11th Cir 1984).
[24] 273 SC 181, 255 SE2d 451 (1979).

Anti-Consolidation Clause

In *Del E. Webb Construction v Richardson Hospital Authority*,[25] a contractor demanded arbitration against the owner of a hospital and the supervising architect. The court ordered that all claims between the three parties be resolved in a single arbitration. HELD: the architect was not compelled to arbitrate its disputes with the contractor, since the architect had never signed a document agreeing to do so. The architect agreed to arbitrate disputes with the owner, but the arbitration clause provided that the architect would not participate in consolidated proceedings without written consent. Since the architect did not consent, the court should not have ordered the consolidation.

One disadvantage of arbitration in the construction field is that it may not be possible to bring all of the parties before the same tribunal, with the result of serial or concurrent arbitration, litigation, or both. For example, suppose the contractor commences arbitration proceedings against the owner, seeking compensation for extra work. The owner may contend that the extra work, if any, was caused by the malpractice of the architect. Unless the architect has agreed to join in the arbitration proceedings between the contractor and the owner, there is no positive way to enforce the joinder. The owner may be put to a separate arbitration, or a separate lawsuit, to determine the responsibility of the architect.

When separate proceedings are necessary, there is an inherent danger that the results of those proceedings may be inconsistent. For example, in a proceeding between a contractor and an owner, the arbitrators may find that the architect was at fault. However, in subsequent arbitration or litigation between the owner and the architect, the tribunal may decide that the contractor was at fault. This clearly does an injustice to the owner, since both tribunals have decided that the owner has suffered a wrong, but each has put the responsibility on a stranger to the proceeding.

From a tactical point of view, an architect would prefer not to become involved as a party to arbitration proceedings between a contractor and an owner. The architect would prefer to participate as a witness for, or an advisor to, the owner, without risking an enforceable adverse award. It is presumably for this reason that Article 13.2 of the American Institute of Architects general conditions to the contract between owner and the contractor prohibit joinder of the architect in arbitration proceedings between owner and contractor.

This provision should be changed. Whether in litigation or arbitration, the owner should not be forced to go through two separate sets of hearings to determine responsibility for the same flaw.

---

[25] 823 F2d 145 (5th Cir 1987).

§14.06 —Joinder and Consolidation

The policy of the courts is to avoid duplication and conflict, so the decisions favor *consolidated* arbitration proceedings. Decisions that have considered the question have found means to require an architect to join in arbitration proceedings with the owner and the contractor, even though the arbitration clause did not specifically require consolidated proceedings.

In *Verdex Steel & Construction Co v Board of Supervisors*,[26] the court employed a theory of waiver. An architect designed a gymnasium for a school district. The design required the fabrication and erection of steel arches. During construction, three arches collapsed, injuring employees of the contractor.

The contractor and the school district had executed a construction contract prepared by the architect on a standard American Institute of Architects (AIA) form. The contract included an arbitration clause that called for arbitration by the school district and the contractor, but not by the architect.

The contractor commenced arbitration proceedings against the school district and the architect. At first the architect took the position that there was no contractual obligation which required him to submit to arbitration. Nevertheless, the architect's participation in the proceedings was extensive. The architect never consented in writing to be bound by the arbitration award, but also did not "disavow that he was an active participant willing to be bound by the arbitrator's award."[27]

The award was in favor of the contractor and against the school district and the architect. The contractor filed an action to confirm the award. The trial court refused to enforce the award against the architect on the ground that the architect did not consent to the arbitration proceedings. REVERSED. One who voluntarily participates in arbitration proceedings without making a clear record disengaging himself from their effect is bound by the award, even though that person signed no arbitration agreement.[28] The factual background raised a debatable issue as to whether the architect participated in the arbitration proceeding to such a degree that he was bound by the award. However, since the architect did not file a brief on appeal, he made a *confession of error*, and the trial court was directed to confirm the award in favor of the contractor and against the architect.

The decision reflects the policy that a party will not be allowed to participate in arbitration proceedings, speculate on the award, and then spurn the award if it is disappointing. By participating in arbitration proceedings without driving home the point that it does not intend to be bound by the proceedings, a party waives the right to deny the validity of the proceedings.

---

[26] 19 Ariz App 547, 509 P2d 240 (1973).
[27] *Id* at 549, 509 P2d at 242.
[28] Ariz Rev Stat Ann §12-1512(a)(5) (1956).

Joint Arbitration Ordered

In *Grover-Dimond Associates v American Arbitration Assn*,[29] the court ordered consolidated arbitration proceedings despite the architect's objection. The owner demanded arbitration with the architect and the general contractor, contending that each of them contributed to a cost overrun of $1,476,759.09. The contractor consented to joint proceedings, but the architect filed a motion to prohibit it. Both the contractor and the architect had signed separate agreements with the owner, each of which contained an arbitration clause. The arbitration clauses did not require joint arbitration, and neither did the Minnesota statute. The Minnesota Supreme Court ordered the architect to proceed with joint arbitration. This avoided the time and expense of separate proceedings and avoided the possibility of conflicting awards. Minnesota policy encourages arbitration, and the effect of the order was not to require the architect to arbitrate directly against the contractor, but to require both the architect and the contractor to arbitrate with the owner in a single proceeding.

The court pointed out that New York and the Second Circuit had approved consolidated arbitration proceedings, and that New Jersey courts had taken the opposite view.

In *McCandliss v Ward W. Ross, Inc*,[30] both the contractor and the architect had signed standard AIA forms of contract with the owner, each of which contained an arbitration clause. The contractor signed a form requiring arbitration in accordance with the construction industry arbitration rules of the American Arbitration Association (AAA). The architect signed an old form requiring arbitration according to the standard form of arbitration procedure of the AIA. (The AIA standard form of arbitration procedure now requires that the arbitration proceed according to the AAA rules.)

The owner commenced an action against the contractor and the architect in the circuit court, which ordered arbitration.

The arbitrator granted the owner a sum of money against the contractor to correct defective items and reduced the balance owing to the architect for its fees. The owner, dissatisfied with the award, appealed from the trial court's judgment confirming the award. The Michigan Court of Appeals AFFIRMED the award, without discussion of consolidation.

The courts have shown a surprising ability to devise means for ordering consolidation of arbitration proceedings. In *Robinson v Warner*,[31] the court stated that a consolidated arbitration would be the preferred proceeding when the separate arbitration clauses in the contract between the owner and the

---

[29] 297 Minn 324, 211 NW2d 787 (1973).
[30] 45 Mich App 342, 206 NW2d 455 (1973).
[31] 370 F Supp 828 (DRI 1974).

architect and between the owner and the subcontractor are general and do not specify the manner of selecting arbitrators.

In *Conejo Valley Unified School District v William Bluerock & Partners, Inc*,[32] the California Court of Appeal ordered consolidation of arbitration proceedings for a school district, a contractor, and an architect. The architect objected to consolidation, but the court held that the roughly parallel arbitration clauses in the contract between the owner and the architect and in the contract between the owner and the contractor made it possible to consolidate the proceedings without prejudice to the architect.

Also exhibiting the desire to consolidate proceedings is *Garden Grove Community Church v Pittsburgh-Des Moines Steel Co*,[33] in which an architect was compelled to consolidate an owner's arbitration claim against the architect with the contractor's arbitration claim against the owner, in spite of a provision in the architect's arbitration clause (taken from the standard AIA contract documents) which provided: "No arbitration, arising out of, or relating to this agreement, shall include, by consolidation, joinder or in any other manner, any additional party not a party to this agreement except by written consent containing a specific reference to this agreement and signed by all the parties hereto."

The policy favoring consolidation of arbitration proceedings was followed in *Sullivan County v Edward L. Nezelek, Inc.*[34] In 1968, the county community college had contracted with the architect to design college buildings. In 1970, the county employed a contractor to construct the buildings. Both contracts contained broad arbitration clauses calling for arbitration under the construction industry arbitration rules of the AAA. In 1975, the college demanded arbitration of the disputes with the architect. Thereafter, the contractor demanded arbitration of disputes with the college. Both the architect and the college moved to stay arbitration proceedings. After the college's motion to stay was denied, both the college and the county moved for consolidation of the proceedings. The lower court granted the motion to consolidate, and the architect appealed. AFFIRMED. Courts have the power to order the consolidation of arbitration proceedings even without specific contract provisions permitting consolidation. Although consolidation might complicate the proceedings and expose the parties to additional claims, it is important to assure that the awards in two separate, but interrelated, disputes will be consistent with each other.

---

[32] 111 Cal App 3d 983, 169 Cal Rptr 102 (1980).
[33] 140 Cal App 3d 251, 191 Cal Rptr 15 (1983).
[34] 42 NY2d 123, 366 NE2d 72, 397 NYS2d 371 (1977).

Collateral Estoppel

In *Sarton v Superior Court (Marin County)*,[35] a nonconsolidation clause contained in a services contract prevented Mrs. Jeffrey from joining the three individual architects of an architectural/engineering firm as defendants to claims of fraud, misrepresentation, and breach of contract. The arbitrator determined that the architectural/engineering firm named was not liable. Following confirmation of the award, Mrs. Jeffrey brought suit against the individual architects, alleging essentially the same facts.

The California Court of Appeal applied the concept of collateral estoppel and held that since the issues decided in the arbitration proceeding against the firm were identical with the ones to be pursued against the individual architects, the ruling of the arbitrator was binding. The individual architects could have taken advantage of the arbitrator's award even though they would not have been bound by the award. They were not parties to the proceeding or in privity with a party to it. The court stated: "It is the policy of this state to give effect to arbitration agreements. The application of collateral estoppel, under the circumstances shown to exist in this proceeding, will promote that policy."[36]

§14.07 —Vouching In

Vouching in is a procedure sometimes called for in an agreement between a prime contractor and a subcontractor, or in an agreement between an architect and its consultants. The typical provision is to the effect that in the event of arbitration proceedings between the architect and the owner, the architect will give the consultant an opportunity to participate in the proceedings, and the consultant will then be bound by the award.

In *Perkins & Will Partnership v Syska & Hennessy & Garfinkel*,[37] a contractor commenced arbitration proceedings against a hospital for delay and extra work. The hospital in turn demanded arbitration against the architect. The proceedings were consolidated. Before the arbitrators were selected or any hearings were held, the architect gave written notice to the mechanical engineer pursuant to their contract, which provided that in the event of arbitration proceedings between the hospital and the architect, any decision would be binding on the mechanical engineer provided it was afforded an opportunity to participate in the arbitration proceedings. HELD: this *vouching in* gave the consultant an opportunity to participate in the arbitration proceedings, and any dispute between the architect and the consultant would be determined in those

---

[35] 136 Cal App 3d 322, 187 Cal Rptr 247 (1982).
[36] *Id* at 328, 187 Cal Rptr at 250.
[37] 50 AD2d 226, 376 NYS2d 533 (1975), *affd*, 364 NE2d 832, 396 NYS2d 167 (1977).

proceedings. Therefore, it was improper for the architect to demand a separate indemnification arbitration proceeding with the consultant.

In *Perkins & Will Partnership v Syska & Hennessy*,[38] the arbitration clause between the architect and its consulting engineers provided: "Any decision or determination resulting from arbitration between the architect and the owner which relates to the consultant's services shall be binding upon the consultant, providing that the consultant has been afforded the opportunity to participate in the arbitration."

The owner made a claim against the architect, and the architect then demanded arbitration against the engineers. The court vacated the architect's demand for arbitration. The arbitration clause did not establish an independent arbitration proceeding between the architect and the consulting engineers. The architect's exclusive access to arbitration proceedings would have been "to vouch in the engineers in the ongoing arbitration between the owner and the architects."[39]

In *In re Perkins & Will Partnership (W.J. Barney Corp)*,[40] a contractor demanded arbitration against a hospital, asserting that the project architect had caused $1.7 million in delay damages. The hospital wrote to the architect, vouching it into the arbitration proceeding. The architect moved to stay arbitration proceedings, showing that its arbitration agreement with the owner contained a clause prohibiting consolidation with any other arbitration proceeding. HELD: since arbitration involves the loss of the right to a jury trial, a party cannot be bound to arbitrate absent express agreement. In the absence of a contract permitting vouching in, or possibly a statute to the same effect, an indemnitor may not be vouched into an arbitration proceeding.

The rules of the American Arbitration Association (AAA) permit an arbitrator to order the joinder of parties in arbitration proceedings. As to a party who by writing has agreed to be bound by those rules, the order would doubtless be enforceable, but the order could not be enforced against a stranger to the arbitration agreement. To do so would deprive the stranger of its right to trial without its consent. The judicial policy to avoid duplication and conflict inclines the courts to imply consent when it is possible to do so.

§14.08 Selection of Arbitrator

The methods which may be employed in the selection of arbitrators are limited only by the ingenuity of the draftsperson. A common pattern is for each

---

[38] 41 NY2d 1045, 364 NE2d 832, 396 NYS2d 167 (1977).

[39] *Id* at 1045, 364 NE2d at 832, 396 NYS2d at 167.

[40] 131 Misc 2d 286, 502 NYS2d 318 (Sup Ct 1985), *affd*, 119 AD2d 1015, 501 NYS2d 290 (1986).

party to select an arbitrator, and the two so selected to select the third. If the two arbitrators cannot agree on a third, the third arbitrator will be appointed by the court.

Most arbitration statutes provide that if the method designated by the parties for the selection of the arbitrators should for any reason fail, the arbitrator will be appointed by the court.

Under some contracts, the arbitrator is appointed from a preselected panel, or by a trade association. In proceedings held under the rules of the American Arbitration Association (AAA), arbitrators are usually selected from a panel maintained by the association and submitted to the parties. The parties may strike from the list any they deem objectionable, and the appointment is made from those remaining. In minor cases, one arbitrator is employed; in larger cases, a tribunal of three arbitrators is employed. In a proceeding between an architect and an owner, the tribunal would usually contain one architect, one lawyer, and one owner.

The arbitration statutes recognize that arbitrators appointed by the parties are not likely to be impartial. Therefore, the third arbitrator is deemed to be neutral, and settles questions of procedure and evidence. The parties may find it expedient to dispense with party-appointed arbitrators and have the dispute determined by the neutral arbitrator alone.

It should go without saying that the selection of arbitrators is crucial to the outcome of a dispute. Before accepting or rejecting a proposed arbitrator, the lawyer should carefully study the nominee's background and experience.

§14.09 Conduct of Arbitration Hearing

Under the arbitration statutes adopted by the states, hearings are usually conducted on dates and at places designated by the arbitrators, or by the neutral arbitrator. They may be conducted at the offices of the arbitrator, at the offices of one of the parties, or at the job site. The American Arbitration Association (AAA) furnishes hearing rooms with appropriate furnishings.

Proceedings that require several days of hearings are usually subject to adjournments or continuances, since the parties and the arbitrators usually have conflicting business and personal obligations. The arbitrators have the discretion to grant or deny adjournments or continuances, but due process requires that they give every party a reasonable opportunity to be heard.

Most states give arbitrators the power to subpoena witnesses and documents, but a party must apply to a court for enforcement procedures.

Arbitrators are not bound by formal rules of evidence, and they may choose to receive, or exclude, hearsay. It is customary to receive hearsay, and to receive much evidence without foundation. If a tribunal consists of three arbitrators, one of whom is a lawyer, the lawyer usually acts as chairman and rules on questions of procedure and evidence.

The examination and cross-examination proceed very much as in court. Testimony is given under oath. The arbitrators receive and mark exhibits. The parties (or a party) may or may not provide a court reporter.

At the conclusion of hearings, the arbitrators issue a written award, signed by a majority. If the loser does not voluntarily comply with the award, the winner applies to court for confirmation.

§14.10 Considerations in Selecting Arbitration

Arbitration differs from litigation in many crucial ways. When a lawyer has an opportunity to select or reject arbitration as a means for settling a dispute, the lawyer should review the differences and determine whether each is to the advantage of the client. This leads to a balancing of favorable factors against those deemed unfavorable to determine whether the client should be advised to select arbitration or litigation.

Time

Arbitration is usually much faster than litigation. Hearings normally commence two or three months after the demand for arbitration is filed. The time factor may be crucial when a project is under construction. Arbitrators may be able to visit the job site and examine evidence that would later be concealed.

After commencement, however, arbitration proceedings may be drawn out by continuances necessitated by conflicting business of the parties or the arbitrators. Nevertheless, the time lapse between the commencement and termination of proceedings is usually much less in arbitration than it would be in litigation.

Appeal

Every judgment can be appealed. A litigant is entitled to a trial free from error. Except in a very limited sense, this is not true of arbitration proceedings. Arbitrators are not required to follow the law. Error in law is no ground for upsetting an arbitrator's award. An award can be vacated only for fundamental error which, in effect, deprives a party of a fair hearing: for example, failure to receive relevant evidence, failure to notify a party of the time and place of a hearing, corruption, or failure of an arbitrator to disclose a pecuniary interest in the success of a party. An award may be vacated if an arbitrator fails to decide the question submitted or decides questions that were not submitted to arbitration or are not arbitrable under the arbitration agreement.

The usual absence of grounds for appeal, of course, plays its part in reducing the lapse of time between the commencement of proceedings and the rendition of a final determination.

Expense

Whether arbitration is more expensive than litigation depends on the length of the proceedings. Judges are paid by the public, but arbitrators must be paid by the parties. Arbitrators may serve one or two days without pay, as a matter of public service. After that, they usually require payment. A customary rate is $500 per day for each arbitrator.

American Arbitration Association Fees

Court filing fees are usually modest. Arbitration under the rules of the American Arbitration Association (AAA) may be considerably more expensive, depending upon the amount in controversy. A filing fee of $300 will be paid when a case is filed. The balance of the administrative fee is based on the amount of each claim or counterclaim as disclosed when the claim or counterclaim is filed. This balance is due and payable 60 days after the AAA's commencement of administration, or prior to the date of the first hearing, whichever occurs first. If at any time a claim or counterclaim is settled or withdrawn, the balance of the administrative fee remains due and the Refund Schedule shall then be applied. When oral hearings are waived under Section 37, the Administrative Fee Schedule shall still apply.

Amount of Claim or Counterclaim	Fee
Up to $10,000	$300
$10,000 to $25,000	3%
$25,000 to $50,000	$750, plus 2% of excess over $25,000
$50,000 to $100,000	$1,250, plus 1% of excess over $50,000
$100,000 to $500,000	$1,750, plus 1/2% of excess over $100,000
$500,000 to $5,000,000	$3,750, plus 1/4% of excess over $500,000
$5,000,000 to $50,000,000	$15,000, plus 1/10% of excess over $5,000,000

Where the claim or counterclaim exceeds $50 million, there is no additional administrative fee.

When no amount can be stated at the time of filing, the administrative fee is $1,000, subject to adjustment in accordance with the above schedule as soon as an amount can be disclosed.

An appropriate administrative fee will be determined by the AAA for claims and counterclaims that are not for a monetary amount.

If there are more than two parties represented in the arbitration, an additional 10 per cent of the administrative fee will be due for each additional represented party.

The minimum administrative fee for a case heard by three arbitrators is $1,500, payable by the party requesting same.

Postponement Fees

Sole-Arbitrator Cases:

$100 is payable by a party causing its first postponement of any scheduled hearing.

$200 is payable by a party causing its second or subsequent postponement of any scheduled hearing.

Three-Arbitrator Cases:

$150 is payable by a party causing its first postponement of any scheduled hearing.

$300 is payable by a party causing its second or subsequent postponement of any scheduled hearing.

Additional Hearing Fee

$75 is payable by each party for each hearing after the first hearing that is clerked by the AAA.

Hearing-Room Rental

Hearing rooms for second and subsequent hearings are available on a rental basis at AAA offices. Check with your local office for specific availability and rates.

Refund Schedule

The Refund Schedule is based on the administrative fee due on a claim or counterclaim asserted by a party.

If the AAA is notified that a claim or counterclaim has been settled or withdrawn before a list of arbitrators has been sent out, all of the fee in excess of $300 will be refunded.

If the AAA is notified that a claim or counterclaim has been settled or withdrawn after a list of arbitrators has been sent out but before the original due date for the return of the first list, two-thirds of the fee in excess of $300 will be refunded.

If the AAA is notified that a claim or counterclaim has been settled or withdrawn after the original due date for the return of the first list but at least two business days before the initial date and time set for the first scheduled hearing, one-third of the fee in excess of $300 will be refunded.

There will be no refund after any hearing or mediation conference has been held; where a claim or counterclaim was filed as an undetermined/undisclosed claim and remained so at the time of settlement or withdrawal; where a consent award was issued by the arbitrator; or where a determination was made by the arbitrator resulting in the closing of the file.

Other Cost Factors

If the parties want a court reporter, the reporter will have to be paid by the parties rather than by the public. Thus, protracted arbitration hearings probably cost the parties more than court proceedings.

On the other hand, arbitration can produce some cost savings. The parties avoid jury fees. Since there is no law and motions work, the parties avoid legal fees which could be incurred. In most states, the arbitration statute does not require or permit depositions or interrogatories, so the cost and annoyance of discovery proceedings are avoided.

In some cases, arbitration is more efficient than litigation because the arbitrators may be willing to work longer hours. Arbitrators may also be technically qualified to understand evidence without extensive expert testimony. Arbitration will almost invariably save the high cost of an appeal. Of course, a judgment confirming an arbitrator's award is appealable, but error in a confirmation proceeding is unusual. An appeal from a judgment confirming an award costs less than an appeal from a trial judgment, since the record is usually extremely limited.

Privacy

Court hearings are public; arbitration proceedings are private.

Discovery

A party to a dispute may need depositions or interrogatories or may wish to avoid them. In a proceeding between an architect and an owner, the architect usually has possession of most of the facts and therefore would not be as likely as the owner to need discovery proceedings.

The statement that discovery is not available in arbitration proceedings needs some elaboration. In some states, in certain types of cases, discovery is available. The arbitrators, to save time, may suggest that the parties disclose their records or even give depositions. If the arbitrators make such a suggestion, the parties usually find it expedient to comply.

Although discovery is a valuable right, experience shows that it can often be used as a device to embarrass and harass a party. This is much less likely to occur in arbitration proceedings than in litigation.

Legal Error

Arbitrators are not required to know the law or to follow the law. Therefore, a case which would be lost on demurrer or summary judgment in court can be won in arbitration.

It must be added, though, that arbitrators usually do follow the law even though they are not required to do so. However, in a particular case, an arbitrator may reject a rule of law if it thinks it is unfair or inequitable.

"The arbitrator looks to what is equitable, the judge to what is law; and it was for this purpose that arbitration was introduced, namely, that equity might prevail."[41]

> The case books are full of reports of cases where lay arbitrators have found contracts to be frustrated and the court has held they were wrong. Lawyers have even been more prone than merchants to cling to the letter of the contract; see, for example, Shylock v Antonio, a case which might have been decided on grounds of public policy but, in fact, turned on a pure question of construction.[42]

A lawyer with a solid legal, though technical, defense would usually rather have the defense decided by a court than by an arbitrator.

Evidence Rules

Arbitrators may follow rules of evidence, though they usually do not. Therefore, the lawyer who wants to exclude hearsay may favor litigation, while the lawyer whose case depends on hearsay may decide on arbitration.

In arbitration proceedings, reams of photocopies of documents may be introduced without foundation and without regard to whether they contain opinion or hearsay evidence. This method of introducing evidence is efficient. Depending on the circumstances it may help or hurt the client's case.

Statute of Limitations

In *Skidmore, Owings & Merrill v Connecticut General Life Insurance Co*,[43] an architect entered into a contract to design an office building in May of 1953; it delivered heating and air conditioning plans in February 1955; the building was occupied in 1957; and the owner became aware of defects in 1960. The owner demanded arbitration in 1962, and the architect sought declaratory relief that the proceeding was barred by the statute of limitations. The Connecticut statute of limitations barred *bringing an action*. HELD: arbitration is not a common law action, and the institution of arbitration proceedings is not the bringing of an action under any statute of limitations. Even assuming that the commencement of arbitration proceedings does constitute the bringing of an action, the application of the statute is to be determined by the arbitrators, and not by the court.

---

[41] Aristotle, Rhetoric, Book 1, ch 13.
[42] Tsakiroglou v Noblee Throl, 2 WLR 179, 185, 186 (1959).
[43] 25 Conn Supp 76, 197 A2d 83 (1963).

In some states, therefore, a case that would be barred by the statute of limitations may still be arbitrable.

Provisional Remedies

Provisional remedies may or may not be available in arbitration, depending on state law. The lawyer should determine whether the client needs or wishes to avoid provisional remedies such as attachment, mechanics lien, stop notice, notice of *lis pendens*, temporary restraining order, or a receiver. If the availability of provisional remedies is significant, state law should be checked to determine which, if any, may be available in arbitration. (It would seem that an arbitration clause could be drafted to preserve the availability of some provisional remedies.)

Multiple Parties

As has been seen, it may not be possible for the owner to join both the architect and the contractor in an arbitration proceeding.[44] This consideration may compel the owner to waive arbitration and select litigation. Otherwise, the owner runs the risk of inconsistent decisions: for example, an arbitrator might render an award in favor of the architect on the ground that the contractor was at fault; while a court, in a separate decision, might enter judgment in favor of the contractor on the ground that the architect was at fault. Thus the owner could be put to the expense of two separate proceedings and lose each proceeding, even though if it had been able to join the contractor and the architect in a single proceeding, the owner would have recovered from one or the other. Joinder and consolidation could, however, be facilitated by a properly drawn arbitration clause.

Expertise

Depending on circumstances, the client may find it advantageous, or disadvantageous, to have the dispute decided by an expert contractor, engineer, or architect.

Lawyers

A party will find it easier to proceed without a lawyer in arbitration than in court. However, parties usually find it to their advantage to employ lawyers in arbitration proceedings, even though they are not required.

Pretrial and Settlement

Judges are disposed to persuade parties to settle their disputes rather than consume the court's time. Many courts have established special proceedings designed to encourage settlement. Arbitrators are not so likely to actively encourage settlement.

---

[44] *See* §14.05.

They also usually tend to listen to all evidence, rather than attempt to expedite the proceedings, since one of the grounds for upsetting an award is the unjustified refusal to hear relevant evidence.

Other Factors

To decide whether to advise arbitration or litigation, it is necessary to examine the impact of the factors summarized here, and more. Are the personal qualities of the chief witnesses such as would be more impressive to a jury, a judge, or an arbitrator? Will a rigorous cross-examination of the opposing witnesses be more effective in the formal atmosphere of a court? Is the expert witness a person of towering reputation among architects, but little known outside the field?

It is readily seen that a factor that favors one party will almost by definition be unfavorable to the opponent. For example, if the claimant desires a speedy settlement, the respondent may want to delay resolution as long as possible. If the respondent is basically ignorant of the facts of the case and needs depositions and discovery, and the claimant is in possession of most of the facts, then the claimant may select arbitration in order to deny the opponent the advantage and save itself the trouble of discovery proceedings. If the respondent has a good chance of winning the case on a technical point of law, but the equities favor the claimant, then the respondent wants a judge to decide the case, while the claimant wants an arbitrator.

Finally, some persons are predisposed in favor of, and others against, arbitration. It is natural for an experienced courtroom lawyer, who has had little to do with arbitration proceedings, to feel more comfortable with litigation than arbitration. This feeling may be translated into a strong predisposition to avoid arbitration whenever it is possible to do so. But the careful lawyer will decide whether to seek arbitration or litigation based upon an analysis of the advantages and disadvantages of each procedure under the circumstances of the particular case.

§14.11 Mediation

The context of arbitration proceedings offers opportunities for mediation. Whether mediation can be instituted depends on the personal qualities of the lawyers, the disputants, and the arbitrators. Mediation is an extremely effective device when employed while a job is in progress.

Commencement of arbitration proceedings while a job is still in progress reflects (if it does not create) strained relationships among the parties. The economic interests of all parties are served by a harmonious relationship among architect, owner, and contractor. If the contractor disputes the owner's instructions or the architect's decisions during the progress of the job, the work may suffer to the detriment of all parties.

In this situation, an arbitrator (especially an architect, an engineer, or a contractor) may be able to do service as mediator. An arbitrator who has the confidence of the parties may be able to visit the job on a regular basis and dispose of an agenda of recommendations on the spot. The parties may find it in their interest to go along with this informal procedure and yet leave the arbitrator (or the arbitration tribunal in case there are three arbitrators) with the authority to make final and binding decisions on issues which cannot be resolved through the mediation process.[45]

§14.12 Enforcement of Award

An arbitrator derives from its position no power to enforce an award. The arbitrator cannot command the sheriff. Therefore, the award, if not voluntarily respected by the parties, must be converted into a judgment. Arbitrators usually attempt to bring the award down to monetary terms: one party will pay the other a specified sum. Regardless of whether the award is for money, or in the nature of an injunction or a restraining order, it must be enforced by application to a court.

Arbitration statutes provide for summary proceedings leading to the confirmation or vacation of an award. If an award is confirmed, it is entered like any other judgment and enforceable by writ of execution, writ of enforcement, or other process. The confirmation is handled as a law and motions matter, which usually means prompt disposition rather than waiting for a spot on the court's trial calendar.

§14.13 Vacation of Award

Arbitration statutes provide that a party dissatisfied with an award may move to vacate. Typical statutory grounds are: corruption, failure of the arbitrator to receive relevant evidence, failure of the arbitrator to disclose a pecuniary interest in the outcome of the proceedings, failure of the arbitrator to decide the issue submitted, rendering an award that goes beyond the scope of the arbitration clause or the submission agreement, and failure to give a party to the arbitration notice of hearings and an opportunity to be heard. It has also been held that a court will not confirm an award if the effect would be to enforce an illegal contract. Thus most courts would not confirm an award enforcing a gambling contract or granting relief to an unlicensed architect or contractor.

---

[45] *See Presenting Construction Cases Before Nonlawyer Arbitrators*, 3, No 2 Shepard's Cal Constr L Rep 25 (Mar 1993).

In a California case, an owner who submitted a controversy with an architect to arbitration and lost could not vacate the award on the ground that the owner was not fluent in the English language.[46]

---

[46] Kemper v Schardt, 143 Cal App 3d 557, 192 Cal Rptr 46 (1983).

Trial and Hearing Techniques

15

§15.01 Generally
§15.02 Fact Summary
§15.03 Delay Chart
§15.04 Witness Outline
§15.05 Document File
§15.06 Deposition Summary
§15.07 Expert Witnesses
 Local Standard Not Established
 Expert from a Different Profession
 Safety Expert
 Hypothetical Questions
 Expert Relies on Hearsay
 Attorney Work Product
 Attorney-Client Privilege
 Qualifications of Expert
§15.08 Law Notes
§15.09 "Trial Book"
§15.10 Proposed Award

§15.01 Generally

Every lawyer develops a technique and style for the preparation and trial of a disputed issue. Just as many lawyers regard their own methods with distinct satisfaction, despite the bountiful literature on the subject, it is doubtful that most experienced lawyers need, or will accept, much advice on trial technique. Yet it remains a favorite subject of legal writers.

§15.02 Fact Summary

It is a distinctive feature of construction cases that they contain many facts. Usually hundreds, sometimes thousands, of facts are relevant. They are culled from correspondence files, contract files, job diaries, inspection reports, minutes of job meetings, payment requests, payment certificates, change orders, and the memories of witnesses.

The lawyer's first job in understanding the case is to review all the documents that he or she can obtain and determine from them which facts are significant. The facts should be arranged in abbreviated style and chronological order.

This can be done with card files, computers, or dictation equipment. The objective is a physical end-product useful to understanding the case and helpful during the trial. A convenient format for the courtroom (or the hearing room) is 8-1/2 x 11-inch sheets with wide margins, typed on one side, and bound at the top with a fastener. Top binding is preferable to side binding for courtroom work, since it enables the lawyer to employ only one hand to work with the file while moving about the room.

The fact summary contains a list of dates followed by brief, sometimes shorthand, descriptions of events. A left margin is used to note new facts or testimony. To facilitate this, ruled paper may be used.

There are many advantages to reviewing documents at the client's office, rather than at the lawyer's office. This gives the lawyer some insight into the client's method of operation and helps avoid the possibility of overlooking pertinent material. During the review of documents, the lawyer may dictate the dates and facts which are pertinent. The material is then transcribed and arranged in chronological order. The following fact summary is illustrative:

1/2/76	First meeting, architect/owner.
1/2/76	Preliminary sketch delivered.
1/8/76	Three sheets of sketches delivered.
1/20/76	Architect-owner contract.
1/29/76	Sheets 1, 2, and 3 prepared.
2/8/76	Consultant contract.
2/12/76	Calcs prepared.
2/15/76	Calcs reviewed.
3/8/76	Owner to architect: revising square footage requirement.
3/10/76	Preliminaries submitted.
8/5/76	Plan check.
8/7/76	Plan checker requires more calcs.
8/11/76	Revised calcs submitted.
9/1/76	Invitation to bid.

10/4/76	Bid opening.
10/11/76	Owner-contractor contract.
10/14/76	Contractor to owner: suggest post-tension slab.
10/18/76	Owner to architect: is post-tensioning feasible.

§15.03 Delay Chart

Delay may be displayed on a chart that plots causes of delay against a date line. This enables visualization of the length of delays and their overlapping nature. Computer generated PERT (Performance, Evaluation, and Review Technique) charts can be most useful, whether composed by the lawyer or supplied by the client.

It is important to develop a rational way to evaluate delay. In a typical job, delay is caused by the owner, by the architect, and by the contractor. Some causes of delay affect only a small portion of the work, while others may affect the whole job.

One approach is to multiply the number of days of delay against a percentage factor which represents the expert's judgment as to the percentage of the work that was affected by the delay. For example, if the architect delays approval of plumbing shop drawings for 20 days and the expert judges that the plumbing work held up by the delay constitutes 15 per cent of the job, then the weight accorded to the delay would be 0.15 x 20 = 3 days.

On the other hand, if the architect shut down the entire job for three days because of safety violations by the contractor, then the weight accorded to that delay would be 1.0 x 3 = 3 days.

Causes of delay can be arranged in tabular form with the percentage, number of days, and weight displayed for each cause.

§15.04 Witness Outline

The lawyer should outline the testimony he or she expects to elicit from each witness, friendly and hostile. The fact summary assists the lawyer in preparing witness sheets. In reviewing the fact summary, the lawyer decides which facts should be established and which document or witness will be used to establish each fact. The facts to be established are then transposed to the witness outlines, and the lawyer asks questions appropriate to elicit the facts.

The format of the witness outline can be similar to that of the fact summary: ruled paper, wide margin for notes, bound at the top.

§15.05 Document File

A construction case may require the introduction of dozens, hundreds, or thousands of documents. If the lawyer elicits testimony from a witness to lay the foundation for each document, much time is consumed, and the chronological development of the facts is lost when the order of introduction is governed by the witness on the stand rather than by logical considerations. Another method should be considered: The lawyer arranges photocopies of the documents in chronological order and binds them at the top. The document file is then paginated. The lawyer seeks a stipulation that it may be introduced as a single exhibit. (In arbitration proceedings, no stipulation is necessary. The document file will be received as a matter of course.)

Copies of the file are provided to opposing counsel, client, and arbitrators or judge. Thus, all have a single frame of reference for the important documents that affect the proceeding.

This method does have a disadvantage. The very process of laying a foundation for the introduction of a document may endow it with drama or importance. The judge would be able to read the document while the foundation is being laid. At the very least, the document comes to the hands of the judge on its own feet, so to speak, and under those circumstances, the judge may be more inclined to read it and assign to it the importance that it truly deserves.

On the other hand, the process of laying a foundation for and eliciting testimony about a document may frustrate the impact of the document. Typically, the lawyer has the document marked for identification and hands it to the witness, but the judge has never seen it. Even after the document is received in evidence, it may be unceremoniously snatched from the judge's hand so the lawyer (or the witness) can read it. It would be better if the judge, the opposing counsel, the witness, the client, and the proponent of the evidence all had a copy before them.

§15.06 Deposition Summary

Depositions should be summarized in a format similar to the fact summary. The page and line where the testimony appears in the deposition is substituted for the date, thus:

3/14	Engineering degree, UCLA.
5/2	Previously designed warehouse for same owner.
7/13	Has designed and supervised about 30 tilt-up structures.

Appropriate material from the deposition summaries is interpolated into the fact summary and the witness outlines. The wide left margin is available to note supporting or conflicting testimony or documentation.

§15.07 Expert Witnesses

The standard of care applicable to a professional must almost always be established by expert testimony.[1] Generally speaking, a malpractice case cannot be won by the plaintiff without expert testimony which persuades the judge that the defendant failed to meet the appropriate standard of care.[2] For example, the common knowledge that water runs downhill does not give a jury the ability to understand the technically complicated excavation, grading, and drainage plans of a gymnasium construction project.[3]

In limited circumstances a trial judge can determine malpractice without expert testimony. In *City of Eveleth v Ruble*,[4] an engineer was employed by a city to design a revision of its water system. The city's purpose was to increase the capacity of the system. However, as designed, the capacity was still insufficient.

The plaintiff did not offer any expert testimony. The court of appeal held that the trial judge was qualified to determine that the failure to design adequate intake capacity under the circumstances was malpractice.

The trial judge in the same case was deemed not qualified to determine without expert testimony an issue as to the design of the high-service pumps. Although the pumps caused sudden surges and water hammer, the engineer did not guarantee that they would be trouble-free. Therefore, liability of the engineer was not based upon breach of contract, but upon the failure to meet the standard of care applicable in the community. Liability for a breach of that standard of care would have to be based on the opinions of experts. Since there was no expert testimony, the portion of the judgment awarding damages for the defective design of the high-service pumps was VACATED.

A poorly prepared expert can lose a case on appeal. In *Paxton v Alameda County*,[5] an injured worker obtained a judgment of $25,000 against an architect. The court of appeal REVERSED on the ground that the expert testimony was too insubstantial to support the verdict. A roofer was injured after breaking through the sheathing of an animal exhibition shed at a fairground. The architect had specified 1 x 6-inch Douglas fir, select merchantable seasoned sheathing laid solid horizontally on 2 x 4-inch rafters on 32-inch centers. This was permitted by the building code, and several contractors and architects testified that it was customary.

The architect testified that it had computed the stress and allowed a large margin of safety. An architect expert witness, however, testified that the

---

[1] Allied Properties v John A. Blume & Assocs, 25 Cal App 3d 848, 102 Cal Rptr 259 (1972).

[2] Van Ornum v Otter Tail Power Co, 210 NW2d 188 (ND 1973).

[3] Seaman Unified Sch Dist No 345 v Casson Constr Co, 3 Kan App 2d 289, 594 P2d 241 (1979).

[4] 302 Minn 249, 225 NW2d 521 (1974).

[5] 119 Cal App 2d 393, 259 P2d 934 (1953).

application was not customary in Alameda County. This expert had not examined the plans or specifications, just photographs. Moreover, the expert had not read the code and had not figured the stress. HELD: this expert's testimony was too insubstantial to support an implied finding that the architect negligently specified the material. An opinion is worth no more than the reasons on which it is based. The expert had never figured the stress; but those who did figure it testified that the application was safe.

In *Herkert v Stauber*,[6] the plaintiff commenced a breach of contract action against an architectural corporation, claiming that it failed to provide the documents necessary to complete an application for the financing of a project. The plaintiff further alleged that the individual architects employed by the corporation were jointly and severally liable for the breach, since the contract was for the rendition of professional services. The court refused to impose personal liability. The record did not contain evidence establishing that it was customary for professional architects to assist a client in securing financing for a construction project. The plaintiff failed to present evidence establishing the standard of care owed by a professional who attempts to perform services beyond its expertise or training. Without such evidence, it was error to impose personal liability for contractual obligations which exceeded the expertise of professional architects.

Local Standard Not Established

In *Maloney v Oak Builders, Inc*,[7] the plaintiff's experts failed to establish the standard of care and skill "required by others engaged in the same profession in the same locality." An architect does not guarantee that the plans will be perfect or lead to a satisfactory result. Liability rests upon unskillfulness or negligence, and not merely on errors of judgment. Four expert witnesses who appeared at the trial expressed opinions as to the quality of the defendant architect's work (some positive, some negative), but none of them established a local prevailing standard of architectural competence. In view of such a defect in the plaintiff's evidence, it was impossible to judge the performance of the architect. The burden of establishing the standard of practice was on the plaintiff. Therefore, the trial court's judgment finding no evidence of professional malpractice was AFFIRMED.

In *A.F. Blair Co v Mason*,[8] the plaintiff alleged that the architects had negligently caused certificates of payment to be issued when the construction contract conditions had not been fulfilled. The lower court dismissed the plaintiff's claim. AFFIRMED. The court could not conclude from the evidence

---

[6] 106 Wis 2d 545, 317 NW2d 834 (1982).

[7] 224 So 2d 161 (La Ct App 1969), *revd in part*, 256 La 85, 235 So 2d 386 (1970).

[8] 406 So 2d 6 (La Ct App 1981), *cert denied*, 410 So 2d 1132 (La 1982).

in the record that the architects were negligent. The plaintiff failed to introduce evidence of the degree of professional care and skill customarily employed by other architects in the local area. (The dissenting opinion criticized the majority's reliance upon the locality rule, suggesting that a nationwide standard now applies to all professions.)

Expert from a Different Profession

In *National Cash Register Co v Haak*,[9] the court held that it is not necessarily imperative to obtain the expert testimony of an architect as to the standard of practice for an architect; in some cases, the opinions of engineers or geologists may suffice. In this case, an architect had designed dry wells to dissipate water from a building site. The dry wells, in collecting percolating water, caused sink holes (the collapse of surface ground caused by erosion of underlying structures). The owner filed suit against the architect for improper design. The trial court granted a nonsuit on the ground that the plaintiff's case lacked essential expert testimony. REVERSED. Expert testimony is needed where *special experience* is required, and experience regarding the design of water disposal systems is not limited to architects. Engineers and geologists are also knowledgeable in this field. One geologist had testified that no one in the area ever recommended dry wells. This established a standard of local practice against which to measure the defendant's action. Therefore, the case should have gone to the jury.

Similarly, in a Texas case, in order to overcome budget problems, architects suggested the use of "C-Tile." Many problems arose. The developer relied on an expert witness with a degree in civil engineering. HELD: the fields of engineering and architecture overlap and are intertwined on the questions and issues testified to here. Therefore, it was proper to have a civil engineer testify as to the alleged negligence of an architect.[10]

The jury should be permitted to consider expert testimony as to the diminution in value of real estate resulting from defective construction, as well as evidence regarding the cost of correction.[11]

In *Perlmutter v Flickinger*,[12] shopping center skylights continued to leak after repeated attempts to repair them. The court of appeal AFFIRMED a trial court judgment against the architect and the installer based on the testimony of two experts: one a chemical engineer specializing in plastics with 20 years experience in design and fabrication of skylights in the Denver area; the other

---

[9] 233 Pa Super 562, 335 A2d 407 (1975).

[10] White Budd Van Ness Partnership v Major-Gladys Drive Joint Venture, 798 SW2d 805 (Tex Ct App 1990), *cert denied*, 112 S Ct 180 (1991).

[11] Rosos Litho Supply Corp v Hansen, 123 Ill App 3d 290, 462 NE2d 566 (1984).

[12] 520 P2d 596 (Colo Ct App 1974).

a contractor with 23 years experience in waterproofing and roofing that devoted 25 per cent of its business to the fabrication and repair of skylights. They were competent to give expert opinion on the adequacy of the skylight design. The crucial factor was the possession of peculiar skill or knowledge, and such skill or knowledge was not restricted to architects practicing in the locality where the damage occurred.

Safety Expert

A plaintiff's attempt to elicit testimony that a defendant's conduct is *unsafe* may be met by the objection that this subverts the function of the jury by taking away their ultimate decision as to liability. In *Cantrell v Dendahl*,[13] the plaintiff fell on a single step in a commercial mall. The court refused to allow the experts to express an opinion as to whether the step was safe or unsafe. Plaintiff appealed from a defense verdict. AFFIRMED. The admission or exclusion of expert testimony is peculiarly within the discretion of the trial court, and there was no abuse of discretion here.

Hypothetical Questions

Hypothetical questions to experts should contain facts supported by the evidence. However, if the opinion is based on disputed facts, the jury may ignore the hypothetical if it disbelieves the assumed facts. In *Board of Trustees v Lee Electric Co*,[14] an apartment house burned down three weeks after it was occupied. The plaintiff's expert asserted that the fire was caused by improper waterproofing which allowed moisture to enter a breaker box. The jury brought in a defense verdict, and the court held that, since the expert's opinion was based upon hypothetical questions which assumed disputed facts, the jury was entitled to ignore the opinion if it found the facts to be otherwise than stated in the hypothetical question.

Expert Relies on Hearsay

An expert witness may rely on hearsay or other nonrecord evidence in reaching a conclusion. The data underlying the expert's opinion need not be admitted in evidence.[15]

Attorney Work Product

In *Jasper Construction, Inc v Foothill Jr College District*,[16] judgment against the architect was REVERSED on the ground that the trial court had improperly

---

[13] 83 NM 583, 494 P2d 1400 (1972).
[14] 198 So 2d 231 (Miss 1967).
[15] Tiffany v Christman Co, 93 Mich App 267, 287 NW2d 199 (1979).
[16] 91 Cal App 3d 1, 153 Cal Rptr 767 (1979).

excluded evidence offered by an expert consulting engineer. (1) The engineer's testimony was excluded under the "work product" privilege. This privilege is applicable only to pre-trial discovery and is not applicable to prevent testimony of an expert at the trial. (2) The attorney-client privilege does not apply merely because a consulting engineer's findings were communicated to an attorney. The court stated, quoting from *City of San Francisco v Superior Court (City & County of San Francisco)*:[17] "[A] litigant cannot silence a witness by having him reveal his knowledge to the litigant's attorney."

Attorney-Client Privilege

Certain statements made by engineers or architects to an attorney may be protected from disclosure. In *Macey v Rollins Environmental Services, Inc*,[18] the corporation's project engineer prepared a statement, at the request of general counsel, regarding a fire and explosion at the corporation's plant. The statement by the engineer was protected from disclosure by the attorney-client privilege since such privilege extends to corporations who act through their agents, including corporate officers and employees.[19]

Qualifications of Expert

In *Farmers Insurance Co v Smith*,[20] the defendant challenged the qualifications of plaintiff's expert witness. The dispute involved responsibility for a fire in a mobile home. The court found that the engineer was: (1) fully qualified as an expert witness; (2) a licensed engineer with training in electrical engineering; (3) teaching an engineering course at the university; (4) a senior partner in an engineering firm which had extensive consulting business in the area of mobile homes; (5) had previously investigated fires and testified as an expert on such issues; and (6) was authorized by the state of Kansas to certify electrical systems in mobile homes.

The qualifications of an expert witness were also challenged in *Seese v Volkswagenwerk AG*.[21] Passengers of a Volkswagen van suffered injuries when they were thrown from the van through a window which popped out during a single-car *rollover* accident. The district court entered a jury verdict for the plaintiffs based on strict liability and negligent design of the window retention system. The court of appeals concluded that the trial court did not abuse its discretion by admitting the testimony of the plaintiff's witness. The court

---

[17] 37 Cal 2d 227, 237, 231 P2d 26, 31 (1951).
[18] 179 NJ Super 535, 432 A2d 960 (1981).
[19] Rules of Evidence, Rule 1-26, NJ Stat Ann §§2A:84A-1 to -20 (West).
[20] 219 Kan 680, 549 P2d 1026 (1976).
[21] 648 F2d 833 (3d Cir), *cert denied*, 454 US 867 (1981).

rejected Volkswagenwerk's assertion that Dr. Brenner was an *accident reconstructionist* and unqualified to provide testimony: "As an auto safety engineer, with substantial credentials, Brenner was clearly qualified to testify as an expert on alternative, practical, safe designs for the van's window retention system, particularly since he had an extensive background in the development of safety performance standards for automobiles."[22]

The cases speak for themselves. The plaintiff will usually lose if it fails to present competent and convincing expert testimony to establish that the defendant failed to meet the local standard of practice. Therefore, the plaintiff's lawyer should seek an expert of impeccable reputation and convincing demeanor and should be certain to produce testimony establishing the local standard of practice, not just an opinion that the defendant was careless.

§15.08   Law Notes

The basic currency of legal knowledge is the decisions of appellate courts, so the lawyer should develop a rational method to keep track of current cases. The method should allow the lawyer, or other members of the firm, to retrieve the information developed in one case for application to another case.

One way to do this is through the use of *abstracts*. The object is to summarize, in 100 to 200 words, the essential facts and rules of law established by a case, in a format that can be indexed and retrieved.

Index words and the citation may be displayed at the top of the paper, followed by the facts and the decision of the trial court, and the holding and reasoning of the appellate court. The lawyer can keep these at hand, alphabetically indexed in notebooks. They may be distributed to other members of the firm. They may be copied and bound into a trial book. They may also be used to prepare trial and appellate briefs and legal opinions, and for day-to-day advice to clients.

A computerized database program can be utilized for the storage and retrieval of abstracts. This system is contrasted to a typical, but less efficient, system in which a law clerk is asked to research a point and produce a memorandum of law. The memorandum of law will probably contain the clerk's opinion and will not necessarily include the facts, holding, and reasoning of the applicable cases. Once the memorandum has disappeared into a file, its value for future legal work has probably been lost.

Moreover, a mere citation supporting a legal proposition in a law memorandum is of little practical use to the lawyer. The lawyer needs to know the facts, the holding, and the reasoning. A citation is practically useless without a law library; but an abstract, for many practical purposes, supplants the library.

---

[22] *Id* 844.

§15.09 "Trial Book"

The trial book may be a three-ring notebook or a compatible series of flip-flop files with letter-size paper bound at the top. The "book" includes the fact summary, deposition summaries, witness outlines, and law abstracts. Blank sheets are added for argument, notes, and other needs.

An argument sheet is kept up-to-date with notes developed during the trial of evidence and testimony that should be included in the argument. Some night these can be organized for orderly presentation.

On another sheet are typed the names, addresses, and home and business telephone numbers of witnesses and opposing and co-counsel.

At trial, the lawyer should be able to concentrate on questions, objections, the demeanor and testimony of the witnesses, and the judge's state of mind. Good organization of material helps prevent distraction from the crucial issues.

§15.10 Proposed Award

It is a maxim of trial practice that the lawyer should ask the jury for exactly what is wanted. In arbitration proceedings, the lawyer should consider preparing a written proposed award for submission to the arbitrators. The case may actually be decided several days after it is submitted, and it is no more than elementary good sense to be certain that the arbitrators are in no doubt as to the contents of the award desired by the client.

Appendix A
Persons Protected

Owner
Remote Owner
Tenant
Neighbor
Patron
Lender
Third Party
Vehicle Occupant
Infant
Worker
Contractor
Subcontractor
Surety
Architect
Supplier

    The subject of the malpractice of architects is distinguished by the extraordinary variety of claimants. The primary duty of the architect is considered to be, and doubtless is, to the client. The architect is a fiduciary to the client and owes to the client the utmost diligence and fidelity.

    The architect is denied the comfortable simplicity which characterizes the lawyer's duty. In fulfilling that duty to the client, the lawyer is permitted to disregard the interests (though not the rights) of others. Most of the third parties who come into the ambit of the lawyer's practice must protect their own interests.

    However, the legal environment in which the architect practices is a perplexing welter of parties, some nearby and others remote, to each of whom it seems the architect owes a duty of care. Indeed, when the architect interprets the contract documents and decides questions arising between the contractor and the owner, the architect is expected to put aside the interests of the client and rise to the stature of an arbitrator. This function, indeed, is said to be the highest pinnacle of the profession of the architect.

The architect is bound to respect the rights not only of the contractor, but also of the other job site participants: subcontractors, sureties, other architects, and workers. The duty extends not only to the present owner of the immediate project, but also to future owners and occupants and to neighboring owners and their successors. The legal drama of the architect is played out with a large cast.

Owner

This discussion includes a collection of cases in which the owner asserted a claim of malpractice against an architect. In some of the cases, the owner is the plaintiff; in others, the owner asserts the malpractice claim as an offset against the architect's action for a fee. The following summaries list the grievances alleged by the owner against the architect. In some cases the grievances were not proved or were held not to be a breach of any duty owed by the architect to the owner.

Note that all of the cases herein, dealing with projects which cost more than estimated by the architect, are cases in which the complaining party is the owner or a tenant.

United States

Roof did not meet the architectural requirement for the Danish ambience of St. Croix. *General Trading Corp v Burnup & Sims, Inc*, 523 F2d 98 (3d Cir 1975).

The contract called for the architect to certify monthly payments to the contractor "upon invoices presented by the contractor and approved by the architect." Instead of demanding invoices, the architect accepted monthly *estimates* by the contractor. The contractor defaulted. *Hall v Union Indemnity Co*, 61 F2d 85 (8th Cir), *cert denied*, 287 US 663 (1932). (*See* **Surety's Guarantee,** below.)

Air conditioning system did not function properly. *Frank M. Dorsey & Sons v Frishman*, 291 F Supp 794 (DDC 1968).

Alabama

The storm drain plan was not adequate to handle storm water on a subdivision. *Broyles v Brown Engineering Co*, 275 Ala 35, 151 So 2d 767 (1963).

Arizona

Defendant designed and built a 30-foot fence to screen light from a drive-in theatre. A week after completion, it fell down. *Rosell v Silver Crest Enterprises*, 7 Ariz App 137, 436 P2d 915 (1968).

California

The owner employed a driller to test soil for fill; the driller reported 12 to 16 inches of fill rather than the 3 to 6 feet actually present. *Gagne v Bertran*, 43 Cal 2d 481, 275 P2d 15 (1954).

Architect circulated slanderous reports that the members of the board of supervisors took bribes and secretly employed an agent who pretended to give the board of supervisors unbiased advice to employ the architect. *Hall v City of Los Angeles*, 74 Cal 502, 16 P 131 (1888).

Soil engineer permitted installation of inadequate compacted fill. *Oakes v McCarthy Co*, 267 Cal App 2d 231, 73 Cal Rptr 127 (1968).

Closets only 18 inches wide, floor uneven, doors too complicated to be fabricated by local artisans, sliding doors stuck, and fireplace cracked. *Bayuk v Edson*, 236 Cal App 2d 309, 46 Cal Rptr 49 (1965).

Celery fields were flooded with sewage from manhole when the Salinas River reached 47 feet above sea level. *Alisal Sanitary District v Kennedy*, 180 Cal App 2d 69, 4 Cal Rptr 379 (1960).

The engineer estimated 51,000 cubic yards of dirt, the court found the correct figure was 15,802 cubic yards. *Roberts v Karr*, 178 Cal App 2d 535, 3 Cal Rptr 98 (1960).

The slab floor on a residence was poorly constructed. *Pancoast v Russell*, 148 Cal App 2d 909, 307 P2d 719 (1957).

After moving into a completed house, the owners discovered the floors were not level, the plaster was cracked, and the foundations had been installed on loose fill rather than solid earth. *Alexander v Hammarberg*, 103 Cal App 2d 872, 230 P2d 399 (1951).

Architect designed inadequate space for receptionist, inadequate air conditioning, soundproofing, door locks, and other unsuitable items for medical building. *Goldberg v Underhill*, 95 Cal App 2d 700, 213 P2d 516 (1950).

Court-appointed surveyor negligently laid out a boundary. *Kingsbury v Tevco, Inc*, 79 Cal App 3d 314, 144 Cal Rptr 773 (1978).

Colorado

Grain storage bin collapsed. *Balcom Industries v Nelson*, 169 Colo 128, 454 P2d 599 (1969).

Surveyor located owner's home on government's land. *Doyle v Linn*, 37 Colo App 214, 547 P2d 257 (1975).

Architect failed to specify water softeners. *Jim Arnott, Inc v L&E, Inc*, 539 P2d 1333 (Colo Ct App 1975) not officially published.

Skylights leaked. *Perlmutter v Flickinger*, 520 P2d 596 (Colo Ct App 1974).

District of Columbia

The defendant building material dealer designed a residential heating and air conditioning system at the request of the builder; the system malfunctioned. *Robitscher v United Clay Products Co*, 143 A2d 99 (DC 1958).

Florida

Houses were not rainproof. *Bayshore Development Co v Bonfoey*, 75 Fla 445, 78 So 507 (1918).

Water line under river installed six feet above the depth required by the contract documents. *Lee County v Southern Waters Contractors, Inc*, 298 So 2d 518 (Fla Dist Ct App 1974).

Georgia

Water seepage in basement. *Block v Happ*, 144 Ga 145, 86 SE 316 (1915).

Water pipes froze. *Wheat Street Two, Inc v James C. Wise, Simpson, Aiken & Associates*, 132 Ga App 548, 208 SE2d 359 (1974).

Roof collapsed. *Wellston Co v Sam N. Hodges Jr & Co*, 114 Ga App 424, 151 SE2d 481 (1966).

Illinois

Architect selected an incompetent and impoverished heating contractor. *Morse v Michaelson, Rabig & Ramp*, 10 Ill App 2d 366, 243 NE2d 271 (1968).

Indiana

Architect conspired with builder to increase the cost of the project. *Rice v Caldwell*, 87 Ind App 616, 161 NE 651 (1928).

Iowa

Defective foundation caused cracks in brick hotel building. *Schreiner v Miller*, 67 Iowa 91, 24 NW 738 (1885).

Kansas

Architect permitted contractor to build according to alternate, rather than basic plan. *School District No 5 v Ferrier*, 122 Kan 15, 251 P 425 (1926).

Louisiana

Because of latent, unstable soil conditions, foundation piles were displaced. Despite the contractor's warning, the engineer went forward with a floating slab foundation on the piles, and settlement occurred. *Pittman Construction Co v City of New Orleans*, 178 So 2d 312 (La Ct App), *appeal denied*, 248 La 434, 179 So 2d 274 (1965).

Designer-builder recommended and installed *super-rock*, which cracked. *Barraque v Neff*, 202 La 360, 11 So 2d 697 (1942).

A surveyor employed to *confirm* an earlier survey failed to discover a mistake in the computation of acreage: the survey called out 13.6 acres; actual was 11.26. *Jenkins v J.J. Krebs & Sons*, 322 So 2d 426 (La Ct App 1975), *writ denied*, 325 So 2d 611 (La 1976).

Warehouse walls cracked because the architect failed to design iron lintels over arches. *Louisiana Molasses Co v Le Sassier*, 52 La Ann 2070, 28 So 217, *affd*, 52 La Ann 1768, 28 So 223 (1900).

Maryland

Surveyor failed to obtain maximum lot yield and erroneously staked corners. *Mattingly v Hopkins*, 254 Md 88, 253 A2d 904 (1969).

Massachusetts

An underground concrete fuel tank floated. *Simpson Brothers Corp v Merrimac Chemical Co*, 248 Mass 346, 142 NE 922 (1924).

Architect falsely represented the value of the work done by the builder and issued a payment certificate even though the work was faulty. *Corey v Eastman*, 166 Mass 279, 44 NE 217 (1896).

Michigan

Owner alleged the engineer delayed in preparing plans for slag-crushing plant. *Giffels & Vallet, Inc v Edward C. Levy Co*, 337 Mich 177, 58 NW2d 899 (1953).

Defective cornice, coping, stairway, elevator, and chimney flue. *Chapel v Clark*, 117 Mich 638, 76 NW 62 (1898).

Minnesota

Defendant represented he had 17 years experience in the building business, he left the business because of ill health, he was an engineer, his net worth was $75,000, and he would be able to obtain a performance bond. In reality he left the building business because of bankruptcy, he was not an engineer, his net worth was $45,000, and because of the bankruptcy, he was not bondable. The house budgeted for $38,000 cost $79,300. *Strouth v Wilkison*, 302 Minn 297, 224 NW2d 511 (1974).

Cracks appeared in bridge abutment walls because piling which was driven under the inspection of architect, designed to carry 15 tons, would only support load of 7 to 13 tons. *Cowles v City of Minneapolis*, 128 Minn 452, 151 NW 184 (1915).

Mississippi

The engineer certified payment at the rate of $15 per linear foot rather than $1.50 per linear foot. *Newton Investment Co v Barnard & Burk, Inc*, 220 So 2d 822 (Miss 1969).

The walls cracked and buckled, the roof leaked, and cracks appeared in the floor slab because of the introduction of drainage water into the expansive Yazoo clay strata. *Dickerson Construction Co v Process Engineering Co*, 341 So 2d 646 (Miss 1977).

Missouri

The entrance to a mule barn was 30 inches above the curb, making it difficult to bring loads of feed into the barn; the floor of the mule alley was inclined. *Dysart-Cook Mule Co v Reed & Heckenlively*, 114 Mo App 296, 89 SW 591 (1905).

Nebraska

The house leaked, floors were uneven, and doors would not open and close. *Lincoln Stone & Supply Co v Ludwig*, 94 Neb 722, 144 NW 782 (1913).

New Mexico

Roof leak. *Board of Education School District No 16 v Standhardt*, 80 NM 543, 458 P2d 795 (1969).

Architect was employed by the contractor, not the owner. He designed a radiant heating system that did not work. *Staley v New*, 56 NM 756, 250 P2d 893 (1952).

New York

Undersized chimney flue. *Hubert v Aitken*, 15 Daly 237, 2 NYS 711 (CP 1888), *affd*, 123 NY 655, 25 NE 954 (1890).

Defective masonry work (height and appearance of windows and stoop). *Petersen v Rawson*, 34 NY 370 (1866), *revd*, 15 NY Sup Ct 234 (1857).

Flood. *Thomas E. Hoar, Inc v Jobco, Inc*, 30 AD2d 541, 291 NYS2d 380 (1968).

Architect failed to detect attachment of floor beams to a stud partition (a violation of the building code) because the contractor concealed the deviation. *Straus v Buchman*, 96 AD 270, 89 NYS 226 (1904), *affd*, 184 NY 545, 76 NE 1109 (1906).

Leaks. *Broome County v Vincent J. Smith, Inc*, 78 Misc 2d 889, 358 NYS2d 998 (Sup Ct 1974).

Trespass. *Henneberger v Herman Schwabe, Inc*, 58 Misc 2d 986, 297 NYS2d 381 (Sup Ct 1968).

Owner versus surveyor for encroachment. *Seger v Cornwell*, 44 Misc 2d 994, 255 NYS2d 744 (Sup Ct 1964).

Woodwork in a residence shrunk. *Lindeberg v Hodgens*, 89 Misc 454, 152 NYS 229 (Sup Ct 1915).

Architect allowed builder to install work which did not comply with the contract documents. *Schwartz v Kuhn*, 71 Misc 149, 126 NYS 568 (Sup Ct 1911).

North Carolina

An architect negligently certified the amount of work completed on a project. *Browning v Maurice B. Levien & Co*, 44 NC App 701, 262 SE2d 355, *review denied*, 300 NC 371, 267 SE2d 673 (1980).

Oklahoma

Improper design of an auxiliary solar heating system for a home. *Keel v Titan Construction Corp*, 639 P2d 1228 (Okla 1981).

Roof leak. *Wills v Black & West Architects*, 344 P2d 581 (Okla 1959).

Oregon

The engineer reviewed plans for viaduct shoring system prepared by plaintiff but failed to discover defects. *Pacific Form Corp v Burgstahler*, 263 Or 266, 501 P2d 308 (1972).

Building improperly located on lot, parking lot too small. *Bales for Food, Inc v Poole*, 246 Or 253, 424 P2d 892 (1967).

Building settled, and it was necessary to shore up the walls with jack screws. *White v Pallay*, 119 Or 97, 247 P 316 (1926).

Pennsylvania

A weaving mill was designed for a constant temperature of 80 and humidity of 60 per cent. Fiberglass insulation collected moisture and became soggy, causing condensation on roof. The owner had to replace the roof. *Bloomsburg Mills, Inc v Sordoni Construction Co*, 401 Pa 358, 164 A2d 201 (1960).

Architect failed to deliver residence plans on time. *Edwards v Hall*, 293 Pa 97, 141 A 638 (1928).

Delay in preparing plan details. *Osterling v Frick*, 284 Pa 397, 131 A 250 (1925).

Collapse of earth embankment. *Trinity Area School District v Dickson*, 223 Pa Super 546, 302 A2d 481 (1973). (*See* **Infant,** *below.*)

Four homeowners stated a cause of action in negligence against a surveyor hired to set boundary lines for lots and streets, lay plans for the sewage and drainage lines in the development, and supervise the excavation of drainage ditches. *Wicks v Milzoco Builders, Inc*, 291 Pa Super 345, 435 A2d 1260 (1981), *vacated on other grounds*, 503 Pa 614, 470 A2d 86 (1983).

Rhode Island

The architect visited the job every day before work began and after it was finished, but not during working hours. *Chiaverini v Vail*, 61 RI 117, 200 A 462 (1938).

South Carolina

Within a few weeks after the cooling process was turned on in a frozen food plant, cracks appeared in the floor, the floor bulged, the walls cracked, and the plant became useless. *Hill v Polar Pantries*, 219 SC 263, 64 SE2d 885 (1951).

Plaster fell from house. *Avent v Proffitt*, 109 SC 48, 95 SE 134 (1918).

Tennessee

Boiler exploded. *Wheeler v Fred Wright Construction Co*, 57 Tenn App 77, 415 SW2d 156 (1966).

Texas

House too big for the lot. *Newell v Mosley*, 469 SW2d 481 (Tex Civ App 1971).

Architect issued payment certificates to contractor although work was defective. *Pierson v Tyndall*, 28 SW 232 (Tex Civ App 1894).

Stove flues in courthouse would not draw smoke. *Larrimore v Comanche County*, 32 SW 367 (Tex Civ App 1895).

Utah

A heavy valve pulled loose from a tank in a gas compression system, causing an explosion. *Uinta Pipeline Corp v White Superior Co*, 546 P2d 885 (Utah 1976).

The home designed by defendant would not fit the lot, violated setback requirements, and did not obtain the desired view. *Quagliana v Exquisite Home Builders, Inc*, 538 P2d 301 (Utah 1975).

Virginia

The heating and air conditioning systems did not work properly: ducts filled with water. *Willner v Woodward*, 201 Va 104, 109 SE2d 132 (1959).

The complicated steel sliding roof of a ballroom did not work. *Surf Realty Corp v Standing*, 195 Va 431, 78 SE2d 901 (1953).

Washington

The soil under an ice rink froze, threatening the foundations. *Prier v Refrigeration Engineering Co*, 74 Wash 2d 25, 442 P2d 621 (1968).

The cantilever retaining wall deflected, bulged, and cracked. *McGuire v United Brotherhood of Carpenters & Joiners of America*, 50 Wash 699, 314 P2d 439 (1957).

Plans for eight-story building violated building code. *Bebb v Jordan*, 111 Wash 73, 189 P 553 (1920).

Roof collapsed under heavy load of snow. *School District No 172 v Josenhans*, 88 Wash 624, 153 P 326 (1915).

Wisconsin

Insufficient heat in hospital. *Milwaukee County v Schmidt, Garden & Erikson*, 43 Wis 2d 445, 168 NW2d 559 (1969).

Remote Owner

There follows a collection of cases where the party complaining of the alleged malpractice was not the architect's client, but one who purchased the project from the architect's client, or from an intermediate owner. The duty of the architect extends beyond his or her immediate client to future owners of the project who may foreseeably be damaged by the negligent performance of the architect's functions.

Alabama

In *Howe v Bishop*, 446 So 2d 11 (Ala 1984), it was held that subsequent purchasers of an apartment complex, not in privity with the original builder, were not entitled to assert a malpractice cause of action against the architect and the engineer who designed the building. It was not reasonably foreseeable that anyone other than the original builder would own the apartments. There was no duty owed to subsequent purchasers.

California

Father and two children asphyxiated by carbon monoxide from gas heater. *Dow v Holly Manufacturing Co*, 49 Cal 2d 720, 321 P2d 736 (1958).

The condominium project as built was hazardous, subject to structural failure, a firetrap, and a poor investment. *Cooper v Jevne*, 56 Cal App 3d 860, 128 Cal Rptr 724 (1976).

Surveyor prepared lot split; encroachment developed. *Kent v Bartlett*, 49 Cal App 3d 724, 122 Cal Rptr 615 (1975).

Soil settlement. *Swett v Gribaldo, Jones & Associates*, 40 Cal App 3d 573, 115 Cal Rptr 99 (1974).

Florida

Action brought against architects by the condominium association on behalf of its owners. *Parliament Towers Condominium v Parliament House Realty, Inc*, 377 So 2d 976 (Fla Dist Ct App 1979).

Georgia

The surveyor used an improperly prepared preexisting plat furnished by the owner as reference for determining the disputed boundary line. Purchaser was damaged when she relied upon the surveyor's certified plat. *Hutchinson v Dubeau*, 161 Ga App 65, 289 SE2d 4 (1982).

Illinois

Relying on a survey prepared by defendant, the plaintiff built a garage and driveway which encroached on property belonging to a neighbor. *Rozny v Marnal*, 43 Ill 2d 54, 250 NE2d 656 (1969).

Massachusetts

Lot flooded with effluent from septic system; defendant had performed a percolation test. *McDonough v Whalen*, 365 Mass 506, 313 NE2d 435 (1974).

New Jersey

Sewage flooded plaintiffs' basements because of an inadequately designed sewer system. *Panepinto v Edmart, Inc*, 129 NJ Super 319, 323 A2d 533, *cert denied*, 66 NJ 333, 331 A2d 33 (1974).

New York

Engineers prepared a grading plan for a subdivision. The land was thereafter sold to builders. When they commenced construction, the city revoked subdivision approval on the ground that storm water would damage a preexisting house. *Vandewater & Lapp v Sacks Builders, Inc*, 20 Misc 2d 677, 186 NYS2d 103 (Sup Ct 1959).

Inconsequential defects. *Sard v Berman*, 47 AD2d 892, 367 NYS2d 266 (1975).

South Dakota

Although a corner monument was incorrectly placed, the surveyor certified the subdivision plat as being accurate. A subsequent purchaser relied upon the corner monument which the surveyor failed to remove after learning of the error. The purchaser properly alleged negligent misrepresentation of the corner monument's location; breach of the warranty of accuracy contained in the certification of the survey; and the purchaser was a third-party beneficiary. *Nichols v Brady Consultants, Inc*, 305 NW2d 849 (SD 1981).

Tenant

United States

Twenty-two-month-old child fell to his death from the balcony of a fifth floor apartment. Distance between vertical rails was five inches; gap between the bottom rail and the floor was six and three-quarters inches; top rail was 42 inches high. *Noble v Worthy*, 378 A2d 674 (DC 1977).

Shopping center was flooded. *Stromberg's v Victor Gruen & Associates*, 384 F2d 163 (10th Cir 1967).

California

Eighteen-month-old child, who resided with her mother at the Harbor Towers apartments, sustained injuries when she fell through the second floor railing to the ground. *Grimmer v Harbor Towers*, 133 Cal App 3d 88, 183 Cal Rptr 634 (1982).

Delaware

Shopping center tenant sustained damage when flood waters entered the building. *Seiler v Levitz Furniture Co*, 367 A2d 999 (Del Super Ct 1976).

Georgia

The engineer designed a novel roof system in 1957. In 1961, he learned that a similar roof had collapsed but did not notify the owner. In 1963, the plaintiff leased the building, and shortly thereafter, the roof collapsed. *Hunt v Star Photo Finishing Co*, 115 Ga App 1, 153 SE2d 602 (1967).

Idaho

Tenant slipped and fell on stairway without handrail. *Stephens v Sterns*, 106 Idaho 249, 678 P2d 41 (1984).

New Jersey

Part of the piping for the heating system was designed in a ladderlike arrangement. Three-year-old plaintiff was burned after trying to climb piping. *Totten v Gruzen*, 52 NJ 202, 245 A2d 1 (1968). (*See* **Infant,** *below.*)

New York

Apartment house tenant fell and was injured in the laundry room of a building completed in 1973. HELD: statute of limitations ran from the time of injury in 1974. *Cubito v Kreisberg*, 69 AD2d 738, 419 NYS2d 578 (1979), *affd*, 51 NY2d 900, 415 NE2d 979, 434 NYS2d 991 (1980).

Wisconsin

Soil settlement. *A.E. Investment Corp v Link Builders, Inc*, 62 Wis 2d 479, 214 NW2d 764 (1974).

Neighbor

United States

The retaining wall supporting an embankment of an excavation collapsed, damaging an adjoining stone sidewalk. *United States v Peachy*, 36 F 160 (D Ohio 1888).

California

Lower landowner filed an action against an engineer employed by an upper landowner to prepare plans for correction of slope damage. *Shurpin v Elmhirst*, 148 Cal App 3d 94, 195 Cal Rptr 737 (1983).

Dam burst, neighbor downstream. *Boswell v Laird*, 8 Cal 469 (1857).

The water system in a residential area was not adequate for fire fighting. *Stuart v Crestview Mutual Water Co*, 34 Cal App 3d 802, 110 Cal Rptr 543 (1973).

Dam burst, plaintiff downstream. *Diamond Springs Lime Co v American River Constructions*, 16 Cal App 3d 581, 94 Cal Rptr 200 (1971).

Florida

Surveyor, who entered land in the practice of his profession, damaged vegetation. *Ragland v Clarson*, 259 So 2d 757 (Fla Dist Ct App 1972).

Georgia

Architect designed a church project and changed the drainage pattern of storm water which then entered plaintiff's land, flooding basement and causing other damage. *Bodin v Gill*, 216 Ga 467, 117 SE2d 325 (1960).

A T-joint slipped off a 24-inch pipe in a pumping station from the pressure of water stored in an adjoining reservoir. This allowed millions of gallons of water to flow onto plaintiff's land. *Covil v Robert & Co*, 112 Ga App 163, 144 SE2d 450 (1965).

Condominium developer charged with damage from diversion of surface water; developer brought a third-party claim against the engineer. *Ponce de Leon Condos v DiGirolamo*, 238 Ga 188, 232 SE2d 62 (1977).

Illinois

Construction of subdivision diverted surface water, causing damage to neighboring property. *Elliott v Nordlof*, 83 Ill App 279, 227 NE2d 547 (1967).

Iowa

Storm waters from school site damaged nearby home; householder complained, architect ignored the problem. *McCarthy v J.P. Cullen & Son Corp*, 199 NW2d 362 (Iowa 1972).

Kentucky

Installation of sanitary sewer disrupted flow of storm sewer, flooding neighbor. *Seaman v Castellini*, 415 SW2d 612 (Ky 1967).

Maryland

Landowner brought an action against neighbor and neighbor's surveyor for continuing trespass and negligent preparation of boundary survey. *Carlotta v T.R. Stark & Associates*, 57 Md App 467, 470 A2d 838 (1984).

New Mexico

During excavation, damage occurred to surrounding buildings and roads. The contractor's insurer paid for the damage and filed suit against the architect, alleging negligent preparation of plans and specifications for excavation, sheet piling, and compaction. *Fireman's Fund American Insurance Co v Phillips, Carter Reister & Associates*, 89 NM 7, 546 P2d 72, cert denied, 89 NM 5, 546 P2d 70 (1976).

Storm waters escaping from school site flooded nearby home. *Martin v Board of Education*, 79 NM 636, 447 P2d 516 (1968).

Texas

Neighboring landowner damaged by storm water from subdivision. *Kraft v Langford*, 565 SW2d 223 (Tex 1978).

Utah

Neighbor charged surveyor with encroachment. *Bushnell v Sillitoe*, 550 P2d 1284 (Utah 1976).

Patron

United States

A theater-goer was killed when the Knickerbocker Theatre collapsed. *Geare v Sturgis*, 56 App DC 364, 14 F2d 256 (1926), *overruled*, *Hannah v Fletcher*, 97 US App DC 310, 231 F2d 469 (1956).

A spectator was injured in the clubhouse at the racetrack when a heating duct dislodged from the ceiling. The supervising architect had not detected that the duct was attached to the ceiling rather than to the ceiling joists. *Pastorelli v Associated Engineers, Inc*, 176 F Supp 159 (DRI 1959).

Motel guest injured after walking into a glass door. *Karna v Byron Reed Syndicate No 4*, 374 F Supp 687, 689 (D Neb 1974).

Plaintiff fell on steps surrounding the fountain area of the Smithsonian Institution. *Watt v United States*, 444 F Supp 1191 (DDC 1978).

California

The plaintiff fell while descending a staircase. She contended the handrail was too short. *Montijo v Swift*, 219 Cal App 2d 351, 33 Cal Rptr 133 (1963).

Florida

A metal counter-weight dislodged from a ceiling fan in a restaurant and struck a patron. *Mai Kai, Inc v Colucci*, 205 So 2d 291 (Fla 1967).

Plaintiff slipped and fell at shopping center mall. *LeMay v United States H. Properties, Inc*, 338 So 2d 1143 (Fla Dist Ct App 1976).

Drama student fell into a pit created by a lowered stage area in a theater auditorium. *Erwine v Gamble, Pownal & Gilroy Architects & Engineers*, 343 So 2d 859 (Fla Dist Ct App 1976).

Illinois

Restaurant patron suffered cuts when the glass portion of an interior restaurant door broke as she exerted force upon it. *Rhodes v Mill Race Inn, Inc*, 126 Ill App 3d 1024, 467 NE2d 915 (1984), *appeal denied* (Jan Term 1985).

Plaintiff was entering a building when a piling was dislodged by a severe windstorm. *Laukkanen v Jewel Tea Co*, 78 Ill App 2d 153, 222 NE2d 584 (1966).

Indiana

An airport patron was blown from pedestrian ramp by the blast of a jet aircraft. HELD: lack of privity between the architect and the injured party did not bar suit. *Hiatt v Brown*, 422 NE2d 736 (Ind Ct App 1981).

Iowa

Plaintiff sustained injuries when she ran into a window in the vestibule area of hospital. *Fox v Stanley J. How & Associates*, 309 NW2d 520 (Iowa Ct App 1981).

Kansas

Plaintiff fell on hospital stairway. *Russell v Community Hospital Assn*, 199 Kan 251, 428 P2d 783 (1967).

Louisiana

A warehouse was designed on a *floating slab*. It contained specially designed racks for tile storage. The racks collapsed, destroying the tile. *Home Insurance Co v A.J. Warehouse, Inc*, 210 So 2d 544 (La Ct App 1968).

New Jersey

A bath house erected in 1927 collapsed in 1940. *State v Ireland*, 126 NJL 444, 20 A2d 69 (1941).

New York

A fire of incendiary origin killed 11 people and injured others trapped on the fourth floor. Inflammable plastic panel exacerbated the fire. *Greenberg v City of Yonkers*, 45 AD2d 314, 358 NYS2d 453 (1974), *affd*, 37 NY2d 907, 340 NE2d 744, 378 NYS2d 382 (1975).

Student injured by glass panel adjoining door in dormitory building. *Coffey v Dormitory Authority*, 26 AD2d 1, 270 NYS2d 255 (1966).

Wisconsin

Nine-year-old plaintiff fell from a four-foot-high railing and struck a window of a school building. *Mlynarski v St Rita's Congregation*, 31 Wis 2d 54, 142 NW2d 207 (1966).

Upon entering a building, the plaintiff fell over an inner step in the lobby. She alleged the step was too close to the door. *Hommel v Badger State Investment Co*, 166 Wis 235, 165 NW 20 (1917).

Lender

California

The engineer conducted soil tests; differential settlement caused the foundations to fail. *United States Finances v Sullivan*, 37 Cal App 3d 5, 112 Cal Rptr 18 (1974).

Florida

The endorser of a note secured by a mortgage was damaged when the engineer negligently inspected and rendered reports on work completed, causing the mortgagee to wrongfully disburse loan proceeds to the mortgagor-developer. *Hobbs v Florida First National Bank*, 406 So 2d 63 (Fla Dist Ct App 1981).

Illinois

The lender alleged impairment of its security interest when a housing development for the elderly suffered a water leakage problem causing substantial interior and exterior damage. *Illinois Housing Development Authority v Sjostron & Sons*, 105 Ill App 3d 247, 433 NE2d 1350 (1982).

Tennessee

The engineer accepted the assurances of the builder and subcontractor that the fill was controlled but made no independent investigation; the foundations failed. *Cooper v Cordova Sand & Gravel Co*, 485 SW2d 261 (Tenn Ct App 1971).

Washington

In *Haberman v Washington Public Power Supply Systems*, 109 Wash 2d 107, 744 P2d 1032 (1987), purchasers of revenue bonds issued to finance nuclear power plants brought an action against engineers who had given opinions as to the structural feasibility of the project. The opinions of the engineers were used in the bond prospectus. HELD: the bondholders were entitled to maintain a claim for misrepresentation, since the engineers knew, or had reason to know, that their opinions would be used in the bond prospectus and that the plaintiffs would rely on the information. The bondholders were also entitled to prosecute a fraud claim against the engineers, since the engineers gave their information to the power company knowing that it would be passed on to investors.

West Virginia

City housing authority filed suit against its architect, alleging negligence, fraud, and breach of implied and express warranties. The architect claimed that the Department of Housing & Urban Development was the real party in interest because it exercised extensive rights of supervision over the project and the architect and furnished all the funds for the construction of the project. *Housing Authority v E.T. Boggess Architect, Inc*, 160 W Va 303, 233 SE2d 740 (1977).

Third Party

Maryland

Surveyor computed the size of a parcel to be 22.075 acres; it was actually 19.58 acres. Plaintiff relied on the computation in determining the purchase price of the property. *Reighard v Downs*, 261 Md 26, 273 A2d 109 (1971), *appeal after remand*, 265 Md 344, 289 A2d 299 (1972).

A 35-year-old guest at a swimming party dove from the diving board and struck his head on the bottom which was seven feet deep; the standard recommended by the American Public Health Association was eight feet. *Telak v Maszczenski*, 248 Md 476, 237 A2d 434 (1968).

Oregon

The county lowered the grade of a road, which undermined the handrail post at the bottom of a stairway leading from plaintiff's house. Plaintiff fell when it collapsed. *Ogle v Billick*, 253 Or 92, 453 P2d 677 (1969).

A masonry wall was not constructed according to code. It collapsed on plaintiff in a windstorm. *Johnson v Salem Title Co*, 246 Or 409, 425 P2d 519 (1967).

Vehicle Occupant

United States

Plaintiffs were thrown from a Volkswagen van when the windows popped out during a single-car rollover accident. *Seese v Volkswagenwerk AG*, 648 F2d 833 (3d Cir), *cert denied*, 454 US 867 (1981).

Kentucky

The engineering consultant failed to recommend guardrails; auto crashed against bridge pier. *Rigsby v Brighton Engineering Co*, 464 SW2d 279 (Ky 1970).

Wisconsin

District engineer permitted curve warning sign to be placed 794-1/2 feet from the intersection. *Chart v Dvorak*, 57 Wis 2d 92, 203 NW2d 673 (1973).

Infant

California

Nine-year-old guest spilled gasoline which was ignited by a gas-fired water heater in the garage; the heater was designed so that the pilot light was about six inches from the floor. *Hyman v Gordon*, 35 Cal App 3d 769, 111 Cal Rptr 262 (1973).

Florida

Child, a social guest, injured by sliding glass door. *Hutchings v Harry*, 242 So 2d 153 (Fla Dist Ct App 1970).

Eleven-year-old motel guest drowned after his arm could not be freed from the suction of a swimming pool drain pump. *Henry v Britt*, 220 So 2d 917 (Fla Dist Ct App), *cert denied*, 229 So 2d 867 (Fla 1969).

Louisiana

Fourteen-year-old guest injured by sliding glass door. *Natal v Phoenix Assurance Co*, 286 So 2d 738 (La Ct App 1973), *revd as to other parties*, 305 So 2d 438 (La 1974).

Mississippi

A child sustained injuries when he thrust his arm through a glass door while leaving a school building. *Anderson v Fred Wagner*, 402 So 2d 320 (Miss 1981).

New Jersey

Heating pipe was designed like a ladder; a three-year-old was burned climbing pipe. *Totten v Gruzen*, 52 NJ 202, 245 A2d 1 (1968). (*See* **Tenant,** *above*.)

An infant was scalded by water from the hot-water tap, which was connected to the radiant heating system containing 190-degree water. A mixing valve was available at a cost of $3.60 to reduce the temperature but was not specified. *Schipper v Levitt & Sons*, 44 NJ 70, 207 A2d 314 (1965).

New York

A two-year-old tenant fell from the stoop; there was no protective railing, and the arc made by the door when opened might force a person close to the edge where the step did not extend the full length of the stoop. *Inman v Binghamton Housing Authority*, 3 NY2d 137, 143 NE2d 895, 164 NYS2d 699 (1957).

Pennsylvania

A school child fell down at a basement entry after being pushed by another child and tripping over a three-inch curb. *Trinity Area School District v Dickson*, 223 Pa Super 546, 302 A2d 481 (1973) (*See* **Owner,** *above.*)

Worker

The reader will note the sudden proliferation of worker versus architect cases in the decades of the 1960s and 1970s. The explanation seems to be that lawyers representing workers have only recently recognized the architect as a potential defendant, and in most cases, a good one.

For a collection of decisions commenting that the architect is exonerated from liability in an unexpectedly large number of cases, see Sweet, *Site Architects & Construction Workers: Brothers and Keepers or Strangers?*, 28 Emory LJ 290 (1980).

United States

A worker contracted silicosis by inhaling heavy clouds of silica dust which were raised during the process of mucking for the Washington Metro Subway System. Bechtel, Inc. contracted to supply safety engineering services, to enforce safety codes, and to inspect the job site for violations. *Caldwell v Bechtel, Inc*, 203 US App DC 407, 631 F2d 989 (1980).

A wheel slipped from the track of a hoist, spilling a load on plaintiff truck driver; the hoist allegedly lacked sufficient wheels. *Coons v Washington Mirror Works, Inc*, 477 F2d 864 (2d Cir 1973).

The engineer designed and supervised the operation of a chemical-manufacturing plant, including loading a catalyst in the form of pellets coated with vanadium into a reactor. Some vanadium dust was inhaled by decedent, causing cancer. *La Rossa v Scientific Design Co*, 402 F2d 937 (3d Cir 1968).

Electric shock. *Associated Engineerrs, Inc v Job*, 370 F2d 633 (8th Cir 1966), *cert denied*, 389 US 823 (1967).

An employee of the general contractor fell through a hole in the roof. *Bruemmer v Clark Equipment Co*, 341 F2d 23 (7th Cir 1965).

Building collapsed during construction. *United Gas Improvement Co v Larsen*, 182 F 620 (CC Pa 1910).

Alabama

Widow of decedent worker sued an engineer for failure to specify a guard to shield the nip point of the head pulley in plans and specifications for modifying the bulk-loading facility at the state docks. *Plant v R.L. Reid, Inc*, 365 So 2d 305 (Ala 1978).

Alaska

Two brothers were killed by a rock slide while working as heavy equipment operators on a state highway project. A wrongful death action was brought against the state, alleging that the state had failed to discharge its affirmative duty to assure job safety as owner of the premises and employer of the excavation contractor for whom the brothers worked. *Moloso v State*, 644 P2d 205 (Alaska 1982).

Arizona

Injured worker brought suit against the contractor, architect, and soil engineer for wrongful death and personal injury sustained as a result of a cave-in during construction on a school campus. *Jackson v Sergent, Hauskins & Beckwith Engineers, Inc*, 20 Ariz App 330, 512 P2d 862 (1973).

Worker fell from scaffolding installed by contractor for church ceiling work. *Parks v Atkinson*, 19 Ariz App 111, 505 P2d 279 (1973).

Steel arches collapsed. *Reber v Chandler High School District No 202*, 13 Ariz App 133, 474 P2d 852 (1970).

Arkansas

Hook-up worker injured when crane contacted overhead power line, energizing the cable. *Heslep v Forrest & Cotton, Inc*, 247 Ark 1066, 449 SW2d 181 (1970).

A 17-foot deep excavation for a building collapsed. The architect knew it was inadequately shored and had demanded correction but had not stopped the job. *Erhart v Hummunds*, 232 Ark 133, 334 SW2d 869 (1960).

California

Worker fell because of stipulated negligence of contractor; engineer was managing the project. *Stilson v Moulton-Niguel Water District*, 21 Cal App 3d 928, 98 Cal Rptr 914 (1971).

The architect knew that underground electrical lines existed on the building site but did not know exactly where they were and did not indicate their location on the plans. Worker was electrocuted when operating jack hammer. *Mallow v Tucker, Sadler & Bennett, Architects & Engineers, Inc,* 245 Cal App 2d 700, 54 Cal Rptr 174 (1966).

A roofer fell through the sheathing on the roof because inferior lumber was used. *Paxton v Alameda County,* 119 Cal App 2d 393, 259 P2d 934 (1953).

Colorado

A worker was injured when the roof on which he was working collapsed during construction because of insufficient bracing and shoring. *Wheeler & Lewis v Slifer,* 195 Colo 291, 577 P2d 1092 (1978), *rehg denied* (May 15, 1978).

Delaware

Ditch designed by architect collapsed. *Seeney v Dover Country Club Apartments, Inc,* 318 A2d 619 (Del Super Ct 1974).

Florida

Employee of general contractor fell while walking on concrete form. Code required guardrails; they were not installed. Architect was to provide supervision to comply with the requirements of regulatory agencies. *Geer v Bennett,* 237 So 2d 311 (Fla Dist Ct App 1970).

Illinois

A vertical support was removed from scaffolding with the knowledge of the engineer; the scaffolding collapsed. *Voss v Kingdon & Naven, Inc,* 60 Ill 2d 520, 328 NE2d 297 (1975).

The roof of a gymnasium building collapsed because the architect failed to provide sufficient steel scaffolding to support the roof during the removal of a proscenium truss. *Miller v DeWitt,* 37 Ill 2d 273, 226 NE2d 630 (1967).

Employee of subcontractor fell from third-floor walkway lacking safety rails. The worker was leaving the job site. *White v Morris Handler Co,* 7 Ill App 3d 199, 287 NE2d 203 (1972).

A worker fell from a scaffold and brought an action against the supervising architect under the Illinois Structural Work Act, contending that the architect was a person *in charge* of the work. *McGovern v Standish,* 65 Ill 2d 54, 357 NE2d 1134 (1976).

A worker injured while moving scaffolding brought an action against the architect under the Illinois Structural Work Act for failure to stop work when necessary for the proper performance of the contract. *Emberton v State Farm Mutual Auto Insurance Co*, 71 Ill 2d 111, 373 NE2d 1348 (1978).

Iowa

A worker on the sixth floor dislodged a chunk of concrete which fractured a bricklayer's skull. *Manton v H.L. Stevens & Co*, 170 Iowa 495, 153 NW 87 (1915).

Louisiana

The architect approved shop drawings for a boiler which later exploded when the subcontractor fired the system to check his own work. *Day v National United States Radiator Corp*, 241 La 288, 128 So 2d 660 (1961).

Maryland

The architect ordered a new concrete pier when it was discovered that some steel beams were short. The concrete base failed, and steel fell, killing a worker. Concrete was poured in freezing weather; no safety cables on steel. *Cutlip v Lucky Stores, Inc*, 22 Md App 673, 325 A2d 432 (1974).

For a scholarly review of cases discussing architects' responsibilities for injuries to a worker for unsafe working conditions, see *Krieger v J.E. Greiner Co*, 282 Md 50, 382 A2d 1069 (1978) (worker injured when iron reinforcement bars, approximately 50 feet long and weighing approximately 780 pounds, toppled over).

Michigan

Employee of the manager of engineering and construction on a project was seriously injured when struck by a crate which fell from a forklift truck. *Caldwell v Cleveland-Cliffs Co*, 111 Mich App 721, 315 NW2d 186 (1981), *appeal denied*, 417 Mich 914, 330 NW2d 854 (1983).

Excavation collapsed; architect had duty to inspect and authority to stop work. Architect was aware that the excavation was not properly shored and was cracking because of wet clay but did not stop job. *Swarthout v Beard*, 33 Mich App 395, 190 NW2d 373 (1971), *revd as to damages, Smith v City of Detroit*, 388 Mich 637, 202 NW2d 300 (1972).

Building undergoing a test to determine structural soundness collapsed; the engineer had noticed cracks in concrete planks but later represented that the building was structurally sound. *Florence v Wm Moors Concrete Products, Inc*, 35 Mich App 613, 193 NW2d 72 (1971).

Building collapsed because the concrete and reinforcing steel were inadequately designed and some reinforcing steel was omitted. *Bayne v Everham*, 197 Mich 181, 163 NW 1002 (1917).

A workers' compensation insurance carrier contracted to provide safety inspections and safety engineering surveys. *Banner v Travelers Insuranc Co*, 31 Mich App 608, 188 NW2d 51 (1971).

The decedent was overcome by methane gas in a manhole, fell into water, and drowned. The engineer had not warned of the danger. *Vannoy v City of Warren*, 15 Mich App 158, 166 NW2d 486 (1968).

Missouri

The wall of a building under construction collapsed. It was supported by tubular girders resting on cast-iron pillars. *Lottman v Barnett*, 62 Mo 159 (1876).

Montana

Inadequate shoring caused cave-in. *Wells v Stanley J. Thill & Associates*, 153 Mont 28, 452 P2d 1015 (1969).

A steamfitter fell from a ladder providing access to a turbine pit in a paper mill which was under construction; the ladder was allegedly defectively designed. *Hackley v Waldorf-Hoerner Paper Products Co*, 149 Mont 286, 425 P2d 712 (1967).

Nebraska

A steamfitter fell through an opening in the concrete deck and was impaled on reinforcing steel below. The engineer held safety meetings and made safety inspections. The contractors were not cooperative with the engineer. Code required that openings in the deck be boxed or covered. This was not done. *Simon v Omaha Public Power District*, 189 Neb 183, 202 NW2d 157 (1972).

New Jersey

The engineer had supervision of a sewer job; trench collapsed. *Atlantic Mutual Insurance Co v Continental National American Insurance Co*, 123 NJ Super 241, 302 A2d 177 (1973).

New York

A heavy drill placed near a platform supporting a vibrating air compressor fell, striking a worker. *Olsen v Chase Manhattan Bank*, 10 AD2d 539, 205 NYS2d 60 (1960), *affd*, 9 NY2d 829, 175 NE2d 350, 215 NYS2d 773 (1961).

The architect authorized a reduction in thickness of the concrete foundation from 18 inches to 12 inches and failed to detect an old cistern under the project. A column resting on the cistern collapsed, killing a workman. *Burke v Ireland*, 166 NY 305, 59 NE 914 (1910).

Trench collapsed. *Scavone v State University Construction Fund*, 46 AD2d 895, 362 NYS2d 22 (1974).

Electrician slipped on icy ramp. *Hamill v Foster-Lipkins Corp*, 41 AD2d 361, 342 NYS2d 539 (1973).

Gas bottle fell from crane, injuring worker. The crane was rigged by the general contractor. *Ortiz v Uhl*, 39 AD2d 143, 332 NYS2d 583 (1972), *affd*, 33 NY2d 989, 316 NE2d 886, 353 NYS2d 962 (1974).

Temporary forms collapsed on highway project. *Ramos v Shumavon*, 21 AD2d 4, 247 NYS2d 699, *affd*, 15 NY2d 610, 203 NE2d 912, 255 NYS2d 658 (1964).

Carpenter injured when wall of building under construction collapsed. *Potter v Gilbert*, 130 AD 632, 115 NYS 425, *affd*, 196 NY 576, 90 NE 1165 (1909).

Building collapsed because foundations were greatly overloaded; building code violated. *Pitcher v Lennon*, 12 AD 356, 42 NYS 156 (1896).

Oregon

Worker was killed when vehicle collided with a barricade on a highway job. *St Paul Fire & Marine Insurance Co v United States National Bank*, 251 Or 377, 446 P2d 103 (1968).

Utah

Floating scaffolding, suspended from eye-bolts in a dome, fell, killing worker. *Peterson v Fowler*, 27 Utah 2d 159, 493 P2d 997 (1972).

Worker trenching for service tunnel, trench collapsed. *Nauman v Harold K. Beecher & Associates*, 19 Utah 2d 101, 426 P2d 621 (1967).

Washington

Concrete forms collapsed and spilled workers into the Columbia River along with wet concrete. *Loyland v Stone & Webster Engineering Corp*, 9 Wash App 682, 514 P2d 184 (1973), *review denied*, 83 Wash 2d 1007 (1974).

Contractor

After the owner and the worker, it seems that the prime contractor is the most likely to be the plaintiff in a malpractice action against an architect. During the progress of the job, the architect is often called upon to determine whether the contractor's performance is up to the standards required by the contract documents. Indeed the architect, in deciding questions that arise between the owner and the contractor, is by some cases accorded the status of an arbitrator with like immunity from suit.

It is said that the architect reaches the pinnacle of the profession when, to do justice to the contractor, he or she must decide questions against the client:

> He occupies a position of trust and confidence. When he acts under a contract as the official interpreter of its conditions and the judge of its performance, he should favor neither side, but exercise impartial judgment.

Macomber v State, 250 Cal App 2d 391, 58 Cal Rptr 393 (1967).

To add to the delicacy of the situation, the contractor or the owner may contend that the problem which has arisen between them was caused by the negligence of the architect in preparing the drawings and specifications. Thus the architect may be far from disinterested in the outcome of the dispute which he or she is called upon to arbitrate between the owner and the contractor.

It is only human for the contractor to infer from the realities of the situation that the judgment of the architect in interpreting the contract documents may be unbalanced by the interest of the client, or by self-interest. When the architect occupies a position of power, including the right to reject work, the right to have work removed and replaced, and the power to stop the job, the courts have held that power to impose responsibility to respect the legal interests of the contractor.

United States

Architect-engineer knew that a construction site contained subsurface debris, but failed to disclose the existence of the debris in plans and specifications for construction of a new project. HELD: general contractor is entitled to an action for negligent misrepresentation based on allegations that architect-engineer supplied false information which caused extra expense and that contractor allegedly relied reasonably on the false information. *Gulf Contracting v Bibb County*, 795 F2d 980 (11th Cir 1986).

Tile installed in the owner's store was defective. The contractor filed a third-party claim against the architect alleging negligent selection of the tile. *R.H. Macy & Co v Williams Tile & Terrazzo Co*, 585 F Supp 175 (ND Ga 1984). (*See* **Supplier,** below.)

An unanticipated spring tide, more than three feet above the previous record, caused water to enter a tunnel project; the contractor alleged inadequate and faulty inspection design. *C.W. Regan, Inc v Parsons, Brinckerhoff, Quade & Douglas*, 411 F2d 1379 (4th Cir 1969).

Contractor alleged the architect negligently misinterpreted test results and thereby allowed defective concrete to be introduced into the job. This had to be removed at the expense of the contractor. *United States v Rogers & Rogers*, 161 F Supp 132 (SD Cal 1958).

General contractor charged architect with negligent preparation of drainage plan which caused accumulation of water on construction site, thereby increasing costs. *Owen v Dodd*, 431 F Supp 1239 (ND Miss 1977).

General contractor brought an action against the architect on New Orleans Port Commission project, alleging damages because of improperly prepared plans, late delivery of plans, and delay in processing change orders. *C.H. Leavell & Co v Glantz Contracting Corp*, 322 F Supp 779 (ED La 1971).

Alabama

Surveyor prepared a plan for excavation of a retention basin. After the contractor excavated the basin, it was determined to be only one-half the size called for in the contract documents. *Paragon Engineering, Inc v Rhodes*, 451 So 2d 274 (Ala 1984).

The contractor alleged that the engineer on a city water system job prevented performance by the contractor and required installations not called for under the contract documents. *Wilder v Crook*, 250 Ala 424, 34 So 2d 832 (1948).

Arizona

Architect required layout and carpenter work not called for under the contract documents and permitted dumping of building materials so as to obstruct the job. *Craviolini v Scholer & Fuller Associated Architects*, 101 Ariz 33, 415 P2d 456 (1966).

Contractor alleged that he pointed out mistakes on the architects' drawing. This enraged the architects who thereafter required the contractor to cover up their blunder, delayed inspections, substituted materials, interfered with subcontractors, withheld funds, and vilified the contractor. *Craviolini v Scholer & Fuller Associated Architects*, 89 Ariz 24, 357 P2d 611 (1960).

The contractor alleged that the architect wrongfully refused to issue a certificate of final payment. *Blecick v School District No 18*, 2 Ariz App 115, 406 P2d 750 (1965).

Arkansas

The contractor followed the engineer's blasting schedule and, as a result, damaged a water intake structure that had been constructed by the contractor. *Carroll-Boone Water District v M&P Equipment Co*, 280 Ark 560, 661 SW2d 345 (1983).

California

Contractor alleged that the soil test engineer employed by the sanitary district negligently failed to disclose unstable material. *M. Miller Co v Central Contra Costa Sanitary District*, 198 Cal App 2d 305, 18 Cal Rptr 13 (1961).

Contractor alleged the engineer negligently prepared inaccurate grade sheets. *Bilich v Barnett*, 103 Cal App 2d Supp 921, 229 P2d 492 (1951).

Florida

Contractor alleged that the engineer negligently designed an inadequate foundation system, which caused delay in the completion of the project and much corrective work. *Palm Bay Towers Corp v Crain & Crouse, Inc*, 303 So 2d 380 (Fla 1974).

On questions submitted to the Florida Supreme Court by the United States Court of Appeals, the Florida Supreme Court stated that an architect may have professional liability to a general contractor absent privity of contract. However, an architect is liable to a general contractor on a third-party beneficiary contractual theory only if the contract was intended for the benefit of the contractor. *A.R. Moyer, Inc v Graham*, 285 So 2d 397 (Fla 1973).

Illinois

General contractor alleged damages resulting from the failure of the supervising engineer to properly stake the project, failure to timely respond to requests for instructions, and failure to complete details of the plans. HELD: privity of contract was not necessary in order to impose a duty of care on the supervising engineer vis-a-vis the general contractor. *Normoyle-Berg & Associates v Village of Deer Creek*, 39 Ill App 3d 744, 350 NE2d 559 (1976).

Contractor alleged that the architect negligently omitted grid points from the site plan. *Mississippi Meadows, Inc v Hodson*, 13 Ill App 3d 24, 299 NE2d 359 (1973).

Indiana

An excavation subcontractor underestimated the amount of work required based on an erroneous estimate submitted by the engineer; the subcontractor went broke and quit the job; prime contractor incurred additional expense to finish the project and alleged the engineer was responsible for this expense. *Peyronnin Construction Co v Weiss*, 137 Ind App 417, 208 NE2d 489 (1965).

Louisiana

Surveyor's crew staked locations for pilings for school buildings; they were driven, then it was discovered that they allowed only 37 feet between the buildings, whereas the plans required 48 feet. *Charles Carter & Co v McGee*, 213 So 2d 89 (La Ct App 1968).

Massachusetts

Engineer erroneously placed survey stakes and recklessly misrepresented soil conditions and land contours. *Craig v Everett M. Brooks Co*, 351 Mass 497, 222 NE2d 752 (1967).

Minnesota

Unlicensed engineer failed to disclose important information on drawings, including subsurface obstructions and the presence of a state highway within the project boundaries. *Zontelli & Sons v City of Nashwauk*, 373 NW2d 744 (Minn 1965).

Architect negligently refused to issue change order. *Grazzini Brothers & Co v Builders Clinic, Inc*, 280 Minn 540, 160 NW2d 259 (1968).

Mississippi

A protective levy surrounding a wastewater treatment plant construction site failed, and the city brought an action against the architect-engineer and the contractor. The contractor filed a cross-claim against the architect-engineer. *Mayor & City Council v Clark-Dietz & Associates-Engineers*, 550 F Supp 610 (ND Miss 1982).

New Jersey

Lack of privity between the architect and general contractor does not prevent a general contractor from recovering extra costs caused by the architect's negligence. *Conforti & Eisele, Inc v John C Morris Associates*, 175 NJ Super 341, 418 A2d 1290 (1980), *affd*, 199 NJ Super 498, 489 A2d 1233 (1985).

The general contractor alleged that the architect interfered with performance of the contract and failed to coordinate and supervise the work, causing 11 months delay on a 400-day school job. *Gherardi v Board of Education*, 53 NJ Super 349, 147 A2d 535 (1958).

North Carolina

An architect owes a duty of due care to persons who foreseeably and reasonably rely upon his or her professional performance, including contractors. *Shoffner Industries v W.B. Lloyd Construction Co*, 42 NC App 259, 257 SE2d 50, *review denied*, 298 NC 296, 259 SE2d 301 (1979).

A general contractor on a public project filed an action against the architect and engineer. HELD: even without privity of contract, an architect, surveyor, or civil engineer may be liable to a general contractor for economic loss from breach of a common law duty of care. *Davidson & Jones, Inc v New Hanover County*, 41 NC App 661, 255 SE2d 580, *review denied*, 298 NC 295, 259 SE2d 911 (1979).

Oregon

Contractor alleged the engineer employed by the city performed tests to disclose the presence of ground water but released only the favorable information and concealed the unfavorable. *Salem Sand & Gravel Co v City of Salem*, 260 Or 630, 492 P2d 271 (1971).

Texas

The electrical contractor alleged that the architect turned down requests for payment for extra work because of self-interest, in that the architect was a stockholder in the owner and had personally guaranteed the owner that if the project cost more than budgeted, the architect would forfeit $50,000 to the owner. *Manett-Seastrunk & Buckner v Terminal Building Corp*, 120 Tex 374, 39 SW2d 1 (1931).

Action by general contractor against architect for refusal to issue certificate of final inspection dismissed for lack of justiciable controversy. HELD: an actual conflict between the contractor and the owner exists because the owner failed to pay for the work, but the controversy between the contractor and the architect is only potential, based on a possible claim by the owner against the contractor for failure to supply a workable system. *Sub-Surface Construction Co v Bryant-Curington, Inc*, 533 SW2d 452 (Tex Civ App 1976).

Wisconsin

Contractor alleged that the architect designed the roof joist system negligently so that it collapsed during construction. *Vonasek v Hirsch & Stevens, Inc*, 6 Wis 2d 1, 221 NW2d 815 (1974).

Subcontractor

The relationship between the architect and subcontractors on a project is almost as sensitive as that between the architect and the prime contractor. Although it is the prime contractor who actually prepares requests for payment, he or she prepares those requests for work done by his or her own forces, and also for work done by subcontractors. In fact, the typical request for payment form is a document which classifies the total prime contract price into 20 or more categories, each of which represents the portion of the work to be done by a particular subtrade. There is also space for work to be performed by the prime contractor personally, and the sum of the categories equals the total prime contract price. The prime contractor submits the request for payment monthly. The request for payment indicates the percentage of completion opposite each subtrade, and the architect certifies payment for each category according to his or her determination as to the percentage of completion.

There is often some amount of debate among the subcontractor, the prime contractor, and the architect as to the percentage of completion for a particular trade. The subcontractor's estimate as to his or her percentage of completion tends to exceed the amount estimated by the architect. It is the architect's part to see that all the subcontractors and the prime contractors receive fair payment for work accomplished, and also to see that the owner does not overpay. Overpayment jeopardizes the interests of the owner, since it tends to destroy the economic motivation for the contractors to continue with the construction of the project. Obviously, if the prime contractor has been paid 80 per cent of the contract price at a time when the project is only 60 per cent complete, it becomes a financial detriment to finish the job, since the contractor will be paid only 20 per cent of the contract price for accomplishing 40 per cent of the work.

It is the architect's role to wield vast economic power over the subcontractors, as well as the prime contractor. If the architect condemns a subcontractor's work, the subcontractor will have to replace it. If the architect cuts down the percentage of completion asserted by the subcontractor, the subcontractor will receive a smaller payment. Any number of decisions made by the architect during the progress of the job may increase or reduce the cost of the subcontractor's performance.

United States

Electrical subcontractor stated a good cause of action against architect for delay damages resulting from architect's alleged negligence in erroneously rejecting certain fixtures and procrastination in making decisions. General contractor was likewise entitled to recover such damages from architect. *E.C. Ernst v Manhattan Construction Co*, 551 F2d 1026 (5th Cir 1977), *cert denied*, 434 US 106 (1978).

Subcontractor brought an action against architect alleging that the architect approved the subcontractor's proposal to substitute grooved pipe for welded or threaded pipe but later ordered the subcontractor to stop work and replace the grooved pipe with welded pipe. HELD: privity of contract is not necessary for a subcontractor to recover from an architect, provided the subcontractor can establish the existence of a duty between the parties, defendant's breach of this duty, and proximate cause. *Detweiler Brothers v John Graham & Co*, 412 F Supp 416 (ED Wash 1976).

Alabama

Pile specifications required architect approval of mix design provided by subcontractor. The mix was stamped by the architect, "furnished as noted." The piles failed load tests and the subcontractor was required to make repairs. *Berkel & Co Contractors, Inc v Providence Hospital*, 454 So 2d 496 (Ala 1984).

California

An engineer employed to inspect the concrete mix at the batch plant voluntarily assisted in mixing the concrete but used the wrong additive. The concrete did not meet the requirements of the specifications, so the prime contractor recovered damages from the subcontractor who sought indemnity from the engineer. *Walnut Creek Aggregates Co v Testing Engineers, Inc*, 248 Cal App 2d 690, 56 Cal Rptr 700 (1967).

Florida

In *Montgomery Industries International, Inc v Southern Baptist Hospital, Inc*, 362 So 2d 145 (Fla Dist Ct App 1978), the court recognized that a subcontractor may have a cause of action against an architect; however, proximate cause is required. "There is nothing in *Moyer*, or for that matter any of the cases relied upon by appellants, which states that a subcontractor may unilaterally alter an architect's plans and sue the architect when the resulting construction becomes deficient."

Georgia

Earth-moving equipment of subcontractor struck a concealed natural gas line, causing an explosion and fire which damaged the equipment. The subcontractor alleged the architect, engineer, and surveyor were negligent for failing to note the concealed pipeline on the drawings. *Chastain v Atlanta Gas Light Co*, 122 Ga App 90, 176 SE2d 487 (1970).

Illinois

A subcontractor may state a cause of action against an engineering firm for negligent design of a sewer treatment plant which causes delay and economic loss to the subcontractor. *Bates & Rogers Construction v North Shore Sanitary District*, 92 Ill App 3d 90, 414 NE2d 1274 (1980), *aff'd*, 109 Ill 2d 225, 486 NE2d 902 (1985).

Iowa

Subcontractor alleged that the architect sent false and slanderous letters to the general contractor and the owner implying that subcontractor was incompetent. As a result, the prime contractor canceled the subcontract. *Vojak v Jensen*, 161 NW2d 100 (Iowa 1968).

Louisiana

The architect specified butyl rubber as waterproofing material for a complex roof consisting of interlocking domes with skylights. The roof leaked, and the owner sued the roofing contractor, who in turn sought indemnity from the architect. *New Orleans Unity Society of Practical Christianity v Standard Roofing Co*, 224 So 2d 60 (La Ct App), *rehg denied*, 254 La 811, 227 So 2d 146 (1969).

Mississippi

The prime contractor went bankrupt, so the subcontractors were not paid. Subcontractor filed suit against the architect, alleging the architect was negligent by certifying the prime contractor's inaccurate and dishonest applications for payment. *Engle Acoustic & Tile, Inc v Grenfell*, 223 So 2d 613 (Miss 1969).

New York

Subcontractor versus architect for damages incurred when the subcontractor had to replace pipe that did not confirm with the requirements of the contract documents. *Haseley Trucking Co v Great Lakes Pipe Co*, 101 AD2d 1019, 476 NYS2d 702 (1984). (*See* **Supplier,** below.)

Subcontractor alleged that the engineers "maliciously, fraudulently and with an intent to injure subcontractor" refused to certify payment. *Unity Sheet Metal Works v Farrell Lines*, 101 NYS2d 1000 (Sup Ct 1950).

Surety

One of the most surprising extensions of liability for the malpractice of architects is the doctrine that an architect can be liable to the prime contractor's surety, or even to that surety's indemnitor.

Most public work must, by statute, be awarded to the lowest responsible bidder, and the bidder must furnish the public entity with a performance bond. Many private owners also require performance bonds.

Surety's Guarantee

The surety guarantees the owner that the prime contractor will perform all of his or her obligations under the contract. Therefore, if the contractor defaults or becomes bankrupt, it becomes the obligation of the surety to complete the prime contractor's performance. If the surety refuses to complete the performance, the owner usually employs other contractors to finish the job and claims the amount by which the cost of the job exceeds the contract price as damages from the surety.

Sometimes prime contractors require that a subcontractor provide a performance bond under which the surety guarantees to the prime contractor that the subcontractor will perform all of his or her obligations under the contract.

The interests of the surety are distinctly affected by the actions of the architect, particularly in certifying, or refusing to certify, payment. If the architect certifies a payment which is too great, the contractor may be induced to default in further performance. A contractor who has been overpaid part way through the job lacks economic motivation to continue with the project. This tends to induce the prime contractor to default, so that the surety becomes liable to the owner for the completion of the project.

On the other hand, if the architect certifies payments for less than the value of work performed by the prime contractor, this itself may cause a default because the prime contractor may be unable to finance the completion of the job. This also would make the surety liable to the owner for the completion of the project. Therefore, from the surety's point of view the architect should certify neither excessive payment nor inadequate payment: the amount certified should be exactly right.

The rule that an architect can be held liable to a contractor's surety for that contractor's breach of contract, adopted in some of the cases, is of doubtful validity. The surety chose to guarantee the contractor's performance, presumably after an investigation of the financial and moral responsibility of its principal. The surety received a fee to guarantee that the contractor would not default. But the architect cannot, like the surety, select the risk. The architect has little influence in the selection of the prime contractor on private projects, and almost none on public projects where the contract must be awarded to the lowest responsible bidder.

United States

Surety, as subrogee of owner, contended that the architect should have warned the owner about legal pitfalls arising out of a contract under which the contractor assembled student housing modules at its factory. The contractor filed a petition in bankruptcy and the trustee in bankruptcy successfully laid claim to the work in progress. *Travelers Indemnity Co v Ewing, Cole, Erdman & Eubank*, 711 F2d 14 (3d Cir 1983), *cert denied*, 464 US 104 (1984).

On an airport project, the surety alleged that the architect negligently allowed the contractor to misalign forms, failed to test backfill, caused delay, and failed to determine how the prime contractor was using the progress payments after receiving reports that subcontractors were not being paid for their work. *Aetna Insurance Co v Helmuth, Obata & Kassabaum, Inc*, 392 F2d 472 (8th Cir 1968).

The contract called for the architect to certify monthly payments "upon invoices presented by the contractor and approved by the architect." Instead, the architect certified monthly *estimates* not supported by invoices. The contractor went broke and defaulted, and the claim against the contractor's surety ensued. *Hall v Union Indemnity Co*, 61 F2d 85 (8th Cir), *cert denied*, 287 US 663 (1932). (*See* **Contractor,** above.)

Architect certified payment prematurely. *Peerless Insurance Co v Cerny & Associates*, 199 F Supp 951 (D Minn 1961).

Louisiana

The surety on a contract between city and contractor brought an action against the engineering company for overestimating the value of the contractor's work and against the city for overpayment to the contractor. *American Fidelity*

Fire Insurance Co v Pavia-Byrne Engineering Corp, 393 So 2d 830, *writ denied*, 397 So 2d 1362 (La Ct App 1981).

The surety claimed that the owner and architect negligently caused certificates of payment to be issued when both knew that construction contract conditions had not been fulfilled. *A.F. Blair Co v Mason*, 406 So 2d 6 (La Ct App 1981), *cert denied*, 410 So 2d 1132 (La 1982).

Missouri

The indemnitor of the prime contractor's surety alleged that the architect certified payments for $23,000 in excess of work performed on a $325,000 church job. *Westerhold v Carroll*, 419 SW2d 73 (Mo 1967).

Montana

Surety alleged that the owner failed to provide a qualified architect with full supervisory authority. *Garden City Floral Co v Hunt*, 126 Mont 537, 255 P2d 352 (1953).

North Carolina

Surety complained that the supervising engineers negligently permitted the prime contractor to install defective wiring in a sewage plant. *City of Durham v Reidsville Engineering Co*, 255 NC 98, 120 SE2d 564 (1961).

Washington

The electrical subcontractor's surety alleged that the architects and electrical engineers negligently failed to discover that the electrical subcontractor improperly performed the contract. *J&J Electric, Inc v Gilbert H. Moen Co*, 9 Wash App 954, 516 P2d 217 (1973), *writ denied*, 83 Wash 2d 1088 (1974).

Architect

United States

In *Bell v Jones*, 523 A2d 982 (DC 1986), an architect employed a surveyor to locate property lines and corner angles and relied on the survey in preparing plans. The court held that the architect could recover damages suffered because of inaccurate survey.

The architect employed a structural engineer as a consultant to design a university student union and dormitory. The engineer designed steel-and-concrete structures known as umbrellas but failed to follow the building code, and one collapsed. *Burran v Dambold*, 422 F2d 133 (10th Cir 1970).

In *Mardirosian v American Institute of Architects*, 474 F Supp 628 (DDC 1979), the American Institute of Architects (AIA) imposed sanctions on an architect for disregarding Standard 9 and taking over the design of refurbishing Union Station. Standard 9 of the AIA Code of Ethics provides:

> An architect shall not attempt to obtain, offer or undertake or accept a commission for which the architect knows another legally qualified architect or firm has been selected or employed, until the architect has evidence that the latter's agreement has been terminated and the architect gives the latter written notice that the architect is so doing.

Id 634. HELD: the ethical standard prohibiting an architect from seeking a commission for which another architect has been selected violates the Sherman Act (15 USC §1) as an unreasonable restraint on trade. Whereas competition is not always conducive to ethical behavior, that is not a reason for doing away with competition. Based upon the *Mardirosian* decision, the AIA has repealed its Code of Ethics.

New York

Defendant engineer prepared a report that was critical of plaintiff architect's plans and specifications for upgrading and expanding a private sewer treatment plant. In the architect's action for defamation, summary judgment dismissing the complaint was AFFIRMED. *Lapar v Morris*, 119 AD2d 635, 501 NYS2d 82 (1986).

Oregon

The owner of a manufacturing plant particularly specified that he wanted a superior floor. The structural engineer designed a system of *keycold* joints, which developed many cracks. The architects contributed $108,200 to settle the owner's claim and filed suit against the structural engineer for indemnity. *Owings v Rose*, 262 Or 247, 497 P2d 1183 (1972).

Supplier

United States

A manufacturer of concrete pipe filed an action against a materials testing laboratory for damages sustained when the testing laboratory notified the project engineer on a sewer project that the manufacturer's pipes did not meet contract specifications. HELD: a testing laboratory has a duty to a manufacturer of construction materials to perform the testing with due care since it is clearly foreseeable that the interests of the material supplier would be injured if tests incorrectly indicate that the materials do not meet specifications. The manufacturer was entitled to recover lost profits, the costs of procuring independent tests, and carrying charges on the rejected pipe. *Doran-Maine, Inc v American Engineering & Testing, Inc*, 608 F Supp 609 (D Me 1985).

Tile installed in the owner's store failed. The tile supplier filed a cross-claim against the architect, contending that the architect negligently failed to have the tile tested. *R.H. Macy & Co v Williams Tile & Terrazzo Co*, 585 F Supp 175 (ND Ga 1984). (*See* **Contractor,** above.)

New York

Subcontractor was required to replace pipe that did not meet the requirements of the contract documents. Supplier filed a cross-claim against the architect, seeking contribution. *Haseley Trucking Co v Great Lakes Pipe Co*, 101 AD2d 1019, 476 NYS2d 702 (1984). (*See* **Subcontractor,** above.)

Appendix B
Fact Situations

Septic, Sewer
Underground Obstruction
Cave-In
Soils
Slab
Bulge
Collapse
Mechanical Heating, Ventilating, and Air Conditioning
Mechanical
Roof Leak
Leaks
Explosion
Cracks
Fire
Glass Door
Falling Object
Flood and Storm Water
Dam Burst
Fall
Bodily Injury: Third Party
Traffic Accident
Asphyxiation
Electrocution
Defective Plans
Multiple Defects in Plans
Plans Violate Code
Negligent Selection of Contractor
Delay

Safety Inspection
Dirt Estimate
Bribery
Misrepresentation
Extra Work
Payment Certificate
Survey
Water and Percolation Tests
Miscellaneous

This material classifies the many fact situations which have produced architect malpractice decisions. The cases are organized by state within each classification. The summaries will help the lawyer to locate cases factually (as well as legally) apposite.

Septic, Sewer

Massachusetts

The homeowner's lot became flooded with water from a septic system. It developed that the leach field had been installed within four feet of the water table, contrary to code. The engineer had designed the system and performed a percolation test. *McDonough v Whalen*, 365 Mass 506, 313 NE2d 435 (1974).

Minnesota

A county health inspector negligently advised owner to build a "mound" septic system rather than a "pressurized" system. *Gilbert v Billman Construction, Inc*, 371 NW2d 542 (Minn 1985).

New Jersey

Material from sewer lines backed up and flooded the basements of homeowners who had purchased homes from a developer in 1965 and 1966. It was determined that the lines had been improperly placed and had to be changed. *Panepinto v Edmart, Inc*, 129 NJ Super 319, 323 A2d 533, *cert denied*, 66 NJ 333, 331 A2d 33 (1974).

Underground Obstruction

California

A worker was electrocuted when he struck a high-voltage line with a jackhammer. The line was not shown on the drawings. *Mallow v Tucker, Sadler*

& *Bennett, Architects & Engineers, Inc*, 245 Cal App 2d 700, 54 Cal Rptr 174 (1966) (*see* **Electrocution,** below).

Florida

The engineers certified that a water main installed in the bed of a river was installed according to the contract documents which required six feet of earth cover. The line was broken by an unrelated dredging operation. There was evidence that the pipe was four to six feet too high and that the engineer had used an inaccurate method of measurement (man in a boat with a stick). *Lee County v Southern Waters Contractors, Inc*, 298 So 2d 518 (Fla Dist Ct App 1974).

Louisiana

Some bystanders were killed and others injured when a bulldozer ruptured a gas pipeline. Engineers for the road construction project were required to show the location of utilities on preliminary plans and transmit them to utility companies for verification. The engineers noted the location but failed to determine the depth and failed to send plans to the utility company. *Womack v Travelers Insurance Co*, 251 So 2d 463 (La Ct App 1971) (*see* **Explosion,** below).

Maryland

The contractor broke an existing waterline not shown on the drawings prepared by the engineer. *Crockett v Crothers*, 264 Md 222, 285 A2d 612 (1972).

Cave-In

United States

A water tunnel was completed in 1966. In 1974, six cave-ins were discovered. *City of Aurora v Bechtel Corp*, 599 F2d 382 (10th Cir 1979).

The excavation for a J. C. Penney's building was 17 feet deep and was supported by perpendicular shoring. The field supervisor for the architect said the shoring was inadequate, was *like whitewash*, and *was not worth a damn*. The architect threatened to stop work unless the contractor furnished a new superintendent. The new superintendent arrived Friday and promised to rebuild the shoring Monday morning. It rained over the weekend. Monday morning, while the field supervisor was driving near the edge of the excavation, the shoring gave way and three workers were killed. *Fidelity & Casualty Co v J.A. Jones Construction Co*, 325 F2d 605 (8th Cir 1963).

An excavation supported by a retaining wall collapsed. *United States v Peachy*, 36 F 160 (D Ohio 1888).

Alaska

Two heavy equipment operators were killed by a rock slide while working on a state highway project. *Moloso v State*, 644 P2d 205 (Alaska 1982).

Delaware

Worker injured when ditch collapsed; the location and depth of the ditch were specified on plans prepared by the architect. *Seeney v Dover Country Club Apartments, Inc*, 318 A2d 619 (Del Super Ct 1974).

Indiana

Walls of trench for sewer pipe collapsed, killing worker. *Clyde E. Williams & Associates v Boatman*, 176 Ind App 430, 375 NE2d 1138 (1978).

Michigan

Contractor excavated for a library job without shoring or sloping. The project engineer protested to an employee of the architect that the condition was dangerous. The bank was cracking because of wet clay. The architect's employee agreed that the condition should be corrected. The architect had the authority to shut down the job. An employee of the general contractor was killed when the excavation collapsed. *Swarthout v Beard*, 33 Mich App 395, 190 NW2d 373 (1971), *revd as to damages, Smith v City of Detroit*, 388 Mich 637, 202 NW2d 300 (1972).

Montana

Trench was not shored with timber in compliance with state safety regulations; worker injured. *Wells v Stanley J. Thill & Associates*, 153 Mont 28, 452 P2d 1015 (1969).

New Jersey

Workers were injured when the contractor violated safety regulations and a sewer trench collapsed. *Atlantic Mutual Insurance Co v Continental National American Insurance Co*, 123 NJ Super 241, 302 A2d 177 (1973).

New York

A plumber was injured when a trench dug by a backhoe operator collapsed. *Scavone v State University Construction Fund*, 46 AD2d 895, 362 NYS2d 22 (1974).

Utah

Worker was injured while digging a trench, which caved in. The trench did not comply with state safety regulations, and the architect allegedly knew of the condition but failed to shut down the job. *Nauman v Harold K. Beecher & Associates*, 19 Utah 2d 101, 426 P2d 621 (1967).

Washington

Ditch for sewer line caved in on worker. *Porter v Stevens, Thompson & Runyan, Inc*, 24 Wash App 624, 602 P2d 1192 (1979), *review denied*, 93 Wash 2d 1010 (1980).

Wisconsin

Excavation was allegedly improperly shored, and it collapsed, injuring worker. *Luterbach v Mochon, Schutte, Hackworthy, Juerisson, Inc*, 84 Wis 2d 1, 267 NW2d 13 (1978).

Soils

United States

In *Miller v City of Broken Arrow Okla*, 660 F2d 450 (10th Cir 1981), *cert denied*, 455 US 1020 (1982), the contractor encountered unstable soil on a sewer line installation project. The contractor repeatedly requested advice from the engineer, but was told to use crushed rock to stabilize the soil and, when this failed, was only told to "keep trying."

Architect-engineer intentionally failed to note subsurface debris on plans and specifications relied upon by prime contractor in bidding construction project. *Gulf Contracting v Bibb County*, 795 F2d 980 (11th Cir 1986).

An engineering company decided to spread excess dirt in a swampy area near the project boundary. This raised the surface of the land 10 feet and created pressure on weak subsoil in an adjoining swampy area. This caused a spreading of soil which bent several oil pipelines located on adjoining property. The lines broke, spilling oil into the harbor. *First Insurance Co v Continental Casualty Co*, 466 F2d 807 (9th Cir 1972).

California

A prospective purchaser of two lots employed defendant at $10 per hour to dig test holes and advise purchaser whether there were any soil problems. The advice was: "nothing to worry about, 12 to 16 inches of fill is about all." Plaintiff bought the lots, only to discover that they contained 3 to 6 feet of fill.

Even the drill rig operator had observed 4 to 5 feet of fill during the testing procedure. *Gagne v Bertran*, 43 Cal 2d 481, 275 P2d 15 (1954).

Soils in a residential subdivision settled so much that eventually repair of the houses became economically unfeasible. The soil engineer had been employed in an advisory capacity and was paid by the hour. *Swett v Gribaldo, Jones & Associates*, 40 Cal App 3d 573, 115 Cal Rptr 99 (1974).

In a residential subdivision, where defendant engineer had conducted soil tests, differential settlement occurred which caused the failure of foundation, cracks in walls, and other damage. *United States Finances v Sullivan*, 37 Cal App 3d 5, 112 Cal Rptr 18 (1974).

In a residential subdivision, plaintiff's house was constructed on permeable fill. The house was damaged extensively. Defendant was a California soil engineer. *Oakes v McCarthy Co*, 267 Cal App 2d 231, 73 Cal Rptr 127 (1968).

A soil engineer was employed by a sanitary district to perform testing and to assist in the preparation of contract documents. The contractors relied on the test data in bidding, but the test data failed to disclose unstable material. *M. Miller Co v Central Contra Costa Sanitary District*, 198 Cal App 2d 305, 18 Cal Rptr 13 (1961).

Residence settled because it was constructed on loose fill rather than solid earth. *Alexander v Hammarberg*, 103 Cal App 2d 872, 230 P2d 399 (1951).

Colorado

The purchaser of an undeveloped lot filed an action against the developer and the soils engineer because of subsidence and soil movement under the home subsequently constructed on the lot. *Rusch v Lincoln-Devore Testing Lab, Inc*, 698 P2d 832 (Colo Ct App 1984).

Florida

The contractor on a sewer project sued the Water and Sewer Authority (WASA) to recover the increased costs of working in more difficult subsurface conditions than those described in WASA's bid request. WASA, in turn, brought a third-party action against the engineering firm that conducted the soil tests relied upon by the contractor. *Lisbon Contractors, Inc v Miami-Dade Water & Sewer Authority*, 537 F Supp 175 (SD Fla 1982).

Plaintiff alleged the engineer employed by the contractor performed soil tests negligently. *Luciani v High*, 372 So 2d 530 (Fla Dist Ct App 1979).

Georgia

Owners of land adjoining a construction site brought a trespass action against the architect, claiming that inadequate erosion control plans caused their property to be damaged by mud and silt. *Tomberlin Associates Architects, Inc v Free*, 174 Ga App 167, 329 SE2d 296 (1985), *cert denied* (May 1, 1985).

Illinois

Building settled and cracked because of rubble under the foundation. *Pollock v Hafner*, 108 Ill App 3d 410, 439 NE2d 85 (1982).

Louisiana

On a city incinerator project, latent unstable soil conditions caused displacement of foundation piles. Remedial work was ordered, including a floating concrete slab which settled. *Pittman Construction Co v City of New Orleans*, 178 So 2d 312 (La Ct App), *appeal denied*, 248 La 434, 179 So 2d 274 (1965).

Mississippi

Commercial building suffered extensive damage because of expansion of Yazoo clay. *Dickerson Construction Co v Process Engineering Co*, 341 So 2d 646 (Miss 1977).

Oregon

Building began to settle, and it was necessary to shore up the walls using jack screws. *White v Pallay*, 119 Or 97, 247 P 316 (1926).

Pennsylvania

The architect recommended dry wells to dispose of surface water. The dry wells caused erosion, creating sink holes. *National Cash Register Co v Haak*, 233 Pa Super 562, 335 A2d 407 (1975).

South Dakota

A contractor and an architect designed and constructed an auditorium on fill which was unsuitable and inadequately compacted. The architect knowingly misrepresented the actual condition of the fill when the building was completed by issuing a final certificate assuring its acceptability. To preserve the building, plaintiff replaced the fill and poured a new concrete floor. *Holy Cross Parish v Huether*, 308 NW2d 575 (SD 1981).

Tennessee

The owner of a tract of land intentionally misrepresented to the engineer that it consisted of a controlled, compacted fill. The engineer then certified the foundations for a brick house for a fee of $25 to $30 without making an independent investigation. *Cooper v Cordova Sand & Gravel Co*, 485 SW2d 261 (Tenn Ct App 1971).

Virginia

Settlement of swimming pool caused water pipes to break, soil eroded under house foundation. HELD: architect out of privity with homeowner is not liable for economic loss. *Sensenbrenner v Rust, Orling & Neals Architects, Inc*, 236 Va 419, 374 SE2d 55 (1988).

Wisconsin

The architect failed to diagnose the condition of the subsoil when designing a supermarket, and differential settlement eventually made it untenable. *A.E. Investment Corp v Link Builders, Inc*, 62 Wis 2d 479, 214 NW2d 764 (1974).

Wyoming

Soils engineer stated in his report that the building should be designed to account for the high swell potential of the soil. His recommendation was ignored. Dismissal of the claim against the soils engineer was AFFIRMED. The report was accurate and the engineer was under no duty to specify how adjustment should be made in constructing the building; that was the job of the architect and the structural engineer. *Reiman Construction Co v Jerry Hiller Co*, 709 P2d 1271 (Wyo 1985).

Slab

California

The architect was responsible for supervision on a ranch house job. The space between pours on the slab was big enough so that the owner could reach through and touch duct work. The owner removed and rebuilt the floor. *Pancoast v Russell*, 148 Cal App 2d 909, 307 P2d 719 (1957).

Oregon

The owner wanted a particularly superior floor for a manufacturing plant. The design called for a slab floor 350 x 390 feet, poured in panels, 6 inches thick and 30 feet square, with rebar on 12-inch centers running both ways. Each square was joined to the next by *keycold* joints, with reinforcing bars extending 12 inches to the adjoining slabs. The floor cracked. *Owings v Rose*, 262 Or 247, 497 P2d 1183 (1972).

Bulge

New York

Building completed in 1965, began to show cracks and bulges; suit was commenced in 1971. *Sosnow v Paul*, 43 AD2d 978, 352 NYS2d 502 (1974), *affd*, 36 NY2d 780, 330 NE2d 643, 369 NYS2d 693 (1975).

South Carolina

Plaintiff employed the operator of a frozen food locker plant to design a layout for such a plant and render advice as to equipment, controls, and insulation. Plans and specifications were prepared in accordance with defendant's design and advice, but within a few weeks after the plant was activated, cracks appeared in the floor, eventually the floor bulged, the walls cracked, and the plant became unusable. *Hill v Polar Pantries*, 219 SC 263, 64 SE2d 885 (1951).

Washington

The architects designed a cantilever retaining wall to contain structural fill. It was designed to equally deflect, but since the north and south ends of the wall were restrained, the deflection became unequal, with the center as much as four inches out of plumb. *McGuire v United Brotherhood of Carpenters & Joiners of America*, 50 Wash 699, 314 P2d 439 (1957).

Collapse

United States

An embankment of a cooling water reservoir suddenly collapsed, resulting in a suit by the power company against the engineer. *Florida Power & Light Co v Mid-Valley, Inc*, 763 F2d 1316 (11th Cir 1985).

A steel-and-concrete structure known as an *umbrella* collapsed; the structural engineer had violated the building code. *Burran v Dambold*, 422 F2d 133 (10th Cir 1970).

The Knickerbocker Theatre in Washington, D.C. collapsed, killing a patron. *Geare v Sturgis*, 56 App DC 364, 14 F2d 256 (1926), *overruled*, *Hannah v Fletcher*, 97 US App DC 310, 231 F2d 469 (1956).

A building under modification collapsed, killing a worker employed by a subcontractor. *United Gas Improvement Co v Larsen*, 182 F 620 (CC Pa 1910).

Alabama

New roof on a church building collapsed. *Campbell v Southern Roof Deck Applicators, Inc*, 406 So 2d 910 (Ala 1981).

Grandstand collapsed, worker injured. No proper permanent bracing was provided. *Looker v Gulf Coast Fair*, 203 Ala 42, 81 So 832 (1919).

Arizona

Arches in gymnasium building collapsed while under construction, injuring workers. *Reber v Chandler High School District No 202*, 13 Ariz App 133, 474 P2d 852 (1970).

The defendant designed and built a fence at a drive-in theater. The purpose of the fence was to protect the theater screen from interfering lights. Within a week after it was completed, the fence fell down. *Rosell v Silver Crest Enterprise*, 7 Ariz App 137, 436 P2d 915 (1968).

Colorado

The owner alleged that a grain storage bin collapsed because it was improperly designed, but the design had not been followed. Only 11 walers had been installed instead of 12, the walers were lapped instead of continuous, rebar was not correctly tied, and roof rafters were not lapped to the studs. *Balcom Industries v Nelson*, 169 Colo 128, 454 P2d 599 (1969).

Florida

In *Grossman v Sea Air Towers Ltd*, 513 So 2d 686 (Fla Dist Ct App 1987), *review denied*, 520 So 2d 584 (Fla 1988), an engineer designed a deck between a high rise apartment building's entrance and an upper level service facility. The work was completed in 1970, cracks, leakage and vibrations occurred, and the deck collapsed in 1981. Meanwhile the engineer inspected the work and said there was no problem with the structure. The jury verdict assessed $540,000 damages, 80 per cent against the engineer and 20 per cent against the architect.

Georgia

The designer provided a novel roof design which at that time had been used on only one other building. In 1961, the roof of the other building collapsed. The designer was informed of this but did not notify the owner of the potential danger. In 1963, plaintiff tenant leased a portion of the building from the owner, and shortly thereafter the roof collapsed. *Hunt v Star Photo Finishing Co*, 115 Ga App 1, 153 SE2d 602 (1967).

The building was finished in late 1957. The roof slab began to sag and shift and partially collapse in February 1961. *Wellston Co v Sam N. Hodges Jr & Co*, 114 Ga App 424, 151 SE2d 481 (1966).

Illinois

A construction worker on a city sewer improvement project injured his knee when escaping from a collapsing trench. *Bisset v Joseph A. Schudt & Associates*, 133 Ill App 3d 356, 478 NE2d 911 (1985).

Scaffolding at sewage disposal plant collapsed because vertical support was removed. The resident engineer had the power to stop work. The engineer knew the function of the vertical support and knew it had been removed earlier in the day. A worker was injured. *Voss v Kingdon & Naven, Inc*, 60 Ill 2d 520, 328 NE2d 297 (1975).

During the remodeling of a gymnasium, a proscenium truss was to be removed. During the process, the roof collapsed. The architects had not included a safety factor in calculating the amount of steel scaffolding needed to shore the truss. They failed to prevent the contractor from using inadequate shoring methods. *Miller v DeWitt*, 37 Ill 2d 273, 226 NE2d 630 (1967).

The plaintiff was injured when a piling designed by the engineer was dislodged during a windstorm. The contract documents did not specify the type of concrete block to be used. The owner had utilized a light-weight aggregate block which failed to withstand the rigors of the storm. *Laukkanen v Jewel Tea Co*, 78 Ill App 2d 153, 222 NE2d 584 (1966).

Iowa

Engineer employed by city for design and on-site review of sewer project had no duty to adjacent property owner. (Owner's building was damaged when contractor failed to install sheeting and backfill to stabilize land.) *Shepard Components, Inc v Brice Petrides-Donohue & Associates*, 473 NW2d 612 (Iowa 1991).

Louisiana

A warehouse was designed to be supported by a floating slab of concrete which also acted as the floor. After construction was commenced, the owner contracted to use the warehouse to store tile and employed a manufacturer to design and produce racks to support the tile. After eight months, the racks collapsed, destroying the tile. *Home Insurance Co v A.J. Warehouse, Inc*, 210 So 2d 544 (La Ct App 1968).

Maine

The contractor prepared drawings and constructed a fire wall according to the owner's specifications. The improper use of the unsupported fire wall caused it to collapse. *Marine Colloids, Inc v M.D. Hardy, Inc*, 433 A2d 402 (Me 1981).

Maryland

Iron reinforcing bars erected during the construction of a bridge were allegedly erected in unsafe manner. Thirty-two bars toppled and fell, injuring a worker. *Krieger v J.E. Greiner Co*, 282 Md 50, 381 A2d 1069 (1978).

Steel beams were too short, but rather than have them refabricated, the architect ordered a new concrete pier. This collapsed, possibly because of inadequate curing. No safety cables were used during the steel erection, and a worker was killed. *Cutlip v Lucky Stores, Inc*, 22 Md App 673, 325 A2d 432 (1974).

Michigan

A building collapsed, killing several workers. The engineer had questioned the use of some concrete planks which had cracked but had certified to the city inspector that they were nevertheless structurally sound. *Florence v Wm Moors Concrete Products, Inc*, 35 Mich App 613, 193 NW2d 72 (1971).

A carpenter was killed when a building collapsed allegedly because of defective steel and concrete plans. *Bayne v Everham*, 197 Mich 181, 163 NW 1002 (1917).

Minnesota

A chicken barn collapsed resulting in a judgment apportioning responsibility 55 per cent to the designer, 15 per cent to the manufacturer, and 30 per cent to the owner. *Jack Frost, Inc v Engineered Building Components Co*, 304 NW2d 346 (Minn 1981).

Foundation wall of hospital wing gave way, causing entire wing to collapse 10 years after completion of the project. *Caledonia Community Hospital v Liebenberg, Smiley, Glotter & Associates*, 308 Minn 255, 248 NW2d 279 (1976).

Manufacturing and warehouse building erected on unstable soil with inadequate foundations began to collapse and was partially repaired. *Northern Petrochemical Co v Thorsen & Thorshov, Inc*, 297 Minn 118, 211 NW2d 159 (1973).

A *poll-type* grain storage building collapsed because cables, turnbuckles, and hooks were of insufficient strength. *Robertson Lumber Co v Stephen Farmers Co-op Elevator Co*, 274 Minn 17, 143 NW2d 622 (1966).

Missouri

A carpenter was killed when a wall of a building under construction collapsed while a cast-iron pillar supporting a tubular girder was being raised by jack screws. *Lottman v Barnett*, 62 Mo 159 (1876).

New Jersey

A bathhouse which was designed in violation of the city building code was erected in 1927 and collapsed in 1940. The architect was indicted for manslaughter. *State v Ireland*, 126 NJL 444, 20 A2d 69 (1941).

New York

In *Board of Education v Mars Associates*, 133 AD2d 800, 520 NYS2d 181 (1987), exterior masonry on a school building collapsed.

When digging for concrete foundations, workers encountered an old circular cistern, and the footing for one of the columns was apparently laid in the cistern although this was unknown to the architect. The concrete footings were also reduced to 12 inches from the 18 inches called for in the contract documents. During construction, a column resting on this foundation collapsed, causing part of the building to fall and killing a construction worker, among others. *Burke v Ireland*, 166 NY 305, 59 NE 914 (1910).

The plans called for an arch in an opera house to be constructed of stone, but brick was used. It collapsed. *Lake v McElfatrick*, 139 NY 349, 34 NE 922 (1893).

Two workers were killed and one was injured when forms on a highway project collapsed; defendant was the engineer employed by the state for supervision. *Ramos v Shumavon*, 21 AD2d 4, 247 NYS2d 699, *affd*, 15 NY2d 610, 203 NE2d 912, 255 NYS2d 658 (1964) (memorandum opinion).

Carpenter was killed when a wall of a building under construction collapsed. *Potter v Gilbert*, 130 AD 632, 115 NYS 425, *affd*, 196 NY 576, 90 NE 1165 (1909) (memorandum opinion).

The architect failed to discover that part of the foundation of an 8-story building rested on the wall of an old cistern. The foundation design called for a row of cast-iron columns to rest on a concrete slab 18 inches thick and 9 feet 6 inches square. The architect instructed the contractor to reduce the thickness of the slab to 12 inches and failed to perceive that the part of the foundation resting on the cistern would, because of differential settlement, become its weakest point. *Fox v Ireland*, 46 AD 541, 61 NYS 1061 (1900).

The building code permitted a load of 11-1/2 tons per foot on a lime and mortar wall. The load imposed by the building was 60 to 90 tons. The building collapsed, killing a worker. *Pitcher v Lennon*, 12 AD 356, 42 NYS 156 (1896).

Oregon

Church under construction collapsed during a windstorm. *Northwestern Mutual Insurance Co v Peterson*, 280 Or 773, 572 P2d 1023 (1977).

A radio and television transmission tower constructed in 1954 collapsed in 1971 because of a defective guy line insulator assembly. *Mount Hood Radio & Television Broadcasting Corp v Dresser Industry*, 270 Or 690, 530 P2d 72 (1974).

A roof lasted for 17 years, then it collapsed. *Josephs v Burns*, 260 Or 493, 491 P2d 203 (1971).

A masonry wall collapsed in a hurricane, injuring a pedestrian. The design of the wall did not comply with the building code. *Johnson v Salem Title Co*, 246 Or 409, 425 P2d 519 (1967).

Pennsylvania

An earth embankment collapsed on a school project. *Trinity Area School District v Dickson*, 223 Pa Super 546, 302 A2d 481 (1973).

Washington

The roof of a school building collapsed under a heavy load of snow. The architect knew the contractor had deviated from the plans but nevertheless certified the work. *School District No 172 v Josenhans*, 88 Wash 624, 153 P 326 (1915).

A form broke, spilling 200 tons of concrete, along with workers, into the Columbia River. *Loyland v Stone & Webster Engineering Corp*, 9 Wash App 682, 514 P2d 184 (1973), *review denied*, 83 Wash 2d 1007 (1974).

An engineer designed a retaining wall for a rockery. The owner later constructed the rockery to a height of 22 feet rather than the designed 16 feet. It collapsed. *Weston v New Bethel Missionary Baptist Church*, 23 Wash App 747, 598 P2d 411 (1978).

Wisconsin

A gymnasium roof with a clear span of 100 feet was supported by 26 steel joists on 4-foot centers connected by horizontal bridging. The steel erector failed to fully tie down the first joist before proceeding to the next, and so on. During construction, the roof system collapsed. *Vonasek v Hirsch & Stevens, Inc*, 6 Wis 2d 1, 221 NW2d 815 (1974).

Mechanical Heating, Ventilating, and Air Conditioning

United States

A duct 20 feet long weighing 500 pounds fell on plaintiff, a horse-racing fan. The duct had been attached by hangers to a 7/8-inch ceiling sheathing in the club house. The sheathing was nailed to the joists. There was no direct attachment to the joists. The architect did not climb the ladder to determine the method of fixture. *Pastorelli v Associated Engineers, Inc*, 176 F Supp 159 (DRI 1959).

Subcontractor alleged that the architect failed to prepare proper specifications for emergency generator system and failed to promptly act on submittals. *E.C. Ernst v Manhattan Construction Co*, 551 F2d 1026 (5th Cir 1977), *cert denied*, 434 US 106 (1978) (*see* **Delay,** below).

California

A legal secretary died of pneumonia contracted while working in a building where the heating and air conditioning system functioned improperly. *Baker v Walker & Walker, Inc*, 133 Cal App 3d 746, 184 Cal Rptr 245 (1982).

Connecticut

Copper pipes used in the heating, ventilating, and air conditioning system corroded because of the chemical content of water drawn from wells on the premises and specifically designed to be used as a cooling agent for the system. Building was occupied in 1957, owner demanded arbitration in 1962. *Skidmore, Owings & Merrill v Connecticut General Life Insurance Co*, 25 Conn Supp 76, 197 A2d 83 (1963).

District of Columbia

The builder purchased a heating and air conditioning unit from a dealer who also provided a schematic layout for the ducts and registers. The system did not operate properly. *Robitscher v United Clay Products Co*, 143 A2d 99 (DC 1958).

Louisiana

The mechanical engineer designed a heating and cooling system based upon the size and placement of the units chosen by the general contractor. One unit of the size selected by the contractor proved to be inadequate for the building. *Segall Co v W.D. Glassell Co*, 401 So 2d 483 (La Ct App 1981).

New Mexico

The homeowner's agent recommended radiant heating and asked an architect to prepare drawings for a radiant heating system. These were sent by mail to the agent, employed in the house, and paid for by the general contractor. The system did not work. *Staley v New*, 56 NM 756, 250 P2d 893 (1952).

New York

The engineer approved manufacturer's shop drawings for heat exchangers that included noncompatible metals, causing galvanic corrosion. *John Grace & Co v State University Construction Fund*, 99 AD2d 860, 472 NYS2d 757, *affd*, 64 NY2d 709, 475 NE2d 105, 485 NYS2d 734 (1984) (*see* **Shop Drawings,** below).

Oklahoma

The owners brought an action against the contractor and the contractor's architect, alleging improper design of an auxiliary solar heating system for a home. *Keel v Titan Construction Corp*, 639 P2d 1228 (Okla 1981).

Virginia

The architect designed a radiant heating system for a home, but a salesman convinced the homeowner that a combination heating and air conditioning system could be installed at little extra cost. The salesman redesigned the system after consulting with the architect. The system would not work; the ducts filled with water after rain; the architect did not inspect the duct work but relied on the design furnished by the plumbing contractor-salesman. *Willner v Woodward*, 201 Va 104, 109 SE2d 132 (1959).

Wisconsin

Hospital with inadequate heat. *Milwaukee County v Schmidt, Garden & Erikson*, 43 Wis 2d 445, 168 NW2d 559 (1969).

Mechanical

United States

A load fell on a truck driver when the wheels slipped off the track of a hoist. *Coons v Washington Mirror Works, Inc*, 477 F2d 864 (2d Cir 1973).

Georgia

A water pumping station contained a 24-inch pipe connected together by a T-joint (suction header). Pressure from water stored in an adjoining reservoir caused the T-joint to slip from the pipe and allowed millions of gallons of water to flow on plaintiff's land. It was alleged that the T-joint was inadequately braced. *Covil v Robert & Co Associates*, 112 Ga App 163, 144 SE2d 450 (1965).

Hawaii

Architect-engineer did not violate professional standards in failing to foresee the need for baffles on window air conditioners, where the manufacturer's literature validated design and where testimony of a mechanical engineer showed that the only technique for assuring performance of the units would have been trial and error. *R.G. Wood & Associates Ltd*, 85-1 BCA (CCH) 17,898 (1985).

Washington

The soil under a skating rink froze to a depth of four feet, threatening the foundations. It was necessary to provide hot air ventilation beneath the floor to correct this condition. *Prier v Refrigeration Engineering Co*, 74 Wash 2d 25, 442 P2d 621 (1968).

Roof Leak

United States

Barrett 20-year roof began leaking soon after construction because of the deterioration of the roof system. *Deville Furniture Co v Jesco, Inc*, 697 F2d 609 (5th Cir 1983).

Arkansas

A school building was completed in 1968, and the roof began to leak almost immediately. From 1968 until 1975 numerous repairs were attempted; in 1975 the architect advised the school district that the roofing system was a failure and would have to be replaced. *Little Rock School District v Celotex Corp*, 264 Ark 757, 574 SW2d 669 (1978).

Florida

Three schools developed roof leaks that were frequently repaired under warranty. After expiration of the warranty period, the leaks became increasingly severe. It was alleged that the architect failed to design proper expansion joints, resulting in the leakage. *School Board v GAF Corp*, 413 So 2d 1208 (Fla Dist Ct App 1982), *opinion quashed by Kelley v School Board*, 435 So 2d 804 (Fla 1983) (*see* **Leaks,** below).

Illinois

The new roof of the math-science building developed leaks, allegedly because it was constructed of materials different from those indicated in the architect's original specifications. Various repairs were performed on the roof over a four-year period, until finally the entire roof membrane and insulation were replaced. *Knox College v Celotex Corp*, 88 Ill 2d 407, 430 NE 976 (1981).

Louisiana

The design for a church called for two interlocking domes with skylights at the apex of each dome. The roofing contractor urged the architect to employ butyl rubber. He did. Since the architect was unfamiliar with the material, the plans and specifications were prepared by the supplier. Within a year, the roof deteriorated and began to leak. The owner filed suit against the roofing contractor on his guarantee, and the contractor sought indemnity from the architect. *New Orleans Unity Society of Practical Christianity v Standard Roofing Co*, 224 So 2d 60 (La Ct App), *rehg denied*, 254 La 811, 227 So 2d 146 (1969).

Missouri

A dome roof, designed by an architect and revised by Butler Manufacturing Company for a school gymnasium, leaked from day one. *Linn Reorganized School District No 2 v Butler Manufacturing Co*, 672 SW2d 340 (Mo 1984).

New Mexico

The plans were defective in that the architect failed to provide a 10-year guaranteed roof. The roof was intended to protect against nuclear fallout and was constructed on concrete slabs caulked with waterproofing compound, but it leaked. *Board of Education School District No 16 v Standhardt*, 80 NM 543, 458 P2d 795 (1969).

New York

A school project was completed in September 1970, and a roof leak was discovered at the same time. In February 1974, the roof was still leaking, and in June 1974, the school district demanded arbitration. *Naetzker v Brocton Cent School District*, 50 AD2d 142, 376 NYS2d 300 (1975), *revd*, 41 NY2d 929, 363 NE2d 351, 394 NYS2d 627 (1977).

Oklahoma

The building was completed in 1946, and the roof began to leak soon thereafter, worsening over the years and requiring frequent repairs. The owner sued the architect in 1955. *Wills v Black & West Architects*, 344 P2d 581 (Okla 1959).

Vermont

School roof was completed in 1961, leaks discovered in 1966. *South Burlington School District v Goodrich*, 135 Vt 601, 382 A2d 220 (1977).

Wisconsin

An apartment complex was completed in 1970. In 1977, plaintiff filed suit against the architect, alleging that the roof began to leak "within the last four years." *Crawford v Shepherd*, 86 Wis 2d 362, 272 NW2d 401 (1978).

Leaks

Alabama

Water leaked through window panels in university dormitory. *United States Fidelity & Guarantee Co v Jacksonville State University*, 357 So 2d 952 (Ala 1978).

Colorado

Skylights in a shopping center continued to leak even after repeated attempts to repair. *Perlmutter v Flickinger*, 520 P2d 596 (Colo Ct App 1974).

Florida

Major leaks were caused by architect's failure to include flashings in the plans and specifications for a medical office complex. *Pearce & Pearce, Inc v Kroh Brothers Development Co*, 474 So 2d 369 (Fla Dist Ct App 1985).

For five years after plaintiff discovered leaks in a newly built school roof, the designer and construction supervisor repeatedly attempted to correct the problem, assuring plaintiff that it was reparable. Plaintiff filed suit when defendant refused to make further repairs. *School Board v GAF Corp*, 413 So 2d 1208 (Fla Dist Ct App 1982), *opinion quashed by Kelley v School Board*, 435 So 2d 804 (Fla 1983) (*see* **Roof Leak,** above).

Illinois

Water leakage in 13-floor residential building for the elderly caused substantial interior and exterior damage. *Illinois Housing Development Authority v Sjostron & Sons*, 105 Ill App 3d 247, 433 NE2d 1350 (1982).

Interior and exterior walls of courthouse separated and tilted; leaks occurred. *Corbetta Construction v Lake City Public Building Commission*, 64 Ill App 3d 313, 381 NE2d 758 (1978).

Iowa

Windows of luxury apartment building leaked. *Roland A. Wilson & Associates v Forty-O-Four Grand Corp*, 246 NW2d 922 (Iowa 1976).

Louisiana

Roof leak in metal building was partly caused by faulty design and partly caused by faulty construction. *Bewley Furniture Co v Maryland Casualty Co*, 285 So 2d 216 (La 1973).

New York

Inferior materials caused leaks in the chilled water system. *State University Construction Fund v United Technology Corp*, 78 Ad2d 748, 432 NYS2d 653 (1980).

A building was completed in June 1968, and for the next three years the architect worked with the owner attempting to correct leaks. Suit was filed in September 1971. *Broome County v Vincent J. Smith, Inc*, 78 Misc 2d 889, 358 NYS2d 998 (Sup Ct 1974).

Explosion

United States

Boiler in heating plant in university exploded during testing, allegedly because consulting engineer insisted that a dual timer burner control system be utilized. *Dresco Mechanical Contractors, Inc v Todd-CEA, Inc*, 531 F2d 1292 (5th Cir 1976).

One pipe line was installed over another, and the weight of the new line caused the old to rupture. Leaking gas from the ruptured line exploded, injuring the plaintiff. *Becker v Black & Veatch Consulting Engineers*, 509 F2d 42 (8th Cir 1974).

Arkansas

The contractor followed the engineer's blasting schedule and, as a result, damaged a water intake structure that had been constructed by the contractor. *Carroll-Boone Water District v M&P Equipment Co*, 280 Ark 560, 661 SW2d 345 (1983).

Georgia

The excavation subcontractor struck a concealed natural gas pipeline, which exploded, damaging the subcontractor's equipment. Subcontractor filed an action against the architect, the engineer, and the surveyor. The line was not located on the drawings. *Chastain v Atlanta Gas Light Co*, 122 Ga App 90, 176 SE2d 487 (1970).

Louisiana

Plaintiff was burned when the rake of a bulldozer he was operating struck a submerged butane tank. *Alexander v State Through Department of Highways*, 347 So 2d 1249 (La Ct App), *writ denied*, 350 So 2d 1224 (La 1977).

A boiler exploded shortly after it was first fired. Investigation showed that the plumbing subcontractor had failed to install either a thermostat or a pressure relief valve on the boiler; he mistakenly installed them on the hot-water storage tank. Thus, the boiler was bound to explode. Under the contract documents, the architect was required to check shop drawings and to furnish adequate supervision to reasonably insure strict conformity with the contract documents. The architect approved a brochure submitted by the plumbing subcontractor "as noted" without referring it to the mechanical engineer. *Day v National United States Radiator Corp*, 241 La 288, 128 So 2d 660 (1961).

Some bystanders were killed and others injured when a bulldozer ruptured a gas pipeline. Engineers for the road construction project were required to show the location of utilities on preliminary plans and transmit them to utility companies for verification. The engineers noted the location but failed to determine the depth and failed to send plans to the utility company. *Womack v Traveler's Insurance Co*, 251 So 2d 463 (La Ct App 1971) (*see* **Underground Obstruction,** above).

Tennessee

Four and one-half years after installation, a boiler installed in a church exploded, damaging the building. *Wheeler v Fred Wright Construction Co*, 57 Tenn App 77, 415 SW2d 156 (1966).

Cracks

United States

Georgetown College brought suit against architects, structural engineers, general contractors, masonry subcontractor, and a surety company for breach of contract and negligence in the construction of a dormitory. The dormitory was substantially completed in 1966, and in 1976 the college discovered that the surface brick was cracking and bulging and that the design and construction of the dormitory was otherwise defective. *Presidents & Directors of Georgetown College v Madden*, 660 F2d 91 (4th Cir 1981).

Georgia

In 1976, plaintiff purchased a building which had been constructed in 1949, with floors added in 1954. When severe cracks were discovered in the building in 1979, the structure was evacuated and refurbished. Plaintiff brought suit against the architects who designed the structure and addition. *U-Haul Co v Abrea & Robeson, Inc*, 247 Ga 565, 277 SE 497 (1981).

Illinois

The architect approved a pour, after which the slab cracked because of frost in the fill. *Rosos Litho Supply Corp v Hansen*, 123 Ill App 3d 290, 462 NE2d 566 (1984).

The school job was completed in 1963, and the owner soon noticed cracks in the plaster. The architect assured the owner it was a maintenance problem; costly repairs were made. In 1969, it was determined that the problem was faulty design: the architect failed to provide expansion joints. The owner filed suit against the architect in 1970, six years after the building was finished. *Society of Mt Carmel v Fox*, 90 Ill App 3d 537, 413 NE2d 480 (1980).

Iowa

Brick hotel building developed cracks in wall. The architect contended it was because of defective construction: the owner claimed it was because of a defective foundation. *Schreiner v Miller*, 67 Iowa 91, 24 NW 738 (1885).

Louisiana

Designer-builder specified and installed *super-rock* composed of cement and cinder. This material absorbed moisture, expanded, and contracted, causing serious cracks. *Barraque v Neff*, 202 La 360, 11 So 2d 697 (1942).

The project was a five-story warehouse building containing arches. Cracks appeared in the front wall. The testimony showed that the arches alone were insufficient: they should have been supported by beams or lintels above the arches to help carry the load. *Louisiana Molasses Co v Le Sassier*, 52 La Ann 2070, 28 So 217, *aff'd*, 52 La Ann 1768, 28 So 223 (1900).

New York

Cracks in ramp system for parking structure. *Sears Roebuck & Co v Enco Associates*, 43 NY2d 389, 372 NE2d 555, 401 NYS2d 767 (1977).

South Dakota

Cracks in the exterior of a school house were allegedly caused by including calcium chloride in the concrete mix. *Canton Lutheran Church v Sovik, Mathre, Sathrum & Quanbeck*, 507 F Supp 873 (DSD 1981).

Fire

California

An engineer designed a water distribution system which was allegedly inadequate to protect residential property owners from fire. *Stuart v Crestview Mutual Water Co*, 34 Cal App 3d 802, 110 Cal Rptr 543 (1973).

Florida

A fire occurred in the waste disposal system of a hospital allegedly because of defects in the plans and specifications. *Montgomery Industries International, Inc v Southern Baptist Hospital, Inc*, 362 So 2d 145 (Fla Dist Ct App 1978).

Georgia

A fire in a shopping center destroyed several stores. The owner filed suit against the architect, who in turn filed a third-party complaint against the consulting engineer, charging him with negligence (violation of the building code). The engineer failed to specify a fire sprinkler system. *Waddey v Davis*, 149 Ga App 308, 254 SE2d 465 (1979) (*see* **Plans Violate Code,** below).

Mississippi

Within three weeks after occupancy, a one-story, five-unit apartment house was damaged by fire. The owner alleged that the architect failed to immobilize electrical conduit, allowing water to enter the circuit breaker box. *Board of Trustees v Lee Electric Co*, 198 So 2d 231 (Miss 1967).

New York

A firefighter was injured when a ladder collapsed while fighting a fire that was allegedly caused by the negligence of the architect. *City of Utica v Holt*, 88 Misc 2d 206, 387 NYS2d 377 (NY Sup 1976).

A fire of incendiary origin killed 11 people and injured others trapped on the fourth floor; flammable plastic panels used as decorative screening around the third-floor balcony had ignited. *Greenberg v City of Yonkers*, 45 AD2d 314, 358 NYS2d 453 (1974), *affd*, 37 NY2d 907, 340 NE2d 744, 378 NYS2d 382 (1975) (memorandum opinion).

Utah

Engineers designed a compressor system connected to a natural gas well. The design included a 12-pound valve on the bottom of the tank. Fire completely destroyed the installation, and the owner claimed it was because the valve vibrated, its threads sheared, and it fell, releasing gas. The owner alleged the valve should have been supported. The engineer testified support was unnecessary. *Uinta Pipeline Corp v White Superior Co*, 546 P2d 885 (Utah 1976).

Glass Door

United States

Plaintiff, a guest at a motel, was injured when he turned away from a check-in desk and ran into a glass door. *Karna v Byron Reed Syndicate No 4*, 374 F Supp 687, 689 (D Neb 1974).

Illinois

Restaurant patron suffered cuts when the glass portion of an interior restaurant door broke as she exerted force upon it. *Rhodes v Mill Race Inn, Inc*, 126 Ill App 3d 1024, 467 NE2d 915 (1984), *appeal denied* (Jan Term 1985).

Indiana

Student fell or was pushed through a glass wall between entrance doors at a school. *Beecher v White*, 447 NE2d 622 (Ind Ct App 1983).

Iowa

Plaintiff sustained injuries when she ran into a window in the vestibule area of hospital. *Fox v Stanley J. How & Associates*, 309 NW2d 520 (Iowa Ct App 1981).

Louisiana

Fourteen-year-old guest walked through a sliding glass door in a residence; panels were three feet wide, framed by aluminum. *Natal v Phoenix Assurance Co*, 286 So 2d 738 (La Ct App 1973), *revd as to other parties*, 305 So 2d 438 (La 1974).

Maine

The outer door of a building at a student center struck plaintiff and caused plate glass panels in the floor to shatter. *Klein v Catalono*, 386 Mass 701, 437 NE2d 514 (1982).

Mississippi

A minor and parents sued the architect and contractor of a school building for injuries sustained when the child thrust his arm through a glass door while leaving the school. *Anderson v Fred Wagner*, 402 So 2d 320 (Miss 1981).

New Jersey

Plaintiff, an infant, was injured in 1967 by a glass sidelight adjoining a glass door in a lobby. *O'Connor v Altus*, 123 NJ Super 379, 303 A2d 329 (1973), *affd in part, revd in part*, 67 NJ 106, 335 A2d 545 (1975).

New York

A student who occupied a dormitory was injured when he collided with a clear, glass panel adjacent to a door. *Coffey v Dormitory Authority*, 26 AD2d 1, 270 NYS2d 255 (1966).

Falling Object

Florida

A restaurant patron was injured when a metal counter-weight dislodged from a ceiling fan because of defective welding. The architect had designed the fan, but not the counter-weight. *Mai Kai, Inc v Colucci*, 205 So 2d 291 (Fla 1967).

Iowa

The skull of a bricklayer was fractured when a member of a wrecking gang kicked a piece of concrete from the sixth floor. The gang was stripping wooden forms from concrete. *Manton v H.L. Stevens & Co*, 170 Iowa 495, 153 NW 87 (1915).

Louisiana

Worker was injured when piling fell from a lead line of a pile driver. *Thomas v Fromherz Engineers*, 159 So 2d 612 (La Ct App), *writ refused*, 245 La 799, 161 So 2d 276 (1964).

Michigan

An employee of the manager of engineering and construction on a project to expand an iron ore mine was seriously injured when a crate fell from a forklift truck. *Caldwell v Cleveland-Cliffs Co*, 111 Mich App 721, 315 NW2d 186 (1981), *appeal denied*, 417 Mich 914, 330 NW2d 854 (1983).

New York

A worker employed by the general contractor was injured when a gas bottle, negligently rigged, fell from a crane. The engineer was responsible for the design and supervision of the project and had a staff of safety personnel on the job site. However, the engineer retained no control over the contractor's methods of construction. *Ortiz v Uhl*, 39 AD2d 143, 332 NYS2d 583 (1972), *affd*, 33 NY2d 989, 316 NE2d 886, 353 NYS2d 962 (1974) (*see* **Miscellaneous, Crane,** below).

A worker constructing a foundation was injured when an object fell from a temporary platform 30 feet above. The contract gave the contractor control of all personnel. The temporary platform was not designed by the architect or engineer, but by the contractor. *Olsen v Chase Manhattan Bank*, 10 AD2d 539, 205 NYS2d 60 (1960), *affd*, 9 NY2d 829, 175 NE2d 350, 215 NYS2d 773 (1961) (memorandum opinion).

A construction worker was injured when a crane dropped a bucket filled with sand bags on the worker's head. *Conti v Pettibone Cos*, 111 Misc 2d 772, 445 NYS2d 943 (1981).

Wisconsin

Plaintiff was injured when struck by a piece of lumber which apparently blew off the top of a building. *Hortman v Becker Constr Co*, 92 Wis 2d 210, 284 NW2d 621 (1979).

Pedestrian injured by brick which fell from partially completed building. *Smith v Milwaukee Builders & Traders Exchange*, 91 Wis 360, 64 NW 1041 (1895).

Flood and Storm Water

United States

Construction of subdivision increased the flow of surface water over the land that was thereby made unfit for growing strawberries. *Breiner v C&P Home Builders, Inc*, 536 F2d 27 (3d Cir 1976).

Neighboring homeowners were flooded by water escaping through breaches in an irrigation canal. *Salt River Valley Water Users Assn v Giglio*, 113 Ariz 190, 549 P2d 162 (1976).

One and one-half years after the tenant moved into a new shopping center, he was flooded out by a heavy rain storm. *Stromberg's v Victor Gruen & Associates*, 384 F2d 163 (10th Cir 1967).

Alabama

Defendant engineering corporation designed the drainage system for a residential subdivision; the storm drain system was inadequate and caused periodic flooding. *Broyles v Brown Engineering Co*, 275 Ala 35, 151 So 2d 767 (1963).

Georgia

Development of condominium allegedly diverted surface water to neighbor's land. *Ponce de Leon Condos v DiGirolamo*, 238 Ga 188, 232 SE2d 62 (1977).

During construction, the contours of the church building site were changed, causing mud, silt, debris, and rain water to enter the plaintiff's property in greater quantities and in different places than before; at the suggestion of the architect, a log-brake-type dam was built, which just diverted water to other parts of the plaintiff's property. *Bodin v Gill*, 216 Ga 467, 117 SE2d 325 (1960).

Illinois

Homeowners, who brought an action against a civil engineer who designed a water drainage system for a subdivision, sought compensation for damage to their home caused by flooding. The engineer, however, had not established the foundation grade level for the project and was, therefore, not liable. *Ferentchak v Village of Frankfort*, 105 Ill 2d 474, 475 NE2d 822 (1985).

Neighbors damaged by storm water filed action against subdivider and engineer. *Elliott v Nordlof*, 83 Ill App 279, 227 NE2d 547 (1967).

Iowa

A cloudburst caused a creek to flood, floating aeration tanks in a sewer project. *Schlitz v Cullen-Schlitz & Associates*, 228 NW2d 10 (Iowa 1975).

After construction started on the neighboring high school, the plaintiffs and their seven children had to move upstairs because their first floor was flooded. This meant putting five girls in one bedroom and two boys in the other. They complained to the contractor and the architect, but neither did anything effective to help. *McCarthy v J.P. Cullen & Son Corp*, 199 NW2d 362 (Iowa 1972).

Kansas

Heavy rains caused flooding, which damaged gymnasium floor. *Seaman Unified School District No 345 v Casson Construction Co*, 3 Kan App 2d 289, 594 P2d 241 (1979).

New Mexico

The architect on a school job designed a culvert to carry 100 cubic feet per second more than the peak from any rain during the preceding 73 years. On August 10, 1963, rainfall exceeded that peak by more than 100 cubic feet per second, and the resulting flood damaged the neighboring homeowners. *Martin v Board of Education*, 79 NM 636, 447 P2d 516 (1968).

New York

A hydraulic pump was used to fill a swamp with sand. This caused water to percolate onto nearby property. *Doundoulakis v Town of Hempstead*, 51 AD2d 302, 381 NYS2d 287 (1976), *revd*, 42 NY2d 440, 368 NE2d 24, 398 NYS2d 401 (1977).

The engineers prepared a drainage plan for a subdivision which was approved by the village authorities, but the approval was later rescinded when it was found that if the drainage plan were followed, the run-off would damage a preexisting house. *Vandewater & Lapp v Sacks Builders, Inc*, 20 Misc 2d 677, 186 NYS2d 103 (Sup Ct 1959).

North Dakota

The residence was built low to the ground, and the first floor became flooded. *Dobler v Malloy*, 214 NW2d 510 (ND 1973).

Rain water drained from a trailer park designed by defendant architect, damaging the neighbor's home. *Jones v Boeing Co*, 153 NW2d 897 (ND 1967).

Pennsylvania

Improperly prepared plans for drainage and sewage facilities resulted in damage when the drainage water was diverted into homes built in the development. *Wicks v Milzoco Builders, Inc*, 291 Pa Super 345, 435 A2d 1260 (1981), *vacated on other grounds*, 503 Pa 614, 470 A2d 86 (1983).

South Carolina

Development of upper riparian owner's land reduced the absorption, seepage, and percolation rate of the land and, therefore, increased the amount of water entering lower riparian landowner's lake through preexisting drainage systems. *Irwin v Michelin Tire Corp*, 288 SC 221, 341 SE2d 783 (1986).

Texas

Construction of subdivision caused an increase in the natural diversion of surface water onto plaintiff's land. *Kraft v Langford*, 565 SW2d 223 (Tex 1978).

Dam Burst

United States

A protective levee surrounding the construction site of a wastewater treatment plant failed. *Mayor & City Council v Clark-Dietz & Associates-Engineers*, 550 F Supp 610 (ND Miss 1982), *appeal denied*, 702 F2d 67 (5th Cir 1983).

Arizona

After a dam burst, plaintiff contractor filed suit against the state engineer, claiming the engineer had approved an inadequate design. A state statute provided that no action shall be brought against the state or its employees for damages sustained through failure of any dam. *Turner v Superior Court (Pima County)*, 3 Ariz App 414, 415 P2d 129 (1966).

California

In 1856, an architect-contractor constructed a dam 40 feet high on Dear Creek to accumulate 100 acres of water for mining. The dam broke while under construction, damaging a downstream owner. *Boswell v Laird*, 8 Cal 469 (1857).

Fall

United States

Plaintiff slipped and fell in the emergency room of a hospital which had been flooded after a heavy rain. The plaintiff claimed the floor was improperly sloped inward. *Brown v McBro Planning & Development Co*, 660 F Supp 1333 (DVI 1987).

A piece of fiberboard roof decking gave way under the weight of a worker, and he fell about 40 feet to the gymnasium floor of a high school under construction. *Bartak v Bell-Gallyardt & Wells, Inc*, 473 F Supp 737 (DSD 1979), *revd*, 629 F2d 523 (8th Cir 1980).

Hotel guest injured in fall on spiral staircase. *Gravely v Providence Partnership*, 549 F2d 958 (4th Cir 1977).

Pedestrian fell on steps surrounding fountain area of Smithsonian Institution. *Watt v United States*, 444 F Supp 1191 (DDC 1978).

Steamfitter, working on a nuclear plant, was injured when the steam line failed, causing him to fall to the ground. *Horn v Burns & Roe*, 536 F2d 251 (8th Cir 1976).

An employee of the general contractor fell through a hole in the roof built by a subcontractor. *Bruemmer v Clark Equipment Co*, 341 F2d 23 (7th Cir 1965).

Arizona

An apprentice carpenter fell from scaffolding while repairing the ceiling in a church. The scaffolding was designed and erected by the contractor; the architect supervised the work. *Parks v Atkinson*, 19 Ariz App 111, 505 P2d 279 (1973).

California

Plaintiff fell through the roof of a house on which he was working. *Martinez v Traubner*, 32 Cal 3d 755, 653 P2d 1046, 187 Cal Rptr 251 (1982).

An 18-month-old child sustained injuries when she fell through the second-floor railing of an apartment. *Grimmer v Harbor Towers*, 133 Cal App 3d 88, 183 Cal Rptr 634 (1982).

An employee of the general contractor was injured in a fall on a water tank job. It was stipulated that the fall was caused by inadequate safety precautions of the general contractor. Defendant was the supervising engineer. *Stilson v Moulton-Niguel Water District*, 21 Cal App 3d 928, 98 Cal Rptr 914 (1971).

A roofer was carrying hot tar on a roof constructed of sheathing on rafters on 32-inch centers. The specifications called for Douglas fir, select merchantable seasoned sheathing laid solid, horizontally, across 2 x 4-inch rafters. The architect had observed inferior sheathing when it was delivered to the job site and condemned it. By his next visit, the inferior sheathing had been installed and covered with tar and gravel. The architect failed to make another inspection. *Paxton v Alameda County*, 119 Cal App 2d 393, 259 P2d 934 (1953).

Colorado

A woman lost her balance and fell over a radiator and through a hotel window to her death. *Yarbro v Hilton Hotels Corp*, 655 P2d 822 (Colo 1982).

District of Columbia

Eight-year-old boy fell from an apartment house stairway after slipping in a puddle. Handrail allegedly negligently designed. *Hill v McDonald*, 442 A2d 133 (DC 1982).

Twenty-two-month-old unattended child killed when he fell from balcony of fifth-floor apartment. *Noble v Worthy*, 378 A2d 674 (DC 1977).

Florida

Worker was injured in a high fall on a project where temporary flooring and safety nets mandated by safety regulations were not provided. HELD:

the architect was not responsible because it had no duty to supervise the methods of construction. *Swartz v Ford, Bacon & Davis Construction Corp*, 469 So 2d 232 (Fla Dist Ct App 1985).

Worker was injured by fall from beam. *Moore v P.R.C. Engineering, Inc*, 565 So 2d 817 (Fla Dist Ct App 1990).

Student fell into pit created by lowered area of stage in a theater auditorium. *Erwine v Gamble, Pownal & Gilroy Architects & Engineers*, 343 So 2d 859 (Fla Dist Ct App 1976).

Slip and fall allegedly caused by differing floor levels at shopping mall. *LeMay v United States H. Properties, Inc*, 338 So 2d 1143 (Fla Dist Ct App 1976).

A worker died when a scaffold broke and he plunged 17 stories. *Conklin v Cohen*, 287 So 2d 56 (Fla 1973).

An employee of the general contractor fell when a slab was being poured. He was walking along a wooden form on the outside of a recently poured section of the slab. There were no guardrails. The contract required the architect to supervise the work and to assure that it would be done in accordance with the requirements of regulatory agencies. Safety regulations required guardrails. The architect instructed the contractor to install guardrails, but allegedly with the architect's knowledge, the contractor failed to do so. *Geer v Bennett*, 237 So 2d 311 (Fla Dist Ct App 1970).

Georgia

A worker was killed when a load being hoisted from one floor to another knocked him into an elevator shaft. *Hutcheson v Eastern Engineering Co*, 132 Ga App 885, 209 SE2d 680 (1974).

Idaho

Tenant slipped and fell on stairway without handrail. *Stephens v Sterns*, 106 Idaho 249, 678 P2d 41 (1984).

Illinois

Worker fell from scaffold. *Getz v Del E. Webb Corp*, 38 Ill App 3d 880, 349 NE2d 682 (1976).

Electrician, pulling backward on electrical wire protruding from ground, fell when the wire came lose. *Podraza v H.H. Hall Construction Co*, 50 Ill App 3d 643, 365 NE2d 944 (1977).

Decedent went to a hospital for medical treatment and somehow entered a portion of the hospital that was under construction. He fell or jumped from the sixth floor. *Kelly v Northwest Community Hospital*, 66 Ill App 3d 679, 384 NE2d 102 (1978).

Iron worker fell from a beam at a construction site. *Fruzyna v Walter C. Carlson & Associates*, 78 Ill App 3d 1050, 398 NE2d 60 (1979).

Homeowner fell when she stepped on a furnace grating which gave way. *Colbert v Holland Furnace Co*, 333 Ill 78, 164 NE 162 (1928).

The employee of a subcontractor fell from a third-floor walkway without safety rails. At the time of the fall, he was in the process of leaving the job site. *White v Morris Handler Co*, 7 Ill App 3d 199, 287 NE2d 203 (1972).

Worker sustained injuries in fall from loading dock. Summary judgment for architect was affirmed. Architect was not responsible for the design or construction of rubber bumper strips that caused the fall. *Hansen v Ruby Construction Co*, 155 Ill App 3d 475, 508 NE2d 301 (1987).

Indiana

By instructing workers to observe obvious safety precautions an architect did not become "an on site baby-sitter." *Teitge v Remy Construction Co*, 526 NE2d 1008 (Ind Ct App 1988).

Worker stepped on the bottom panel of a heating and ventilating unit which gave way, causing him to fall 30 feet. *Walters v Kellam & Foley*, 172 Ind App 207, 360 NE2d 199 (1977).

Decedent fell from the top of bleacher upon which the back railing had not been installed. *Lukowski v Vecta Education Corp*, 401 NE2d 781 (Ind Ct App 1980).

A schoolboy fell down the outside entry to a basement in the school after being pushed by another child and tripping over a three-inch curb near the entrance. *Sherman v Miller Construction Co*, 90 Ind App 462, 158 NE 255 (1927).

Kansas

Plaintiff fell on the steps leading from the hospital to the parking lot. *Russell v Community Hospital Assn*, 199 Kan 251, 428 P2d 783 (1967).

Louisiana

A worker tripped over a guardrail brace, fell in the water, and drowned. *Burmaster v Gravity Drainage District No 2*, 366 So 2d 1381 (La 1978).

Michigan

A foundry worker was injured when he stepped on a roof hatch; it gave way and caused him to fall 40 feet. Defendant was the sheet metal contractor which designed and built the hatch. *Barger v Sheet Metal Industry*, 48 Mich App 1, 209 NW2d 877 (1973).

Workers were attempting to connect steel beams in a double connection when one beam pulled away from the column and the workers fell. *Tiffany v Christman Co*, 93 Mich App 267, 287 NW2d 199 (1979).

Missouri

Worker fell through a hole in the roof of a building under construction. The hole had been left in the incompleted roof to permit insulation of duct work. *Brown v Gamble Construction Co*, 537 SW2d 685 (Mo Ct App 1976).

Nebraska

Worker fell from scaffold that violated safety standards. *Belgum v Mitsuo Kawamoto & Associates*, 236 Neb 127, 459 NW2d 226 (1990).

The contract called for the architect to supervise the entire construction, perform all managerial functions, and protect the owner's interest in safety. Architect made twice daily safety inspections. The state safety inspector had complained to the architect about holes in the deck. Contractors were uncooperative in eliminating job site hazards. Architect held weekly safety meetings. A piping subcontractor left a hole three and one-quarter feet by three and one-half feet in the deck without boxing or covering. A steamfitter fell through the hole while helping to carry a section of pipe 40 to 60 feet long. The hole had been open and unguarded for three months. The steamfitter was impaled on unprotected reinforcing steel bars projecting from the slab below. They had been unprotected for a year. State safety regulations required that all floor openings be covered with planks and guarded by rails. *Simon v Omaha Public Power District*, 189 Neb 183, 202 NW2d 157 (1972).

New York

Plaintiff fell on a slippery floor in the laundry room of apartment complex. *Cubito v Kreisberg*, 94 Misc 2d 56, 404 NYS2d 69 (1978), *affd*, 51 NY2d 900, 415 NE2d 979, 434 NYS2d 991 (1980).

An electrician, employee of a subcontractor, slipped and fell on an icy ramp. *Hamill v Foster-Lipkins Corp*, 41 AD2d 361, 342 NYS2d 539 (1973).

North Carolina

A hotel guest fell to his death when he was pushed backwards through a window which allegedly lacked sufficient strength or protective devices. *Lamb v Wedgewood South Corp*, 308 NC 419, 302 SE2d 868 (1983).

Oregon

The county lowered the grade of a road at the bottom of a stairway, thus undermining a handrail post which collapsed, causing the plaintiff to fall. *Ogle v Billick*, 253 Or 92, 453 P2d 677 (1969).

Pennsylvania

Worker fell through a hole in drywall enclosure around elevator shaft. HELD: architect was not responsible. Architect's only duty was to make periodic visits to the site; contract imposed no safety-related duties on architect. *Young v Eastern Engineering & Elevator Co*, 381 Pa Super 428, 554 A2d 77, *appeal denied*, 524 Pa 611, 569 A2d 1369 (1989).

A laborer stepped onto a steel beam which was being dismantled from a construction project. It gave way and he fell 20 feet to the ground, after which the beam landed on his legs, causing severe injuries. The jury found that the owner and the engineer were jointly and severally liable. REVERSED. The engineer's safety responsibilities were removed from the contract. *Marshall v Port Authority of Allegheny County*, 106 Pa Commw 131, 525 A2d 857 (1987), *affd*, 524 Pa 1, 568 A2d 931 (1990).

The railroad station contained a raised step four-feet wide and nine-inches high which extended the entire length of the platform between the train and the exit. Plaintiff did not see it, and fell. *Graham v Pennsylvania Co*, 139 Pa 149, 21 A 151 (1891).

South Carolina

Plaintiff sought damages from architect and manufacturer after she caught her foot on a raised threshold. *Broome v Truluck*, 270 SC 277, 241 SE2d 739 (1978).

South Dakota

An iron worker fell when a temporary guardrail failed to support his weight. Highrise housing development. *Duncan v Pennington City Housing Authority*, 283 NW2d 546 (SD 1979).

A University of South Dakota student sustained serious personal injury when she fell down the stairwell in a dormitory. The student brought suit against the state and the architectural firm which designed the structure, alleging that the height of the stairwell railing was insufficient to provide adequate protection. *McMacken v State*, 320 NW2d 131 (SD 1982).

Texas

Plaintiff was injured when the back of a chair installed by defendant contractor at a lunch counter of a hotel broke, causing the plaintiff to fall to the floor. The hotel was undergoing remodeling. *S. Blickman, Inc v Chilton*, 114 SW2d 646 (Tex Civ App 1938).

Utah

Employee of subcontractor was killed when *floating scaffolding* collapsed. He was cleaning the beams of a dome in a sports arena which had become dirty since installation; the original scaffolding used for erecting the dome had been removed, and the subcontractor had installed floating scaffolding suspended from "I" bolts in the dome. The type of scaffolding was not selected by the architect. *Peterson v Fowler*, 27 Utah 2d 159, 493 P2d 997 (1972).

Washington

Plaintiff fell when her heel became lodged in a water-return threshold of a school lounge. *Hull v Enger Construction Co*, 15 Wash App 511, 550 P2d 692, review denied, 87 Wash 2d 1012 (1976).

A skier fell and slid into the steel support of a ski lift tower. *Pinneo v Stevens Pass, Inc*, 14 Wash App 848, 545 P2d 1207, review denied, 87 Wash 2d 1006 (1976).

Wisconsin

A nine-year-old school girl was balancing on a four-foot high railing when she fell and struck a school building window approximately four feet from the railing. Defendant was the architect for the school building. *Mlynarski v St Rita's Congregation*, 31 Wis 2d 54, 142 NW2d 207 (1966).

The plaintiff tripped on an inner step located inside the building next to the inside doors and fell to the lobby floor. Expert testified that the location of the step was not in accordance with good architectural practice. *Hommel v Badger State Investment Co*, 166 Wis 235, 165 NW 20 (1917).

Bodily Injury: Third Party

California

The nine-year-old plaintiff was playing in his friend's garage; the children knocked over an open can of gasoline left by the father to clean paint brushes. Gas fumes were ignited by a nearby water heater. *Hyman v Gordon*, 35 Cal App 3d 769, 111 Cal Rptr 262 (1973).

A woman carrying a suitcase down a flight of steps in a bus station was injured when she fell. She was 80 years old and overweight. The handrail did not extend all the way to the bottom of the stairway, and the construction was such as to give the illusion that the stairs ended one step before they actually did. *Montijo v Swift*, 219 Cal App 2d 351, 33 Cal Rptr 133 (1963).

Maryland

At a swimming party in 1962, the 35-year-old plaintiff dove from a diving board into a 7-foot deep plastic pool. The American Public Health Association recommends minimum depth of 8 feet. *Telak v Maszczenski*, 248 Md 476, 237 A2d 434 (1968).

New Jersey

A housing project was erected in the late 1940s. In 1961, a three-year-old plaintiff was burned on the leg when he touched hot piping leading to a radiator. The piping system formed a ladderlike arrangement less than a foot from the floor, and the child was burned when he tried to climb it. *Totten v Gruzen*, 52 NJ 202, 245 A2d 1 (1968).

An infant was scalded by a hot-water tap in a residence. The design called for hot water to be drawn from the water supply for the radiant heating system at 190 degrees Fahrenheit. A mixing valve, recommended by the manufacturer to reduce temperature and available for $3.60 wholesale, was not specified. *Schipper v Levitt & Sons*, 44 NJ 70, 207 A2d 314 (1965).

New York

The two-year-old tenant fell from a stoop. It was alleged that there was no hand railing, that the arc made by the door when opened almost intersected the edge of the stoop, and that the step did not extend the full length. *Inman v Binghamton Housing Authority*, 3 NY2d 137, 143 NE2d 895, 164 NYS2d 699 (1957).

A basketball spectator was injured when pushed against a metal railing protruding from bleachers. *DiPerna v Roman Catholic Diocese*, 30 AD2d 249, 292 NYS2d 177 (1968).

Traffic Accident

California

Vehicle struck guardrail in front of a concrete pillar supporting an overpass on a state highway. *Erfurt v State*, 141 Cal App 3d 837, 190 Cal Rptr 569 (1983).

Hawaii

Car left road and struck bridge abutment. *Lagua v State*, 65 Haw 7702, 649 P2d 1135 (1982).

Louisiana

Two men were killed while their car was standing near a major intersection and struck by another car driven at 75 to 80 miles per hour. Plaintiff alleged an "entrapping traffic control system." Defendant was the parish traffic engineer. *Snell v Stein*, 201 So 2d 876 (La Ct App), *writ refused*, 251 La 35, 202 So 2d 652 (La 1967).

Michigan

Plaintiff was injured when a truck tipped over on an "S-curve" on a federal highway (statute of limitations case). *O'Brien v Hazlet & Erdal*, 84 Mich App 764, 270 NW2d 690 (1978), *affd*, 410 Mich 1, 299 NW2d 336 (1980).

New Mexico

One-car accident on curve. *Terry v New Mexico State Highway Commission*, 98 NM 119, 645 P2d 1375 (1982).

Motorcyclist/intersection accident. *Blackburn v State*, 98 NM 34, 644 P2d 548 (1982).

Oregon

An employee of a contractor was killed when his vehicle collided with a barricade installed by the contractor to exclude traffic from a highway construction site. *St Paul Fire & Marine Insurance Co v United States National Bank*, 251 Or 377, 446 P2d 103 (1968).

Pennsylvania

A motor vehicle accident resulted from the negligent design and construction of a highway's guardrails, lights, signs, and directional signals. *Keller v Pennsylvania Department of Transportation*, 56 Pa Commw 236, 424 A2d 614 (1981).

Wisconsin

Plaintiff, speeding, missed a curve on a state highway. A warning sign with an arrow showing a curve and calling for 20 miles per hour had been posted 708 feet from the beginning of the curve. The defendants were the district chief maintenance engineer and the district traffic supervisor. The job description required them to determine when warning signs were necessary. A directive in the state highway commission's manual required that a warning sign be placed 750 feet in advance of a hazard. *Chart v Dvorak*, 57 Wis 2d 92, 203 NW2d 673 (1973).

Asphyxiation

California

The general contractor designed and built a home for Muth, who sold to Petty, who sold to Dow. Dow and two children died from asphyxiation caused by carbon monoxide entering the house from two 25,000 B.T.U. gas heaters installed by a subcontractor. The heaters were defective because the gas orifices were too large and secondary heat exchangers caused the collection of soot and allowed carbon monoxide to enter the room. *Dow v Holly Manufacturing Co*, 49 Cal 2d 720, 321 P2d 736 (1958).

Illinois

Leaking refrigerant gas from an air conditioning system entered a boiler room and corroded the gas burners; this allowed toxic quantities of carbon monoxide to enter the room, killing the decedent. The village ordinance and national safety standards required ventilation; the design omitted any provision for ventilation. *Skinner v Anderson*, 38 Ill 2d 455, 231 NE2d 588 (1967) (*see* **Plans Violate Code,** below).

Michigan

The decedent worker was killed when he entered a manhole and, overcome by methane gas, fell into 7 to 10 feet of water. *Vannoy v City of Warren*, 15 Mich App 158, 166 NW2d 486 (1968).

New York

Worker smothered in underground structure. *Persichilli v Triborough Bridge & Tunnel Authority*, 21 AD2d 819, 251 NYS2d 733 (1964), *modified*, 16 NY2d 136, 209 NE2d 802, 262 NYS2d 476 (1965).

Electrocution

United States

Worker injured by electric shock on job site. *Associated Engineers, Inc v Job*, 370 F2d 633 (8th Cir 1966), *cert denied*, 389 US 823 (1967).

Arkansas

A hook-up worker for a mobile crane was injured when the boom and cable were energized by contact with power lines while the plaintiff was trying to hook the cable to a joint of pipe. Defendant was the supervising engineer. *Heslep v Forrest & Cotton, Inc*, 247 Ark 1066, 449 SW2d 181 (1970).

California

Worker struck underground high-voltage line with jack-hammer and was electrocuted. Architect knew the line was there but did not show it on the contract documents. *Mallow v Tucker, Sadler & Bennett, Architects & Engineers, Inc*, 245 Cal App 2d 700, 54 Cal Rptr 174 (1966) (*see* **Underground Obstruction,** above).

Louisiana

A worker on a metal building job was electrocuted when a 20-foot section of gutter that he was holding came into contact with an uninsulated electric line. *Patin v Industrial Enterprises*, 421 So 2d 362 (La Ct App), *writ denied*, 423 So 2d 1166 (La 1982).

Massachusetts

Electrician was injured by an "arc-over" while testing a panel that, unknown to the electrician, contained 2,300 volts. There was no "Danger—High Voltage" label. *Parent v Stone & Webster Engineering Corp*, 408 Mass 108, 556 NE2d 1009 (1990).

Montana

A student was electrocuted in university whirlpool bath. *Reeves v Ille Electric Co*, 170 Mont 104, 551 P2d 647 (1976).

Nevada

A swimmer died from electrocution, allegedly because the color coding of wires was incorrect, causing them to be attached in such a way as to permit electrical current to flow into the pool rather than into the pool lights. *Nevada Lake Shore Co v Diamond Electric, Inc*, 89 Nev 293, 511 P2d 113 (1973).

New York

A worker was electrocuted while troubleshooting a problem in a parking lot lighting system. *Jaroszewicz v Facilities Development Corp*, 115 AD2d 159, 495 NYS2d 498 (1985).

Defective Plans

United States

The subcontractor alleged that defective plans resulted in increased construction costs. *Harbor Mechanical, Inc v Arizona Electric Power Co-op, Inc*, 496 F Supp 681 (D Ariz 1980) (*see* **Misrepresentation,** below).

California

The structural engineer signed and sealed the plans but omitted details concerning electrical work, mechanical piping, grading, and drainage. *Wynner v Buxton*, 97 Cal App 3d 166, 158 Cal Rptr 587 (1979).

Contractor alleged the plans were defective because they failed to indicate that the concrete was to be poured by *wall-to-wall* method rather than the customary *floor-to-floor* method. *Jasper Construction, Inc v Foothill Jr College District*, 91 Cal App 3d 1, 153 Cal Rptr 767 (1979).

Engineer prepared inaccurate grade sheets for sewer line. *Bilich v Barnett*, 103 Cal App 2d Supp 921, 229 P2d 492 (1951).

Illinois

The plaintiff alleged that it was negligence for the architect to omit grid points on the grading plan. *Mississippi Meadows, Inc v Hodson*, 13 Ill App 3d 24, 299 NE2d 359 (1973).

Contractor and subcontractor alleged that the drawings were so defective that the electrical equipment for a sewage treatment plant could not be manufactured and installed. *Bates & Rogers Construction v North Shore Sanitary District*, 92 Ill App 3d 90, 414 NE2d 1274 (1980), *affd*, 109 Ill 2d 225, 486 NE2d 902 (1985).

Kentucky

The contractor alleged that the contract documents for the roof, walls, flooring, and painting were defective. *Kortz v Kimberlin*, 158 Ky 566, 165 SW 654 (1914).

Oklahoma

A motorist lost consciousness and propelled his automobile over a curb, through a three-foot brick wall, and onto the street below a parking garage. He alleged that the drawings and plans were defective. *Minor v Zidell Trust*, 618 P2d 392 (Okla 1980).

Oregon

The contractor alleged that the engineers dug several test trenches and test holes to determine ground water conditions but disclosed only the favorable data to bidders, withholding the unfavorable data. *Salem Sand & Gravel Co v City of Salem*, 260 Or 630, 492 P2d 271 (1971).

South Carolina

Architect was liable to condominium association for defective design of condominium project. Action was not barred by the economic loss rule. *Beachwalk Villas Condo Associates v Martin*, 305 SC 144, 406 SE2d 372 (1991).

Multiple Defects in Plans

Arizona

Road plan did not adequately provide for disposal of storm water or sewer effluent. *Henningson, Durham & Richardson v Prochnow*, 13 Ariz App 411,

477 P2d 285 (1970), *review denied*, 107 Ariz 222, 485 P2d 547 (1971) (*see* **Miscellaneous, Shop Drawings,** below).

California

The medical building as planned by defendant had inadequate space for the receptionist, unsuitable door locks, and inadequate soundproofing, and the air conditioning system was inadequate. *Goldberg v Underhill*, 95 Cal App 2d 700, 213 P2d 516 (1950).

Florida

Chimneys were defective, stucco was faulty, and the buildings were not rainproof. *Bayshore Development Co v Bonfoey*, 75 Fla 445, 78 So 507 (1918).

Iowa

The opera house was designed so that private boxes had no view of the stage. It was necessary to lower the balcony. Walls sustaining the arch bulged. *Trunk & Gordon v Clark*, 163 Iowa 620, 145 NW 277 (1914).

Louisiana

On a street job, there were substantial failures in the base, defects in curbs and gutters, and other flaws. The cost of repair would be about $175,000. The owner alleged that the engineer employed an incompetent resident engineer. *Town of Winnsboro v Barnard & Burke, Inc*, 294 So 2d 867 (La Ct App 1974).

Michigan

The owner alleged that the plans were unskillfully drawn causing defects in the sewer, cornice, coping for towers, stairway, elevator, and chimney flue. *Chapel v Clark*, 117 Mich 638, 76 NW 62 (1898).

Missouri

The elevations of a two-story mule barn were unsatisfactory; the entrance was 30 inches above the curb which made it difficult to load feed into the barn; the mule alley was inclined, not level. *Dysart-Cook Mule Co v Reed & Heckenlively*, 114 Mo App 296, 89 SW 591 (1905).

Nebraska

There were cracks throughout the house, it leaked, the floors were uneven, and the house settled in such a way that the doors would not close properly. *Lincoln Stone & Supply Co v Ludwig*, 94 Neb 722, 144 NW 782 (1913).

New York

The architect agreed to prepare plans for $600, $100 of which was paid on account. They were defective in many respects. No dimensions were noted; the figures and scales were inaccurate; necessary items were omitted. The plans were not usable, and the owner discarded them. *Dunne v Robinson*, 53 Misc 545, 103 NYS 878 (1907).

Plans Violate Code

United States

The architect knew that the planning board on the Island of St. Croix required a hip roof to harmonize with the Danish village architectural style. He submitted an acceptable design to the planning board but then allowed the contractor to build a flat roof. He certified the work even though he was aware that the roof was incorrect. This delayed completion of the project until the roof was revised. *General Trading Corp v Burnup & Sims, Inc*, 523 F2d 98 (3d Cir 1975).

California

Failure of the plans to comply with the requirements of the Uniform Building Code is negligence per se; therefore, expert testimony as to the standard of professional practice is not required. *Huang v Garner*, 157 Cal App 3d 404, 203 Cal Rptr 800 (1984).

A licensed building designer prepared plans for a laundromat to be constructed in an area where laundromat use was not permitted by the zoning ordinance. *Chaplis v Monterey County*, 97 Cal App 3d 249, 158 Cal Rptr 395 (1979).

Florida

Architect designed building that violated city zoning requirements. *Graulich v Frederic H. Berlowe & Associates*, 338 So 2d 1109 (Fla Dist Ct App 1976).

Architect designed building that failed to comply with building codes and zoning ordinances. *Robsol, Inc v Garris*, 358 So 2d 865 (Fla Dist Ct App 1978).

Architects allegedly falsely represented that zoning problems (off-street parking requirements) had been resolved. *Forte v Tripp & Skrip*, 339 So 2d 698 (Fla Dist Ct App 1976).

Architect followed the advice of owner's lawyer regarding zoning requirements; the plan, when prepared, failed to conform with the zoning ordinance. *Krestow v Wooster*, 360 So 2d 32 (Fla Dist Ct App 1978).

Premanufactured wall units failed to comply with the Southern Standard Building Code because they did not provide fire resistance. *Atlantic National Bank v Modular Age, Inc*, 363 So 2d 1152 (Fla Dist Ct App 1978), *cert denied*, 372 So 2d 466 (Fla 1979).

Georgia

The architect and engineer failed to specify the fire sprinkler system required by the building code. *Waddey v Davis*, 149 Ga App 308, 254 SE2d 465 (1979) (*see* **Fire,** above).

Illinois

Hospital required extensive corrective work when it was discovered that the wooden wall paneling specified by the architect failed to comply with the Chicago Building Code "Flame Spread Rating" requirements. *St Joseph Hospital v Corbetta Construction Co*, 21 Ill App 3d 925, 316 NE2d 51 (1974).

Engineer was aware of controversy regarding the interpretation of the code but nevertheless specified installation of telephone wires in open cable tray. This was ultimately determined to be a fire hazard, and therefore a code violation. *Himmel Corp v Stade*, 52 Ill App 3d 294, 367 NE2d 411 (1977).

Leaking refrigerant gas from an air conditioning system entered a boiler room and corroded the gas burners; this allowed toxic quantities of carbon monoxide to enter the room, killing the decedent. The village ordinance and national safety standards required ventilation; the design omitted any provision for ventilation. *Skinner v Anderson*, 38 Ill 2d 455, 231 NE2d 588 (1967) (*see* **Asphyxiation,** above).

Indiana

At the request of the owner, the architect revised the plan so as to provide only one fire exit; two were required. *Greenhaven Corp v Hutchcraft & Associates*, 463 NE2d 283 (Ind Ct App 1984).

Louisiana

Walls failed to meet wind load requirements of municipal code. *State v Wilco Construction Co*, 393 So 2d 885 (La Ct App), *writ denied*, 400 So 2d 905 (La 1981).

New York

Architect attempted to file plans with the city building department on October 16 in order to avoid more stringent zoning requirements which were to become effective the next day. The city refused to accept the plans. *530 East 89*

Corp v Unger, 54 AD2d 848, 388 NYS2d 284 (1976), *affd*, 43 NY2d 776, 373 NE2d 276, 402 NYS2d 382 (1977).

The contract documents called for brick walls 12 inches thick, but the building code required a minimum of 16 inches. *Burger v Roelsch*, 77 Hun 44, 28 NYS 460 (1894).

South Carolina

Engineer failed to apply for a permit from the Department of Health and Environmental Control, then concealed from developer objections lodged by the department. *Foxfire Village, Inc v Black & Veatch, Inc*, 304 SC 366, 404 SE2d 912 (Ct App 1991), *cert denied* (Aug 15, 1991).

Utah

Plaintiff told the designer he wanted a house with a view, and the designer assured plaintiff that he could produce this; in reliance, the plaintiff bought a lot. After the house was laid out, it was discovered that the building code required an *average* setback. The restrictive covenants required a 30-foot setback. However, whether the average setback or the 30-foot setback was used, the house would not have a view. *Quagliana v Exquisite Home Builders, Inc*, 538 P2d 301 (Utah 1975).

Virginia

The plans could not be used because they violated setback requirements. *Bott v Moser*, 175 Va 11, 7 SE2d 217 (1940).

Washington

The plans for an eight-story building violated the building ordinance. *Bebb v Jordan*, 111 Wash 73, 189 P 553 (1920).

Negligent Selection of Contractor

California

Evidence was introduced that the architect failed to require mechanics lien releases. The prime contractor went bankrupt during the job at a cost to the owner of about $15,000. The owner alleged a conflict of interest, in that the contractor was a client of the architect on a different job. *Palmer v Brown*, 127 Cal App 2d 44, 273 P2d 306 (1954).

Florida

The owner alleged that the architect gave negligent advice as to the selection of a general contractor who subsequently abandoned the job. *MacIntyre v Green's Pool Service, Inc*, 347 So 2d 1081 (Fla Dist Ct App 1977) (*see* **Payment Certificate,** below).

Illinois

Evidence was introduced that the architect selected an incompetent, impoverished heating contractor who was on the verge of going bankrupt. *Morse v Michaelson, Rabig & Ramp*, 10 Ill App 2d 366, 243 NE2d 271 (1968).

Minnesota

After accepting a written proposal from an electrical subcontractor, the general contractor notified the subcontractor that he was *unacceptable* for the job because the state's consulting engineer determined that the subcontractor did not have sufficient experience or equipment. *Electric Service Co v Lakehead Electric Co*, 291 Minn 22, 189 NW2d 489 (1971).

Delay

United States

Subcontractor alleged that architect failed to act promptly on submittals. *EC Ernst v Manhattan Construction Co*, 551 F2d 1026 (5th Cir 1977), *cert denied*, 434 US 106 (1978) (*see* **Mechanical Heating, Ventilating, and Air Conditioning,** above).

Subcontractor alleged that defendants failed to follow the construction schedule. *Danny's Construction Co v Havens Steel Co*, 437 F Supp 91 (D Neb 1977).

The contractor alleged that the city engineer delayed progress on the job by failure to have necessary engineering ready on time, delay in locating the site, and discrepancies in contract documents. *Cox v City of Freeman*, 321 F2d 887 (8th Cir 1963).

Alabama

The contractor alleged that the city engineer fraudulently and corruptly prevented him from finishing work by demanding performance not required by the contract. *Wilder v Crook*, 250 Ala 424, 34 So 2d 832 (1948).

Alaska

Engineer's negligence allegedly caused delay in construction of a sewage treatment plant. *Clark v City of Seward*, 659 P2d 1227 (Alaska 1983).

Arkansas

An engineer contracted to prepare plans for a wastewater treatment facility within 135 days. When the plans were not ready on time, the city's entitlement to funding fell from 75 per cent to 55 per cent. *W. Wm Graham, Inc v City of Cave City*, 289 Ark 105, 709 SW2d 94 (1986).

Illinois

Engineer allegedly failed to complete timely details of the plans and failed to respond timely to requests for instructions. *Normoyle-Berg & Associates v Village of Deer Creek*, 39 Ill App 3d 744, 350 NE2d 559 (1976).

Michigan

Owner alleged the engineer delayed in the delivery of drawings and specifications for a slag-handling plant. Engineer denied the client had set any deadline. *Giffels & Vallet, Inc v Edward C. Levy Co*, 337 Mich 177, 58 NW2d 899 (1953).

New Jersey

The contractor alleged that the architect, through improper supervision and coordination, delayed the completion of a school project for 11 months. *Gherardi v Board of Education*, 53 NJ Super 349, 147 A2d 535 (1958).

New York

Property owners charged that architect failed to respond timely to objections raised by the city building department to plans prepared by architect. *530 East 89 Corp v Unger*, 43 NY2d 776, 373 NE2d 276, 402 NYS2d 382 (1977).

Pennsylvania

Architect delayed in delivering plans for residences. *Edwards v Hall*, 293 Pa 97, 141 A 638 (1928).

The building was scheduled for completion in May 1916 but was not finished until August 1917. Much delay was caused by changes made by the owner, but there was also evidence that the architects failed to promptly provide large-scale details from which the subcontractors could prepare shop drawings. *Osterling v Frick*, 284 Pa 397, 131 A 250 (1925).

Safety Inspection

Michigan

A workers' compensation insurance company agreed to provide safety inspections and safety engineering surveys; plaintiff was injured on the job. *Banner v Travelers Insurance Co*, 31 Mich App 608, 188 NW2d 51 (1971).

A workers' compensation insurance carrier voluntarily undertook to provide safety inspection; worker lost hand operating a punch press. *Ray v Transamerica Insurance Co*, 10 Mich App 55, 158 NW2d 786 (1968).

Nebraska

Plaintiff suffered severe injuries on the job and received workers' compensation; he then sued the workers' compensation insurance carrier seeking recovery for the same injuries on the ground that the insurance carrier negligently performed its agreement with the employer to provide safety engineering inspection. *Pettigrew v Home Insurance Co*, 191 Neb 312, 214 NW2d 920 (1974).

New Mexico

An architect was employed by a homeowner to inspect the completed project and concluded that nothing in the construction of the stairs operated to create a dangerous condition. *Oschwald v Chrisie*, 95 NM 251, 620 P2d 1276 (1980).

Dirt Estimate

California

The engineer prepared a grading plan for hillside property. The plan showed a 33-lot subdivision, and the engineer advised the client that it was a *tight plan*. In the end, there was a surplus of dirt on the project, and it was necessary to leave the last portion of the project higher than designed. As a result, the 3 lots planned for that area were reduced to 2 lots. *Bonadiman-McCain, Inc v Snow*, 183 Cal App 2d 58, 6 Cal Rptr 52 (1960).

A surveyor estimated that a tract of land contained 51,000 cubic yards of excess dirt. He had set his instruments erroneously; there were only 15,802 cubic yards. Relying on the report, plaintiff, who owned the tract, sold it for $100,000 plus the excess value of the dirt over the cost of grading. *Roberts v Karr*, 178 Cal App 2d 535, 3 Cal Rptr 98 (1960).

Indiana

A subcontractor submitted a bid for excavation based on dirt quantities estimated by an engineer employed by the subcontractor. It was alleged that the engineer underestimated the quantities as a result of which the subcontractor defaulted on the contract with the prime contractor. The prime contractor filed suit against the engineer. *Peyronnin Construction Co v Weiss*, 137 Ind App 417, 208 NE2d 489 (1965).

Louisiana

The contractor alleged that the engineer negligently misrepresented the amount of excavation necessary to complete an airport job. *Delta Construction Co v City of Jackson*, 198 So 2d 592 (Miss 1967).

Bribery

Kansas

An architect was indicted for conspiracy to bribe a public employee to award an architectural contract for a medical center. *State v Campbell*, 217 Kan 756, 539 P2d 329, *cert denied*, 423 US 1017 (1975).

New York

Architect alleged to have offered to secure a zoning variance to permit a coffee house for $6,000, half of which would be used to bribe members of the New York City Bureau of Standards and Appeals. *Daub v Board of Regents of University of New York*, 33 AD2d 964, 306 NYS2d 869 (1970).

Misrepresentation

United States

Under Arizona law, a contractor may allege an action against an engineer based on negligent misrepresentation, even though his or her case against the engineer for negligent performance of the contract is barred by lack of privity. *Harbor Mechanical, Inc v Arizona Elec Power Co-op, Inc*, 496 F Supp 681 (D Ariz 1980) (*see* **Defective Plans,** above).

Florida

The architect employed a window sign listing himself as being in architectural partnership with draftsman who was not a registered architect. After the draftsman prepared drawings, the architect checked them, and they were published under the architect's name and seal. *Markel v Florida State Board of Architecture*, 268 So 2d 374 (Fla 1972).

Iowa

Engineer designed a building to accept a snow load of 17.5 pounds per square foot then represented to the building inspector that the roof would hold 30 pounds per square foot. *Wright v State Board of Engineering Examiners*, 250 NW2d 412 (Iowa 1977).

Minnesota

Defendant represented he had 17 years experience in the building business; he had stopped because of ill health; he was an engineer; his net worth was $75,000; he would be able to obtain a performance bond. In truth, defendant stopped the construction business because he became bankrupt; he was not an engineer, he could not get a bond; and his net worth was $45,000. The house he designed cost $79,300, rather than the budgeted $38,000. *Strouth v Wilkison*, 302 Minn 297, 224 NW2d 511 (1974).

Montana

A surveyor falsely testified to the Board of Professional Engineers and Land Surveyors that a boundary survey had been properly monumented. *In re Shaw*, 189 Mont 310, 615 P2d 910 (1980).

Extra Work

California

The architect instructed the contractor to install additional concrete; the owner refused to pay for it, claiming the architect was not authorized to order the extra work. *Scribante v Edwards*, 40 Cal App 561, 181 P 75 (1919).

Minnesota

The contractor alleged that the city's architect and engineer negligently failed to authorize an appropriate change order for extra work. *Grazzini Brothers & Co v Builders Clinic, Inc*, 280 Minn 540, 160 NW2d 259 (1968).

Nebraska

The architect required the contractor to perform extra grading which was necessitated by the architect's error. *Erskine v Johnson*, 23 Neb 261, 36 NW 510 (1888).

Payment Certificate

United States

Architect continued to certify progress payments after discovering that subcontractors and suppliers were unpaid. *Aetna Insurance Co v Helmuth, Obata & Kassabaum, Inc*, 392 F2d 472 (8th Cir 1968).

The contract required monthly payments to be made "upon invoices presented by the Contractor and approved by the Architects, in the sum of . . .

85% of all materials delivered and paid for and work incorporated in the building." Instead of submitting invoices, the contractor submitted mere estimates of the value of work accomplished, which the architect approved. This resulted in overpayments to the contractor, who defaulted. *Hall v Union Indemnity Co*, 61 F2d 85 (8th Cir), *cert denied*, 287 US 663 (1932).

The architect certified the contractor's application for final payment at a time when the contractor had not presented adequate proof that all laborers and material suppliers had been paid for their work or material. The architect also certified final payment when construction was incomplete. The surety finished the job and filed suit against the architect. *Peerless Insurance Co v Cerny & Associates*, 199 F Supp 951 (DC Minn 1961).

Arizona

The contractor alleged that the architect arbitrarily refused to issue a payment certificate. *Blecick v School District No 18*, 2 Ariz App 115, 406 P2d 750 (1965).

Florida

Owner alleged that architect gave negligent advice as to construction progress payments. *MacIntyre v Green's Pool Service, Inc*, 347 So 2d 1081 (Fla Dist Ct App 1977) (*see* **Negligent Selection of Contractor,** above).

Inaccurate reports of the work completed on the project submitted by the engineering inspector caused the mortgagee to wrongfully disburse loan proceeds to the developer-mortgagor. *Hobbs v Florida First National Bank*, 406 So 2d 63 (Fla Dist Ct App 1981), *dismissed without opinion*, 412 So 2d 466 (Fla 1982).

Indiana

The owner alleged that the architect negligently issued a payment certificate. *Bump v McGrannahan*, 61 Ind App 136, 111 NE 640 (1916).

Louisiana

An engineer was held liable to the contractor's surety because the engineer negligently certified overpayment of progress payments. As a result, materialmen and subcontractors recorded mechanics liens. *American Fidelity Fire Insurance Co v Pavia-Byrne Engineering Corp*, 393 So 2d 830, *writ denied*, 397 So 2d 1362 (La Ct App 1981).

Massachusetts

The architect certified payment. The homeowner complained that the work did not comply with the contract documents, but the architect said the work done was worth more than that for which the owner contracted. Relying on that, the owner paid the contractor, who thereupon abandoned the project, insolvent. *Corey v Eastman*, 166 Mass 279, 44 NE 217 (1896).

Mississippi

A subcontractor filed suit against an architect on the theory that the architect was negligent when he certified the prime contractor's inaccurate and dishonest applications for payment, so the prime contractor became bankrupt and the subcontractor was not paid for his work. *Engle Acoustic & Tile, Inc v Grenfell*, 223 So 2d 613 (Miss 1969).

The contractor's bid contained a unit price of $1.50 per linear foot for installation of drainage pipe, but the extension of the price on the same line was calculated at the rate of $15 per foot. The engineer certified payment at $15 per foot and failed to invoke a $50-per-day penalty for delay. *Newton Investment Co v Barnard & Burk, Inc*, 220 So 2d 822 (Miss 1969).

Missouri

In the absence of a contractual provision, an architect who issues payment certificates is not responsible for checking the adequacy of mechanics lien releases. *Fabe v W.V.P. Corp*, 760 SW2d 490 (Mo Ct App 1988).

It was alleged that the architect certified payments for $23,000 in excess of the value of work performed on a $325,000 church job. The plaintiff was the surety of the prime contractor. *Westerhold v Carroll*, 419 SW2d 73 (Mo 1967).

New York

Although the architect withheld the final certificate, he issued payment certificates to a masonry contractor at a time when defective work had been performed. *Petersen v Rawson*, 34 NY 370 (1866), *revd*, 15 NY Sup Ct 234 (1857).

The subcontractor alleged that the engineers "maliciously, fraudulently and with intent to injure" refused to certify payment. *Unity Sheet Metal Works v Farrell Lines*, 101 NYS2d 1000 (Sup Ct 1950).

North Carolina

Owner alleged negligence by architect in preparing progress reports before progress payments were made to contractor. *People's Center, Inc v Anderson*, 32 NC App 746, 233 SE2d 694 (1977).

Bank agreed to lend money to a partnership to finance the construction of an apartment complex and employed an architect to supervise the project and certify the amount of work completed. The architect negligently overcertified the construction project, and the partnership brought suit to recover damages.

Browning v Maurice B. Levien & Co, 44 NC App 701, 262 SE2d 355, *review denied*, 300 NC 371, 267 SE2d 673 (1980).

Texas

Contractor alleged that engineer improperly refused to issue certificate of completion. *Sub-Surface Construction Co v Bryant-Curington, Inc*, 533 SW2d 452 (Tex Civ App 1976).

The architect issued a certificate of completion even though he knew that the work did not comply with the contract documents. *Pierson v Tyndall*, 28 SW 232 (Tex Civ App 1894).

Survey

Alabama

Surveyor prepared a plan for excavation of a retention basin. After the contractor excavated the basin it was determined to be only one-half the size called for in the contract documents. *Paragon Engineering, Inc v Rhodes*, 451 So 2d 274 (Ala 1984).

Surveyor unintentionally stepped across a boundary line, trespassing on the neighbor's property during a boundary survey. *Johnson v Martin*, 423 So 2d 868 (Ala Civ App 1982).

California

A surveyor prepared a lot split, the original owner died, and plaintiff bought a lot from the estate. An encroachment ensued because of an error in the survey. *Kent v Bartlett*, 49 Cal App 3d 724, 122 Cal Rptr 615 (1975).

Colorado

The owners had to move their house when it was discovered that, because of surveyor's negligence, it occupied land belonging to the government. *Doyle v Linn*, 37 Colo App 214, 547 P2d 257 (1975).

District of Columbia

In *Bell v Jones*, 523 A2d 982 (DC 1986), a surveyor negligently certified that he had carefully surveyed the property when he had not actually done so. This negligence proximately caused increased construction costs to the architect. The court asserted that the standard of practice for surveyors was a national standard, not a local or regional one.

Florida

Surveyor transposed 138-foot boundary measurement to read 183. *Jacobs v Petrino*, 351 So 2d 1036 (Fla Dist Ct App 1976), *cert denied*, 349 So 2d 1231 (Fla 1977).

Professional land surveyors were named in a suit for malpractice and breach of contract for improper preparation of a plat. *Lauren v Grant*, 407 So 2d 395 (Fla Dist Ct App 1981).

Illinois

A surveyor was employed to survey three separate 3-acre parcels out of a master 27-acre parcel. The surveyor failed to detect that the master parcel had been erroneously calculated by a previous survey to contain 30 acres. *Barnes v Rakow*, 78 Ill App 3d 404, 396 NE2d 1168 (1979).

Defendant surveyed a vacant lot for S&S Builders in 1953; they sold to Nash, which sold to plaintiffs. Plaintiffs built a driveway and garage which encroached because of the survey error. The plat said: "This plat of survey carries our absolute guarantee for accuracy." *Rozny v Marnal*, 43 Ill 2d 54, 250 NE2d 656 (1969).

Indiana

Inaccurate survey allegedly damaged remote owner not in privity. *Essex v Ryan*, 446 NE2d 368 (Ind Ct App 1983).

Louisiana

In *Crawford v Gray & Associates*, 493 So 2d 734 (La Ct App), *writ denied*, 497 So 2d 1013 (La 1986), a surveyor negligently failed to inquire about the width of a right of way and incorrectly furnished the plaintiff with a plat which revealed no servitudes, easements, or rights of way.

The survey inaccurately reflected the number of acres enclosed within the boundary. Broussard v Continental Casualty Co, 421 So 2d 341 (La Ct App), *writ denied*, 423 So 2d 1165 (1982).

Home purchaser suffered mental anguish because of incorrect survey. *Guthrie v Rudy Brown Builders, Inc*, 416 So 2d 590 (La Ct App), *writ denied*, 420 So 2d 455 (La 1982).

Surveyor certified he had staked an oil well site even though he had never been there. Well was staked and drilled on the wrong land. *Hogan Exploration, Inc v Monroe Engineering Associates*, 430 So 2d 696 (La Ct App 1983).

Survey showed a drain pipe on the owner's property; it was actually located on adjoining property. *Lawyers Title Insurance Co v Carey Hodges & Associates*, 358 So 2d 964 (La Ct App 1978).

The surveyor was employed to *confirm* an earlier survey. He found that the courses and dimensions were correct but failed to check the accuracy of a note that the tract contained 13.16 acres. In fact, it only contained 11.26 acres. *Jenkins v J.J. Krebs & Sons*, 322 So 2d 426 (La Ct App 1975), *writ denied*, 325 So 2d 611 (La 1976).

The architect, performing services for a school board, relied on an erroneous topographical survey provided by a school board member. *Jacka v Ouachita Parish School Board*, 249 La 223, 186 So 2d 571 (1966).

The surveyor's crew staked the locations for pilings for school buildings allowing only a 37-foot space between the buildings rather than the intended 48 feet. The drawings were ambiguous because of an overhang. The contractor was required to relocate the pilings. The surveyor had obtained some information from the contractor's foreman. *Charles Carter & Co v McGee*, 213 So 2d 89 (La Ct App 1968).

Maryland

Landowner brought action against neighbor and neighbor's surveyor for continuing trespass and negligent preparation of boundary survey. *Carlotta v T.R. Stark & Associates*, 57 Md App 467, 470 A2d 838 (1984).

Because of the negligence of the surveyor, the buyer received 19.5 acres when he thought he was going to receive 22 acres. *Reighard v Downs*, 261 Md 26, 273 A2d 109 (1971), *appeal after remand*, 265 Md 344, 289 A2d 299 (1972).

The owner alleged that the surveyor erroneously staked lot corners and failed to obtain the maximum lot yield. *Mattingly v Hopkins*, 254 Md 88, 253 A2d 904 (1969).

Massachusetts

The contractor sued the engineer employed by the owner for negligent misplacement of offset stakes. *Craig v Everett M. Brooks Co*, 351 Mass 497, 222 NE2d 752 (1967).

New Hampshire

The surveyor mislocated the town's main water line with reference to a boundary survey, relying on information supplied by the seller and by an independent engineer. *Rabe v Carnaby*, 120 NH 809, 423 A2d 610 (1980).

New Jersey

As a result of an erroneous survey, the truck docks were only 35 feet from the boundary, instead of 55 feet. This left insufficient room for the trucks to unload. *E.A. Williams, Inc v Russo Development Corp*, 82 NJ 160, 411 A2d 697 (1980).

New York

Survey errors in plot plan, building setback, and property description. *Tool v Boutelle*, 91 Misc 2d 464, 398 NYS2d 128 (Sup Ct 1977).

Petitioner's license as a land surveyor was revoked and his license as a professional engineer was suspended for one year for the following violations: incorrect calculation of a boundary line, traverse closure errors, incorrect description of square footage of certain land parcel, inaccurate outline of a structure, faulty descriptions on a topographic survey, and false advertising representing that petitioner was associated in his engineering and land surveying firm with other licensed professional engineers and land surveyors. *Brew v State Education Department*, 73 AD2d 743, 423 NYS2d 271 (1979).

Land surveyor subdivided a plot of land, setting out a strip along the northern boundary to provide access to the highway. Plaintiffs purchased the property with the belief that a road suitable for vehicles could be built in the access strip for the cost of the road itself. Greater expenditures were required because a moving brook, not properly indicated in the subdivision map, crossed the potential road. *Wetzler v O'Brien*, 81 AD2d 517, 437 NYS2d 343 (1981).

Surveyor mislocated a building, causing an encroachment. *Seger v Cornwell*, 44 Misc 2d 994, 255 NYS2d 744 (Sup Ct 1964).

Oregon

Surveying error caused two-foot shortage in lot. *Kashmir Corp v Barnes*, 278 Or 433, 564 P2d 693 (1977).

A surveyor failed to follow the Bureau of Land Management Manual and was disciplined by the Board of Engineering Examiners. *Hambleton v Board of Engineering Examiners*, 40 Or App 9, 594 P2d 416 (1979); *accord Voelz v Board of Engg Examiners*, 37 Or App 113, 586 P2d 807 (1978), *review denied*, 285 Or 479 (1979).

The building was mislocated, reducing the size of the parking lot. *Bales for Food, Inc v Poole*, 246 Or 253, 424 P2d 892 (1967).

South Dakota

The surveyor who prepared the residential subdivision plat acknowledged that a corner monument was inaccurately represented but failed to remove the corner monument. *Nichols v Brady Consultants, Inc*, 305 NW2d 849 (SD 1981).

Texas

Architect designed a house which would not fit the lot. *Newell v Mosley*, 469 SW2d 481 (Tex Civ App 1971).

Washington

Faulty survey caused encroachments. *Kundahl v Barnett*, 5 Wash App 227, 486 P2d 1164, *review denied*, 80 Wash 2d 1001 (1971).

Water and Percolation Tests

Georgia

Engineer was liable to remote purchaser for negligently performed percolation tests. *Southeast Consultants, Inc v O'Pry*, 199 Ga App 125, 404 SE2d 299 (1991), *cert denied* (May 15, 1991).

Massachusetts

A surveyor failed to warn purchasers of the existence of a high water table. *Nei v Boston Survey Consultants, Inc*, 388 Mass 320, 446 NE2d 681 (1983).

Miscellaneous

Bidding: After the bids were opened, the architect allowed one bidder to correct its bid. Negotiations ensued and the job was awarded to the bidder that had been permitted to make corrections. The low bidder filed suit against the architect. *Commercial Industrial Construction, Inc v Anderson*, 683 P2d 378 (Colo Ct App 1984).

Blast Furnace: A worker was injured when his hand was pinned between the rails of a skip bridge and the wheel of a car at a blast furnace unit used in a steel plant. *Abdul Warith v Arthur G. McKee & Co*, 488 F Supp 306 (ED Pa 1980).

Bricks: Bricks used in construction peeled, fell apart, and disintegrated. *Henderson Clay Products, Inc v Edgar Wood & Associates*, 122 NH 800, 451 A2d 174 (1982).

Burn: A new tenant, who was a paraplegic, suffered second- and third-degree burns in bathwater by not first testing water temperature. *Tirella v American Properties Team, Inc*, 145 AD2d 724, 535 NYS2d 252 (1988).

Carcinogenic dust: A final step in the construction of a chemical-processing plant was installation of a catalyst in the form of pellets coated with vanadium. The operation generated vanadium dust which penetrated the respirator mask employed by plaintiff, allegedly causing his death from throat cancer. *La Rossa v Scientific Design Co*, 402 F2d 937 (3d Cir 1968).

Concrete mix: The engineer's inspector at the batch plant volunteered to help mix the concrete. He poured the wrong admixture. As a result, the concrete had to be removed, and the prime contractor sued the subcontractor, who in turn sued the engineer who employed the negligent inspector. *Walnut Creek Aggregates Co v Testing Engineers, Inc*, 248 Cal App 2d 690, 56 Cal Rptr 700 (1967).

Conspiracy: Taxpayer's suit accused an architect of conspiracy to give a favored contractor an unfair advantage in bidding a public job. *Grieb v Citizens Casualty*, 33 Wis 2d 552, 148 NW2d 103 (1967).

Contract Documents: Architect informed public works bidder that a $9,000 contingency allowance would be removed from the contract documents by addendum. The contingency allowance was never removed. *Godrey, Bassett & Kuykendall Architects, Ltd v Huntington Lumber & Supply Co*, 584 So 2d 1254, 1259 (Miss 1991).

A dispute arose between a contractor and a school district as to who was responsible to pay for utility charges. The school district claimed that the architect was negligent in failing to specify in the contract documents which party would be responsible. *Overland Constructors, Inc v Millard School District*, 220 Neb 220, 369 NW2d 69 (1985).

Crane: Worker was injured by a gas bottle which fell from a crane operated by the contractor. The engineer had responsibility for supervision of the project and had a staff of safety personnel on the job site. Fall was caused by the general contractor's negligent procedures in rigging bottles to the crane. *Ortiz v Uhl*, 39 AD2d 143, 332 NYS2d 583 (1972), *affd*, 33 NY2d 989, 316 NE2d 886, 353 NYS2d 962 (1974) (*see* **Falling Object,** above).

Deflection: In remodeling a partially completed building, it was necessary to make way for a new stairwell. Floor joists were shortened and reattached to a cross beam. This violated the building code, which provided that "in no case shall either end of a beam or beams rest on stud partitions." The floor deflected. The architect visited the site every day but did not catch the error because it had been floored over and covered before the architect had an opportunity to inspect. *Straus v Buchman*, 96 AD 270, 89 NYS 226 (1904), *affd*, 184 NY 545, 76 NE 1109 (1906).

Drainage ditch: The widening and deepening of an existing drainage ditch located east of plaintiff's premises resulted in damage to a well which was fed by percolating waters. *Lee v City of Pontiac*, 99 Ill App 3d 982, 426 NE2d 300 (1981).

Forklift: Forklift overturned when a metal grating became dislodged. *Shibuya v Architects Hawaii, Ltd*, 65 Haw 26, 647 P2d 276 (1982).

Foundation: The engineer provided inspection on a bridge project but failed to detect that the pilings would not support the required load of 15 tons each. *Cowles v City of Minneapolis*, 128 Minn 452, 151 NW 184 (1915).

Frozen pipes: Water piping in an apartment building froze. *Wheat Street Two, Inc v James C Wise, Simpson, Aiken & Associates*, 132 Ga App 548, 208 SE2d 359 (1974).

Grant: Engineer allegedly misrepresented that a grant would be forthcoming from the Environmental Protection Agency for construction under the Water Pollution Prevention and Control Act. *Jaillet v Hill & Hill*, 460 F Supp 1075 (WD Pa 1978).

Ground Water: The high water table forced the purchaser of a home to install a sewage ejection system. The engineer had reported that the water table was at seven feet; it was actually at one and one-half feet. *Greco v Mancini*, 476 A2d 522 (RI 1984).

Interference with contract relations: The contractor alleged that he called attention to defects in the contract documents. The architect became enraged at this criticism and began to harass the contractor on the job. The architect delayed inspections, substituted materials, interfered with subcontractors, withheld funds, vilified the contractor to his bonding company, tied up progress payments, and required the contractor to cover up blunders. *Craviolini v Scholer & Fuller Associated Architects*, 89 Ariz 24, 357 P2d 611 (1960).

Ladder: A steamfitter working on the job fell from a permanent ladder installed to provide access to a turbine pit in a paper mill. *Hackley v Waldorf-Hoerner Paper Products Co*, 149 Mont 286, 425 P2d 712 (1967).

Model rejected: The contractor constructed a model of the Smithsonian Institution. The architect allegedly wrongfully rejected the model, causing the government to require the contractor to build a new model. *Piracci Construction Co v Skidmore, Owings & Merrill*, 490 F Supp 314 (SDNY), *affd*, 646 F2d 562 (2d Cir 1980).

Pedestrian ramp: Passenger blown from pedestrian ramp by jet blast. *Hiatt v Brown*, 422 NE2d 736 (Ind Ct App 1981).

Piping: Subcontractor alleged that architect approved its submittal to substitute grooved piping for welded and later stopped the work and ordered the subcontractor to replace the grooved piping with welded. *Detweiler Brothers v John Graham & Co*, 412 F Supp 416 (ED Wash 1976).

Plaster: Plaster fell from a home ceiling. *Avent v Proffitt*, 109 SC 48, 95 SE 134 (1918).

After completion of the Bronson-Mulholland house, the plaster began to peel away from the plaster wallboard. *Shepherd v City of Palatka*, 399 So 2d 1044 (Fla Dist Ct App 1981).

Prison design: Failed to provide stronghold against inmate uprising. *State v Gatham-Matotan Architects*, 98 NM 790, 653 P2d 166 (1982).

Puddles: There were low spots on the concrete roof of a six-story building, causing puddles. *Home Furniture, Inc v Brunzell Construction Co*, 84 Nev 309, 440 P2d 398 (1968).

Radiant heating: An architect employed a heating engineer to design and construct a radiant heating system for a hospital. The original design called for copper tubing, but it was not available (Korean War); steel tubing was used. After about 18 months, the system began to leak. The steel corroded. *Scott v Potomac Insurance Co*, 217 Or 323, 341 P2d 1083 (1959).

Recreation area: Eleven-year-old boy killed when his sled hit a metal post anchored in concrete in a recreational area under construction. *Caine v New Castle County*, 379 A2d 1112 (Del Super Ct 1977).

Refrigerator system: Employee sustained severe personal injuries when liquid ammonia in a refrigerator system escaped from a storage tank located in a separate refrigeration building. *Harmon v Angus R. Jessup Associates*, 619 SW2d 522 (Tenn 1981).

Roof: Windstorm blew the roof off a school building. *Moundsview Independent School District No 621 v Buetow & Associates*, 253 NW2d 836 (Minn 1977).

Rough water: The owners of the Biltmore Hotel in Santa Barbara employed engineers to study the feasibility of installing a small boat pier in front of the hotel. After the pier was completed, it developed that the hotel customers would not use the pier. The wave action in the open roadstead was too severe. *Allied Properties v John A. Blume & Associates*, 25 Cal App 3d 848, 102 Cal Rptr 259 (1972).

S-hook: A porch swing collapsed when an S-hook that held the chain to the swing frame straightened. *Melancon v American Hardware Mutual Insurance Co*, 392 So 2d 159 (La Ct App 1980).

Silica Dust: A worker contracted silicosis from breathing heavy clouds of silica dust raised in mucking for the Washington Metro Subway System. *Caldwell v Bechtel, Inc*, 203 US App DC 407, 631 F2d 989 (1980).

Shop Drawings: An architect approved shop drawings of a stairway from which the subcontractor had omitted angle supports and deviated as to the gauge of the steel. The architect stamped the drawing: "furnished as noted . . . this review is for general conformance with design concept only. Any deviation from plans or specifications not clearly noted by the contractor has not been reviewed. Review shall not constitute a complete check of all detailed dimensions or count or serve to relieve the contractor of contractual responsibility for any error or deviation from contract requirements." *Henningson, Durham & Richardson v Prochnow*, 13 Ariz App 411, 477 P2d 285 (1970), *review denied*, 107 Ariz 222, 485 P2d 547 (1971) (*see* **Multiple Defects in Plans,** above).

Pile specifications required architect approval of mix design provided by subcontractor. The mix was stamped by the architect, "furnished as noted." The piles failed load tests, and the subcontractor was required to make repairs. *Berkel & Co Contractors, Inc v Providence Hospital*, 454 So 2d 496 (Ala 1984).

The engineer approved manufacturers shop drawings for heat exchangers that included noncompatible metals, causing galvanic corrosion. *John Grace & Co v State University Construction Fund*, 99 AD2d 860, 472 NYS2d 757, *affd*, 64 NY2d 709, 475 NE2d 105, 485 NYS2d 734 (1984) (*see* **Mechanical Heating, Ventilating, and Air Conditioning,** above).

Supplier prepared shop drawings for large louvered panels for subcontractor, who passed them onto prime contractor, who passed them onto the engineer for approval. The engineer approved the shop drawings, but they were defective. Judgment for subcontractor against engineer was REVERSED. Subcontractor was responsible to submit proper shop drawings. Subcontractor could not transfer responsibility to the engineer on the ground that the engineer failed to catch mistakes made by subcontractor's supplier. *Lutz Engineering Co v Industrial Louvers, Inc*, 585 A2d 631 (RI 1991).

Skylights: The plans called for "C-45-D" skylights, but "C-54-D" skylights were actually required, and the architects rejected the "C-45-Ds" after delivery to the job site but before installation. *Associated Architects & Engineers v Lubbock Glass & Mirror Co*, 422 SW2d 942 (Tex Civ App 1967).

Sliding roof: The sliding roof designed by architect for a ballroom would not work. It was 120 feet high and was designed to move in cantilevered beam tracks. The architect also failed to discover that the steel fabricator had inadvertently changed six-inch columns to four-inch columns. *Surf Realty Corp v Standing*, 195 Va 431, 78 SE2d 901 (1953).

Soil: Golf course architect specified a two-inch layer of manure to be tilled into soil to a depth of six inches. The grass did not grow. *Loup-Miller v Brauer & Associates Rocky Mountain, Inc*, 40 Colo App 67, 572 P2d 845 (1977).

Stove flue: Stove flues would not draw smoke. *Larrimore v Comanche County*, 32 SW 367 (Tex Civ App 1895).

Suicide: Decedent hung himself from a heating and air conditioning grill in his prison cell. *La Bombarde v Phillips Swager Associates*, 130 Ill App 3d 896, 474 NE2d 942, *appeal denied* (May Term 1985).

Surface Water: Neighbors brought a negligence action against an architect for damage resulting from improper surface drainage in a subdivision. *Ferentchak v Village of Frankfort*, 121 Ill App 3d 599, 459 NE2d 1085 (1984), *affd in part, revd in part*, 105 Ill 2d 474, 475 NE2d 822 (1985).

Surge tank: Workers were injured when hot oil erupted or overflowed from a delayed coking unit and surge tank at an oil refinery. *McClanahan v American Gilsonite Co*, 494 F Supp 1334 (D Colo 1980).

Swimming pool drain: An 11-year-old boy drowned when his arm became lodged in the main drain outlet of a swimming pool. He could not be released until the pump had been turned off. *Henry v Britt*, 220 So 2d 917 (Fla Dist Ct App), *cert denied*, 229 So 2d 867 (Fla 1969).

Tank float: The contractor designed and built an underground concrete fuel storage tank, which floated. *Simpson Bros Corp v Merrimac Chemical Co*, 248 Mass 346, 142 NE 922 (1924).

Taxi-way: A wide-bodied jet slid off a negligently designed taxi-way at Anchorage International Airport, causing substantial damage to the aircraft. *Japan Airlines Co v State*, 628 P2d 934 (Alaska 1981).

Testing: The contractor alleged that the architect misinterpreted test reports and allowed defective concrete to be installed on the job. *United States v Rogers & Rogers*, 161 F Supp 132 (SD Cal 1958).

A testing laboratory negligently tested concrete pipes manufactured for a sewer project and advised the project engineer that the pipes did not meet specification requirements. *Doran-Maine, Inc v American Engineering & Testing, Inc*, 608 F Supp 609 (D Me 1985).

Toxic Waste: Engineer designed a plan for cleanup of subsurface toxic oils and prepared a report in February 1979 showing that all but traces of the toxic substances had been removed. Four years later, it was discovered that heavy contamination existed. Workers employed by the owner to work at the toxic site brought an action against the engineer. Summary judgment for engineer was REVERSED. Material questions of fact existed as to whether engineer should have foreseen the possibility of harm to such workers. *Henshaw v Edward E. Clark Engineers-Scientists*, 490 So 2d 161 (Fla Dist Ct App 1986).

Tree: A large tree standing in the median of Interstate 10 fell and struck a vehicle, killing its driver. The consulting engineers on the project were charged with designing and constructing the highway so that it impeded the flow of groundwater and formed a small lake in the area where the tree stood. *Bullard v State Department of Transportation & Development*, 413 So 2d 606 (La Ct App 1982).

Tunnel: A tunnel under a river was flooded while under construction because of an unanticipated spring tide, more than three feet above any previously recorded spring tide. The water entered the tunnel in three places: through the ventilating building, through a steel tide gate, and through a wooden bulkhead. The tide gate was under the control of the engineer. The wooden bulkhead was designed by a fellow contractor and approved by the engineer. The steel tide gate would not close completely because of air and water lines installed by contractors. The bulkhead contained holes for pipes and wires, and the caulking was inadequate. *C.W. Regan, Inc v Parsons, Brinckerhoff, Quade & Douglas*, 411 F2d 1379 (4th Cir 1969).

Vapor seal: A weaving mill required a constant temperature of 80 and 60 per cent humidity. The vapor seal at the roof leaked, insulation retained moisture and became soggy which caused condensation on the roof, which had to be replaced. *Bloomsburg Mills, Inc v Sordoni Construction Co*, 401 Pa 358, 164 A2d 201 (1960).

Vegetation damaged by surveyor: The school board was considering plaintiff's farm as a school site and employed defendant to survey the site. The statute gave the surveyor the right to enter the land, but not the right to destroy, injure, damage, or move anything without the written permission of the owner. The surveyor and his crew had to cut some vegetation. *Ragland v Clarson*, 259 So 2d 757 (Fla Dist Ct App 1972).

Visits to job site: The architect visited the job each morning before work commenced and each evening after work stopped. The owner contended this did not constitute supervision. *Chiaverini v Vail*, 61 RI 117, 200 A 462 (1938).

Walls: School building walls were damaged by efflorescence (deterioration caused by moisture within the walls). *Board of Education v Del Biano & Associates*, 57 Ill App 3d 302, 372 NE2d 953 (1978).

Water seepage: Water in city hall basement. *City of Mounds View v Walijarvi*, 263 NW2d 420 (Minn 1978).

Water system: The intake capacity of a city water system designed by defendant was insufficient. *City of Eveleth v Ruble*, 302 Minn 249, 225 NW2d 521 (1974).

Appendix C
Contract Forms

Agreement between Owner and Architect for the Provision of Architectural Services

For many years the American Institute of Architects (AIA) has published, revised, and republished construction industry forms. Some of them are widely accepted. The B141 "Standard Form of Agreement between Owner and Architect" is very popular and frequently used.

The use of published forms is to be recommended because they are carefully drawn and reflect, as well as create, standard construction industry practice. The forms, naturally, however, do not meet the requirements of all users. In recent years, published forms have been modified to reduce the exposure of architects to liability for job site injuries and construction defects and delays. Some such protection is afforded by reducing the role of the architect from *job site supervision and inspection* to the *observation of construction*. The published forms also avoid giving the architect the power to stop the work and thereby reduce the architect's responsibility for job site safety.

The primary differences between the following form and AIA Document B141 are: first, the broadly worded arbitration clause which permits arbitration of multiple party disputes, so that the owner, contractor, architect, and other parties may be joined in the same arbitration proceeding (AIA Document B141 does not permit the architect to be joined in an arbitration proceeding with parties other than the owner, except by the architect's consent); second, the form contains an attorneys' fees clause, which AIA Document B141 does not.

It is important that the form of agreement between the owner and the architect be consistent with the provisions of the contract between the owner and the general contractor, so that there will be no misunderstanding between owner, architect, and contractor as to the scope of the services to be provided by the architect.

The author is indebted to Arthur F. O'Leary, F.A.I.A., for consultation and advice as to the following form of agreement between architect and owner.

AGREEMENT BETWEEN OWNER AND ARCHITECT FOR THE PROVISION OF ARCHITECTURAL SERVICES

THIS AGREEMENT is between _____ _____, owner, and _____ _____, architect. The owner has acquired or is in the process of acquiring land described as: _____

_____

Owner wants to develop, on the land, the following project: _____

_____

Owner employs architect to perform, and architect agrees to perform, the following services:

1. *Programming and Schematics.* Owner will provide architect with programming information, to inform architect as to the use of the structures to be designed and the amount of space needed to be devoted to various purposes, and will supply architect with as much detailed information as possible as to the characteristics of the project desired by owner. Owner will take the time and trouble to provide architect with specific and detailed information as to the owner's criteria for the project, both economic and aesthetic. Owner will supply architect with all information and documents in owner's possession as to zoning, governmental restrictions, permits, variances, conditional uses, title, surveys, construction financing, recorded covenants, conditions, restrictions, and all other information that is known to owner and would be relevant to the proper performance of architect's duties under this contract. The architect will then propose, for the consideration of owner, a scheme of design as to the location, structure, appearance, and function of the project. Owner will in turn provide architect with detailed reactions to the architect's scheme, and the architect will supply a gross estimate as to the cost of the project. If owner is operating under financing or budget constraints, owner will inform architect of such constraints, in writing, as early as possible. Owner acknowledges that many desirable architectural features are costly and that design requires compromise. Architect will supply owner with schematic drawings that will display the general characteristics, appearance, and dimensions of the project.

2. *Preliminary Drawings.* After owner and architect have agreed as to the philosophy of design and after owner has approved the schematics, the architect will proceed with preliminary drawings. The purpose of the preliminary

drawings is to totally describe the general characteristics of the project as to the size and location of buildings, size and location of rooms and other spaces within the buildings, the general characteristics of the architectural design, the general characteristics of the structural and roof design, and the allocation of interior and exterior functions and spaces. Architect will not proceed with working drawings until owner has approved, in writing, the preliminary drawings. Based on the preliminary drawings, architect will supply owner with a written preliminary estimate of the cost of constructing the project. The preliminary estimate is subject to a substantial margin of error, because of the preliminary nature of the design, cost fluctuations, and the limited sources of cost data that are available to architect. If owner needs a more accurate estimate, owner will employ an independent estimating service to provide detailed information.

3. *Working Drawings.* Architect will produce working drawings and specifications for the construction of the project. Architect will submit the drawings to all applicable governmental agencies for approval, and will make any corrections that are necessary to obtain all necessary governmental approval. Owner will commit the time that is necessary to carefully and promptly check the drawings and specifications for conformance to owner's aesthetic, functional, and economic requirements. Architect will perform revisions and redesign necessary to meet owner's requirements. If owner requires architect to change drawings that owner has already approved or agreed to, architect's fee will be equitably adjusted.

4. *Contracts and Bidding.* Architect will consult with owner as to the various systems available for the employment of a contractor or contractors for the construction of the project, and will provide appropriate forms of agreement. Owner will provide review of the forms of agreement by a lawyer selected by owner. Architect will advise owner as to the reputations (if known) of contractors and subcontractors who are under consideration. If competitive bidding is to be employed, it will be from a select bid list approved by owner and architect, and bidding and bid opening will be supervised by architect.

5. *Inspection and Observation.* During the progress of the job, the architect will visit the job site at appropriate intervals and observe the progress of the work. The architect's inspection will be as to those features of the project that can be observed without intrusive or destructive techniques. Intrusive, destructive, chemical, mechanical, and laboratory testing will be performed by appropriate agencies employed by owner upon the recommendation of architect. Architect will act as owner's agent, and will deal, as such, with the contractor in order to protect the interests of owner against deviation from the contract documents or acceptable standards of construction. If architect determines that work performed by the contractor does not comply with the requirements of the contract documents, architect will notify owner and contractor of such deviation in writing, and owner will take such measures as it deems desirable to secure compliance. If legal assistance is needed to obtain proper performance from the

prime contractor or subcontractors, owner will employ a lawyer for that purpose.

6. *Progress Payments.* Architect will recommend documents and an appropriate system for processing progress payments to the contractor, and will issue certificates for payment, as appropriate under the contract documents, based on information obtained by architect by inspection of the progress of the work.

7. *Change Orders.* Architect will recommend a procedure for processing change orders, will check pricing of change orders, and will recommend appropriate change orders for signature by owner. Owner will avoid dealing directly with the contractor and will process change orders through architect.

8. *Job Site Discipline and Safety.* Within the constraints of periodic inspection and observation, architect will use its best efforts, as the agent of owner, to require the contractor to maintain a disciplined, orderly, and safe job site. Architect is not, however, responsible for activities that are beyond its control, or that occur when architect is not present on the site, or for activities or conditions that are not reasonably observable by architect when present on the site. If architect determines that the job is being conducted in an unsafe manner, it will inform the contractor and owner in writing, and owner will take such measures as are necessary to require the contractor to proceed safely.

9. *Shop Drawings, Submittals, Selections.* Architect will process shop drawings and other submittals and will make color and material selections, and will promptly respond to reasonable requests for information from contractor.

10. *Completion and Occupancy.* When the project is substantially complete, architect will make a detailed inspection, and will prepare a punch list. Architect will determine when the project is substantially complete, and when it is ready for occupancy.

11. *Repairs and Warranties.* Architect will assist the owner in processing warranty claims, repairs, and corrections, and will use its best efforts, as the agent of the owner, to require contractors, subcontractors, and suppliers to correct improper work and to make good their warranties. If legal action is required to secure corrective or warranty work, owner will employ a lawyer for that purpose.

12. *Payment.* For the architect's services, owner shall make payments as follows:

>(a) *Creation of Design Concept and Philosophy.* For the creation of the design concept and philosophy, including schematic drawings, owner will pay a retainer fee of $ _____ in advance. Upon the completion of the schematic drawings, owner will pay a design fee of $ _____ .
>
>(b) *Working Drawings and Specifications.* For the preparation of working drawings and specifications, owner will pay architect, against monthly billings, according to Schedule A which is attached hereto and incorporated herein.

(c) *Consultants' Fees.* Owner will reimburse architect, monthly as billed, for the fees of consultants employed by architect for mechanical, electrical, and structural services.

(d) *Survey, Testing, Reproduction, and Incidentals.* Owner will reimburse architect, monthly as billed, for surveying, testing, inspection, reproduction, and incidental fees and expenses incurred by architect, including any moneys laid out by architect for permits, inspections, materials, services, or necessary travel or subsistence.

(e) *Bidding, Change Orders, Redesign, and Other Services.* For all other services rendered by architect, including services in connection with bidding, rebidding, change orders, redesign, supervision, inspection, warranty, and corrective work, owner will pay architect in accordance with the rates established by Schedule A attached hereto.

(f) *Extra Services.* If architect provides extra services at the request of owner, architect will bill monthly for such services, which will be compensated by owner on an equitable basis. Examples of extra services are feasibility studies, surveys, appearances before governmental agencies, preparing documents for alternates, providing continuous on site supervision, interior design, tenant improvements, making revisions requested by owner, providing consultant and testing services, serving as an expert witness, or providing services made necessary by default of the contractor.

13. *Errors and Omissions.* Architect will use its best efforts to guard against errors or omissions in the performance of its services under this agreement, and will carefully prepare the drawings, contract documents, and instruments of service. Architect will not be responsible for negligence, errors, omissions, mistakes, or breaches of warranty, and the risk of damage from such causes rests with owner. Owner may elect to make architect responsible for negligence, errors, omissions, mistakes, and breaches of warranty that may be committed by architect in exchange for a surcharge of 15 per cent in addition to all of the charges specified in Paragraph 12. The initials of owner and architect at the end of this paragraph indicate owner's election to pay the surcharge and architect's agreement to extend its liability.

☐ ☐
Initials   Initials

14. *Disputes.* If a dispute should arise between owner and the contractor, architect shall determine the dispute by a written decision. Architect's written decision shall be subject to review by appropriate arbitration or court proceedings. Architect shall give each party an opportunity to produce evidence and argument supporting its side of the dispute.

15. *Attorneys' Fees.* If architect or owner should become involved in litigation or arbitration proceedings as a result of this agreement, or the construction of

the project, the court or arbitration tribunal shall award reasonable attorneys' fees to the party justly entitled thereto.

16. *Arbitration.* If a dispute should arise between architect and owner relating to this agreement or its performance, it shall be subject to arbitration under the rules of the American Arbitration Association. The contractor and any other party with a direct interest in the dispute may become a party to the arbitration with the permission of the arbitrator. By submitting the dispute to arbitration, the parties do not waive the right to seek provisional remedies from the court, such as restraining orders, attachments, injunctions, and receiverships. The parties authorize the arbitration tribunal to grant equitable, as well as monetary, relief. The arbitration tribunal is authorized to award compensation for the time and trouble of arbitration, including arbitration fees, expert witness fees, and attorneys' fees, to the party or parties justly entitled thereto. If a party, after due notice, fails to participate in an arbitration hearing, the tribunal shall decide the dispute in accordance with evidence introduced by the party or parties who do participate.

DATED: _____

OWNER

_____

ARCHITECT

_____

ALTERNATIVE AND OPTIONAL CONTRACT PROVISIONS

The language of the following paragraphs may be used to replace, or may be used in addition to, provisions of the preceding form.

Ownership of Drawings

All of the drawings produced by architect under this agreement are supplied for the owner's use in constructing the project only, and are not to be reused for any purpose. Architect shall remain the owner of the drawings, and owner shall not have any ownership interest therein.

Ownership of Drawings

The entire product of the architect's services under this agreement shall become the property of owner. Upon the completion of the project, architect will deliver the tracings for all drawings to owner, and owner shall have the right to use and reuse the tracings as owner sees fit.

As-Built Drawings

During the progress of the project, architect will obtain from the contractor marked prints showing as-built information to show the true location of electrical, mechanical, structural, and architectural features. The architect will revise the tracings to incorporate the as-built information, and will deliver a print of the as-built drawings to the owner.

Reimbursements

Owner will reimburse architect for all expenditures laid out for the project including transportation, long distance telephone, permit fees, reproduction costs, and other similar items. Such items will be reimbursed monthly, plus a 10 per cent handling charge, as billed. Expenditures in excess of $ _____ will be paid by owner in advance.

Delay of Project

The fees established by this agreement are based on the assumption that the project will be completed in _____ months. In the event that the completion is delayed, then fees paid for those services rendered after _____ are subject to escalation in accordance with the following formula:

> For services rendered during the year beginning _____ , fees will be 110 per cent of those specified in the agreement. Annually, thereafter, the fees specified in the agreement are subject to an additional 10 per cent increase.

Supervision and Progress Reports

Architect will provide continuous job site observation, inspection, and supervision, and will use its best efforts to cause the contractor to comply with all the requirements of the contract documents and good trade practice. Architect will provide monthly progress reports to owner as to the progress of the work. Architect will use its best efforts to require contractor to correct any defective work. If the contractor refuses to correct defective work, architect will report such failure, in writing, to owner and contractor.

Meetings and Reports

Architect will convene weekly job site meetings to be attended by contractor, subcontractors, and other job site personnel. Architect shall maintain minutes of such meetings, which will be forwarded to owner and contractor. Architect will supply a written job cost progress report to owner each month.

Scheduling

Contractor will prepare a project schedule before the commencement of the work. Architect will monitor the progress of the work for conformance to the schedule. The contractor will revise the schedule at least monthly. Copies of the revisions will be distributed to owner and architect. Architect will use its best efforts to require contractor, subcontractors, and suppliers to comply with the schedule, but will not be responsible for their failure to do so.

Errors and Omissions Insurance

Throughout the duration of the project, architect shall carry professional liability insurance in a standard form with a company admitted to do insurance business in the State of _____ . Such insurance shall be on a project insurance basis, and not on the claims made basis. Owner shall have the right, at any time, to inspect the insurance policy. The insurance shall be written with limits of $ _____ .

Change Orders

After consultation with owner, architect is authorized to issue written change orders to contractor, and owner will pay for such changes when due.

Architect Independent Contractor

In performing duties under this agreement, the architect shall act as an independent contractor and not as the agent of owner.

COMMENT: Courts usually hold that an architect is an independent contractor when he or she prepares contract documents and instruments of service but acts as the agent of the owner in inspecting and supervising job site work. Some cases, however, have found that an architect, supervising job site work, acted as an independent contractor. See §8.03. If evidence shows that the owner exerted actual control of the detailed activities of the architect, the independent contractor language in the contract would not serve to protect the owner from liability.

Impartiality as between Owner and Contractor

In judging the performance of the work, and in issuing payment certificates, the architect shall favor neither the owner nor the contractor but shall act impartially so that the interests of both the owner and the contractor are protected.

Architect as Arbitrator

If a dispute should arise between the owner and the contractor, the architect shall act as arbitrator of the dispute to the extent that the architect is called upon to do so under the contract documents. In making its decision, the architect shall favor neither the owner nor the contractor but shall decide the dispute impartially in accordance with the evidence presented by the parties.

Payment for Schematic and Preliminary Drawings

For the schematic and preliminary drawings, the architect shall be paid monthly for the time of its personnel working on the project in accordance with the following schedule:

Principal	_____
Associate	_____
Draftsperson	_____

The maximum charge for the schematic phase is $ _____ . The maximum charge for the preliminary phase (excluding schematics) is $ _____ . Maximum charges exclude reimbursables.

Computation of Charges

For services provided under this agreement, the owner will pay the architect _____ per cent of the hourly rate for the time expended by architect's personnel on the project. The hourly rate consists of salaries or wages plus fringe benefits and contributions including payroll taxes, workers' compensation insurance, liability insurance, pension benefits, and similar contributions and benefits.

Cases

A

Abdul Warith v Arthur G. McKee & Co, 488 F Supp 306 (ED Pa 1980) §6.08, app B

Acorn Structure, Inc v Swant, 846 F2d 923 (4th Cir 1988) §3.08

Adams v Nelsen, 313 NC 442, 329 SE2d 322 (1985) §14.03

AE Inv Corp v Link Builders, Inc, 62 Wis 2d 479, 214 NW2d 764 (1974) §§1.02, 9.03, 9.04, 10.10, app A, app B

Aetna Ins Co v Helmuth, Obata & Kassabaum, Inc, 392 F2d 472 (8th Cir 1968) §4.03, app A, app B

A.F. Blair Co v Mason, 406 So 2d 6 (La Ct App 1981), *cert denied*, 410 So 2d 1132 (La 1982) §§1.05, 15.07, app A

Akins v Parrish of Jefferson, 591 So 2d 800 (La Ct App 1991), *writ denied*, 592 So 2d 1288 (La 1992) §11.07

Alexander v City of Shelbyville, 575 NE2d 1058 (Ind Ct App 1991) §§1.22, 4.03

Alexander v Hammarberg, 103 Cal App 2d 872, 230 P2d 399 (1951) app A, app B

Alexander v State Through Department of Highways, 347 So 2d 1249 (La Ct App), *writ denied*, 350 So 2d 1224 (La 1977) §9.11, app B

Alfred A. Altimont, Inc v Chaterlain, Samperton & Nolan, 374 A2d 284 (DC 1977) §§2.04, 2.05

Alisal Sanitary Dist v Kennedy, 180 Cal App 2d 69, 4 Cal Rptr 379 (1960) §§12.05, 12.06, app A

Allied Contracting Co v Bennett, 110 Ill App 3d 310, 442 NE2d 326 (1982) §14.01

Allied Properties v John A. Blume & Assocs, 25 Cal App 3d 848, 102 Cal Rptr 259 (1972) §§6.03, 6.07, 15.07, app B

American Employers Ins Co v Continental Casualty Co, 85 NM 346, 512 P2d 674 (1973) §§13.02, 13.03, 13.07, 13.15

American Fidelity Fire Ins Co v Pavia-Byrne Engg Corp, 393 So 2d 830 (La), *writ denied*, 397 So 2d 1362 (La Ct App 1981) §§1.18, 8.06, app A, app B

American Home Assurance v Vecco Concrete Constr Co, 629 F2d 961 (4th Cir 1980) §14.02

American Liberty Ins Co v West & Conyers, Architects & Engrs, 491 So 2d 573 (Fla Dist Ct App 1986) §11.08

American Sur Co v San Antonio Loan & Trust Co, 44 Tex Civ App 367, 98 SW 387 (1906) §§1.04, 8.03

Anderson v Brouwer, 99 Cal App 3d 176, 160 Cal Rptr 65 (1979) §11.02

Anderson v Fred Wagner, 402 So 2d 320 (Miss 1981) §11.08, app A, app B

Anderson-Parrish Assocs v City of St Petersburg Beach, 468 So 2d 507 (Fla Dist Ct App 1985) §14.02

Andry & Feitel v Ewing, 15 La App 272, 130 So 570 (1930) §5.13

A.R. Moyer, Inc v Graham, 285 So 2d 397 (Fla 1973) §§1.20, 4.05, 4.07, 9.04, app A

Ashworth v Cunningham/MSE, 252 Ga 569, 315 SE2d 419 (1984) §4.01

Associated Architects & Engrs v Lubbock Glass & Mirror Co, 422 SW2d 942 (Tex Civ App 1967) app B

Associated Constr Co v Camp, Dresser & McKee, Inc, 646 F Supp 1574 (D Conn 1986) §§9.37, 9.38, 9.41

Associated Engrs, Inc v Job, 370 F2d 633 (8th Cir 1966), *cert denied*, 389 US 823 (1967) §§9.17, 9.25, 12.05, app A, app B

Atlantic Mut Ins Co v Continental Natl Am Ins Co, 123 NJ Super 241, 302 A2d 177 (1973) §§13.02, 13.15, app A, app B

Atlantic Natl Bank v Modular Age, Inc, 363 So 2d 1152 (Fla Dist Ct App 1978), *cert denied*, 372 So 2d 466 (Fla 1979) app B

Audlane Lumber & Builders Supply, Inc v D.E. Britt & Assocs, 168 So 2d 333 (Fla 1964), *cert denied*, 173 So 2d 146 (Fla 1965) §6.03

Aurora, City of v Bechtel Corp, 599 F2d 382 (10th Cir 1979) §§11.02, 11.06, 11.09, app B

Auster v Keck, 31 Ill App 61, 333 NE2d 65, *revd*, 63 Ill 2d 485, 349 NE2d 20 (1975) §11.06

Avent v Proffitt, 109 SC 48, 95 SE 134 (1918) **app A, app B**

Avner v Longridge Estates, 272 Cal App 2d 607, 77 Cal Rptr 633 (1969) §6.05

B

Bacco Constr Co v American Colloid Co, 148 Mich App 397, 384 NW2d 427 (1986) §1.20

Bailey v Jones, 243 Mich 159, 219 NW 629 (1928) §9.21

Bair v School Dist No 141 Smith County, 94 Kan 144, 146 P 347 (1915) §§5.08, 5.17

Baker v Walker & Walker, Inc, 133 Cal App 3d 746, 184 Cal Rptr 245 (1982) §§11.07, 11.10, **app B**

Balagna v Shawnee County, 233 Kan 1068, 668 P2d 157 (1983), *revd on other grounds*, 11 Kan App 2d 357, 720 P2d 1144 (1986) §§1.16, 4.04

Balcom Indus v Nelson, 169 Colo 128, 454 P2d 599 (1969) §9.28, **app A, app B**

Bales for Food, Inc v Poole, 246 Or 253, 424 P2d 892 (1967) §11.02, **app A, app B**

Banner v Travelers Ins Co, 31 Mich App 608, 188 NW2d 51 (1971) §4.06, **app A, app B**

Barger v Sheet Metal Indus, 48 Mich App 1, 209 NW2d 877 (1973) **app B**

Barnes v J.W. Bateson Co, 755 SW2d 518 (Tex Ct App 1988) §11.09

Barnes v Rakow, 78 Ill App 3d 404, 396 NE2d 1168 (1979) §§9.11, 9.18, app B

Barnett v City of Yonkers, 731 F Supp 594 (SDNY 1990) §1.03

Barraque v Neff, 202 La 360, 11 So 2d 697 (1942) §4.02, app A, app B

Bartak v Bell-Gallyardt & Wells, Inc, 473 F Supp 737 (DSD 1979), *revd*, 629 F2d 523 (8th Cir 1980) §1.19, app B

Bartley, Inc v Jefferson Parish Sch Bd, 302 So 2d 280 (La 1974) §14.04

Baskerville-Donovan Engrs, Inc v Pensacola Executive House Condo Assn, 581 So 2d 1301 (Fla 1991) §11.02

Bates & Rogers Constr v North Shore Sanitary Dist, 92 Ill App 3d 90, 414 NE2d 1274 (1980), *affd*, 109 Ill 2d 225, 486 NE2d 902 (1985) §§1.04, 1.17, 6.03, 10.10, app A, app B

Batterbury v Vyse, 2 Hurl C 42, 46 Ex (1863) §8.02

Bay Garden Manor Condominium Assn v James D. Marks Assocs, 576 So 2d 744 (Fla Dist Ct App 1991) §10.10

Baylor Univ v Carlander, 316 SW2d 277 (Tex Civ App 1958) §5.03

Bayne v Everham, 197 Mich 181, 163 NW 1002 (1917) §9.28, app A, app B

Bayshore Dev Co v Bonfoey, 75 Fla 445, 78 So 507 (1918) §§1.04, 10.09, app A, app B

Bayuk v Edson, 236 Cal App 2d 309, 46 Cal Rptr 49 (1965) §§8.05, 10.07, app A

Beacham v Greenville County, 218 SC 181, 62 SE2d 92 (1950) §5.03

Beachwalk Villas Condo Assocs v Martin, 305 SC 144, 406 SE2d 372 (1991) §10.10, app B

Bebb v Jordan, 111 Wash 73, 189 P 553 (1920) §3.03, app A, app B

Becker v Black & Veatch Consulting Engrs, 509 F2d 42 (8th Cir 1974) §§4.03, 12.02, 12.08, app B

Beecher v White, 447 NE2d 622 (Ind Ct App 1983) §11.08, app B

Belgum v Mitsuo Kawamoto & Assocs, 236 Neb 127, 459 NW2d 226 (1990) §§1.14, 1.22, 9.13, app B

Bell v Jones, 523 A2d 982 (DC 1986) §§1.05, 9.15, app A, app B

Benenato v McDougall, 166 Cal 405, 137 P 8 (1913) §§5.12, 9.15

Berkel & Co Contractors, Inc v Providence Hosp, 454 So 2d 496 (Ala 1984) §1.20, app A, app B

Bewley Furniture Co v Maryland Casualty Co, 285 So 2d 216 (La 1973) §13.02, app B

Bilich v Barnett, 103 Cal App 2d Supp 921, 229 P2d 492 (1951) §§1.13, 9.02, app A, app B

Biller v Zeigler, 406 Pa Super 1, 593 A2d 436 (1991) §9.42

Birch v Hale, 99 Cal 299, 33 P 1088 (1893) §8.03

Bisset v Joseph A. Schudt & Assocs, 133 Ill App 3d 356, 478 NE2d 911 (1985) §§3.05, 4.07, 9.23, app B

Bismark, City of v Toltz, King, Duvall, Anderson & Assocs, 855 F2d 580 (8th Cir 1988) §9.42

Blackburn v State, 98 NM 34, 644 P2d 548 (1982) §9.36, app B

Blake Constr Co v Alley, 233 Va 31, 353 SE2d 724 (1987) §§1.20, 7.03, 10.10

Blaske v Smith & Entzeroth, Inc, 821 SW2d 822 (Mo 1991) §11.08

Blecick v School Dist No 18, 2 Ariz App 115, 406 P2d 750 (1965) §§9.09, 9.11, app A, app B

Block v Happ, 144 Ga 145, 86 SE 316 (1915) app A

Bloomsburg Mills, Inc v Sordoni Constr Co, 401 Pa 358, 164 A2d 201 (1960) app A, app B

Board of Educ v Architects Taos, 103 NM 462, 709 P2d 184 (1985) §14.03

Board of Educ v Celotex Corp, 58 NY2d 684, 444 NE2d 1006, 458 NYS2d 542 (1982) §11.10

Board of Educ v Del Biano & Assocs, 57 Ill App 3d 302, 372 NE2d 953 (1978) §4.01, app B

Board of Educ v Fry, Inc, 22 Ohio App 3d 94, 489 NE2d 294 (1984) §12.07

Board of Educ v Joseph J. Duffy Co, 97 Ill App 2d 158, 240 NE2d 5 (1968) §§11.06, 12.08, 12.09

Board of Educ v Mars Assocs, 133 AD2d 800, 520 NYS2d 181 (1987) §12.08, app B

Board of Educ v Perkins & Will Partnership, 119 Ill App 2d 196, 255 NE2d 496 (1970) §§11.03, 11.06

Board of Educ v Sargent, Webster, Crenshaw & Folley, 125 AD2d 27, 511 NYS2d 961, *affd*, 71 NY2d 21, 517 NE2d 1360, 523 NYS2d 475 (1987) §12.08

Board of Educ of Hudson City Sch Dist v Thompson Constr Corp, 111 AD2d 497, 488 NYS2d 880 (1985) §11.11

Board of Educ Sch Dist No 16 v Standhardt, 80 NM 543, 458 P2d 795 (1969) app A, app B

Board of Mgrs of Yardarm Beach Condo v Vector Yardarm Corp, 109 AD2d 684, 487 NYS2d 17 (1985) §11.04

Board of Pub Works v L. Cosby Bernard & Co, 435 NE2d 575 (Ind Ct App 1982) §9.40

Board of Regents v Wilscam Mullins Birge, Inc, 230 Neb 675, 433 NW2d 478 (1988) §11.02

Board of Trustees v Lee Elec Co, 198 So 2d 231 (Miss 1967) §15.07, app B

Bodin v Gill, 216 Ga 467, 117 SE2d 325 (1960) §§1.20, 9.06, app A, app B

Bonadiman-McCain, Inc v Snow, 183 Cal App 2d 58, 6 Cal Rptr 52 (1960) §§1.08, 10.07, app B

Borman's, Inc v Lake State Dev Co, 60 Mich App 175, 230 NW2d 363 (1975) §6.03

Boswell v Laird, 8 Cal 469 (1857) §§8.01, 8.03, 9.06, app A, app B

Bott v Moser, 175 Va 11, 7 SE2d 217 (1940) §1.08, app B

Bouser v Lincoln Park, 83 Mich App 167, 268 NW2d 332 (1978), *affd*, 410 Mich 1, 299 NW2d 336 (1980) §11.08

Breaux v St Paul Fire & Marine Ins Co, 326 So 2d 891 (La Ct App 1976) §13.09

Breiner v C&P Home Builders, Inc, 536 F2d 27 (3d Cir 1976) §1.18, app B

Brew v State Educ Dept, 73 AD2d 743, 423 NYS2d 271 (1979) §3.02, app B

Broome v Truluck, 270 SC 277, 241 SE2d 739 (1978) §11.08, app B

Broome County v Vincent J. Smith, Inc, 78 Misc 2d 889, 358 NYS2d 998 (Sup Ct 1974) §11.11, app A, app B

Broussard v Continental Casualty Co, 421 So 2d 341 (La Ct App), *writ denied*, 423 So 2d 1165 (1982) §10.07, app B

Brown v Cox, 459 SW2d 471 (Tex Civ App 1970) §§5.02, 5.12

Brown v Gamble Constr Co, 537 SW2d 685 (Mo Ct App 1976) §§4.04, 9.30, app B

Brown v McBro Planning & Dev Co, 660 F Supp 1333 (DVI 1987) §9.42, app B

Browning v Maurice B. Levien & Co, 44 NC App 701, 262 SE2d 355, *review denied*, 300 NC 371, 267 SE2d 673 (1980) §§1.21, 9.04, app A, app B

Broyles v Brown Engg Co, 275 Ala 35, 151 So 2d 767 (1963) §6.03, app A, app B

Bruemmer v Clark Equip Co, 341 F2d 23 (7th Cir 1965) §§8.01, 8.03, app A, app B

Bryant Elec Co v City of Fredericksburg, 762 F2d 1192 (4th Cir 1985) §§9.04, 10.10

Bueche v Eickenroht, 220 SW2d 911 (Tex Civ App 1949) §5.12

Bullard v State Dept of Transport & Dev, 413 So 2d 606 (La Ct App 1982) §1.03, app B

Bump v McGrannahan, 61 Ind App 136, 111 NE 640 (1916) §9.10, app B

Burger v Roelsch, 77 Hun 44, 28 NYS 460 (1894) §9.40, app B

Burke v Ireland, 166 NY 305, 59 NE 914 (1910) §§1.22, 8.03, app A, app B

Burmaster v Gravity Drainage Dist No 2, 366 So 2d 1381 (La 1978) §11.08, app B

Burns v DeWitt & Assocs, 826 SW2d 884 (Mo Ct App 1992) §12.08

Burran v Dambold, 422 F2d 133 (10th Cir 1970) §3.03, app A, app B

Burrows v Bidigare, Bublys, Inc, 158 Mich App 175, 404 NW2d 650 (1987) §1.14

Bushnell v Sillitoe, 550 P2d 1284 (Utah 1976) §12.05, app A

C

Caine v New Castle County, 379 A2d 1112 (Del Super Ct 1977) §9.23, app B

Caldwell v Bechtel, Inc, 203 US App DC 407, 631 F2d 989 (1980) §§1.16, 3.06, 4.07, app A, app B

Caldwell v Cleveland-Cliffs Co, 111 Mich App 721, 315 NW2d 186 (1981), *appeal denied*, 417 Mich 914, 330 NW2d 854 (1983) §§8.02, 9.32, app A, app B

Caldwell v United Presbyterian Church, 20 Ohio Op 2d 364, 180 NE2d 638 (1961) §§5.08, 5.09, 5.17

Caledonia Community Hosp v Liebenberg, Smiley, Glotter & Assocs, 308 Minn 255, 248 NW2d 279 (1976) §11.10, app B

Campbell v Southern Roof Deck Applicators, Inc, 406 So 2d 910 (Ala 1981) §12.02, app B

Canton Lutheran Church v Sovik, Mathre, Sathrum & Quanbeck, 507 F Supp 873 (DSD 1981) §11.10, app B

Cantrell v Dendahl, 83 NM 583, 494 P2d 1400 (1972) §15.07

Capital Hotel Co v Rittenberry, 41 SW2d 697 (Tex Civ App 1931), *dismissed w.o.j.* (Mar 23, 1932) §§5.15, 5.17

Carden v Board of Registration for Professional Engrs, 174 Cal App 3d 736, 220 Cal Rptr 416 (1985) §3.02

Carlotta v T.R. Stark & Assocs, 57 Md App 467, 470 A2d 838 (1984) §§1.18, 1.26, app A, app B

Carmania Corp v Hambrecht Terrell Intl, 705 F Supp 936 (SDNY 1989) §10.10

Carroll-Boone Water Dist v M&P Equip Co, 280 Ark 560, 661 SW2d 345 (1983) §1.20, app A, app B

Carter v Deitz, 478 So 2d 996 (La Ct App 1985) §§12.08, 13.09

CCC Builders, Inc v City Council, 237 Ga 589, 229 SE2d 349 (1976) §8.02

Century Ready-Mix Co v Campbell School Dist, 816 P2d 795 (Wyo 1991) §1.14

Chambers v Goldthorpe, 1 KB 624 (1901) §9.09

Chaney Bldg Co v City of Tucson, 148 Ariz 571, 716 P2d 28 (1986) §9.41

Chapel v Clark, 117 Mich 638, 76 NW 62 (1898) app A, app B

Chaplis v Monterey County, 97 Cal App 3d 249, 158 Cal Rptr 395 (1979) §§1.19, 3.03, app B

Chapple v Big Bear Supermarket No 3, 108 Cal App 3d 867, 167 Cal Rptr 103 (1980) §8.03

Charlebois v J.M. Weller Assocs, 72 NY2d 587, 531 NE2d 1288, 535 NYS2d 356 (1988) §3.02

Charles Carter & Co v McGee, 213 So 2d 89 (La Ct App 1968) app A, app B

Charles T. Main, Inc v Fireman's Fund Ins Co, 406 Mass 862, 551 NE2d 28 (1990) §13.08

Chart v Dvorak, 57 Wis 2d 92, 203 NW2d 673 (1973) §§3.03, 4.06, 9.36, app A, app B

Chastain v Atlanta Gas Light Co, 122 Ga App 90, 176 SE2d 487 (1970) §1.20, app A, app B

Chiaverini v Vail, 61 RI 117, 200 A 462 (1938) §1.08, app A, app B

Chisholm v Georgia, 2 US (2 Dall) 419 (1793) §9.34

C.H. Leavell & Co v Glantz Contracting Corp, 322 F Supp 779 (ED La 1971) §9.05, app A

Ciancio v Serafini, 40 Colo App 168, 574 P2d 876 (1977) §11.06

Cincinnati Gas & Elec Co v General Elec Co, 656 F Supp 49 (SD Ohio 1986) §§6.08, 10.10

Cincinnati Riverfront Coliseum, Inc v McNulty Co, 28 Ohio St 3d 333, 504 NE2d 415 (1986) §9.28

Cipriani v Sun Pipe Line Co, 393 Pa Super 471, 574 A2d 706 (1990), *appeal denied*, 527 Pa 668, 593 A2d 843 (1991) §1.19

Clark v City of Seward, 659 P2d 1227 (Alaska 1983) §1.03, app B

Clark v Madeira, 252 Ark 157, 477 SW2d 817 (1972) §5.16

Cliffs Forest Prods Co v Al Disdero Lumber Co, 144 Mich App 215, 375 NW2d 397 (1985), *appeal denied*, 424 Mich 896, 384 NW2d 8 (1986) §11.08

Clinton v Boehm, 139 AD 73, 124 NYS 789 (1910) §9.25

Clyde E. Williams & Assocs v Boatman, 176 Ind App 430, 375 NE2d 1138 (1978) §§1.22, 4.04, 9.23, app B

Coac, Inc v Kennedy Engrs, 67 Cal App 3d 916, 136 Cal Rptr 890 (1977) §4.05

Cobb v Thomas, 565 SW2d 281 (Tex Civ App 1978), *error refused* (Sept 13, 1978) §§5.09, 5.12

Coffey v Dormitory Auth, 26 AD2d 1, 270 NYS2d 255 (1966) §§1.23, 9.07, 12.07, app A, app B

Colbert v BF Carvin Constr Co, 600 So 2d 719 (La Ct App 1992), *rehg denied* (May 21, 1992) §2.05

Colbert v Holland Furnace Co, 333 Ill 78, 164 NE 162 (1928) §§1.18, 9.02, app B

Collins Co v City of Decatur, 533 So 2d 1127 (Ala 1988) §8.03

Commercial Indus Constr, Inc v Anderson, 683 P2d 378 (Colo Ct App 1984) §§2.05, 8.04, app B

Commonwealth Dept of Transport v Upper Providence Township Mun Auth, 55 Pa Commw 398, 423 A2d 769 (1980) §8.06

Commonwealth Land Title Ins Co v Conklin & Assocs, 152 NJ Super 1, 377 A2d 740 (1977), affd, 167 NJ Super 392, 400 AD2d 1208 (1979) §11.03

Comptroller *ex rel* Va Military Inst v King, 217 Va 751, 232 SE2d 895 (1977) §§4.01, 11.04

Comstock Ins Co v Thomas A. Hanson & Assocs, 77 Md App 431, 550 A2d 731 (1988) §§5.07, 13.02

Conejo Valley Unified Sch Dist v Wm Bluerock & Partners, Inc, 111 Cal App 3d 983, 169 Cal Rptr 102 (1980) §14.06

Conforti & Eisele, Inc v John C. Morris Assocs, 175 NJ Super 341, 418 A2d 1290 (1980), affd, 199 NJ Super 498, 489 A2d 1233 (1985) app A

Conklin v Cohen, 287 So 2d 56 (Fla 1973) §§1.17, 9.04, 9.32, app B

Conti v Pettibone Cos, 111 Misc 2d 772, 445 NYS2d 943 (Sup Ct 1981) §§3.03, 3.04, 9.11, 9.30, app B

Continental Casualty Co v Enco Assocs, 66 Mich App 46, 238 NW2d 198 (1975) §13.09

Cook v Oklahoma Bd of Pub Affairs, 736 P2d 140 (Okla 1987) §8.04

Coombs v Beede, 89 Me 187, 36 A 104 (1896) §§1.03, 5.10

Coon v Blaney, 311 So 2d 622 (La Ct App 1975) §11.07

Coons v Washington Mirror Works, Inc, 477 F2d 864 (2d Cir 1973) §§9.17, 12.05, 12.07, app A, app B

Cooper v Cordova Sand & Gravel Co, 485 SW2d 261 (Tenn Ct App 1971) §§9.04, 12.08, app A, app B

Cooper v Jevne, 56 Cal App 3d 860, 128 Cal Rptr 724 (1976) §§1.21, 7.03, 9.04, 9.36, 10.10, app A

Corbetta Constr v Lake City Public Bldg Commn, 64 Ill App 3d 313, 381 NE2d 758 (1978) §9.28, app B

Corey v Eastman, 166 Mass 279, 44 NE 217 (1896) §§1.15, 2.01, 4.01, 9.10, app A, app B

Cornell, Howland, Hays & Merryfield, Inc v Continental Casualty Co, 465 F2d 22 (9th Cir 1972) §13.14

Coulson & CAE, Inc v Lake LBJ Municipal Utility District, 734 SW2d 649 (Tex 1987) §1.15

Council of Co-Owners Atlantis Condo, Inc v Whiting-Turner Contracting Co, 308 Md 18, 517 A2d 336 (1986) §§9.04, 10.10

Covil v Robert & Co, 112 Ga App 163, 144 SE2d 450 (1965) §§1.20, 9.28, app A, app B

Cowles v City of Minneapolis, 128 Minn 452, 151 NW 184 (1915) §§1.08, 1.09, 9.12, 9.27, app A, app B

Cox v City of Freeman, 321 F2d 887 (8th Cir 1963) §§8.04, 9.36, 9.38, app B

Craig v Everett M. Brooks Co, 351 Mass 497, 222 NE2d 752 (1967) §§1.13, 9.03, 10.10, app A, app B

Craviolini v Scholer & Fuller Associated Architects, 89 Ariz 24,

357 P2d 611 (1960) §§2.05, 9.09, app A, app B
Crawford v Gray & Assocs, 493 So 2d 734 (La Ct App), *writ denied*, 497 So 2d 1013 (La 1986) §1.14, app B
Crawford v Shepherd, 86 Wis 2d 362, 272 NW2d 401 (1978) §11.05, app B
Crockett v Crothers, 264 Md 222, 285 A2d 612 (1972) §§12.03, 12.08, app B
Cubito v Kreisberg, 69 AD2d 738, 419 NYS2d 578 (1979), *affd*, 51 NY2d 900, 415 NE2d 979, 434 NYS2d 991 (1980) app A
Cubito v Kreisberg, 94 Misc 2d 56, 404 NYS2d 69 (1978), *affd*, 51 NY2d 900, 415 NE2d 979, 434 NYS2d 991 (1980) §§1.23, 11.05, app B
Cuhaci & Peterson Architects, Inc v Huber Constr Co, 516 So 2d 1096 (Fla Dist Ct App 1987), *review denied*, 525 So 2d 878 (Fla 1988) §12.04
Cutlip v Lucky Stores, Inc, 22 Md App 673, 325 A2d 432 (1974) §§1.22, 9.11, app A, app B
C.W. Regan, Inc v Parsons, Brinckerhoff, Quade & Douglas, 411 F2d 1379 (4th Cir 1969) §§1.20, 4.05, 6.03, 9.03, 9.25, 9.30, app A, app B

D

Daniel, Mann, Johnson & Mendenhall v Hilton Hotels, 98 Nev 113, 642 P2d 1086 (1982) §§1.03, 1.19, 10.09
D'Annunzio Bras v New Jersey Transit Corp, 245 NJ Super 527, 586 A2d 301 (1991) §1.19

Danny's Constr Co v Havens Steel Co, 437 F Supp 91 (D Neb 1977) §12.07, app B
Daub v Board of Regents, 33 AD2d 964, 306 NYS2d 869 (1970) app B
Davidson & Jones, Inc v New Hanover County, 41 NC App 661, 255 SE2d 580, *review denied*, 298 NC 295, 259 SE2d 911 (1979) §§1.16, 1.20, 10.10, app A
Davis v Lenox Sch, 151 AD2d 230, 541 NYS2d 814 (1989) §1.22
Day v National United States Radiator Corp, 241 La 288, 128 So 2d 660 (1961) §§1.02, 9.25, app A, app B
D.C. Consulting Engrs, Inc v Batavia Park Dist, 143 Ill App 3d 60, 492 NE2d 1000 (1986) §9.40
Dehnert v Arrow Sprinklers, Inc, 705 P2d 846 (Wyo 1985) §§2.05, 9.33
Del E. Webb Constr v Richardson Hosp Auth, 823 F2d 145 (5th Cir 1987) §14.05
Della Corte v Incorporated Village of Williston Park, 60 AD2d 639, 400 NYS2d 357 (1977) §9.30
Del Mar Beach Club Owners Assn v Imperial Contracting Co, 123 Cal App 3d 898, 176 Cal Rptr 886 (1981) §6.04
Delmar Vineyard v Timmons, 486 SW2d 914 (Tenn Ct App 1972) §1.01
Delta Constr Co v City of Jackson, 198 So 2d 592 (Miss 1967) §§1.20, 4.01, 8.02, 9.02, app B
Demetriades v Kaufmann, 680 F Supp 658 (SDNY 1988) §3.08
Designed Ventures, Inc v Housing Auth, 132 BR 677 (Bankr DRI 1991) §1.24
Detweiler Bros v John Graham & Co, 412 F Supp 416 (ED Wash

1976) §§1.18, 1.20, 4.05, 9.03, app A, app B
Deville Furniture Co v Jesco, Inc, 697 F2d 609 (5th Cir 1983) §11.09, app B
Diamond Springs Lime Co v Amer River Constrs, 16 Cal App 3d 581, 94 Cal Rptr 200 (1971) app A
Dickerson Constr Co v Pcrocess Engg Co, 341 So 2d 646 (Miss 1977) §§9.22, 10.10, app A, app B
Diomar v Landmark Assocs, 81 Ill App 3d 1135, 401 NE2d 1287 (1980) §3.05
DiPerna v Roman Catholic Diocese, 30 AD2d 249, 292 NYS2d 177 (1968) §9.07, app B
District Moving & Storage Co v Gardiner & Gardiner, Inc, 63 Md App 96, 492 A2d 319, *affd*, 306 Md 286, 508 A2d 487 (1986) §§4.05, 14.02
Dobler v Malloy, 214 NW2d 510 (ND 1973) app B
Donnell & Froom v Baldwin County Bd of Educ, 599 So 2d 1158 (Ala 1992) §1.19
Donnelly Constr Co v Oberg, Hunt & Gilleland, 139 Ariz 184, 677 P2d 1292 (1984) §§1.13, 6.03, 7.03, 9.03, 9.09
Doran-Maine, Inc v American Engg & Testing, Inc, 608 F Supp 609 (D Me 1985) §10.10, app A, app B
Doundoulakis v Town of Hempstead, 51 AD2d 302, 381 NYS2d 287 (1976), *revd*, 42 NY2d 440, 368 NE2d 24, 398 NYS2d 401 (1977) app B
Dow v Holly Mfg Co, 49 Cal 2d 720, 321 P2d 736 (1958) §9.02, app A, app B
Doyle v Linn, 37 Colo App 214, 547 P2d 257 (1975) §11.05, app A, app B

Dresco Mechanical Contractors, Inc v Todd-CEA, Inc, 531 F2d 1292 (5th Cir 1976) §1.19, app B
Drzewinski v Atlantic Scaffold & Ladder Co, 70 NY2d 744, 515 NE2d 902, 521 NYS2d 216 (1987) §12.02
Duggan v Arnold N. May Builders, Inc, 33 Wis 2d 49, 146 NW2d 410 (1966) §9.22
Duncan v Missouri Bd of Architects, 744 SW2d 524 (Mo Ct App 1988) §3.02
Duncan v Pennington City Hous Auth, 283 NW2d 546 (SD 1979) §§1.22, 9.37, app B
Dunne v Robinson, 53 Misc 545, 103 NYS 878 (1907) §1.04, app B
Durand Assocs v Guardian Inv Co, 186 Neb 349, 183 NW2d 246 (1971) §§5.01, 5.02, 5.03, 5.05
Durham, City of v Reidsville Engg Co, 255 NC 98, 120 SE2d 564 (1961) §§1.24, 4.03, 9.09, 9.30, app A
Durring v Reynolds Smith & Hills, 471 So 2d 603 (Fla Dist Ct App 1985) §11.07
Dysart-Cook Mule Co v Reed & Heckenlively, 114 Mo App 296, 89 SW 591 (1905) §1.13, app A, app B
Dyson & Co v Flood Engrs, Architects, Planners, Inc, 523 So 2d 756 (Fla Dist Ct App 1988) §13.04

E

East Moline, City of v Bracke Hayes & Miller, 133 Ill App 3d 136, 478 NE2d 637 (1985) §10.10
E.A. Williams, Inc v Russo Dev Corp, 82 NJ 160, 411 A2d 697 (1980) §11.10, app B

Eberhard v Mehlman, 60 A2d 540 (DC 1948) §5.06

E.C. Ernst v Manhattan Constr Co, 551 F2d 1026 (5th Cir 1977), *cert denied*, 434 US 106 (1978) §1.20, app A, app B

E.C. Goldman, Inc v A/R/C Assocs, 543 So 2d 1268 (Fla Dist Ct App), *review denied*, 551 So 2d 461 (Fla 1989) §§1.18, 4.05

Edward Barron Estate Co v Woodruff Co, 163 Cal 561, 126 P 351 (1912) §§5.04, 5.15, 10.07

Edward B. Fitzpatrick Jr Constr Corp v County of Suffolk, 138 AD2d 446, 525 NYS2d 863 (1988) §§2.04, 4.05, 9.02, 9.05

Edwards v Haeger, 180 Ill 99, 54 NE 176 (1899) §9.42

Edwards v Hall, 293 Pa 97, 141 A 638 (1928) §9.21, app A, app B

Edwin J. Dobson, Jr, Inc v Rutgers State Univ, 157 NJ Super 357, 384 A2d 1121 (1978), *affd*, 90 NJ 253, 447 A2d 906 (1982) §8.03

Eichler Homes, Inc v Anderson, 9 Cal App 3d 224, 87 Cal Rptr 893 (1970) §6.05

EIS, Inc v Connecticut Bd of Registration for Professional Engrs & Land Surveyors, 200 Conn 145, 509 A2d 1056 (1986) §3.02

Electric Serv Co v Lakehead Elec Co, 291 Minn 22, 189 NW2d 489 (1971) app B

Elkhart, City of v Middleton, 346 NE2d 274 (Ind Ct App 1976) §12.07

Elliott v Nordlof, 83 Ill App 279, 227 NE2d 547 (1967) §9.06, app A, app B

Emberton v State Farm Mut Auto Ins Co, 44 Ill App 3d 839, 358 NE2d 1254 (1976), *revd*, 71 Ill 2d 111, 373 NE2d 1348 (1978) §§3.05, 4.07, app A

Engle Acoustic & Tile, Inc v Grenfell, 223 So 2d 613 (Miss 1969) §9.05, app A, app B

Episcopal Hous Corp v Federal Ins Co, 273 SC 181, 255 SE2d 451 (1979) §14.05

Erfurt v State, 141 Cal App 3d 837, 190 Cal Rptr 569 (1983) §9.36, app B

Erhart v Hummunds, 232 Ark 133, 334 SW2d 869 (1960) §§3.03, 4.03, 9.26, app A

Ernest W. Hahn, Inc v Superior Court (Los Angeles County), 108 Cal App 3d 567, 166 Cal Rptr 644 (1980) §11.10

Erskine v Johnson, 23 Neb 261, 36 NW 510 (1888) §8.02, app B

Erwine v Gamble, Pownal & Gilroy Architects & Engrs, 343 So 2d 859 (Fla Dist Ct App 1976) app A, app B

Essex v Ryan, 446 NE2d 368 (Ind Ct App 1983) §9.05, app B

Eveleth, City of v Ruble, 302 Minn 249, 225 NW2d 521 (1974) §15.07, app B

F

Fabe v W.V.P. Corp, 760 SW2d 490 (Mo Ct App 1988) app B

Facilities Dev Co v Miletta, 180 AD2d 97, 584 NYS2d 491 (1992) §§12.03, 12.05

Fairbanks North Star Borough v Roen Design Assocs, 727 P2d 758 (Alaska 1986), *opinion vacated in part on rehg by*, 823 P2d 632 (Alaska 1991) §12.02

Fairfax County Redevelopment & Hous Auth v Hurst & Assocs Consulting Engrs, Inc, 231 Va 164, 343 SE2d 294 (1986) §10.01

Farash Constr Corp v Stanndco Developers, Inc, 139 AD2d 899, 527 NYS2d 940 (1988) §11.03

Farmers Ins Co v Smith, 219 Kan 680, 549 P2d 1026 (1976) §15.07

Farm Fuel Prods Corp v Grain Processing Corp, 429 NW2d 153 (Iowa 1988) §4.03

Farmington Plumbing & Heating Co v Fisher Sand & Aggregate, Inc, 281 NW2d 838 (Minn 1979) §12.03

Farrell Constr Co v Jefferson Parish, 693 F Supp 490 (ED La 1988) §§1.20, 4.03, 9.03, 9.30

Federal Mogul Corp v Universal Constr Co, 376 So 2d 716 (Ala Civ App), *writ denied*, 376 So 2d 726 (Ala 1979) §6.03

Feltham v Sharp, 99 Ga 260, 25 SE 619 (1896) §§5.02, 5.17

Fennell v John J. Nesbitt, Inc, 154 Mich App 644, 398 NW2d 481 (1986) §11.09

Ferentchak v Village of Frankfort, 105 Ill 2d 474, 475 NE2d 822 (1985) §§1.14, 4.03, app B

Ferentchak v Village of Frankfort, 121 Ill App 3d 599, 459 NE2d 1085 (1984), *affd in part, revd in part*, 105 Ill 2d 474, 475 NE2d 822 (1985) §§1.18, 9.02, app B

Fidelity & Casualty Co v J.A. Jones Constr Co, 325 F2d 605 (8th Cir 1963) §§3.01, 9.32, 12.02, 12.08, app B

Financial Bldg Consultant, Inc v Guillebau, Britt & Waldrop, 163 Ga App 607, 295 SE2d 355 (1982) §§8.05, 13.06

Fireman's Fund Am Ins Co v Phillips, Carter Reister & Assocs, 89 NM 7, 546 P2d 72, *cert denied*, 89 NM 5, 546 P2d 70 (1976) §13.16, app A

First Ins Co v Continental Casualty Co, 466 F2d 807 (9th Cir 1972) §§13.03, 13.05, 13.06, app B

530 East 89 Corp v Unger, 54 AD2d 848, 388 NYS2d 284 (1976), *affd*, 43 NY2d 776, 373 NE2d 276, 402 NYS2d 382 (1977) §§1.04, 1.19, 9.12, 9.13, 9.30, app B

Fletcher v Ryland, 1 LR-Ex 265 (1866) §6.04,

Floor Craft Floor Covering, Inc v Parma Community Gen Hosp Assn, 54 Ohio St 3d 1, 560 NE2d 206 (1990) §§1.18, 10.10

Florence v Wm Moors Concrete Prods, Inc, 35 Mich App 613, 193 NW2d 72 (1971) app A, app B

Florida Power & Light Co v Mid-Valley, Inc, 763 F2d 1316 (11th Cir 1985) §12.03, app B

Follansbee Bros v Garrett-Cromwell Engg Co, 48 Pa Super 183 (1911) §4.01

Ford v Robertson, 739 SW2d 3 (Tenn Ct App 1987) §1.23

Forte v Tripp & Skrip, 339 So 2d 698 (Fla Dist Ct App 1976) §2.01, app B

Forte Bros v National Amusement, Inc, 525 A2d 1301 (RI 1987) §§9.04, 10.10

Fox v Jenny Engg Corp, 122 AD2d 532, 505 NYS2d 270 (1986), *affd*, 70 NY2d 761, 514 NE2d 1374, 520 NYS2d 750 (1987) §§4.07, 9.25

Fox v Ireland, 46 AD 541, 61 NYS 1061 (1900) app B

Fox v Stanley J. How & Assocs, 309 NW2d 520 (Iowa Ct App 1981) app A, app B

Foxfire Village, Inc v Black & Veatch, Inc, 304 SC 366, 404 SE2d 912 (Ct App 1991), *cert denied* (Aug 15, 1991) §§1.21, 3.03, app B

Framlau Corp v Kling, 233 Pa Super 175, 334 A2d 780 (1975) §11.12

Francisco v Manson, Jackson & Kane, Inc, 145 Mich App 255, 377 NW2d 313 (1985), *appeal denied* (Jan 28, 1986) §§1.10, 3.06, 9.42

Frank M. Dorsey & Sons v Frishman, 291 F Supp 794 (DDC 1968) §9.28, app A

Freeport Memorial Hosp v Lankton, Ziegele, Terry & Assocs, 170 Ill App 3d 531, 525 NE2d 194 (1988) §§11.06, 11.13

Freezer Storage, Inc v Armstrong Cork Co, 476 Pa 270, 382 A2d 715 (1978) §11.08

French v Jinright & Ryan PC Architects, 735 F2d 433 (11th Cir 1984) §§1.20, 9.41, 14.05

Friedman, Alschuler & Sincere v Arlington Structural Steel Co, 140 Ill App 3d 556, 489 NE2d 308 (1985), *appeal denied* (June 3, 1986) §§12.02, 12.08

Friendship Heights Assocs v Koubek, 785 F2d 1154 (4th Cir 1986) §1.19

Friendship Heights Assocs v Vlastimil Koubek, AIA, 573 F Supp 100 (D Md 1983), *revd*, 785 F2d 1154 (4th Cir 1986) §§1.04, 4.01

Frischertz Elec Co v Housing Auth, 534 So 2d 1310, 1316 (La Ct App 1988), *writ denied*, 536 So 2d 1236 (La 1989) §1.04

Fruzyna v Walter C. Carlson & Assocs, 78 Ill App 3d 1050, 398 NE2d 60 (1979) §§3.05, 4.03, 9.05, 9.23, app B

Fuchs v Parsons Constr Co, 172 Neb 719, 111 NW2d 727 (1961) §§8.01, 8.02

Funk v Wollin Silo & Equip, Inc, 148 Wis 2d 59, 435 NW2d 244 (1989) §11.08

G

Gaastra v Holmes, 36 NM 175, 10 P2d 589 (1932) §§6.03, 9.28

Gagne v Bertran, 43 Cal 2d 481, 275 P2d 15 (1954) §§1.09, 1.13, 6.03, 6.04, 6.07, 9.12, 10.07, app A, app B

Garden City Floral Co v Hunt, 126 Mont 537, 255 P2d 352 (1953) §9.25, app A

Garden Grove Community Church v Pittsburgh-Des Moines Steel Co, 140 Cal App 3d 251, 191 Cal Rptr 15 (1983) §14.06

Geare v Sturgis, 56 App DC 364, 14 F2d 256 (1926), *overruled*, Hannah v Fletcher, 97 US App DC 310, 231 F2d 469 (1956) §§1.18, 9.02, app A, app B

Geer v Bennett, 237 So 2d 311 (Fla Dist Ct App 1970) §§3.06, 4.03, app A, app B

General State Auth v Kline, 29 Pa Commw 232, 370 A2d 402 (1977) §14.02

General Trading Corp v Burnup & Sims, Inc, 523 F2d 98 (3d Cir 1975) §10.03, app A, app B

Georgetowne Ltd Partnership v Geotechnical Services, Inc, 230 Neb 22, 430 NW2d 34 (1988) §11.06

Getz v Del E. Webb Corp, 38 Ill App 3d 880, 349 NE2d 682 (1976) §3.05, app B

Getzschman v Miller Chem, Inc, 232 Neb 885, 443 NW2d 260 (1989) §§5.01, 5.03

Gherardi v Board of Educ, 53 NJ Super 349, 147 A2d 535 (1958) §§2.04, 9.02, 9.30, app A, app B

Giffels & Vallet, Inc v Edward C. Levy Co, 337 Mich 177, 58 NW2d 899 (1953) app A, app B

Gilbert v Billman Constr, Inc, 371 NW2d 542 (Minn 1985) §9.36, app B

Gilbert Engg Co v City of Asheville, 74 NC App 350, 328 SE2d 849, *review denied*, 314 NC 329, 333 SE2d 485 (1985) §1.14

Gilchrist v City of Troy, 113 AD2d 271, 495 NYS2d 781 (1985), *affd*, 67 NY2d 1034, 494 NE2d 1382, 503 NYS2d 717 (1986) §1.09

Gilliland v Elmwood Properties, 301 SC 295, 391 SE2d 577 (1990) §§1.13, 1.19

Godrey, Bassett & Kuykendall Architects, Ltd v Huntington Lumber & Supply Co, 584 So 2d 1254 (Miss 1991) §1.20, app B

Goette v Press Bar & Cafe, Inc, 413 NW2d 854 (Minn Ct App 1987) §9.28

Goldberg v Underhill, 95 Cal App 2d 700, 213 P2d 516 (1950) §§2.01, 5.02, 5.16, app A, app B

Golden Grain Macaroni Co v Klefstad Engg Co, 45 Ill App 3d 77, 358 NE2d 1295 (1976) §11.06

Gomes v Pan Am Assocs, 406 Mass 647, 549 NE2d 1134 (1990) §11.02

Goulette v Babcock, 153 Vt 650, 571 A2d 74 (1990) §12.07

Graham v Pennsylvania Co, 139 Pa 149, 21 A 151 (1891) app B

Graman v Continental Casualty Co, 87 Ill App 3d 896, 409 NE2d 387 (1980) §§13.07, 13.09

Graulich v Frederic H. Berlowe & Assocs, 338 So 2d 1109 (Fla Dist Ct App 1976) §§4.01, 8.05, 12.02, app B

Gravely v Providence Partnership, 549 F2d 958 (4th Cir 1977) §§1.09, 4.04, 6.03, app B

Grazzini Bros & Co v Builders Clinic, Inc, 280 Minn 540, 160 NW2d 259 (1968) app A, app B

Greco v Mancini, 476 A2d 522 (RI 1984) §§2.01, 10.08, app B

Greenberg v City of Yonkers, 45 AD2d 314, 358 NYS2d 453 (1974), *affd*, 37 NY2d 907, 340 NE2d 744, 378 NYS2d 382 (1975) §§1.23, 9.17, app A, app B

Green Constr Co v Williams Form Engg Corp, 506 F Supp 173 (WD Mich 1980) §§9.36, 12.07

Greenhaven Corp v Hutchcraft & Assocs, 463 NE2d 283 (Ind Ct App 1984) §§3.03, 9.21, app B

Greenman v Yuba Power Prods, Inc, 59 Cal 2d 57, 377 P2d 897, 27 Cal Rptr 697 (1963) §6.04

Gribaldo, Jacobs, Jones & Assocs v Agrippina Versicherunges AG, 3 Cal 3d 434, 476 P2d 406, 91 Cal Rptr 6 (1970) §§13.11, 13.12, 13.13

Grieb v Citizens Casualty, 33 Wis 2d 552, 148 NW2d 103 (1967) §§2.02, 13.07, app B

Grimmer v Harbor Towers, 133 Cal App 3d 88, 183 Cal Rptr 634 (1982) §12.09, app A, app B

Grizwold & Rauma Architects, Inc v Aesculapius Corp, 301 Minn 121, 221 NW2d 556 (1974) §§5.02, 5.09, 5.10, 5.11

Grossman v Sea Air Towers Ltd, 513 So 2d 686 (Fla Dist Ct App 1987), *review denied*, 520 So 2d 584 (Fla 1988) §10.03, app B

Grover-Dimond Assocs v American Arbitration Assn, 297 Minn 324, 211 NW2d 787 (1973) §14.06

Guirey, Srnka & Arnold Architects v City of Phoenix, 9 Ariz App 70, 449 P2d 306 (1969) §5.03

Gulf Contracting v Bibb County, 795 F2d 980 (11th Cir 1986) §§1.20, 9.04, app A, app B
Guthrie v Rudy Brown Builders, Inc, 416 So 2d 590 (La Ct App), *writ denied*, 420 So 2d 455 (La 1982) §10.11, app B

H

Haberman v Washington Pub Power Supply Sys, 109 Wash 2d 107, 744 P2d 1032 (1987) §§1.13, 1.25, 2.01, app A
Hackley v Waldorf-Hoerner Paper Products Co, 149 Mont 286, 425 P2d 712 (1967) §9.07, app A, app B
Haines v Bechdolt, 231 Cal App 2d 659, 42 Cal Rptr 53 (1965) §5.08
Hall v City of Los Angeles, 74 Cal 502, 16 P 131 (1888) §2.01, app A
Hall v Union Indem Co, 61 F2d 85 (8th Cir), *cert denied*, 287 US 663 (1932) §8.02, app A, app B
Hambleton v Board of Engg Examiners, 40 Or App 9, 594 P2d 416 (1979) §§3.02, 4.01, app B
Hamby v High Steel Structures, Inc, 134 AD2d 884, 521 NYS2d 926 (1987) §9.23
Hamill v Foster-Lipkins Corp, 41 AD2d 361, 342 NYS2d 539 (1973) §§1.09, 9.05, app A, app B
Hammaker v Schleigh, 157 Md 652, 147 A 790 (1929) §8.02
Hanna v Huer, Johns, Neel, Rivers & Webb, 233 Kan 206, 662 P2d 243 (1983) §§1.16, 4.04
Hansen v Ruby Constr Co, 155 Ill App 3d 475, 508 NE2d 301 (1987) §9.13, app B
Harbor Mechanical, Inc v Arizona Elec Power Co-op, Inc, 496 F Supp 681 (D Ariz 1980) §§1.13, 1.20, 4.05, 9.02, 9.11, 9.30, app B
Harman v CE&M, Inc, 493 NE2d 1319 (Ind Ct App 1986) §§4.05, 9.30
Harmon v Angus R. Jessup Assocs, 619 SW2d 522 (Tenn 1981) app B
Harmon v Christy Lumber, Inc, 402 NW2d 690 (SD 1987) §8.01
Harry Skolnick & Sons v Heyman, 7 Conn App 175, 508 A2d 64, *cert denied*, 200 Conn 803, 510 A2d 191 (1986) §9.09
Hartford Accident & Indem Co v Case Found Co, 10 Ill App 3d 115, 294 NE2d 7 (1973) §13.04
Hartford Elec Applicators of Thermalux, Inc v Alden, 169 Conn 177, 363 A2d 135 (1975) §1.20
Hartford Fire Ins Co v Architectural Management, Inc, 158 Ill App 3d 515, 511 NE2d 706, *appeal denied*, 117 Ill 2d 543, 517 NE2d 1086 (1987) §11.07
Haseley Trucking Co v Great Lakes Pipe Co, 101 AD2d 1019, 476 NYS2d 702 (1984) §9.04, app A
Hastings & Civetta Architects v Burch, 794 SW2d 294 (Mo Ct App 1990) §2.08
Heckert v Commonwealth, Dept of State, Bureau of Professional & Occupational Affairs, 82 Pa Commw 636, 476 A2d 481 (1984) §3.02
H. Elton Thompson & Assocs, PC v Williams, 164 Ga App 571, 298 SE2d 539 (1982) §1.19
Henderson Clay Prods, Inc v Edgar Wood & Assocs, 122 NH 800, 451 A2d 174 (1982) §11.10, app B
Henneberger v Herman Schwabe, Inc, 58 Misc 2d 986, 297 NYS2d 381 (Sup Ct 1968) §12.07, app A

Henningson, Durham & Richardson, Inc v Prochnow, 13 Ariz App 411, 477 P2d 285 (1970), *review denied*, 107 Ariz 222, 485 P2d 547 (1971) **app B**

Henningson, Durham & Richardson, Inc v Swift Bros Constr Co, 739 F2d 1341 (8th Cir 1984) **§§12.02, 12.06, app B**

Henry v Britt, 220 So 2d 917 (Fla Dist Ct App), *cert denied*, 229 So 2d 867 (Fla 1969) **§§1.06, 3.03, 9.14, 9.15, app A, app B**

Henshaw v Edward E. Clark Engineers-Scientists, 490 So 2d 161 (Fla Dist Ct App 1986) **§§1.17, 1.22, app B**

Herkert v Stauber, 106 Wis 2d 545, 317 NW2d 834 (1982) **§§1.19, 15.07**

Heslep v Forrest & Cotton, Inc, 247 Ark 1066, 449 SW2d 181 (1970) **§§3.06, 9.25, app A, app B**

Hiatt v Brown, 422 NE2d 736 (Ind Ct App 1981) **§§1.23, 9.03, app A, app B**

Hill v McDonald, 442 A2d 133 (DC 1982) **§§8.04, 9.37, app B**

Hill v Polar Pantries, 219 SC 263, 64 SE2d 885 (1951) **app A, app B**

Hilliard & Bartko Joint Venture v Fedco Sys, Inc, 309 Md 147, 522 A2d 961 (1987) **§11.04**

Himmel Corp v Stade, 52 Ill App 3d 294, 367 NE2d 411 (1977) **§3.03, app B**

Hobbs v Florida First Natl Bank, 406 So 2d 63 (Fla Dist Ct App 1981), *dismissed without opinion*, 412 So 2d 466 (Fla 1982) **§1.21, app A, app B**

Hogan v Postin, 695 P2d 1042 (Wyo 1985) **§8.04**

Hogan Exploration, Inc v Monroe Engg Assocs, 430 So 2d 696 (La Ct App 1983) **§§1.19, 10.11, app B**

Holy Cross Parish v Huether, 308 NW2d 575 (SD 1981) **§§2.01, 11.06, app B**

Home Furniture, Inc v Brunzell Constr Co, 84 Nev 309, 440 P2d 398 (1968) **app B**

Home Ins Co v A.J. Warehouse, Inc, 210 So 2d 544 (La Ct App 1968) **§1.23, app A**

Hommel v Badger State Inv Co, 166 Wis 235, 165 NW 20 (1917) **§1.23, app A, app B**

Hooper Water Improvement Dist v Reeve, 642 P2d 745 (Utah 1982) **§11.09**

Horgan & Slattery v City of New York, 114 AD 555, 100 NYS 68 (1906) **§§5.05, 5.09, 5.14, 5.17**

Horn v Burns & Roe, 536 F2d 251 (8th Cir 1976) **§11.02, app B**

Hortman v Becker Constr Co, 92 Wis 2d 210, 284 NW2d 621 (1979) **§§3.03, 3.04, 9.05, 9.23, app B**

Horton v Goldminer's Daughter, 785 P2d 1087 (Utah 1989) **§11.08**

Hotel Utica, Inc v Armstrong, 62 AD2d 1147, 404 NYS2d 455 (1978) **§§1.16, 4.01**

Housing Auth v E.T. Boggess Architect, Inc, 160 W Va 303, 233 SE2d 740 (1977) **app A**

Howard, Needles, Tammen & Bergendoff v Stears, Perini & Pomeroy, 312 A2d 621 (Del Super Ct 1973) **§9.32**

Howe v Bishop, 446 So 2d 11 (Ala 1984) **app A**

Howell v Burk, 90 NM 688, 568 P2d 214, *cert denied*, 91 NM 3, 569 P2d 413 (1977) **§11.08**

Huang v Garner, 157 Cal App 3d 404, 203 Cal Rptr 800 (1984) §§1.19, 3.03, 6.04, 6.07, 6.08, 7.03, app B

Huber, Hunt & Nichols, Inc v Moore, 67 Cal App 3d 278, 136 Cal Rptr 603 (1977) §§8.04, 9.20

Hubert v Aitken, 15 Daly 237, 2 NYS 711 (CP 1888), *affd*, 123 NY 655, 25 NE 954 (1890) §§1.05, 1.15, 9.18, app A

Huggins v Atlanta Tile & Marble Co, 98 Ga App 597, 106 SE2d 191 (1958) §8.01

Hughes-Bechtol, Inc v State, 124 BR 1007 (Bankr SD Ohio 1991) §1.18

Hull v Enger Constr Co, 15 Wash App 511, 550 P2d 692, *review denied*, 87 Wash 2d 1012 (1976) §1.19, app B

Hunt v Ellisor & Tanner, Inc, 739 SW2d 933 (Tex Ct App 1987), *error denied* (Mar 23, 1988) §9.17

Hunt v Star Photo Finishing Co, 115 Ga App 1, 153 SE2d 602 (1967) §§1.11, 9.05, app A, app B

Hutcheson v Eastern Engg Co, 132 Ga App 885, 209 SE2d 680 (1974) §9.13, app B

Hutchings v Harry, 242 So 2d 153 (Fla Dist Ct App 1970) §§9.07, 9.13, app A

Hutchinson v Dubeau, 161 Ga App 65, 289 SE2d 4 (1982) §§3.09, 9.18, app A

Hyman v Gordon, 35 Cal App 3d 769, 111 Cal Rptr 262 (1973) §6.07, app A, app B

I

Idaho State Univ v Mitchell, 97 Idaho 724, 552 P2d 776 (1976) §9.41

Illinois Hous Dev Auth v Sjostron & Sons, 105 Ill App 3d 247, 433 NE2d 1350 (1982) §§4.05, 6.02, app A, app B

Impastato v Senner, 190 So 2d 111 (La Ct App 1966) §§5.11, 5.12

Inman v Binghamton Hous Auth, 3 NY2d 137, 143 NE2d 895, 164 NYS2d 699 (1957) §§9.03, 9.07, 12.07, app A, app B

Intamin, Inc v Figley-Wright Contractors, Inc, 608 F Supp 408 (ND Ill 1985) §12.08

Iowa State Bd of Engg Examiners v Olson, 421 NW2d 523 (Iowa 1988) §3.02

Irondequoit Bay Pure Waters Dist v Nalews, Inc, 123 Misc 2d 462, 472 NYS2d 842 (Sup Ct 1984) §12.06

Irwin v Michelin Tire Corp, 288 SC 221, 341 SE2d 783 (1986) §9.42, app B

Italian Economic Corp v Community Engrs, Inc, 135 Misc 2d 209, 514 NYS2d 630 (Sup Ct 1987) §10.03

J

Jacka v Ouachita Parish Sch Bd, 249 La 223, 186 So 2d 571 (1966) §9.18, app B

Jack Frost, Inc v Engineered Bldg Components Co, 304 NW2d 346 (Minn 1981) §9.17, app B

Jackson v Sergent, Hauskins & Beckwith Engrs, Inc, 20 Ariz App 330, 512 P2d 862 (1973) app A

Jacobs v Petrino, 351 So 2d 1036 (Fla Dist Ct App 1976), *cert denied*, 349 So 2d 1231 (Fla 1977) §6.03, app B

Jaillet v Hill & Hill, 460 F Supp 1075 (WD Pa 1978) §9.42, app B

J&J Electric, Inc v Gilbert H. Moen Co, 9 Wash App 954, 516 P2d

217 (1973), *writ denied*, 83 Wash 2d 1088 (1974) §§9.30, 9.31, app A
Japan Airlines Co v State, 628 P2d 934 (Alaska 1981) §9.36, app B
Jaquin Fla Distilling Co v Reynolds, Smith & Hills Architects-Engrs-Planners, Inc, 319 So 2d 604 (Fla Dist Ct App 1975) §5.13
Jaroszewicz v Facilities Dev Corp, 115 AD2d 159, 495 NYS2d 498 (1985) §§3.03, 3.04, 9.06, 9.23, app B
Jasper Constr, Inc v Foothill Jr College Dist, 91 Cal App 3d 1, 153 Cal Rptr 767 (1979) §15.07, app B
Jefferson Mills, Inc v Gregson, 124 Ga App 96, 183 SE2d 529 (1971) §§9.37, 13.12
Jenkins v J.J. Krebs & Sons, 322 So 2d 426 (La Ct App 1975), *writ denied*, 325 So 2d 611 (La 1976) §§1.16, 10.04, app A, app B
Jewish Bd of Guardians v Grumman Allied Instruments, Inc, 62 NY2d 684, 465 NE2d 42, 476 NYS2d 535 (1984) §§9.11, 9.22
Jim Arnott, Inc v L&E, Inc, 539 P2d 1333 (Colo Ct App 1975) not officially published §§5.09, 10.03, app A
John Grace & Co v State Univ Constr Fund, 99 AD2d 860, 472 NYS2d 757, *affd*, 64 NY2d 709, 475 NE2d 105, 485 NYS2d 734 (1984) §12.06, app B
John Martin Co v Morse/Diesel, Inc, 819 SW2d 428 (Tenn 1991) §9.04
Johnson v Martin, 423 So 2d 868 (Ala Civ App 1982) §§2.06, 9.13, 10.11, app B
Johnson v Salem Title Co, 246 Or 409, 425 P2d 519 (1967) §§1.12, 3.03, 8.05, 9.19, app A, app B

Johnson, Voiland, Archuleta, Inc v Roark Assocs, 40 Colo App 269, 572 P2d 1220 (1977) §6.03
John W. Johnson, Inc v Basic Constr Co, 139 US App DC 85, 429 F2d 764 (1970) §1.20
Jones v Boeing Co, 153 NW2d 897 (ND 1967) §12.02, app B
Jones v Continental Casualty Co, 123 NJ Super 353, 303 A2d 91 (1973) §13.10
Jones v McGuffin, 454 So 2d 509 (Ala 1984) §§1.13, 4.05
Josephs v Burns, 260 Or 493, 491 P2d 203 (1971) §11.09, app B

K

Kaltenbrun v City of Port Wash, 156 Wis 2d 634, 457 NW2d 527 (1990) §§3.03, 3.04, 9.11
Karna v Byron Reed Syndicate No 4, 374 F Supp 687, 689 (D Neb 1974) §1.17, app A, app B
Kashmir Corp v Barnes, 278 Or 433, 564 P2d 693 (1977) §11.05, app B
Kaufman v Leard, 356 Mass 163, 248 NE2d 480 (1969) §§5.07, 5.15
Kecko Piping Co v Town of Monroe, 172 Conn 197, 374 A2d 179 (1977) §2.04
Keel v Titan Constr Corp, 721 P2d 828 (Okla Ct App 1986) §§1.19, 9.28
Keel v Titan Constr Corp, 639 P2d 1228 (Okla 1981) §§4.01, 4.05, app A, app B
Keeler v Pennsylvania Dept of Trans, 56 Pa Commw 236, 424 A2d 614 (1981) §11.09, app B
Kellogg v Pizza Oven, Inc, 157 Colo 295, 402 P2d 633 (1965) §§5.09, 5.15

Kelly v Northwest Community Hosp, 66 Ill App 3d 679, 384 NE2d 102 (1978) §§3.05, 4.03, 9.23, app B

Kemper v Schardt, 143 Cal App 3d 557, 192 Cal Rptr 46 (1983) §14.13

Kemper Architects, PC v McFall, Konkel & Kimball Consulting Engrs, Inc, 843 P2d 1178 (Wyo 1992) §6.03

Kennedy v Columbia Lumber & Mfg Co, 299 SC 335, 384 SE2d 730 (1989) §10.10

Kent v Bartlett, 49 Cal App 3d 724, 122 Cal Rptr 615 (1975) §9.04, app A, app B

Kerr v Rochester Gas & Elec Corp, 113 AD2d 412, 496 NYS2d 880 (1985) §9.23

Kevin Roche-John Dinkelo & Assocs v City of New Haven, 205 Conn 741, 535 A2d 1287 (1988) §10.02

Key Intl Mfg, Inc v Morse/Diesel, Inc, 142 AD2d 448, 536 NYS2d 792 (1988) §4.05

Kingsbury v Tevco, Inc, 79 Cal App 3d 314, 144 Cal Rptr 773 (1978) §9.41, app A

Kirk v Walter E. Deuchler Assocs, 79 Ill App 3d 416, 398 NE2d 603 (1979) §§3.05, 4.03

Kittson County v Wells, Denbrook & Assocs, 308 Minn 237, 241 NW2d 799 (1976) §§11.02, 11.10

Kleb v Wendling, 67 Ill App 3d 1016, 385 NE2d 346 (1978) §§1.07, 9.30

Klein v Allen, 470 So 2d 224 (La Ct App 1985) §11.09

Klein v Catalono, 386 Mass 701, 437 NE2d 514 (1982) §§1.09, 11.08, app B

K-Mart Corp v Midcon Realty Groups, Ltd, 489 F Supp 813 (D Conn 1980) §6.04

Knox College v Celotex Corp, 88 Ill 2d 407, 430 NE 976 (1981) §11.06, app B

Kortz v Kimberlin, 158 Ky 566, 165 SW 654 (1914) §1.07, app B

Kostohryz v McGuire, 298 Minn 513, 212 NW2d 850 (1973) §5.16

Kraft v Langford, 565 SW2d 223 (Tex 1978) §3.07, app A, app B

Krestow v Wooster, 360 So 2d 32 (Fla Dist Ct App 1978) §9.18, app B

Krieger v J.E. Greiner Co, 282 Md 50, 382 A2d 1069 (1978) §§4.04, 4.07, 9.25, app A, app B

Kriegler v Eichler Homes, Inc, 269 Cal App 2d 224, 74 Cal Rptr 749 (1969) §6.05

Kundahl v Barnett, 5 Wash App 227, 486 P2d 1164, *review denied*, 80 Wash 2d 1001 (1971) §11.06, app B

Kurz v Quincy Post No 37 Am Legion, 5 Ill App 3d 412, 283 NE2d 8 (1972) §§5.08, 5.11

L

La Bombarde v Phillips Swager Assocs, 130 Ill App 3d 896, 474 NE2d 942 (1985), *appeal denied* (May Term 1985) §1.01, app B

Lagerstrom v Beers Constr Co, 157 Ga App 396, 277 SE2d 765 (1981) §§8.03, 12.02

Lagua v State, 65 Haw 7702, 649 P2d 1135 (1982) app B

Lake v McElfatrick, 139 NY 349, 34 NE 922 (1893) §9.28, app B

Lake Placid Club Attached Lodges v Elizabethtown Builders, Inc, 131 AD2d 159, 521 NYS2d 165 (1987) §§4.05, 10.10

Lamb v Wedgewood South Corp, 308 NC 419, 302 SE2d 868 (1983) §11.09, app B

Lamb v Wedgewood South Corp, 55 NC App 686, 286 SE2d 876 (1982), *affd*, 308 NC 419, 302 SE2d 868 (1983) §12.09

Lane v Geiger-Berger Assocs, 608 F2d 1148 (8th Cir 1979) §12.07

Lane v Inhabitants of Town of Harmony, 112 Me 25, 90 A 546 (1914) §5.04

Lapar v Morris, 119 AD2d 635, 501 NYS2d 82 (1986) **§2.04, app A**

Lapierre, Litchfield & Partners v Continental Casualty Co, 32 AD2d 353, 302 NYS2d 370 (1969) **§§13.07, 13.09**

La Rossa v Scientific Design Co, 402 F2d 937 (3d Cir 1968) **§§6.02, 6.03, 6.08, app A, app B**

Larrimore v Comanche County, 32 SW 367 (Tex Civ App 1895) **§10.02, app A, app B**

Laukkanen v Jewel Tea Co, 78 Ill App 2d 153, 222 NE2d 584 (1966) **§§1.23, 9.03, 9.11, app A, app B**

Lauren v Grant, 407 So 2d 395 (Fla Dist Ct App 1981) **app B**

Lawyers Title Ins Co v Carey Hodges & Assocs, 358 So 2d 964 (La Ct App 1978) **§1.19, app B**

Layton v Allen, 246 A2d 794 (Del Super Ct 1969) §11.03

Lee v City of Pontiac, 99 Ill App 3d 982, 426 NE2d 300 (1981) **§9.42, app B**

Lee County v Southern Waters Contractors, Inc, 298 So 2d 518 (Fla Dist Ct App 1974) **§1.20, app A, app B**

Leeper v Hiller Group, Architects, Planners PA, 543 A2d 258 (RI 1988) §11.09

LeMay v United States H Properties, Inc, 338 So 2d 1143 (Fla Dist Ct App 1976) **app A, app B**

Lembert v Gilmore, 312 A2d 335 (Del Super Ct 1973) §11.03

Lemmon, Freeth, Haines & Jones, Architects Ltd, v Underwriters at Lloyd's, 52 Haw 614, 484 P2d 141 (1971) §13.09

Lewis v Axinn, 100 AD2d 617, 473 NYS2d 575 (1984) **§§2.01, 11.07**

Lincoln Pulp & Paper Co v Dravo Corp, 436 F Supp 262 (D Me 1977) §9.30

Lincoln Stone & Supply Co v Ludwig, 94 Neb 722, 144 NW 782 (1913) **§4.02, app A, app B**

Lindeberg v Hodgens, 89 Misc 454, 152 NYS 229 (Sup Ct 1915) **§1.15, app A**

Linde Enters, Inc v Hazelton City Auth, 602 A2d 878 (Pa Super Ct 1992) §1.20

Linn Reorganized Sch Dist No 2 v Butler Mfg Co, 672 SW2d 340 (Mo 1984) **§11.05, app B**

Lisbon Contractors, Inc v Miami-Dade Water & Sewer Auth, 537 F Supp 175 (SD Fla 1982) **§§3.01, 11.02, 11.06, app B**

Little Rock Sch Dist v Celotex Corp, 264 Ark 757, 574 SW2d 669 (1978) **app B**

Livingston Parish Sch Bd v Fireman's Fund Am Ins Co, 263 So 2d 356 (La Ct App 1972), *affd*, 282 So 2d 478 (La 1973) §13.09

Long Island Lighting Co v IMO Delaval, Inc, 668 F Supp 237 (SDNY 1987) **§§9.30, 10.10**

Looker v Gulf Coast Fair, 203 Ala 42, 81 So 832 (1919) **§6.07, app B**

Lottman v Barnett, 62 Mo 159 (1876) **§§1.22, 9.42, app A, app B**

Louisiana Molasses Co v Le Sassier, 52 La Ann 2070, 28 So 217, *affd*, 52 La Ann 1768, 28 So 223 (1900) **§4.02, app A, app B**

Loup-Miller v Brauer & Assocs Rocky Mountain, Inc, 40 Colo App 67, 572 P2d 845 (1977) §§9.14, 9.17, app B
Loyland v Stone & Webster Engg Corp, 9 Wash App 682, 514 P2d 184 (1973), *review denied*, 83 Wash 2d 1007 (1974) §§1.10, 3.03, 4.03, 9.26, app A, app B
Luciani v High, 372 So 2d 530 (Fla Dist Ct App 1979) §9.04, app B
Lukowski v Vecta Educ Corp, 401 NE2d 781, 786 (Ind Ct App 1980) §§1.04, 9.12, 9.28, app B
Lundgren v Freeman, 307 F2d 104 (9th Cir 1962) §§2.04, 2.05, 9.09
Luterbach v Mochon, Schutte, Hackworthy, Juerisson, Inc, 84 Wis 2d 1, 267 NW2d 13 (1978) §§4.07, 9.30, app B
Lutz Engg Co v Industrial Louvers, Inc, 585 A2d 631 (RI 1991) §1.20, app B

M

MacDonnell v Dreyfous, 144 La 891, 81 So 383 (1919) §5.17
Macey v Rollins Environmental Services, Inc, 179 NJ Super 535, 432 A2d 960 (1981) §15.07
MacIntyre v Green's Pool Serv, Inc, 347 So 2d 1081 (Fla Dist Ct App 1977) §§1.08, 9.11, app B
MacKay v Benjamin Franklin Realty & Holding Co, 288 Pa 207, 135 A 613 (1927) §8.03
Macomber v State, 250 Cal App 2d 391, 58 Cal Rptr 393 (1967) §2.03, app A
MacPherson v Buick Motor Co, 217 NY 382, 111 NE 1050 (1916) §§6.04, 9.02, 9.03
Magnolia Constr Co v Mississippi Gulf South Engrs, Inc, 518 So 2d 1194 (Miss 1988) §§1.20, 4.03

Mai Kai, Inc v Colucci, 205 So 2d 291 (Fla 1967) §§1.23, 9.13, app A, app B
Major v Leary, 241 AD 606, 268 NYS 413 (1934) §9.20
Mallow v Tucker, Sadler & Bennett, Architects & Engrs, Inc, 245 Cal App 2d 700, 54 Cal Rptr 174 (1966) app A, app B
Malo v Gilman, 177 Ind App 365, 379 NE2d 554 (1978) §§5.02, 5.08, 5.17
Maloney v Oak Builders, Inc, 224 So 2d 161 (La Ct App 1969), *revd in part*, 256 La 85, 235 So 2d 386 (1970) §§9.12, 15.07
Malta Constr Co v Henningson, Durham & Richardson, Inc, 694 F Supp 902 (ND Ga 1988) §§1.20, 10.10
Manett-Seastrunk & Buckner v Terminal Bldg Corp, 120 Tex 374, 39 SW2d 1 (1931) app A
Manning Engg, Inc v Hudson County Park Commn, 74 NJ 113, 376 A2d 1194 (1977) §§2.01, 9.40
Manton v H.L. Stevens & Co, 170 Iowa 495, 153 NW 87 (1915) §§8.01, 8.04, app A, app B
Mardirosian v American Inst of Architects, 474 F Supp 628 (DDC 1979) §9.40, app A
Marine Colloids, Inc v M.D. Hardy, Inc, 433 A2d 402 (Me 1981) §9.18, app B
Maritime Constr Co v Benda, 262 So 2d 20 (Fla Dist Ct App 1972) §4.01
Markel v Florida State Bd of Architecture, 268 So 2d 374 (Fla 1972) app B
Marlborough, City of v Cybulski Ohnemus & Assocs, 370 Mass 157, 346 NE2d 716 (1976) §9.40
Marshall v Port Auth of Allegheny County, 106 Pa Commw 131, 525

A2d 857 (1987), *affd*, 524 Pa 1, 568 A2d 931 (1990) §4.07, app B

Marshall-Schule Assocs v Goldman, 137 Misc 2d 1024, 523 NYS2d 16 (Civ Ct 1987) §9.39

Marszalk v Van Volkenburg, 24 Wash App 646, 604 P2d 501 (1979) §8.06

Martin v Board of Educ, 79 NM 636, 447 P2d 516 (1968) §1.07, app A, app B

Martinez v Traubner, 32 Cal 3d 755, 653 P2d 1046, 187 Cal Rptr 251 (1982) §11.10, app B

Matthews v Neal, Green & Clark, 177 Ga App 26, 338 SE2d 496 (1985) §5.03

Mattingly v Hopkins, 254 Md 88, 253 A2d 904 (1969) §11.06, app A, app B

Mayor & City Council v Clark-Dietz & Assocs-Engrs, 550 F Supp 610 (ND Miss 1982), *appeal denied*, 702 F2d 67 (5th Cir 1983) §§1.12, 1.20, app A, app B

Mayor & City of Albany v Cunliff, 2 NY 165 (1849) §9.02

MBA Commercial Constr, Inc v Roy J. Hannaford Co, 818 P2d 469 (Okla 1991), *rehg denied* (Oct 29, 1991) §11.05

McCandliss v Ward W Ross, Inc, 45 Mich App 342, 206 NW2d 455 (1973) §14.06

McCarthy v J.P. Cullen & Son Corp, 199 NW2d 362 (Iowa 1972) §§9.26, 9.30, 9.31, 12.07, app A, app B

McClanahan v American Gilsonite Co, 494 F Supp 1334 (D Colo 1980) §§6.04, 11.08, 11.10, app B

McCloskey & Co v Wright, 363 F Supp 223 (ED Va 1973) §§11.03, 11.05

McDermott v TENDUM Constrs, 211 NJ Super 196, 511 A2d 690 (1986) §§1.04, 9.35

McDonough v Whalen, 365 Mass 506, 313 NE2d 435 (1974) §§1.02, 3.03, 7.02, 9.03, 9.35, 9.36, app A, app B

McElvy, Jennewein, Stefany, Howard, Inc v Arlington Elec, Inc, 582 So 2d 47 (Fla Dist Ct App 1991), *rehg denied* (July 11, 1991) §1.20

McGovern v Standish, 65 Ill 2d 54, 357 NE2d 1134 (1976) §§3.05, 4.07, 9.23, app A

McGuire v United Bhd of Carpenters & Joiners of Am, 50 Wash 699, 314 P2d 439 (1957) §9.28, app A, app B

McKee v City of Cohoes Bd of Educ, 99 AD2d 923, 473 NYS2d 269 (1984) §9.40

McKee v City of Pleasanton, 242 Kan 649, 750 P2d 1007 (1988) §1.19

McKeen Homeowners Assn v Oliver, 586 So 2d 679 (La Ct App 1991) §1.25

McKinney Drilling Co v Nello Teer Co, 38 NC App 472, 248 SE2d 444 (1978) §§2.05, 9.04

McMacken v State, 320 NW2d 131 (SD 1982) §11.08, app B

Mears Park Holding Corp v Morse/Diesel, Inc, 427 NW2d 281 (Minn Ct App 1988) §§1.02, 1.21

Medak v Cox, 12 Cal App 3d 70, 90 Cal Rptr 452 (1970) §9.39

Medoff v Fisher, 257 Pa 126, 101 A 471 (1917) §§3.03, 9.40

Meek v Spinney, Coady & Parker Architects, Inc, 50 Ill App 3d 919, 365 NE2d 1378 (1977) §§3.05, 4.04, 4.07

Melancon v American Hardware Mut Ins Co, 392 So 2d 159 (La Ct App 1980) app B

Merchants Natl Bank & Trust Co v Smith, Hinchman & Grylls Assocs, 876 F2d 1202 (5th Cir 1989) §11.02

Mercury Constr Corp v Moses H. Cone Memorial Hosp, 656 F2d 933 (4th Cir 1981), *affd*, 460 US 1 (1983) §14.02

Mercy Hosp v Hansen, Lind & Meyer PC, 456 NW2d 666 (Iowa 1990) §§2.01, 9.17

Midland, City of v Helger Constr Co, 157 Mich App 736, 403 NW2d 218 (1987) §§11.02, 11.13

Miller v City of Broken Arrow Okla, 660 F2d 450 (10th Cir 1981), *cert denied*, 455 US 1020 (1982) §§1.14, 12.07, app B

Miller v DeWitt, 37 Ill 2d 273, 226 NE2d 630 (1967) §§3.05, 9.26, 9.32, 12.08, app A, app B

Miller v Los Angeles County Flood Control Dist, 8 Cal 3d 689, 505 P2d 193, 106 Cal Rptr 1 (1973) §6.05

Milligan v Tibbitts Engg Corp, 391 Mass 364, 461 NE2d 808 (1984) §11.02

Milwaukee County v Schmidt, Garden & Erikson, 43 Wis 2d 445, 168 NW2d 559 (1969) §§11.02, 11.03, app A, app B

Minor v Zidell Trust, 618 P2d 392 (Okla 1980) §§1.17, 9.13, 9.17, app B

Mississippi Meadows, Inc v Hodson, 13 Ill App 3d 24, 299 NE2d 359 (1973) app A, app B

M.J. Womack, Inc v House of Representatives of State, 509 So 2d 62 (La Ct App), *writ denied*, 513 So 2d 1211 (La 1987) §§1.19, 8.03

Mlynarski v St Rita's Congregation, 31 Wis 2d 54, 142 NW2d 207 (1966) §§1.23, 3.03, 3.04, app A, app B

M. Miller Co v Central Contra Cesta Sanitary Dist, 198 Cal App 2d 305, 18 Cal Rptr 13 (1961) §§9.03, 9.30, app A, app B

Moloso v State, 644 P2d 205 (Alaska 1982) §8.03, app A, app B

Montaup Elec Co v Ohio Brass Corp, 561 F Supp 740 (DRI 1983) §§11.09, 12.09

Montgomery Indus Intl, Inc v Southern Baptist Hosp, Inc, 362 So 2d 145 (Fla Dist Ct App 1978) §§9.13, 9.28, app A, app B

Montijo v Swift, 219 Cal App 2d 351, 33 Cal Rptr 133 (1963) §§1.23, 9.03, 9.07, app A, app B

Moore v Bolton, 480 SW2d 805 (Tex Civ App 1972) §5.03

Moore v PRC Engg, Inc, 565 So 2d 817 (Fla Dist Ct App 1990) §§1.18, 4.06, app B

Moorman Mfg Co v National Tank Co, 91 Ill 2d 69, 435 NE2d 443 (1982) §§1.15, 4.01, 6.01, 6.04, 7.03, 10.03

Moossy v Huckabay Hosp, Inc, 283 So 2d 699 (La 1973) §5.08

Morrison-Maierle, Inc v Selsco, 186 Mont 180, 606 P2d 1085 (1980) §§1.09, 1.19, 9.12

Morse v Michaelson, Rabig & Ramp, 10 Ill App 2d 366, 243 NE2d 271 (1968) app A, app B

Morse/Diesel, Inc v Trinity Indus, 859 F2d 242 (2d Cir 1988) §9.02

Morton Z. Levine & Assocs Chartered v Van Deree, 334 So 2d 287 (Fla Dist Ct App 1976) §14.02

Moseley v Abrams, 170 Cal App 3d 355, 216 Cal Rptr 40 (1985), *review denied* (Oct 23, 1985) §11.07

Mound Bayou, City of v Roy Collins Constr Co, 499 So 2d 1354 (Miss 1986) §2.07

Mounds View, City of v Walijarvi, 263 NW2d 420 (Minn 1978) §§1.04, 6.03, 6.04, 6.07, app B

Moundsview Indepe6ndent Sch Dist No 621 v Buetow & Assocs, 253 NW2d 836 (Minn 1977) §§4.04, 9.30, app B

Mount Hood Radio & Television Broadcasting Corp v Dresser Indus, 270 Or 690, 530 P2d 72 (1974) §11.09, app B

Mozzetti v City of Brisbane, 67 Cal App 3d 565, 136 Cal Rptr 751 (1977) §10.03

Muehlstedt v City of Lino Lakes, 473 NW2d 892 (Minn Ct App 1991), *review denied* (Sept 25, 1991) §10.12

Mullis v Southern Cos Servs, Inc, 250 Ga 90, 296 SE2d 579 (1982) §11.09

Mulverhill v Mulverhill, 78 AD2d 748, 432 NYS 654 (1980) §§12.08, 12.09

Murphy v City of Brockton, 364 Mass 377, 305 NE2d 103 (1973) §9.40

Mutual Serv Life Ins Co v Galaxy Builders, Inc, 435 NW2d 136 (Minn Ct App 1989), *review denied* (Apr 19, 1989) §11.06

N

Naetzker v Brocton Cent Sch Dist, 50 AD2d 142, 376 NYS2d 300 (1975), *revd*, 41 NY2d 929, 363 NE2d 351, 394 NYS2d 627 (1977) §§11.02, 11.04, app B

Natal v Phoenix Assurance Co, 286 So 2d 738 (La Ct App 1973), *revd as to other parties*, 305 So 2d 438 (La 1974) §9.07, 9.23, app A, app B

National Cash Register Co v Haak, 233 Pa Super 562, 335 A2d 407 (1975) §15.07, app B

National Hous Indus v E.L. Jones Dev Co, 118 Ariz 374, 576 P2d 1374 (1978) §§1.08, 1.19

Nauman v Harold K. Beecher & Assocs, 19 Utah 2d 101, 426 P2d 621 (1967) §§1.22, 3.06, app A, app B

Navajo Circle, Inc v Development Concepts Corp, 373 So 2d 689 (Fla Dist Ct App 1979) §§1.16, 4.01, 4.03, 9.04

Nei v Boston Survey Consultants, Inc, 388 Mass 320, 446 NE2d 681 (1983) §§1.10, 1.13, 2.01, app B

Nelson v Commonwealth, 235 Va 228, 368 SE2d 239 (1988) §§1.19, 11.03

Nevada Lake Shore Co v Diamond Elec, Inc, 89 Nev 293, 511 P2d 113 (1973) §11.09, app B

Newell v Mosley, 469 SW2d 481 (Tex Civ App 1971) §1.15, app A, app B

New Orleans Unity Socy of Practical Christianity v Standard Roofing Co, 224 So 2d 60 (La Ct App), *rehg denied*, 254 La 811, 227 So 2d 146 (1969) §§1.20, 9.15, app A, app B

Newton Inv Co v Barnard & Burk, Inc, 220 So 2d 822 (Miss 1969) §9.20, app A, app B

New York Facilities Dev Corp v Kallman & McKinnell, Russo & Sonder, 121 AD2d 805, 504 NYS2d 557 (1986) §12.08

Nichols v Brady Consultants, Inc, 305 NW2d 849 (SD 1981) **app A, app B**

Nicholson-Brown, Inc v City of San Jose, 62 Cal App 3d 526, 113 Cal Rptr 159 (1976) **§§11.02, 12.02**

Niver v Nash, 7 Wash 558, 35 P 380 (1893) **§§1.13, 6.02**

Noble v Worthy, 378 A2d 674 (DC 1977) **§1.19, app A, app B**

Norair Engg Corp v St Joseph's Hosp, Inc, 147 Ga App 595, 249 SE2d 642 (1978) **§8.03**

Normoyle-Berg & Assocs v Village of Deer Creek, 39 Ill App 3d 744, 350 NE2d 559 (1976) **§9.03, app A, app B**

Northern Montana Hosp v Knight, 248 Mont 310, 811 P2d 1276 (1991) **§11.11**

Northern Petrochemical Co v Thorsen & Thorshov, Inc, 297 Minn 118, 211 NW2d 159 (1973) **§10.07, app B**

Northrup Contracting, Inc v Village of Bergen, 139 Misc 2d 435, 527 NYS2d 670 (Sup Ct 1986) **§§1.20, 2.05, 9.05**

Northwestern Mut Ins Co v Peterson, 280 Or 773, 572 P2d 1023 (1977) **§9.42, app B**

O

Oakes v McCarthy Co, 267 Cal App 2d 231, 73 Cal Rptr 127 (1968) **§§9.03, 11.05, app A, app B**

O'Brien v Hazlet & Erdal, 84 Mich App 764, 270 NW2d 690 (1978), *affd*, 410 Mich 1, 299 NW2d 336 (1980) **§11.08, app B**

O'Connor v Altus, 123 NJ Super 379, 303 A2d 329 (1973), *affd in part, revd in part*, 67 NJ 106, 335 A2d 545 (1975) **§9.07, 11.09, app B**

Ogle v Billick, 253 Or 92, 453 P2d 677 (1969) **§§1.20, 9.35, app A, app B**

Ohio River Pipeline Corp v Landrum, 580 SW2d 713 (Ky Ct App 1979) **§§9.18, 12.03, 12.07**

O'Kon & Co v Riedel, 588 So 2d 1025 (Fla Dist Ct App 1991) **§3.02**

Oldenburg v Hagemann, 159 Ill App 3d 631, 512 NE2d 718 (1987), *appeal denied*, 188 Ill 2d 546, 520 NE2d 387 (1988) **§10.10**

Olsen v Chase Manhattan Bank, 10 AD2d 539, 205 NYS2d 60 (1960), *affd*, 9 NY2d 829, 175 NE2d 350, 215 NYS2d 773 (1961) **§9.11, 9.25, app A, app B**

Omaha, City of v Hellmuth, Obata & Kassabaum Inc, 767 F2d 457 (8th Cir 1985) **§11.02**

Orleans Parish Sch Bd v Pittman Constr, 261 La 665, 260 So 2d 661 (1972) **§11.06**

Ortiz v Uhl, 39 AD2d 143, 332 NYS2d 583 (1972), *affd*, 33 NY2d 989, 316 NE2d 886, 353 NYS2d 962 (1974) **app A, app B**

Oschwald v Chrisie, 95 NM 251, 620 P2d 1276 (1980) **app B**

Ossining Union Free Sch Dist v Anderson La Roca Anderson, 73 NY2d 417, 539 NE2d 91, 541 NYS2d 335 (1989) **§§4.01, 9.04**

Osterling v Frick, 284 Pa 397, 131 A 250 (1925) **app A, app B**

Overland Constr Co v Sirmons, 369 So 2d 572 (Fla 1979) **§§11.08, 11.10, app B**

Overland Constructors, Inc v Millard Sch Dist, 220 Neb 220, 369 NW2d 69 (1985) **§§1.19, 14.02, app B**

Owen v Dodd, 431 F Supp 1239 (ND Miss 1977) **§9.03, app A**

Owings v Rose, 262 Or 247, 497 P2d 1183 (1972) §§12.08, 12.09, app A, app B

P

Pacific Form Corp v Burgstahler, 263 Or 266, 501 P2d 308 (1972) §§1.17, 9.15, app A

Palm Bay Towers Corp v Crain & Crouse, Inc, 303 So 2d 380 (Fla 1974) §1.20, app A

Palmer v Brown, 127 Cal App 2d 44, 273 P2d 306 (1954) §§2.03, 9.39, app B

Palsgraf v Long Island RR, 248 NY 339, 162 NE 99, *rearg denied*, 249 NY 511, 164 NE 564 (1928) §1.02

Pancoast v Russell, 148 Cal App 2d 909, 307 P2d 719 (1957) app A, app B

Panepinto v Edmart, Inc, 129 NJ Super 319, 323 A2d 533, *cert denied*, 66 NJ 333, 331 A2d 33 (1974) §9.35, app A, app B

Paragon Engg, Inc v Rhodes, 451 So 2d 274 (Ala 1984) §1.19, app A, app B

Parent v Stone & Webster Engg Corp, 408 Mass 108, 556 NE2d 1009 (1990) §§1.22, 9.11, 11.07, app B

Parks v Atkinson, 19 Ariz App 111, 505 P2d 279 (1973) §§1.22, 9.23, 9.25, app A, app B

Parliament Towers Condominium v Parliament House Realty, Inc, 377 So 2d 976 (Fla Dist Ct App 1979) §§6.03, 9.04, app A

Parrish v Tahtaras, 7 Utah 2d 87, 318 P2d 642 (1957) §§5.05, 5.10

Pastorelli v Associated Engs, Inc, 176 F Supp 159 (DRI 1959) §1.18, app A, app B

Patin v Industrial Enterprises, Inc, 421 So 2d 362 (La Ct App), *writ denied*, 423 So 2d 1166 (La 1982) §9.19, app B

Patton v United States, 549 F Supp 36 (WD Mont 1982) §9.35

Paver & Wildfoerster v Catholic High Sch Assn, 38 NY2d 669, 345 NE2d 565, 382 NYS2d 22 (1976) §§11.02, 11.12

Paxton v Alameda County, 119 Cal App 2d 393, 259 P2d 934 (1953) §§1.04, 1.09, 9.15, 9.27, 15.07, app A, app B

Pearce & Pearce, Inc v Kroh Bros Dev Co, 474 So 2d 369 (Fla Dist Ct App 1985) §§1.14, 10.03, app B

Peerless Ins Co v Cerny & Assocs, 199 F Supp 951 (DC Minn 1961) §1.24, app A, app B

People v Connolly, 253 NY 330, 171 NE 393 (1930) §2.02

People *ex rel* Resnik v Curtis & Davis, Architects & Planners, Inc, 78 Ill 2d 381, 400 NE2d 918 (1980) §4.05

People's Center, Inc v Anderson, 32 NC App 746, 233 SE2d 694 (1977) §9.13, app B

Perkins & Will Partnership v Syska & Hennessy, 41 NY2d 1045, 364 NE2d 832, 396 NYS2d 167 (1977) §§12.08, 14.07

Perkins & Will Partnership v Syska & Hennessy & Garfinkel, 50 AD2d 226, 376 NYS2d 533 (1975), *affd*, 364 NE2d 832, 396 NYS2d 167 (1977) §14.07

Perkins & Will Partnership (W.J. Barney Corp), *In re*, 131 Misc 2d 286, 502 NYS2d 318 (Sup Ct 1985), *affd*, 119 AD2d 1015, 501 NYS2d 290 (1986) §14.07

Perkis v Northeastern Log Homes, 808 SW2d 809 (Ky 1991) §11.07

Perlmutter v Flickinger, 520 P2d 596 (Colo Ct App 1974) §15.07, **app A, app B**

Persichilli v Triborough Bridge & Tunnel Auth, 21 AD2d 819, 251 NYS2d 733 (1964), *modified*, 16 NY2d 136, 209 NE2d 802, 262 NYS2d 476 (1965) **§9.23, app B**

Peteet v Fogarty, 297 SC 226, 375 SE2d 527 (1988) §5.01

Petersen v Rawson, 34 NY 370 (1866), *revd*, 15 NY Sup Ct 234 (1857) **§1.07, app A, app B**

Peterson v Fowler, 27 Utah 2d 159, 493 P2d 997 (1972) **§9.25, app A, app B**

Pettigrew v Home Ins Co, 191 Neb 312, 214 NW2d 920 (1974) **§§4.06, 9.32, app B**

Peyronnin Constr Co v Weiss, 137 Ind App 417, 208 NE2d 489 (1965) **§§9.02, 9.15, app A, app B**

Phillips v ABC Builders, Inc, 611 P2d 821 (Wyo 1980), *affd*, 632 P2d 925 (Wyo 1981) §11.08

Pickard & Anderson v Young Men's Christian Assn, 119 AD2d 976, 500 NYS2d 874 (1986) §5.04

Pieri v Rosebrook, 128 Cal App 2d 250, 275 P2d 67 (1954) **§§5.07, 5.12**

Pierson v Tyndall, 28 SW 232 (Tex Civ App 1894) **§§1.15, 4.01, 9.10, 9.20, app A, app B**

Pinneo v Stevens Pass, Inc, 14 Wash App 848, 545 P2d 1207, *review denied*, 87 Wash 2d 1006 (1976) **§11.09, app B**

Pipe Welding Supply Co v Haskell, Conner & Frost, 61 NY2d 884, 462 NE2d 1190, 474 NYS2d 472 (1984) §5.07

Piracci Constr Co v Skidmore, Owings & Merrill, 490 F Supp 314 (SDNY), *affd*, 646 F2d 562 (2d Cir 1980) **§§2.05, 11.03, 11.11, app B**

Pitcher v Lennon, 12 AD 356, 42 NYS 156 (1896) **§3.03, app A, app B**

Pittman Constr Co v City of New Orleans, 178 So 2d 312 (La Ct App), *appeal denied*, 248 La 434, 179 So 2d 274 (1965) **§§1.04, 1.07, 1.19, 9.14, app A, app B**

Plant v R.L. Reid, Inc, 365 So 2d 305 (Ala 1978) **§1.07, app A**

Podraza v H.H. Hall Constr Co, 50 Ill App 3d 643, 365 NE2d 944 (1977) **§§4.07, 9.13, 9.15, app B**

Pokora v Wabash Ry, 292 US 98 (1934) §1.06

Pollock v Hafner, 108 Ill App 3d 410, 439 NE2d 85 (1982) **§11.06, app B**

Polycon Indus v Hercules, Inc, 471 F Supp 1316 (ED Wis 1979) §6.04

Ponce de Leon Condos v DiGirolamo, 238 Ga 188, 232 SE2d 62 (1977) **§1.19, app A, app B**

Porter v Stevens, Thompson & Runyan, Inc, 24 Wash App 624, 602 P2d 1192 (1979), *review denied*, 93 Wash 2d 1010 (1980) **§§4.03, 4.04, 9.23, app B**

Potter v Gilbert, 130 AD 632, 115 NYS 425, *affd*, 196 NY 576, 90 NE 1165 (1909) **§1.22, 9.42, app A, app B**

Presidents & Directors of Georgetown College v Madden, 660 F2d 91 (4th Cir 1981) **§11.09, app B**

Prichard Bros v Grady Co, 436 NW2d 460 (Minn Ct App 1989), *review denied* (May 2, 1989) **§§1.19, 8.03**

Prier v Refrigeration Engg Co, 74 Wash 2d 25, 442 P2d 621 (1968) **§§6.03, 10.03, 10.06, app A, app B**

Pugh v Butler Tel Co, 512 So 2d 1317 (Ala 1987) §9.22
Pyramid Condo Assn v Morgan, 606 F Supp 592 (D Md 1985), affd, 823 F2d 548 (4th Cir 1987) §§12.06, 12.08
Pytko v State, 28 Conn Supp 173, 255 A2d 640 (1969) §14.02

Q

Quagliana v Exquisite Home Builders, Inc, 538 P2d 301 (Utah 1975) app A, app B
Quail Hollow East Condominium Assn v Donald J. Scholz Co, 47 NC App 518, 268 SE2d 12 (1975), review denied, 301 NC 527, 273 SE2d 454 (1980) §§1.18, 1.23
Queensbury Union Free Sch Dist v Jim Walter Corp, 91 Misc 2d 804, 398 NYS2d 832 (Sup Ct 1977) §§6.03, 6.07

R

Rabe v Carnaby, 120 NH 809, 423 A2d 610 (1980) §9.18, app B
RA Civitello Co v City of New Haven, 6 Conn App 212, 504 A2d 542 (1986) §11.02
Raffel v Perley, 14 Mass App 242, 437 NE2d 1082 (1982) §§6.03, 11.10
Ragland v Clarson, 259 So 2d 757 (Fla Dist Ct App 1972) §§2.06, 10.05, app A, app B
Ralph M. Parsons Co v Combustion Equip Assocs, 172 Cal App 3d 211, 218 Cal Rptr 170 (1985) §9.28
Ramos v Shumavon, 21 AD2d 4, 247 NYS2d 699, affd, 15 NY2d 610, 203 NE2d 912, 255 NYS2d 658 (1964) §4.03, app A, app B
Ransburg v Haase, 224 Ill App 3d 681, 586 NE2d 1295 (1992), rehg denied, (Mar 10, 1992) §3.02
Ray v Transamerica Ins Co, 10 Mich App 55, 158 NW2d 786 (1968) §4.06, app B
Reber v Chandler High Sch Dist No 202, 13 Ariz App 133, 474 P2d 852 (1970) §§1.22, 3.01, 9.11, 9.25, app A, app B
Reeves v Ille Elec Co, 170 Mont 104, 551 P2d 647 (1976) §11.08, app B
Regency Wood Condo, Inc v Dessent, Hammach & Ruckman, Inc, 405 So 2d 440 (Fla Dist Ct App 1981) §11.03
Reich v Jesco, Inc, 526 So 2d 550 (Miss 1988) §11.08
Reighard v Downs, 261 Md 26, 273 A2d 109 (1971), appeal after remand, 265 Md 344, 289 A2d 299 (1972) §§1.16, 10.04, app A, app B
Reiman Constr Co v Jerry Hiller Co, 709 P2d 1271 (Wyo 1985) §9.11, app B
Ressler v Nielsen, 76 NW2d 157 (ND 1956) §§1.04, 9.12, 9.28
R.G. Wood & Assocs Ltd, 85-1 BCA (CCH) [0014]17,898 (1985) §1.19, app B
R.H. Macy & Co v Williams Tile & Terrazzo Co, 585 F Supp 175 (ND Ga 1984) §§9.02, 9.05, 12.06, app A
Rhodes v Mill Race Inn, Inc, 126 Ill App 3d 1024, 467 NE2d 915 (1984), appeal denied (Jan Term 1985) §§3.06, 6.07, app A, app B
R.H. Sanbar Projects, Inc v Gruzen Partnership, 148 AD2d 316, 538 NYS2d 532 (1989) §8.01

Rian v Imperial Mun Servs Group, Inc, 768 P2d 1260 (Colo Ct App 1988) §4.04

Riblet Tramway Co v Ericksen Assocs, 665 F Supp 81 (DNH 1987) §2.04

Rice v Caldwell, 87 Ind App 616, 161 NE 651 (1928) §§2.01, 2.02, 2.03, app A

Richards & Assocs v Boney, 604 F Supp 1214 (EDNC 1985) §§1.01, 1.20

Rigsby v Brighton Engg Co, 464 SW2d 279 (Ky 1970) §§1.23, 3.03, 9.36, 9.42, app A

Robert & Co Assocs v Rhodes-Haverty Partnership, 250 Ga 680, 300 SE2d 503 (1983) §1.13

Robert R. Jones Assocs v Nino Homes, 858 F2d 274 (6th Cir 1988), *rehg denied* (Nov 7, 1988) §3.08

Roberts v Karr, 178 Cal App 2d 535, 3 Cal Rptr 98 (1960) §§1.13, 4.01, 10.07, app A, app B

Robertson v Swindell-Dressler Co, 82 Mich App 382, 267 NW2d 131 (1978) §§12.02, 12.04

Robertson Lumber Co v Stephen Farmers Co-op Elevator Co, 274 Minn 17, 143 NW2d 622 (1966) §6.03, app B

Robinson v Warner, 370 F Supp 828 (DRI 1974) §14.06

Robinson Redevelopment Co v Anderson, 155 AD2d 755, 547 NYS2d 458 (1989) §§1.14, 4.03

Robitscher v United Clay Prods Co, 143 A2d 99 (DC 1958) §9.02, app A, app B

Robsol, Inc v Garris, 358 So 2d 865 (Fla Dist Ct App 1978) app B

Roland A. Wilson & Assocs v Forty-O-Four Grand Corp, 246 NW2d 922 (Iowa 1976) §§4.04, 10.01, app B

Rose v Shearrer, 431 SW2d 939 (Tex Civ App 1968) §§5.05, 5.17

Rosell v Silver Crest Enter, 7 Ariz App 137, 436 P2d 915 (1968) §4.02, app A, app B

Rosenberg v Town of North Bergen, 61 NJ 190, 293 A2d 662 (1972) §11.09

Rosenthal v Kurtz, 62 Wis 2d 1, 213 NW2d 741, *rehg denied*, 62 Wis 2d 1, 216 NW2d 252 (1974) §11.09

Rosos Litho Supply Corp v Hansen, 123 Ill App 3d 290, 462 NE2d 566 (1984) §§1.13, 7.03, 10.03, 10.08, 15.07, app B

Rotwein v General Accident Group, 103 NJ Super 406, 247 A2d 370 (1968) §13.10

Rowell v Crow, 93 Cal App 2d 500, 209 P2d 149 (1949) §5.17

Rozny v Marnal, 43 Ill 2d 54, 250 NE2d 656 (1969) §§1.13, 9.04, 10.10, 11.06, app A, app B

Rusch v Lincoln-Devore Testing Lab, Inc, 698 P2d 832 (Colo Ct App 1984) §6.03, app B

Russell v Community Hosp Assn, 199 Kan 251, 428 P2d 783 (1967) §§1.23, 12.05, 12.07, app A, app B

Russell v GAF Corp, 422 A2d 989 (DC 1980) §1.10

Ryan v Morgan Spear Assocs, 546 SW2d 678 (Tex Civ App 1977) §1.09, 6.03

S

St John Pub Sch Dist v Engrs-Architects PC, 414 NW2d 285 (ND 1987) §9.22

St Joseph Hosp v Corbetta Constr Co, 21 Ill App 3d 925, 316 NE2d 51 (1974) §§3.03, 12.02, 12.03, app B

St Paul Fire & Marine Ins Co v United States Natl Bank, 251 Or 377, 446 P2d 103 (1968) §§12.02, 12.03, app A, app B

Salem Sand & Gravel Co v City of Salem, 260 Or 630, 492 P2d 271 (1971) §§2.01, 9.36, 11.06, app A, app B

Salley v Charles R. Perry Constr, Inc, 403 So 2d 556 (Fla Dist Ct App 1981) §12.08

Salt River Valley Water Users Assn v Giglio, 113 Ariz 190, 549 P2d 162 (1976) §12.05, app B

Sams v Kendall Constr Co, 499 So 2d 370 (La Ct App 1986) §1.19

Samuel N. Zarpas, Inc v Morrow, 215 F Supp 887 (DNJ 1963) §13.09

Sandy v Superior Court (Daon Corp), 201 Cal App 3d 1277, 247 Cal Rptr 677 (1988) §11.09

San Francisco, City of v Superior Court (City & County of San Francisco), 37 Cal 2d 227, 237, 231 P2d 26, 31 (1951) §15.07

San Juan Dupont Plaza Hotel Fire Litigation, *In re*, 687 F Supp 716 (DPR 1988) §11.08

San Pedro Properties, Inc v Sayre & Toso, Inc, 203 Cal App 2d 750, 21 Cal Rptr 844 (1962) §13.08

Santucci Constr Co v Baxter & Woodman, Inc, 151 Ill App 3d 547, 502 NE2d 1134 (1986), *appeal denied*, 115 Ill 2d 550, 511 NE2d 437 (1987) §§2.05, 4.05, 10.10

Sard v Berman, 47 AD2d 892, 367 NYS2d 266 (1975) §10.07, app A

Sargent v Johnson, 601 F2d 964 (8th Cir 1979) §12.03

Sarton v Superior Court (Marin County), 136 Cal App 3d 322, 187 Cal Rptr 247 (1982) §14.06

S. Blickman, Inc v Chilton, 114 SW2d 646 (Tex Civ App 1938) §§8.01, 8.02, app B

Scavone v State Univ Constr Fund, 46 AD2d 895, 362 NYS2d 22 (1974) §9.23, app A, app B

Schenburn v Lehner Assocs, 22 Mich App 534, 177 NW2d 699 (1970) §§7.02, 7.03, 11.02

Schiavone Constr Co v Nassau County, 717 F2d 747 (2d Cir 1983) §12.02

Schiltz v Cullen-Schiltz & Assocs, 228 NW2d 10 (Iowa 1975) §9.15

Schipper v Levitt & Sons, 44 NJ 70, 207 A2d 314 (1965) §§1.23, 6.05, 6.07, 9.07, app A, app B

Schlitz v Cullen-Schiltz & Assocs, 228 NW2d 10 (Iowa 1975) §§1.20, 10.03, app B

School Bd v G.A.F. Corp, 413 So 2d 1208 (Fla Dist Ct App 1982), *opinion quashed by* Kelley v School Bd, 435 So 2d 804 (Fla 1983) §11.11, app B

School Dist No 5 v Ferrier, 122 Kan 15, 251 P 425 (1926) §2.01, app A

School Dist No 11 v Sverdrup, Parcel & Assoc, 797 F2d 651 (8th Cir 1986) §§1.19, 10.01

School Dist No 172 v Josenhans, 88 Wash 624, 153 P 326 (1915) §10.02, app A, app B

Schreiner v Miller, 67 Iowa 91, 24 NW 738 (1885) §1.14, app A, app B

Schwartz v Kuhn, 71 Misc 149, 126 NYS 568 (Sup Ct 1911) §§9.21, 10.03, app A

Schwender v Schraft, 246 Mass 149, 141 NE 511 (1923) §5.12

Scott v Potomac Ins Co, 217 Or 323, 341 P2d 1083 (1959) §§8.01, 8.05, 13.11, app B

Scribante v Edwards, 40 Cal App 561, 181 P 75 (1919) §8.02, app B

Seaman v Castellini, 415 SW2d 612 (Ky 1967) §1.20, app A

Seaman Unified Sch Dist No 345 v Casson Constr Co, 3 Kan App 2d 289, 594 P2d 241 (1979) §§1.19, 15.07, app B

Sears Roebuck & Co v Enco Assocs, 43 NY2d 389, 372 NE2d 555, 401 NYS2d 767 (1977) §§11.02, 11.04, app B

Seattle Western Indus v David A. Mowat Co, 110 Wash 2d 1, 750 P2d 245 (1988) §§1.25, 9.37, 10.10

Securities-Intermountain, Inc v Sunset Fuel Co, 289 Or 243, 611 P2d 1158 (1980) §11.02

Seeney v Dover Country Club Apartments, Inc, 318 A2d 619 (Del Super 1974) §§1.10, 9.23, 9.25, app A, app B

Seese v Volkswagenwerk AG, 648 F2d 833 (3d Cir), *cert denied*, 454 US 867 (1981) §15.07, app A

Segall Co v W.D. Glassell Co, 401 So 2d 483 (La Ct App 1981) §9.18, app B

Seger v Cornwell, 44 Misc 2d 994, 255 NYS2d 744 (Sup Ct 1964) §11.03, app A, app B

Seiler v Levitz Furniture Co, 367 A2d 999 (Del Super Ct 1976) §§1.19, 10.03, app A

Seiler v Ostarly, 525 So 2d 1207 (La Ct App 1988) §1.03

Senior Housing, Inc v Nakawatase, Rutkowski, Wyns & Yi, Inc, 192 Ill App 3d 766, 549 NE2d 604 (1989) §11.01

Sensenbrenner v Rust, Orling & Neals Architects, Inc, 236 Va 419, 374 SE2d 55 (1988) §10.10, app B

Sevilla v Stearns-Roger, Inc, 101 Cal App 3d 608, 161 Cal Rptr 700 (1980) §11.10

Shapiro v Board of Regents, 29 AD2d 801, 286 NYS2d 1001 (1968) §3.02

Shaver v Continental Casualty Co, 210 Kan 189, 499 P2d 513 (1972) §§13.13, 13.15

Shaw, *In re*, 189 Mont 310, 615 P2d 910 (1980) §§2.01, 3.02, app B

Shaw v Aetna Casualty & Sur Co, 407 F2d 813 (7th Cir 1969) §§13.03, 13.07

Shea v Bay State Gas Co, 383 Mass 218, 418 NE2d 597 (1981) §12.02

Shepard Components, Inc v Brice Petrides-Donohue & Assocs, 473 NW2d 612 (Iowa 1991) §1.08, app B

Shepherd v City of Palatka, 399 So 2d 1044 (Fla Dist Ct App 1981) §9.30, app B

Sheppard, Morgan & Schwaab, Inc v United States Fidelity & Guar Co, 44 Ill App 3d 481, 358 NE2d 305 (1976) §§13.02, 13.03, 13.07

Sherman v Miller Constr Co, 90 Ind App 462, 158 NE 255 (1927) §§1.23, 9.06, app B

Sherwood v Omega Constr Co, 657 F Supp 345 (SDNY 1987) §9.23

Shibuya v Architects Hawaii, Ltd, 65 Haw 26, 647 P2d 276 (1982) §11.10, app B

Shoffner Indus v W.B. Lloyd Constr Co, 42 NC App 259, 257 SE2d 50, *review denied*, 298 NC 296, 259 SE2d 301 (1979) app A

Shurpin v Elmhirst, 148 Cal App 3d 94, 195 Cal Rptr 737 (1983) §§1.26, 2.01, 4.05, app A

Simon v Omaha Pub Power Dist, 189 Neb 183, 202 NW2d 157 (1972) §§4.05, 4.06, 9.04, app A, app B

Simoniz v J. Emil Anderson & Sons, 81 Ill App 2d 428, 225 NE2d 161 (1967) §11.06

Simpson Bros Corp v Merrimac Chem Co, 248 Mass 346, 142 NE 922 (1924) §§1.20, 9.21, app A, app B

65th Center, Inc v Copeland, 825 SW2d 574 (Ark 1992) §11.01

Skidmore, Owings & Merrill v Connecticut Gen Life Ins Co, 25 Conn Supp 76, 197 A2d 83 (1963) §§11.02, 11.12, 14.10, app B

Skidmore, Owings & Merrill v Volpe Constr Co, 511 So 2d 642 (Fla Dist Ct App 1987), *review denied*, 520 So 2d 586 (Fla 1988) §12.02

Skinner v Anderson, 38 Ill 2d 455, 231 NE2d 588 (1967) §11.10, app B

Skinner v F.G.M., Inc, 166 Ill App 3d 802, 502 NE2d 1024, *appeal denied*, 122 Ill 2d 593, 530 NE2d 263 (1988) §10.10

Skinner v Graham, 170 Ill App 3d 417, 524 NE2d 642 (1988) §§10.10, 11.06

S.K. Whitty & Co v Laurence L. Lambert & Assocs, 576 So 2d 599, 601 (La Ct App), *writ denied*, 580 So 2d 928 (La 1991) §9.30

Smith v City of Detroit, 388 Mich 637, 202 NW2d 300 (1972) §9.04

Smith v Dickey, 74 Tex 71, 11 SW 1049 (1889) §5.09

Smith v Goff, 325 P2d 1061 (Okla 1958) §5.10

Smith v Milwaukee Builders & Traders Exch, 91 Wis 360, 64 NW 1041 (1895) §8.03, app B

Smithhart v AAA Contracting Co, 260 So 2d 8 (La Ct App), *rehg denied*, 261 La 1051, 262 So 2d 38 (1972) §4.06

Snell v Stein, 201 So 2d 876 (La Ct App), *writ refused*, 251 La 35, 202 So 2d 652 (La 1967) §9.35, app B

Society of Mt Carmel v Fox, 90 Ill App 3d 537, 413 NE2d 480 (1980) §11.06, app B

Soriano v Hunton, Shivers, Brady & Assocs, 524 So 2d 488 (Fla Dist Ct App), *review denied*, 534 So 2d 399 (Fla 1988) §§8.05, 12.01

Sosnow v Paul, 43 AD2d 978, 352 NYS2d 502 (1974), *affd*, 36 NY2d 780, 330 NE2d 643, 369 NYS2d 693 (1975) §§11.03, 11.04, app B

South Burlington Sch Dist v Goodrich, 135 Vt 601, 382 A2d 220 (1977) §§11.02, 11.03, app B

South Dakota Bldg Auth v Geiger-Berger Assocs PC, 414 NW2d 15 (SD 1987) §12.07

Southeast Consultants, Inc v O'Pry, 199 Ga App 125, 404 SE2d 299 (1991), *cert denied* (May 15, 1991) §§1.25, 9.05, app B

South Union Ltd v George Parker & Assocs AIA, 29 Ohio App 3d 197, 504 NE2d 1131 (1985) §§8.02, 10.03

Spainhour v B. Aubrey Huffman & Assocs, 237 Va 340, 377 SE2d 615 (1989) §1.03

Spielvogel v Merrill, Lynch, Pierce, Fenner & Smith, Inc, 127 AD2d 532, 512 NYS2d 75 (1987) §1.01

Spitz v Brickhouse, 3 Ill App 2d 536, 123 NE2d 117 (1954) §§5.08, 5.17

Spurgeon v Buchter, 192 Cal App 2d 198, 13 Cal Rptr 354 (1961) §5.05

Staley v New, 56 NM 756, 250 P2d 893 (1952) §§6.03, 9.02, app A, app B

Standhardt v Flintkote Co, 84 NM 796, 508 P2d 1283 (1973) §§1.10, 12.08

State v Campbell, 217 Kan 756, 539 P2d 329, *cert denied*, 423 US 1017 (1975) §2.02, app B

State v Gatham-Matotan Architects, 98 NM 790, 653 P2d 166 (1982) §6.03, app B

State v Ireland, 126 NJL 444, 20 A2d 69 (1941) §11.05, app A, app B

State v Robert E. McKee, Inc, 584 So 2d 1205 (La Ct App 1991) §11.02

State v Wilco Constr Co, 393 So 2d 885 (La Ct App), *writ denied*, 400 So 2d 905 (La 1981) §3.03, app B

State Bd of Registration v Rogers, 239 Miss 35, 120 So 2d 772 (1960) §§8.05, 9.39

State Department of Human Resources v Williams, 12 Or App 133, 505 P2d 936 (1973) §14.02

State *ex rel* Love v Howell, 281 SC 463, 316 SE2d 381 (1984) §3.02

State *ex rel* Love v Howell, 285 SC 53, 328 SE2d 77 (1985) §3.02

State *ex rel* State Community College Bd v Sergent, Hauskins & Beckwith, Inc, 27 Ariz App 469, 556 P2d 23 (1976) §11.02

State Farm Fire & Casualty Co v All Elec, Inc, 99 Nev 222, 660 P2d 995 (1983) §11.10

State Univ Constr Fund v United Technology Corp, 78 AD2d 748, 432 NYS2d 653 (1980) app B

Steiner v Wenning, 43 NY2d 831, 373 NE2d 366, 402 NYS2d 567 (1977) §11.02

Stein, Hinkle, Dawe & Assocs v Continental Casualty Co, 110 Mich App 410, 313 NW2d 299 (1981) §13.09

Stephens v Sterns, 106 Idaho 249, 678 P2d 41 (1984) §§1.23, 11.02, app A, app B

Sterns-Roger Corp v Hartford Accident & Indem Co, 117 Ariz 162, 571 P2d 659 (1977) §13.02

Stevens v Fanning, 59 Ill App 2d 285, 207 NE2d 136 (1965) §§5.08, 5.11, 5.17

Stilson v Moulton-Niguel Water Dist, 21 Cal App 3d 928, 98 Cal Rptr 914 (1971) §1.12, app A, app B

Stine v Continental Casualty Co, 419 Mich 89, 349 NW2d 127 (1984) §13.08

Stine v Continental Casualty Co, 112 Mich App 174, 315 NW2d 887 (1982) §13.09

Straus v Buchman, 96 AD 270, 89 NYS 226 (1904), *affd*, 184 NY 545, 76 NE 1109 (1906) §§1.09, 3.03, 4.01, app A, app B

Strauss Veal Feeds, Inc v Mead & Hunt, Inc, 538 NE2d 299, 303 (Ind Ct App 1989), *transfer denied* (Feb 8, 1990) §1.03

Stromberg's v Victor Gruen & Assocs, 384 F2d 163 (10th Cir 1967) app A, app B

Strouth v Wilkison, 302 Minn 297, 224 NW2d 511 (1974) §§2.01, 5.04, 10.07, app A, app B

Stuart v Crestview Mut Water Co, 34 Cal App 3d 802, 110 Cal Rptr 543 (1973) §§1.20, 6.07, app A, app B

Sub-Surface Constr Co v Bryant-Curington, Inc, 533 SW2d 452 (Tex Civ App 1976) app A, app B

Sullivan County v Edward L. Nezelek, Inc, 42 NY2d 123, 366 NE2d 72, 397 NYS2d 371 (1977) §14.06

Surf Realty Corp v Standing, 195 Va 431, 78 SE2d 901 (1953) §§1.08, 4.01, 9.12, app A, app B

Swarthout v Beard, 33 Mich App 395, 190 NW2d 373 (1971), *revd as to damages by*, Smith v City of Detroit, 388 Mich 637, 202 NW2d 300 (1972) §§1.22, 9.04, app A, app B

Swartz v Ford, Bacon & Davis Constr Corp, 469 So 2d 232 (Fla Dist Ct App 1985) §9.25, app B

Swett v Gribaldo, Jones & Assocs, 40 Cal App 3d 573, 115 Cal Rptr 99 (1974) §§1.20, 1.21, 6.02, 6.07, 9.12, app A, app B

T

Tamarac Dev Co v Delameter, Freund & Assocs PA, 234 Kan 618, 675 P2d 361 (1984) §§1.15, 6.03

Tamblyn v Mickey & Fox, Inc, 195 Colo 354, 578 P2d 641 (1978) §11.02

Tampa Elec Co v Stone & Webster Engg Corp, 367 F Supp 27 (MD Fla 1973) §13.03

Taylor, Thon, Thompson & Peterson v Cannaday, 230 Mont 151, 749 P2d 63 (1988) §§1.03, 3.03

Teachers Credit Union v Horner, 487 F Supp 246 (WD Mo 1980) §9.41

Teitge v Remy Constr Co, 526 NE2d 1008, 1041 (Ind Ct App 1988) §1.09, app B

Telak v Maszczenski, 248 Md 476, 237 A2d 434 (1968) §3.06, app A, app B

Terry v New Mexico State Highway Commn, 98 NM 119, 645 P2d 1375 (1982) §11.10, app B

The TJ Hooper, 60 F2d 737 (2d Cir 1932) §1.06

Thomas v Fromherz Engrs, 159 So 2d 612 (La Ct App), *writ refused*, 245 La 799, 161 So 2d 276 (1964) §§9.23, 9.25, app B

Thomas E. Hoar, Inc v Jobco, Inc, 30 AD2d 541, 291 NYS2d 380 (1968) §9.19, app A

Thomas Haverty Co v Jones, 185 Cal 285, 197 P 105 (1921) §10.08

Three Affiliated Tribes of the Fort Berthold Reservation v Wold Engg PC, 419 NW2d 920 (ND 1988) §§1.09, 9.12, 9.13

Tiffany v Christman Co, 93 Mich App 267, 287 NW2d 199 (1979) §§12.08, 15.07, app B

Tirella v American Properties Team, Inc, 145 AD2d 724, 535 NYS2d 252 (1988) §1.19, app B

Tittle v Giattina, Fisher & Co Architects, Inc, 597 So 2d 679 (Ala 1992) §9.11

Tomberlin Assocs Architects, Inc v Free, 174 Ga App 167, 329 SE2d 296, *cert denied* (May 1, 1985) §§1.19, 2.06, 10.12, app B

Tool v Boutelle, 91 Misc 2d 464, 398 NYS2d 128 (Sup Ct 1977) §11.11, app B

Torres v Jarmon, 501 SW2d 369 (Tex Civ App 1973) §§5.14, 5.17

Totten v Gruzen, 52 NJ 202, 245 A2d 1 (1968) §§1.23, 9.06, 9.07, app A, app B

Trane Co v Gilbert, 267 Cal App 2d 720, 73 Cal Rptr 279 (1968) §§8.01, 8.02

Travelers Indem Co v Ewing, Cole, Erdman & Eubank, 711 F2d 14 (3d Cir 1983), *cert denied*, 464 US 104 (1984) §§1.08, 9.11, app A

Tri-City Constr Co v A.C. Kirkwood & Assocs, 738 SW2d 925 (Mo Ct App 1987) §§8.04, 9.37

Trinity Area Sch Dist v Dickson, 223 Pa Super 546, 302 A2d 481 (1973) §§1.14, 4.01, **app A, app B**

Troy & Stalder Co v Continental Casualty Co, 206 Neb 28, 290 NW2d 809 (1980) §13.08

Trulove, *In re*, 54 NC App 218, 282 SE2d 544 (1981), *review denied*, 304 NC 727, 288 SE2d 808 (1982) §3.02

Trunk & Gordon v Clark, 163 Iowa 620, 145 NW 277 (1914) §§1.17, 10.08, **app B**

Trus Joist Corp v Safeco Ins Co of Am, 153 Ariz 95, 735 P2d 125 (1986) §13.02

Trustees of Rowan Technical College v J. Hyatt Hammond Assocs, 313 NC 230, 328 SE2d 274 (1985) §11.02

Turner v Superior Court (Pima County), 3 Ariz App 414, 415 P2d 129 (1966) **§9.35, app B**

Turner, Collie & Braden, Inc v Brookhollow, Inc, 624 SW2d 203 (Tex Civ App 1981) §12.07

Turner Constr Co v Scales, 752 P2d 467 (Alaska 1988) §11.08

Twelker v Shannon & Wilson, Inc, 88 Wash 2d 473, 564 P2d 1131 (1977) §2.04

Twin Falls Clinic & Hosp Bldg v Hamill, 103 Idaho 19, 644 P2d 341 (1982) §11.08

2314 Lincoln Park West Condo Assn v Mann, Gin, Ebel & Frazier Ltd, 136 Ill 2d 302, 555 NE2d 346 (1990) §§7.03, 10.10

U

Uinta Pipeline Corp v White Superior Co, 546 P2d 885 (Utah 1976) §§1.06, 1.19, 4.01, **app A, app B**

U-Haul Co v Abrea & Robeson, Inc, 247 Ga 565, 277 SE 497 (1981) §11.03, **app B**

Ultramares Corp v Touche, 255 NY 170, 174 NE 441 (1931) §9.05

Umpqua River Navigation Co v Crescent City Harbor Dist, 618 F2d 588 (9th Cir 1980) §4.05

Union College v Kennerly, Slomanson & Smith, 167 NJ Super 311, 400 A2d 850 (1979) §§6.03, 6.04

Union Sch Dist No 20 v Lench, 134 Vt 424, 365 A2d 508 (1976) §11.06

United Gas Improvement Co v Larsen, 182 F 620 (CC Pa 1910) §§1.22, 9.25, **app A, app B**

United States v Burton, 580 F Supp 660 (ED Mich 1984) §§11.02, 12.09

United States v Peachy, 36 F 160 (DC Ohio 1888) §§1.07, 8.02, 9.12, **app A, app B**

United States v Rogers & Rogers, 161 F Supp 132 (SD Cal 1958) §§1.20, 7.03, **app A, app B**

United States v United States Fidelity & Guar Co, 601 F2d 1136 (10th Cir 1979) §§13.03, 13.07

United States Fidelity & Guar Co v Continental Casualty Co, 153 Ill App 3d 185, 505 NE2d 1072 (1987) §13.02

United States Fidelity & Guar Co v Jacksonville State Univ, 357 So 2d 952 (Ala 1978) §6.03, **app B**

United States Fin v Sullivan, 37 Cal App 3d 5, 112 Cal Rptr 18 (1974) §§1.21, 6.08, **app A, app B**

Unity Sheet Metal Works v Farrell Lines, 101 NYS2d 1000 (Sup Ct 1950) §§2.01, 9.10, **app A, app B**

Urania, Town of v M.P. Dumesnil Constr Co, 492 So 2d 888 (La Ct App 1986) §9.28

Urbandale, City of v
Frevert-Ramsey-Cobes,
Architects-Engrs, Inc, 435 NW2d
400 (Iowa Ct App 1988) §1.03
URS Co v Gulfport-Biloxi Regional
Airport Auth, 544 So 2d 824
(Miss 1989) §§1.24, 4.03
Utica, City of v Holt, 88 Misc 2d
206, 387 NYS2d 377 (Sup Ct
1976) §§11.02, 11.05, 12.05,
app B

V

Vaky v Phelps, 194 SW 601 (Tex
Civ App 1917), *error refused* (Nov
21, 1917) §5.09
Vandervoort v Levy, 396 So 2d 480
(La Ct App 1981) §8.02
Vandewater & Lapp v Sacks Builders,
Inc, 20 Misc 2d 677, 186 NYS2d
103 (Sup Ct 1959) §§4.05, 11.02,
app A, app B
Vannoy v City of Warren, 15 Mich
App 158, 166 NW2d 486 (1968)
§§8.01, 8.05, 9.23, app A, app B
Van Ornum v Otter Tail Power Co,
210 NW2d 188 (ND 1973)
§§6.07, 15.07
V.C. Edwards Contracting Co v Port
of Tacoma, 7 Wash App 883, 503
P2d 1133 (1972), *affd*, 83 Wash 2d
7, 514 P2d 1381 (1973) §9.18
Vee See Constr Co v Jensen &
Halstead, Ltd, 79 Ill App 3d 1084,
399 NE2d 278 (1979) §2.04
Verdex Steel & Constr Co v Board of
Supervisors, 19 Ariz App 547, 509
P2d 240 (1973) §14.06
Victor M. Solis Underground Util &
Paving Co v City of Laredo, 751
SW2d 532 (Tex Ct App 1988),
error denied (June 28, 1989) §2.04
Vivian v Examining Bd of Architects,
61 Wis 2d 627, 213 NW2d 359
(1974) §3.02

Voelz v Board of Engg Examiners, 37
Or App 113, 586 P2d 807 (1978),
review denied, 285 Or 479 (1979)
§3.02, app B
Vojak v Jensen, 161 NW2d 100
(Iowa 1968) §§2.04, 9.33, app A
Vonasek v Hirsch & Stevens, Inc, 6
Wis 2d 1, 221 NW2d 815 (1974)
§9.22, app A, app B
Vorndran v Wright, 367 So 2d 1070
(Fla Dist Ct App), *cert denied*, 378
So 2d 350 (Fla 1979) §§3.06, 9.23
Voss v Kingdon & Naven, Inc, 60 Ill
2d 520, 328 NE2d 297 (1975)
§3.05, app A, app B
VTN Consolidated, Inc v Northbrook
Ins Co, 92 Cal App 3d 888, 155
Cal Rptr 172 (1979) §13.09

W

Waddey v Davis, 149 Ga App 308,
254 SE2d 465 (1979) §11.04,
app B
Waggoner v W&W Steel Co, 657
P2d 147 (Okla 1982) §9.11
Wagner v Modulars by Design, Inc,
163 AD2d 676, 558 NYS2d 194
(1990) §1.19
Waldor Pump & Equipment Co v
Orr-Schelen-Mayeron & Assocs,
386 NW2d 375 (Minn Ct App
1986) §1.20
Walker v Wittenberg, Delony &
Davidson, Inc, 241 Ark 525, 412
SW2d 621 (1966) §9.22
Walnut Creek Aggregates Co v
Testing Engrs, Inc, 248 Cal App
2d 690, 56 Cal Rptr 700 (1967)
§1.20, app A, app B
Walsh v Gowing, 494 A2d 543 (RI
1985) §11.07
Walters v Kellam & Foley, 172 Ind
App 207, 360 NE2d 199 (1977)
§§1.22, 4.04, 9.22, 9.25, app B

Waterford Condo Assn v Dunbar Corp, 104 Ill App 3d 371, 432 NE2d 1009 (1982) §§2.01, 4.05, 6.03, 9.04, 11.06

Watson, Watson & Rutland, Architects, Inc v Montgomery County Board of Educ, 559 So 2d 168 (Ala 1990) §§1.19, 11.06

Watt v United States, 444 F Supp 1191 (DDC 1978) §8.02, app A, app B

Wausau Paper Mills Co v Charles T. Main, Inc, 789 F Supp 968 (WD Wis 1992) §1.18

Weill Constr Co v Thibodeaux, 491 So 2d 166 (La Ct App 1986) §1.03

Wells v City of Vancouver, 77 Wash 2d 800, 467 P2d 292 (1970) §1.07

Wells v Stanley J. Thill & Assocs, 153 Mont 28, 452 P2d 1015 (1969) §§1.11, 3.06, 9.25, app A, app B

Wellston Co v Sam N Hodges Jr & Co, 114 Ga App 424, 151 SE2d 481 (1966) §11.03, app A, app B

Wenatchee Wenoka Growers Assn v Krack Corp, 89 Wash 2d 847, 576 P2d 388 (1978) §12.05

Wenke v Amoco Chem Corp, 290 A2d 670 (Del Super Ct 1972) §12.04

Westerhold v Carroll, 419 SW2d 73 (Mo 1967) §§1.24, 4.03, 9.04, 9.10, app A, app B

Western Technologies, Inc v Neal, 159 Ariz 433, 768 P2d 165 (1988) §2.04

Western Technologies, Inc v Sverdrup & Parcel, Inc, 154 Ariz 1, 739 P2d 1318 (1986) §§2.04, 2.05

Westmount Intl Hotels, Inc v Sear-Brown Assocs Professional Corp, 65 NY2d 618, 480 NE2d 739, 491 NYS2d 150 (1985) §1.14

Weston v New Bethel Missionary Baptist Church, 23 Wash App 747, 598 P2d 411 (1978) §§1.07, 9.28, 12.01, app B

Wetzel v Roberts, 296 Mich 114, 295 NW 580 (1941) §§5.05, 5.17

Wetzler v O'Brien, 81 AD2d 517, 437 NYS2d 343 (1981) app B

Wheat Street Two, Inc v James C. Wise, Simpson, Aiken & Assocs, 132 Ga App 548, 208 SE2d 359 (1974) §§9.17, 9.28, app A, app B

Wheeler v Aetna Casualty & Sur Co, 57 Ill 2d 184, 311 NE2d 134 (1974) §13.03

Wheeler v Bucksteel Co, 73 Or App 495, 698 P2d 995, *review denied*, 299 Or 583, 704 P2d 513 (1985) §3.02

Wheeler v Fred Wright Constr Co, 57 Tenn App 77, 415 SW2d 156 (1966) §3.01, app A, app B

Wheeler & Lewis v Slifer, 195 Colo 291, 577 P2d 1092 (1978), *rehg denied* (May 15, 1978) §§4.04, 9.23, app A

White v Green, 82 SW 329 (Tex Civ App 1904) §§1.11, 8.03

White v Morris Handler Co, 7 Ill App 3d 199, 287 NE2d 203 (1972) §§9.32, 12.02, 12.04, app A, app B

White v Pallay, 119 Or 97, 247 P 316 (1926) §§1.08, 1.17, 9.12, app A, app B

White Budd Van Ness Partnership v Major-Gladys Drive Joint Venture, 798 SW2d 805 (Tex Ct App 1990), *cert denied*, 112 S Ct 180 (1991) §§6.03, 15.07

White Constr Co v Commonwealth, 81 Mass App 640, 418 NE2d 357 (1981) §9.30

Wicks v Milzoco Builders, Inc, 291 Pa Super 345, 435 A2d 1260 (1981), *vacated on other grounds*,

503 Pa 614, 470 A2d 86 (1983) §1.02, app A, app B
Widett v United States Fidelity & Guar Co, 815 F2d 885 (2d Cir 1987) §9.04
Wilder v Crook, 250 Ala 424, 34 So 2d 832 (1948) §§9.09, 9.10, app A, app B
William Dorsky Assocs v Highlands County Title & Guar Land Co, 528 So 2d 411 (Fla Dist Ct App 1988) §2.01
Williams Engg, Inc v Goodyear. 480 So 2d 772 (La Ct App 1985), *affd*, 496 So 2d 1012 (La 1986) §5.15
Willner v Woodward, 201 Va 104, 109 SE2d 132 (1959) §1.16, app A, app B
Wills v Black & West Architects, 344 P2d 581 (Okla 1959) §11.04, app A, app B
Winnsboro, Town of v Barnard & Burke, Inc, 294 So 2d 867 (La Ct App 1974) §§1.08, 4.01, app B
Winterbottom v Wright, 10 M&W 109, 152 Eng Rep 402 (1842) §§6.04, 7.01, 9.02, 9.16
Witherspoon v Sides Constr Co, 219 Neb 117, 362 NW2d 35 (1985) §11.07
Womack v Travelers Ins Co, 251 So 2d 463 (La Ct App 1971) §13.03, app B
Wood Bros Constr Co v Simons-Eastern Co, 193 Ga App 874, 389 SE2d 382 (1989), *cert denied* (Jan 25, 1990) §§1.18, 9.02
Woodsum v Pemberton Township, 177 NJ Super 639, 427 A2d 615 (1981) §9.35

Wright v State Bd of Engg Examiners, 250 NW2d 412 (Iowa 1977) app B
W. Wm Graham, Inc v City of Cave City, 289 Ark 105, 709 SW2d 94 (1986) §§4.01, 9.30, app B
Wynner v Buxton, 97 Cal App 3d 166, 158 Cal Rptr 587 (1979) §3.09, app B

Y

Yarbro v Hilton Hotels Corp, 655 P2d 822 (Colo 1982) §§3.02, 11.08, app B
Young v Eastern Engg & Elevator Co, 381 Pa Super 428, 554 A2d 77, *appeal denied*, 524 Pa 611, 569 A2d 1369 (1989) §9.11, app B
Yow v Hussey, Gay, Bell & Deyoung Intl, Inc, 201 Ga App 857, 412 SE2d 565 (1991), *rehg denied* (Nov 19, 1991) §4.01

Z

Zannoth v Booth Radio Stations, 333 Mich 233, 52 NW2d 678 (1952) §§5.03, 5.05, 5.06, 5.14, 5.17
Zontelli & Sons v City of Nashwauk, 373 NW2d 744 (Minn 1965) §§1.19, 12.07, app A
Zukowski v Howard, Needles, Tammen & Bergendoff, Inc, 657 F Supp 926 (D Colo 1987) §§4.05, 10.11

Statutes

Ala Code §6-5-101 §1.13
Ariz Rev Stat Ann §12-1512(a)(5) (1956) §14.06
Ariz Rev Stat Ann §32-142 (1976) §§9.11, 9.25
Ariz Rev Stat Ann §45-715 (1956) §9.35
Cal Bus & Prof Code §5537 (West 1974) §9.39
Cal Civ Code §2778(4) (West 1983) §13.13
Cal Civ Code §3479 §1.26
Cal Civ Proc Code §330(1) (West 1982) §11.02
Cal Civ Proc Code §337 §11.02
Cal Civ Proc Code §337(1)(a) (West 1982) §11.02
Cal Civ Proc Code §337.1 (West 1982) §11.10
Cal Civ Proc Code §337.15 (West 1982) §§11.02, 11.10, 12.09
Colo Rev Stat §13-21-111 (1973) §§9.14, 9.17
Colo Rev Stat §13-80-110 (1973) §§11.02, 11.06
Colo Rev Stat §13-80-127 (1973) §§11.02, 11.10
Conn Gen Stat §52-417 §9.09
Conn Gen Stat §52-584 §11.02
Conn Gen Stat Ann §52-417 §14.01
Del Code Ann tit 6 §2704(a) §12.04
Del Code Ann tit 10, §8106 (1975) §11.03
Fla Stat Ann §95.11 (West 1980) §11.08
Fla Stat Ann §95.11(3)(c) (1975) §11.10
Fla Stat Ann §472.14 (West) §10.05
Fla Stat Ann §725.06 §12.04
Ga Code Ann §3-706 §11.04
Ga Code Ann §51-1-11 (Harrison 1981) §§9.02, 9.05, 12.06
Ga Code Ann §56-408-1 (1963) §§9.37, 13.12
Ga Code Ann §84-2121 (1976) §9.18
Ill Rev Stat ch 10, §101 *et seq* (1981) §14.01
Ill Rev Stat ch 48, 69 (1971) §9.23
Ill Rev Stat ch 48 (1977) §9.05
Ill Rev Stat ch 48, para 60 (1979) §9.23
Ill Rev Stat ch 111 1/2, §3101 *et seq* (1972) §6.07
Ind Code Ann §§20-301 to -307 (Burns 1950) §8.03
La Rev Stat Ann §9:2772 (West 1964) §11.08
Mass Gen L ch 260, §2 B amended 1973 Stat ch 777, §2 §11.02

Mich Comp Laws Ann §691.991 §§**12.02, 12.04**
Mich Stat Ann §26.1146(1) §§**12.02, 12.04**
Mich Stat Ann §893.155 §**11.09**
Miss Code Ann §15-1-41 (1972) §**11.09**
NC Const, art 1, §19 §**11.09**
Nev Rev Stat §11.205 (1979) §**11.10**
NJ Stat Ann §2A:14-11 (West 1952) §**11.03**
NJ Stat Ann §§2A:84A-1 to -20 (West) §**15.07**
NY Civ Prac Law §214(4) (1978) §§**2.05, 11.03**
NY Civ Prac Law §7502(b) §**11.11**
NY Lab Law §241 §**9.06**
Or Rev Stat §12.110(1) §**11.06**
Or Rev Stat §33.240 (1976) §**14.02**
SD Codified Laws Ann §56-3-16 (1980) §**12.02**
SD Comp Laws Ann §15-2-9 (1967) §**11.08**
US Const, amend XIV §**11.09**
Va Code Ann §8.01-223 §**7.03**
Wash Rev Code §4.22.010 §**12.05**
Wis Stat §101.11(1) §**9.23**
Wis Stat Ann §893.19(5) §**11.03**
Wis Stat Ann §101.01(2)(b)-(d) (West) §**9.05**

Index

A

ABANDONED PROJECT
Estimate liability §5.10
ACCRUAL, NEGLIGENT ACT
Limitations. See LIMITATIONS
ACTIVE NEGLIGENCE, NONFEASANCE IS
Indemnity §12.08
ACTIVE/PASSIVE
Indemnity §§12.07, 12.08
ACTIVE/PASSIVE DISTINCTION
Indemnity §12.06
ACTIVE/PASSIVE, EARLY DEVELOPMENT
Indemnity §12.06
ACTUAL KNOWLEDGE
Agency liability §8.02
AGENCY
Liability arising from contract §4.07
AGENCY DEFENSE
Intentional torts §2.05
AGENCY LIABILITY
Generally §8.01
Agency relationship as defense to architect §8.04
Liability for acts of consultant §8.05

AGENCY LIABILITY, *continued*
Liability of partnerships and corporations §8.06
Owner bound by acts or knowledge of agent §8.02
Owner not bound by acts of architect §8.03
AGENCY RELATIONSHIP
Agency liability §8.01
AGENCY RELATIONSHIP AS DEFENSE TO ARCHITECT
Agency liability §8.04
AGENT, DELEGATION OF DUTIES OF
Agency liability §8.01
AGENT FOR DESIGN
Agency liability §8.02
AGENT FOR TRANSACTION
Agency liability §8.03
AGENT, LIABILITY FOR ACTS OF
Agency liability §8.01
AGENT, LIMITATION ON AUTHORITY OF
Agency liability §8.02
AGENT VERSUS INDEPENDENT CONTRACTOR
Agency liability §8.01

AMBIGUOUS CLAUSE
Indemnity §12.02
AMERICAN ARBITRATION ASSOCIATION (AAA)
Arbitration §14.03
AMERICAN ARBITRATION ASSOCIATION (AAA) FEES
Arbitration §14.10
ANTI-CONSOLIDATION CLAUSE
Arbitration §14.05
APPEALS
Arbitration §14.10
APPLICABLE PERIOD
Limitations §11.02
APPLICATION CRITICIZED
Warranty law §6.09
ARBITRATION
Generally §14.01
Arbitration, conditions precedent to §14.04
Arbitration, considerations in selecting §14.10
Arbitration hearing, conduct of §14.09
Arbitration, right to compel §14.02
Arbitrator, selection of §14.08
Award, enforcement of §14.12
Award, vacation of §14.13
Limitations §11.12
Mediation §14.11
Multiple parties
–generally §14.05
–joinder and consolidation §14.06
–vouching in §14.07
Waivers §14.03
ARBITRATION AGREEMENTS UNENFORCEABLE
Arbitration §14.02
ARBITRATION, CONDITIONS PRECEDENT TO
Arbitration §14.04
ARBITRATION, CONSIDERATIONS IN SELECTING
Arbitration §14.10

ARBITRATION HEARING, CONDUCT OF
Arbitration §14.09
ARBITRATION, RIGHT TO COMPEL
Arbitration §14.02
ARBITRATOR, NOT AGENT
Agency liability §8.03
ARBITRATOR, SELECTION OF
Arbitration §14.08
ARCHITECT ACTIVELY NEGLIGENT
Indemnity §12.08
ARCHITECT AS ARBITRATOR
Arbitration §14.01
ARCHITECT INDEMNIFYING OWNER
Indemnity §12.02
ARCHITECT LIABLE
Negligence liability §1.09
ARCHITECT, NO INDEMNITY FOR
Indemnity §12.02
ARCHITECT NOT LIABLE TO LENDER
Negligence liability §1.21
ARCHITECTS
Warranty law §6.07
ARCHITECT'S DUTY
Negligence liability §1.08
ARCHITECT'S LACK OF AUTHORITY
Liability arising from contract §4.07
ARCHITECT VERSUS STATE
Arbitration §14.02
ARCHITECT VERSUS SUPPLIER
Indemnity §12.08
ATTORNEY-CLIENT PRIVILEGE
Trial and hearing techniques §15.07

INDEX

ATTORNEYS AND ATTORNEYS FEES
Arbitration §14.10
Indemnity §12.02

ATTORNEY WORK PRODUCT
Trial and hearing techniques §15.07

AUTO ACCIDENT
Limitations §11.07

AWARD, ENFORCEMENT OF
Arbitration §14.12

AWARD, PROPOSED
Trial and hearing techniques §15.10

AWARD, VACATION OF
Arbitration §14.13

B

BAD FAITH
Insurance §13.02
Intentional torts §2.07

BENEFIT-OF-THE-BARGAIN DAMAGES
Estimate liability §5.15

BENEFIT-OF-THE-BARGAIN DAMAGES INAPPLICABLE
Warranty law §6.03

BETTERMENT
Damages §10.03

BODILY INJURY
Limitations §§11.02, 11.07

BONDHOLDERS
Negligence liability §1.25

BOX SCORE
Limitations §11.08

BREACH OF CONTRACT
Estimate liability §5.05
Liability arising from contract §4.01
Negligence liability §1.16

BREACH OF CONTRACT ENFORCED
Insurance §13.02

BREACH OF CONTRACT, INTENTIONAL
Estimate liability §5.05

BROAD CONSTRUCTION
Indemnity §12.03

BROAD SCOPE
Arbitration §14.02

BUDGET, DUTY TO ESTABLISH
Estimate liability §5.03

BUDGET ESTABLISHED BY LAW
Estimate liability §5.03

BUDGET NOT ESTABLISHED
Estimate liability §5.03

BUILDERS RISK
Insurance §13.04

BUILDING CODE, COMPLIANCE FAILURE
Statutory liability §3.03

C

CARRIER'S RESPONSIBILITY WHERE INSURED LOSES OR FORGIVES FEE
Insurance §13.12

CHANGES, MAJOR
Estimate liability §5.02

CLAIM AFTER POLICY EXPIRED
Insurance §13.08

CLAIM COVERED
Insurance §13.03

CLAIM EXCLUDED
Insurance §13.03

CLAIM, PRIOR KNOWLEDGE OF
Insurance §13.09

CLAIMS MADE DURING POLICY PERIOD
Insurance. See INSURANCE

COLLAPSE
Statutory liability §3.02

COLLATERAL ESTOPPEL
    Arbitration §§14.05, 14.06
COMFORT
    Damages §10.05
COMMON LAW INDEMNITY, FAULT DESTROYS RIGHT TO
    Indemnity §12.08
COMMON LAW OBLIGATION
    Liability arising from contract §4.07
COMMON WRONG
    Indemnity §12.08
COMPARATIVE NEGLIGENCE
    Defenses. See DEFENSES
COMPENDIUM
    Limitations §11.01
COMPLIANCE DEFENSE
    Statutory liability §3.03
COMPREHENSIVE LIABILITY COVERAGE
    Insurance §13.02
COMPREHENSIVE VERSUS PROFESSIONAL
    Insurance §13.02
CONCEALMENT, FRAUDULENT
    Intentional torts §2.01
CONFLICT OF INTEREST
    Intentional torts §2.03
CONSEQUENTIAL DAMAGES
    Damages §10.01
CONSOLIDATION
    Arbitration §14.05
CONSPIRACY
    Intentional torts §2.02
CONSTITUTIONAL CONSIDERATIONS
    Limitations §11.08
CONSTRUCTION, COMPLETION OF
    Limitations §11.09
CONTRACT ACTION
    Limitations §11.07
CONTRACT AS CREATING DUTY
    Liability arising from contract §4.03
CONTRACT, DUTIES IMPOSED BY
    Liability arising from contract §4.01
CONTRACT, DUTY ARISING FROM
    Liability arising from contract §4.01
CONTRACT DUTY VERSUS CONTRIBUTORY NEGLIGENCE
    Liability arising from contract §4.01
CONTRACT INTERFERENCE
    Intentional torts §2.05
CONTRACTOR AS THIRD-PARTY BENEFICIARY
    Liability arising from contract §4.05
CONTRACTOR INDEMNIFYING ENGINEER
    Indemnity §12.02
CONTRACTOR NOT AS THIRD-PARTY BENEFICIARY
    Liability arising from contract §4.05
CONTRACTOR NOT RELYING ON ARCHITECT
    Limitations §11.11
CONTRACTOR VERSUS ENGINEER
    Liability arising from contract §4.03
CONTRACTS
    Limitations §11.02
CONTRACTS AND TORTS
    Limitations §11.02
CONTRACT STANDARDS
    Negligence liability §1.08
CONTRACT STATUTE APPLIED
    Limitations §11.02

INDEX

CONTRACTUAL INDEMNITY
  Indemnity §12.02
CONTRACT UNCERTAINTY
  Estimate liability §5.08
CONTRACT VERSUS MALPRACTICE
  Limitations §11.02
CONTRACT VERSUS TORT LIABILITY
  Negligence liability §1.15
CONTRIBUTION PERMITTED
  Indemnity §12.08
CONTRIBUTION STATUTE, ECONOMIC LOSS
  Indemnity §12.08
CONTRIBUTORY FAULT OF OWNER
  Estimate liability §5.12
CONTRIBUTORY NEGLIGENCE
  Contract duty versus contributory negligence. See CONTRACT DUTY VERSUS CONTRIBUTORY NEGLIGENCE
  Estimate liability §5.07
CONTROL
  No control. See NO CONTROL
CONVENIENCE
  Damages §10.05
CONVENTIONAL STANDARD APPLIED
  Negligence liability §1.07
CONVENTIONAL STANDARD CRITICIZED
  Negligence liability §1.06
CONVERSION
  Intentional torts §2.08
COPYRIGHT
  Statutory liability §3.08
COST FACTORS, OTHER
  Arbitration §14.10

COST OF CORRECTION
  Damages §10.03
COST OF CORRECTION UNECONOMIC
  Damages §10.08
COST OF REPAIR
  Damages §10.03
COST SAVING OR VALUE
  Damages §10.03
COVERAGE, EXOTIC
  Insurance §13.04
CRIMINAL PROSECUTION
  Limitations §11.05
CRITICISM
  Limitations §11.01

D

DAMAGE, PAYMENT AS
  Limitations §11.05
DAMAGES
  Generally §10.01
  Comfort §10.05
  Convenience §10.05
  Cost of correction uneconomic §10.08
  Economic damage. See ECONOMIC DAMAGE
  Economic loss §10.10
  Enjoyment §10.05
  Loss-of-fee damages. See LOSS-OF-FEE DAMAGES
  Mental anguish §10.11
  Misrepresentation, damages for. See MISREPRESENTATION, DAMAGES FOR
  Negligent survey §10.04
  Niggardly damages. See NIGGARDLY DAMAGES
  No damage cases. See NO DAMAGE CASES
  Out-of-pocket damages. See OUT-OF-POCKET DAMAGES

DAMAGES, *continued*
  Out-of-pocket damages, development of
  —generally §10.06
  —application §10.07
  Public project, cost of correction of
  —generally §10.02
  —private project §10.03
  Punitive damages §10.12
  Quantum meruit damages, effect of. See QUANTUM MERUIT DAMAGES, EFFECT OF
  Rental value §10.09
  Tenant's damages. See TENANT'S DAMAGES
  Warranty law §6.03

DAMAGES, APPROACHES TO
  Damages §10.01

DAMAGES, MEASURE CRITICIZED
  Estimate liability §5.15

DAMAGES, MEASURE OF
  Estimate liability §5.05

DAMAGE TO PROJECT
  Limitations §11.02

DECISIONS, CONFLICTING
  Damages §10.10

DEDUCTIBLE
  Insurance §13.13

DEFECTIVE DESIGN, INDEMNITY FOR
  Indemnity §12.07

DEFENSE, REJECTION OF
  Negligence liability §1.18

DEFENSES
  Generally §9.01
  Accord and satisfaction §9.38
  Architect no insurer §9.12
  Building department approval §9.19
  Comparative negligence
  —generally §9.16
  —application §9.17
  Completion and acceptance §9.06
  Contributory negligence §9.15
  Defective work concealed §9.27

DEFENSES, *continued*
  Deviation from plans §9.28
  Economic loss
  —generally §9.04
  —continuing application of privity defense §9.05
  Exclusive remedy §9.32
  Exculpatory clauses
  —generally §9.29
  —application §9.30
  —criticism §9.31
  Immunity, architect as arbitrator
  —generally §9.08
  —application §9.09
  —criticism §9.10
  Information furnished by others, reliance on §9.18
  No causation §9.13
  No control
  —generally §9.23
  —application §9.25
  —construction methods §9.24
  —rejection §9.26
  No duty §9.11
  No license §9.39
  No supervision §9.22
  Owner approval §9.21
  Patent defect §9.07
  Privilege §9.33
  Privity of contract
  —generally §9.02
  —rejection §9.03
  Release §9.37
  Risk, assumption of §9.14
  Sovereign immunity
  —generally §9.34
  —application §9.35
  —rejection §9.36
  Waiver and estoppel §9.20

DELAY CHART
  Trial and hearing techniques §15.03

DEPOSITION SUMMARY
  Trial and hearing techniques §15.06

INDEX

DESIGN-BUILD
  Agency liability §8.01
DESIGN-BUILD CONTRACT
  Statutory liability §3.02
DESIGN COMPLIANCE DEFENSE OF DESIGNER-BUILDER
  Liability arising from contract §4.02
DESIGN VERSUS MALPRACTICE
  Limitations §11.02
DEVELOPERS AND CONSTRUCTION LENDERS
  Negligence liability §1.21
DIFFERENCE MINUS FEE
  Damages §10.04
DISCOVERY
  Arbitration §14.10
DISCOVERY EXTENSION
  Limitations §11.07
DISCOVERY, PURSUIT OF
  Arbitration §14.03
DISCOVERY RULE
  Limitations §11.06
DISCOVERY VERSUS OCCURRENCE POLICY
  Insurance §13.09
DISPROPORTIONATE FAULT
  Indemnity §12.07
DOCTRINE, HISTORY OF
  Warranty law §6.06
DOCTRINE REJECTED
  Damages §10.10
DOCUMENT FILE
  Trial and hearing techniques §15.05
DUTY
  No duty. See NO DUTY
DUTY CREATED BY CONTRACT
  Third-party beneficiary versus duty created by contract. See THIRD-PARTY BENEFICIARY VERSUS DUTY CREATED BY CONTRACT
DUTY FOUND
  Liability arising from contract §4.04
DUTY, LACK OF
  Negligence liability §1.18
DUTY OF DISCLOSURE, INSURER'S
  Insurance §13.09
DUTY TO DEFEND
  Insurance §13.07
DUTY TO DEFEND NOT EXCLUDED
  Insurance §13.03
DUTY TO NOTIFY CARRIER
  Insurance §13.06
DUTY TO SUPERVISE
  Liability arising from contract §4.04
DUTY VERSUS NEGLIGENCE
  Negligence liability §1.02

E

ECONOMIC DAMAGE
  No damage cases §7.03
ECONOMIC DAMAGES, NO INDEMNITY FOR
  Indemnity §12.02
ECONOMIC LOSS
  Damages §10.10
  Defenses. See DEFENSES
  Liability arising from contract §4.03
  Limitations §11.02
ECONOMIC LOSS AWARDED
  Damages §10.10
ECONOMIC LOSS RULE
  Negligence liability §1.18
ENGINEER
  Contractor versus engineer. See CONTRACTOR VERSUS ENGINEER

ENGINEER NOT STRICTLY LIABLE
Warranty law §6.08

ENGINEER'S DUTY
Negligence liability §1.08

ENJOYMENT
Damages §10.05

ERROR OR OMISSION, KNOWN
Insurance §13.07

ESTIMATE LIABILITY
Benefit-of-the-bargain damages §5.15
Breach of contract §5.05
Budget, duty to establish §5.03
Contributory fault of owner §5.12
Exculpatory clauses §5.11
Loss-of-fee damages §5.17
Misrepresentation §5.04
Negligence §5.07
Out-of-pocket damages §5.16
Parol evidence rule §5.08
Pervasive problem of §5.01
Recoverability of fee §5.02
Redesign §5.10
Substantial accuracy §5.09
Unjust enrichment §5.14
Waivers §5.13
Willful overrun §5.06

ESTOPPEL
Agency liability §8.02
Limitations §11.01
Waiver and estoppel. See WAIVER AND ESTOPPEL

EVIDENCE RULES
Arbitration §14.10

EXCESS CLAUSE
Insurance §13.15

EXCESS CLAUSE VERSUS PRO RATA CLAUSE
Insurance §13.15

EXCLUSION APPLIED
Insurance §13.03

EXCULPATORY CLAUSE AS DEFENSE TO THIRD-PARTY ACTION
Liability arising from contract §4.03

EXCULPATORY CLAUSES
Defenses. See DEFENSES
Estimate liability §5.11
Liability arising from contract §4.01

EXPENSES
Arbitration §14.10

EXPERT FROM DIFFERENT PROFESSION
Trial and hearing techniques §15.07

EXPERTISE
Arbitration §14.10

EXPERT QUALIFICATIONS
Trial and hearing techniques §15.07

EXPERT TESTIMONY
Negligence liability §1.19

EXPERT TESTIMONY REQUIRED
Estimate liability §5.07

EXPERT WITNESSES
Statutory liability §3.02
Trial and hearing techniques §15.07

EXPRESS WARRANTY
Warranty law §6.02

EXTRA WORK
Agency liability §8.02

F

FACT SUMMARY
Trial and hearing techniques §15.02

FAILURE TO WARN
Negligence liability §1.10

FALSE PAYMENT CERTIFICATE
Intentional torts §2.01

FEE ESTIMATES
  Estimate liability §5.04
FEE SIZE, LIABILITY LIMITED BY
  Negligence liability §1.09
FLAWED JURY INSTRUCTION
  Damages §10.10
FORESEEABILITY
  Negligence liability §1.17
FRAUD
  Intentional torts §2.01
FRAUD CLAIM
  Limitations §11.07
FRAUD THEORY
  Estimate liability §5.15
FREEDOM OF CONTRACT
  Insurance §13.10

G

GUARANTEES
  Negligence liability §1.17
GUESS VERSUS ESTIMATE
  Estimate liability §5.03

H

HEARING TECHNIQUES
  See TRIAL AND HEARING TECHNIQUES
HEARSAY, EXPERT RELYING ON
  Trial and hearing techniques §15.07
HYPOTHETICAL QUESTIONS
  Trial and hearing techniques §15.07

I

ILLEGALITY
  Statutory liability §3.03
IMMUNITY, ARCHITECT AS ARBITRATOR
  Defenses. See DEFENSES
IMMUNITY OF ARBITRATOR
  Intentional torts §2.05
IMPLIED CONDITIONS
  Liability arising from contract §4.01
IMPLIED EQUITABLE INDEMNITY, DEVELOPMENT
  Indemnity. See INDEMNITY
IMPLIED WARRANTY
  Warranty law §6.03
IMPLIED WARRANTY, INDEMNITY BASED ON
  Indemnity §12.07
IMPLIED WARRANTY OF BUILDER
  Warranty law §6.03
INDEMNITORS
  Negligence liability §1.24
INDEMNITY
  Generally §12.01
  Contractual indemnity §12.02
  Implied equitable indemnity, development
  —generally §12.06
  —sought by architect or engineer §12.08
  —sought from architect or engineer §12.07
  Limitations §§11.02, 12.09
  Negligence, indemnity against own §12.03
  No contribution §12.05
  Statute annulling indemnity provision §12.04
INDEMNITY ACTION
  Limitations §11.09
INDEMNITY AGAINST ARCHITECT
  Indemnity §12.02
INDEMNITY ENFORCED
  Indemnity §12.07

INDEMNITY, RELEASE BARRING
  Indemnity §12.08
INDEMNITY TO ACTIVELY NEGLIGENT ENGINEER
  Indemnity §12.08
INDEPENDENT CONTRACTORS
  Agency liability §8.03
INDEPENDENT WRONGS, NO INDEMNITY
  Indemnity §12.08
INDUCEMENT
  Negligence liability §1.13
INJURIES
  Liability arising from contract §4.03
  Statutory liability §3.06
INNOCENT CONSTRUCTION RULE
  Intentional torts §2.04
INSPECTION AND SUPERVISION
  Statutory liability §3.01
INSPECTIONS, CONTINUING
  Limitations §11.11
INSUBSTANTIAL ERROR
  Estimate liability §5.09
INSURANCE
  Generally §13.01
  Carrier's responsibility where insured loses or forgives fee §13.12
  Claims made during policy period
    –generally §13.08
    –application §13.09
    –policy arguments §13.10
  Comprehensive liability coverage §13.02
  Coverage, exotic §13.04
  Deductible §13.13
  Duty to defend §13.07
  Excess clause §13.15
  Professional liability insurance §13.06
  Professional services exclusion §13.03

INSURANCE, *continued*
  Settlement by insured §13.11
  Subrogation §13.16
  Subsurface exclusion §13.05
INSURANCE CARRIER NOT LIABLE
  Liability arising from contract §4.06
INSURANCE EXTENDED BY CONTRACT
  Insurance §13.02
INTENTIONAL TORTS
  Bad faith §2.07
  Conflict of interest §2.03
  Conspiracy §2.02
  Contract interference §2.05
  Conversion §2.08
  Fraud §2.01
  Slander §2.04
  Trespass §2.06
INTENTIONAL WRONGDOING
  Insurance §13.07
INVITEES
  Negligence liability §1.23

J

JOINT ARBITRATION ORDERED
  Arbitration §14.06
JOINT FAULT
  Indemnity §§12.05, 12.07
JOINT NEGLIGENCE
  Indemnity §12.02
JOINT VENTURE
  Liability arising from contract §4.03

L

LACK OF PRIVITY NO DEFENSE
  Liability arising from contract §4.01

LATENT DEFECT
  Limitations §11.07
LATE PRESENTATION OF CLAIM
  Insurance §13.07
LATE REPORT
  Insurance §§13.09, 13.09
LAW NOTES
  Trial and hearing techniques §15.08
LAWYERS
  See ATTORNEYS AND ATTORNEYS FEES
LEGAL ERROR
  Arbitration §14.10
LENDERS NOT AS THIRD-PARTY BENEFICIARY
  Liability arising from contract §4.05
LIABILITY
  Agency liability. See AGENCY LIABILITY
  Estimate liability. See ESTIMATE LIABILITY
  Intentional torts. See INTENTIONAL TORTS
  Liability arising from contract. See LIABILITY ARISING FROM CONTRACT
  Negligence liability. See NEGLIGENCE LIABILITY
  Statutory liability. See STATUTORY LIABILITY
  Strict liability versus express warranty. See STRICT LIABILITY VERSUS EXPRESS WARRANTY
  Warranty law. See WARRANTY LAW
LIABILITY ARISING FROM CONTRACT
  Breach of contract §4.01
  Contract as creating duty §4.03
  Design compliance defense of designer-builder §4.02
  Duty to supervise §4.04

LIABILITY ARISING FROM CONTRACT, *continued*
  Negligence §4.01
  Safety engineering §4.06
  Third-party beneficiaries §4.05
  Work stoppage §4.07
LIABILITY FOR ACTS OF CONSULTANT
  Agency liability §8.05
LIABILITY OF PARTNERSHIPS AND CORPORATIONS
  Agency liability §8.06
LIBEL PER SE
  Intentional torts §2.04
LICENSING STATUTES
  Statutory liability §3.02
LIMITATIONS
  Generally §11.01
  Accrual, negligent act
  –generally §11.03
  –application of statute rejected §11.10
  –constitutional considerations §11.08
  –discovery rule §11.06
  –statute of repose applied §11.09
  –statutes of repose §11.07
  –time of completion §11.04
  –when damage occurs §11.05
  Applicable period §11.02
  Arbitration §11.12
  Continuous services §11.11
  Indemnity §12.09
  Remedial efforts §11.13
  Statutory liability §3.02
LIMITED SCOPE
  Arbitration §14.02
LITIGATION PRIVILEGE
  Intentional torts §2.05
LOCAL STANDARD NOT ESTABLISHED
  Trial and hearing techniques §15.07
LOSS-OF-FEE DAMAGES
  Estimate liability §5.17

650   INDEX

LOST PROFIT DENIED
   Damages §10.04

M

MALICE, REQUIREMENT OF
   Intentional torts §2.05
MALPRACTICE
   Contract versus malpractice. See
      CONTRACT VERSUS
      MALPRACTICE
   Design versus malpractice. See
      DESIGN VERSUS
      MALPRACTICE
   Limitations §11.02
   Negligence liability §1.01
MARKET VALUE
   Damages §10.01
MASS HOME BUILDERS
   Warranty law §6.05
MECHANICS LIENS
   Indemnity §12.02
MEDIATION
   Arbitration §14.11
MENTAL ANGUISH
   Damages §10.11
   No damage cases §7.02
MISREPRESENTATION
   Estimate liability §5.04
   Warranty versus misrepresentation.
      See WARRANTY VERSUS
      MISREPRESENTATION
MISREPRESENTATION, DAMAGES
     FOR
   Estimate liability §5.04
MISREPRESENTATION,
     FRAUDULENT
   Intentional torts §2.01
MISREPRESENTATION,
     INTENTIONAL
   Estimate liability §5.04
MISREPRESENTATION VOIDS
     CONTRACT
   Estimate liability §5.04

MOORMAN DOCTRINE
   Damages §§10.03, 10.10
MULTIPLE CLAIMS
   Insurance §13.07
MULTIPLE PARTIES
   Arbitration. See ARBITRATION

N

NARROW CONSTRUCTION
   Indemnity §12.03
NEGLIGENCE
   Estimate liability §5.07
   Liability arising from contract
      §4.01
   Statute of repose versus negligence.
      See STATUTE OF REPOSE
      VERSUS NEGLIGENCE
   Statutory liability §3.03
NEGLIGENCE, ACTIVE
   Liability arising from contract
      §4.03
NEGLIGENCE, ACTIVE OR
     AFFIRMATIVE
   Indemnity §12.07
NEGLIGENCE, INDEMNITY
     AGAINST OWN
   Indemnity §12.03
NEGLIGENCE LIABILITY
   Duty versus negligence §1.02
   Failure to warn §1.10
   Intrinsically dangerous §1.11
   Malpractice §1.01
   Negligence
   –generally §1.14
   –contract versus tort liability §1.15
   –expert testimony §1.19
   –negligence and breach of contract
      §1.16
   –privity of contract §1.18
   –reasonable skill required §1.17
   Negligent misrepresentation
     inducement §1.13
   No insurer §1.09
   Nondelegable duty §1.12

INDEX

NEGLIGENCE LIABILITY, *continued*
  Real estate law, liability arising from §1.26
  Standard of practice
  –generally §1.03
  –conventional standard applied §1.07
  –conventional standard criticized §1.06
  –not a warrantor §1.04
  –reasonable skill and knowledge §1.05
  –required duty §1.08
  Third-party liability, contractors
  –generally §1.20
  –developers and construction lenders §1.21
  –invitees, patrons, and occupants §1.23
  –remote parties, other §1.25
  –sureties and indemnitors §1.24
  –workers §1.22

NEGLIGENCE PER SE
  Statutory liability §3.03

NEGLIGENCE STATUTE APPLIED
  Limitations §11.02

NEGLIGENT APPROVAL
  Indemnity §12.07

NEGLIGENT APPROVAL OF ESTIMATES EXONERATES BOND
  Agency liability §8.02

NEGLIGENT MISREPRESENTATION INDUCEMENT
  Negligence liability §1.13

NEGLIGENT, MORE VERSUS LESS
  Indemnity §12.08

NEGLIGENT PARTIES, NO INDEMNITY FOR
  Indemnity §12.07

NEGLIGENT SURVEY
  Damages §10.04

NEW YORK RULE
  Limitations §11.03

NIGGARDLY DAMAGES
  Estimate liability §5.02

NO CONTRACTUAL DUTY
  Liability arising from contract §4.03

NO DAMAGE CASES
  Generally §7.01
  Economic damage §7.03
  Mental anguish §7.02

NO-DAMAGE-FOR-DELAY
  Intentional torts §2.05

NO DUTY
  Indemnity §12.07

NO DUTY OF CONTRACTOR TO ENGINEER
  Indemnity §12.08

NO DUTY TO WORKERS
  Liability arising from contract §4.04

NONDELEGABLE DUTY
  Agency liability §8.05
  Negligence liability §1.12
  Statutory liability §3.03

NO RIGHT OF CONTROL
  Agency liability §8.03

NOTICE TO EXCESS CARRIER
  Insurance §13.08

O

OCCUPANTS
  Negligence liability §1.23

OLD RULE
  Negligence liability §1.18

ORAL CONDITION
  Estimate liability §5.08

OUT-OF-POCKET DAMAGES
  Estimate liability §5.16

OUT-OF-POCKET DAMAGES, DEVELOPMENT OF
  Damages. See DAMAGES

OWNER AS THIRD-PARTY BENEFICIARY
Liability arising from contract §4.05
OWNER BOUND BY ACTS OR KNOWLEDGE OF AGENT
Agency liability §8.02
OWNER, COLLUSION WITH
Agency liability §8.02
OWNER, COST INCREASES BY
Estimate liability §5.12
OWNER, KNOWLEDGE OF ARCHITECT ATTRIBUTED TO
Agency liability §8.02
OWNER NOT AS THIRD-PARTY BENEFICIARY
Liability arising from contract §4.05
OWNER NOT BOUND BY ACTS OF ARCHITECT
Agency liability §8.03
OWNERS
Negligence liability §1.22

P

PAROLE EVIDENCE RECEIVED
Estimate liability §5.08
PAROL EVIDENCE CONTRADICTING CONTRACT
Estimate liability §5.08
PAROL EVIDENCE REFUSED
Estimate liability §5.08
PAROL EVIDENCE RULE
Estimate liability §5.08
PARTIES IN PARI DELICTO, NO INDEMNITY FOR
Indemnity §12.07
PATRONS
Liability arising from contract §4.04
Negligence liability §1.23

PERFORMANCE, PREVENTION OF
Estimate liability §5.05
PERFORMANCE, SPECIFIC
Liability arising from contract §4.01
PRETRIAL AND SETTLEMENT
Arbitration §14.10
PRIMARY FAULT
Indemnity §12.07
PRIVACY
Arbitration §14.10
PRIVATE PROJECT
Damages §10.03
PRIVILEGE NOT SHOWN
Intentional torts §2.05
PRIVITY
Liability arising from contract §4.03
PRIVITY DEFENSE
Warranty law §6.04
PRIVITY DEFENSE, LACK OF
Liability arising from contract §4.01
PRIVITY OF CONTRACT
Defenses. See DEFENSES
Negligence liability §1.18
PRIVITY OF CONTRACT DEFENSE
Intentional torts §2.05
PRIVITY, STATUTE OF LIMITATIONS
Warranty law §6.03
PROFESSIONAL ASSURANCES
Limitations §11.11
PROFESSIONAL LIABILITY INSURANCE
Insurance §13.06
PROFESSIONAL SERVICE
Limitations §11.02
PROFESSIONAL SERVICES EXCLUSION
Insurance §§13.02, 13.03
PRO RATA CLAUSE
Excess clause versus pro rata clause. See EXCESS CLAUSE VERSUS PRO RATA CLAUSE

PROXIMATE CAUSE
  Negligence liability §1.17
PUBLIC PROJECT, COST OF CORRECTION OF
  Damages. See DAMAGES
PUNITIVE DAMAGES
  Damages §10.12

Q

QUALIFIED IMMUNITY
  Intentional torts §2.04
QUALIFIED PRIVILEGE
  Intentional torts §2.05
QUANTUM MERUIT DAMAGES, EFFECT OF
  Estimate liability §5.15
QUANTUM MERUIT RECOVERY
  Estimate liability §5.09

R

REAL ESTATE LAW, LIABILITY ARISING FROM
  Negligence liability §1.26
REAL PROPERTY, IMPROVEMENT TO
  Limitations §11.09
REASONABLE CARE STANDARD
  Negligence liability §1.14
REASONABLE SKILL AND KNOWLEDGE
  Negligence liability §1.05
REASONABLE SKILL REQUIRED
  Negligence liability §1.17
RECOVERABILITY OF FEE
  Estimate liability §5.02
RECOVERY OF FEE, NONLICENSURE PREVENTING
  Statutory liability §3.02

REDESIGN
  Estimate liability §5.10
RELATIONSHIP, REQUIRED
  Indemnity §12.08
REMEDIAL EFFORTS
  Limitations §11.13
REMEDIES, PROVISIONAL
  Arbitration §14.10
REMEDY DEFENSE, EXCLUSIVE
  Indemnity §12.08
REMOTE OWNER AS THIRD-PARTY BENEFICIARY
  Liability arising from contract §4.05
REMOTE OWNER NOT AS THIRD-PARTY BENEFICIARY
  Liability arising from contract §4.05
REMOTE PARTIES, OTHER
  Negligence liability §1.25
RENTAL VALUE
  Damages §10.09
RENT PLUS INTEREST
  Damages §10.09
RENT VERSUS INTEREST
  Damages §10.09
REPAIR, ASSURANCES OF
  Limitations §11.11
REPAIRS, ATTEMPTED
  Limitations §11.11
REQUIRED DUTY
  Negligence liability §1.08
RETROSPECTIVE EFFECT
  Limitations §11.07

S

SAFE PLACE STATUTES
  Statutory liability §3.04
SAFETY ENGINEERING
  Liability arising from contract §4.06

SAFETY EXPERTS
Trial and hearing techniques §15.07
SAFETY INSPECTIONS, VOLUNTARY
Liability arising from contract §4.06
SAFETY REGULATIONS
Statutory liability §3.06
"SCAFFOLD ACTS"
Statutory liability §3.05
SEALS
Statutory liability §3.09
SERVICES, COMPLETION OF
Limitations §11.07
SERVICES, CONTINUOUS
Limitations §11.11
SERVICES, GAP IN
Limitations §11.11
SETOFFS
Negligence liability §1.15
SETTLEMENT BY INSURED
Insurance §13.11
SLANDER
Intentional torts §2.04
SLANDER CLAIM COVERED
Insurance §13.06
SOVEREIGN IMMUNITY
Defenses. See DEFENSES
STANDARD OF CARE, EVIDENCE OF
Statutory liability §3.06
STANDARD OF PRACTICE
Negligence liability. See NEGLIGENCE LIABILITY
STATUTE ANNULLING INDEMNITY PROVISION
Indemnity §12.04
STATUTE OF LIMITATIONS
Arbitration §14.10
Intentional torts §2.05

STATUTE OF LIMITATIONS, PRIVITY
Warranty law §6.03
STATUTE OF REPOSE APPLIED
Limitations §11.09
STATUTE OF REPOSE HELD UNCONSTITUTIONAL
Limitations §11.08
STATUTE OF REPOSE NOT EXTENDING TIME TO SUE
Limitations §11.07
STATUTE OF REPOSE VERSUS NEGLIGENCE
Limitations §11.02
STATUTE REJECTED, APPLICATION OF
Limitations §11.10
STATUTES OF REPOSE
Indemnity §12.09
Limitations §11.07
STATUTES, OTHER
Indemnity §12.09
STATUTE UPHELD, CONSTITUTIONALITY OF
Limitations §11.08
STATUTORY LIABILITY
Building code, compliance failure §3.03
Copyright §3.08
Inspection and supervision §3.01
Licensing statutes §3.02
Safe place statutes §3.04
Safety regulations §3.06
"Scaffold acts" §3.05
Seals §3.09
Water, intentional diversion of §3.07
STAY OF LITIGATION PENDING ARBITRATION
Arbitration §14.02
STRICT LIABILITY
Warranty law. See WARRANTY LAW

STRICT LIABILITY REJECTED
  Warranty law §6.07
STRICT LIABILITY VERSUS
    EXPRESS WARRANTY
  Warranty law §6.02
SUBROGATION
  Insurance §13.16
  Liability arising from contract
    §4.03
SUBROGATION TO INDEMNITY
  Indemnity §12.02
SUBSEQUENT PURCHASERS
  Negligence liability §1.25
SUBSTANTIAL ACCURACY
  Estimate liability §5.09
SUBSTANTIAL ERROR
  Estimate liability §5.09
SUB-SUBCONTRACTORS
  Negligence liability §1.25
SUBSURFACE EXCLUSION
  Insurance §13.05
SUPERVISION
  No supervision. See NO
    SUPERVISION
SURETIES
  Negligence liability §1.24
SURETY'S INDEMNITEE
    PROTECTED
  Liability arising from contract
    §4.03
SURVEYORS
  Statutory liability §3.02

T

TARDY NOTICES
  Insurance §13.08
TELEPHONE, CLAIM BY
  Insurance §13.09
TENANT'S DAMAGES
  Estimate liability §5.15

THIRD-PARTY BENEFICIARIES
  Arbitration §14.02
  Liability arising from contract
    §4.05
  Limitations §11.02
THIRD-PARTY BENEFICIARY
    VERSUS DUTY CREATED BY
    CONTRACT
  Liability arising from contract
    §4.03
THIRD-PARTY LIABILITY,
    CONTRACTORS
  Negligence liability. See
    NEGLIGENCE LIABILITY
TIME
  Arbitration §14.10
TIME OF COMPLETION
  Limitations §11.04
TORTFEASOR, NO INDEMNITY
    TO ACTIVE
  Indemnity §12.07
TORTIOUS INTERFERENCE
  Intentional torts §2.05
TORTS
  Limitations §11.02
TORTS OF AGENT
  Agency liability §8.02
TORTS VERSUS CONTRACTS
  Limitations §11.02
TORTS VERSUS CONTRACTS
    VERSUS PROPERTY DAMAGE
  Limitations §11.02
TRADE PRACTICE
  Statutory liability §3.03
TRESPASS
  Intentional torts §2.06
TRIAL AND HEARING
    TECHNIQUES
  Generally §15.01
  Award, proposed §15.10
  Delay chart §15.03
  Deposition summary §15.06
  Document file §15.05
  Expert witnesses §15.07

TRIAL AND HEARING
    TECHNIQUES, *continued*
  Fact summary §15.02
  Law notes §15.08
  "Trial book" §15.09
  Witness outline §15.04
"TRIAL BOOK"
  Trial and hearing techniques
    §15.09

U

UNJUST ENRICHMENT
  Estimate liability §5.14

V

VOUCHING IN
  Indemnity §12.08

W

WAIVER AND ESTOPPEL
  Insurance §13.14
WAIVERS
  Arbitration §14.03
  Estimate liability §5.13
WAIVERS, AMBIGUOUS
  Estimate liability §5.13
WARRANTORS
  Estimate liability §5.10
  Negligence liability §1.04
WARRANTY FOUND
  Warranty law §6.03

WARRANTY IMPLIED IN FAVOR
    OF OWNER
  Warranty law §6.03
WARRANTY LAW
  Generally §6.01
  Express warranty §6.02
  Implied warranty §6.03
  Strict liability
    –generally §6.04
    –application criticized §6.09
    –architects §6.07
    –engineers §6.08
    –history of doctrine §6.06
    –mass home builders §6.05
WATER, INTENTIONAL
    DIVERSION OF
  Statutory liability §3.07
WILLFUL OVERRUN
  Estimate liability §5.06
WITNESS OUTLINE
  Trial and hearing techniques
    §15.04
WORKERS
  Negligence liability §1.22
WORKERS NOT AS THIRD-PARTY
    BENEFICIARY
  Liability arising from contract
    §4.05
WORK STOPPAGE
  Liability arising from contract
    §4.07
WRAPUP POLICY
  Insurance §13.04
WRITTEN NOTICE, LACK OF
  Insurance §13.09
WRONG ADDRESSES
  Insurance §13.08